A. P. Giannini

A. P. Giannini

Banker of America

Felice A. Bonadio

UNIVERSITY OF CALIFORNIA PRESS

Berkeley / Los Angeles / London

University of California Press
Berkeley and Los Angeles, California

University of California Press, Ltd.
London, England

© 1994 by
The Regents of the University of California

Library of Congress Cataloging-in-Publication Data
Bonadio, Felice A.
    A.P. Giannini : Banker of America / Felice A. Bonadio.
      p. cm.
    Includes bibliographical references and index.
    ISBN 0-520-08249-4 (alk. paper)
    1. Giannini, Amadeo Peter, 1870–1949.   2. Bankers—United States—
Biography.   3. Bank of America—History.   4. Banks and banking—
United States—History.   I. Title.
HG2463.G5B66 1994
332.1'23'092—dc20
[B]
                                                93-25768
                                                  CIP

Printed in the United States of America
9 8 7 6 5 4 3 2 1

The paper used in this publication meets the minimum requirements of
American National Standard for Information Sciences—Permanence
of Paper for Printed Library Materials, ANSI Z39.48-1984.

For my grandchildren—Carson, Colin, Connor, and Clare—who brighten my days

Contents

Illustrations

Preface

This book is about the life and career of one of the most extraordinary figures in the history of American finance—Amadeo Peter Giannini. Giannini's influence on the conduct of banking in the country was enormous, perhaps greater than that of the legendary J. P. Morgan. Certainly no other banker succeeded in creating a financial institution that directly affected the lives of so many people. Consider a few facts. In 1945, at the height of its power as the world's largest bank, Giannini's Bank of America had a total of nearly four million customers and held about 40 percent of the total deposits of California. With its five hundred or so branch offices located in more than three hundred California communities, Bank of America seemed to most people as familiar and as vital as the neighborhood grocery. The reward for Giannini was enormous. Among all other banks, Bank of America stood out as the richest and most influential financial institution in the country.

Giannini's spectacular rise to power is all the more dramatic because four decades earlier his Bank of Italy had been a one-room affair catering primarily to San Francisco's working-class Italians. The phenomenal leap that Giannini made to the apex of financial power is all the more remarkable because Bank of America was largely a one-man show—the triumph of talent, ambition, and imagination, qualities he possessed in abundance even in an age of heroic entrepreneurs. The Giannini "miracle," as it was called, was based on a set of ideas that were as revolutionary as they were rooted in the essentials of democracy. Briefly

stated, he believed that the great mass of ordinary people were entitled to the services of professional banking; that the combined deposits
of small savers could be used to fund loans to farmers, consumers, and
small businesses; and that this free transfer of money could give new
opportunities to communities to promote economic growth. So in
1909, only five years after opening Bank of Italy, Giannini made a
move that would have an immense impact on banking in the United
States: he opened his first branch office in San Jose, thus embarking on
a rapidly expanding network of banks that would turn him into a figure both feared and respected in the financial world.

The reaction of Giannini's competitors was swift and brutal. By
soliciting deposits and making loans among the tens of thousands of
society's "little people," Giannini was challenging the power and the
financial assumptions of traditional bankers. Banks in general were
indifferent to the credit needs of the many, preferring to serve the
financial interests of the few who possessed all the comforts and privileges of the well-born. In California a phalanx of independent bankers
and their big-city allies rose up to crush Giannini's expansionist ambitions. Outside the state, the opponents of branch banking did their best
to help. Giannini, shrewd and strong-willed, counterattacked with
equal ferocity. For forty years, from Wall Street and the corridors of
power in Washington to the cities and towns of California, the battle
raged. The larger the Giannini empire grew, the more determined was
the response of his opposition. These public battles and behind-the-
scenes maneuverings for strategic advantage gave Giannini his reputation as California's "best loved and best hated banker."

Even before the battles were over, it was clear that Giannini had
forever changed the landscape of banking in the United States. What
Giannini had done was to create the first privately owned bank that
tried to make the business of lending money both more efficient and
more democratic, thereby giving to large numbers of ordinary Americans the opportunity to satisfy their own needs and aspirations. Giannini's achievement is largely overlooked in our histories.

In writing this book, I did not intend to deal in a technical way
with the intricacies of branch banking in California, although I hope
the book provides the general reader with an understanding of how
Giannini's branch system spread throughout the state and why it prospered. My intention, simply, was to introduce a new generation of
Americans to the life of a remarkable businessman whose success in

creating the world's first "department store of finance" continues to affect us all today.

The Bank of America Archives in San Francisco are a mine of source material on the history of the bank during the Giannini years, thanks in large part to the prodigious efforts of the late Bessie James, who with Marquis James published *Biography of a Bank: The Story of Bank of America N.T. and S.A.* in 1954. I have drawn heavily on the official records, private and business correspondence, and the newspaper and magazine clippings collected by Bessie James.

I wish to express my appreciation to a succession of archivists and staff members at Bank of America Archives for their help and cooperation: Orv Wilson, James Babbitt, Theresa Hickey, Marilyn Ghausi, and John Donofrio. I am also grateful to Duncan Knowles, Bank of America's vice-president of organizational communications, for furnishing me with valuable assistance.

In my pursuit of documentary material, I benefited greatly from the courtesy and research services provided by the professional staffs at numerous libraries, most notably the Bancroft Library of the University of California, Berkeley; the Department of Special Collections at the University of California, Los Angeles; the California Historical Society of San Francisco; the Federal Reserve Bank, San Francisco; the Manuscript Division, Stanford University; the Manuscript Division, Library of Congress; the National Archives; the Baker Library at the School of Business, Harvard University; and the Marriner Eccles Collection, University of Utah.

For permission to reproduce photographs, I am grateful to Bank of America Archives, the San Francisco Public Library, the California Historical Society of San Francisco, the San Mateo Historical Society, the San Jose Historical Society, and the Academy of Motion Picture Arts and Sciences, Los Angeles.

I owe a special debt of gratitude to Mrs. Claire Giannini Hoffman, who talked with me about her father on numerous occasions and over many hours at her home in San Mateo. She was, characteristically, unflinchingly candid in her opinions, intelligent in her assessment of the events of her father's life, and generous with her time and energy.

Former Bank of America executives and directors under Giannini's leadership have dwindled to a small group. I am most grateful to those who agreed to be interviewed, including Jake Fischer, Angelo Scampini, Roland Pierotti, Russell Smith, Keith Carver, Francis Herwood, Harry M. Bardt, Joseph Garcia, Margaret Dickson, and the late Virgil Dardi.

For their suggestions in improving the manuscript, I am indebted to Robert Middlekauff, Robin Winks, and Dr. James Fisher. I also wish to thank Brian Sullivan and Steve Adams for interrupting their own work to send me some highly useful Giannini material.

My brother, the Reverend Joseph Bonadio, and the Sulpician Order at St. Patrick's Seminary, Menlo Park, provided me with a home away from home on my research trips to San Francisco. I am grateful to them for their generosity.

I wish to express my heartfelt gratitude to James Clark, director of the University of California Press, not only for his enthusiasm for the Giannini biography but also for his unfailing patience and wise counsel. He made all the frustrations endurable. I would also like to thank as well his associate, Valeurie Friedman, and Scott Norton, production editor at the University of California Press, who helped me greatly in a variety of ways during the final stage of the book's completion. Dan Gunter, who took on the task of copyeditor, was responsible for numerous valuable changes in the manuscript. I am extremely grateful to him for his professional advice.

I owe the profoundest debt of all to my wife, Betty, who saw me through the writing of this book, as she has seen me through our life together, with love, support, and encouragement.

Prologue

Early in the morning of October 15, 1969, blustery, rain-swollen clouds swept in unannounced from the horizon of San Francisco Bay, blotting out the calm, predawn sky. On the massive plaza at the intersection of California and Kearny Streets, in the heart of San Francisco's financial center, reporters and photographers huddled under umbrellas to witness the unveiling of the 200-ton black granite abstract by the Japanese sculpture Masayuku Nagare. Towering high above the plaza itself was Bank of America's handsome new headquarters, a dark-red fifty-two-story structure, the tallest west of the Rockies. Like the founder of the bank—Amadeo Peter Giannini, for whom the plaza was being dedicated that day—the building was bold, uncompromising, monumental.

Watching the dedication ceremonies through the ground-floor windows of Bank of America's football-field-length mezzanine stood a large gathering of the bank's senior executives, politicians, civic leaders, and invited guests. Among them was Claire Giannini Hoffman, Giannini's daughter, who had assumed her father's place on the board of directors after his death two decades earlier. She felt a special (some said nearly fanatical) obligation to keep her father's memory alive to a generation of Californians who hardly knew his name. At age sixty-three, her graying hair pulled back in a bun, she also bore a striking resemblance to him: the same heavy-lidded eyes, the same prominent cheekbones, the same aggressive chin.[1]

An unkind fate had dictated that the Giannini show of numbers at the dedication ceremony would be small. Only three of Giannini's eight children had survived to reach adulthood. Two of the remaining children—Virgil Thomas and Lawrence Mario, both hemophiliacs— had suffered severe complications and cast a shadow of collective sorrow on the family's life. Virgil, the younger of the two, thin, frail, and seriously crippled by the nightmarish effects of his illness, had held a number of minor positions in the bank, but grew weaker as the years passed. On September 24, 1938, at age thirty-eight, he slipped and fell in his apartment, hitting his head against the hard edge of a chair. Three days later he was dead.

The bright promise of the family had been Lawrence Mario. He was, Giannini had often remarked, "my trusted lieutenant, someone who can take over the bank when I am no longer around." Mario had graduated from the Hastings Law School at the University of California to emerge in the late 1920s as one of the nation's savviest investment bankers. Later he served as president of Transamerica Corporation, the giant bank holding company that his father had created in 1931; still later he was president of Bank of America. Despite the chronic pain in his body and the episodes of spontaneous bleeding that frequently put him in the hospital, Mario worked harder than any other of Giannini's executives, the possibility of a potentially fatal medical emergency never far from his thoughts. In March 1952, three years after his father's death, he was rushed to a San Francisco hospital. He never recovered.

In 1930 Claire had married Clifford "Biff" Hoffman, a star athlete at Stanford who had been named to the nation's All-American football team. Fearful of the genetic abnormality by which hemophilia is transmitted by the female from one generation to the next, she decided against having children. Her marriage to Biff Hoffman was marred by family acrimony. His casual habits and penchant for the locker-room camaraderie of other men did not mix well with her father's relentless ambition and seriousness of purpose. There were bitter arguments and lingering resentments. At fifty-three, his middle years spent in unrealized goals and alcoholism, Biff Hoffman too was dead.

Now, in 1969, Claire Hoffman had sat on Bank of America's board of directors for a decade and a half. Throughout this long period she had been acutely aware of her position as the lone survivor in a family diminished by so much death and tragedy, the solitary Giannini with a direct link to her father's vast financial creation. And this isolation had wearied her, tested her.

Only a handful of people at the dedication ceremony knew how close in recent months Claire Hoffman had come to resigning from the board. Bank of America's management and board of directors had not been in favor of the ceremony and, in fact, had opposed the idea of memorializing her father in so conspicuous a way. Her clash with the board had taken place at a directors' meeting six months earlier, when she urged that Bank of America's new headquarters building be named after her father as a monument to the man who had founded the bank at the turn of the century and had almost single-handedly directed its growth. But the men who were now managing the bank were of a very different sort and of a different generation from the handful of Italian immigrants and first-generation Italian Americans who were at its core in the beginning. With only one dissenting vote, Claire Hoffman's own, the board had rejected her proposal.[2]

This was not Claire Hoffman's first disagreement with the board, but it was clearly the most personal, involving as it did close family ties and obligations. Increasingly she had come to believe, rightly or wrongly, that Bank of America's chief executive officers were caught up in the frantic pursuit of personal ambition and growth for the sake of growth; because of their fixation on the world's financial markets, they had neglected the bank's small clients at the branch level in California. The board's rejection of her recommendation was another reminder to her of the great difference that had developed between the old Bank of America of her father and the new Bank of America of pin-striped executives for whom the "human touch" seemed outmoded and irrelevant.

Within days of the board meeting, letters and telegrams protesting the board's decision poured into San Francisco from prominent Italians throughout the state—politicians, business leaders, and professionals— as well as from a growing number of Italian organizations.[3] Bank of America executives were certain they knew who was behind the protest and who had made the outside world privy to the board's confidential deliberations. For weeks the battle raged on behind the scenes. Rudolph Peterson, Bank of America's suave, handsome, Swedish-born president, was particularly concerned. Peterson believed that it was only a matter of time before the controversy would be thrust into the full glare of the public, embarrassing the board and damaging the bank's reputation.

After months of recrimination and harsh words on both sides, the board eventually compromised. Bank of America's new corporate headquarters would be dedicated as Bank of America World Headquarters Building, while the plaza that seemed to serve as a giant pedestal for the building's marble facade would be named the A. P. Giannini Plaza.[4] Although many on the board were satisfied with the outcome of the controversy, the personal bitterness left a sour taste, increasing the tension that had developed over the years between Claire Hoffman and Bank of America's management.

The power struggle between Claire Giannini Hoffman and the board was in keeping with the life and career of the man who had founded the bank. Few figures in American business history generated as much controversy, fought as bitterly with their opposition, and made as many powerful enemies as did Amadeo Peter Giannini. To his critics he was a man obsessed with grandiose ambitions, an intimidating, hot-tempered financial maverick who brought to his branch banking operations in California a fierce competitive drive and the urge to dominate others. To his admirers he was a legendary figure—bold, imaginative, unorthodox, the classic underdog who seemed blessed with the Midas touch. His undisputed achievement was to bring the services of professional banking to millions of ordinary people. "He did for banking what Henry Ford did for the automobile," one industry observer said years later.[5]

The son of Italian immigrant parents, Giannini left school in 1885, at the age of fifteen, to become a clerk in his stepfather's produce firm on the San Francisco waterfront. At thirty-four he quit the produce business to open the Bank of Italy in the city's North Beach district—a "people's bank" he called it—which catered primarily to working-class Italians. Over the next half century, and in the face of powerful opposition, he roamed the cities and towns of California, buying more and more banks and converting them into branch offices. By the end of World War II his Bank of America branch banking empire had become the largest and richest privately owned financial institution in the world.

To many, this achievement seemed as predictable as it was extraordinary. No one who knew Giannini over the forty-five years he ran Bank of America ever doubted his single-minded purpose—to give California the biggest bank in the world, "whether California wanted it or not."[6] He was passionate about California, its people, climate, resources, energy, habits of mind, and economic future. Years later one close aide would remember traveling by car on a trip with Giannini and several Bank of America senior executive vice-presidents. The monotony of the long highway drive soon gave way to lazy conversation.

Sitting in the front seat of the car, silent and aloof from the others, Giannini twice interrupted with the comment, "You can't hold California back." Heads nodded in silent agreement and the conversation resumed. Several minutes later came the roar, "YOU CAN'T HOLD CALIFORNIA BACK." Everyone spent the remainder of the trip enthusiastically discussing Giannini's observation.[7]

The reach and power of Giannini's branch banking empire in California was extraordinary, beyond the comprehension of people living outside the state. "I still can't realize that in forty years a man has built something out here that compels the awe—that's the right word, awe—of all New York," said an East Coast financial writer on his first trip to San Francisco in the late 1940s.[8] With 504 branches and four million individual customers, Bank of America held the savings deposits of one out of every three Californians, or 40 percent of the state's total bank deposits. "The Gianninis have so much power," one industry observer remarked, "that they could start a depression throughout the West simply by going 'conservative'—that is calling in their loans and putting the bank's money in Treasury bonds."[9]

Giannini always remained the bank's most energetic booster. He would go to extremes to attract new depositors and to keep them as customers. He did this partly to reaffirm Bank of America's relentlessly promoted image as a "people's bank" and partly out of his own fierce competitive urge; there was no such thing as an unimportant customer. "When you sell people," he was fond of saying, "keep them sold."

As successful as Giannini was, nothing generated more public comment than his disregard for his own wealth. He saw no point in accumulating money or in surrounding himself with the signs of material success. The home in which he lived until the end of his life was the one he had purchased when he was selling fruits and vegetables on the San Francisco waterfront. The wardrobe of the man whom *Fortune* would include in its Hall of Fame of America's ten greatest businessmen consisted of four off-the-rack suits, three pairs of shoes, and a handful of shirts and ties. "My hardest job," he said on one occasion, "was to keep from becoming a millionaire."[10] When he died in 1949 at age seventy-nine, he left an estate valued at $489,278. Considering depreciation, that was less than he had been worth before he went into the banking business.

Although Giannini's name was associated with the concentration of enormous financial power, the Giannini family collectively owned less than one half of 1 percent of Transamerica's more than twenty million shares. His strength lay in the force of his personality and in the fierce loyalty of millions of small stockholders, among whom he had distributed the corporation's shares as widely as possible. "He had power without ownership," as Adolf Berle and Gardiner Means explained in *The Corporation and Private Property*.[11] He was one of the very first American businessmen to promote employee ownership and profit sharing. At the time of his death nearly 40 percent of Bank of America's shares were owned by its employees.

His personal honesty was beyond question. He refused to accept gifts from admirers or Bank of America clients. When Louis B. Mayer, head of Metro-Goldwyn-Mayer, sent Giannini's daughter a lifetime gold pass to the studio's productions, Giannini insisted she send it back. If, as occasionally happened, one of his executives used his financial transactions with a client to obtain gifts or favors, Giannini was quick to take action, regardless of how high the executive's position in the organization. "From the day of its original founding," Giannini told a reporter for the *Wall Street Journal,* "it has been an undeviating policy of Bank of America that no employee should seek to feather his own nest by taking advantage of his position or of any outside information; that no employee should engage in any outside financial interests which might get him into trouble."[12]

Giannini was fond of calling Bank of America employees his "boys and girls," and he demanded total loyalty from them. He also insisted that those who held positions of authority within the organization adhere to the same unbending ethical standards he imposed on himself. The bank's executives were prohibited from sitting on the boards of other major corporations and from having a financial interest in any outside business venture. Divorce was frowned upon; gambling and attendance at the horsetrack were forbidden. Only the most foolish would ever let it be known that they had a fondness for highballs and the glamour and excitement of San Francisco night life. At even a hint of impropriety, Giannini would hire private detectives to watch the alleged offender around the clock.

He was sensitive to his status as a member of an ethnic minority in a financial world dominated by the elite of the nation's Protestant establishment, symbolized at the time by Wall Street's most prestigious bank investment firm, J. P. Morgan and Company. He knew that they were contemptuous of his "retail bank" for the many, that they regarded him less as an equal among the nation's most powerful financiers than as a promoter and a schemer—a huckster. "We were wops and dagos," his daughter would remember.[13] Early in his banking career Giannini applied unsuccessfully for admission into San Francisco's exclusive Pacific Union Club on Nob Hill. The speculation inside Bank of America was that beneath his inexhaustible drive and monumental ambition smoldered a lifetime of resentments, which made him eager to push Bank of America into the position of a financial superpower, in a class by itself. His sense of persecution may also have sprung from his continual struggles as an innovative outsider in an industry not generally known for innovation.

A physically intimidating man, Giannini thrived on incessant controversy and enjoyed nothing so much as a good fight. The more powerful and well connected the opposition, the better he liked it. He could assault those whom he viewed as his enemies in language so violent as to frighten them into hiring personal bodyguards. He was obsessive about defending his branch banking empire in California against enemies, whom he located primarily in Washington and on Wall Street. In the face of threats, real or imaginary, he could not be satisfied with anything less than total victory. In the words of one critic, "Giannini [was] inclined to wars of extermination."

He could be immensely charming and self-effacing, a man without social pretensions who was at the same time supremely confident of his own abilities, with more than a touch of self-righteous arrogance. He had an intuitive sense about people, their vanities, ambitions, and vulnerabilities. He grew up not only with a powerful urge to succeed but with great skill as an observer of other's talents; he learned to recognize the personal weaknesses of other men and women, and he placed great emphasis on his ability to anticipate their behavior. Having decided on a course of action, he moved swiftly, so certain of the correctness of his actions that anyone who got in his way became the target of his fierce rage. "There are only two ways of doing things," he once told a prominent member of the New Deal, "the wrong way and my way." Asked by a reporter toward the end of his life if he had ever made a mistake, Giannini promptly answered "No."[14]

He was the archetype of the driven businessman. Aside from Sunday dinner with his family, he had no personal life outside the bank. His capacity for work was legendary. His day began at five in the morning and ended, as he liked to say, "in sleep."[15] Gifted with a remarkable memory and extraordinary powers of concentration, he could digest huge amounts of technical and financial information at breakneck speed. "He was a natural mathematician," one associate remembered. "He could figure swiftly and keep totals and percentages in his recollection, even though a balanced personal checkbook was beyond him. He could remember the balance sheet figures of scores of banks from year to year, even though he never knew how much money was in his bank account."[16]

Behind his desk, which he placed on the open floor of the bank, he was a figure of unremitting energy. He avoided the protective environment of a private office and a personal secretary, answered his own phone, and frequently saw as many as one hundred people in a single afternoon on a first-come, first-serve basis. His conversations with them were of necessity rapid-fire and to the point, none lasting more than a few minutes, all held within the hearing of other people. "You can't learn anything from a secretary," he once told a visiting reporter from New York. "The people who come to see me tell me what's going on. I figure I get at least five times more business done with personal contacts than I could handle by other methods."[17]

He surrounded himself with the best talent he could find and drove his executives to the limit. In return, he gave them a free hand in running their departments. "Come to me for advice, if that's what you want, but don't come to me for a decision," he would instruct them. "If a decision is involved, bring it with you." He had no patience with committees, organizational flow charts, and the mechanisms of corporate management. He delighted in tossing out unconventional ideas in the company of his executives, suspicious of those who seemed overly eager to agree with him. "Are you yessing me?" he would shout in a hoarse voice that some compared to the sound of a howitzer; he would then demand that his supporters explain why they thought he was right.[18] He could tolerate mistakes, but never lazy or careless mistakes. He did not easily forgive those whom he judged guilty of incompetence, and he would let them know of their deficiencies in devastatingly brutal language.

"I see nothing wrong with a man putting all his eggs in one basket," Giannini remarked on one occasion. "But watch that basket!" He did not just build a financial empire bigger, richer, and more powerful than any other. He slept, lived, and breathed the bank, which he referred to as "my baby." He cared more about the bank than anything else. "For God's sake, Amadeo," his wife complained over dinner one night, "can't you talk about something else?" When, in conversation with friends and associates, the talk turned to an entirely different subject, he grew visibly impatient. He knew what he wanted and he went after it, as he liked to say, "hammer and tongs." Rather than spend precious time shaving at home, he relied instead on a barbershop in downtown San Francisco. Sitting in a barber's chair, transacting business with two or three of his senior executives, he had found a more productive way to make use of the time.[19]

He was, above all else, a visionary whose raw force and empire-building megalomania made few allowances for the power and prominence of other men. Russell Smith, Bank of America's senior executive vice-president, would remember the time he was traveling with Giannini in Italy at the end of World War II. After viewing the devastation caused by the war, the two men were granted a twenty-minute audience with Pope Pius XII. "I think the Holy Father had been talking for five minutes when Giannini suddenly interrupted him, holding up a peremptory arm," Smith said. "'Pope, now you listen to my friend Russell.' He explained who I was and said I could tell him the truth about the situation in Italy and what should be done to restore people's confidence. At the end of twenty minutes I turned to A. P., told him our time had run out and that we must leave now. 'Never mind, Russ,' Giannini retorted, 'we've plenty of time,' . . . never hesitating to hand out personal advice to the Pontiff, whom he kept calling 'Pope.'"[20]

Bold, bombastic, irreverent, iconoclastic, controversial, ever on the lookout to expand Bank of America's power and influence—that was A. P. Giannini.

ONE

Waterfront Entrepreneur

I

Normally a blunt, outspoken man, given to great bouts of uninhibited conversation with friends and associates, A. P. Giannini seldom talked at any length about his childhood on the California frontier. On those few occasions when he did, however, he claimed that it had been one of the most decisive experiences in his life. "San Jose had a population of about fourteen thousand," he said toward the end of his life. "It was located in the Santa Clara Valley about fifty miles from San Francisco. Back in the days of the gold rush, it had been a pretty rough town. But then things settled down and families began moving in to buy land on which to farm. . . . I didn't care very much for farming, but it is sincere, honest work which is the best recipe for happiness I know."[1]

When Giannini's father, Luigi Giannini, settled in San Jose with his wife in the fall of 1869, it was with the hope of exchanging the poverty of his native Favale di Malvaro, a small mountain village high above the Ligurian coast thirty miles northeast of Genoa, for a new life of work and prosperity in the United States. Luigi Giannini had been to California six years earlier, part of a steady migration of Italian and other European immigrants to the gold fields north of San Francisco in search of riches. Like most of the others, he was soon disappointed; the work was hard and dangerous, life in the fields was lonely, and only the luckiest found enough gold to make their efforts worthwhile.[2]

While Luigi poured out his energies digging for gold, he began to notice another side to California that was much more familiar to him: its agricultural lands. On occasional trips away from the mines, he joined groups of other Italian immigrants who traveled throughout the surrounding region, eager to explore their new environment. Like them, he was fascinated by the resemblance between California and Italy: the sunny climate, the mountains, the blue waters of the Pacific. He was particularly attracted by the state's vast abundance of fertile land. He looked into the possibility of buying a farm just south of San Francisco and later told friends that California seemed an ideal place for a man to settle and raise a family.[3]

Late one evening in the spring of 1869, Luigi was sitting around a campfire beside two brothers and mining companions who had come from Chivaki, a mountain village near his own on the Ligurian coast. He listened carefully as they began reading the latest letter from home written by their youngest sister, Virginia DeMartini. Nearly three quarters of a century later, Virginia's older sister, Teresa, then the mother superior of a convent outside of Genoa, would remember what happened next.

"Luigi was a friend of my brothers," she wrote. "Being friendly they often discussed the news that came from Italy. Virginia's style of letter writing revealed her good qualities and energetic strength, so much so, that one fine day, without letting anyone know, Luigi left America and came to Italy with the intention of marrying Virginia. He left America with a double money belt, which he wore next to his skin, and which contained a large number of $20 gold pieces. During the trip through the Panamanian peninsula, he came down with the small pox but was able to keep the vest so well hidden that he succeeded in bringing it to Italy. The belt was later ripped [open] by us."[4]

Details are sparse, but Luigi's gold coins and obvious sincerity were apparently enough to convince Virginia's parents that he was a young man of considerable promise and ambition. Thus began a six-week courtship that ended when Luigi proposed marriage and Virginia accepted. They were married before a parish priest in Chivaki on August 10, 1869, a few months after Virginia's fifteenth birthday. Scores of relatives and neighbors attended the reception in the village square following the ceremony. "It was the most exciting celebration we had ever seen," Virginia's sister would remember. "Virginia wore a white hat to the wedding, a gift from Luigi from America. The hat attracted much attention among the wedding guests. They had never seen one before."[5]

A few weeks later Luigi and his wife took passage in a third-class cabin in a sailing ship bound for New York; he was taking her to a world she knew only from his enthusiastic and frequently repeated descriptions. This time they were able to avoid the overland route across the Isthmus of Panama, with its jungle, disease, and suffocating heat, traveling instead from New York to California over the nation's newly completed transcontinental railroad. Toward the end of September 1869 the couple arrived in San Jose, a frontier farm town of thirteen thousand on the southernmost tip of the San Francisco peninsula.[6]

San Jose, county seat of Santa Clara, had spent nearly a decade in the economic doldrums but was now in the midst of a vigorous comeback. Formerly the state capital, San Jose had lost much of its glamour after state legislators moved the capital to Sacramento and the gold rush ended. But thanks to a railroad connecting San Jose to San Francisco, it suddenly became a busy market center for the scores of smaller farm communities scattered throughout the rich and fertile Santa Clara Valley. On the outskirts of town, smoke billowed from a half-dozen or so flour mills, lumberyards, and meat-packing firms, which had sprung up to supply the needs of the local population. By the time the Gianninis moved into town, the economy was expanding and generating opportunity and San Jose was bustling with the presence of ten thousand new residents, most of whom had arrived in less than a single decade.[7]

Once in San Jose, Luigi concentrated on rebuilding his diminishing finances. He used the last of his savings to lease the Swiss Hotel, a two-story, white clapboard building on San Jose's dusty, crowded Market Street, the town's main thoroughfare. There, on May 6, 1870, seven months after their arrival in California, Virginia gave birth to the Gianninis' first son. He was christened Amadeo Peter Giannini.[8]

Word spread quickly that the Swiss Hotel had passed into new hands. Before long it became a boardinghouse for other Italian immigrants who worked in and around San Jose as sharecroppers, day laborers, or migrant workers. Most were young, single men, unable to speak the language of their new country, unfamiliar with its habits and cultural mores. Like Luigi, they had first traveled to California hoping to strike it rich in the mines. But they continued to come long after the gold was gone, because it seemed to be a place where ambitious, hard-working men might find success.[9]

According to several accounts, Luigi was something of a conspicuous figure among the thousands of transplanted, largely midwestern farmers who swarmed into San Jose in the decades after the gold rush.[10] Tall, handsome, broad-shouldered, with pale blue eyes and a dark handlebar mustache, he was remembered by neighbors many years later as a quiet man of few opinions and even fewer words. These traits undoubtedly had something to do with the racial prejudices of San Jose's Anglo-American residents, many of whom objected to the presence of foreigners. The Chinese were the town's most racially despised inhabitants and the frequent victims of punitive legislation and savage mob violence. But Italians also faced a good deal of hostility, and the local press went so far as to warn city officials about too large an increase in their numbers. Luigi undoubtedly knew better than to risk more than a brief conversation with anyone outside of his circle of Italian boarders at the Swiss Hotel.[11]

After spending two years as the proprietor of the Swiss, Luigi sold his lease on the hotel and purchased forty acres of orchard land in Alviso, a hamlet eight miles north of San Jose. Not long after the Gianninis settled on the farm, the family increased to four when, in July 1874, their second son, Attilio Henry, was born. Luigi, now an independent farmer with a wife and two young sons, energetically set about the task of raising his own fruits and vegetables and selling them to the growing number of commission firms in San Francisco. Over the next two years the family prospered, and Luigi began preparations to clear more land and plant more trees.

Then, on the afternoon of August 14, 1876, tragedy struck. Luigi was shot and killed by a transient farm worker, Jose Ferrari, who had acquired something of a reputation in San Jose as a moody, hot-tempered man eager to take offense. Luigi had hired Ferrari the week before to assist him in picking fruit from his orchard. A quarrel between the two men broke out when Ferrari collected his wages and complained that he had received two dollars less than he thought he had earned. One week later Ferrari returned to the Giannini farm armed with a shotgun, confronted Luigi a few yards from the front door of the home, and settled his grievance with violence. The facts about the disagreement between the two men were related to the police by Luigi Giannini himself, who regained consciousness long enough to name his assailant. Ferrari was apprehended outside of San Jose a few days later, convicted of murder, and sent to prison.[12]

With Luigi gone, the next two years were a grim time for the Giannini family. At the age of twenty-two, living in an isolated and not always hospitable community with two small children, Virginia was now obliged to assume all the daily responsibilities of the farm. To make matters worse, at the time of her husband's death Virginia was pregnant; George, the third of the Giannini sons, was born six months later. But through strenuous efforts she nevertheless managed to survive the tragedy of her husband's sudden and violent death. Neighbors were impressed by her courage and genial disposition in the face of adversity. "A remarkable woman," characteristically "unafraid and intelligent," one of them would remember.[13]

Occasionally Giannini accompanied his mother on her periodic trips to the San Francisco waterfront to sell fruits and vegetables. In those days such a journey required precarious navigation along the rocky shoals of the peninsula's coast.[14] Many years later John Leale, captain of the bay steamer *Reform*, left a vivid description of California's emerging coastal trade in farm commodities.[15] "It was always an adventure," Leale wrote. "Some of us would be checking off sacks of vegetables with marks scratched in the dirt with a stick. When the job was done, the steamer would take in its plank, back out into the slough, and go on to the next stop." Leale went on to remember the two Gianninis: a pleasant, attractive widowed woman and her small son sitting quietly together on the crowded deck of his boat as it moved through the cold, predawn darkness of the bay.[16]

In the summer of 1880 the family's prospects changed for the better when Virginia remarried. Lorenzo Scatena, a native of Genoa, had arrived in San Jose in the 1850s at the age of twelve. For the next ten years he found work hauling produce for local farmers and later for a commission firm on the San Francisco waterfront; it was there that he met Virginia. Scatena was an eager, conscientious worker and made a modest living, but at the time of his marriage to Virginia he was pushing thirty, still looking to find his niche.[17] Stocky, barrel-chested, with luminous large eyes and a ready smile, Scatena was a gentle, soft-spoken man who soon became the focus of immense admiration by Virginia's three children. "Pretty soon we were calling him 'Pop' or 'Boss,'" Giannini would recall, "bestowing on him a nickname which his friends used until the end of his days."[18]

When Giannini was old enough, he attended a one-room schoolhouse in Alviso. His classmates were the children of the town's polyglot

immigrant population, and he remembered the experience with pleasure in later years. "I studied with children of many nationalities," he
said, "Portuguese, French, German, Armenian, Spanish, Japanese, and
Americans. Unable to pronounce my Italian name, they called me
'Amador Jenning.' I had a good time at school, learning as quickly as
any of the pupils and establishing friendships which endured through
life."[19]

If things seemed to come easily at school to young Giannini, they
did not come so easily to his stepfather on the farm. For a time Scatena
was successful, but for reasons he never made clear later in life, it didn't
last. It may well have been the consequence of the "terrible seventies"—
the farmer's bitter description of California's five-year-long drought in
that decade. Many growers in the region were bankrupted by the
devastating drought.[20] In addition, by 1882 the family had increased to
seven with the birth of two Scatena children, placing an additional
financial strain on the family's modest budget. Whatever the reason,
Lorenzo decided to abandon the Alviso farm, taking Virginia and the
children back to San Jose. Once again he resumed the kind of work he
knew best: hauling produce.

But Virginia had other ideas. "She was a shrewd judge of people and
places and had bright plans for the family," one close friend would
remember.[21] On her business trips to San Francisco she had taken a keen
interest in the activities of the city's hard-bargaining commission merchants. Like her, most of these merchants were immigrants: Italians,
Greeks, Russians, and other Europeans, whose wholesale firms stood
jammed next to one another along the wooden piers that jutted out like
giant fingers into the waters of the San Francisco Bay.[22] They were the
middlemen of California's rapidly developing production of agricultural commodities, paying farmers for goods shipped to San Francisco
and then reselling them to the city's proliferating neighborhood groceries, restaurants, street markets, and pushcart peddlers. It was a
tough, brutally competitive business, but the profits from the commission trade were far greater than could ever be realized from farming.[23]

Scatena was reluctant to try his hand as a commission clerk, but
Virginia persisted in her efforts. Finally, toward the end of 1882, Scatena
returned home one night and announced that he had taken a job with
A. Galli and Company, one of the largest and most influential commission firms on the San Francisco waterfront. After selling the Alviso
farm, Scatena moved the family into a rented house on Jackson Street,

near the waterfront and only a few blocks from the city's infamous Barbary Coast district.[24]

2

    Scatena plunged into his duties as a commission clerk for the Galli firm, working sixteen hours a day from midnight until early the next afternoon. Only when the last shipment of produce had been unloaded and the last crate sold did he return home for a hot meal and sleep. "Those were the days when it was necessary for us to get to work early to buy, sell, and handle our produce," he later remembered. "If we did not get down there early we could not sell, and we would have lost the produce we had bought. We left home at midnight. One A.M. was a late hour—often too late—to show up on the docks."[25]

Although the hours were long and the work backbreaking, Scatena brought considerable talent to the wholesale trade in produce. Soon he was earning more than his share of profits for the Galli firm, which, in recognition of his dedication and competitive skills, increased his salary from $100 to $250 a month. "Ask for $300," Virginia urged him over his customary "breakfast" late one night. "Your services are now worth much more than that."[26]

Scatena asked for the increase and disappointedly heard his boss refuse. He was, he was told, being paid salary enough for a relatively new man in the firm. "Quit your job," Virginia replied when she heard the news. "Open your own wholesale house. You can make more money working for yourself." A few weeks later the firm of L. Scatena and Company opened for business in a rented wooden shed on Davis and Washington Streets, about four blocks from the waterfront. Virginia's prophecy was fulfilled. By the end of his first month in business, Scatena had earned $1,500.[27]

Encouraged by his success, Scatena moved his family into the noisy, congested bustle of the city's North Beach district, then one of the nation's largest communities of Italians. They settled into a two-story, brown-shingled house at 411 Green Street, along the southern base of Telegraph Hill, where Giannini shared a bed with his younger brother Attilio. Though similar to the cluster of ramshackle, weathered frame buildings that crept up the unpaved streets of the hill's steep slope, the home boasted a spacious bay window. Many years later Giannini recalled with pride the meaning of that bay window to San Francisco residents, "old or new, Nob Hill or North Beach": it was an outward sign of personal achievement and prosperity.[28]

Spreading down from Telegraph Hill to the narrow strip of valley below and then out toward the waterfront, North Beach was one square mile of groceries, butcher shops, commercial buildings, sidewalk cafés, and crowded streets. During the gold rush era, it had been home for the Irish, Germans, and French who settled around the slopes of the hill. But in the early 1860s a steady stream of Italians began moving into the district, attracted by its cheap rents, access to the vast waters of the bay, and isolation from the rest of the city. A sizable number were itinerant merchants and former miners who had gravitated to the city in the years following the gold rush, but a great many more were recent immigrants who had come directly from Italy.[29]

At the time the Gianninis moved into the district, North Beach's Italian population had increased to nearly ten thousand, and thousands more were arriving each year. The great majority were from northern Italy—Tuscany, Piedmont, Liguria—but a considerable number were Sicilians with names like Alioto and Tarantino. They worked as laborers, stonemasons, shoemakers, fishermen, longshoremen, pushcart peddlers, or shopkeepers; some, like Scatena, sold produce. Most of them lived in small fishing shacks and red-tiled cottages along narrow cobblestone streets that staggered down from Telegraph Hill in row upon row. To outsiders, North Beach resembled nothing so much as a colorful Mediterranean seaside village.[30] But to the Italians who lived there, it was *un piccolo canto della patria*: "a small corner of the mother country."[31]

In North Beach, Giannini resumed his education at the Washington Street Grammar School. He was a good student and excelled in spelling and penmanship. He was remembered by his teachers as a friendly and serious-minded boy with a conspicuous streak of stubborn independence; he avoided the temptations of schoolyard pranks and displayed a nearly obsessive determination to be at the top of his class. In later years, reminiscing with associates, Giannini used to smile with satisfaction when describing his "running battles" with other students "to uphold the honors of the class."[32]

Giannini's grades at school were as surprising to his parents as they were welcome. He seemed far more interested in promoting his step-father's business than he was in his own promotion at school. On one occasion Lorenzo came home from work with the happy news that he was suddenly receiving orders from growers whose business he had not solicited. He was at a loss to explain it until an employee furnished him with the reason. Though only twelve, Giannini had been spending his afternoons away from school hunched over his stepfather's desk on the docks, writing neat, exuberant sales pitches about the advantages of doing business with the firm. Growers within a wide radius of San Francisco had received letters promising "honest prices on the barrel-head and quick service" if they dealt exclusively with the firm of L. Scatena and Company. It was the first time anyone had ever solicited their business directly by mail, and they had responded to the novelty.[33]

Soon Giannini began turning up on the waterfront late at night during the peak hours of business. Such behavior naturally worried his mother. Aside from the threat to his health and the hazards of the docks, the waterfront was not an environment likely to encourage an interest in a good education, which she wanted for her children. Despite his mother's objections, Giannini persisted. "I used to carry my shoes till I got out of the house and down on the sidewalk, and put them on there, so I wouldn't worry her," he told an interviewer years later. "When the drays came by I would jump on and ride down to the commission district. I went from work to school, and got along all right."[34]

The commission docks were crowded and noisy, worked by men— Italians, Jews, Greeks, Armenians, Syrians, Portuguese—who cursed and shouted in their multifarious languages to outbid the others for the huge sacks of produce carried by paddle-wheel steamers from river ports north of San Francisco. Giannini later claimed that these nightly transactions deepened his addiction to business.[35] He enjoyed watching the rough give-and-take among rival merchants, which he later said taught him a good deal about the art of survival in the world of commerce. "The old waterfront commission business was a pretty stiff school for men," he remembered. "I used to study them down there and I suppose I picked up the knack of sizing up men."[36]

One day late in the spring of 1885, Giannini came home from the docks and announced that he had decided to leave school. Despite all of Virginia's hopes for her son's education, she realized he had made up his mind. To soften the blow to her expectations for him, Giannini enrolled in a three-month course in accounting at Herald's Business School in downtown San Francisco. Too impatient to attend the full three months, he petitioned for an early examination after six weeks, passed it, and joined his stepfather's commission firm on the waterfront. "It was ambition, I guess," Giannini later said of his decision to leave school. "I wanted to get ahead. That was the kind of work I wanted to do. There wasn't any sense in putting it off."[37]

The commission trade in which Giannini entered was no place for those unable to withstand the daily struggle of fierce competition. Its prerequisites were an unerring sense for favorable prices and the ability to make rapid decisions. When word got out that a bay steamer loaded with produce was entering the harbor, a crowd of wholesalers would gather near the end of the wharf. Under the smoky glow of oil lamps, the bidding and buying at these late night auctions was loud and frenzied. At stake was a wholesaler's survival. If he bought at prices either too high or too low, it could mean a serious loss of money as well as the loss of an opportunity to gain on his competitors. Later, when selling his produce to the city's retail merchants or restaurants, the wholesaler engaged in a second round of intense negotiations over prices. The commission trade in produce, in short, made success a combination of hard work and talent and a willingness to gamble.[38]

As it turned out, Giannini had all three. Along with shrewd negotiating skills, he seemed to possess an uncanny ability to come up with the right prices to ensure that his stepfather's warehouse of perishable goods would be empty by the time the last buyer had left the waterfront. "He never had a carryover," Scatena would recall years later.[39] These impressive talents, along with an unrelenting drive and seemingly inexhaustible energy, combined to make him an extremely formidable competitor. "I don't think he ever lost an account or a contest of any kind," one rival merchant would remember. "No one could bluff, intimidate, or out-general him. In those price wars, he had an extraordinary faculty for gauging just how long the other fellow could stand the gaff. No such salesman was ever known on the waterfront."[40]

Giannini was at work by eleven every night, rubbing shoulders with some of the toughest and sharpest operators on the San Francisco waterfront. The noise, the long hours, the bitter and sometimes bloody rivalries—the commission trade in produce appeared calculated to test the energy and spirit of men who worked in it. Giannini, however, seemed to thrive in its unrestrained atmosphere of incessant activity and entrepreneurial warfare. Gradually he earned the reputation as a bright, savvy, enormously aggressive young man who could more than hold his own. "Young Scatena," his competitors began calling him, but more commonly "A. P.," a nickname that would stay with him for the rest of his life.[41]

At sixteen Giannini was also growing into a commanding physical presence: six feet two and a half inches tall, powerfully built, with thick black hair and dark, penetrating eyes set deep in a large, ruddy face. George Webster, a rival wholesaler of his acquaintance, admired his friend's drive and resourcefulness. But what impressed Webster even more was Giannini's cool—some would say excessive—self-assurance and remarkable powers of persuasion. "There was something about his self confidence . . . that had us licked before we started fighting," Webster later recalled. "I've seen men go up to him, after having rehearsed to themselves why they should buy beans at 3 cents a pound under his price; but before the story ever stumbled past their lips they would be signing their names to an order at his figure—which was probably a perfectly fair one."[42]

Giannini was fond of telling people later in life that he had no patience with leisure pursuits or social occasions of any kind. Both activities, he liked to say, were "a damn waste of time." But he enjoyed the company of others and was sometimes described as a "mixer . . . a talented and fascinating individual who could be quite charming when he wanted to be."[43] Already, too, there was a good deal of the glad-handing, self-effacing gregariousness about him that would later make him a popular figure to millions. In the end, however, it was business that consumed nearly the whole of his life. "I kept working hard and not paying attention to anything else like hanging around with the boys and going to parties and dances," he would remember. "I decided what I wanted and then went after it hammer and tongs."[44]

Giannini already knew the kind of men he wanted to meet. They were the farmers whose success or failure in cultivating their vast acres of fruits and vegetables was so closely tied to the firm's profits. On horseback, away from the waterfront, he traveled from farmhouse to farmhouse throughout the surrounding countryside to talk with growers about their plans for the upcoming season, about soil and weather conditions, or just about anything else they thought might affect the market. "His curiosity about local conditions was insatiable," an associate later commented. "He never tired of stopping strangers in remote farm towns to ask them question after question, until he was satisfied he knew almost as much about the economic life of the community as they did."[45]

With each year L. Scatena and Company grew more prosperous. Net profits by the end of Giannini's first year with the firm were

$10,000, and they climbed to $15,000 the following year. Largely because of his stepson's efforts, Scatena was forced to move his operations to larger quarters and, still later, into larger facilities at 300 Washington Street, the heart of the city's smelly, congested produce district. This kind of progress, however, did not satisfy Giannini. If anything, he worked even more frantically, impatient for greater profits, more customers, and a larger share of the market. Most of all, as he told friends, he longed for the freedom to move about on his own and to take bigger risks.[46] One family member later said that he was enormously "impatient, . . . high-strung and crazy with ideas. I felt he had a new idea every time he moved."[47]

In the summer of 1887, when Giannini was seventeen, he found the opportunity. Certain that there would be a shortage of pears in the fall harvest, he persuaded Scatena to entrust him on a buying trip to the Sacramento Valley, north of San Francisco. Saying nothing about his intentions to his stepfather, he signed consignment orders with growers for all the pears he could find. The stakes were high, but just as he had anticipated, there was a shortage of pears and the price climbed to more than twice its expected value. "It was a big gamble," Giannini later remembered, "but I guessed right. I made $50,000 for the Scatena firm with that deal. For weeks, everybody in North Beach talked about it."[48]

Giannini would later claim that his stepfather was so impressed by his coup that he gave him the responsibility for purchasing all of the firm's produce from growers in the Sacramento Valley. Although this comment is plausible, a more likely explanation is that Scatena's decision was based on his growing awareness that in his stepson he had an enormously ambitious salesman of considerable talent and determination whose need to play a more decisive role in the affairs of the firm had to be satisfied. Giannini accepted the responsibility bursting with ambition. "I had my own ideas how a commission house should be run," he would remember. "The ideas were different from those of others in the trade. Mine were sound and they won. Besides, I backed them to win."[49]

3

During the years he spent on the road for the Scatena firm, Giannini drove himself mercilessly. Salesman by day and into the night, he would set out from boarding homes before sunrise, crisscrossing the vast, rolling sweep of the Sacramento Valley on horseback in a tireless pursuit of business. "I used to take a loaf of bread and a big Italian cheese along with me for my lunch and supper," he later remembered. "I never aimed to arrive at a place when they were having meals. It would have meant a serious loss of time." No sooner had he succeeded in hammering out an agreement than he was off again, heedless of invitations to rest and exchange gossip. As he later explained, "I wasn't a bit interested in anything whatsoever not connected with my business. I had an object in view, and I went after that object just as straight as I could."[50]

Soliciting consignment orders from valley farmers was no easy matter. The Sacramento River itself was a challenge. Running south from the snowcapped peaks of the Sierra Nevada, the river cut a muddy, tortuous, two hundred mile long path through the wide valleys expanding below. On the succession of "islands" that ran nearly the length of the Sacramento, ranches of pears, plums, cantaloupes, corn, turnips, potatoes, and sugar beets could be found wherever one looked, each protected from high waters by irrigation ditches and thick dikes. River steamers, their stacks belching smoke, zigzagged across the river picking up produce from the various ranch landings. That a place could be so rugged yet so fertile struck visitors as a miracle of nature.[51]

Given the ruggedness of the land, travel from one valley town to the next was difficult and often dangerous. But the real threat, as Giannini later recalled, came from other consignment merchants. They were tough, violent men who had few illusions about their work and the hard-nosed methods it took to survive in it. Inevitably, more than a few of them resented the intrusion of a newcomer, especially one so young and aggressive who seemed to thrive on competition and possessed an ambition greater than their own. Stories were told of insults, threats, and occasional bloody fights on remote country roads. Giannini refused to deny or confirm these stories later in life, saying only that he "never let anyone intimidate me."[52]

Giannini prided himself on his incessant work habits, which he defended with one of his frequently repeated aphorisms, "Be first in everything."[53] Once, on horseback to solicit a consignment order from one of the valley's biggest growers, he suddenly spotted a competitor's team in the distance headed in the same direction. Remembering a deep slough that stood between him and the farm, he quickly cut across the field, tethered his horse to a tree, and swam to the other side. Then he ran the rest of the way to the farmhouse. By the time the other merchant had arrived, Giannini was negotiating a deal with the grower.[54] "He never let anyone take a customer away from him if he could help it," one competitor recalled. "Salesmanship of that sort just gets under your skin."[55]

Because farmers had little or no control over the marketing of their goods, they were often exploited. The commission trade had more than its share of con men and swindlers who either refused to honor their contracts or to send farmers all the money their crops had earned in San Francisco.[56] In sharp contrast to these practices, Giannini quickly established a remarkable reputation for personal integrity and honest business practices. Instead of keeping farmers in the dark about prices, he would bring along a list of prices for produce in San Francisco. Although his own prices were firm, they invariably reflected fair market value. Moreover, farmers always got their earnings in cash and on time.[57]

Besides his integrity, Giannini was also famous for his remarkable memory for names, dates, and faces, even after the passage of many years. On one occasion toward the end of his life, a customer from his commission days walked up to Giannini at an airport, thrust out his hand, and started to introduce himself. Before he could get his words out, Giannini called out his name and then proceeded to recite the names of his wife and three children. He had a similar talent with numbers. This astonishing ability for nearly total recall convinced many who came into contact with him that Giannini was a genius.[58]

By 1891 the Scatena firm was earning an annual net profit of over $100,000, most of which was the result of new business Giannini had brought to the firm. Before the year was out, Scatena had made him a partner. The partnership opened up new vistas for Giannini: outside the Sacramento and San Joaquin Valleys were the fertile valleys of the Salinas and the Santa Clara. Below the Tehachapi, the great range of mountains that split the state into its northern and southern halves, the soil was just as rich, if not richer, in farm communities like Santa Barbara, Los Angeles, and San Diego. No waterfront merchant had ever ventured much beyond a two-hundred-mile radius of San Francisco to purchase produce directly from farmers, but Giannini was eager to conquer new territories.[59]

At twenty-two Giannini had won a reputation that was beginning to spread beyond the confines of the waterfront. On the morning of January 1, 1892, a friend of Giannini's mother was standing inside the front window of her home when she suddenly spotted Giannini passing by on the street below. He was wearing a top hat, gloves, and a Prince Albert coat. His walking stick and neatly trimmed handlebar mustache added to the impressiveness of his appearance. Watching him as he made his way on the traditional round of New Year's Day visits, as she later recalled, there was no doubt in her mind that she was looking at the "handsomest man in North Beach" and a young man with a very bright future.[60]

One holiday call Giannini undoubtedly made that New Year's Day was at the Bay Street home of Clorinda Agnes Cuneo. She was both attractive and gifted, a small, graceful, demure woman with large brown eyes and a warm, expressive smile, well known in North Beach social circles as a talented vocalist. At twenty-two, the same age as Giannini, Clorinda was the youngest of the fourteen children of Joseph Cuneo, whose climb from itinerant miner to highly successful businessman made him something of a local exemplar of the American dream of success. After spending ten years in the gold fields, in the 1860s Cuneo gravitated to North Beach, where he opened a grocery. Cuneo could neither read nor write, but he could recognize an opportunity when he saw it. With the profits from his neighborhood business, he began investing in real estate—apartments, vacant lots, commercial buildings. Eventually he acquired more than a hundred pieces of property, which residents said made him the richest man in North Beach.[61]

Giannini told an interviewer later in life that he saw Clorinda one Sunday morning at mass where she sang in the choir and immediately "made up his mind he would never marry any other woman." As far as is known, she was Giannini's first infatuation, and his romantic pursuit of her turned out to have more than its share of difficulties. His nightly routine on the waterfront hampered his courtship, as did the fact that Clorinda was engaged to another man. Her fiancé, a North Beach resident and recent medical school graduate, was in Germany doing postgraduate work in the field of childhood diseases. They had made plans to marry as soon as he returned to San Francisco.[62]

Undeterred, Giannini spent the next six months wooing Clorinda with relentless determination. Her engagement was, in fact, a "challenge," as he later described it, which he set about to overcome with much the same single-minded intensity that accompanied his pursuit of business in the Sacramento. "My courting days were strenuous affairs," Giannini later remembered. "I used to dress up mighty fancy and have never dressed up as fancy since. Many a time I went home after leaving her after a dance and changed to go to work—in those days we wore black formal clothes, long tails and all. But she was engaged to a doctor who went to Europe, and the big job I had then was to get her away from him."[63]

According to some family members, Clorinda was not immediately attracted to him, but she was fascinated by his harried charm and by the great force of his personality. He was, she later said, unassuming and sentimental, yet excessively ambitious and supremely confident of his own power and abilities, a man who seemed destined to achieve considerable success. Eventually she succumbed to his persistent pursuit and expressions of love. Silencing the gossip that was making the rounds in North Beach community circles about the romantic "triangle" that had now developed, she broke off the engagement to her fiancé that summer and agreed to marry Giannini.[64]

They were married on September 12, 1892, in Old St. Mary's Church, the handsome, stately, red-brick parish church of the Paulist fathers in San Francisco. After the wedding the couple attended a reception given by family members at Clorinda's home in North Beach and then boarded a train later that same day for a two-week honeymoon to Carmel, an idyllic retreat of white beaches and pine-covered slopes along the Monterey peninsula.

TWO

A New Career

I

Early in the fall of 1892 the Gianninis moved into a comfortably furnished brownstone just a few miles beyond North Beach. Not long after, they took up residence in a Victorian-style frame house at 1022 Green Street near the crest of Russian Hill, only a short distance from the waterfront. Following the custom on both sides of the young couple's family, the home soon began filling up with children. A son, Amadeo Peter Giannini, Jr., was born in the first year of the Gianninis' marriage. Then came, at intervals of two years, Lloyd Thomas, Lawrence Mario, two other children who died in infancy, and Agnes Rose.[1] Another son and daughter, Virgil David and Claire Evelyn, were to come later.

California's booming economy in agricultural production did not give Giannini much time for family matters. In the 1890s the state began the most astonishing record of agricultural production in the nation's history. In the 1880s the first carload of California grapefruit reached New York. Refrigeration and rail connections to the East Coast made possible the transcontinental shipment of perishable goods. Eastern markets were hungry for the extraordinary variety of the state's specialty crops. The bonanza was, as one local historian put it, "the gold rush relived."[2]

Excited by the new opportunities to increase business, Giannini seemed to be everywhere at once. He bought tomatoes in Decanto, apples and strawberries in Watsonville, peppers, lettuce, and artichokes in Santa Cruz. Before long he was venturing into remote farm communities south of the Tehachapi. One day a shipment of oranges arrived at the L. Scatena and Company warehouse in San Francisco. They had come from two growers who gave as their address Beverly Hills, then a dusty, sleepy farm town with fewer than five hundred inhabitants.[3]

As Giannini moved into the small, predominantly Protestant farm towns of southern California, the competition got rougher. His presence aroused a good deal of resentment among local wholesalers who were not accustomed to losing business to an outsider. The wholesale trade in most rural communities in those days was in fact controlled by two or three local merchants whose price-fixing arrangements and other noncompetitive practices operated to the disadvantage of farmers. Rumors soon began to circulate that Giannini was a foreigner and an agent of the pope. Other stories had it that he was a member of the Mafia and had close personal ties with mobsters outside the state. Giannini was aware of these efforts to discredit him but made it a practice to say nothing publicly about them.[4]

The methods Giannini used to break these small, local monopolies anticipated those he would later use to expand his branch banking system throughout the state. Instead of scattering his efforts, he preferred to concentrate on one or two large growers, offering them higher prices, faster results, and superior services. Once the grower had switched his business to L. Scatena and Company, Giannini made it a special point to deliver on what he had promised. As news of his dependability and better prices got out, more and more farmers began to consider the advantages of doing business with the Scatena firm instead of maintaining their attachment to the local wholesaler. By the end of the decade Giannini's reputation was building him a large and enthusiastic following among hundreds of growers in the southern half of the state.

Giannini's dedication and aggressiveness in attracting new customers paid off. By 1899 L. Scatena and Company had become the largest wholesale firm in produce on the San Francisco waterfront and was prospering as never before. "Profits were being made that until then were unheard of in the commission business," one rival merchant later recalled. "New employees were hired, many of whom were former competitors who had sold out to join the Scatena firm." In a business that was as tough, risky, and furiously competitive as any around, Giannini was "king of the San Francisco waterfront."[5]

On the waterfront and in North Beach commercial circles, the spectacular rise of the Scatena firm earned Giannini a good deal of attention. Within the larger North Beach community, however, only a relatively small number of people had heard of him. He had only occasionally spent time in its busy, densely populated neighborhoods, and even then, according to his own admission, he visited simply to transact business with the firm's ever-increasing number of retailers and street market clients. "Outside of the business in which he was engaged," one San Francisco reporter later commented, "he was practically unknown."[6]

All that began to change in the early fall of 1899, when Dr. Louis Bacigalupi, a prominent North Beach physician and San Francisco councilman, asked Giannini for his help in a grass-roots political movement that was beginning to take shape in the city. Giannini agreed, stepping out of the shadows of the city's influential but socially restricted world of wholesale entrepreneurs for the first time in his career. Before the year was over, almost everyone in North Beach would know the identity of one of the community's youngest *prominenti* and the waterfront's most successful commission merchant.[7]

2

By the turn of the century, San Francisco had the unenviable reputation of being the most "corrupt city in the nation," the result in large part of some twenty years of boss rule by Christopher "Christ Himself" Buckley. A shrewd, dapper, scrappy, Irish saloonkeeper, Buckley, blind since his early thirties, had settled in San Francisco in the 1860s with a powerful urge to run its politics like "a small family business."[8] He succeeded in putting together the most powerful political machine in the city's history. From the regular Democratic organization to the city council to the courthouse and fire and police departments, Buckley and his allies enjoyed all the rewards and privileges of municipal "bossism," and the influence of his power was felt everywhere.[9]

Giannini's own congressional district had little to offer its predominantly Italian voters besides its reputation as a pocket borough that had never once challenged the power of the Buckley machine.[10] For years it had been run by two of Buckley's closest cronies, George Maxwell, who sat on the city's fire commission, and George Ryan, a one-time prize-fighter now turned deputy sheriff. Aided by a retinue of bodyguards, both men used a combination of corruption and physical intimidation to ensure a healthy majority in the district for Buckley's candidates. Given this situation, most North Beach voters ignored political issues entirely and simply stayed away from the polls, a development that only enhanced Buckley's control.[11]

In the fall of 1899, however, Buckley faced a serious challenge to his power. James Phelan, a young, civic-minded millionaire businessman who had been elected mayor of San Francisco three years earlier as a reform Democrat, wanted to broaden the base of his support and make efficient municipal government an important force throughout the city.[12] He saw his opportunity in a bipartisan proposal for a revised city charter, which would increase the power of the mayor's office and diminish the ability of Buckley's lieutenants to "deliver" the vote of their districts. Phelan opened his "good government" campaign by calling on businessmen and concerned citizens from all over the city to help win approval of the new city charter in the upcoming municipal elections and bring centralized authority and "civic efficiency to San Francisco."[13]

Giannini later recalled that he joined Phelan's "good government" campaign in part because he was restless and in part because he saw an opportunity to rid North Beach of Buckley's political influence. "October and November were quiet months in the commission business," he said. "I got into politics because of a desire to help Phelan. It was a diversion. I had lots of energy and this gave me an outlet."[14] Others sensed, however, that Giannini's decision to enter the campaign was not altogether as casual as he liked to claim: he was, in their estimation, a man of considerable ambition and egoism who possessed a strong desire for wider public acclaim.

Within days of joining Phelan's campaign, Giannini had rented the upper floor of a three-story building near the base of Telegraph Hill. Huge green-and-white signs announcing the headquarters of North Beach's "reform Democrats" hung from the sides of the building. Giannini now spent nearly all of his time in meetings with local officials and volunteers, organizing rallies in support of the party's delegates to the upcoming county convention. Energized by his obvious abilities for leadership and organization, voters were soon flocking to his office from all over the district. As one party worker recalled, "He had a psychological something. Whatever it was, he could look a man in the eye and convince him that almost anything was possible."[15]

Weeks went by in almost continuous speechmaking as Giannini toured the district with the party's candidates, a task he performed with obvious enthusiasm. As he had demonstrated in the commission trade, his particular skill was in mobilizing a personal following. "We were selling good government," he later remembered. "I wanted the candidates to meet the voters and to convince them the same way a businessman does to buy goods."[16] Giannini would first deliver a speech in Italian and then introduce voters to the candidates amid plenty of handshaking and backslapping. "We discussed the issues," one reform candidate later commented, "but Giannini was chiefly interested in getting us to shake hands and to know the voters face to face."[17]

Angered by Giannini's apparent success in organizing North Beach voters behind Phelan's candidacy, Buckley's forces responded with well-publicized threats of physical violence against voters who turned out at the polls on election day. Giannini immediately hired seventy-five wagons with his own money and recruited a small force of men armed with rifles. He personally escorted the wagons carrying voters to the polls. Other "Giannini guards"—as the San Francisco press promptly dubbed them—patrolled the district's streets and polling places. As one North Beach reform Democrat would recall, "Giannini made sure there would be no danger of a count out."[18]

The results of the election stunned the district. All of the Democratic party's "good government" delegates were elected by majorities of six to one. The final indignity for the Buckley forces came one week later at the county convention. By the end of the evening the crowds of sweating, yelling delegates packed into North Beach's Native Sons Hall had endorsed all of the party's reform candidates in the upcoming municipal elections.[19]

After the election Giannini demonstrated just how well he had learned the art of successful salesmanship. He went back over the district to personally thank voters for their support and to make certain they understood how important their participation had been in the party's victory. "I passed out more cigars after the election than before," he would remember. "We exhibited friendliness when we were seeking nothing. The result was that when election time came around next time we were remembered. When you sell people keep them sold. That applies to politics as well as business."[20]

Despite the heavy cost in time and energy, Giannini's involvement in the campaign had positive repercussions for him personally. He had shown himself willing to take bold action in challenging the power of the Buckley machine, even at some risk to his own safety. He had succeeded, as Phelan later remarked, in appealing to and uniting the core interests of the district's fragmented base of voters. And he had elicited from North Beach's Italian residents the same admiration for his charm, savvy, and raw energy that he had been receiving from his competitors in the commission trade for years.

As Giannini's reputation increased, so did the size of his family. Two months after he resumed his work on the waterfront, Clorinda gave birth to the Gianninis' fifth child in their eight years of marriage, a boy christened Virgil David. Giannini was well on his way to becoming a financially comfortable man and a respected civic leader, and his friends and relatives looked with admiration not only at his business success but also at his obvious good fortune in his marriage and succession of children.[21]

Late in 1900, however, Giannini shocked his friends by announcing that the time had come for him to get out of the wholesale business and to try something new.[22] He later claimed that his decision was prompted by boredom with the routine duties of a career that had lost its excitement and ceased being a challenge to him personally. "Our firm had absorbed or driven out of business all of the big commission houses," he said. "I suppose that's why I quit the produce business. There wasn't anyone around to fight me anymore."[23]

Although Giannini was far from being wealthy, he could certainly afford to indulge his appetite for a change. His shares in the firm were valued at $200,000, and he owned several pieces of property in and around San Francisco. Overall, he valued his net worth at approximately $300,000, much more than he needed to support his family until he broke into a new line of work. A few months later Giannini invested $20,000 in a handsome two-story, wood and brick Tudor-style house in San Mateo, a quiet suburban community on the peninsula about fifteen miles south of San Francisco. One of the most charming features of the property was a thick grove of oak trees that stood near the entrance to the house, which prompted the Gianninis to christen their new home "Seven Oaks."[24]

After selling his shares in the Scatena firm to a handful of its employees, Giannini decided to plunge into the precarious but potentially lucrative world of San Francisco real estate. He had taken an interest in the real estate market during his years in the commission trade, and with property values in the city climbing, he considered the possibility of opening his own office. To learn more about the business, Giannini rented a desk at Madison and Burke, one of the city's oldest and most respected real estate firms. Then, in the summer of 1902, six months into his work at Madison and Burke, Giannini's career took another sudden turn, one that would change his life forever.[25]

3

In June 1902, at the age of ninety-one, Giannini's father-in-law died. Joseph Cuneo left no will behind, but he did leave a widow, eleven children, and an estate valued at approximately $1 million.[26] Cuneo's immediate heirs could have simply divided the money among themselves and gone their separate ways. Instead, they decided to keep their father's estate intact and to place its management in Giannini's hands for a period of ten years. Since Cuneo had grown sons, nearly all of them in business for themselves, this decision seemed to some outsiders like an odd arrangement. But Giannini's sharp intelligence and seemingly unlimited knack for making money convinced Cuneo's widow that in time he could turn the value of the estate into something much bigger.[27]

Giannini accepted the job. He had more than one hundred separate pieces of property to look after, and he promptly began the process of updating their value.[28] In addition to real estate, there were other holdings in the Cuneo estate, among them a large block of shares in a small Italian North Beach bank called the Columbus Savings and Loan. As a major stockholder in the bank, Cuneo had served as one of its directors. It seemed only logical to the bank's principal owners and directors that Giannini would succeed to his father-in-law's place on the board.[29]

When Giannini took his seat at the directors' table of Columbus Savings and Loan, the institution was controlled by its founder, John F. Fugazi. Like so many other early Italian immigrants to California, Fugazi had settled in North Beach in the 1850s after an unsuccessful fling as a miner. A succession of jobs followed until eventually he became an agent for the White Star Lines. Later he opened his own travel agency in North Beach—the Agenzia Fugazi—which proved so successful that he soon began expanding its operations to other cities across the country.[30] As an accommodation to some of his North Beach clients, Fugazi, who owned one of the few iron safes in the community, became a "banker"—accepting their gold for safekeeping or for remittance to relatives in Italy. In 1893 Fugazi emulated the careers of other "ethnic" businessmen in San Francisco when he opened the Columbus Savings and Loan.[31]

As well as being North Beach's first Italian bank, the Columbus Savings and Loan was a rigidly conservative institution. Fugazi and the bank's board of directors were clearly more comfortable making large loans to the community's more prosperous residents than in offering small amounts of credit to ordinary Italians. In addition, according to the recollections of one director, the bank's capital was frequently used for investments with a few favored clients in which Fugazi and other board members had a personal financial interest. Not surprisingly, at age sixty-five Fugazi had formed a strong attachment to the restrictive lending practices that had proved profitable to the bank and to its officers and directors.[32]

Meanwhile, Fugazi's policy of paying only perfunctory attention to the credit needs of the larger community had encouraged other local Italian businessmen to fill the vacuum. In 1899 Alfred Sbarboro opened the Italian American to give North Beach its second Italian bank.[33] A critic of unrestrained capitalism who flirted with socialist principles, Sbarboro had arrived in North Beach from Genoa in the 1850s; he eventually became an elementary school teacher, then founder of the Italian-Swiss wine colony, and finally a banker.[34] Gradually he managed to build a small but loyal following in the community by making small loans to borrowers who wanted to buy their own homes. Although Sbarboro's attempt to enter the home mortgage market was modest, it was an important step away from Fugazi's practice of catering primarily to people who already owned money.[35]

Although Giannini had only scant knowledge of the banking business, he soon began expressing dissatisfaction with Fugazi's management of the Columbus Savings and Loan. He wanted Fugazi and the others to pursue a bold new strategy of deposit building and aggressive lending while maintaining the bank's close ties to the community's more prosperous residents. North Beach had a population of nearly twenty-five thousand Italians and was growing at a rate of two thousand Italian immigrants each year.[36] Most of them were poor and uneducated, but nearly all were thrifty, ambitious, and hard-working. They had made a choice for a new life by immigrating to California. Giannini insisted that what the Columbus Savings and Loan had to do to increase its size and influence was to win their friendship and support by becoming their bank, to become their patron in the style of financial institutions for the rich and powerful.[37]

Aside from raising embarrassing questions about Fugazi's tight-fisted control of the bank, Giannini's proposals exposed a serious flaw in San Francisco's financial machinery as well.[38] San Francisco, then a city of just under 450,000, was the "emporium of a new world" to the wildly extravagant railroad barons and bonanza kings whose magnificent "wooden castles" sat like a "gilded crown" on Nob Hill; it was also fast becoming the money capital of the West Coast.[39] By the early 1900s the city's most prestigious banks—Crocker-Woolworth, Anglo-California, Wells-Fargo Nevada National—were pouring vast sums of money into mining, real estate, and public works projects not only in downstate cities like Los Angeles but also in the nearby states of Oregon, Washington, Nevada, and far beyond.[40] In 1903 alone, for example, San Francisco's biggest banks financed loans totaling over $30 million for overseas investments in London and Paris.[41]

None of this activity had any practical meaning in the lives of San Francisco's working-class citizens. The big banks were not interested in soliciting their business, particularly if they were foreigners.[42] Small loans were a nuisance, not worth the time or the profit that banks could expect to receive from them. Compounding this indifference, many of North Beach's residents were unable to read or write English and, in any case, were intimidated by the ornate marble and brass interiors and cold formality of the city's old established banks.[43] As a result, most did without the services of banks, turning for their credit needs instead to loan sharks who forced them to pay four and five times above the prevailing interest rates.[44]

Giannini tried to persuade Fugazi to move Columbus Savings and Loan into a more prominent position by taking advantage of the social and economic forces that were transforming North Beach. He called for an aggressive program of direct solicitation of new customers, particularly from among the steadily expanding numbers of ordinary Italians. Such a program would require the bank to loan its money, as he said during one directors' meeting, "right up to the hilt." This recommendation, however, represented a radical departure from Fugazi's style of doing business. He promptly turned it down, replying matter-of-factly that the bank had managed well enough before Giannini's appearance on the board.

By the end of 1903 the disagreement between Giannini and the board had escalated into an all-out war. Monthly directors' meetings rarely survived more than a few minutes of routine discussion without a heated exchange between Giannini and the bank's management. Impressed by Giannini's arguments, three directors eventually changed their minds and agreed to support his recommendations. Fugazi, alarmed at these defections and annoyed by Giannini's persistence, angrily accused him of being "a young ambitious hotshot . . . infatuated with big plans and crazy ideas." Several directors arranged a private meeting between Giannini and Fugazi to patch things up, but nothing was settled.[45]

At a monthly directors' meeting in the summer of 1904, Giannini decided to bring matters to a head: if the board continued in its opposition to his recommendations, he would resign. Once again his criticism of the way the bank was being run touched off a furor.[46] The meeting broke up when Giannini angrily announced his resignation and walked out. "I might never have gone into the banking business if I hadn't gotten so damn mad at those directors," he later recalled.[47]

After leaving the meeting, Giannini hurried over to the Market Street office of James J. Fagan, the short, stocky, well-regarded vice-president of the American National Bank.[48] Fagan's bank handled the account of the Scatena firm, and the association between the two men dated back to Giannini's earliest years on the waterfront. Fagan was aware of Giannini's dissatisfaction with Fugazi's management of the Columbus Savings and Loan and had occasionally joked with him about it. But in the aftermath of what had just taken place, Giannini was in no mood for good-natured bantering. As Fagan later recalled, he was sitting at his desk when the door suddenly opened and Giannini burst into his office. "Giacomo," he shouted, "I'm going to start a bank. Tell me how to do it."[49]

Over the next several weeks there were other meetings in Fagan's office and in the North Beach law office of James Cavagnaro, one of three directors who had resigned from the Columbus Savings and Loan with Giannini.[50] With two Italian banks already in North Beach, Giannini needed all the help he could get. Two men he regularly escorted to Cavagnaro's office were Charles Grondona, a local realtor, and George Caglieri, an accountant and part owner of Fugazi's travel agency.[51] In addition to his stepfather, five others whom Giannini recruited to the board included an undertaker, a wholesale grocer, a confectioner, and an importer. Fagan, who also agreed to serve as a director, was the board's only non-Italian.

Throughout the summer of 1904 the scheme went forward in absolute secrecy. Convinced that if Fugazi got wind of what was happening
he would do all that he could to sabotage the plans, Giannini moved
the locations of his meetings with Cavagnaro, Grondona, and the others
from the home of one North Beach friend to another.[52] In final form,
the bank was capitalized at $300,000, which was divided into three
thousand shares at $100 each. Ownership was limited to 100 shares for
each officer and director. The remaining shares would be offered to the
public and distributed as widely as possible. "We don't want a situation
in which any individual can promote his own interest over those of the
bank," Giannini reportedly told the others.[53]

In August 1904 Giannini sent Grondona to the state capital in Sacramento to obtain a certificate of incorporation for what he and the others
had agreed to call the Italian Bank of California. When word leaked out
about Grondona's mission, Sbarboro, president of the Italian American,
complained to state banking officials that the name of North Beach's
newest bank was too much like that of his own.[54] By now, however,
even Giannini was having second thoughts. Confident that his "baby
bank," as he began to call it, would one day expand beyond its present
location, he nevertheless understood that it would first have to prove
itself in North Beach. To give the bank a stronger identification with
the community's preponderance of Italians, he sent Grondona back to
Sacramento with the name "Bank of Italy."[55]

As in every other phase of the bank's formation, Giannini assumed
the job of finding a home for it. In this objective he showed his usual
combativeness and well-developed sense of vendetta. He quickly settled
on a North Beach saloon whose owner had decided to retire. The saloon
had a promising location at the intersection of Washington Street and
Columbus Avenue, a traffic-crowded artery of small shops and commercial buildings. The saloon held other attractions for Giannini aside
from its strategic location: it stood next to the four-story Drexler
Building, the first floor of which was occupied by Fugazi's Columbus
Savings and Loan.[56]

Without saying much even to his directors, Giannini persuaded the
owner of the Drexler to lease him the entire building.[57] Fugazi arrived
at his bank one morning to discover a crew of carpenters renovating
the saloon to make way for Giannini's bank and to learn that he was
now the tenant of his former director.[58] The other thing Fugazi learned
was that Giannini had tripled the rent on his lease. Fugazi was so

infuriated that by the end of the month he had moved his bank across the street. Nevertheless, it was the Bank of Italy that now occupied one corner of North Beach's busiest intersection.

Giannini proceeded to add insult to injury. He hired as chief cashier in his bank a young, recent arrival to North Beach, Armando Pedrini, who had worked as the assistant cashier in Fugazi's bank.[59] Tall, trim, handsome—almost as handsome as Giannini himself, in the judgment of the young women of North Beach—the energetic Pedrini had learned his banking skills in Latin America before immigrating to San Francisco. Giannini was impressed not only with Pedrini's intelligence but also with his courtesy in dealing with customers. ("The women are crazy about him and he gives a man in overalls as much attention as a big depositor," he said.) Pedrini left his job in Fugazi's bank after Giannini agreed to double his salary.[60]

On the morning of October 15, 1904, Giannini stood at the front entrance to his bank in what was basically a medium-sized room with three wooden desks and a few chairs. There were no private offices, no marble foyer, no brass railings, and no uniformed guards—just a Burrough's adding machine, an iron safe, and a single teller's window. At exactly nine o'clock he turned to Victor Calagieri, a young North Beach accountant whom he had hired to assist Pedrini. "Vic," he said, "you may now open the door."[61]

THREE

A People's Bank

I

Not surprisingly, many customers who opened savings accounts during Bank of Italy's first day of business were friends and relatives of its small group of Italian officers and directors. Giannini's mother deposited one thousand dollars and Rose Cuneo, a sister-in-law, sixty dollars. Maria Custo, the wife of one of the bank's directors, put in eight hundred dollars.[1] The largest part of the first day's deposits, however, came from North Beach's fish merchants. After making his own deposit, Grondona slipped out of the bank and hurried over to a nearby fish market. A popular figure in the community's commercial circles, Grondona knew most of the merchants on a first-name basis.[2] He soon returned to the bank accompanied by more than a dozen men in hip boots and leather aprons, each of whom opened a savings account. At the end of the day the Bank of Italy had a total of $8,780 in deposits.[3]

As most people who met him quickly discovered, Giannini had an enormous capacity for work. But in the months immediately following Bank of Italy's opening, he embarked on a hectic campaign to increase business that for sheer physical exertion startled even those closest to him. Duplicating the determination and high-pressure tactics that had characterized his career as a commission clerk with L. Scatena and Company, he pounded the docks and street markets along the city's waterfront district, badgering his friends in the wholesale trade into becoming Bank of Italy customers. At night, after the bank had closed, he and Grondona would fan out into the larger North Beach community, moving from door to door, explaining the advantages of interest-bearing savings accounts to the Italian residents.[4]

Giannini knew from the start that persuading North Beach Italians to deposit their savings in his bank would be an uphill battle. In addition to their preference for dealing strictly in gold, most were deeply suspicious of banks and lacked confidence in the people who either owned or managed them. North Beach Italians had ample reason for their distrust of financial institutions. Back in 1878, for example, a small neighborhood bank, the French Mutual, went into bankruptcy, wiping out the hard-earned savings of scores of Italian depositors. This calamity left a deep impression on the collective memory of the community. Rather than put their trust in a bank, most North Beach residents preferred to keep their savings safely at home, where it was hoarded in cans, jars, and mattresses.[5]

Despite, or perhaps because of, these obstacles, Giannini's pursuit of depositors was relentless. He was by temperament and experience a consummate salesman, driven nearly as much by an intense personal satisfaction in his ability to attract new business as by his excitement in the possibilities for growth of the bank itself. Few North Beach residents managed to avoid becoming a target of his repeated efforts to solicit deposits. "We knew they had the money because I made any number of real estate sales for which I was paid the full amount in gold," Grondona later recalled. "I'd turn around to my gold paying client and try to get him to bring the rest of his hoard to the Bank of Italy to start an account. If I didn't succeed, A. P. or someone else would call on him. It was impossible to escape us."[6]

Nor did Giannini confine his promotional efforts to North Beach. Retracing the roads he had traveled as a commission merchant, he embarked on a search for customers in the towns and on the farms of the Sacramento and Santa Clara Valleys.[7] This naturally meant grueling hours of travel to and from San Francisco, but to Giannini it was worth the effort. Although credit was the lifeblood of a farmer's survival, not nearly enough of it was being furnished by California's independent bankers, and the credit that was offered was not on the most favorable terms.[8] By contrast, Giannini viewed the state's vast sweep of heavily populated farm towns as a reservoir of untapped business, particularly in the energy and ambition of the "mixed multitudes" of immigrants who had settled in them. "Hell," he replied to one associate who marveled at his driving pace, "we've got to let people know about our bank."[9]

Not many San Francisco bankers noticed the appearance of North Beach's newest Italian bank. The few who did were scornful of Giannini's direct solicitation of business. Such practices were thought to be vulgar, unethical, and demeaning to the staid traditions of the banking profession.[10] Giannini, however, had no such inhibitions, and he later offered this "lack" as one reason why he encountered so much opposition from rival bankers to his branch-building operations. "They thought I was undignified," he would remember. "I could never figure it out. I always thought that if business was worth having, it was worth going after. How can people know what a bank can do for them unless they're told?"[11]

Meanwhile, news of Giannini's aggressive lending policy spread rapidly through the North Beach community. Scores of residents eagerly responded. Pursuing the unorthodox recommendations he had tried unsuccessfully to persuade Fugazi and the board of Columbus Savings and Loan into adopting, Giannini devoted the bulk of Bank of Italy's capital to individual real estate loans. More risky were the bank's unsecured personal loans to neighborhood friends and their families. "Character loans," Giannini called them, often made with no more collateral than the fact that he knew the borrower personally to be a good risk.[12] "I found it impossible to clear the top of my desk with so many people coming in," Grondona later remembered.[13] Eighteen months after Bank of Italy opened its doors, its loans exceeded deposits by more than $200,000.[14]

Among North Beach's Italians, the sale of Bank of Italy's stock grew faster than Giannini had expected.[15] To placate the Italians who felt cheated at having been left out, Giannini persuaded four of the bank's directors to surrender part of their own shares to carry out his policy of wide distribution. He was particularly pleased with the hundreds of small investors who bought two, three, or four shares each. Aiming at a broadly based ownership, he eventually spread more than half the bank's stock among 1,620 shareholders, the majority of whom held fewer than ten shares.[16] In doing so, Giannini was laying the foundation for a large, highly disciplined army of small stockholders who were fiercely dedicated to him personally and who would one day make him a powerful force in the nation's banking community.

Though continuing for several months more with his work at Madison and Burke, Giannini found himself spending less and less time with his real estate activities. Lights burned late through Bank of Italy's windows. The front doors were seldom locked, and it was not unusual for customers to wander in at night and on weekends.[17] The bank owned a small iron safe sufficient to impress its customers, but which Giannini would later describe as "little more than a tin box without a top."[18] To avoid the possibility of a late-night robbery, he made arrangements to store the bank's overnight cash in the stronger and better-protected vaults at the Crocker-Woolworth.[19]

Throughout the months of 1905 the Bank of Italy grew faster than ever. As Giannini had expected, the opportunity to buy a home financed at prevailing bank rates proved to be immensely popular to hundreds of North Beach residents. At the same time, total deposits climbed to over $700,000, much of which was the result of Giannini's door-to-door solicitation of business. Moreover, the bank was achieving this impressive growth while maintaining the highest ratio of loans to total assets of any other bank in the state.[20] So successful had Giannini been in putting new business on the books that several Bank of Italy board members expressed serious misgivings about his aggressive lending policies and urged him to slow down. Giannini, however, brushed their concerns aside.[21]

2

Events were moving swiftly for Giannini, but no more so than in the months immediately following San Francisco's greatest natural disaster. As Giannini would remember years later, in the early morning hours of April 18, 1906, he was suddenly thrown out of bed by a violent upheaval in the earth whose vibrations shook his house in San Mateo to its foundations. An earthquake had hit San Francisco with such force that the chimney on Seven Oaks collapsed, taking part of the roof with it.[22] Giannini calmed his wife, now expecting their eighth child, and dressed quickly. After first making arrangements with neighbors for his family's safety, he set out for the city not knowing the extent of the damage, but fearing the worst.

Giannini's fears increased when he learned that he would be unable to reach San Francisco via the peninsula railroad line from San Mateo. The earthquake had wrenched the rails from the ground at several points along the line, making travel by train impossible.[23] After leaving the

San Mateo depot, Giannini headed north on foot over the San Bruno road, the great circle course that would bring him to the northern boundaries of the city. Soon he ran into a procession of wagons carrying frightened people fleeing the city, many of them clutching salvaged possessions. The stories they told had a depressing similarity of physical destruction unparalleled in the history of the city. "I had seen so much panic on the faces of the people I had met," Giannini later remembered, "that I didn't have much hope for the bank."[24]

After walking the seventeen miles to San Francisco, Giannini got his first look at the earthquake's damage. Block after block of the city was buried in a mass of brick, mortar, and splintered wood.[25] Gas mains had burst, and broken water pipes shot geysers thirty feet in the air. To make matters worse, fires from overturned stoves and broken electric wires burned uncontrollably in scores of different locations. Without water, firemen were helpless and had resorted to using dynamite to stop the inferno before it swept everything in its path. Along city streets, people rushed frantically back and forth dragging trunks and other containers, making use of every available means to move their personal possessions to safety.[26]

Giannini reached his bank around noon. He was surprised to find that it had not suffered any major damage. Fortunately, two employees had rescued from the vaults of the Crocker-Woolworth the overnight cash, approximately $80,000 in gold and silver, which they had locked inside Bank of Italy.[27] Pedrini suddenly showed up with the report that the fire was rapidly moving westward and threatened to consume the whole of the city that stood between Market Street and the waterfront district, including North Beach.[28] Giannini moved quickly. "I figured we had about two hours to get out of there," he later recalled. "At the rate the fire was spreading, I realized that no place in San Francisco could be a safe storage spot for the money. I decided to take it home to San Mateo."[29]

Aided by Pedrini and a brother-in-law, Clarence Cuneo, Giannini loaded two wagons with Bank of Italy's money, books, and furniture. The heat was intense. To reduce the risk of being robbed by roving bands of hoodlums who had begun looting abandoned homes and office buildings, Giannini decided to camouflage the contents of the wagons with crates of oranges. "We didn't have any guards," he later recalled. "All the police were busy fighting the fire. It was extremely difficult to disguise the load we were carrying and I thought I saw would-be robbers on every street corner. The idea of the crates worked, but for weeks after the earthquake the bank's money smelled like orange juice."[30]

After leaving San Francisco late that night, the wagons reached San Mateo as dawn broke. With the possibility of robbery still on his mind, Giannini and the others carried the pouches of gold and silver into the house, where they buried them in the ash trap of the living room fireplace. Giannini stationed Pedrini and Cuneo at the upstairs window while he and his brother stood guard over the money on the first floor. As Giannini later remembered, "None of us got much sleep, only one or two hours. But I wouldn't risk leaving the fireplace. We were all grateful when the hours went by and nothing happened."[31]

The next day Giannini returned to San Francisco. Bank of Italy was a mass of charred rubble. The fire had consumed nearly all of the 500 block area from the neighborhoods south of Market Street to the waterfront beyond North Beach, whose old wooden shanties and frame houses had been the least defensible against the fire.[32] Fewer than three hundred of North Beach's four thousand homes and buildings were still standing—the greatest devastation of any district in the city. Estimates of property loss throughout the city ranged between $350 and $500 million. More than 200,000 people were homeless, many of them living in tents and makeshift shelters in Golden Gate Park.[33]

On Saturday, April 21, Giannini attended an emergency meeting of prominent businessmen at the home of Henry C. Scott, a director of the Crocker-Woolworth. The mood of the meeting was grim.[34] Few of the bankers who attended thought it would be possible to reopen their banks for at least five or six weeks. Aside from the structural damage to the buildings themselves, the fire had heated vaults to a white-hot intensity, which meant they could not be opened safely for several weeks. Across San Francisco Bay, banks in Oakland had opened for business, but with little in the way of cash reserves to pay out to customers. Withdrawals were limited to thirty dollars.[35]

Responsibility for preventing a financial panic was in the hands of Governor George Pardee. Hoping to calm public fears and give bankers time to resume normal operations, Pardee had proclaimed a bank holiday.[36] Speculation preceded the meeting in Scott's home that the legal holiday was only the start of a banking moratorium that might last until the early fall. One distraught banker who attended the meeting described his colleagues as a "thoroughly dispirited" group of men. "We appeared to be conscious," he wrote later, "but really our brains were in a fog and our actions were those of sleepwalkers."[37]

The story of what happened next would be celebrated by Bank of Italy executives for decades to come. According to the most heroic and well-publicized version, while other San Francisco bankers watched in paralyzing fear and uncertainty, Bank of Italy became the city's first financial institution to reopen its doors, offering loans to people who wanted to rebuild their homes.[38] This version was an exaggeration, although Giannini did his best over the years to promote the story as a symbol of Bank of Italy's commitment to serving the needs of the general public, in good times as well as bad. In reality, despite the much-talked-about moratorium, a number of San Francisco banks, including the Crocker-Woolworth, reopened for business on a limited basis in the days immediately following the earthquake.[39] What is undoubtedly true, however, is that no banker reacted to the disaster so quickly, so aggressively, and so conspicuously as did Giannini.

Giannini, in fact, pursued two courses of action, both of which demonstrated his lifelong proclivity for responding to immediate crises with the unexpected and the dramatic. Two days after the earthquake he inserted a boxed notice in the front page of the *San Francisco Chronicle:* "Bank of Italy Now Opened for Regular Business." The notice went on to inform the bank's depositors that their money was safe and available for withdrawal.[40] Giannini then took the unprecedented— though illegal—step of having a desk set out at the foot of the Washington Street wharf. On top of the desk, he placed a bag of gold on prominent display. Nearby, a handmade banner announced Bank of Italy's temporary home.[41]

News of Giannini's sudden and dramatic appearance on the waterfront made the rounds of North Beach in a matter of hours.[42] As scores of people whose homes had been destroyed in the fire showed up, they found him shaking hands with customers and would-be customers, a figure of strength and confidence. One North Beach resident attracted by the crowd later remembered Giannini standing at the foot of the wharf exhorting a group of Italians: "We're going to rebuild San Francisco and it will be better than ever."[43] They responded to his offer of help in overwhelming numbers.[44] As Grondona later remembered, "All of us kept out of his way in those days. He was too busy to do anything except take care of customers."[45]

Giannini was not so busy that he missed an opportunity to use the crisis to Bank of Italy's advantage. Remembering the gold that still lay hidden in cans and mattresses in the homes of numerous families, he devised a method for getting at it. As promised, Giannini made hundreds of loans to North Beach's grief-stricken residents, but only for half of what they requested, and on the condition that they first raise the other half. By this means he unleashed scores of borrowers who persuaded friends and relatives to dig up their savings. "The hoarded money came from the most unlikely of places," Grondona later recalled.[46]

In addition to individual loans, Giannini also took steps to ensure that borrowers would have the material to rebuild their homes and businesses as soon as possible. While other bankers waited for insurance companies to pay their claims, he contacted a number of bay ship captains and urged them to bring lumber and other building materials from Oregon and Washington, advancing them loans from Bank of Italy to do so. Shipowners who followed his advice generally had the lumber sold before their boats returned to San Francisco, making good profits on their investment, although Giannini did not share in them. "He could have made a fortune for himself out of the disaster," one associate later commented. "Instead, he passed the idea along to others."[47]

Although a number of events were playing into Giannini's hands, his bold and unhesitating actions during the crisis benefited the North Beach community immensely. When San Francisco's rebuilding boom got under way three months later, North Beach's residents had already begun the task of replacing their homes and businesses, and with material acquired at considerably lower prices. Less than a year later North Beach became the first of the city's large residential districts to rebuild itself from the destruction of the earthquake and fire.[48]

Hailed as a local hero by North Beach Italians, Giannini was now beginning to attract attention outside the confines of the city's "Latin quarter." L'Italia, San Francisco's largest Italian-language newspaper, called him North Beach's "most progressive businessman" and praised him for "bringing hope and confidence to so many people who had lost their homes in the fire."[49] Others went further. After noting that the first shipments of building materials to reach the city were paid for with unsecured loans from Bank of Italy, the San Francisco Call praised Giannini's courage and imagination as "one of the most inspiring stories to come out of the disaster."[50]

As soon as business returned to normal, Giannini turned to the task of rebuilding his bank. By now he had become dissatisfied with its identification as a strictly "Italian neighborhood" institution and was ready for bigger things. Never one to think small, he persuaded Bank of Italy's board of directors to approve the purchase of an empty lot on the southeast corner of Clay and Montgomery Streets, only a few blocks beyond North Beach itself but close to the heart of the city's downtown financial center.[51] Work soon began on the construction of a nine-story granite-and-limestone building that the *San Francisco Chronicle* would later call "among the most handsome and modern of its kind in the city."[52]

In January 1907, with construction of the building under way, Giannini decided to take a trip with his wife to New York for the first real vacation of their married life. The trip was important to Giannini, who saw an opportunity to meet and talk with bankers in the nation's financial capital and to establish personal contacts with civic and business leaders among the city's many Italians. The Gianninis left San Francisco by train on an itinerary that would include stopovers in Chicago, Pittsburgh, and Philadelphia. Three weeks later they arrived in New York.[53]

Over the next several weeks Giannini toured Wall Street and spent a good deal of time meeting with prominent Italian businessmen. He was distressed by what he heard. Despite record annual earnings, New York's largest banks were short of money, the result in part of an unprecedented worldwide prosperity that had seriously diminished the nation's supply of gold.[54] Some financiers were warning that gold reserves had fallen so low that large withdrawals of funds would lead to a wave of failures. In December 1905 Jacob Schiff, a prominent Wall Street banker, had warned a group of New York businessmen: "If the currency conditions of the country are not changed materially, I predict a panic as will make all previous panics look like child's play."[55]

Equally worrisome to many New York financiers was the general weakness in the structure of the nation's banking system. The problem, as some experts perceived it, rested squarely with the system itself, a sprawling hodgepodge of thirty thousand banks, each independent of the other, each competing furiously against the other for loans and deposits. What was worse, with no powerful central bank, as in England, the inability of bankers themselves to control the expansion, contraction, or free flow of money from one part of the country to another could become a serious problem.[56] If the economy suddenly turned sour, many state banks could find themselves in desperate trouble, particularly if they had made too many loans or had failed to keep adequate reserves.[57]

As Giannini went to more meetings, he seemed to encounter nothing but gloom.[58] "I didn't say much," he would remember, "but I could see that they were depressed and down in the mouth."[59] Cutting his vacation short, Giannini packed and headed back to the West Coast. He and Grondona had worked hard at overcoming the suspicions of North Beach's Italians toward banks.[60] If, in the event of a major financial panic, Bank of Italy proved itself unable to withstand the pressure of heavy withdrawals, he could lose the respect and confidence of the entire community. He might even face a run on his bank. With everything he had worked for hanging in the balance, Giannini wanted to be in San Francisco.

FOUR

On the Move

I

Back in San Francisco, Giannini called a special meeting of the board to inform his directors of what he had seen and heard in New York. Convinced that an economic collapse was coming, he proposed an immediate cutback on real estate loans and a crash program to increase deposits.[1] Not every member of the board agreed with his proposals. Fagan, whose years of experience in banking lent weight to his opinions, vigorously objected and accused Giannini of being unnecessarily alarmist. The disagreement between the two men degenerated into what one director would later remember as a series of "hot arguments," but Giannini refused to back down.[2] The more he thought about the possibility of a full-scale panic, as he later recalled, the more he wanted the bank to be literally "bursting with gold" if and when it arrived.[3]

Throughout the summer of 1907 Giannini proved adept at building up the bank's supply of gold.[4] Still not a member of the San Francisco Clearing House, the Bank of Italy cleared its checks each day through Fagan's own bank, the Crocker-Woolworth. The usual procedure was for Giannini's brother-in-law, Clarence Cuneo, to show up at the Crocker each evening with a bag containing the bank's daily supply of cash; by mutual agreement, the bag ordinarily contained a specified amount of gold. Without bothering to inform officials at the Crocker-Woolworth, Giannini instructed Cuneo to replace the biggest part of this gold with paper money.[5] The subtracted gold was then placed in Giannini's private hoard at Bank of Italy. Although the amount of hard currency obtained this way was modest, Giannini felt it would eventually be useful.[6]

Giannini's stockpiling activities did not interfere with his pursuit of business. Early in the fall of 1907 he jumped outside North Beach to open a "branch" of his Bank of Italy in San Francisco's Mission District, a heavily populated working-class neighborhood of Irish and Germans south of Market Street. Unlike most other parts of the city, the Mission District had been untouched by the fire, a fact that had prompted several downtown department stores to open temporary quarters there.[7] In the months immediately following the earthquake, it had also attracted a sizable number of Italians, most of whom had moved from their burned-out homes on the steep hillsides of North Beach for a "safer" part of the city.[8]

Although Giannini's branch outside North Beach was no innovation in banking, it did establish a pattern that he would use again and again in his early drive toward building a statewide system of branches: locate a town or city where sizable numbers of Italians had settled and bring them into Bank of Italy as depositors and stockholders. With this nucleus of small but loyal customers, he would then reach out to other minorities from among California's "mixed-multitudes" of immigrants—Greeks, Yugoslavians, Armenians, Russians, Chinese, Japanese, Mexicans—who had by then become the state's leading source of population growth.[9]

With his move to the Mission District, Giannini was ahead of his competitors in other respects as well. Sensing the potential of mass advertising as a vehicle for increasing business for the bank, he hired Bank of Italy's first public relations personnel and covered the neighborhood with promotional fliers.[10] "It is never easy to save money," one such flier said, "but when you do, place it in a safe bank, instead of hiding it in a mattress where thieves can steal it, or fire can destroy it." Another urged potential home buyers to "put aside a certain amount each week or each month. In a short while you will be surprised to see that your savings have accumulated interest amounting to hundreds of dollars."[11] The fliers turned out to be Giannini's most effective promotional device and encouraged him to put more of the bank's money into professional advertising.

Meanwhile, the economic crisis that Fagan had dismissed as mischievous speculation suddenly hit New York's financial district with devastating force. On October 10, 1907, prices on the New York Stock Exchange dropped sharply.[12] Less than two weeks later a frantic run began on the Knickerbocker Trust, forcing the company to close its doors. Runs on other banks in the city quickly followed, triggering the worst financial panic in the nation's history to that time. The crisis spread steadily westward. On a single day both the Pittsburgh and New Orleans stock exchanges suspended operations. There were ugly riots in a dozen different cities. More than 130 banks across the country closed their doors. The failure to keep reserves anywhere near legal limits pushed many into bankruptcy.[13]

One week after the collapse of the Knickerbocker, the panic reached San Francisco. Within days the California Safe Deposit and Trust—the city's largest trust company—closed its doors.[14] With public fear spreading, the state's small correspondent banks began calling on San Francisco's large banks to return their deposits. Given the lack of currency in the East, however, it was impossible for these metropolitan banks to oblige without endangering their own survival. On October 31, 1907, in an effort to prevent a depositors' stampede from pushing other financial institutions into bankruptcy, Governor James Gillette declared a bank holiday. Soon after, San Francisco's largest banks began issuing clearinghouse script—"funny money," some critics called it—to make up for the lack of gold.[15]

Giannini's months of quiet preparations paid off in increased prestige for Bank of Italy. No sooner had the panic hit San Francisco than Giannini passed the word among the bank's customers that he was ready to pay gold on demand to depositors who wanted to withdraw their savings. If some who hurried over to the bank were skeptical, they were soon disabused of their doubts. To their great relief, Giannini and three of his employees were waiting with the biggest part of the gold he had been accumulating stacked behind the cages of the tellers' windows for everyone to see.[16] The result, as a reporter for the *San Francisco News* commented later, was that "Mr. Giannini and his Bank of Italy were once again the talk of San Francisco."[17]

Elsewhere in the city, banks suffered a severe drain on their re-sources. Some of these losses were so great as to assume the proportion of runs.[18] The Crocker-Woolworth, San Francisco's largest bank, lost $7 million in withdrawals. Unable to meet the frightened demands of their depositors, sixteen of the city's smaller banks failed completely, leaving behind over $8 million in unprotected losses. By the time the worst of the panic had run its course, San Francisco banks had lost nearly $17 million in deposits.[19]

2

The months immediately following the panic were marked by intense debate among politicians and bankers over the state's credit system.[20] Like states in other parts of the country, California had emerged from the gold rush decades with a loosely regulated mixture of state and national banks, only a small number of which operated with the trust and smooth efficiency necessary for public confidence. An investigation by Sacramento legislators into the spectacular collapse of the California Safe Deposit and Trust, for example, disclosed that the corporation's chief executive officers and directors were guilty of massive self-lending. Loans to one principal director, in fact, totaled some $4 million. All in all, the estimated total loss was $16 million in unsecured loans, the largest in California history.

Yet in a number of critical ways, California differed from the rest of the nation. Perhaps in no other region of the country had any state experienced such rapid economic growth. Beginning in 1900 and continuing over the next two decades, a total of 29,793 new corporations came into existence. The state's farm production during this same period more than doubled; by 1920 California was supplying two-thirds of the nation's fruits and vegetables.[21] The consequence was a soaring demand for credit and better service by farmers, businessmen, and industrialists, who were dissatisfied with the chronic instability of the state's existing banking system. As the president of the Los Angeles Clearinghouse put it, too many banks were "of a mushroom character, illy [sic] organized as to personnel, undercapitalized, addicted to unethical methods."[22]

Giannini played virtually no part in these discussions, preferring instead to reach his own conclusions about the mediocre performance of so many California banks during the crisis. He was particularly impressed by the relative ease with which the San Francisco–based branches of two large Canadian banks—the Canadian Bank of Commerce and the Bank of British Columbia—had come through the panic. The Bank of British Columbia, for instance, had maintained a branch in the city since the 1860s. On the eve of the 1907 panic, it had assets of $100 million and had earned the reputation in business and financial circles as one of California's three most outstanding banks.[23] This kind of performance interested Giannini.[24]

Late in the spring of 1908 Giannini left San Francisco on a trip to the western provinces of Canada for a firsthand look at the country's branch banking system. For three weeks or more he traveled from one remote prairie town to another. He was immediately intrigued by the way in which the powerful resources of parent banks in large metropolitan cities like Montreal and Toronto were made available through branches to people clustered in small frontier communities thousands of miles away, and how well their needs were being served by them.[25] Compared to the unreliable and loosely run operations of a great many California banks with their excessive risk and mismanagement, the Canadian system seemed a model of efficiency.[26]

Sooner and certainly more clearly than any other banker in California, Giannini recognized the harmony of interests between branch banking and the state's abundant and varied agricultural economy. As he would later recall, few small-town bankers could appreciate the extent to which their crushing monopoly over local credit frustrated an expanding economy.[27] There was, first of all, the risk of making too many loans beyond the ability of banks to support them. In addition, since the amount of money a local bank could loan was limited by the resources of the town in which it was located, most country bankers preferred a steady level in the demand for credit. What they faced instead (and were invariably unable to satisfy) was a widely fluctuating demand, the result of the highly seasonal character of California's agricultural production.[28]

Giannini was confident that branch banking offered solutions to complaints he had heard from farmers during his years as a commission merchant. By using the superior resources of his bank in San Francisco, he could shift large amounts of money from one branch to another, according to the credit needs of the various communities.[29] Giannini was intent on changing the rules of the game, but he was also attracted to branch banking because, as an "ethnic" outsider, he resented the men who made up much of the state's banking community—men whom he perceived as "aloof . . . silk hat" elitists, who were always eager to provide "wholesale advantages for the few" but paid scant attention to the money needs of the many.[30] "By opening branches," he said later, "I saw that we could give better service to everybody. Each branch would be a business-getter for the institution, but each branch likewise would have behind it the resources the bank possessed. We would be able to care for the needs of any customer."[31]

Unlike other states, California had no laws specifically prohibiting branch banking. From the 1860s to the early years of the twentieth century, branch banking in the state had been carried on without statutory authority, under the discretion of the attorney general's office in Sacramento.[32] During these uncertain years a handful of small rural banks had opened branches, usually in neighboring towns, but only a few other banks followed their example. Two factors contributed to this reluctance. One was the moral legitimacy and "time-honored tradition" of the small-town independent bank, a tradition deeply rooted in American culture. The other was the failure of bankers to see the economic potential in the building of a branch system. On the eve of the 1907 panic, California banks were operating a total of only five branches throughout the state, none of which was prepared to accommodate the credit needs of the communities in which they were located.[33]

As it turned out, Giannini's enthusiasm for branch banking came at a time when events in Sacramento seemed to be moving in his favor. Hoping to embarrass the Republican administration of Governor James Gillette, reform-minded Democrats in the legislature began to exploit to the fullest the poor performance of banks during the 1907 panic. With the governor's political appointees as their chief target, they charged the state board of banking commissioners with incompetence and failure to use its powers in the public interest.[34] Gillette reacted swiftly, calling for the establishment of a legislative commission, as he expressed it, "to investigate the methods of doing banking business in the state . . . so as to protect depositors."[35]

Bankers from across the state saw immediately that reform legislation might hamper their activities and create serious problems for the industry. Official delegations from the California Bankers Association lobbied energetically in Sacramento to influence the direction of the commission's recommendations. They were successful in persuading the commission to adopt proposals that were in many ways less hostile and threatening than others that had been considered. The recommendations were embodied in the Banking Act of 1909, which was enacted in March of that year.[36] The act provided that the authority to regulate the industry be directed by a superintendent of banking appointed by the governor. To ensure the safety of money entrusted to banks by their depositors, the act also prohibited banks from loaning money to their officers and established procedures for more stringent and frequent examinations of banks in the state.[37]

Far more interesting as far as Giannini was concerned—indeed, of major importance to his branch banking ambitions as a whole—was a provision prohibiting bankers from opening branches "outside their principal place of business" without first obtaining approval of the superintendent of banking.[38] The obvious intention of this provision had been to give statutory recognition to a seldom-used practice that had previously been conducted on a relatively informal basis: that is, its fundamental purpose was to make certain that the new superintendent of banking had discretionary authority over every aspect of the state's financial system.

The more Giannini studied this provision, however, the more it took on a much wider meaning for him. Rather than seeing it as a simple regulatory restraint, as the commission itself did, he interpreted it to mean legislative approval for the development of statewide branch banking. It was all the encouragement he needed. Early in the spring of 1909, at a regular monthly meeting of the board, he announced his intention to open branches of the bank outside San Francisco. Although several directors expressed their astonishment at the brashness of his proposal, the entire board nevertheless deferred to his judgment. With that accomplished, Giannini now waited for the right opportunity.[39]

3

On the morning of October 12, 1909, Giannini was in San Jose to attend a Columbus Day celebration with some friends from the city's Italian community.[40] San Jose had changed a good deal from the days when he had lived there as a boy nearly forty years earlier. With its rail connections to the East Coast, San Jose had become the busiest and most vital fruit-packing and distributing center in the state. Shops, hotels, restaurants, a theater, and sycamore trees lined the paved sidewalk along the town's main thoroughfare. The population had increased to more than fifty thousand, many of whom worked in the two dozen or more fruit canneries and shipping firms that were San Jose's biggest source of employment.[41] As an editorial in the *San Jose Mercury and Herald* put it, the city's "great leap in a single generation has been too great to be either fully understood or appreciated."[42]

Giannini had more on his mind this Columbus Day than simply watching a parade. Two weeks earlier Gus Lion, the vice-president of San Jose's oldest and largest bank, the Commercial and Savings, and son of the bank's president, Lazard Lion, had arrived unexpectedly in San Francisco to discuss an urgent matter with him. As Lion explained it, a compelling reason had developed for his father to consider the possibility of selling the bank and persuading its directors and major stockholders to go along with his decision. The Commercial and Savings was sinking in a swamp of bad debts, primarily in unpaid real estate loans, and lacked even the capital to satisfy the state's minimum requirements.[43]

According to Lion, the Commercial and Savings' troubles had begun twenty years earlier under the bank's previous president, Bernard Murphy, scion of a land-rich family and one of San Jose's most respected citizens. Over the years Murphy and the bank's directors had arranged unsecured loans totaling hundreds of thousands of dollars for their friends from among the valley's landowning gentry, mostly for highly speculative purposes. But the largest share of these generous loans by far had gone to Murphy himself and to various members of his family.[44] Unable to repay the money, Murphy resigned, leaving behind a vast number of bad debts that threatened the bank's solvency. Despite Lion's best efforts, he had not succeeded in improving the bank's deteriorating condition.[45] He asked Giannini if he was interested in purchasing the bank.

Giannini jumped at the opportunity. All around him he saw Italians and immigrants of other nationalities working their farms on some of the best land in California. Some had prospered better than others, but few, in his opinion, had done nearly as well as they might have hoped or expected.[46] The fault, as Giannini perceived it, rested squarely with those small-town "neighborhood" bankers, like Murphy, whose self-serving policies had led them to ignore the needs and aspirations of people, as Giannini later recalled, who had nothing to offer in the way of collateral "but their own imagination and ambition."[47]

Much as Giannini coveted ownership of the Commercial and Savings, there was one problem: the banking act of 1909 prohibited one bank from acquiring the stock of another. Giannini turned for advice to James Bacigalupi, a recent graduate of the Hastings Law School in San Francisco who had opened a private practice in an office above the Bank of Italy. Tall, lean, somber, with thick black hair combed straight back and deep-set, mournful eyes, Bacigalupi was the son of Italian immigrant parents who had settled in the Santa Clara Valley nearly thirty years earlier.[48] Personally recruited by Giannini, who was impressed by his quickness of mind and considerable oratorical skills, Bacigalupi had become accustomed to providing him with legal advice from time to time. Even though it would be several years more before Bacigalupi would join the Bank of Italy on a full-time basis, Giannini was soon throwing so much legal business his way that for all practical purposes he had assumed the position as its official attorney.[49]

Bacigalupi's solution was simplicity itself and became the method whereby Giannini would acquire scores of other banks on his march toward creating his banking empire in California. A handful of Giannini executives, led by one of the bank's directors, would combine in a "stockholders' auxiliary" to purchase in their own names as *individuals* a controlling number of shares in the Commercial and Savings.[50] The Bank of Italy, as a *corporation,* would then buy nearly all of the Commercial's assets, as distinct from its stock. Once this transaction had been completed, the two banks would then be consolidated, enabling Giannini's majority stockholders to exchange their shares in the Commercial for Bank of Italy stock.[51]

Bacigalupi's scheme went forward as smoothly as he said it would, and on November 18, 1909, Giannini opened the doors to his San Jose branch office, his first outside San Francisco.[52] In a printed notice inserted in the *San Jose Mercury and Herald* four days earlier, Giannini had left no doubt in anyone's mind that much more was involved in his purchase of the Commercial and Savings than a simple change in ownership. After announcing Bank of Italy's presence in San Jose in bold type, the notice went on to say that the new management "planned to pay special attention to the affairs of people who speak English with difficulty and will have employees who speak the French, Italian, Spanish, and Portuguese languages."[53]

Over the next several months Giannini was an almost constant presence in San Jose, drumming up business.[54] As always, he appealed directly to the city's immigrant, working-class population. One such meeting was arranged by L. S. Slavich, a popular local figure whose restaurant in the center of town was a favorite hangout for the city's sizable number of Yugoslavian residents. Slavich's nephew, a waiter in the restaurant, later remembered Giannini's first meeting with his uncle's friends and relatives. "I knew something important was going on," he said, "because my uncle pushed closed the sliding door to cut off the diners from the private room. Once the door opened and I heard one of the men say, 'We'll get the Portuguese, the Italians and the Slavs—and we'll give them a bank that can help them.'"[55]

With his move into San Jose, Giannini adopted two organizational practices that he would later use with great effectiveness in the creation of his other branches. The first was to retain the services of the Commercial and Savings former employees; he thus avoided alienating local residents by staffing the branch with unfamiliar faces brought out from San Francisco. The second was to insist that at least one employee in the branch be fluent in Italian; other branch employees who spoke only English were encouraged to attend evening classes to learn the language of one or more of the other large immigrant groups residing in the area. To help boost Bank of Italy's business in the community, Giannini also appointed an advisory committee for the branch composed of prominent civic and business leaders from a variety of immigrant groups. The committee's primary function was to oversee the branch's lending practices and to bring in new customers.

To manage the San Jose branch, Giannini named his brother, Attilio, a San Francisco physician who left his medical practice in 1907 for an executive career in Bank of Italy. An intense, volatile, dark-complexioned man of medium height with quick, dark eyes behind steel-rimmed glasses, Attilio, or "Doc" as he was called, was a man of unquestioned ability and a success story in his own right. With his medical degree from the University of California, he had served with distinction in a field hospital in the Philippines during the Spanish-American War. Back in San Francisco, he went into private practice, joined various civic and charitable organizations, and later sat on San Francisco's board of supervisors. During a smallpox epidemic he attained public praise and received an award from city officials for his courage in volunteering to treat patients in the charity hospital.[56]

Urbane and dignified in his three-piece suits, but harsh and intimidating in his relationships with subordinates and possessed of a hair-trigger temper, Attilio was fond of moving in wealthy circles and counted among his friends many of San Francisco's most powerful and socially prominent figures. As one Giannini aide later recalled, "Doc thought of himself as a self-made man in his own right."[57]

Bank of Italy's San Jose branch soon exceeded Giannini's expectations. On November 17, 1909, Bacigalupi informed him excitedly that the branch had attracted hundreds of new customers "of the ready and desirable classes of Latin blood" and that the future looked bright.[58] Encouraged by the news, Giannini was ready now to push aggressively ahead with plans for the purchase of additional banks and their conversion into Bank of Italy branches. The following year he opened three more branches, two in San Francisco, the other in San Mateo.[59] By the end of 1910 Giannini's branch banking operations extended along a fifty-mile corridor from San Francisco in the north to the southern tip of the San Francisco peninsula.

Not long after he opened his San Mateo branch, Giannini began considering the possibility of jumping clear across the country to duplicate the success of his "people's bank" in New York. This was an audacious move. He had spent only limited time in New York, and his hard-earned reputation could suffer badly if his efforts to establish himself in the city ended in failure. Nevertheless, some who knew Giannini well later claimed that on the basis of his success thus far, he had already begun envisioning the possibility of expanding his California-based Bank of Italy into a nationwide network of banks stretching all the way to New York.[60]

If that was Giannini's intention, he concealed it well. A more likely explanation is that he was attracted by the demographic changes that had further strengthened New York's reputation as the immigrant capital of the country. This development was most conspicuous with the flood of Italians into the city. In 1910 alone, for example, more than 300,000 Italians passed through Ellis Island, many of them settling in the congested quarters of the Bronx and New York's Lower East Side. Ten years later the number of Italians in New York had expanded to 800,000—nearly twice the entire population of San Francisco.[61]

James Cavagnaro, vice-president of a small Brooklyn bank called the East River National, provided Giannini with the opportunity. Cavagnaro had met Giannini on his trip to New York six years earlier and had watched the rapid success of Bank of Italy with admiring interest. In January 1913 he informed Giannini that the East River National faced more problems than its current management could handle and was available for purchase. In addition to arranging for the sale of the bank, Cavagnaro said, he had succeeded in putting together a group of "small capitalists," nearly all of them Italians, who were eager to become stockholders in a reorganized institution.[62]

Seizing on Cavagnaro's offer, Giannini sent Pedrini to New York to work out the details of an agreement. By this time Pedrini, now a senior executive vice-president, had emerged as one of Giannini's closest and most trusted associates, soliciting new business and running Bank of Italy's recently formed Italian Department. In New York the negotiations with Cavagnaro and the others went smoothly, and Pedrini returned to San Francisco confident the deal would go through.[63] Giannini immediately authorized a press release calling attention to his plans. "It will be a matter of only a few months," the *Coast Banker* reported, "when the management of the Bank of Italy will be invited to go East to organize and direct the policy of a new Italian bank there."[64]

In the end, however, the deal fell through. Cavagnaro and his circle of "small capitalists" concluded that if the new bank was going to follow successfully in the Bank of Italy's footsteps, Giannini's presence in New York on a full-time basis would be indispensable.[65] Preoccupied with his branch expansion plans in California, Giannini offered to send an associate "trained in Bank of Italy methods" to run the East River National, but he declined the invitation to go himself. Informed of this decision, Cavagnaro and the others canceled the agreement.[66] Giannini and Cavagnaro tried several more times to reach an agreement, but without success.[67]

In January 1913, meanwhile, Giannini doubled the bank's capitalization to $2 million by selling 10,000 new shares of stock and made room for eleven new members on the bank's board of directors. Everyone involved said later that they were uncertain at the time exactly what he was up to. Whatever it was, though, they were certain it would be big.

FIVE

Going South

I

    Booms had come and gone in Los Angeles, but nothing could compare with the seemingly endless number of people who settled in the city during the first two decades of the twentieth century. In 1900 the population was 102,000; ten years later it had increased to 300,000.[1] Subdivisions were opening in what had been empty tracts of land and fruit orchards, generally "closer to the surrounding hills than to the city itself." And still they came—midwestern farmers, mostly, people who wanted to live and work in a city that seemed infinitely more attractive to them than any in Iowa, Kansas, or Nebraska. "Like a swarm of invading locusts," one regional historian later wrote, "migrants crept in all over the roads. Often they came with no funds or prospects . . . apparently trusting that heaven would provide for them. They camped on the outskirts of town, and their camps became suburbs."[2]

    The attraction for the most part was climate: a subtropical paradise of hot sun and cool ocean breezes. Demand for citrus fruits in eastern markets was then soaring—up by 50 percent over a decade earlier—a development that would soon turn Los Angeles into the nation's single most productive agricultural county.[3] The other, equally important development was the spectacular growth of the oil industry. In 1909 fabulous oil deposits were discovered in and around Los Angeles, generating new excitement to the unprecedented influx of people; in the space of a decade the city would grow to be larger even than San Francisco. "Outside the city, rows of derricks competed with rows of orange trees as totems of prosperity."[4] By 1920 Los Angeles County was producing 105 million barrels of oil a year, up from 89 million barrels in 1914. "No California generation had ever seen its equal before; none is ever likely to see its counterpart again."[5]

In San Francisco, Giannini watched these whirlwind developments with intensifying interest. But Los Angeles held other attractions for him aside from its explosive growth. The Panama Canal was scheduled for completion in 1915, less than two years away. No one at the time knew exactly how many new immigrants this new route would add to the population of the city. Estimates ranged from the tens of thousands to a virtual deluge. But nearly everyone agreed they would come primarily from southern and eastern Europe, including "a tremendous increase in population of people of Latin birth."[6] Certain that a huge financial market for the kind of "people's bank" he had established in San Francisco was about to arrive in Los Angeles, Giannini wanted to be on the scene when it did.[7]

There were, however, a number of obvious risks. The overwhelmingly Protestant population of Los Angeles made it the most ethnically homogeneous city in the state. Giannini could not expect the same immediate and enthusiastic response to a Bank of Italy branch as had come from the heavily populated immigrant communities in and around San Francisco.[8] In addition, Los Angeles was already home to thirty-nine banks, foremost among them the "Big Seven": Security Trust and Savings, Farmers and Merchants, First National, and four others that controlled three-fourths of the city's total banking resources.[9] The most powerful of these financial institutions was Security Trust and Savings, with resources of approximately $50 million—nearly four times the size of Bank of Italy.[10]

Along with the transcending wealth and superior size of his competition, Giannini faced another major problem. Excited by the emergent potential for economic growth, Los Angeles's business leaders had developed "a civic ambition comparable to the high provincial security of San Francisco."[11] The presence of a Bank of Italy branch in their midst was almost certain to generate a good deal of resentment among men of strictly local prominence anxious to establish a reputation for themselves as well as the city itself independent of San Francisco.

Undeterred by these obstacles, Giannini traveled to Los Angeles with Fagan in the spring of 1913 to look the situation over. He soon found a bank available for purchase: a small, neighborhood institution called the Park Bank, whose principal owner, James C. Kays, was anxious to sell.[12] Although the Park Bank did a thriving business and had total resources of close to $2 million, it was in poor shape financially, the consequence primarily of sloppy lending practices and bad investments. To compound these difficulties, Kays had tried to cover up the bank's losses with fictitious profits and had been threatened by state banking officials in Sacramento with stiff regulatory action.[13]

Word of Giannini's plans to purchase the Park caused an uproar in Los Angeles's banking community. Joseph Sartori, the cautious, extremely successful, and highly regarded president of Security Trust and Savings, was so angered that he rushed to Sacramento for a private meeting with the state superintendent of banking, William Williams, to express his objections.[14] Sartori told Williams that it would be a serious mistake to allow Giannini to open a branch of Bank of Italy in Los Angeles. Giannini's restless ambitions were "too grandiose for his own good" and a "serious menace to the banking profession." Once Giannini moved into the city, Sartori warned, he would inaugurate a campaign of "cutthroat competition" that would disrupt its financial community for years to come.[15]

The solemn, soft-spoken Williams, then forty-two years old, had been appointed superintendent of banking two years earlier by California's "progressive" governor, the flamboyant Hiram Johnson, who had instructed him to use the full power of his office to bring stability and public confidence to the state's banking system.[16] Nevertheless, as Williams told Sartori, he was "embarrassed" by his lack of authority under the state's existing banking laws to regulate the expansion of branch banks. In giving statutory approval to branch banking, California lawmakers had unfortunately failed to make clear where and just how far any banker could go in opening branches. Faced with these unresolved difficulties, Williams said, there was little he could do to prevent Giannini from moving into Los Angeles.[17]

If Williams was outwardly doing his best to soothe Sartori's outraged feelings, privately he was uneasy over the aggressive and unprecedented way Giannini had set about buying small independent banks and converting them into Bank of Italy branches. In Giannini, whom he had met briefly and informally on several occasions, Williams saw a man obsessed by his objective—one whose expansionist ambitions would not be satisfied with the half dozen or so branches he had already established.[18] "I was willing for him to move fast, but I had to check him until new legislation got on the books," Williams would remember. "To A. P. the law was a business competitor who stood in his way. When it blocked his progress, he went after it, as he went after any business competitor who stood in his way. If evasion was the best way to overcome it, then he evaded."[19]

A few weeks later Williams granted Giannini a permit to open a Bank of Italy branch in Los Angeles. Giannini hurried back to the city to conclude his deal with Kays.[20] Giannini's modus operandi for acquiring banks made the outcome of his meeting with Kays certain. Strong-willed, imperious, and motivated by a powerful urge to dominate others, Giannini did not like giving anyone the opportunity of turning him down to his face. Instead, he relied on his associates to handle the complex negotiations and to hammer out the terms of a final settlement. Only when an agreement had been reached would he make an appearance, pen in hand, ready to sign. "The final act in the drama was always Giannini's," one observer would later write.[21]

As Giannini had anticipated, his takeover of the Park Bank produced a storm of local resentment.[22] The May 2, 1913, edition of the *Los Angeles Daily Tribune* announced the purchase in a bold, six-word headline that resonated with overtones of xenophobic indignation: "Italians Take over Park Bank."[23] The city's banking establishment was outraged and responded with sharply worded criticism. One prominent banker condemned Bank of Italy's presence in the community as a "shocking and unwelcome development." Giannini himself was variously characterized in business circles as an agent of the pope, a member of the Sicilian Mafia, and a leader in a mysterious international organization whose aims and clandestine activities posed a serious threat to American society. Whatever the content of these stories, the message they conveyed was the same: doing business with the Bank of Italy was at best risky and at worst unpatriotic.[24]

To get his Bank of Italy branch off the ground, Giannini turned to the promotional techniques that he had used with so much success in San Francisco: an aggressive and heavily financed public relations campaign extolling Bank of Italy's "friendly service and dependable management." On July 26, a quarter-page Bank of Italy advertisement in the *Los Angeles Daily Tribune* informed readers that "the small wage-owner or business man who deposits his savings regularly, no matter how small the amount, is the most valuable client our bank can have."[25] Another advertisement asked the eye-catching question: "Would money help you?" At one point Giannini displayed a large sign in the front window of the branch that proclaimed the bank's fluency in seven different languages: "Tobopn Ce Cphckn; Govori Se Hrvatski; On parle français; Si parla italiano; Se habla español; Man spricht Deutsch; Ome Laoymai Emhnika."[26] "We had money to sell and we went direct to the people to sell it," Giannini would recall. "We were not offering that money to a favored few, but we were offering it to all the people."[27]

As it turned out, Giannini's promotional efforts were not sufficient. Five months after the bold move into Los Angeles, there were signs that his Bank of Italy branch was in serious trouble. For all the printed neighborhood fliers and flashy advertising in local newspapers, Giannini had succeeded in coaxing only a small number of new customers into opening accounts. Even more discouraging was the branch's commercial loan portfolio, which totaled just over $2 million—$100,000 *less* than it had been when he acquired the Park.[28] To Giannini, who was inclined to see hostile machinations all around him, the implication of these dismal figures seemed clear: his competition had put together a well-organized campaign "to steer business to other banks."[29]

Giannini was not entirely wrong in his judgment, but a more basic reason for the lackluster performance of his Los Angeles branch was the continuing decline in the nation's economy. Beginning in the East and spreading rapidly across the country, the downward momentum reached California late in November. Farm prices, which did not come anywhere near their high, pre-1907 panic levels, fell to a new low with the growing prospect of a war in Europe. Throughout the fall and winter of 1913 most banks in the state experienced a severe loss in deposits, occasioned in large part by tight credit and a decrease in profits.[30] By the end of the year, for example, Sartori's Security Trust and Savings had lost nearly $2 million in withdrawals. For Giannini, the steep decline could not have come at a worse time. Unable to make headway in Los Angeles when times were good, the prospects of turning things around with the economy in a slump were dismal.

Desperate to salvage the situation, Giannini returned to Los Angeles to assume personal control over the branch's day-to-day operations. Taking a room in a downtown hotel, he worked frantically over the next several months to boost business, choosing as his primary target some newly opened subdivisions on the outskirts of the city. When some of the branch's employees complained about the long hours and punishing routine, he responded harshly by summoning them to a meeting and denouncing them as a "bunch of damn seat warmers."[31]

He turned instead to his North Beach veterans, Pedrini and Michatetti, who hurried down from San Francisco. Within hours both men had familiarized themselves with a map of the city and had begun knocking on doors in search of customers.[32]

Meanwhile, back in San Francisco, Bank of Italy's directors watched the mounting crisis in Los Angeles with alarm. Fagan, who had played a major role in persuading the board to go along with the move, was increasingly disenchanted. The problem, as he saw it, was Giannini's insistence on continuing the struggle to establish a foothold in Los Angeles long after the effort had obviously become a losing proposition. Other directors expressed doubts about the wisdom of having gone into Los Angeles in the first place. There were complaints that Giannini was so preoccupied with various schemes to save the Los Angeles branch that he was finding it impossible to devote any attention to those branches in the north that had shown themselves to be profitable.[33]

Word of the board's dissatisfaction soon reached Giannini. Early in December 1913 he returned to San Francisco to meet with his nervous directors. Still certain that he had made the right decision, Giannini made it clear that he had no intention of acquiescing to their doubts and abandoning the venture. What was at stake in Los Angeles, he told his directors at a special meeting of the board on December 14, was not simply Bank of Italy's prestige but the key to the development of branch banking in the state. Giannini had little patience with the board's concern over the branch's poor showing. Things would get worse in Los Angeles before they got better, he said. Branch expansion on the kind of aggressive and vastly expansive scale he envisioned for Bank of Italy was unfamiliar, unprecedented, and invariably controversial. As such, it was bound to be an uphill struggle.

Giannini startled the board with his next announcement. Claiming that part of the difficulty in Los Angeles was the bank's "out of touch" location, he proposed moving it to the corner of Seventh and Broadway, the very heart of the city's busy downtown shopping district.[34] The move was a gamble, he admitted, but the most promising way to expand the bank's business was with a more prominent and strategically located position. In addition to the proposal itself, what also stunned board members was the price Giannini was willing to pay to lease the new location—$60,000 a year, or nearly four times the amount the bank was paying for the branch's present location.[35]

Giannini was shocked and deeply disappointed when the meeting adjourned with no recommendation of support.[36] The board's response was partly the result of the continuing skepticism about the entire venture. Far more critical to the timid reluctance of many directors, however, was the result of a recently completed internal audit of Bank of Italy's expenditures in Los Angeles. Board members were devastated to learn that the bank had spent $2 million to support a single branch that in nine months of operations had returned an average monthly profit of exactly $1,187.[37] Panic gripped the board when, on the morning of January 13, 1914, it again met to discuss the rapidly deteriorating situation in Los Angeles.

Rather than insist that the board yield to his proposals, Giannini pursued a different course. He claimed that he could no longer handle the burden of keeping the Los Angeles branch from going under, for it was clear that the board no longer had confidence in his business judgment; he would therefore resign from the bank at the end of the year. "The strain of having personally to continue to stand practically responsible for the management of the bank is in my best judgement too severe—at least for me in an exhausted physical state," he said. Consequently, he "deemed it but fair . . . to afford you the notice that *under no condition* will I accept the position of director or officer of the bank at the next annual meeting of stockholders."[38]

Board members were startled. Although Giannini had talked privately with several directors in the days just prior to the meeting, he had given no indication that he was prepared to go this far out of his disappointment with the board's opposition to his recommendations. How could he walk away from the management of a bank that he himself had founded and guided to such a promising position? Had the board failed to appreciate the extent to which Giannini had committed himself to Bank of Italy's expansion through a statewide system of local branches?

Bacigalupi and a handful of other directors argued and pleaded with Giannini to reconsider, but without success. His decision to resign, he said, was final.[39] He walked away from the directors' table, then turned to board members and wished them "success and even greater prosperity" in the years ahead. Later that month Giannini and his family left San Francisco on an extended vacation trip to the West Indies.

In Giannini's absence, his supporters on the board did what they could to overcome the objections to his proposals. Gradually the attitude of three or four directors began to change. Then, on March 12, 1914, at a monthly directors' meeting, Attilio Giannini asked the board to adopt a formal position in support of his brother's recommendations. Fagan again took the lead in opposing a continued effort. To deal with a "losing proposition" by throwing more money into it, he protested, "made no sense in light of the poor returns from Los Angeles." Sensing the possibility that Attilio had the votes he needed, Fagan and two other directors then got up and left the room. In the absence of a quorum, the motion was defeated.[40]

In early April 1914 Giannini returned to San Francisco. He immediately met with Bacigalupi, who filled him in on what had occurred at the March 12 directors' meeting. A few days later Giannini returned to Los Angeles, where he found conditions much the same as he had left them. With business still in a slump and credit tight, almost every bank in the city was losing deposits, few more heavily than his own. Even more discouraging, during his three-month absence the branch had lost an additional $200,000 in deposits, bringing the total loss to more than $500,000. As one Bank of Italy executive would remember, "To put it mildly the situation in the south was far from rosy."[41]

With developments in Los Angeles going from bad to worse, Giannini settled on a bold course of action. The turning point came on the morning of November 14, 1914, at a meeting of the board called at Giannini's request. Despite the continuing grim news from Los Angeles, Giannini appeared in a smiling, confident, even cocksure mood. After reviewing business conditions in the south with the board, he noted that only a few months remained before his resignation took effect. Consequently, he said, he wanted the opportunity to defend himself against the accusation of his critics that he had wasted millions of dollars of Bank of Italy's money on a wildly ambitious venture that some believed had turned into a calamity. "I do not," he said, "want any director to feel that I have abandoned the ship, leaving behind as a legacy to those who remain any other than solid and solvent holdings."[42]

Giannini rejected the view that the move into Los Angeles had been a mistake and pointed to the "disheartening odds" the bank faced in its efforts to establish a foothold in the city. To retreat from the struggle now "would stamp as an error or mistake the branch system theretofore adopted by the bank," he said. "The Bank of Italy was launched and has had its remarkable record growth on the policy of energetic and enthusiastic optimism. The institution has never known and should never know the word 'failure' in any matter large or small; nor will 'cold feet' ever bring it enduring or any sort of success."[43]

Then, to the astonishment of everyone in the room, Giannini announced that he had put together a group of unnamed investors who were prepared to take control of the Los Angeles branch if the board was still unwilling to go along with his recommendations. "In the event the board decides to dispose of the branch," he said, "there will be no difficulty in disposing of it." In addition, he was ready to reimburse Bank of Italy for all the money the board had thus far thrown into Los Angeles.[44] "In other words," Giannini said, "I desire it distinctly understood at this time that I have no desire to leave in the hands of the Bank of Italy anything for which I may have been directly or indirectly responsible, which I am not now ready and willing to assume myself and to back up with every dollar in the possession of myself and my estate."[45]

Giannini's offer to purchase the Los Angeles branch was a clever maneuver. Board members were visibly impressed not only by the confidence he expressed in his ability to overcome the odds in Los Angeles but also by his determination to carry on, even if that meant turning for financial assistance to outside investors. By offering to reimburse Bank of Italy for its losses, Giannini also deprived his small core of critics on the board of their most discrediting objection. As one director would recall, Giannini's dramatic and supremely forceful performance was designed to put as much pressure as possible on board members "to whip them into line."[46]

Whether bluffing or not, Giannini succeeded brilliantly. No sooner had he completed his remarks than George Caglieri, one of Bank of Italy's original directors, offered a motion urging the board to support Giannini's recommendations. Fagan, realizing that Giannini now had the momentum in his hands, did a complete about-face. "I now believe that making a larger effort in the city will be in the best interest of the bank," Fagan said.[47] With that, Giannini's opposition collapsed and the board unanimously endorsed Caglieri's motion. Giannini did not bother to appear at a directors' meeting a few days later when the board unanimously voted to reject his resignation. As one director recalled, "Giannini never said another word about retiring."[48]

On the morning of April 5, 1916, Giannini and a small contingent of his directors gathered in Los Angeles to celebrate the opening of Bank of Italy's new branch office at Seventh and Broadway. A large crowd of local reporters, customers, and the merely curious sipped punch and sampled hors d'oeuvres from a buffet set in the center of the glimmering white marble and brass lobby. As always Giannini worked the crowd, shaking hands, exchanging smiles and small talk, escorting one group of customers after another on a triumphal tour of the building. It was the kind of public display of financial showmanship and blatant self-promotion that so infuriated his competition and confirmed their opinion of him as a vulgar "dago huckster." But Giannini had more in mind than a public relations gimmick. As one aide would remember, "The less obvious purpose of the celebration was to let his competitors know that the Bank of Italy was in Los Angeles to stay."[49]

2

With the much-debated move into Los Angeles now settled to his satisfaction, Giannini hurried to open additional Bank of Italy branches throughout the California countryside. He had good reason to move quickly. The outbreak of war in Europe had created a soaring demand for the state's agricultural production. In 1916, the second full year of the war, the annual cash value of California's field crops jumped to approximately $350 million—a staggering increase over previous years.[50] With the price of major farm goods climbing to higher and higher levels, farmers in all parts of the state felt as if they had struck a bonanza. "Everybody was running around looking for a piece of land to irrigate," one Sacramento rancher would remember.[51]

Notwithstanding their great dependence on credit, most farmers found the task of borrowing money from local banks far more difficult—and riskier—than the business of farming itself. Many county banks charged unreasonably high rates of interest—up to 12 percent in remote farm towns, five points higher than the national average.[52] Others tied up the bulk of their money in loans to a few large growers in the community, often for purposes in which the bank's directors and officers had a piece of the action. Still others preferred making loans through a "credit broker," which meant that farmers had to contend with the "services" of a third party at an additional cost.[53] The result, as one farmer put it, was that borrowing money from a local bank "was like living with a delivery system which was full of rusted plugs and padlocked faucets."[54]

Excited by the opportunity the boom presented for Bank of Italy's expansion, Giannini embarked on a hectic campaign to buy more banks and convert them into branches. He made his initial move into the Santa Clara Valley, where his San Jose branch was experiencing an impressive growth in depositors. Early in 1916 he bought a small bank in the town of Santa Clara itself, then still more local banks in a half-dozen or so farm towns scattered along the valley's northern edge.[55] Over the next three years Giannini kept buying more banks and opening more branches. Soon he had jumped into the San Joaquin Valley, whose twenty million acres of rich farmland stretching three hundred miles through the central part of the state had grown into a thriving network of densely populated farm centers.[56] Once again Giannini personally assumed the task of promoting his bank with a determination that amounted almost to an obsession.[57]

Giannini's methods for acquiring banks ranged from the conventional to the ethically dubious. During the 1920s he was particularly successful in acquiring banks that found themselves in serious financial difficulty. He received scores of letters from small-town bankers pleading with him to purchase their banks, which had failed because officers and directors had mismanaged the banks or had misused the bank's money and feared the consequences of public exposure. In 1921, for example, Giannini purchased the National Bank of Visalia after its president repeatedly urged him to rescue the institution from bankruptcy.[58] What these and other bankers in similar circumstances got in return for selling out to Giannini was the avoidance of a public scandal and the opportunity to join his Bank of Italy "family" as loyal stockholders.

Small-town bankers who were reluctant to sell out were treated to a combination of lucrative financial offers and incessant pressure. Although frugal in his personal life, Giannini often offered to pay more than a bank was worth in order to acquire it. If this approach proved unsuccessful, he was quick to resort to hard and intimidating tactics. One close aide later remembered the time when he and Giannini drove to a small town in southern California. They parked directly across the street from a local bank whose owner had repeatedly rejected Giannini's purchase offer. As the aide described it, "Giannini had me get out of the car, walk back and forth, and pretend I was measuring distances with my feet. When the owner of the bank came out to ask what was going on, I told him the man seated in the back of the car was A. P. Giannini, and that he was planning to open a branch of his bank on the corner." Faced with the prospect of having to compete with the Bank of Italy, the owner sold out.[59]

Sensitive to the ethnic and anti-Catholic bigotry that prevailed throughout the countryside, Giannini relied more heavily than ever before on Bank of Italy's non-Italian executives to conduct his face-to-face negotiations for him. One of these was Prentice Hale, the son of San Francisco department store owner Marshall Hale, who had joined the bank as a director in 1922.[60] Stocky and distinguished looking, with white wavy hair and patrician manners, Hale looked the part, as Giannini would recall, of a "respectable Yankee banker."[61] Once the take-over had been completed, carpenters and sign painters were brought in late at night to make the necessary alterations. Not until the bank opened its doors the following morning did most local residents learn that their familiar "hometown" bank had become a branch of Giannini's Bank of Italy. As one Giannini executive would remember, "Speed was essential to reduce avoidable shifts in deposits."[62]

To accommodate the busy schedule of local farmers, Giannini took the unprecedented step of keeping his branches open until eight o'clock in the evenings and on weekends.[63] More important was his insistence that employees treat each customer with the same courtesy and consideration that his competitors reserved for their wealthiest clients, no matter how small their deposits. He based his strategy for attracting working-class depositors on personal and high-quality service. "The little fellow is the best customer that a bank can have," he was fond of telling his branch managers. "He starts with you and stays to the end; whereas the big fellow is only with you so long as he can get something out of you, and when he cannot, he is not for you anymore."[64]

Giannini offered money to borrowers at two, three, and even five percentage points lower than what other banks were then charging.[65] This strategy naturally provoked howls of protest from local bankers, who accused him of engaging in the most vicious kind of cutthroat competition. But the more his competitors complained, the more Giannini pushed ahead with his aggressive lending program. "The glad hand is all right in sunshine, but it's the helping hand on a dark day that folks remember to the end of time," he liked to say.[66] Customers who were paying on loans from the bank's previous owners were astonished to learn that their interest had been reduced to the 7 percent his Bank of Italy was then charging.[67] "You are putting borrowers out of business if you charge 10 or 12 percent," Giannini told one local reporter.[68]

Not surprisingly, news of Giannini's liberal lending policy spread quickly from one farm town to another. In addition to making banking more competitive locally by forcing his opposition to meet Bank of Italy's interest rates, Giannini also won praise in the rural press for his policy of financing strictly local development.[69] Farmers, of course, were delighted by the lower interest rates and by his willingness to satisfy the credit needs of anyone in the community who needed a loan. As one Fresno rancher later remembered, "After the arrival of Giannini's bank, we had a breather. We thought we could afford to borrow money for the first time."[70]

As the number of Giannini's branches increased, so did his days on the road. Then, as in later years, he was Bank of Italy's most energetic booster, dropping in at the homes of local farmers, talking, persuading, opening new accounts, selling stock in the bank. He would go to remarkable lengths to recruit new depositors and to keep them as customers. Once, driving through a rainstorm at the end of a long and exhausting day, Giannini was informed by an aide that an elderly woman in a town a hundred miles away had withdrawn her $1,000 savings account from the local branch of his bank and transferred it to one of his competitors. No one seemed to know the reason why. Late that night, after a three-hour drive over dark, muddy country roads, Giannini showed up at the woman's home. By the time he left, he had convinced her to transfer the money back to his bank.[71]

Giannini's capacity for work was extraordinary. He was at his desk in the bank from seven in the morning until nine or ten at night. "My day began early and ended late," he would recall years later. "In fact, it never ended at all except in sleep. And at night I did my planning for the next day, the next week and the next year; in fact, the next ten years."[72] It was about this time that Giannini bought a black Packard touring car. Valley farmers soon came to know him by sight, an energetic, oversized figure seated next to his driver, roaring along dusty county roads from one farm town to the next.

Occasionally Giannini would take his wife along with him. "If he passed some farmer he knew," one observer wrote later, "some acquaintance of his commission days, A. P. would stop and invite the man for a ride. He would sit in the jump seat, while the poor farmer would be placed like some honored guest beside Mrs. Giannini."[73] Sunday drives in the countryside with his family invariably turned into scouting missions in search of new locations for a Bank of Italy branch.

"Travel on those dusty, bumpy roads was difficult then," his daughter Claire would remember. "The car was always breaking down. We had to plead with our father to stop. By then it was usually late at night and we would be forced to share a single room in some godawful place. All of us would complain, but my father never did."[74]

Giannini's ever-proliferating network of branches soon began paying impressive dividends. In less than two years Bank of Italy's total resources climbed from $11 million to just over $22 million. Nowhere was this growth more evident than in farm towns, where Giannini's branches were attracting more and more customers, many of whom had never before been inside a bank. At the end of 1917, for example, Bank of Italy's annual earnings from its Santa Rosa branch office were $1,700; one year later they had climbed to $11,000. Annual profits from the Fresno branch went from $9,449 to $104,515 during the same period. Easily the most successful of Giannini's branch banks was the one in Stockton, whose annual profits went from $23,000 to $132,000 in just three years.[75]

3

In the 1910s, when Giannini began his branch expansion program, he relied on Bacigalupi's formula for buying banks: an indirect method designed to get around the state's banking law prohibiting one bank from purchasing the stock of another bank. Although cumbersome, this method had worked reasonably well—as long as Giannini was buying a single bank. But when he began acquiring three and four banks at a time, the financial risk to individual Bank of Italy directors was staggering. On the acquisition of his branch in the town of Napa, for example, the financial obligation of one director was $800,000.[76] Giannini had to find a better method for acquiring banks, one that entailed far less personal risk. Otherwise, he would be forced to buy banks at longer intervals, thus slowing him down in the expansion of his branch banking system.[77]

As it happened, Giannini had less difficulty overcoming this problem than he had expected. On May 20, 1917, he approved plans for the creation of a holding company that was later incorporated under the name of the Stockholders Auxiliary. The incorporation papers showed that even though this new corporation was beneficially owned, share by share, by Giannini's Bank of Italy stockholders, it was a separate entity independent of the bank. More important, it had the power to do what the Bank of Italy could not do—buy stock in other banks.[78]

Giannini later admitted that it was William Williams who first suggested the holding company device to him. Although there was nothing illegal about Williams's advice, the fact that he had offered it at all was an indication that the two men enjoyed an unusually close relationship.[79] The most persistent rumor in financial circles was that Williams had ambitions that went beyond the superintendent's office and that Giannini had promised him a top position in the bank in return for favorable treatment. Giannini vigorously denied the allegation, but the rumors persisted. "Sure we were angry," one of Giannini's competitors said later. "We all knew that Giannini was Williams' pet."[80]

Regardless of the question of conflict of interest, the Stockholders Auxiliary offered Giannini the solution he had been looking for. Late in May 1917, in a hastily written letter from the Biltmore Hotel in Santa Barbara, Giannini urged Bacigalupi to take the necessary legal steps for the creation of the corporation as quickly as possible. Excited by the opportunities for expanding his operations, Giannini told Bacigalupi that he was ready to embark on a path that would turn Bank of Italy into a financial powerhouse. "Just think what this new arrangement could mean," he wrote. "Try and get it as soon as you can." He added in a postscript: "Go to it Jim. It's no dream, I assure you—never was I more serious on a proposition."[81]

It had been slightly more than ten years since Giannini had opened his first branch in San Jose, and his achievements in that time dazzled his supporters and critics alike. By the end of 1919 he had opened 24 Bank of Italy branches in 18 towns and cities from the tidewaters of the San Joaquin in the northern part of the state to Los Angeles in the south. At the same time, the bank's total resources had climbed from $22 million to $100 million.[82] This made the Bank of Italy the fourth largest financial institution in the state. Far more important, as far as Giannini was concerned, he had succeeded in creating the first statewide branch banking system anywhere in the country.

SIX

A Storm of Opposition

I

As Giannini kept buying more and more banks and converting them into branches, he inevitably became the object of a great
deal of resentment. California's small-town independent bankers expressed the most alarm. They complained most often about being
forced to compete against the Bank of Italy's superior resources, which
they claimed would drive many of them out of business. The independents also feared that Giannini's branches would drain money from
the countryside to finance the large metropolitan centers like San Francisco and Los Angeles.[1] "Branch banking is in essence monopolistic
and a threat to the established American way of banking," one enraged
independent told a legislative committee in Sacramento on January
15, 1915. "Steps should be taken now to eradicate it before a condition develops which would invite great harm to individuals and
communities."[2]

Giannini seldom responded publicly to these protests. Privately he
viewed local independents as "village blacksmiths, . . . horse and
buggy bankers" whose rhetoric about "friendly hometown service"
was seldom matched by a genuine concern for the larger credit needs
of the community or by a willingness to make loans in the interest of
economic progress.[3] Far more important to him was the attitude of the
state's department of banking. Since California law prohibited banks
from acquiring branches without first obtaining approval of the state

superintendent of banking, much of his expansionist ambitions depended on not being frustrated by unfavorable decisions made in Sacramento. So far, this had not been much of a problem. From 1913 on, Giannini had found a sympathetic ally in William Williams, who had been generous in approving his requests for permits to open branches.[4] But now, in the summer of 1918, all that was about to change.

The reason was William D. Stephens, the pudgy, smooth-talking former mayor of Los Angeles and two-term Republican congressman who had succeeded Hiram Johnson as governor of California in 1917.[5] Ever since Stephens had begun consolidating the base of his political power in southern California—aided by his personal and business connections as the former president of the Los Angeles Chamber of Commerce—he had been increasingly critical of Giannini's branch banking operations. After his election as governor, Stephens privately informed his political allies in Los Angeles that he intended to put an immediate halt to the Bank of Italy's expansion.[6] Stephens later defended his policy on grounds of "safe banking" and said that for a San Francisco bank to operate a branch as far away as Los Angeles was both "risky and undesirable."[7]

According to Bank of Italy executives, Stephens was motivated in his opposition to Giannini by much more than concern for "safe and sound" banking practices. They charged that Stephens had, during his two terms in Congress, given new and unambiguous meaning to the word "deadbeat" in his financial transactions with various Los Angeles banks. When his personal needs required it—and they often did— Stephens would take out loans for modest amounts of money and then neglect to repay them. To avoid the publicity and embarrassment in bringing a lawsuit against a local incumbent congressman, Los Angeles bankers had long since adopted the practice of simply writing off their losses to "goodwill."[8]

By the oddest of events, among the notes Giannini inherited when he took over the Park Bank in 1913 was an overdue loan to Stephens. Unlike other Los Angeles bankers who had accommodated the congressman, Giannini refused to write off the loan. On two occasions he sent letters to Stephens requesting repayment, but without success. Giannini persisted, finally sending an associate to Washington with instructions to pursue Stephens "into the very halls of Congress if necessary" to collect the money.[9] Eventually Stephens paid up, but he let it be known to aides that he bitterly resented the indignity he had been forced to suffer.

Then, in the spring of 1919, Giannini took a step that his executives warned would result in serious political repercussions. Shortly after Stephens took over the governor's office, Williams resigned as superintendent of banking and promptly accepted an offer from Giannini to join Bank of Italy as chief cashier.[10] Stephens reacted as if he had been betrayed and humiliated. After Stephens replaced Williams with Charles Stern, the state's former commissioner of highways, rumors began circulating in Sacramento that Stern would soon move to "tame" Giannini's branch banking ambitions once and for all. As one Giannini associate recalled, "The hiring of Williams was a mistake and was certainly . . . a poor investment politically."[11]

Giannini soon found out just how poor. When he applied to the bank superintendent's office for permission to open a branch in Santa Rosa, a small town just north of San Francisco, Stern turned him down.[12] After calling the Bank of Italy a financial institution "unique in American banking," Stern informed Giannini in a letter on June 23, 1919, that he was "frankly disappointed" with the rapid expansion of so many widely scattered branches. Among other things, Stern charged that the loose coordination between "this mosaic of many units" had resulted in a number of unsound banking practices. Stern ended his letter by accusing Giannini of exposing Bank of Italy to potentially grave problems. "We are not only deeply disappointed but we are very seriously concerned with the situation that we find from the standpoint of the safety and ultimate solvency of your institution."[13]

Characteristically, Giannini viewed these criticisms as an attack against him personally, but there was more to Stern's hostile attitude than mere vindictiveness.[14] Giannini, in fact, was more vulnerable to criticism of his banking practices than he was willing to admit. Examiners complained that in Giannini's haste to acquire branches, Bank of Italy's bookkeeping methods were at best sloppy. Pressure to achieve rapid growth pushed branch officers into approving loans unsupported by financial statements, while a good many other loans were allowed to run past maturity. The bank's earnings statements were frequently inflated. In addition, Bank of Italy's local advisory boards—another Giannini innovation—set the policy agenda for each branch and reviewed loans before they had been committed, compounding what examiners perceived as a severe fragmentation of authority within the lower echelons of the organization.[15]

Hoping to smooth things over, Giannini sent Bacigalupi to Sacramento in June 1919 with instructions to reach some sort of accommodation with Stern. Bacigalupi's efforts got nowhere. Bacigalupi told Giannini that during his meeting with Stern the superintendent had "likened our bank to a house of cards" and had bitterly denounced branch banking generally as "European in principle . . . [and] diametrically opposed to the splendid system of unit banking consistently followed in the United States since the birth of the nation under which our country has grown to its position of world supremacy." Stern warned Bacigalupi in no uncertain terms that unless Bank of Italy took prompt action in dealing with the problems uncovered by examiners, "he felt it his duty, by the use of the 'strong arm' if necessary, to arrest our further expansion."[16]

As always when confronted by personal criticism or obstacles to his ambitions, Giannini immediately struck back, ignoring the warnings of Bacigalupi and others who urged him not to respond to Stern's threats. In a move widely interpreted in the banking community as a public challenge to Stern's authority, Giannini issued a statement in the pages of *Bankitaly Life,* a house organ for Bank of Italy employees. After claiming that Bank of Italy's rapid growth had aroused the envy and hostility of many "powerful people in the state," Giannini concluded: "Should official attitude toward branch banking prevent the Bank of Italy from establishing additional branches, nothing will deter it from lawfully benefiting the residents of any and every part of California."[17]

Giannini's determination to push ahead in the face of political resistance in Sacramento was no doubt intended in part to intimidate state banking officials. His low opinion of government officials was exceeded only by his contempt for lawyers, politicians, and bureaucrats, whom he privately characterized as venal, pliant, and invariably corrupt, among society's least honorable and productive members. But such public and defiant behavior was bound to have self-defeating consequences. Whatever the political benefits Giannini may have derived from his close relationship with Williams over the years, they would almost certainly be more than offset by Stern's ability to cripple Giannini's plans for expanding Bank of Italy.

As Bacigalupi and others had expected, Stern was quick to respond. "I cannot believe," he wrote to Giannini a short time later, "that the . . . public advantage can be promoted by a theory of banking that, when its ultimate has been reached, four, or three or one Bank of Italy controls the finances of California." Consequently, Stern said, "While this department holds its present point of view, you may not go forward with further branch expansion."[18]

To meet this challenge, Giannini countered with a different course of action that caught his competitors off guard and would further arouse their anger. Late in 1913 he joined the nation's newly created Federal Reserve System.[19] Giannini's strategy was to use his affiliate, the Stockholders Auxiliary, to acquire additional banks, which he would then convert into national banks, distinct from his state-chartered Bank of Italy. The difficulty, of course, was that he would be forced to operate two different banking systems in California at the same time—one state, the other national. But this arrangement hardly mattered to Giannini. What mattered more was that he would be free to continue with his expansionist ambitions without being blocked and frustrated by state banking officials in Sacramento.[20]

Giannini was soon buying small county banks whenever and wherever the opportunity presented itself. Within two years he had moved into two dozen or more farm towns like Sunnyvale, Hayward, Los Banos, King City, Paso Robles, and Lompoc.[21] Then he purchased four banks in San Francisco itself. To the great outrage of his competitors, Giannini did not pretend for one moment that his newly acquired string of national banks was "independent" of Bank of Italy; indeed, he infuriated state banking officials by notifying the public in press releases and printed inserts in local newspapers that for all practical purposes they were one and the same. As one Giannini executive would recall, "In all but name only, the new acquisitions were branches of the Bank of Italy."[22]

It was now that Giannini's reputation for cunning and financial legerdemain began to spread across the state. To his well-known image as a financial "wizard" was added the reputation of a fiercely determined individual who would allow nothing or no one to stand in his way. He had exploited loopholes in the law or else ignored the intent of the law entirely in his relentless pursuit of branches, thus demonstrating his skill at outmaneuvering his opposition and making it clear that it was he who intended to control the initiatives to use against his critics, and not the other way around. As one financial writer later put it, all this "increased the fear and mystification people in California felt about Giannini, who seemed to be operating *sub rosa*—through secret agents."[23]

Meanwhile, the Bank of Italy was matching the ever-expanding number of its branches with wealth and power. One year after Giannini opened his branches in northern California, deposits had increased by nearly $42 million. That brought the Bank of Italy's total assets to

$142 million, enough to make it the third largest financial institution west of Chicago.[24] By now the combined number of Bank of Italy depositors had climbed to two hundred thousand. This growth conjured up in the minds of many the image of a financial leviathan whose full authority was yet to be felt. As the *San Francisco Chronicle* commented, "By every sign the really frightening thing to his competitors is that Giannini's drive for the financial domination of California is only just getting under way."[25]

2

Even as Giannini was busy expanding his branch banking system in California, the idea of opening a bank in New York was never far from his mind.[26] During the summer of 1919 Cavagnaro and his small group of Italian investors again appealed to Giannini to purchase the East River National. This time they expressed their willingness to have a high-level Bank of Italy executive run the bank while Giannini himself remained in San Francisco. Giannini agreed, but on the condition that Cavagnaro and the others raise at least $1.5 million to get the bank off the ground. To assist Cavagnaro in this effort, Giannini sent Bacigalupi to New York with instructions to pull out all stops in the campaign to attract investors.[27]

Always the best promoter for his own ventures, Giannini directed Bacigalupi's activities from San Francisco by means of a constant stream of letters and telegrams. "Don't forget to point out what an Italian institution properly organized can do for the upbuilding, development, and prosperity of the Italian business men—particularly small ones— and laboring men," he wrote in one such telegram.[28] "There is one thing, Jim, if we have anything to do with the organization of an Italian institution in New York. We would see to it that the managing officers, from the president on down, were put out in front and in the open. . . . They all should be just where everybody could have a chance to approach them," he said in another.[29]

In October 1919, after signing up approximately one thousand investors, Giannini purchased the East River National. Ownership of the bank was placed under a holding company he created for that purpose called Bancitaly Corporation. A team of veteran solicitors sent out from San Francisco was soon searching for depositors in Brooklyn, the Bronx, and other boroughs where wave after wave of Italian immigrants had settled in the congested sprawl of New York's Lower East Side.[30] They quickly discovered that pounding the streets of the city's two dozen or more "Italian colonies" was much more difficult than it had been in San Francisco. Soon, however, they were ringing doorbells in nearby cities like Newark, Hoboken, and Jersey City.[31]

To manage the East River National, Giannini named his brother, Attilio. It was, in some ways, a curious move. The relationship between the two men, never close, had grown increasingly more strained and distant. Some, including Giannini family members, thought that the antagonism between the two was the result of long-standing resentments. Giannini had spent his early adult years struggling to make a success of his stepfather's firm on the waterfront. By contrast, Attilio had traveled a relatively untroubled path through his undergraduate and medical school years at the University of California, a good part of which Giannini had financed out of his profits in the commission trade. Attilio prided himself on his college education and his familiarity with literature; he thought of himself as something of an intellectual and enjoyed flaunting his learning. Giannini, who had no interest in books and was suspicious of any man who did, was scornful of Attilio's intellectual pretensions and what he perceived as a lack of appreciation for the contribution he had made to his brother's success.[32]

Others believed that the two men were temperamentally opposed. Giannini was the ascetic, unpretentious, hard-driving businessman whose daily life was consumed by the bank and little else; Attilio was his mirror. Shortly after leaving his medical practice in 1907 to join Bank of Italy, Attilio married the daughter of a wealthy Los Angeles businessman, moved to the fashionable suburb of Atherton, and soon became a prominent figure in some of the finest restaurants and private clubs in the city. Unlike Giannini, who had no interest in the whirl of celebrity recognition or executive rewards of any kind, Attilio loved the spotlight and found the prerogatives of corporate office irresistible. Giannini referred to his brother privately as the "prima donna" and viewed him as an immature, self-centered, "spoiled little boy" whose claims to business ability were overrated.[33]

But Giannini valued his brother's close personal and business friendships with the socially powerful and his ability to move easily in sophisticated circles—traits he thought might serve Bank of Italy well in New York. Thanks in large part to the aggressive groundwork of the bank's New York solicitors, the East River National grew faster and faster. When Giannini took over the bank, its assets were $3.5 million;

nine months later they had climbed to nearly $13 million, a remarkable increase for a small Brooklyn bank whose customers were predominantly working-class Jews and Italians.[34] Giannini moved swiftly to broaden the bank's appeal. "No favorites," he cabled Bacigalupi. "The bank to deal with all classes, particularly foreign element 100% of the public—Italians, Poles, Swiss, Slavonians, Spanish, etc. etc."[35]

Giannini then stunned his critics with his next move. No sooner had he taken control of the East River National than he sent Pedrini across the Atlantic to buy the Banca dell'Italia Meridiorale, a medium-sized bank in Naples that was on the edge of financial disaster.[36] Within weeks of arriving in Naples, Pedrini had fired most of the bank's executives and their staffs, reorganized its operations, and introduced efficient management policies in an environment where personal greed and incompetence had once prevailed.[37] Before long the Banca dell'Italia Meridiorale had regained the confidence of its depositors and had begun expanding its operations into other Italian cities.[38] In just over a decade after opening his first Bank of Italy branch in San Jose, Giannini had laid the foundations for an intercontinental network of banks extending from Italy to New York to California.[39]

In California, meanwhile, opposition to the expansion of Giannini's branch banking system was beginning to enter a more bitterly contested phase. Nothing demonstrated this more than an event in Santa Rosa, a farm town fifty miles north of San Francisco. On the morning of January 7, 1921, Bacigalupi was sitting at his desk in San Francisco when the phone rang and he heard the voice of Glen Murdock, manager of Bank of Italy's branch in Santa Rosa. Speaking with difficulty, Murdock informed Bacigalupi that a run on the branch was in progress.[40] Preliminary reports were not encouraging, Murdock said. The police were trying to keep order, but the bank was virtually under siege by hundreds of panic-stricken customers demanding the return of their savings.[41] In less than two hours the bank had used up nearly half its total cash reserve of $150,000. Outside the building a surging mass of people waited to enter and withdraw their deposits.[42]

With Giannini out of the city, Bacigalupi called Cuneo, Scatena, and two aides to his office and filled them in on the situation. Together they packed $500,000 in gold and silver coins into an old suitcase and some canvas bags, which they then placed in the back of Cuneo's car— enough, Bacigalupi thought, to handle the run until the bank closed for the day.[43] Accompanied by armed guards, the car sped through city streets toward the waterfront and the ferry to Sausalito, across the bay. As soon as the car hit the main highway outside Sausalito, Cuneo pushed his foot to the floor for the dusty, winding, one-hour ride to Santa Rosa.[44]

Bacigalupi, fearful that the excitement of events in Santa Rosa had the potential for sensational front-page headlines that could affect the entire organization, immediately made arrangements to increase the behind-the-counter money of Bank of Italy's other branches.[45] "By tomorrow morning you will receive an extra supply of currency," he cabled each of the bank's branch managers. "Keep a stiff upper lip and let every man wear a big smile. Do business in the usual manner and honor every legitimate demand without asking questions. Remember, A. P. is counting on you."[46]

By the time Scatena and the others reached Santa Rosa, news of the run had spread to the surrounding countryside. "The crowd was becoming more and more excited," he later remembered.[47] Struggling through the pandemonium, they carried the suitcase and canvas bags into the bank's crowded lobby. To everyone's surprise, Scatena promptly dumped the $500,000 in gold and silver across a table. "You can have your money," he shouted. "This bank is as safe as the Rock of Gibraltar."[48]

It was nearly six that evening before the bank closed its doors. Even so, lights inside the bank burned far into the night. While employees prepared for a continuation of the run the following morning, Scatena and Murdock counted the losses.[49] The result of their audit was shocking. Withdrawals on the first day of the run totaled $500,000, a staggering loss for a small-town bank.[50]

As it turned out, when the bank opened in the morning, things went much better than anyone had expected. By this time Giannini had been informed of the run and had hurried up to Santa Rosa, bringing with him an additional $3 million in gold. Moving through the crowd that had gathered outside the bank, his thunderous voice conveying authority and confidence, he reassured customers that their deposits were safe.[51] The rest of the morning was anticlimactic. As the *Santa Rosa Republican* informed its readers later that day, "The Bank of Italy is safe and sound in every way," adding, "If there is any weakness at all then Jack Dempsey is tubercular and Sampson was a weakling."[52]

An investigation by local officials later determined that the run had resulted from the hysteria generated by two of Bank of Italy's own customers.[53] According to an official report filed by Santa Rosa's chief of police, during the late afternoon on the day preceding the run most local banks and businesses had closed their doors during the funeral of the town's former mayor. As fate would have it, two elderly women had chosen that time to show up at the branch to make a deposit. Terrified at the "Bank Closed" sign in the window, they had rushed back to their homes to tell their neighbors that the bank had gone out of business. Within hours, news of Bank of Italy's "failure" had spread like wildfire through town.[54]

Giannini, however, was not satisfied with this explanation. Back in San Francisco a few days later, he launched his own investigation. A team of private detectives from the Pinkerton Agency spearheaded the effort. Among other things, investigators claimed to have found hard evidence to prove that confidential reports critical of Bank of Italy's banking practices had been "leaked" to Giannini's opposition by officials in the office of the superintendent of banking. "The rumors were that we had grown too fast and that we were 'riding for a fall,'" Giannini would recall. "Our competitors apparently had the most intimate knowledge of the lack of harmony existing between the department and the bank." The implication was that Stern had served as a conduit to Giannini's opposition, supplying them with potentially damaging information that they had used to smear the bank's reputation whenever the opportunity presented itself.[55]

Other Pinkerton reports, too, hinted at some high-level conspiracy, suggesting the possibility that Giannini's opposition had hired agents to spread damaging stories about him and the bank in valley towns where he had located branches of Bank of Italy. According to one report, rumors had been circulating in the city of Stockton weeks before the Santa Rosa run that "the Bank of Italy had loaned large sums of money to the King or Governor of Italy and that the paper was no good and that the Bank had loaned large sums to Hindoos on crops . . . and would lose all this money."[56] Another rumor offered the "confidential" information that "the Bank of Italy was in serious financial trouble and about to fail."[57]

This threat only heightened Giannini's determination to push ahead with Bank of Italy's penetration into the state's agricultural valleys. He redoubled his efforts in appealing to the credit needs of California farmers. A series of notices placed in small-town newspapers announced that the Bank of Italy had "plenty of money available at seven percent" to farmers who needed it.[58] Local residents were also informed that the bank had a policy of "no entangling or conflicting outside interests on the part of its officers or employees." In time the Santa Rosa branch would recover most of its losses. But Giannini would never forget the Bank of Italy's tarnished reputation nor the intrigue of his enemies whom he held personally responsible for it.

3

The fear and resentment of Giannini's opposition was not difficult to understand. By the early 1920s the Bank of Italy had emerged as an immensely powerful force in the state. A crucial factor was the activity of the bank's Italian Department, which Giannini had established some years earlier and then placed under the direction of Armando Pedrini. Sharing the department's duties and responsibilities with Pedrini was Robert Paganini, a young, energetic, and demanding North Beach businessman who had owned an Italian-language newspaper in Sacramento before joining Bank of Italy.[59] Paganini directed the activities of the department's corps of handpicked solicitors, or "missionaries" as they were called, all of them Italians, whose job was to turn every Italian resident of California into a depositor and stockholder in the Bank of Italy.

During the early years of the department's activities, Paganini's missionaries limited their activities to a wide radius around San Francisco. Eventually, however, they began combing Italian communities in towns and cities south of the Tehachapi, in places like San Luis Obispo, Santa Maria, Santa Barbara, Los Angeles, and as far south as San Diego.[60] In contrast to the East Coast, where ethnic minorities were located primarily in urban centers, the California countryside had attracted a large and heterogeneous population of first-generation immigrants with cheap land and the promise of economic success. Paganini's expectations for the department knew no limits and reflected the goals and values with which Giannini had imbued his organization. "The Bank of Italy is continuing and will continue in the future under your splendid leadership," Paganini reported to Giannini on one occasion, "and nothing and nobody can stop it."[61]

Under Paganini's merciless direction, the department's missionaries canvassed the state with a messianic intensity that had by now become a marked characteristic of Bank of Italy executives.[62] Under pressure from Giannini to show results and certain of his backing, Paganini drove his missionaries to brutal, almost unbearable extremes. They responded by pushing themselves harder, reaching for higher and higher goals, and thus increasing the number of new Italian depositors. "It is raining very hard and it may snow during the night," a missionary in the Sierra Nevada region of the state reported to Paganini in one of his reports. "There are no lights in the hotel and I am writing this report by the aid of my flashlight. This does not discourage me, but it makes me fight that much harder."[63] Another missionary informed Paganini that he "was on the job and . . . doing more than I really ought to," adding his assurance that "the institution is going to benefit through my endeavors."[64]

More than just a promotional arm of the bank, the Italian Department was a sophisticated, highly disciplined, and well-organized system of private financial information. In San Francisco the department maintained an "Italian index file" consisting of three-by-five cards on which were typed the names and addresses of every Italian living in California on a town-by-town and county-by-county basis.[65] Missionaries in the field were instructed to use these cards to track down local Italians and to collect confidential information concerning their "moral and financial standing in the community."[66]

Out of this flow of information the Italian Department put together, long before centralized credit files became fashionable, "an ingenious and confidential intelligence system of its own making" to assist Bank of Italy officials in determining who among the state's population of Italians was a good credit risk.[67] The existence of these files was not generally known to the public, allowing Giannini to go on pretending that the bank owed its remarkable success to his "faith in the honesty of the common man."[68]

Giannini's bank held other attractions for Italians aside from its access to credit. It also functioned as a voluntary social service agency to assist them in nonfinancial matters. On Giannini's instructions, the department's missionaries encouraged Italian aliens to become American citizens and arranged for evening classes in local branch offices to prepare them for their naturalization examination. "Mr. Giannini wants all good Italians to become American citizens," Paganini instructed his missionaries.[69] They found jobs for the unemployed, visited the sick, translated official documents into Italian or English, and paid grocery bills for the needy. Occasionally they were called on to settle domestic arguments. Before long the Bank of Italy became almost as well known among California Italians for its social as for its financial services.[70]

With so much at stake, Paganini's missionaries did not hesitate to go beyond acceptable limits of behavior in soliciting the business of Italians. Not only by direct inquiries, but by enlisting the secret cooperation of rival employees, they obtained the names of Italians who deposited their savings in other banks. Through a variety of methods, including personal visits by a local missionary or pressure from employers and family members, attempts were made to persuade them to shift their accounts to a local branch of the Bank of Italy.[71] These high-pressure tactics were remarkably successful. As one of Paganini's missionaries who worked the farm towns along the Monterey peninsula reported, "The greatest part of our Italian depositors that were dealing with other local banks . . . left those institutions entirely, and all their business is now being transacted through us."[72]

This combination of ceaseless effort and roughneck tactics infuriated rival bankers and often created problems for state banking officials. After investigating a complaint filed by one Italian businessman, for example, an official in the bank superintendent's office reported: "The solicitation of the Italian representatives of the Bank of Italy had been so offensive and insistent that he had been obliged to give them a deposit in self-defense."[73] Such charges were, of course, denied by Bank of Italy executives. Nevertheless, it was the one aspect of Giannini's promotional activities that most confirmed his critics' view of him as a brazen, ruthless, and vindictive aggrandizer, prepared, if necessary, to use almost any means in his relentless drive for power.[74]

A man driven by results, Paganini placed exhausting demands on his missionaries. Daily reports were mandatory. If a report was late or missing, Paganini usually interpreted that to mean that the missionary was loafing—and that meant an immediate reprimand.[75] "During the last four days, we have not received a report from you," he wrote one of his missionaries on the San Francisco peninsula. "Whether you are on the road traveling from town to town, taking a rest or ill, a report should come daily to the department showing how your time has been occupied," he wrote. "In other words, we should receive a report from all the solicitors for each 365 days of the year. I do not want to repeat these instructions to you again."[76]

Nothing escaped Paganini's scrutiny. He could run his watchful eyes over a report, wondering why new accounts were down or why a missionary had not covered more territory. If he suspected a missionary of giving less than his duties required, he was quick to take action. "In checking over the accounts I noticed that you are amongst the last on the list," he wrote to one of his missionaries. "Only seven to your credit. I am sorry to say this, but it seems you do not care to assist me in my undertaking."[77] Even when the results were good, Paganini kept the pressure on. "I feel ashamed to repeat over and over again . . . I have no new business to show," the department's missionary in Monterey reported. "This is mainly due to the fact that all the Italians of this territory are already our customers."[78] Paganini's reply was typical. "You already have a good percentage of the Italian business, but I am sure there are some good prospects in the hills and near the coast."[79]

In addition to building an Italian clientele on the basis of loans and deposits, Paganini's missionaries also devoted a considerable part of their time to promoting the sale of Bank of Italy stock.[80] "Sell as much Bank of Italy stock as possible," Paganini wrote in one of his directives.[81] Tens of thousands of Italians eagerly responded. Giannini was delighted with the department's stock promotion activities. "Chart showing distribution of stockholders of Bank of Italy proved very interesting to me," he wrote to Pedrini on April 27, 1923. "The most pleasing thing I notice is the large number of stockholders owning from one to five shares. . . . We have practically all of the good Italian element in the State of California under our banner."[82]

Paganini's missionaries were only a minority among the bank's many "foreign divisions," but their efforts proved remarkably successful. Less than five years after the department began operations, nearly 40,000 Italians had become Bank of Italy depositors, a figure that translated into 20 percent of the bank's total number. The sale of stock grew at a rate faster than that of depositors. By the end of the 1920s, 40 percent of the bank's more than 100,000 stockholders were Italians, the vast majority of whom lived in California.[83]

Other foreign departments grew right along with the Italian—Yugoslavian, Russian, Portuguese, Greek, Mexican, Spanish, Chinese.[84] Strictly speaking, there was thus no single Bank of Italy but a financial world in itself, complex and comprehensive, exerting enormous influence in the lives of millions of people.[85] From the outside the bank looked monolithic. Inside, however, it was a confederation of banks, each rigorously disciplined and organized, each aggressively tracking down scattered communities of the foreign-born—all designed to reach the greatest number of people.[86]

Giannini liked to boast that Bank of Italy was a "people's bank" whose purpose was to serve the financial needs of those other banks had chosen to ignore. As early as 1911 he announced that San Francisco's

Board of Education had named Bank of Italy the "official" depository for the savings of school children.[87] "Let's not talk about thrift," he told a local reporter. "Let's give children a sample of it."[88] What Giannini could have added, but didn't, was that each school-age child who opened a "one penny account" in the Bank of Italy was likely to remain a customer for the rest of his or her life.[89]

Bank of Italy employees were soon collecting savings from children in 1,200 classes in some 86 San Francisco schools.[90] Within five years the bank had expanded its school savings program outside San Francisco to more than 160 schools in 41 towns and cities throughout the state.[91] Other banks hurried to mimic Giannini's school savings program, but with far less success. As so often in the past, he had been a step ahead of the competition. The results, though modest by industry standards, were nonetheless impressive. By the end of 1918, the bank had more than 22,000 school-age customers and deposits of nearly $1 million—and a bridgehead of customers from one generation of Californians to the next.[92]

Nor was Giannini content to limit his business extension activities to ethnic groups and school children. By 1921 he was ready to promote the bank's services among women. The idea of catering to women was not new. A number of banks in the country had already adopted the practice of advising women on money matters, usually with a single teller's window set aside for that purpose. To Giannini, however, these "windows" were just that—a convenience provided to women who specifically asked for it. Giannini had different ideas. One was to create a bank devoted exclusively to the financial interests of women. The other was to staff the bank entirely with women and to appoint a woman to run it.

Giannini's "Women's Bank" opened in June of 1921. Taking up the entire upper floor of the bank's headquarters building in San Francisco, it was equipped with tasteful furnishings, conference rooms, and a staff of twelve female officers and employees.[93] The purpose of the bank, as women were informed through brochures distributed across the state, was to promote their "economic independence" by providing them with the full range of professional banking services.[94] To assist the uninitiated, the bank conducted free evening classes on business and financial matters, a practice that brought Giannini a windfall of favorable publicity from women's civic and professional groups in California as well as other parts of the country.[95]

The Women's Bank was slow to get off the ground, but it didn't take long for news of its existence to circulate. By the end of 1923 it had ten thousand customers and $1.5 million in deposits.[96] The bank's annual report for that year also showed that on the commercial side (wills, trusts, deeds, and investments) it had done more than $5 million in business.[97] As one woman writer in Boston put it, the great success of the "only bank in America that is administered, staffed, and maintained solely by women . . . should give every male banker in the country deep pause."[98]

Whatever Giannini's critics might charge about his haste to add new branches to his banking operations, there was no mystery about Bank of Italy's sudden rise to prominence. In 1921 alone, he added 100,000 new depositors, bringing the total to 400,000, the highest number of any bank in the country.

Although few Americans outside of California had heard of him, by the early 1920s Giannini was slowly making a name for himself that was beginning to reach well beyond the limits of the state. "You would never guess which of all the banking institutions in America has the largest number of depositors," the financial editor of the *New York Herald Tribune* informed his readers. "This bank is not located in New York or Chicago or Philadelphia or St. Louis or Detroit. The institution enjoying this unique distinction is the Bank of Italy with headquarters in San Francisco. This phenomenal achievement prompted me to delve into how it was done. The answer might be summed up thus: A. P. Giannini."[99]

SEVEN

Winning at Any Cost

I

By 1920, as the profit-making opportunity as well as the superior advantages of branch banking in promoting economic growth demonstrated themselves, big-city bankers in every region of the state moved eagerly to share in Giannini's success.[1] Small, independently owned unit banks became prime targets for acquisition and conversion into branches. Among the earliest and most prominent converts to branch banking were Herbert Fleishhacker, vice-president of the San Francisco–based Anglo-California, and Joseph Sartori, founder of Security Trust and Savings.[2] Next to Sartori, the most powerful voice in the Los Angeles banking community making the shift to branch banking belonged to Henry Robinson, president of the First National. A former corporation lawyer and longtime personal friend of Herbert Hoover, Robinson was linked by political and business interests to the city's Republican establishment and occupied a "conspicuous place in the financial and social world of southern California."[3]

In Sacramento, Stern's office was flooded with formal applications for acquisitions and branch permits. On the whole Stern responded favorably, but not indiscriminately. During the two-year period from 1919 to the end of 1920 he granted a total of seventy-one branching permits to Sartori, Robinson, Fleishhacker, and a small number of the state's other converts to branch banking. By contrast, Bank of Italy received only two permits, neither of which involved the opening of new branches.[4]

Giannini concluded—correctly, as it turned out—that Stern had joined forces with his branch banking rivals in Los Angeles in an effort to keep Bank of Italy "boxed up" in the northern half of the state. Stern admitted as much many years later. "When I became superintendent," Stern told an interviewer, "bankers beat a path to my office to complain about the monopolistic tendency of the bank. The more I thought about it, the clearer it became to me that the south should be left to southern bankers and the northern banks would stay in their part of the state."[5]

Whatever the obstacles Stern had decided to make for him, Giannini nonetheless had a considerable advantage. Moving cautiously, his major competitors like Sartori, Robinson, and Fleishhacker confined their acquisition of branches to the cities in which their own parent banks were located.[6] Giannini was still the only banker in California who had scattered his branch banking operations in an increasingly powerful interlocking network of local offices far from Bank of Italy's headquarters in San Francisco. With forty-one branches in some thirty towns and cities and $100 million in deposits, he was far ahead of the competition. Catching up with him would not be easy.[7]

Symbolic of Giannini's growing financial power was the opening in June 1921 at 1 Powell Street of Bank of Italy's new headquarters building, a seven-story, neoclassical, white-granite structure located a few blocks from the center of San Francisco's downtown shopping district. Giannini's public invitation to a three-day "housewarming" drew large and enthusiastic crowds of more than seventy thousand to inspect the splendor of the new surroundings that the *San Francisco Examiner* hailed as "the largest building devoted exclusively to banking on the North American continent."[8] Giannini himself remembered the occasion as "the only fear" he had ever experienced in business. "My thoughts were all directed toward wondering whether I made a blunder moving from the place where all my success had been laid. I wondered if old friends and associates would believe we were mainly putting on the dog."[9]

Giannini had other reasons to celebrate. A few days earlier Stern had announced that he was resigning as the state superintendent of banking to join Henry Robinson's Los Angeles Trust and Savings, an affiliate of First National, as a senior executive vice-president.[10] Stern was replaced by Jonathan Dodge, a Los Angeles lawyer and former chairman of the city's board of supervisors, who was rumored to be building a power base outside Los Angeles in an effort to capture the Republican gubernatorial nomination in two years' time. Although Dodge was known to have close personal connections to the Los Angeles business establishment, Giannini was hopeful that he would be more sympathetic to Bank of Italy's expansion than Stern had been. As it developed, Giannini's hopes were never completely realized, but at the time it seemed that they might.[11]

Indeed, no sooner had Dodge taken control of the bank superintendent's office than Giannini moved quickly to "make up" for the discriminatory treatment he felt he had suffered under Stern. This time the target of his expansionist ambitions was the city of Sacramento, seventy miles north of San Francisco, whose surrounding acres of flat, rich farmland he had canvassed during his years in the Scatena firm as a commission merchant.[12] News of Giannini's intentions soon reached the ears of Sacramento bankers. They reacted by organizing a whispering campaign designed to mobilize public opinion against the "threat" of Bank of Italy's presence and in favor of the city's "home-town" bankers. "All kinds of propaganda appears to be in circulation," a Giannini aide wrote from Sacramento. "They have a kind of non-union rumore [sic] in effect . . . that the Bank of Italy uses cutthroat methods."[13]

Confronted by the organized opposition of Sacramento's banking community, Giannini countered with a campaign of his own. He sent two dozen Bank of Italy employees to the city to gather signatures on a petition urging Dodge to approve his application for a branch permit. Knocking on doors, they canvassed the city's working-class neighborhoods with the fervor of visiting evangelists. Within three days they managed to collect eight thousand signatures, the vast majority of which came from Sacramento's sizable number of Italians and Portuguese.[14] "We have worked this town to a finish," one of Giannini's associates informed him. Letters and telegrams expressing support for the proposed branch poured into Dodge's office. "Please no more," an exasperated Dodge wired Giannini.[15] He approved the permit.

While rival bankers in Sacramento fumed over Dodge's action, other towns in the region reacted excitedly to the possibility that Giannini would soon be opening branches of Bank of Italy in their communities. The scores of letters Giannini received gave evidence of the extent of the bank's reputation as a financial institution that served the credit needs and economic well-being of small customers.[16] The overwhelming majority of these letters came from ordinary residents who lived in dusty farm towns far removed from San Francisco. "When is the Bank of Italy coming to Eureka?" a dairy farmer wrote in one such letter. "Many people are forced to transact business under conditions not of their choosing. We need a Bank of Italy branch here."[17]

Giannini needed no coaxing. Approval of his Sacramento permit, his first in two years, gave him the opening he had been waiting for. He quickly purchased a string of small county banks in the Sacramento Valley, converting them as rapidly as he could into branches of his Bank of Italy. By the end of 1921 he had opened still more branches in such Central Valley farm communities as Chico and Woodland in the north and Fresno, Bakersfield, Shafter, and Taft in the south. Along the way he expanded the number of Bank of Italy's branches in large cities like Oakland, San Diego, and San Francisco.[18] "Everywhere Giannini was seizing leadership from his rich, long established competitors," one financial writer commented later. "And by every sign, his drive was just getting underway."[19]

One reason why Giannini was racing to expand his banking operations was the growing competition from his rivals. By this time Sartori, Robinson, Fleishhacker, and other big-city bankers had embarked on an astonishing surge of branch expansion unprecedented in the state's financial history.[20] Henry Robinson's Los Angeles Trust and Savings, for example, increased the number of its branch offices from three in 1920 to thirteen one year later. Dodge's office was swamped with applications for permits, mergers, and consolidations. Although Giannini's competitors continued to confine their activities to their own home cities, most industry observers agreed it was only a matter of time before they would begin to zero in on independent banks in neighboring communities.[21]

California's small independent bankers howled in protest. If the unrestrained pace of acquisitions and branch expansion was allowed to continue, they argued, the traditional small-town "neighborhood" bank would cease to exist. Calling branch banking the "menace of the hour," they bitterly announced their intention to fight back, using whatever means they had at their disposal.[22] Not surprisingly, with his larger and far more powerful branch banking system, it was Giannini and the Bank of Italy that became the chief target of their fear and resentment.

As word of Bank of Italy's continuing advance spread throughout the state, the independents formed themselves into an organization called the California League of Independent Bankers. By the end of 1922 the league had enlisted as members nearly all of the state's more than five hundred independent bankers.[23] In small, closed-door meetings held in scores of rural outposts and valley towns, league members took a solemn oath never to sell out to Giannini, no matter how attractive the offer. More important to their hopes of putting a halt to Bank of Italy's advance was the league's intense lobbying efforts in Sacramento for legislation to restrict the further spread of branch banking. In committee hearings and strongly worded resolutions introduced by their political allies in the state legislature, Bank of Italy was portrayed as an "undemocratic . . . European-type bank" that posed a serious threat to "the true principles of American democracy."[24]

Attacks came from other quarters, most prominently from small-town fundamentalist ministers in southern California, a stronghold of anti-Catholic bigotry. The Reverend Robert Schuler used his popular weekly radio sermons to unleash a steady flow of inflammatory statements—a propaganda whose spread was secretly financed by the League of Independent Bankers and Giannini's branch banking rivals, particularly in Los Angeles. "There is no question," Schuler informed his radio audience, "but what the Bank of Italy was founded and is controlled by Roman Catholic Italians, who . . . by some slick work . . . have gained control of most of the banks of California." Schuler warned that if the people of the state did not take immediate steps to end the spread of Bank of Italy branches, Giannini would succeed in "consummating his plan toward controlling the entire West, both financially and politically."[25]

Confronted by renewed protests from Giannini's branch banking rivals in Los Angeles and by growing pressure from the independents and their hometown allies, Dodge adopted a more stringent position on the granting of additional Bank of Italy branch permits. In a letter to Giannini on July 12, 1921, he severely criticized Bank of Italy's organizational "inefficiency," which he attributed to its "domination by an official family." Dodge went on: "This control is held so closely by President Giannini and his immediate associates that insofar as such a thing is possible in an institution of your size, your management may be likened to . . . a one man bank."[26] Dodge warned that unless Giannini took prompt steps to "put his house in order" and diminish Bank of Italy's aggressive management style and excessive control at the top, he would refuse permission to open additional branches.[27]

Before Giannini had a chance to respond to these charges, Dodge called a press conference to announce a major change in the department's policy regarding the continuing growth of branch banking. In the future, Dodge said, banks could open new, or *de novo,* branches only in those cities in which their "principal place of business" was located. Elsewhere, however, branches would have to be established out of existing banks that had been specifically acquired for that purpose. Dodge made it clear that permission to open other than strictly de novo branches would be granted only in "exceptional cases . . . in which the bank superintendent in his discretion shall find that the public convenience and advantage shall require it."[28]

Despite warnings, Dodge's de novo ruling angered Giannini, suspecting as he did that it was aimed directly at him personally.[29] He was essentially correct. Although Dodge defended his policy on grounds of protecting small-town "neighborhood" banks against the competitive spread of branch banking, the appearance of regulatory evenhandedness was deceptive. Since Giannini's major branch banking rivals like Sartori, Fleishhacker, and Robinson had no immediate plans to push their branch-building operations beyond the boundaries of their own home cities, Dodge's de novo ruling had no damaging short-term effect on them. The situation for Giannini, however, was far different. Given the fact that he alone had embarked on an ambitious plan to build a statewide system of branches, the de novo ruling had the effect of freezing him in place.[30]

Although Dodge assumed full responsibility for his de novo policy, he had been supported behind the scenes by John Perrin, a former Los Angeles investment banker who was now governor of San Francisco's Federal Reserve Bank (FRB).[31] In San Francisco and Washington, FRB officials were growing increasingly concerned about the steady loss of nationally chartered banks from the banking system, primarily because federal law prohibited banks from engaging in branch activity.[32] In 1921 alone, the Twelfth Federal Reserve District, which comprised the states of California, Washington, Oregon, Nevada, and Arizona, lost twenty-six member banks through mergers and consolidations.[33] One year later this figure had doubled—a clear sign that growing numbers of national banks were finding it more and more difficult to compete against state-chartered banks with powerful branch systems.[34]

Giannini was already in front of Washington's changing mood. Anticipating the possibility that Dodge would respond to pressure from the FRB and Bank of Italy's politically influential competitors in Los Angeles, he embarked on a bold scheme. His strategy called for the establishment of an entirely new state bank with a branch system of its own, which could operate beyond the limits of the northern half of the state where Dodge's de novo ruling had been designed to restrict him.[35] Under this arrangement, Giannini, who had a high regard for his own ability at finding ways to outmaneuver his opposition, would have the freedom to expand his banking operations into towns and cities where he had been prohibited by state officials from opening additional Bank of Italy branches.

Late in the summer of 1921 Giannini's Liberty Bank opened its doors in downtown San Francisco, one block north of the city's financial center.[36] Although there was no doubt in anyone's mind about who actually controlled the bank, Giannini created the public impression— or at least tried to do so—that Bank of Italy's "official family" had only a relatively marginal interest in the establishment of San Francisco's newest bank. He stacked Liberty Bank's management and board of directors with non-Italians—men with names like Hale, Wood, Webster, Miller, Olsen, Murphy, and Buckley.[37] "I thought that by organizing the Liberty Bank with a new crowd they'd think we had little to do with it," Giannini said later.[38] Convinced of the correctness of his actions, Giannini seldom entertained the possibility that he might be risking regulatory disapproval by overreaching himself.

Sputtering with rage, Perrin summoned Giannini to his office at the San Francisco FRB (SFFRB). During a heated argument he accused Giannini of endangering the financial health of California by creating a complex network of banks, subsidiaries, and affiliates whose ability to ensure the safety of the money entrusted to them by depositors was entirely dependent on his leadership.[39] According to Bacigalupi, who accompanied Giannini to the meeting, "The burden of his [Perrin's] general remarks was a deep concern as to what would happen if Giannini were to be 'hit by an automobile.' Giannini was told that the Bank of Italy was a 'one man bank'; that although Giannini was not exactly an experienced banker he was nevertheless the 'whole show'; that if he died suddenly, there wasn't a man in the world who could step in and take his place."[40]

But Giannini had no more intention of relinquishing his hold on the Liberty Bank in the face of Perrin's heated objections than he had of cooperating with Dodge in adhering to the spirit of the de novo ruling. Indeed, in the weeks following Dodge's announcement of the de novo policy, Giannini further angered his critics in Sacramento and Washington by acquiring four new national banks, running them in all but name as part of his network of Bank of Italy branch offices.[41] Rejecting Perrin's allegations about the bank's "one man" management style as "groundless," Giannini replied that there "was not the slightest chance that an institution the size of the Bank of Italy could possibly be run by one man or a dozen unless it was well organized and staffed with competent executives."[42]

Giannini's response left little doubt in Perrin's mind that something needed to be done to prevent other banks from becoming takeover targets for Bank of Italy's expansion. In a sharply worded letter of November 25, 1921, Perrin informed Giannini that henceforth he would need the approval of the FRB "before proceeding to acquire any bank for the Bank of Italy, or any corporation affiliated with it."[43] This meant that Giannini's days of using the Stockholders Auxiliary to purchase banks for the purpose of turning them into branches were over.[44] To Giannini, that translated into a policy of virtually no expansion at all. As Bacigalupi remarked years later, "Perrin's idea of branch expansion was at the rate of one branch addition each year."[45]

Perrin's injunction came as a blow to Giannini.[46] Los Angeles was growing as never before. Local banks were experiencing an increase in deposits and a heavy demand for loans. He wanted to boost Bank of Italy's presence in the city, making him at least an equal partner with Sartori and Robinson in grabbing a share of the booming credit market. From Giannini's perspective, Perrin, who was rumored to have set his sights on the Republican gubernatorial nomination in 1922, was trying to ingratiate himself with Sartori and Robinson. Beyond the role he had played in formulating the de novo ruling, Giannini told Bacigalupi, Perrin's objective was to "discredit us" with FRB officials in Washington in the hope of frustrating Bank of Italy's chances of acquiring a larger presence in Los Angeles.[47]

Whatever the merits of Giannini's suspicions, there was a good deal more to the FRB's hostility toward his branch-building ambitions than an uncritical acceptance of Perrin's recommendations. The rapid spread of branch banking had come at an enormous cost to the nation's banking system.[48] From independent bankers across the country there came loud and angry outcries for some kind of federal protection in their one-sided competition with state-chartered branch banking systems. They found a friend in Washington at the highest level of the government's regulatory agencies. He was Henry M. Dawes, comptroller of the currency, ex officio member of the FRB, and an outspoken critic of branch banking. Dawes called for strict limitations on branch banking and urged the passage of legislation in Congress that would halt the spread of "such monopolistic practices."[49]

With state and federal officials bearing down on him as never before, Giannini pursued two courses. The first was to reach outside Bank of Italy's own legal staff to hire an experienced attorney who had the expertise and the right political connections in Washington to negotiate a compromise with the FRB. He was William G. McAdoo, a former chairman of the FRB who had served as secretary of the treasury in the administration of his father-in-law, Woodrow Wilson. After resigning from the Treasury Department in 1919, McAdoo moved to Los Angeles three years later to open his own law firm, McAdoo, Neblett, and O'Connor.[50] A tall, thin, sharp-featured man, with a considerable talent for self-promotion, McAdoo was a smooth political operator and had close personal ties to many influential policymakers in Washington. Giannini believed that if anyone could help repair his strained relations with the FRB, McAdoo was the man.[51]

Giannini had another objective: to alter the public perception that Bank of Italy was strictly a one-man show. Early in the spring of 1922 he left San Francisco with his family for a year-long vacation in Europe. "He made that trip to prove to the world that the bank could continue to operate, keep clean and prosper without him," Bacigalupi would remember.[52] During Giannini's absence the bank's executives did their best to convey the impression that he had removed himself completely from Bank of Italy's day-to-day operations and had assigned to them responsibility for running the bank. In fact, Giannini kept in close contact with Bacigalupi, Pedrini, and his other senior executives via a steady flow of letters and cablegrams across the Atlantic.[53]

As Giannini had hoped, McAdoo had soon negotiated a settlement with FRB officials in Washington. In January 1922 the board handed Giannini a much-desired objective by approving branch licenses for the dozen or more banks he had acquired over the preceding two years through his Stockholders Auxiliary.[54] For his part, Giannini agreed to first seek approval from the FRB before he "promoted the establishment of any new bank" and to limit Bank of Italy's "direct or indirect participation" in the ownership of other banks to 20 percent of their stock.[55] With this settlement, board members believed they had succeeded in putting the brakes on the spread of Giannini's Bank of Italy branches. In time they would come to understand how wrong they had been in that assumption.

2

    In spring 1923 Giannini returned to San Francisco to some unexpectedly welcome news. Californians had elected a new governor, Friend Richardson, the colorless, mediocre, special-interest candidate of the Republican party's ultraconservative wing.[56] Richardson replaced Dodge as superintendent of banking with a Los Angeles businessman, J. Franklin Johnson.[57] The state's former deputy treasurer, the politically ambitious Johnson had played a key role in Richardson's election and had friends and influential supporters at every level of the party organization. Among them was John Chambers, manager of Bank of Italy's branch office in Sacramento. Chambers told Giannini that in a private meeting with Johnson, the new superintendent of banking had expressed his willingness to establish a more cooperative relationship between his office and Bank of Italy.[58]

    Giannini was excited. He quickly mobilized Bank of Italy's resources for a new expansionist drive, beginning with San Luis Obispo, a farm town located among low, rolling hills about 250 miles south of San Francisco.[59] For more than a year Giannini orchestrated a quiet campaign to buy a controlling interest in the Union National, one of San Luis Obispo's two local banks. When the Union National's principal owners finally became aware of what was happening, they succeeded in mobilizing strong support among the bank's stockholders in opposition to the takeover. In the battle for control that followed, Union National officials thought the matter so desperate that they enlisted the secret aid of Giannini's branch banking rivals in Los Angeles, who were alarmed at the prospect of Bank of Italy assuming a larger presence in the southern half of the state.[60]

    Their efforts, however, were not good enough. As it happened, one of the Union National's largest shareholders died.[61] For reasons that later became a source of gossip among local residents, his widow decided to sell the stock to Giannini, giving him control of the bank. Furious Union National officers and stockholders denounced the takeover bitterly.[62] When a team of Bank of Italy officials from San Francisco arrived in San Luis Obispo several days later to begin the conversion process, they were shocked by what they found. The bank's windows were broken, office furniture smashed, and books and records pulled out of file cabinets and scattered. "Everything was turned upside down," one Giannini aide recalled. "It was a glorious mess."[63]

Not long after he moved into San Luis Obispo, Giannini turned his sights on the neighboring town of Santa Maria, sixty miles to the south, whose fertile valley of dairies and sugar beet farms had attracted sizable numbers of Swiss Italians and Portuguese.[64] The banking situation there was similar to what it had been in San Luis Obispo. Although Santa Maria already had three banks, all were controlled by a small, tightly knit group of the town's first-generation settlers, the most influential of whom was Paul Teitzen, president of the Bank of Santa Maria.[65]

Accounts of what happened next differ. According to Bacigalupi, Teitzen showed up unexpectedly in San Francisco one day in the spring of 1921 with an offer to sell the Bank of Santa Maria to Giannini. As Bacigalupi remembered, "Mr. Teitzen represented to us that he was getting along in years and was desirous of getting out of the banking business." Bacigalupi drew up a preliminary purchase agreement, which Teitzen and Giannini then signed several days later.[66] A short time later, without warning, Teitzen suddenly broke off negotiations, telling Bacigalupi that he had changed his mind. Teitzen eventually sold his bank to Henry Robinson's Los Angeles Trust, which had begun laying the groundwork for a network of branches outside of Los Angeles.[67]

Teitzen told a much different story. According to Teitzen, Giannini had been badgering him for more than two years to sell the Bank of Santa Maria, but each time he had refused. Then, in the spring of 1921, Teitzen said, he became seriously ill and was taken to a hospital in San Francisco. One day, while "hovering near death," Teitzen received a visit by "an agent from the Bank of Italy" who inquired about the state of his health and then "demanded" that he reconsider Giannini's offer. Once again Teitzen held his ground and refused.[68]

Concluding that he was getting nowhere in his efforts to purchase the Bank of Santa Maria, according to Teitzen's account, Giannini adopted stronger measures. As the bank's cashier remembered: "When Mr. Teitzen refused to be brow-beaten, the Bank of Italy employed certain officers . . . and sent them through the Santa Maria county buying up the pass books on that bank. On one occasion, these men, agents of the Bank of Italy, had saved up some 85 of such pass books and took them into the Bank of Santa Maria in a lump, laid them down on the counter and demanded the money." Returning to the bank the next morning, Giannini's aides asked the cashier how "his boss" had liked that "wallop" and warned that if Teitzen did not sell out to Giannini, "the Bank of Italy had many more such wallops to administer."[69]

Some months later Teitzen's allegations became the focus of the House Committee on Banking, which had opened hearings in Washington on the issue of branch banking. Giannini's most militant critics from among the ranks of California's independent bankers seized on Teitzen's accusations to make Giannini's "ruthlessness" a weapon in their campaign to stop the spread of branch banking. A hush settled over the committee as witness after witness told of threats, harassment, and cold contempt for "fair and honest business dealings" on the part of Bank of Italy officials in Giannini's efforts to expand his branch system into Santa Maria.[70] "There is not room for two banks in Santa Maria and it won't be the Bank of Italy that will go broke," Giannini was quoted as angrily telling one Teitzen supporter.[71]

Under questioning from committee members, Bacigalupi, who represented Giannini at the hearings, denied that Bank of Italy had committed any wrongdoing.[72] Bacigalupi called Teitzen's allegations "wholly unjustifiable . . . and a complete surprise," the product of Teitzen's determination to "dominate the banking situation in Santa Maria." In a lengthy letter to the committee soon after his return to San Francisco, Bacigalupi said that there was "positively nothing in the conduct of the Bank of Italy in its efforts to enter the Santa Maria field . . . that was in any way unethical or censurable."[73]

Despite his claims of innocence, Bacigalupi did not deny that a team of Bank of Italy employees sent into Santa Maria had made personal calls on scores of local residents and succeeded in persuading them to transfer more than $100,000 in deposits from Teitzen's bank in Santa Maria to Giannini's Bank of Italy branch in San Luis Obispo. Nor did he deny that this same team of employees had managed to purchase an unspecified number of savings account books from Bank of Santa Maria depositors and taken them to the cashier in Teitzen's bank for repayment. Giannini was always eager to publicize the "dirty tricks" of his opposition, but when it came to getting what he wanted, he had no difficulty tolerating excesses by his own employees.

Unable to buy one of Santa Maria's three existing banks, Giannini then submitted a formal application to Sacramento for a de novo permit to open a branch of his Bank of Italy in Santa Maria. On March 6, 1921, he instructed Chambers to meet with Johnson and either persuade him to acquiesce in a new bank permit or confront him with the prospect of having to wage a bloody battle in court over the legality of the de novo rule itself. After a private meeting with Johnson in Sacramento, Chambers was able to give Giannini some encouraging news. "Mr. Johnson is a friend of the Bank of Italy and he happens to be a personal and a Masonic friend of my own. My impression is that you will be granted a permit in Santa Maria."[74]

Word of the Johnson-Chambers meeting quickly got out, sending one delegation of independents after another racing to the state capital to express their opposition. In the months that followed, Johnson would face mounting pressure from the opposing forces—on the one side, small-town bankers from across the state joined by Giannini's branch banking competitors in Los Angeles pushing for containment; on the other, Giannini.[75]

In Santa Maria, meanwhile, a powerful coalition of local agribusiness interests and Giannini's anti-branch-banking opponents from across the state organized protest meetings and spread damaging accusations against Bank of Italy. Residents who were known to favor the presence of a Bank of Italy branch in Santa Maria were threatened with violence; others were informed that their "access to credit in town would be denied them for good" if they persisted in allying themselves with Giannini.[76] Giannini's supporters, primarily small businessmen and working-class Italians and Portuguese, counterattacked with protest meetings of their own and with a flood of petitions to Sacramento protesting the monopolistic and discriminatory practices of Santa Maria's three local banks. "We find ourselves under the influence of a small clique," one typical petition said. "Those who do not have a friend at court are simply out of luck, that's all."[77]

The battle raged for months. Giannini, who had maintained a low profile while there appeared to be any chance for a favorable decision from Sacramento on his de novo permit, grew increasingly annoyed and frustrated by the long delay. As was so often the case when deterred from his empire-building objectives, his public manner as a warm and friendly businessman was capable of turning quickly into dark and uncontrollable anger. At one point he stormed into Johnson's office, waved his fist in the face of an official in the department, and demanded an immediate answer. It was a terrifying performance that exposed, in the eyes of many, Giannini's willingness to resort to intimidation to achieve his objectives. Badly shaken and personally embarrassed by

Giannini's intemperate outburst, Johnson sent word to Bacigalupi that "if it happened again everything would be off."[78]

Finally, in July 1923, Johnson informed Giannini that he had decided to approve his de novo permit for a Bank of Italy branch in Santa Maria. At a press conference in Sacramento, Johnson defended his decision by saying that he had been persuaded by a careful review of the evidence that "the public convenience and advantage of the city of Santa Maria would be promoted by the opening of a Bank of Italy branch."[79] Infuriated, independent bankers from across the state denounced Johnson's action and accused him of having capitulated in the face of what they alleged had been a Giannini-inspired campaign of fear and intimidation.[80] There was an intensified demand for legislative intervention from Sacramento to halt the spread of branch banking.[81]

In San Francisco, meanwhile, congratulatory letters and telegrams flowed into Bank of Italy headquarters. Most came from Santa Maria residents who claimed that the town's vital economic interests had never been served by Teitzen's Bank of Santa Maria. "Hurrah!" one such resident wrote. "I am surely delighted. This section has great possibilities ready to be developed and I feel very sure that when the Bank of Italy is located here, we will come into our own."[82] Giannini, who seldom paused in his branch-building pursuits to savor the gratifications of victory, had already put plans in motion for his next offensive. Soon after he had learned that Johnson was prepared to comply with his request for a permit in Santa Maria, he ordered his executives to begin preparing the necessary papers for de novo permits in at least half a dozen other communities along the state's south-central coast.[83]

Despite the victory, Giannini's two-year struggle to break into Santa Maria harmed him immensely. Stories about the brutal methods he was alleged to have used against Teitzen as well as other small-town independent bankers whose banks he coveted spread rapidly throughout the state and outside California as well. The image that his critics projected of him was that of a ruthless competitor of limitless ambition who would not hesitate to resort to the most ethically indefensible tactics against anyone who dared to challenge the spread of Bank of Italy branches. In time the events surrounding Giannini's acquisition of a branch in Santa Maria confirmed what his harshest critics had long been warning: Giannini was the most dangerous banker in the country.

As it developed, Giannini's excitement over his de novo permit in Santa Maria was short-lived. After reviewing Bank of Italy's application for formal approval of the permit, FRB officials in Washington declined to take action.[84] This move was partly the result of the succession of horror stories that board members had heard about the tactics Giannini was alleged to have adopted in his struggle to break into Santa Maria. For a majority of the board members, however, the issues went deeper still, to a national banking system whose difficulty in competing with state-chartered branch banks had reached near-crisis proportions. Dawes, who left the comptroller's office in 1925 to become chairman of the FRB, issued a statement prior to his departure calling branch banking "essentially monopolistic" and "destructive of sound banking principles."[85]

3

Although deeply disappointed by the FRB's action, Giannini had no intention of allowing federal banking officials to slow his momentum. Early in 1923 he moved his New York–based Bancitaly Corporation into a newly completed twelve-story building on Seventh and Olive in the center of Los Angeles's financial district.[86] Blocked from expanding his Bank of Italy branch system outside northern California, he now intended to use Bancitaly as a vehicle to do what Dodge's de novo ruling prevented his Stockholders Auxiliary from doing: acquiring more banks.

Moving quickly, Giannini purchased two large Los Angeles banks. One was Bank of America, the city's third largest financial institution with a string of twenty-five branches, which he merged and placed under the control of a new holding company called Americommercial Corporation. Within six months Americommercial was operating thirty-five branches, the vast majority of which were located in Los Angeles.[87] Under the Americommercial umbrella, Giannini later formed two state-chartered branch banking systems in southern California, one of which he called Bank of America of Los Angeles.

Giannini's achievements with Bancitaly in southern California were stunning. He had disregarded totally the intent of the de novo ruling, moved with a combination of brilliantly calculated maneuvers and astonishing speed that had been overwhelming, and emerged with a banking system in Los Angeles larger and more powerful than any possessed by the city's well-established financial institutions. As the *San Francisco Chronicle* put it, "Giannini has at last invaded Los Angeles with a banking combination of unquestioned strength. What Los Angeles thinks, we know not and we venture the opinion that Giannini is not worried what anyone thinks of the latest banking consolidation. Well, it has been no secret that Giannini for many a day has been anxiously awaiting the opportunity of going to Los Angeles. He is there."[88]

Before his competitors had time to recover from this unanticipated shock, Giannini resumed the offensive.[89] He startled his opposition in the northern half of the state by expanding the base of his Liberty Bank, which he had been holding in reserve since its founding in 1921.[90] Beginning in the fall of 1923 and continuing over the next two years, Giannini conducted a financial blitzkrieg in the northern California countryside. One town after another saw the establishment of a Liberty Bank branch: Turlock, Daly City, Palo Alto, Salinas, Vallejo, Crescent City, Roseville. Before long Giannini had scattered a string of Liberty Bank branches from as far north as the Oregon border to the outer edges of the San Joaquin Valley, three hundred miles south of San Francisco.[91]

The net result of Giannini's nearly twenty years of branch building was staggering. Counting all of the various subdivisions—Bank of Italy, Commercial National, Bank of America of Los Angeles, Liberty Bank—Giannini's hydra-headed banking empire now consisted of 155 local offices scattered across the state from the Oregon border in the north to the Mexican border in the south and holding more than $470 million in deposits. One observer wrote, "Giannini has succeeded in creating a huge financial octopus which threatens to wipe independent banks out of existence."[92]

Given this remarkable achievement, it came as a surprise to many when, on January 4, 1924, Giannini announced his intention to resign as Bank of Italy's president on the twentieth anniversary of the bank later that year. Acting on Giannini's recommendation, the bank's board of directors met a few days later to name James Bacigalupi as his successor. "I will not conceal the fact," Bacigalupi wrote to Giannini, "that I was made very happy on receiving the news of your flattering offer. I desire only to be certain of the goodwill of my leader."[93]

Giannini broke the news of his "retirement" at a press conference in San Francisco. He told reporters that the time had come for him to make way for younger executives who would be given the opportunity to set the strategy for Bank of Italy's future.[94] "I want the men here to feel that this isn't simply a one-man institution," he said. "There's a place for everybody and a chance to hit the top mark if they come up to the qualifications. I just thought I'd step out before I got so old that I'd have to be put out."[95]

Giannini's decision to place more of the responsibility for running Bank of Italy in the hands of his top executives was no doubt sincere. But Bacigalupi, Pedrini, and others in the organization saw what a number of industry observers also thought they saw: Giannini wanted to put some distance between himself and Bank of Italy in order to pursue a larger, bolder, and far more ambitious strategy. As the financial editor of the *San Francisco Chronicle* speculated in commenting on this "retirement," "Giannini is an idealist but an idealist who has the faculty, the stamina and the persistence to transform his ambitious dreams into successful realities."[96]

EIGHT

The Octopus

I

Throughout the late spring and summer of 1926, Giannini concentrated on one objective: the merger of Bank of Italy and all his subsidiary state-chartered banks into a single, unified, statewide branch banking system. The great stumbling block, of course, was Dodge's de novo rule, which Johnson, as the new superintendent of banking, had publicly pledged himself to uphold. On April 30, 1926, Bank of Italy attorneys petitioned the California Supreme Court for a writ of mandamus to force Johnson into granting Giannini permits to open a dozen or more Bank of Italy branches. In the petition, they charged that the department of banking's de novo policy was "arbitrary, capricious, and without support in reason."[1]

As a preliminary to this consolidation program, Giannini next instructed Bacigalupi to submit a formal request to the superintendent's office for permission to merge the Liberty Bank and the Bank of America of Los Angeles into a single organization called the Liberty Bank of America.[2] Giannini gave no thought to the possibility that, in view of the public controversy that surrounded his move into Santa Maria, Johnson might respond by rejecting his request. "Institutions with sound policies and excessive capital," Giannini told Bacigalupi, "can't be successfully attacked."[3] As always, Giannini's confidence in the absolute correctness of his position reduced to irrelevance any other consideration.

Months passed before Johnson replied. When he finally did, he tore into Bacigalupi's request with a blistering seventeen-page letter that raised new concerns about the ultimate reach of Giannini's ambitions and accused him of trying to monopolize the banking business in California.[4] "Is it the intention of your banks . . . to circumvent the law when it stands in the way of your expansion by doing indirectly what cannot be done directly?" Johnson wrote. "Is it your intention, with the cooperation of the Bank of Italy, to attempt a monopoly of the banking business of the State of California? Do your intentions go further in this regard, and if so are they national or international in scope? Kindly state, also, at what point, if any, short of the elimination of the independent banker, you propose to stop."[5]

Bacigalupi was stunned by Johnson's innuendos and harsh language. "Incredible . . . what Carlyle called articulate wind," he wrote in a draft reply, which he thought better about sending.[6] The letter Bacigalupi finally did send was only slightly less pugnacious. "The superintendent's duty," he replied, "is to approve the consolidation without further ado or delay . . . since no reason whatever exists upon which to challenge or question the right given us by statute to consolidate. . . . The duty of every bank is to keep its own house in order, to be clean, and ready to meet its obligations. You know from your examinations . . . that the Bank of Italy compares most favorably with any bank in the state of California."[7]

Johnson, who was under heavy pressure from Giannini's branch banking competitors, was angered at being asked to acquiesce in a corporate merger that was simultaneously so remarkably bold and so openly contemptuous of the department's de novo policy. But Johnson also realized that Giannini's mandamus petition to the court raised a number of troublesome legal issues, since there was absolutely nothing in California's banking laws that specifically prohibited a bank in one part of the state from opening branches in another. From a strictly legal point of view, Johnson was vulnerable to the charge of having exceeded his authority, and Bacigalupi knew it.[8]

Bacigalupi went on: "Practically the whole ground of your attack on the Bank of Italy is that it has grown too large, notwithstanding that it had grown under your supervision and in large part through branches many of which you have authorized as it was your duty under the law. Let us suggest . . . that the superintendent has no more right to set apart any particular territory in California as the preserve of any favored group of bankers, than has the bank to evade or circumvent the law."[9]

Just as Giannini was determined to push forward with his consolidation program, so too was Johnson determined not to allow it to happen.[10] On May 22, 1926, Johnson filed a mandamus brief with the court. Charging Giannini with "menacing the financial and political liberty of California," Johnson shifted the controversy from Giannini's complaint of political harassment to an issue of monopolization and the economic health of the state. The essential purpose of the department's de novo policy, he told the court, "was merely to assist me in . . . the exercise of my discretion on the question whether public convenience requires the opening of any proposed branch." The time had come "when the public convenience cannot be promoted by granting to any one of the banks that compose the gigantic Bancitaly chain any more branches or banking power in the State of California."[11]

Whether Giannini would succeed with his petition was uncertain. But with Johnson intent on blocking Bank of Italy's advance outside the northern half of the state, few of Giannini's executives doubted that without a change in the administration in Sacramento, there was little hope he could succeed with his consolidation program.[12] Giannini, who left San Francisco with his family in the spring of 1926 for a three-month vacation to Europe, asked Bacigalupi to look into the matter and to work out a strategy that could be used to defeat his opposition and settle the de novo question once and for all. On July 26, 1926, Bacigalupi sent Giannini a plan of action. He urged Giannini in the strongest terms to oppose Richardson's renomination in the Republican gubernatorial primary later that year.[13]

But Bacigalupi's proposal was far more ambitious than simply denying the nomination to Richardson. As it developed, Richardson was being opposed in the Republican primary by three other candidates, the most highly regarded of whom was a dark horse, Charles C. Young. A former high school teacher and the incumbent lieutenant governor, Young had the support of the party's progressive wing.[14] Bacigalupi suggested that Giannini give serious thought to the possibility of throwing Bank of Italy's political and organizational clout behind Young's candidacy. Despite the heavy odds against Young, Bacigalupi was certain that the outcome of the primary was by no means a foregone conclusion and that the possibility of replacing Johnson with a more sympathetic superintendent of banking was worth the risk. "I think that you personally should, immediately upon returning home, come out openly for Young," Bacigalupi wrote.[15]

Bacigalupi told Giannini that he regretted "seeing the bank forced into politics." But given Richardson's close personal and political ties to Giannini's branch banking rivals, particularly in Los Angeles, he felt there was no other choice. "Our fate cannot be worse than at present and for another four years," Bacigalupi wrote. "The day of stalling is past. Our actions have been and are clean and honorable and we should not fear. Let us take a stand and give them the best we have. . . . If we are called upon to act, let us not hesitate to fight clean and with all our might. You are the *Big Chief,* and we anxiously await your orders, whatever they may be."[16]

Back in San Francisco later that summer, Giannini met privately at Bank of Italy headquarters with John F. Neylan, Young's closest political strategist and a leader of the Republican party's progressive wing in northern California. Bright, young, politically sophisticated, Neylan served as a confidant and personal attorney to the newspaper tycoon William Randolph Hearst and was later destined to play a critical role in the survival of Giannini's banking empire.[17]

Never one to mince words, Giannini told Neylan that he was prepared to support Young in the primary. What he wanted, in return, was a personal pledge from Young to appoint a new superintendent of banking who would cooperate in bringing about the success of his consolidation program. Worried about the possibility of putting Young in a politically embarrassing position, Neylan played it safe. He replied that while Young could certainly profit from Bank of Italy's support, the proposal that he place himself in the service of Giannini's consolidation ambitions, which would risk alienating the anti-branch-banking forces within the ranks of the party's progressive wing, was out of the question. The best that Young could commit himself to was "fair and impartial treatment."[18]

After the meeting, Giannini told Bacigalupi that while Neylan's assurance of fair and impartial treatment was encouraging, it was far less than the positive response he had wanted.[19] Yet his meeting with Neylan had not been without its political benefits. The fact that it had taken place at all, Giannini said, would certainly send a strong signal to the Richardson administration that he was prepared to do everything in his power to ensure the success of his consolidation program.[20]

News of the meeting—some said leaked by Giannini aides—sent a delegation of Richardson lieutenants hurrying to San Francisco. They hastened to assure Giannini that his neutrality during the campaign could be part of a deal in which the governor was prepared to look favorably on his consolidation program once he had been returned to office. Giannini, understandably cautious, wanted assurances from Richardson himself.[21] Days went by. No response from Richardson came. Instead, reports reached Bacigalupi from sources close to the Richardson camp that the governor had no intention of alienating his politically influential fund-raising supporters in Los Angeles by coop-erating with Giannini.[22] The Richardson strategy was to keep Giannini "neutralized" during the campaign with additional promises until it was too late for him to intervene on Young's behalf.[23]

Bacigalupi relayed this information to Giannini, who instructed him to begin mobilizing Bank of Italy's resources behind Young's cam-paign.[24] Giannini had chosen a risky and potentially damaging course of action that would inevitably expose him to public accusations of having acted improperly. But the alternative of sitting passively on the sidelines when there seemed to be a reasonable chance of preventing Richardson from being returned to office was unacceptable. As Gian-nini later recalled, "If Richardson had been reelected, we would have had to undergo four more years of political domination and our devel-opment would have been held back just that much."[25]

Early in September 1926 Bacigalupi summoned three hundred Bank of Italy branch managers and regional executives to a secretly arranged meeting in San Francisco. He told the hushed gathering that Rich-ardson's defeat in the Republican primary was "absolutely essential" in overcoming a political opposition that seriously jeopardized the bank's future growth. "The bank is being discriminated against and not because the people do not want us to come into the district in which they live, but through the arbitrary discretion of one man," he said. Bacigalupi's chief concern was secrecy. If the bank jumped into the campaign too soon, the predictable public backlash could kill Young's chances of winning. Since timing was everything, Bacigalupi warned against talk-ing about the proposed undertaking with anyone until the signal for action had been given from San Francisco.[26]

Throughout the remaining three weeks of the Republican primary, the Richardson campaign moved ahead with mounting confidence, encouraged not only by the governor's superior strength in southern California but also by a split in the ranks of the party's progressive forces that seemed to hurt Young in the northern half of the state.[27] One week before the end of the primary, Giannini decided to move. He instructed

Bacigalupi to pass the word to Bank of Italy's 4,000 employees and 15,000 stockholders via its network of branch managers to throw as much of their time and energy as possible into Young's campaign. Accompanying Bacigalupi's orders was a brief, ominously worded message from Giannini himself: "At stake is the existence and future growth of our institution."[28]

Throughout the state, Bank of Italy branch employees, executives, and advisory board members swung into action. Some made personal calls on the bank's stockholders or contacted them by phone.[29] Others joined Young's campaign as volunteer workers and spent their evenings and weekends canvassing neighborhoods, organizing rallies, and passing out campaign literature.[30] From San Francisco, Giannini kept in daily contact with his statewide network of local and regional executives, dispensing tactical advice and appealing to them by telegram and telephone to pull out all stops in obtaining the results he wanted. "Our efforts are being redoubled," one senior Bank of Italy vice-president in Los Angeles assured him. "Written reports are coming in from our branch managers and associates."[31]

As Giannini and his executives had anticipated, Bank of Italy's last-minute campaign blitz on Young's behalf produced a barrage of criticism from many quarters across the state. On August 25, 1926, Harry Chandler, a prominent Richardson fund-raiser and publisher of the influential and hard-line conservative *Los Angeles Times,* accused Giannini of "unethical behavior" and "rank opportunism."[32] Over the next several days the *Times* stepped up its attack. Angered by what the paper charged was a blatant and self-serving "violation of the state's unwritten law requiring banks to stay neutral in politics," the *Times* editorialized that Bank of Italy's intervention in the primary on Young's behalf was a quid pro quo given for what Giannini hoped would eventually be favorable treatment in Sacramento. "This is a fight against those whose dreams of power prompt them to support a man willing to grant their demands," the editorial said. "There is no place in the banking community for partisanship."[33]

Richardson's campaign leaders picked up the attack with a viciousness that startled everyone. "The contest for the Republican nomination for Governor has been invaded by a powerful banker, A. P. Giannini," began a Richardson campaign advertisement that the *Los Angeles Times* carried two days before the election. "He wants an official who will give him what Governor Richardson has refused to give him, special privileges and favors. If Young is elected, Banker Giannini expects to become the financial dictator of California." The bold caption above the advertisement was clearly intended to translate Bank of Italy's involvement in the campaign into an image of fascist authoritarianism. It said: "California Does Not Need a Mussolini, Financial, Political, or Otherwise."[34]

Meanwhile, throughout the Giannini organization, the frantic business of securing votes for Young continued. Bank of Italy's campaign activities were directed primarily at downstate counties from San Luis Obispo south through Los Angeles, a critical region of the state where Young desperately needed to make inroads into Richardson's political strength.[35] Reports from Giannini's executives in the field grew increasingly optimistic. "Just got solid block of fifteen hundred switched from opposition," a senior Bank of Italy vice-president cabled Giannini from Los Angeles. "It would do your heart good to see how our boys and girls are hitting the ball down here."[36] Equally encouraging was the news that in response to a widely circulated personal appeal from Giannini himself, Italians across the state were planning to vote for Young in overwhelming numbers.[37]

Young won the Republican nomination by the smallest of margins— a plurality of 15,272 out of a total 773,022. One month later he was elected governor.[38] It is difficult to determine just how decisive Bank of Italy's participation in the Republican primary had been in bringing about Young's victory. But most political observers agreed that serious disaffections in Richardson's ranks in southern California, where Giannini had concentrated his efforts, had cost the incumbent governor his renomination. Giannini himself had no doubts. He was certain that Young's upset victory was in large part the result of the campaign waged by his "boys and girls" in the Bank of Italy. He intended to exploit that fact to the fullest advantage as soon as the new administration took office.[39]

Infuriated by the outcome of the election, Richardson supporters responded with indignant letters and telegrams to legislators of both major parties in Sacramento, denouncing Giannini for his audacity and ruthless ambition. Their conclusion was unanimous: unless Giannini's "mad scramble for power" was brought to an abrupt halt, California's financial system would eventually fall under the complete domination of Bank of Italy. In Los Angeles's political and banking community, Giannini was reported to be "the most hated man" in California. "I feel justified in saying," one Bank of Italy senior executive informed him two weeks after the election, "that the ugliness of the opposition here is more apparent than ever."[40]

Simultaneously, as had happened on numerous occasions before, the brash and aggressive path that Giannini had chosen intensified the concerns of anti-branch-banking politicians in Congress. Speaking in defense of "small-town bankers" in the course of a heated debate on the nation's banking system, Democratic senator J. Thomas Heflin of Alabama seized on the Republican primary in California to denounce the "evil power" of branch banking. "Giannini is the most dominant figure in California politics," Heflin told his colleagues in the Senate. "He has gone into politics. He went to a Republican governor and tried to get his authority to extend his branch banking system. When the governor refused, Giannini sent word to his branches to have the people to whom they had loaned money induced to vote against the governor."[41]

Informed by reporters in San Francisco of Heflin's remarks, Giannini angrily denied the senator's accusations. "That's a lie," he said. "I am not in politics, never have been and don't expect to be. Whoever says I am is a liar."[42]

2

Giannini was much too busy pushing ahead with his consolidation program to trade charges and countercharges with his opposition. Certain that the critical role Bank of Italy had played in Young's victory would not be forgotten by the new administration in Sacramento, he embarked on a whirlwind bank-buying campaign to have more banks to consolidate when the merger occurred. In slightly less than three weeks he purchased more than two dozen rural banks with total resources of approximately $80 million.[43] The *San Francisco Chronicle,* commenting on this hectic burst of acquisitions, editorialized that "by all signs Giannini's latest activities are preliminary to the merger of all Bank of Italy properties."[44] On this point, of course, the *Chronicle* was absolutely correct.

Early in January 1927 Young announced the appointment of a new superintendent of banking. He was Will C. Wood, the state's former superintendent of public education and a highly regarded spokesman for the party's progressive wing.[45] Wood soon found out something about the kind of concessions Giannini expected from the new administration.[46] On the morning of January 20, only hours after Wood had been sworn into office, Bacigalupi and Williams were in his office at the state capital. They brought with them an application to consolidate Giannini's smaller "outside" banking systems with his giant Liberty Bank of America. What shocked Wood was not the merger request itself, which he had been warned to expect, but the permits Bacigalupi and Williams had brought with them to open 115 de novo branches, one-third of which were located in Los Angeles.[47]

Giannini had good reason for wanting to move quickly. After months of intense and bitter debate, the U.S. Senate was moving quickly toward passage of the McFadden Act, which had been introduced and pushed through the House five years earlier by its chief sponsor, Congressman John T. McFadden of Pennsylvania. Of critical importance to Giannini's branch banking ambitions as a whole, the McFadden Act opened the way for the nation's fourteen thousand nonmember branch banks to join the Federal Reserve system, but only if their branches were in lawful operation on the date the act actually took effect.[48]

Aside from the deadline of the McFadden Act, Giannini had other reasons to push Wood hard for a decision. Some weeks earlier Giannini had received an important piece of confidential information from Charles Collins, who had left his post as assistant comptroller of the currency in 1920 to join the Giannini organization as Bank of Italy's chief Washington lobbyist. In the weeks following Young's victory in California, Collins had worked hard to gather support for Giannini's consolidation plan from regulatory officials in Washington. He had directed his lobbying efforts at one official in particular: Joseph McIntosh, the comptroller of the currency and an ex officio member of the FRB. Collins told Giannini that McIntosh had promised to use his influence on the board to bring about approval of the merger, provided it had first been approved by banking officials in California.[49]

In Sacramento the pressure on Wood was intense. Faced with the largest corporate merger in California's financial history and with no previous experience in banking, Wood said later that he was "thunderstruck" by the enormous implications of the decision he was being asked to make.[50] The advantages of the merger to Giannini were self-evident: control over a single privately owned and centrally managed financial institution with the size and financial resources to exert enormous influence over the state's entire credit system.

When Wood turned to Young for assistance, the governor saw no need to involve himself in the decision. Wood later quoted Young as saying that "the only thing" he had promised Giannini in return for his help in the primary "was fair and impartial treatment . . . and that I was absolutely free to handle the banking problem as I saw fit."[51] To make matters more difficult for Wood personally, he was regarded by many as a rising star in the Republican party. He could not acquiesce in Giannini's merger request without inflicting a good deal of damage on himself politically. Indeed, Wood said later that close friends and colleagues in the department warned him repeatedly that granting permission for the giant consolidation "was equivalent to signing my political death warrant."[52]

Racing against the clock, Giannini did not give Wood much time for reflection. On February 12, 1926, five days after his initial meeting with Wood, Williams was back in the state capital, accompanied by Louis Ferrari, Bank of Italy's chief legal counsel. Wood later described both men as grim-faced and "visibly agitated."[53] The latest word out of Washington was that the long and acrimonious debate in the Senate over the branch banking provisions in the McFadden Act was winding quickly to a close and that its passage seemed imminent.

Wood's feeling that the decision was his alone to make was confirmed by his chief legal assistant, Albert Rosenshine, who joined the others at the meeting. "Here I was," Wood later recalled, "inexperienced in my new office, without technical knowledge of banking, facing decisions on an application that if granted would create a giant bank. Two men, representing a giant financial interest, sat with eyes fixed on me. I had been urged to grant it; urged not to grant it. . . . The Governor had told me distinctly that I was under no obligation to grant the merger. . . . All these things flashed through my mind as I sat here, with three pairs of eyes on me."[54]

The four men sat in silence for a few moments. Wood then looked calmly at Williams and nodded his approval. "I brushed aside every factor save the fundamental justice involved," Wood said later. "There was a slight stir in the room. Williams . . . gave potent evidence of relief. . . . We went to my office immediately and the necessary documents were signed. The giant merger had been granted."[55]

Williams then left the room to phone Giannini, who was in San Francisco anxiously awaiting word about the outcome of the meeting. It was an exhilarating moment for Giannini. "Consolidated institution expected to commence business," he immediately cabled his wife, who was visiting friends in New York. "Consider ourselves fortunate to have been able to get what we have in such short space time."[56] All that remained to put Giannini in total command of the largest and most powerful branch banking system in both California and the nation was the merger of the Liberty Bank of America with Bank of Italy.

That final step proved easy enough. Having approved the merger, Wood showed himself to be even more generous. On February 9, 1927, Wood revoked Dodge's de novo ruling by announcing that his predecessor's efforts to divide the state into rigid banking zones along north-south lines had been "unjustified and contrary to the laws of California."[57] Five days later, in response to the inevitable and second formal request from Giannini that he knew was coming, Wood approved the merger of the Liberty Bank of America with the Bank of Italy.[58]

Events now moved rapidly. On the morning of February 17, 1926, the FRB met to consider approval of the giant merger. As promised to Collins three weeks earlier, McIntosh spoke forcefully and convincingly for immediate favorable action.[59] Whether individual board members were aware of the private assurances the comptroller of the currency had given to Collins some weeks earlier is uncertain. But at least one member was so angered by McIntosh's enthusiastic recommendation that he walked out of the room before the meeting ended. His absence made no difference. By a vote of four to one, the FRB approved the merger.[60]

Giannini's attention now shifted to the Senate, where a bitterly frustrated bipartisan minority coalition of anti-branch-banking senators was making a last-ditch attempt to defeat the McFadden Act with a filibuster. They did not succeed. On Friday afternoon, February 22, 1927, the Senate passed the bill by an overwhelming vote of seventy-one to seventeen.[61]

With the bill out of the Senate and on its way to the White House for Coolidge's signature, Giannini now hurried to bring his far-flung network of Liberty branch banks into the national banking system and to merge them with Bank of Italy. The weekend went by in a blur of frenzied activity as teams of employees and junior executives were dispatched to scores of communities across the state to complete the consolidation process.[62] Late Monday morning, February 25, sign painters were still putting the finishing touches on their work. Even so, Giannini's Bank of Italy branch system was open for business.

The public reacted to the results of the consolidation with astonishment. Almost overnight Giannini's Bank of Italy appeared as a single, thousand-mile-long chain stretching from Oregon to Mexico, with 276 branches in 199 California towns and cities and nearly $750 million in assets. Only two other banks in the country—National City and the Chase, both located in New York—were bigger and wealthier.[63]

Giannini's stunning achievement was front-page news across the state and outside California as well. Under the heading "GREAT COUP" the *San Francisco Examiner* hailed the emergence of the nation's third-largest bank as an extraordinary achievement and reason enough "to spread Giannini's fame throughout the world." The *San Francisco Call* praised Giannini "for daring to become the world's first financier to make of banking and investment a huge democratic fraternity."[64]

Not everyone either in California or outside the state was similarly enthralled. Some industry observers expressed serious reservations about Bank of Italy's monumental size and power. As the *New York Commercial and Financial Chronicle* expressed it, "Those behind Bank of Italy are restless and ambitious spirits. They will not be satisfied with having conquered the whole State of California. . . . Is this desirable?"[65]

Bank of Italy's rise to financial dominance in California turned Giannini into a figure of national prominence. His face appeared on the cover of *Time, Forbes, Business Week,* and a host of lesser-known publications.[66] Nowhere, however, were his achievements more celebrated than among Americans of Italian descent. They idolized him not only for succeeding in so spectacular a fashion but also for conferring on them a pride and respectability that society at large had long withheld from them. "I was a dago before Giannini," a San Francisco Italian told a visiting reporter from Boston. "Now I am an American."[67] Many Italians regarded him with the same reverence other Americans reserved for movie stars or sports heroes. On one occasion a local writer reported overhearing a clerk in a North Beach market facetiously call a customer "Mr. Giannini." "Don't do that," the Italian owner of the market admonished the clerk. "You mustn't talk like that. That's the greatest man in America. There's magic in his name."[68]

Characteristically, Giannini was not content with his consolidation triumph. All across California he saw scores of bustling rural communities still unconnected to the financial leviathan he had created out of the ashes of his North Beach bank. Prohibited under the provisions of the McFadden Act from adding additional branches to his Bank of Italy system outside of San Francisco, Giannini now embarked on the creation of a new state-chartered branch banking system that would be free to expand without regard to federal banking legislation in Washington.[69]

The results of Giannini's efforts were astonishing. Beginning in the spring of 1927 and continuing to the end of the year, he acquired nearly a hundred banks with total resources of over $200 million, all of which he then merged with one or another subsidiary corporation he had created for that purpose. One of these corporations, the United Bank and Trust, soon had fifty-three branches scattered throughout northern California. By the spring of 1928 Giannini had succeeded in putting together the largest state banking system in California and the second largest in the country, which he would eventually call Bank of America.[70] "A. P. had literally thought of everything," one financial writer commented. "He could now operate in the national or state banking system as it suited his advantage."[71]

3

Back in New York, Attilio Giannini was making headlines of his own by guiding Bank of Italy into new and uncharted waters: film financing. The relationship between Bank of Italy and the movies began in the fall of 1919, when Attilio moved to New York to manage the East River National on 630 Broadway, only a few blocks from "the theater and movie crowd."[72] Attilio's interest in the movie business was both personal and professional. Along with his attraction to the glitz and glamour of show business, he was impressed by the large number of "immigrants and working-class families" who "made up a significant portion of the early moviegoing audience."[73] The business prospects for a small and obscure Brooklyn bank looked promising. "I was a newcomer," Attilio would remember. "I was in a new pasture; there were many grazing herds and the grass was short, and I was obliged to turn to a business that other bankers did not particularly wish to finance."[74]

By 1920 the movie industry was in its tenth year of rapid growth, but it was struggling to overcome a chronic problem: the need to find more dependable and legitimate sources of financing.[75] Certain that movies were a passing fad doomed to oblivion, Wall Street's old-line investment firms were reluctant to advance loans to producers. "I approached different bankers and tried to sell them on the idea of big profits in the motion picture business," one early movie producer would recall. "They wished me luck . . . but they did not see their way clear to participate in this lucrative business."[76] Without access to traditional sources of capital, many producers were forced to deal with loan sharks who charged outrageously high rates of interest, some even demanding a substantial part of a picture's profits.

Attilio, however, was eager to get involved. "What if they do smell like cheese and garlic?" he was reported to have remarked about the movie industry's largely Jewish producers. "They meet their obligations."[77] Attilio soon established close personal and business relationships with a large number of pioneer movie producers who were destined to have a profound influence on the rise of the industry: Cecil B. DeMille, Lewis Selznick, Marcus Lowe, Samuel Goldwyn, Jesse Lasky, Joseph and Nicholas Schenck, and Carl Laemmle.[78]

As Attilio's involvement in the moviemaking business deepened, he quickly emerged as the "angel to the stars," making desperately needed loans to producers like Lowe, Selznick, DeMille, and others—men who were "for the most part from immigrant families or were immigrants themselves."[79] With access to a dependable and sympathetic source of credit, the producers who showed up at Attilio's office in the Bowery and East River National grew more numerous.[80] "We stepped in and made loans to deserving companies, thereby eliminating some of these so-called money lenders," he later recalled. "Our loans were at the current rate of interest. I simply decided that motion pictures were good merchandise, as good as cotton, wheat, or barley."[81]

Starting with one- and two-reel "flicks" for Brooklyn's movie houses, Attilio very quickly began making loans to finance larger productions. In 1919 Bank of Italy loaned Jesse Lasky, Samuel Goldwyn's brother-in-law, $50,000 to start Famous Players–Lasky Studio in Hollywood.[82] The risk was considerable, but Lasky possessed an unusually sharp intelligence and had produced a number of highly successful films. Two years later Bank of Italy made banking and movie history by loaning $250,000 to First National Productions to make *The Kid,* starring Charlie Chaplin and Jackie Coogan. The movie was a box-office hit in 1922–23 and "added new and exciting laurels" to Chaplin's star image as the "King of Comedy."[83]

Besides advancing loans to film producers, Attilio introduced an innovation to banking that proved to be a boon to the film industry. To enable moviemakers to maintain a steady production of films, he adopted the practice of accepting the negative of a completed film as collateral for a loan to begin production on another.[84] State banking examiners reacted to this arrangement with dismay and sent harshly disapproving reports to Sacramento. But where regulators saw an unusual and risky departure from the more traditional forms of collateral, Attilio found sound lending practices. "If a film is offered me starring Doug (Fairbanks), Charlie (Chaplin), or Harold (Lloyd), it's as good as cash," he said.[85] Despite repeated warnings from state banking officials, Bank of Italy continued to accept negatives as collateral.

In San Francisco, Giannini, who shared his brother's enthusiasm for film financing, moved quickly to strengthen Bank of Italy's position in the industry. With the rise of Hollywood as the movie capital in the 1920s, he began the policy of bringing producers, directors, and well-known actors and actresses into the organization as board members and stockholders. Giannini depended on these movie moguls and screen celebrities to serve as Bank of Italy "boosters" in attracting the payroll accounts from Hollywood's major studios and the savings accounts of the industry's tens of thousands of employees.[86]

The list included many of Hollywood's best-known and most talented self-made movie moguls. Among them was Cecil B. DeMille, who had received a $200,000 production loan from Bank of Italy in 1920 to complete his Academy Award–winning *Ten Commandments*. Two years later DeMille became president of Bank of Italy's Culver City branch, only a short distance from many of Hollywood's major studios; the bank's advisory board included Louis B. Mayer, the short, volatile, tyrannical chief of MGM. Joseph and Nicholas Schenck, two of Hollywood's most influential producers, sat on Bank of Italy's board of directors in San Francisco.[87] Other studio heads whom Giannini pulled into the organization as board members included Harry Cohn, Howard Hughes, Sol Lesser, Jack Warner, and Darryl Zanuck.

By the early 1920s Attilio was not the only banker in the country who saw the profit and investment potential in the film industry. But he was the only one who did everything possible to bankroll the industry's growth and to provide moviemakers with personal support and much-needed public legitimacy.[88] With Giannini's authorization, Attilio arranged the financing for the birth of Columbia Pictures in 1920.[89] Later he sat on the studio's board of directors.[90] He arranged screen tests for promising actors, defended the movie industry against some of its sharpest critics, and served as a financial adviser to producers like Louis B. Mayer, Cecil B. DeMille, and Alexander Korda.[91] When Jack Warner's drinking and gambling problems threatened to ruin his career as head of one of Hollywood's largest studios, it was Attilio to whom Warner's wife turned for assistance.[92] "The Doc's been more than a banker to Hollywood," said one movie writer. "Everyone in Hollywood has cried on his shoulders."[93]

4

In California, meanwhile, Giannini had taken the first step toward realizing his most grandiose ambition: the creation of a nationwide network of banks. Early in the spring of 1927 he sent Armando Pedrini and Robert Paganini on a city-by-city, cross-country promotional trip to each of the nation's large communities of Italians. He instructed both men "to make friends with influential Italians and incidentally to sell blocks of Bancitaly stock." Giannini was planning for the day when each of these far-flung Italian settlements would form the nucleus of a Bank of Italy branch—ultimately functioning as parts of a nationwide network of branches.[94]

Six months later, after traveling to more than sixty cities across the country, both men returned to San Francisco vastly encouraged. "We have been successful in establishing nucleuses and groups of new stockholders in all cities visited by us, who will form a large class of stockholders, friends, and boosters throughout the United States," Pedrini wrote in a confidential report to Bacigalupi. "The wonderful vision of our Mr. Giannini to have these nucleuses created will bring good and beneficial results in the future. The trip and the work was not so easy, but we had the satisfaction of blazing the trail for the future of our institution in the United States, as we did in the past for the Bank of Italy."[95]

Giannini's next step was the boldest and potentially most hazardous in his career: a jump clear across the country to New York, the nation's financial capital and the key to the success of his nationwide branch banking ambitions. He had already established a presence in New York with his Bowery and East River National. But that bank, whose clientele consisted largely of working-class Jews and Italians, was inconsequential by industry standards and had attracted little national attention. What Giannini wanted was a larger, far more prestigious bank with strong Wall Street connections, one that could serve as the easternmost bastion for his planned nationwide network of banks.

Late in the spring of 1927 Giannini sent one of his top executives, Leo Belden, to act as his chief emissary to New York's financial community. An adroit and well-connected wheeler-dealer and former stockbroker of immense ambitions, the forty-three-year-old Belden had joined the Bank of Italy in the early 1920s. As a financial officer, then head of the bank's bond department, and in 1923 vice-president of its Los Angeles operations, Belden had risen rapidly in the ranks of the Giannini organization. Within the bank he was regarded by many as a man of considerable ability, although some thought him duplicitous and "slimy."[96] But considering Belden's smooth corporate manners, stock market savvy, and fondness for mixing with the "best people," Giannini felt he had made the logical choice for his New York mission.

Wall Street is no place to keep a secret. Soon after Belden arrived in New York, stories began appearing in the press that Giannini was preparing to "invade New York." The publicity alarmed Giannini. Already the target of anti-branch-banking forces in Washington, he also feared that any premature disclosure of his plans might create problems for him with government regulators and produce an unfavorable reaction on Wall Street. When a reporter for the *New York Herald Tribune* showed up in San Francisco to question him about the rumors, Giannini denied that he had any large ambitions in New York. "I have no such plans," he replied, and added that he was "amused by some of the Wall Street fiction in which I have figured."[97]

Meanwhile, on the tide of Giannini's latest string of successes, Bancitaly's profits climbed to record levels. In December 1924, the year he transferred Bancitaly to Los Angeles, the corporation's annual profits were slightly more than $1.2 million; four years later they had soared to $112 million.[98] Not surprisingly, Bancitaly became one of the most eagerly sought-after stocks on the San Francisco Stock Exchange. As the financial writer for the *San Francisco Examiner* put it, "From all indications, Giannini is just getting a good start. Nothing succeeds like success. Hitch your wagon to a star."[99]

One consequence of Bancitaly's remarkable rise in profits was to make Giannini potentially a very rich man. In 1924, after stepping down as Bank of Italy's president, Giannini accepted no further salary; nor, except for the payment of income taxes and personal and business expenses, did he accept a salary from Bancitaly after assuming the presidency of the holding company he had founded five years earlier.[100] At a board meeting in April 1926, however, Bancitaly's directors voted to compensate him, "in lieu of salary . . . and in recognition of his extraordinary services," 5 percent of the corporation's annual net profits, "with a guaranteed minimum of $100,000 a year."[101] Since the corporation's net profits for 1927 were expected to be around $30 million, this meant that Giannini was entitled to receive approximately $1.5 million.

According to several reliable accounts, Giannini, who had not attended the meeting, was "visibly annoyed" when he learned of the board's action. He made it clear that under no circumstances would he accept the money. "I already have half a million dollars," he was quoted as telling a group of Bancitaly directors over lunch one day. "That's all any man needs."[102]

In a decision that would later embroil Giannini in a long and bitter controversy with the Internal Revenue Service, he recommended that Bancitaly's board of directors donate the money to philanthropy. Specifically, Giannini had in mind the creation of a research institute to improve California agriculture.[103] At a directors' meeting in late January of 1928, Bancitaly's board acquiesced in Giannini's request and voted to donate the $1.5 million to the Berkeley campus at the University of California for the endowment and creation of a school of agricultural research. The purpose of the institute, as stated in the terms of the endowment, was "to rehabilitate and assist agriculture in California."[104]

As Giannini had expected, the donation produced a good deal of favorable publicity. "By forming the foundation and putting his personal wealth to the use of California," the *San Francisco News* editorialized, "Giannini strips himself of the title of millionaire . . . and . . . thus the product of his financial genius has been dedicated to helping all Californians."[105] The most widely publicized reaction came from Will Rogers, then the country's best-known humorist. After learning that Giannini "wanted to die poor," Rogers quipped to a Hollywood reporter, "I put in a bid for a loan . . . and the funny part about it is this feller is on the level. I got the loan, so hurry up, everybody, before he turns banker."[106]

Giannini himself remained silent about the donation. Pursued by the press, however, he told a reporter for the *San Francisco Examiner*, "I don't want any more money. If I had all the millions in the world, I couldn't live better than I do. I enjoy work. What is called high society doesn't mean anything to me. I've always said I would never be a millionaire. Maybe this will convince some of the skeptics that I mean what I say."[107]

NINE

Morgan's Rules

I

Leo Belden spent the late fall and winter of 1927 re-
connoitering New York's financial district in search of a bank available
for Giannini to purchase. Belden liked the glamour and excitement of
Wall Street; he enjoyed negotiating business transactions, cultivating
friendships, rubbing shoulders with the high and mighty. "The game
is played very differently here than in California," he wrote to Giannini
on November 22, 1927, in one of his confidential reports to San Francisco. Sensitive, as all Bank of Italy executives were, to Giannini's
hostility toward Wall Street, Belden hastened to add that he had absolutely no intention of exchanging his "Bank of Italy ideals" for the
personal pursuit of money and power. "I am only telling you this," he
said, "as I thought it would please you to see the boys here following
in your footsteps."[1]

Giannini in turn was "delighted" to learn that Belden was "certainly
true blood in spreading our gospel" on Wall Street. "Maybe California
straight talk and square shooting are just what New York needs."
Giannini cautioned Belden not to underestimate the fraud, chicanery,
and self-serving transactions that lay behind Wall Street's facade of high
financial statesmanship. "We have worked hard in building up this
corporation," he replied, "and are not going to take any chances on a
new crowd coming in and taking it away from the boys and girls of the
Bank of Italy whom we want to have it."[2]

Sometime toward the end of 1927 Belden found the kind of large, well-connected bank he felt certain Giannini was looking for: the 116-year-old Bank of America, successor to the Bank of the United States, which had been founded in 1812 and later grew to financial prominence as one of "the leading banks of New York."[3] Located at 66 Wall Street, Bank of America occupied the lower five floors of its own thirty-two-story, spiral-topped skyscraper that the *New York Times* had described as "the best known in greater New York and an architecture purely American."[4] Although in recent years Bank of America had experienced serious losses, it was still valuable property, primarily because of its historic reputation and eight city branches with total deposits of $100 million.[5]

By the late 1920s Bank of America had lost a good deal of its luster by becoming involved in a fierce internecine battle for control. The bank was owned by a small number of investors, including Ralph Jonas, a talented, street-smart, Brooklyn-born son of Jewish immigrant parents. Jonas had built his own Manufacturers Trust into one of New York's most prominent bank investment firms; along the way he had acquired 45 percent of Bank of America's stock, giving him working control. None of this pleased the bank's management and minority stockholders, who formed a voting trust to prevent him from exercising his control. The struggle between Jonas and the trust had gone on for three years in what the *New York Times* called "the most bitter contest in the country's financial history."[6]

Leading the tightly knit group of stockholders opposed to Jonas was Bank of America's president, Edward C. Delafield. Born to one of New York's socially prominent families and endowed with status, wealth, and a Princeton education, Delafield had been able to recruit in his fight with Jonas a number of Wall Street's most powerful figures.[7] Prominent among them was John P. Morgan, Jr., the tall, husky, bald, sixty-one-year-old son of the legendary Pierpont and, since 1913, president of J. P. Morgan and Company, Wall Street's most powerful and prestigious banking investment firm.[8] The gossip making the rounds was that Morgan, who detested Jews, was actually the driving force behind Delafield and the trust's efforts to squeeze Jonas out.

Confronted by what he believed was a well-organized anti-Semitic assault against him and the steady losses to Bank of America that the internal struggle had produced, Jonas gave in. Toward the end of 1927 he quietly let it be known that he was prepared to sell his controlling interest in the bank if the price was right.[9] Giannini, flushed with his enormous success in California, was eager to seize the opportunity. Acquisition of Bank of America would give him entry into the financial capital of the world and a much greater influence well beyond the distant shores of the Pacific. Of critical importance for his expansionist purposes, he would also have the considerable advantage of being able to use Bank of America as a strategically located financial engine with which he could launch his efforts to build a network of Bancitaly-controlled banks throughout the entire eastern half of the country.

Bank of America held other attractions for Giannini aside from its reputation and prominent Wall Street location: its very name reflected perfectly his long-range branch-building ambitions outside California. Acting on Giannini's instructions, Belden met privately with Jonas on several occasions to discuss the sale of his stock and to negotiate a price. The two men eventually reached a tentative purchase agreement. But a critical question remained: would the "corner" give its informal approval to the transaction? The "corner," of course, was Wall Street's shorthand term for J. P. Morgan and Company, which was widely assumed to have a decisive say in such matters in New York's banking investment world.

On the evening of December 15, 1927, Belden discussed the transaction with Francis Bartow, a junior partner in J. P. Morgan and Company, in Bartow's secluded, English-style, Long Island home.[10] Bartow told Belden that the Morgan firm was anxious to see an end to Bank of America's self-destructive squabbling in favor of Delafield and the voting trust. Giannini's offer to purchase Jonas's controlling interest seemed a promising solution to the problem. At the same time, Bartow said, he as well as other partners in the Morgan firm were troubled by Giannini's well-known reputation as a man who had a fondness for "unorthodox banking practices" and for going his own way without regard to the conventional methods of conducting business. Bartow told Belden that before the firm could give its approval to the Jonas transaction, it first wanted assurances that Giannini would "play by the rules of the Street."[11]

Anxious to dispel Bartow's concerns, Belden replied that allegations of "sinister motives" with regard to Giannini's business practices were unfounded and stemmed largely from the competitive resentments of his branch banking rivals in California. Contrary to the public perception and numerous published reports that Bank of Italy was strictly a one-man show, Belden said, Giannini in fact was "paying no attention to the bank whatever and it was running as well, or better, than it ever did before." ("God forgive me for this misstatement," Belden later wrote to Giannini.) Belden went a step further. He told Bartow that Giannini had completed nearly all that he had set out to accomplish with his branch banking operations in California; he "had no idea of doing things" outside the state that would later cause the Morgan firm to regret its decision to welcome him into Wall Street.[12]

Back in his hotel room in midtown Manhattan later that night, Belden summed up the impressions he had carried away from the meeting in a confidential letter to Giannini. "Bartow is Morgan's eyes and ears and Rock of Gibraltar," he wrote. "I feel that it is perfectly safe to say that this crowd has a real understanding of us now that they never had before. It is my opinion that the real crowd down here in New York, such as Morgan, First National, etc., are a good deal like the English people—they are slow to accept you but when they finally make up their minds that you are all right, they do it one hundred percent."[13]

Over the next several weeks Belden and Bartow established a close and friendly relationship. In addition to their meetings at J. P. Morgan and Company at the corner of Broad and Wall Streets, they spent hours conferring together in Bartow's home and whiled away the weekends playing golf and tennis at his exclusive country club in Glen Cove. As time went by, Belden became increasingly optimistic about the chances of getting Morgan's approval. "Very much gratified," he cabled Giannini after one such weekend. "Our relationship with Morgan is working out. This is going along much better than I had hoped for."[14] Encouraged by this news, Giannini responded: "That's the spirit, Lee. You're some general."[15]

Late in December 1927 Belden informed Giannini that he had succeeded in "rolling out the red carpet" with J. P. Morgan and Company. "I am sure," Belden wrote, "that our relations with them are going to grow closer, and that we are going to, as time goes on, find this association most profitable."[16]

It was the signal Giannini had been waiting for. Accompanied by his wife and daughter, he left San Francisco on the morning of February 14, 1928, for the cross-country train trip to New York to meet with J. P. Morgan personally. "I had to see the House of Morgan first although they were not in any sense owners of the Bank of America," he would recall many years later.[17]

A crowd of reporters was on hand to greet Giannini at Grand Central Station when he arrived in New York four days later. By now rumors had spread that he was in New York to put the finishing touches on a huge financial transaction that would put him in control of one of Wall Street's most prestigious bank investment firms. "Has some Lochinvar come out of the West to challenge the financial honors of New York?" the *New York Herald* would ask later that day, adding that Giannini was "the most interesting and talked about man in the world today."[18] Questioned by reporters about the rumors, Giannini was evasive, saying, "No deal whatsoever has been made."[19] After shaking hands with friends and posing for photographers, he climbed into a taxi and went directly to his room at the Ritz Carlton.

In the lobby of the hotel Giannini was again met by reporters, eagerly looking for the opportunity to arrange a personal interview with California's hugely successful "ex-fruit peddler." Many were struck by the contrast between his commanding physical presence and reputation as the "Wild Bull of Montgomery Street" and his charm, warmth, and unassuming openness.[20] As a reporter for the *New York Times* put it, "Ever skeptical of philanthropic bankers, people are beginning to believe in A. P. Giannini of California. He has not changed the simplicity of his life or activities in any way since millions began to burgeon from his tremendously successful labor. He is a regular knockout of a personality, with a titanic head, a face like a rock, and a voice like a howitzer."[21]

For days Giannini captured the attention of all New York, his empire-building accomplishments in California sensationally publicized in the pages of every newspaper of importance in the city. A front-page story in the *New York City Telegram* treated Giannini like a financial warrior hero and urged its readers, in a bold caption under his photograph, "Get to Know Him. He May Be Your Banker Tomorrow." Readers were promised a three-part serialization of his life, which the *City Telegram* characterized as "a true story . . . stranger and more romantic in some respects than most fiction."[22] Not to be outdone, the *New York Sun* praised Giannini as a "modern day de Medici" and commented, "The great Pacific coast banker whose rise from humble beginnings out where the Pacific rolls in is the wonder of the financial world today."[23]

Two days after arriving in New York, Giannini met with J. P. Morgan and two senior Bank of America executives at Bartow's home. Belden's earlier assurance to San Francisco of a cozy working relationship with the Morgan firm did not fit with the man Giannini now met, nor did he find the friendly, confirmative meeting he had been led to expect.[24] Politely but firmly, Morgan asserted his authority immediately. As a condition to approving Giannini's purchase of Jonas's controlling interest in Bank of America, he insisted on Edward Delafield's retention as president and on veto power for himself over future appointments to the bank's board of directors.[25]

Giannini found these conditions intolerable, but he was careful to disguise his resentment and made no effort to resist them.[26] He wanted no difficulties with Morgan that would lose him the "good feelings" that Belden had spent weeks in promoting or that would cripple his chances for success once he had taken over Bank of America. Uppermost in Giannini's mind was his long-term goal of nationwide branch banking. To come anywhere near accomplishing that objective, he would need to have a powerful Wall Street presence to serve as the hub for his East Coast operations and as the easternmost extension of his branch banking empire in California.

That night the word spread among Bancitaly executives in New York that Morgan had succeeded in intimidating Giannini to a degree that none of them would have thought possible. As one Bancitaly executive would remember, confronted by a series of demands that he would never have accepted in his financial dealings in California, "Giannini was as meek as a lamb."[27]

Giannini learned a good deal more about the reach and power of J. P. Morgan and Company when he met the following morning with officials of the New York Federal Reserve Bank (NYFRB) to discuss the details of the Jonas transaction. At one point in the conversation Giannini mentioned in passing that he was impressed by Jonas's financial ability and had decided to offer him the position as chair of Bank of America's board of directors once the purchase had been completed. Giannini was "stunned," as he would later recall, when NYFRB officials reacted by informing him in no uncertain terms that if he went ahead with the Jonas appointment, the board would refuse to approve his purchase of Bank of America. "All because he was a Jew, although they didn't say it," Giannini told aides later.[28] Eager for the deal to go through, Giannini agreed to abandon the idea. A few weeks later he announced the appointment of his brother, Attilio, as board chairman.

In New York, Bancitaly executives were dissatisfied over the outcome of Giannini's negotiations with Morgan and the NYFRB. Most felt that he had yielded far too much in his desire to break into Wall Street. In San Francisco, Mario Giannini simmered over the personal humiliation he felt his father had been forced to experience. In his mind, at least, it seemed clear that the motivation behind the Morgan firm's decision to approve the Jonas deal came down to one thing: "Morgan chose us in preference to Jonas," he wrote in the margin of a letter to an associate, "because he felt he could dictate."[29]

Giannini, too, felt bitter about the concessions he had made. J. P. Morgan's insistence on Delafield's retention as Bank of America's president annoyed him more perhaps than anything else. But Giannini had no intention of succumbing to the domination of J. P. Morgan and Company any longer than he felt absolutely necessary. He reasoned that once he had consolidated his power in New York and throughout the East Coast generally, he would be in a much stronger position to resist the institutional power of the Morgan firm and to reshape Bank of America's management to his own satisfaction. "Let President Delafield and other officers of the bank start out on their own," he informed Belden in a confidential letter on March 14, 1928. "Later on if we find that things are not progressing as they should we could step in and take charge."[30]

With the issue of his move into Wall Street settled, Giannini moved swiftly to conclude his transaction with Jonas. On February 25, 1928, he purchased Jonas's 78,000 Bank of America shares for $7.50 a share—a total of $17 million.[31] As many had expected, control of the bank was only the first step in Giannini's New York program. Next he set plans in motion to merge the Bowery and East River National and his other smaller New York banks with Bank of America. When finally completed, two months later, Giannini had succeeded in creating a gigantic $406 million financial institution—the third largest in New York.[32]

Public reaction to the purchase was swift and dramatic. "BRANCH BANKING WITH A VENGEANCE," the *New York Herald Tribune* announced in a front-page headline.[33] News of the transaction sent the value of Bank of America stock soaring. Within days the price jumped to over $500 a share; less than a week later it had doubled. "The rise in the value of this stock," the *San Francisco Chronicle* commented, "has been sensational in the extreme . . . setting Wall Street agog. . . . Now that Bancitaly has entered the New York banking field the gossip-makers feel it is necessary to have the California institution buying banks in all four corners of the nation."[34]

Financial observers were not always certain what Giannini was up to; but a few of the more perspicacious among them thought they understood something about the goal Giannini had set for himself in his purchase of Bank of America. As the financial editor of the *San Francisco Bulletin* explained, "The speed with which the mammoth idea was engineered has tended somewhat to diminish its tremendous significance. The alliance will give Giannini three potential places for realization of the hope of establishing throughout the United States a banking system patterned after the Federal Reserve System which has 12 regional bases. . . . The emergence of the Giannini banking interests is potentially the most powerful in America and . . . appears to set the stage for the entrance of A. P. Giannini as the new colossus of world finance."[35]

The day after he completed his deal with Jonas, Giannini had but one thought in mind: to return to San Francisco as quickly as possible. He had originally planned to leave New York for a one-month trip to Italy. But in the midst of his negotiations in New York, he had received some worrisome news from San Francisco. While moving into an apartment at the Mark Hopkins Hotel on Nob Hill, Mario had suddenly collapsed. He was rushed by ambulance to a nearby hospital, where doctors quickly confirmed that he was hemorrhaging badly in the thigh muscles of both legs. Repeated transfusions of fresh blood had finally stabilized the bleeding, but the trauma from another of his spontaneous and life-threatening hemophiliac episodes had left the joints in both legs swollen and excruciatingly painful.

Over the years an extremely close relationship had developed between the two men. At age thirty-two Mario shared the handsome features of his father, the same strong cheekbones and dark, penetrating eyes, the same carefully trimmed mustache. But there the physical similarity ended. The devastating years of frequent hemorrhages and medical treatments had taken a deplorable toll on Mario's body: his hips bent stiff, his legs twisted and crippled, he could walk only with the aid of a cane. At an age when other men found outlets from work in close friendships and weekend leisure pursuits, Mario devoted himself to the interests of his father's banking empire with a total absorption that startled those around him. Once when an aide expressed concern over the brutal work schedule Mario imposed on himself, he shrugged his shoulders and replied, "What else can I do?"[36]

As a teenager Mario had worked after school in Bank of Italy as an unpaid clerk, first in one department and then another, until he was satisfied he had mastered the details of every facet of the bank's operations from the teller's window to the highest echelon of management. Later, after graduating summa cum laude from the University of California at Berkeley and the Hastings School of Law, he joined Bank of Italy as his father's personal assistant.[37] However disabling

Mario's physical condition, no one could dispute the brilliance of his mind—cool, sharp, precise, relentlessly methodical. Although courteous and considerate in his relations with others, Mario, unlike his father, encouraged no intimacies. "He built a solid wall around his innermost self," one Bank of Italy executive would remember. "In effect, he put himself in a sanctuary that no one but a small handful of closest intimates could enter . . . and he would remain . . . a more or less remote being."[38]

Giannini took enormous pride in his son's executive talents and financial acumen; he felt strongly that Mario should be given more public credit for the critical role he played in Bank of Italy's growth and earnings. For his part, Mario was in awe of his father. He was constantly on guard against saying or doing anything that might diminish his father's reputation, even to the point of blaming himself or others for decisions gone wrong that Giannini himself had been responsible for. "A. P. should get all the spotlight," he once confided to an associate, "and as long as Dad is with us no one should dim his luster by sharing it."[39] As one senior Bank of Italy associate would remember, "Every time Mario pulled off something really big that had the banking world buzzing with excitement, he would say, 'Let them give Dad the credit.'"[40]

2

By the time Giannini returned to San Francisco, news of his much-publicized financial transactions in New York had excited the appetite of an overly eager investing public. On the San Francisco Stock Exchange the price of his stocks rose spectacularly; during the first three weeks of March, Bank of America jumped 49 points—to 737—while Bancitaly climbed to a record level; Bank of Italy was selling at $545.[41] The widespread panic buying of Giannini stocks became the major topic of discussion in the nation's financial press. On March 7, 1928, B. C. Forbes, the nationally syndicated financial columnist, wrote: "Stepping off the train on arriving in California I entered a barber's and, as usual, asked 'How's business.' The reply astounded me. 'Poor, very poor. . . . Everybody's saving every cent and buying Bank of Italy stock. Giannini is the big hero in California these days.'"[42]

The press itself contributed significantly to the hysteria. Newspapers delighted in running stories about ordinary Americans who had become wealthy because they had invested in Giannini stocks: a San Francisco accountant who had bought five shares of Bank of Italy stock in 1904 could now afford to retire; a Fresno barber sent one of his shop's chairs to Giannini with a letter of gratitude for his stock profits; a Bakersfield truck driver had increased his personal finances by over $100,000.[43] As a financial writer for the *San Francisco News* put it, "Giannini has made an awful lot of people rich."[44]

To those around him, Giannini appeared genuinely concerned about the tens of thousands of small investors who were borrowing money at "usurious rates" from banks and finance companies to speculate in his stocks. On March 14, 1928, he issued a press release warning investors to pay off their debts and get out of the market: "We want them to own their own shares outright," he said. "We do not want them held as security for loans. We want our stockholders so firmly entrenched that they cannot be forced to sell out at some unfavorable time."[45] Two weeks later he sent an open letter to banks and brokerage firms across the country, urging them to refrain from making loans on Bancitaly stock where the obvious intention of borrowers was to use the money to speculate in his stocks. "The public is attributing to me miracle working powers which I do not have," Giannini said.[46]

While Giannini continued to state for the public record that the speculation must be stopped, in practice his own organization had become a considerable force in contributing to the mania. By now Bank of Italy's various "foreign departments" had become a marvelous stock-promoting machine for the sale of Bancitaly and Bank of Italy stock— the "gold dust twins," as the press dubbed them. Bank of Italy missionaries and local branch mangers were regularly sent monthly quotas with orders from Pedrini to solicit buyers at every available opportunity. Pedrini's missionaries, in turn, resorted to all sorts of "selling gimmicks" in their efforts to encourage small investors to take advantage of the rising market by using their savings, or borrowed money, to purchase Giannini's stocks. A few months later, after the bubble had burst, there would be angry complaints from scores of Bank of Italy customers who felt they had been "pushed" into buying stock.[47]

As March gave way to April, the market reached a frenzy as money to finance the purchase of Giannini stocks poured into San Francisco from every part of the country. Local business leaders estimated the total at $50 million in one two-week period alone.[48] Witnesses marveled at the crush of people who daily arrived before the ten o'clock opening of the San Francisco Stock Exchange for the opportunity to purchase

Bancitaly or Bank of Italy stock. As described by an incredulous reporter for the *San Francisco Chronicle,* "Everyone with a few dollars . . .
[has] taken their place with the bulls and bears. . . . Scavengers and
scrub women, truck drivers and debutantes, peddlers and landladies,
snatch moments from their work or their bridge teas, to gather in front
of the boards. The maddest manifestation of gambling fever that San
Francisco has ever seen. Not even the wild days of the Comstock
witnessed such a plunging, such a fierce rush to get aboard."[49]

Meanwhile, Giannini had completed arrangements to convert his
newly acquired, state-chartered Bank of America into a national bank,
which would also have the authority to engage in trust business.[50] The
issue of trust powers was critical to Giannini; under its New York
charter, Bank of America had engaged in a lucrative trust business that
he was naturally anxious to preserve. Three weeks after his return to
San Francisco, Giannini called a stockholders' meeting to convene in
the city on Monday morning, March 26, 1928, for the purpose of
approving the conversion process. Since none of his intentions regarding Bank of America would come as a particular surprise to anyone in
the nation's financial community, Giannini assumed there would be
few, if any, difficulties.[51]

That assumption turned out to be incorrect. Late Friday afternoon,
March 23, Giannini received a frantic phone call from Belden in New
York with some highly disturbing news. Belden told Giannini that he
had just been informed by Gates McGarrah, agent for the NYFRB, that
the board was very much opposed to holding companies owning stock
in New York banks. Consequently, Bancitaly had six months to transfer
its 45 percent stock interest in Bank of America to individual ownership. McGarrah had gone on to say that unless Giannini agreed to this
arrangement promptly and "in writing," the board would have no
choice but to pass his request for trust powers on to FRB officials in
Washington with an unfavorable recommendation.[52]

Giannini was thunderstruck. Within the boundaries of New York's
third reserve district, he knew of at least four holding companies that
owned a controlling interest of stock in various Wall Street banks,
including Charles Mitchell's National City.[53] None had been required
by the NYFRB to divest their holdings. Giannini naturally viewed the
board's demands as blatantly discriminatory. "I am just wondering if
Federal Reserve Bank in New York is going to compel the National
City . . . to distribute all of their stock as they do in our case," he cabled
Belden later that same afternoon. "Don't know why they ought to com-

pel us to do this when other holding companies in New York . . . are not compelled to do it."[54]

Belden made some phone calls and then got back to Giannini. He was convinced, he said, that NYFRB officials were responding to allegations from Giannini's competitors in California about the aggressive and openly defiant way in which he had gone about creating his Bank of Italy branch system. One reliable Wall Street source informed Belden, "very confidentially," that the board was "very much upset" by an open letter Joseph Sartori had recently sent to each of the nation's twenty-eight thousand bankers. Sartori had warned that unless Giannini's ambitions were promptly checked, Bank of Italy would eventually control nearly the whole of the nation's banking business.[55] "There is no question," Belden said, "that much underhanded work is being done by various people in California with reserve people both here and Washington."[56]

Giannini was skeptical of Belden's explanation. Sartori's complaints were nothing new and, in any event, were based on less than impartial evidence. Furthermore, even supposing that NYFRB officials had been persuaded by the rhetoric of Sartori's dark warnings, why had the board waited more than three weeks before issuing what amounted to an ultimatum?[57] To Giannini it seemed ominously clear that something more than mere coincidence had prompted the board to delay informing him about its stock divestment demands until Friday afternoon on the weekend before the scheduled stockholders' meeting in San Francisco. The more he thought about it, the more convinced he became that J. P. Morgan and Company was behind the board's action.[58]

Giannini was not alone in his suspicions. Collins also believed that the Morgan firm had pressured the NYFRB into issuing the terms under which Bank of America would be granted trust powers.[59] According to Collins, the huge consolidation of financial power that Giannini had put together following his acquisition of Bank of America came as a great shock to Morgan. It made Giannini's private declaration of only "modest ambitions" outside California something less than convincing. The NYFRB's divestiture demands, in short, had been Morgan's way of imposing restrictions on Giannini's freedom of action on Wall Street and diminishing his direct authority over Bank of America.

As Collins and others viewed the situation, McGarrah's phone call had obviously been designed to place Giannini in a difficult position. On the one hand, to reject the NYFRB's demands would undoubtedly result in the denial of trust powers to Bank of America and thus a serious loss of business. On the other hand, to postpone the scheduled stockholders' meeting until an appeal could be filed with the FRB in Washington would create a good deal of anxiety among Bancitaly stockholders and raise doubts about the wisdom of Giannini's decision to acquire Bank of America in the first place. As one Giannini executive later commented, "It was impossible to change the March 26 date without causing confusion, delay and perhaps the impairment of confidence in the institutions involved."[60]

After some hesitation, a bitterly resentful Giannini reluctantly gave in and had Bank of Italy lawyers draw up a letter in which he acquiesced to the terms that McGarrah had relayed to Belden. On the following day, Saturday, March 24, Belden cabled Giannini with the news that the NYFRB had approved his request for trust powers.[61] Belden appeared entirely satisfied with the settlement and extended his congratulations. But in light of what he had been required to surrender in order to obtain what he believed should have been granted him in equity with other bank holding companies operating in New York, Giannini was in no mood for celebration. Privately he accused J. P. Morgan and Company of wanting to freeze him out of Wall Street.[62]

3

Other, not entirely unrelated, problems emerged. On March 10, 1928, soon after his return to San Francisco, Giannini received a letter from Attilio in New York with some disturbing news: Bank of America's highest echelon of senior executive officers, represented by Delafield and Attilio himself, had split into two hostile camps. The blame, according to Attilio, rested squarely with Leo Belden, whom Giannini had appointed as a senior executive vice-president before leaving the city. With Delafield's eager assistance, Attilio said, Belden had formed a clique of "Wall Street types" and was throwing his authority around in ways that Giannini's East River "boys," who had been moved from Brooklyn to Wall Street after the merger, found insulting and demeaning.[63]

Attilio told his brother that he had tried his best to reach an accommodation of sorts with Delafield and Belden, but without success. The insulting behavior persisted, the most blatant display of which was a condescending attitude toward him and Bank of America's other

Italian executives. On one occasion, Attilio said, Delafield "humiliated" him in front of other senior executives by trying to prevent him from presiding over a regular monthly meeting of Bank of America's board of directors. "Will continue to be patient until hear the contrary," Attilio said, "but would like permission to tell them we cannot ignore those who were with us from the start."[64]

As Attilio saw it, Delafield and Belden's poor treatment of the bank's Italian officers reflected the one-sided executive structure that had sprung up in the weeks following the merger.[65] Attilio was "startled" to learn, for example, that Delafield had not even bothered to provide him with an office. After protesting this omission, Attilio said, he was "virtually secluded" in a fifth-floor office in the rear of the building. By leaps and bounds, Attilio told his brother, Delafield and Belden had moved to expand and consolidate their authority. Bank of America had become a hiring ground for Wall Street lawyers and their friends in the financial community. Attilio assured his brother that his complaints were not a matter of "conceit or dignity but simply square deal."[66]

Giannini was cynical about his brother's complaints and concluded —in large part wrongly, as events would develop—that Attilio's difficulties were his own doing: the "ego problem," he called it. "Do the right thing and compose the prima donna situation," Giannini cabled Belden.[67] "Am doing my level best to keep the prima donna situation composed," Belden replied. A few days later Belden informed Giannini that he had spoken with Delafield about the situation and that Attilio now occupied an office "only ten feet from" Delafield's office.[68]

In San Francisco, Giannini was less concerned with the caste system that Attilio charged had developed in New York than with recruiting the "right kind" of outside businessmen to serve on Bank of America's board of directors.[69] Not just anyone from among the nation's constellation of highly regarded corporate leaders would do: he wanted, as he told his brother, "ten-strike executives, . . . good, hard-headed, well-informed, successful men" whose social and professional ties with other prominent and tough-minded businessmen reached deep into the corridors of corporate power across the country. "We want the biggest men who would in each case give us prestige and at the same time mean business for us," Giannini said.[70]

The outside directors Giannini eventually assembled on Bank of America's board of directors included such business luminaries as Bernard Behn, vice-president of International Telephone and Telegraph,

Stanley Moffett, vice-president of Standard Oil of New Jersey, Frank Doon, president of the Borden Company, and American Tobacco Company president George Hill. Giannini was especially anxious to bring Montgomery Ward president George Everitt on the board and made a special trip to the chain store's headquarters in Chicago to talk with him about accepting the position. Everitt agreed, but only after talking with New York and getting J. P. Morgan's approval.[71]

In the months to come, Giannini also appointed some of New York's most prominent Italian businessmen to the board, but not in anything like the numbers who sat on Bank of Italy's board of directors in San Francisco.[72] Of Bank of America's thirty-six directors, only five were Italians. Giannini assured Attilio and his other Italian executives in New York that this departure from traditional Bank of Italy practice was less a matter of "playing favorites" with the "new crowd" than sound business strategy. If he had any hope of succeeding with his East Coast branch building operations, he would need the assistance of men of power and social connections in the world of business, men who were shrewd and informed enough to share the bold vision he would hold out to them.[73]

But Attilio remained unconvinced. The composition of Bank of America's board of directors, he told his brother in a letter on March 16, 1928, was a serious mistake and had generated a good deal of resentment in New York's close-knit Italian community. "Nine years with New York places me in position to sincerely recommend not ignore East River bunch," Attilio said. "Limiting Bank of America board to only five Italians will I think create much unfavorable comment here. Will also give the impression of throwing off old for the new. Preserve good will by sticking to those who helped us start."[74]

Attilio's repeated warnings, however, did nothing to change Giannini's mind. He was certain that once he moved into high gear with his East Coast expansion program, his enemies could almost certainly be expected to respond ruthlessly to prevent him from succeeding. To deal with that challenge, he must himself be surrounded by men of intimidating reputation, tough, innovative, and resourceful enough to withstand the pressure and to strike back. "The time has come," Giannini cabled Attilio, "when we should avail ourselves of the opportunity of lining up with our organization the biggest men possible with a view of once and for all elimination [sic] all opposition from the powers that be. In other words, do that now which will serve to have our competitors at least feel that we are surrounded by men of big affairs."[75]

As for the injured egos of New York's Italian *prominenti,* Giannini said, the eventual success of his New York and East Coast operations would be reward enough for being asked to take a back seat to business-men who could provide Bank of America with the kind of luster and legitimacy he needed to push forward. "The Italians there have gotten rich playing the game with us," Giannini told his brother, "and it is hard to believe that they will so readily drop such a good thing as the Bank of America which is destined to make better progress than has the East River or even the Bank of Italy."[76]

In San Francisco, meanwhile, Giannini continued to deny press re-ports that he was planning to expand his banking operations outside New York. In fact, he had already set plans in motion to send a small team of Bank of Italy acquisition specialists to East Coast cities like Boston, Providence, Philadelphia, Baltimore, and New Haven in search of banks available for purchase.[77] The important thing now, Giannini told Belden in a confidential letter on March 12, 1928, was to push quietly ahead and to say nothing that might arouse the suspicions of J. P. Morgan and Company and FRB officials in Washington. "Even the mention" of his long-range plans, Giannini warned, "would serve to queer us among certain people there and in Washington. We certainly don't want to lose the good opinion of the many people who are now for us."[78]

On April 17, 1928, with San Francisco still in the grip of a runaway market in his stocks, Giannini and his wife left the city for a vacation in Italy. The press and the investing public followed his every move. A brief stopover in Chicago three days later was enough to send the stock value of the city's four largest banks soaring. As the *Chicago Commercial* explained it, "There has developed a speculative interest in the activities of A. P. Giannini that has seldom been seen in financial history. Every move he makes is watched and given significance. . . . If he walks into a bank not already owned by him, word goes out like wildfire that Giannini is buying the bank."[79]

After crossing the Atlantic on the luxury liner *Conte Grande,* the Gianninis reached Paris in late April. Rumors flourished, as they had in Chicago, creating a spectacular rise in the stock of the Banque de Paris and the Pays Bas de Paris, two of the city's largest banks.[80] Four days later the Gianninis reached Milan, their first stop in Italy on their way to Rome, where he was welcomed at the station by an enthusiastic crowd of reporters and local dignitaries.[81] "I came here on a pleasure trip," Giannini told the gathering. "I did not come here for business, but I do not know what the turn of the wheel will bring. If somebody offers me 50 cents for something I know is worth $2 dollars, I might buy it."[82]

As it developed, the "turn of the wheel" came with astonishing speed. Three days after arriving in Rome, Giannini met with reporters to announce the formation of a $25 million corporation called Amer-italia, whose purpose was to finance "the rehabilitation of Italy's old and ailing industries."[83] Press reports generated speculation on Wall Street and in San Francisco that Giannini had set about to supplant J. P. Morgan and Company as the largest foreign investment bank in Italy. The news sent thousands of hungry investors racing to the San Francisco Stock Exchange, desperate to buy shares in Giannini's Banca d'America e d'Italia, his branch banking system in Italy. "They came in droves," the *San Francisco Chronicle* reported, "four clerks being busy taking over the counter sales."[84]

Alarmed by the speculative frenzy, Giannini sent an urgent telegram to Bacigalupi recommending caution: "Stock selling too high. Discourage purchases by our friends there," he said.[85] The next day, May 11, 1928, Bacigalupi issued a press release in which he praised Banca d'America e d'Italia as "a good, sound bank, but nothing phenomenal to justify the sudden and abnormal general willingness to acquire the stock at present prices." Despite Bacigalupi's warnings, Bancitaly's price climbed to still higher levels on the San Francisco and Milan stock exchanges.[86]

By the spring of 1928 Giannini had become a financial figure of national significance and enormous popular appeal. An editorial in the *Wall Street Journal* summed up the attitude of many when it suggested that Giannini's rise to financial power belonged "more to a wonderful tale from the imaginative brain of Robert Louis Stevenson than an actual fact happening in the third decade of the twentieth century."[87] Of course, many more in California held that view. As the *San Francisco Examiner* expressed it, "Day by day in every way those who have pinned their hopes on A. P. Giannini are getting wealthier and wealthier."[88]

TEN

Season of Troubles

I

The Gianninis arrived in Rome to intense public excitement and a barrage of press attention. Crowds waited daily in the lobby of the Excelsior Hotel for the opportunity to meet and shake hands with the man whom the Italian press had begun to call the "Napoleon of high finance." The most extravagant praise came from the *Popolo d'Italia,* the country's leading Fascist newspaper, which Benito Mussolini had founded some years earlier and which was now being edited by the dictator's brother. After announcing Giannini's arrival in a boxed, front-page column, the paper went on to call him "the greatest banker in the world, equal if not greater than Morgan, Rockefeller or Ford with his destiny in the ascendent," adding that "his work here will increase Italy's world prestige."[1]

Two days later Giannini met with Mussolini over lunch at the Palazzo Chigi, the dictator's residence in Rome. Like a good many other well-known Americans in the 1920s, Giannini admired Mussolini and had praised him publicly as "one of the few great men, if not the greatest man, in the world today."[2] Rumors circulated in official circles that high on Mussolini's agenda was an effort to enlist Giannini's aid in a campaign among Americans of Italian descent to furnish his government with much-needed financial support.[3] Whether Giannini cooperated with Mussolini in this objective is not known. But Mussolini certainly benefited directly in the decade of the 1920s from Giannini's financial transactions in Europe. Giannini himself later admitted, "I made a lot of money on French francs and Italian lire. I gave the lire profits to Mussolini."[4]

Soon after his meeting with Mussolini, Giannini's Roman holiday turned suddenly into a personal nightmare. One morning he began to complain of sharp pains in his legs, arms, and shoulders. Over the next several days the pain became increasingly more excruciating until he was unable to get out of bed. Doctors summoned to his room at the Excelsior Hotel diagnosed his illness as polyneuritis, a serious and debilitating inflammation of the nerves and muscles of the body.[5] Unable to eat or sleep, barely able to walk, Giannini was taken for treatment to the home of his personal physician on Lake Nemi, forty miles outside the city.

News of Giannini's illness soon reached San Francisco. Stories began appearing in the press that he was dead or dying. Bank of Italy and Bancitaly stockholders were devastated. There was talk in the financial community that many small investors were thinking seriously of selling out. In an effort to calm their anxiety, Bacigalupi held a press conference at which he called the speculation concerning Giannini's illness a "ridiculous exaggeration." A few days later he issued a reassuring statement to the press saying that Giannini was suffering from a "slight rheumatic attack" and was expected to be back on his feet in a few days.[6] In fact, Giannini was a desperately sick man, and some at his bedside on Lake Nemi began to doubt that he would recover.

Giannini's illness could not have occurred at a worse time. Toward the end of May 1928 there was a sudden drop on the New York Stock Exchange. Giannini's stocks—Bancitaly, Bank of Italy, Bank of America—were particularly hard hit. Over the next several days their price moved steadily downward.[7] On June 8, for example, Bancitaly closed at $195, down 28 points from a previous high of $223. The slump in the market made Giannini's executives in San Francisco increasingly uneasy.[8] Bancitaly and Bank of America had attracted thousands of small, first-time investors who had borrowed heavily from brokers and finance companies on a thin margin to finance their speculation. A further decline in the value of the stocks was bound to set off a wave of selling. The lower the price declined, the more shares would be dumped wholesale on the market, touching off a full-scale panic.[9]

On the afternoon of June 7 Mario Giannini, still undergoing orthopedic treatment in the hospital for his nearly fatal hemophilia episode three months earlier, phoned his father at Lake Nemi.[10] In addition to the decline that had taken Bank of Italy from $308 a share to $284 in just three days, Mario said, rumors were circulating in San Francisco's financial district that "there was going to be a raid on the Bancitaly stock" and that manipulators "were going to drive the price down to $75."[11] Mario presented his father with two options: either allow the wave of liquidation to run its course or mount a coordinated campaign to support the market by buying back large blocs of the corporation's stocks until the situation stabilized. Concerned about the effect that a loss of public confidence could have on his plans for nationwide banking, Giannini chose the latter.[12] It would turn out to be a great mistake.

Acting quickly, Mario assembled a group of inside buyers in San Francisco and New York to handle the secret buy-back operations. On Friday, June 9, the day rumored for the start of the raid, Mario instructed his buyers in New York to purchase 16,000 shares of Bancitaly and an additional 20,000 the following day.[13] Despite these efforts to force the price of the stock up, the selling of Bancitaly and Bank of Italy continued, beating down the previous level of resistance. Although other bank stocks were being hammered, Mario and others concluded that "there seemed to be a well coordinated movement by unknown groups against all of Giannini's stocks."[14]

Emotions were running high when, on Sunday afternoon, June 10, Bacigalupi, Pedrini, and a small number of other Bank of Italy senior executives gathered in Mario's hospital room to reassess the situation. Bacigalupi, who had originally gone along with Giannini's insistence on supporting the market, now felt that a continuation of that policy was potentially disastrous. He argued that far too much of Bancitaly's assets had already been "frozen" in what had obviously turned out to be a futile maneuver.[15] Mario disagreed and urged Bacigalupi, Pedrini, and the others to redouble their efforts at forcing buying pressure into the market—a position that Bacigalupi felt was motivated more by concern for his father's reputation than good business sense.

The disagreement between the two men dragged on, worsening an already tense situation. Lacking agreement on tactics, Mario again phoned his father at Lake Nemi. Giannini responded a few hours later with a terse, somewhat ambiguous, telegram: "Continue support. Stand firm. But if must retreat then make orderly."[16]

Then, on Monday, June 11, 1928—"Blue Monday," as the press later dubbed it—the market opened with a tremendous drive against all Giannini stocks. On the San Francisco Stock Exchange Bancitaly fell to $170, a drop of more than twenty points; three hours later it had declined to $109. The news swept through the city and beyond with gale force, sending thousands of frightened investors into the financial district. As viewed by a reporter for *Barron's,* the scene inside Montgomery Street's brokerage houses was more chaotic than anything he had ever witnessed. "Old men cried, women fainted, brokers were frantic," he wrote. "Many an erstwhile paper-profit millionaire found himself a sadder but wiser amateur in the art of getting rich quick. The wildest, weirdest day . . . in all its history as the financial center of the West."[17]

The market continued its general decline over the next six or seven days and then began to level off. By mid-June prices had stabilized and the market began moving upward in a slow but steady climb. All told, in just over two tumultuous weeks Mario Giannini had thrown $60 million of Bancitaly's capital into the effort to support his father's stocks at a combined total loss to the corporation of approximately $20 million.[18] "No one who was not here can have a full realization of the methods they used in bearing down the stock," Hale cabled Giannini. "Mario has a good head and was quite heroic."[19]

Convalescing in his doctor's villa outside Rome, Giannini had followed the maelstrom over the preceding three weeks with an increasing sense of disappointment.[20] He was particularly unhappy with Bacigalupi's conduct during the crisis, which Hale had privately characterized in his cabled reports to him as "weak and indecisive." Bacigalupi himself admitted as much in an apologetic letter to Giannini on July 25, 1928, in which he called his efforts at dealing with the fluctuations in the market "the most difficult experience" in his life. "It may be well for you to seriously consider getting hold of some 'big gun' (honest and thoroughly familiar with stock market operations) to operate from New York and handle our several issues," Bacigalupi said. "This stock game is some science, and in your absence there is no one in the entire organization . . . capable of handling it."[21]

Bacigalupi pointed the finger of blame for the debacle to everything from the orgy of speculation that had preceded the Blue Monday market panic to the bogus financing of stock purchases.[22] But in a letter on July 25, 1928, Hale asked Giannini to consider the possibility that short sellers had been responsible for driving down the price of his stocks— the object of a well-orchestrated plan devised by his enemies in California and New York to damage the corporation's reputation. "I cannot get away from the feeling," Hale wrote, "that there was a plan . . . to take advantage of a real strong weakness in the general market to drive down the Giannini stocks; and I am under the impression that it was started in San Francisco and taken to New York . . . so that there was a concerted action between New York and San Francisco . . . and no doubt there was more or less sabotage, that is buying in New York and selling in San Francisco, and vice versa."[23]

Giannini—who was given to imagining conspiracies all around him—had already arrived at the same conclusion. He was convinced, he cabled Bacigalupi a few days later, that "certain competitive interests" had been involved in the raid on his stocks. Prominent among them, he said, was Herbert Fleishhacker, vice-president of the Anglo-California and his major competitor in northern California. He accused Fleishhacker of having joined forces with J. P. Morgan and other "Wall Street gangsters . . . to manipulate the market." What his enemies evidently hoped to accomplish, Giannini said, was "a mass of bankrupted small fry" whose widely publicized losses would leave him and his financial empire with a badly tarnished reputation.[24]

Giannini had reached a further conclusion that stunned Bacigalupi and Hale. He accused Belden of having joined Fleishhacker and Morgan as a "co-conspirator" in pushing down the price of his stocks. As Giannini told Bacigalupi and Hale, not long after reports of his illness reached New York, Belden showed up unexpectedly at his doctor's lakeside villa outside Rome. "He took one look at me and asked to be allowed to go to London for a few days and then return to Rome," Giannini said. But instead of returning to Rome, Belden "cabled me for permission to go home from London and who do you suppose he returned with on the same steamer? Mr. Anderson, a Morgan partner." No sooner had Belden arrived back in New York than "the drive was on in full blast."[25] Giannini told Bacigalupi that as soon as he returned to New York, he intended to confront Belden with his "treachery" and fire him.[26]

Shocked by Giannini's accusations, Bacigalupi and Hale came immediately to Belden's defense. Hale told Giannini that while Belden's actions in New York during the crisis had been disappointing, he continued to believe that Belden "has been sincere and conscientious in all he has done." Bacigalupi was more supportive. He cabled Giannini that the circumstances surrounding Belden's curious behavior in Rome were obviously baffling. At the same time, it was entirely possible that the extreme emotional and physical effects of Giannini's illness had combined with his disappointment over the catastrophic events of Blue Monday to lead him momentarily to the wrong conclusion. To fire Belden on what was largely circumstantial evidence, Bacigalupi said, would be unfair and would lower morale among Bancitaly's other senior executives.[27]

Confronted by Bacigalupi and Hale's protests, Giannini decided to postpone a showdown with Belden until he had evidence that would confirm his suspicions. Instead, he cabled Louis Ferrari, Bank of Italy's chief legal counsel, with instructions to pursue the matter of Bancitaly and Bank of Italy's collapse during the June market break with the Justice Department. "Officials Bank of Italy under the impression that short selling of Giannini stocks is result of conspiracy to discredit all Giannini organizations and that this is a violation of common law," Ferrari cabled Collins in Washington. "A conviction is not hoped for but it is believed that investigation will have beneficial result."[28]

Collins had his own reasons for sharing Giannini's suspicions regarding Belden's involvement in an elaborate scheme to drive down the price of Giannini's stocks, but he nevertheless advised against pursuing a government investigation.[29] "In the first place," he told Ferrari in a telegram on June 26, 1928, "there is nothing more difficult to prove than a conspiracy." Then, too, there was the risk of causing further damage. "It might boomerang," Collins said. "In fact, the investigation might fall into the hands of your enemies. No doubt rumors would be circulated that the Justice Department was investigating the Bank of Italy and its affiliates and thus a new crop of irresponsible gossip might be started."[30]

Temporarily stymied, Giannini turned to his favorite method of dealing with his executives whom he suspected of disloyalty to him or to the organization. He directed Mario Giannini in a confidential cable to hire a team of private detectives ("the best and most dependable") to tail Belden around Wall Street and to report on his every activity. "I remain convinced," Giannini said, "that Morgan with the aid of Belden and Fleishhacker were wholly responsible for the June 1928 drive and break."[31]

As the months went by, Giannini continued to believe that Belden had "sold out" to J. P. Morgan for personal gain and the opportunity to run with Wall Street's rich and powerful.[32] Confronted with the accusation two years later, when Giannini demanded and got his resignation, Belden denied everything. Despite his protestations of innocence, the most damaging evidence against Belden emerged five years later as a result of an investigating committee under the chairmanship of John Pecora, congressman from Rhode Island. During the course of the Pecora hearings on Wall Street's manipulations of the securities market, the committee made public J. P. Morgan and Company's "preferred list" of privileged clients to whom the firm sold stock at figures far below prevailing market prices.[33] Included on the list was the name of Leo Belden.

2

Late in August 1928, four months after the start of his vacation to Italy, Giannini boarded the *Ile de France,* bound for New York on the first leg of his return trip home. Bacigalupi, fearful that Giannini would use the occasion of an expected dockside press conference to publicly denounce J. P. Morgan and Company for having "conspired" with his competitors in the bear raid against his stocks, made a hurried trip from San Francisco to be on hand when the ship arrived. With him, Bacigalupi carried a carefully worded statement he had written ("the proper newspaper twist") and sent to Giannini some weeks earlier, in which he called the June market break "regrettable . . . but in accordance to [*sic*] your predictions . . . and justified your repeated warnings against speculation."[34]

On the morning of September 4, when the *Ile de France* reached New York, Giannini was greeted by a large group of reporters. Those who had covered his departure from the city five months earlier were shocked by his appearance. Giannini, who had lost nearly forty pounds, walked with difficulty, and the dark circles under his eyes accentuated the gauntness of his face. As a reporter for the *New York Times* described his arrival, "Giannini plainly shows the results of his long and terrible suffering. He does not stride about with his old-time vigor and aggressiveness."[35]

To Bacigalupi's great relief, Giannini confined his remarks to the press about the Blue Monday disaster to the statement he had written for him.[36] After telling reporters that he was glad to be back from "what I thought was going to be a vacation," Giannini said that what had occurred in the market three months earlier "naturally included our stocks and resulted in the severe decline which I had feared and even predicted in warnings against speculation as far back as last winter." Careful to avoid showing any public sign of disappointment, Giannini closed the press conference by praising the conduct of his executives in their efforts to deal with the crisis. "I am immensely pleased with the

way our people handled things," he said. "We have seen our management subjected to a severe and critical test, from which they have
emerged with flying colors."[37]

Inside a waiting car, however, the smoldering anger that Giannini
had carried with him across the Atlantic suddenly exploded. As one
close aide would remember, "Giannini was beside himself with rage.
He turned on Bacigalupi and accused him of acting with 'cowardly
indecision' during the crisis. 'You have destroyed in twenty-five days
what I took twenty-five years to build up,'" Giannini shouted.[38] Bacigalupi sat glumly in the car and refused to argue, waiting for Giannini's
devastating outburst to pass.

Exhausted and still in considerable pain, Giannini was anxious to
leave New York as quickly as possible for the long cross-country train
trip back to San Francisco. It would not be that easy. During his
transatlantic crossing he had received an urgent radiogram from Belden:
"Bartow anxious to see you on arrival."[39] Belden furnished no explanation for Bartow's request. Although cool to the idea, Giannini, believing he had no choice, agreed to the meeting.

The next morning Giannini, Bacigalupi, and Hale met with Bartow
at Bank of America headquarters, not far from J. P. Morgan and Company. It was a brief and unpleasant session. Bartow made it immediately
clear that the Morgan firm was deeply disappointed with Giannini's
decision to support the market during the June market break and
accused him of having sacrificed a sizable amount of Bancitaly's capital
to personal ambition. In addition, Bartow said, he as well as other
Morgan partners had been informed that Giannini had accused certain
"unnamed enemies" of established reputations in New York and California of having taken advantage of the market slump to drive down
the price of his stocks. Such allegations were not only "groundless,"
Bartow said, but an embarrassment to J. P. Morgan personally. Bartow
warned Giannini not to repeat them to the press on his return to San
Francisco.[40]

Giannini started to argue, responding that Bancitaly's management
and stockholders alone had the responsibility for running the corporation; the Morgan firm was treading where it did not belong.

Bartow brushed aside Giannini's objections. He reminded Giannini
that he had been given the opportunity to establish his presence on
Wall Street in no small part because of the blessing and goodwill of
J. P. Morgan and Company; the firm could just as easily arrange for
another owner of Bank of America. Like it or not, Bartow said, Gian-

nini "would have to play the game their way if he wanted to be right with them."

Giannini was quick to grasp the implications of Bartow's remarks and decided to play a delaying game. He was, he told Bartow, "still weak" from the illness that had struck him in Rome and suggested that the two of them get together in a few weeks' time to discuss their disagreements. "I did all I could to stall things by saying I would return to New York," Giannini wrote later.[41]

On the morning of October 2, 1928, Giannini arrived in Oakland, California, where he was met at the train station by an enthusiastic crowd of friends and employees. He kept his remarks brief. "Thank you for your kindness," he said to the throng of well-wishers. "What I had planned as a summer vacation trip with my family turned out to be a stubborn fight with an attack of neuritis. But I feel fit now to be back in the saddle."[42]

With his wife and daughter beside him, Giannini then turned and climbed into the family car for the fifty-minute drive to San Mateo. During the trip Giannini sat depressed and bitterly angry over the series of personal humiliations that had begun with the events of Blue Monday in the spring and had reached a low point in his meeting with Bartow four days earlier. Suddenly, in a voice husky with emotion, Giannini broke the gloomy silence that had descended over everyone in the car. "Those bastards will never do this to us again," he said to no one in particular.[43]

Back in San Francisco two days later, Giannini summoned Bacigalupi, Mario, and Hale to a meeting at Bank of Italy headquarters. Giannini began by outlining to the others his sense of what needed to be done: some way would have to be found to reorganize Bancitaly's far-flung, immensely complex, and multifaceted operating structure to make his stocks less vulnerable to manipulation in the market.[44] The major problem, as Bacigalupi had defined it in an earlier memorandum to Giannini, was the great difficulty of watching over too many stocks—some five million shares of Bancitaly alone and almost as many more in his four banking systems in California. "Our problems have become so large, many, and widespread that a better and more impersonal organization must be built up," Bacigalupi said.[45]

With Mario taking the lead and working out nearly all of the complex technical details, the group eventually arrived at a solution: the consolidation of Bancitaly, Bank of Italy, Bank of America, and a host of various affiliates and subsidiaries into one giant bank holding company.[46] The advantage of this new organizational structure, as Mario later told the press, was that by consolidating all of the parts of his father's banking and investment operations into a single unit, "it would be simpler to look after the stock of one company than to guard against the fluctuations of four."[47]

There remained a minor problem: what name to give to the corporation. Giannini wanted one that would reflect what he envisioned as its primary purpose: to be the parent corporation of a vast family of branch banks that would eventually stretch from one end of the country to the other. The problem was finally solved by a Bank of Italy secretary, who overheard Ferrari discussing the problem one afternoon with an aide in the legal department. Looking up from her typewriter, she suddenly blurted out, "Why not call it Transamerica?" The name delighted Giannini.[48]

On October 2, 1928, Ferrari traveled to Delaware, where he filed legal documents with the secretary of state's office setting up the corporation. Press reaction to the emergence of the $1.5 billion Transamerica Corporation was heightened by speculation that it would soon become the vehicle for the realization of Giannini's nationwide banking ambitions. As the *New York Tribune* commented, "It has been known for a long time that Giannini has been striving to evolve a plan to take the securities of his banks and other institutions out of the realm of stock market speculation. The new corporation will enable him to do this."[49]

With Transamerica ready, Giannini now embarked on a potentially dangerous course, but one that he believed would solve many of his remaining problems. Convinced that Morgan was doing everything possible directly and indirectly to force him out of Wall Street, Giannini informed his top executives in New York that he planned to bring Bank of America under the direct control of Transamerica.[50] This meant, of course, that he would be compelled to abrogate unilaterally the agreement he had signed with the NYFRB and sent to Gates McGarrah nearly a year earlier. But Giannini had not forgotten the circumstances under which he had signed the agreement in the first place, reason enough in his eyes to consider it invalid.[51]

In New York, news of Giannini's intentions terrified Belden, who pleaded with him to reconsider. "Such a step," he cabled Giannini on January 7, 1929, "would be seen as a direct threat to Morgan's rule on

Wall Street and will probably result in considerable friction."[52] Desperate to impress Giannini with the seriousness of the course he had decided to take, Belden sent a second urgent warning later that same day: "Any break with the Federal would lose us corner and other support."[53]

But Giannini had made up his mind. As he explained to Bacigalupi and his other executives, unless he cut his ties to J. P. Morgan and Company, he would never be in a position to consolidate his control over Bank of America and to push toward his ultimate goal of building a nationwide system of branch banks. On January 8, 1929, Giannini sent a telegram to Belden that shocked everyone in authority over his New York operations. "It seems to me," he wrote, "that we should now transfer all securities we have with Morgan to Bank of America." In what would soon become the full glare of Wall Street, Giannini had made his break with J. P. Morgan and Company complete.[54]

Giannini executives in San Francisco who had predicted a swift and angry reaction from Wall Street were not mistaken. On January 10, 1929, Giannini received a frantic telegram from Belden written partly in code: "Montgomery [Morgan] much exercised. . . . Please tell me what to say to Montgomery."[55]

Ignoring Belden's request, Giannini decided to deal with the outraged feelings of Morgan himself. Accompanied by Hale, Giannini left San Francisco on January 11, 1929, and arrived in New York four days later. The next morning the two men met with Bartow in the Park Avenue home of George Whitney, president of J. P. Morgan and Company. Bartow, barely able to control his anger, insisted that Giannini adhere to the terms of the agreement he had signed with the NYFRB. He warned that the course of action Giannini had set in motion would have serious consequences as far as the Morgan firm's attitude toward his control of Bank of America was concerned. "Right or wrong," Bartow said, "we are for the Federal Reserve Bank."[56]

"I don't feel morally or legally bound by the agreement," Giannini replied. "We are absolutely right in our position. The federal reserve has treated us badly and you and Morgan ought to uphold us and help us."

Bartow eyed Giannini coldly. The Morgan firm had no intention of cooperating with Giannini in violating the terms of a formal agreement he had signed with the NYFRB, Bartow said. "You are obviously not the kind of man who can be counted on to keep his word."

Giannini was incensed. "If anyone questions my integrity I will fight this out to the last ditch," he shouted. Hale, shocked by the level of anger to which the discussion had risen, quickly intervened in an effort to smooth things over. The meeting abruptly ended when Hale suggested that the four of them get together later in the week to resume the discussion.[57]

Still in a rage, Giannini hurried to midtown Manhattan, where he had a luncheon engagement with Jackson Reynolds, the highly regarded president of New York's First National Bank and an old hand on Wall Street. Stunned by Hale's account of the heated argument that had taken place with Bartow in Whitney's home, Jackson warned Giannini that he was stepping over a dangerous line. "Granted for the sake of argument that you have received the worst kind of treatment," Jackson said, "my judgement is that even if you were shanghaied, knocked down and jumped on, I would advise you to divest Transamerica of all stock it holds in Bank of America. The law of the street is that a corporation shall not hold stock in any bank in Wall Street. . . . Time will work out in your favor, but for now go along with what Morgan wants."[58]

"The law of the street has nothing whatsoever to do" with the agreement he felt he had been forced to sign with the NYFRB, Giannini replied. "Morgan is determined to keep us out of Wall Street and not allow us to grow." He would not permit that to happen.[59]

The next day Giannini and Hale left New York to discuss the situation with FRB officials in Washington. Hale wrote later that he and Giannini were "astonished" to learn that the FRB "knew nothing" about Giannini's difficulties with J. P. Morgan and Company and were "surprised" to learn about McGarrah's March 23, 1928, ultimatum.[60] This unexpected piece of information served to confirm Giannini's darkest suspicions: the NYFRB's threat to deny trust powers to the Bank of America, the demand that Giannini agree to divest Bancitaly of its stock interest in Bank of America, the June raid against his stocks—all had been arranged by Morgan and those leading the fight against Bank of Italy in California.[61]

Giannini moved swiftly. Back in New York, he met with Collins at the Ritz Carlton to draft a formal letter of notification to McGarrah, a copy of which he sent to Bartow.[62] "As you are doubtless aware," the letter began, "we have taken the position that Transamerica is not in anyway bound by the terms of the letter written by the Bancitaly Corporation . . . because the letter itself was without any legal or moral force . . . and had been written under duress." In a thinly disguised reference to Charles Mitchell's National City, Giannini told McGarrah that he considered Transamerica Corporation "free to act as every other corporation which has the right and power to hold the stock of banking institutions."[63] No reply came from McGarrah.

Giannini's letter to McGarrah, however, did elicit a response from other quarters. Back in San Francisco five days later, Giannini was informed in a phone call from Belden that Morgan was "very much upset" by his action and considered his continued presence in New York a menace to the entire financial community. It was an ominous message, one that was underscored a few days later when four of Bank of America's outside directors—all of whom J. P. Morgan had personally selected—submitted their resignations from the board. As one Giannini aide would remember, "The breech between the Morgan interests and the Giannini concerns was widening, and the men who represented these interests were lining up on either side."[64]

Morgan wasted no time before making clear that he had all he could stand of Giannini. A few weeks later Belden phoned Giannini with the news that Bartow had arranged for the merger of Bank of America with the Chase National, then the country's largest bank. Belden told Giannini that Chase National president Albert Wiggin had expressed "great interest" in the transaction. For the merger to go forward, however, Wiggin had insisted that he be "given the exclusive right to vote Transamerica's shares . . . and that no one from California, particularly Italians . . . would be allowed on the reorganized board of directors."[65] Giannini rejected the offer. "That son-of-a-bitch, Wiggin," he remarked to an aide.[66]

3

Not coincidentally, in the weeks following Giannini's break with Morgan the split in the executive ranks at Bank of America intensified. Attilio informed his brother in a letter on January 13, 1929, that Delafield and his "gang of Wall Street cronies" had embarked on a vicious campaign of character assassination and were predicting that Morgan would soon "send Giannini packing from Wall Street."[67] At a meeting of Bank of America's executive committee, Attilio said, Delafield complained about Giannini's refusal to "accommodate himself to the ways of Wall Street," charging that "the bank had lost . . . a half million dollar trust account because of the bad influence of the

Gianninis." Delafield's remarks sent Attilio into a fury. "I gave him a very fine dressing down," he said. "I did not spare him or his feelings."[68]

Attilio told his brother that before he could use his authority with greater effectiveness at Bank of America, he would need to crack down hard on the maliciousness and mischief making of its senior core of "Wall Street types." Especially destructive of morale was the brutal treatment of the bank's Italian officials and employees, whom the Delafield side of the organization had taken to insulting "left and right as to our nationality and our religion. . . . Disparaging remarks concerning our clientele are made continuously. . . . If we were to listen to Wall Street we would throw out 95% of our clientele at the branches."[69] Attilio warned his brother that he could no longer afford to delay a confrontation. "You must break up the Delafield and Belden ring in order to succeed in New York," he wrote. "I am on to their curves . . . and am of the opinion that a good talking to them with a firm insistence that we are members of the family and not illegitimate children will do a lot of good."[70]

Giannini rejected his brother's pleas for prompt and decisive intervention, at least temporarily. He explained that too aggressive an approach toward solving the problems at Bank of America would inevitably result in a rancorous internal battle and compound his difficulties in New York, thus disrupting the carefully planned timetable he had devised for himself in his drive toward nationwide branch banking. Giannini urged Attilio instead to be patient until he had consolidated the gains he expected to make with his East Coast banking operations. "We don't control the bank now but we hope to in due course," Giannini wrote. "I think the most important thing now is to get along the best we can until we are in a better position to assert ourselves. Now is not the time."[71]

Despite Giannini's caution, there were limits to what he was willing to tolerate from the Delafield side of his New York organization. After being informed that Delafield had turned away a customer who had tried to open a $200 savings account in Bank of America, Giannini fired off a telegram reprimanding Delafield for what he perceived as an effort on his part to introduce Wall Street's aura of exclusivity into the bank. "You cannot expect to build up much of a savings business if you are going to adhere to any limit," Giannini said. "You should take savings deposits from one dollar up."[72]

Anxious to reestablish the Wall Street connection lost by his break with J. P. Morgan and Company, Giannini began looking for a suitable replacement. To assist him in giving Transamerica a far more prominent position than its identity as a strictly California corporation might allow, he wanted a man of stature and experience, someone whose very name suggested indisputable connections to the elite of the nation's business establishment. Late in the spring of 1929 he was certain he had found the man he was looking for. His name was Elisha Walker.[73]

A tall, trim, formal, immaculately tailored man with small brown eyes, thinning hair, and a neatly trimmed moustache, the fifty-year-old Walker, a native New Yorker, had entered the securities business on Wall Street in 1904 soon after graduation from Yale.[74] Later he joined Blair and Company, one of Wall Street's oldest and most distinguished investment firms, which operated a string of twenty-three securities offices from Paris to New York and as far across the country as Portland, Oregon. In 1921 Walker became the firm's president. One measure of Blair and Company's solid reputation in the nation's financial community was that it was represented on the directorates of more than a hundred major corporations.

Walker welcomed the opportunity to join forces with an organization that commanded capital far in excess of any amount his own Blair and Company could hope to assemble. When finally hammered out, the deal called for Giannini to merge Blair and Company with his New York securities affiliate, Bancamerica, to become the investment arm of Bank of America (New York) called Bancamerica-Blair. Giannini appointed Walker president of the firm and chairman of Bank of America's executive committee at an annual salary of $100,000.[75] For vice-chairman, Giannini selected Walker's close associate, Jean Monnet, the highly regarded French industrial expert and former deputy secretary of the League of Nations who had been the financial brains behind Blair and Company's investment activities in Europe.[76]

Most financial observers agreed that Giannini, in bringing Walker and Monnet into the organization, had taken a crucial step in transforming Transamerica into the nation's premier bank investment corporation. As the *Wall Street Journal* commented, "The admission of Walker and Monnet into the Giannini family is one of Transamerica's fundamental assets."[77] Giannini himself was no less enthusiastic, telling a group of reporters in San Francisco that he now had some of the "best bankers in the country" working for him, "the finest bunch in New York." Walker and Monnet, he said, "know their way around Wall Street."[78]

Giannini pushed aggressively ahead in the months that followed, initiating a campaign to increase the numbers of Transamerica's stockholders to 500,000 by the end of 1930.[79] He reached out for a marketing strategist from Tennessee, Howard Preston, to establish a "selling organization" in New York.[80] Preston quickly recruited a large and aggressive staff of salesmen. Confident that there were large numbers of small investors across the country just waiting for an opportunity to gamble in the market with the right stock, Preston wrote to Giannini: "I hope to see in every small town in the United States . . . a reliable man selling Transamerica stock every day of the year."[81]

News of the stand that Giannini had taken against the Morgan firm and the boldness of his actions in finding new ways to strengthen his position spread throughout the nation's financial community. After the Transamerica and Blair and Company triumphs, many were quick to predict that Giannini had taken the necessary steps toward making Transamerica the nation's preeminent financial institution. As the *San Francisco Examiner* explained it, "There is probably no banker in the country today who is in the advantageous position in which Giannini finds himself. The prospects for the future are startling. It seems extremely probable that future developments affecting Transamerica will attract public interest sooner or later, as great, or even greater, than anything we have ever seen before."[82]

ELEVEN

The Downhill Slide

I

On the evening of October 17, 1929, Bank of Italy's senior executives and board of directors gathered at the Pacific Union Club on Nob Hill for a dinner party in Bacigalupi's honor. Since the early years of the bank's remarkable climb to financial power, Giannini had maintained the practice of rotating his top executives out of their positions every five years to make way for others. "When a man knows he has a chance to go up the ladder instead of having to wait for the chief to die before he can hope for advancement," he liked to say, "it stimulates him to concentrate on his job and to achieve something."[1] Bacigalupi, who was less than three months away from the end of his five years as Bank of Italy's president, had been chosen by Giannini to become vice-chairman of Transamerica's advisory committee.[2]

Amid the smiles and relaxed dinner conversation in the rich, darkly paneled dining room of the club, the mood was nostalgic. An older generation of Bank of Italy executives and directors was passing. Of the nine men who had sat on the bank's board of directors at its founding in 1904, only Giannini, Pedrini, and Scatena remained. Death, retirement, and two resignations had taken away the others. Symbolic of this transition was Giannini's announcement in a press release a few weeks earlier that he planned to step down as Transamerica's president on his sixtieth birthday, less than one year away.[3]

To succeed Bacigalupi, Giannini had named Arnold J. Mount, Bank of Italy's first non-Italian president. A native of California, Mount had gone to work for a small bank in Oakland in 1916 after graduation from Stanford. He eventually caught the attention of Giannini, who recruited him to manage a succession of Bank of Italy branches in and around San Francisco. Later Mount became Bank of Italy's cashier, and then senior vice-president of its regional headquarters in Los Angeles. A stocky, balding, round-faced man with an aloof and somewhat overbearing manner, Mount had risen rapidly in the organization through his own considerable talents and intense efforts and through Giannini's confidence in his abilities.[4]

Before the dinner party was over, Giannini slipped away and hurried across the street to a banquet at the Fairmont Hotel, where more than a thousand employees were celebrating the twenty-fifth anniversary of Bank of Italy's founding. With Pedrini at his side, Giannini entered the grand ballroom to a standing ovation. After slicing into a huge, multi-tiered birthday cake and posing for photographers, Giannini responded to the cheers of the enthusiastic gathering with a prediction of great things ahead for the bank. "On this twenty-fifth anniversary," he said, "we are aware that we stand on the threshold of a new era of even greater prosperity in the Bank of Italy."[5]

Two days after the birthday party, stock market values on the New York Stock Exchange dropped $1 billion in a wave of liquidation. Monday, October 21, 1929, was another grim day as the panic selling brought prices to even lower levels. Throughout the following week the liquidation continued. Sell orders poured in from every part of the country.[6] Then, on Thursday, October 29—"Black Thursday" as the financial press called it—the "great bull market of the 1920s came disastrously to an end" as more than sixteen million shares were dumped on the floor of the New York Stock Exchange, sending prices plunging to an average loss of twenty-five points. In the weeks and months that followed the situation steadily worsened, "a bitter downward spiral of economic activity affecting every phase and aspect of human life."[7]

In San Francisco, Giannini's initial reaction to the debacle was to mount a counteroffensive to defend the value of Transamerica's stock by supporting the market. On October 24, 1929, he purchased nearly all of the 230,000 shares of Transamerica that had been dumped on the San Francisco Stock Exchange. Over the next three days he bought

800,000 additional shares. In the end, Giannini threw more than $68 million of the corporation's capital into the hastily conceived buy-back operation, a precipitous and some said irresponsible action that he would later privately admit to Bank of Italy's board of directors had been a terrible mistake.[8] Confronted by the unprecedented collapse of the market, Giannini withdrew his support.[9] Transamerica promptly fell from $62 to $32 a share—a total market loss of more than $750 million.[10]

Obsessed as always by his expansionist ambitions, Giannini gave no outward sign that he was seriously concerned over the dizzying collapse that had swept Wall Street. He immediately made it clear to his top executives in San Francisco and New York that he had no intention of allowing anything to interfere with his goal of nationwide banking. "You are not to let the recent market slump change our plans," he cabled Howard Preston, head of Interstate Trading, Transamerica's stock distributing affiliate in New York. "Go ahead with the work as if nothing had happened."[11]

In the weeks that followed, Giannini embarked on a number of highly publicized actions designed in large part to shore up investor confidence. To reporters he had summoned to a press conference at Bank of Italy headquarters, he said that it was "absolutely essential for the American people to face the future with optimism." On December 18, 1929, San Francisco newspapers reported that Giannini had purchased the Oakland Bank with eight city branches and had added five branches to his Bank of America system in New York.[12] Ten days later Giannini announced that Bank of Italy had taken over a $41 million bond issue to complete construction of the Hetch Hetchy Aqueduct, San Francisco's water and power supply system.[13] As he had expected, newspaper editorials were quick to praise his action. The *San Francisco Chronicle* called it "a patriotic act and loyalty to the people of San Francisco."[14]

Meanwhile, Giannini began preparing to relinquish his position as president of Transamerica. As many had expected, he decided to offer overall command of the corporation to Elisha Walker and Jean Monnet. Late in November 1929 he sent Mario to New York to work out the contractual arrangements.[15] Things went smoothly at first, but a sticking point in the negotiations soon developed. Walker proposed that he limit his support of nationwide branch banking to a "public declaration."[16] That did not satisfy Giannini. He insisted on and received formal assurances with a secret letter of understanding, signed by both Walker

and Monnet, that committed them to an unqualified pursuit of coast-to-coast branch expansion. The agreement said in part, "Transamerica shall develop its policy of nationwide branch banking."[17]

The contract was signed on January 16, 1930.[18] Walker became Transamerica's chairman of the board and chief executive officer at an annual salary of $100,000; Monnet was named vice-chairman, for which he received a $50,000 contract.[19] Giannini was at the Breakers Hotel in Miami on his annual winter vacation when he received a telegram from Walker full of optimism and good feelings. "Am delighted with the happy closing of our agreement," Walker said. "I am entering my new responsibilities with high hopes of real accomplishment and count on your hearty cooperation. I hope you will take a well earned rest and Monnet joins me in sending you our warmest regards."[20]

Two weeks later, at Transamerica's annual stockholders' meeting in San Francisco, Mario became the corporation's new president—Giannini's choice as his successor. At thirty-five Mario was considered by many to be one of the nation's most talented and respected investment bankers, the man who labored diligently and in relative obscurity in his "office" at the Mark Hopkins Hotel to engineer a considerable share of Giannini's success. "Will endeavor to so conduct myself as to be worthy of the loving trust and confidence which you have reposed in me," he cabled his father the day after the stockholders' meeting. "My one great hope is that I shall prove worthy."[21]

On the morning of February 19, 1930, Walker and Monnet arrived in San Francisco. Mario Giannini met the two men at the train station, then escorted them on a tour of Bank of Italy's headquarters at 1 Powell. Later that same day the three of them went to the St. Francis Hotel, where a packed room of stockholders had gathered to get their first look at the corporation's new chief operating officers. Standing behind a lectern with Monnet at his side, Walker praised Giannini as a visionary and a figure of great courage and innovation in the nation's financial community. He went on to pledge his support of nationwide branch banking. "I will do my best to carry out the policies of A. P. Giannini in making Transamerica the most outstanding institution of its kind in the country," he said. "Transamerica is only starting. Recently it was only a local institution. Now it has the world at its feet. . . . The American people must adopt branch banking."[22]

Mario was impressed by the chairman's remarks—a bold blueprint of ambitious goals and corporation confidence around which Transamerica employees and stockholders could rally. The next day Mario sent a telegram to Preston in New York praising Walker's performance. "Mr. Walker made splendid statement and expressed himself as favoring a continuation of the policies which have made the institution so successful in the past," Mario said. "Prospects for the future are very bright and your organization should feel proud of being part of this gigantic institution."[23]

Not everyone felt the same way. In New York, Attilio was unhappy over his brother's decision to appoint Walker and Monnet as the corporation's chief executive officers. "The Blair crowd is already spreading the word in Wall Street that Giannini is through and they are now in control," he wrote to Pedrini on January 25, 1930. "There is no mention even of Mario assuming the presidency. What A. P. built up seems to have been emasculated overnight."[24] If Attilio's years in New York had taught him anything, it was that Wall Street's old guard of WASP bankers and heads of corporations catered only to their own financial interests and could not be trusted. "This group never cared for our kind and never will. I am on to them. . . . I am not going to permit them to outsmart me. . . . If I cannot do that I am through once and for all."[25]

Even as Walker and Monnet were meeting with Transamerica executives and stockholders in San Francisco, nothing less than a potentially fatal threat to the very survival of the corporation itself was shaping up in Bank of America of California's regional headquarters in Los Angeles. This time the problem arose not from the opposition of Giannini's enemies but from the criminal activities of a handful of Bank of America of California's top executives. To explain this extraordinary development, it is necessary to go back to the spring of 1928.

2

The story began in the spring of 1928 when James C. Byrnes, a well-known San Francisco broker, showed up at Bank of Italy headquarters with a proposition that he was certain Giannini could not refuse. Acting as the agent for a group of "selling interests," Byrnes said, he had been authorized to offer Giannini the opportunity to purchase the Merchants National Trust and Savings Bank of Los Angeles, the city's third largest financial institution, with thirty-five branches and total resources of more than $65 million. In addition to the price of the bank, Byrnes said, certain side issues were involved in the trans-action. As part of the purchase agreement, Giannini would be required to retain the services of the Merchants National Trust and Savings' president and three senior officials in their present executive positions.[26]

The "selling interests" turned out to be the same four executives who expected to join the Giannini organization once the transaction had been completed. Two were brothers, Marco and Irving Hellman, neph-ews of Wells Fargo founder Isaias Hellman; Marco and Irving had inherited Merchants National after the death of their father two years earlier.[27] As descendants of one of the state's most prominent Jewish families, the Hellman brothers enjoyed a socially influential position in Los Angeles—contributing money to various philanthropies and raising campaign funds for the city's Republican establishment. Like the Hellmans, Edward Nolan, the Merchants National president, num-bered among his closest personal friends many of the bank's wealthiest clients. Tall, handsome, silver-haired, and smooth-talking, the forty-seven-year-old Nolan was credited with being the most aggressive member of the group in bringing new business to the bank. Asked by a local reporter on one occasion to explain the secret of his success, Nolan replied: "You asked me about my success, as you call it. Better call it luck; for I am an opportunist, pure and simple."[28]

The fourth member of the group was Charles R. Bell, a Canadian by birth who had emigrated to the United States in 1915 and eventu-ally settled in Los Angeles. After pursuing a career as a stockbroker, Bell moved into real estate in the early 1920s, quickly demonstrating a talent for salesmanship, a sharp eye for identifying new business oppor-tunities, and a willingness to take high risks. Once described by the *Los Angeles Times* as the "boy wonder" of real estate, Bell performed wide-ranging services for Merchants National as a senior vice-president in charge of real estate investments; he mixed easily with the same circle of social and business friends as Nolan and the Hellmans.[29]

As Byrnes had anticipated, Giannini was excited by the opportunity to purchase Merchants National Trust and Savings. He was always on the lookout to expand his banking operations in southern California, and acquisition of the bank, with its string of thirty-five branch offices in and around Los Angeles, would clearly help him accomplish that objective. The merger of this system with his Bank of America of California branch system would move him into a commanding financial presence in Los Angeles, vastly superior to that of Henry Robinson's Los Angeles Savings and Trust and Joseph Sartori's Security First.[30]

Giannini immediately contacted William Snyder, Bank of Italy's chief acquisitions officer, and instructed him to hurry down to Los Angeles in order to enter into preliminary negotiations with the Nolan group.[31]

As discussions with Nolan progressed, however, Snyder began to raise doubts about the wisdom of rushing into an agreement. Attractive as the purchase of Merchants National seemed to be on the surface, Snyder wrote to Giannini, a number of things worried him deeply. One was his feeling—a gut instinct—that Nolan was not the sort of man whom Giannini would want in a position of authority over his branch banking operations in southern California.[32] In addition, Snyder said, he had picked up rumors in the city's financial district that Merchants National was in considerable difficulty, primarily because of its heavy involvement in a number of real estate schemes that had gone bad.[33] "The more I have thought these conditions over," Snyder said, "the more I have considered that we should take ample time to think over the transaction and have it completed in a most careful manner."[34]

Despite Snyder's reservations, Giannini plunged ahead, sending Robert Trengrove, a Bank of Italy examiner, to Los Angeles to conduct a preliminary examination of the Merchants National books and records. Trengrove eventually came up with more than $3.5 million in "doubtful" loans, which Giannini insisted that Nolan, Bell, and the Hellmans assume as losses.[35] Nolan protested and began to hint that perhaps the deal might not go through, but Giannini refused to be intimidated. "Unless they are willing to do business in this way, pack your grip and come home," he cabled Trengrove. "Evidently those fellows down there are trying to put something over on us."[36] To demonstrate that he meant business, Giannini instructed Trengrove to conduct a second examination of the Merchants National books.

Informed of Giannini's threat to withdraw from the negotiations, Nolan quickly backed down and agreed to assume the $3.5 million in losses. A short time later Trengrove sent a memorandum to Bacigalupi recommending that Giannini move ahead with the purchase. Trengrove's recommendation, of course, was based on the assumption that Nolan had furnished him with a complete and accurate record of Merchants National's loans, losses, earnings, and financial statements. In time, Trengrove and others in the Giannini organization would come to see how wrong he had been in that assumption.[37]

On December 28, 1928, both sides came to terms. Giannini paid $40 million to acquire 100,000 of Merchants National 140,000 outstanding shares. As many had expected, Giannini moved quickly to merge Merchants National Trust and Savings with his Bank of America of California system, increasing the number of its branches to 138 statewide. Nolan became president and chief operating officer of Bank of America of California; Bell and the Hellmans were appointed as senior executive vice-presidents. With nearly $360 million in deposits, Bank of America of California became the largest state bank in California and the second largest in the country. Together with his Bank of Italy branch system, the total resources of Giannini's branch banking empire in California now exceeded a staggering $1 billion.[38]

In Los Angeles, Nolan wasted no time in ingratiating himself with Giannini. "Southern crowd behind you strong," he wrote in a telegram praising Giannini for his "wise leadership."[39] Giannini, in turn, flattered Nolan. When Nolan and his wife left Los Angeles soon after the merger for a vacation in New York, Giannini instructed Belden to give him the royal treatment. "They will stop at the St. Regis Hotel," he said. "Will you see to it that he is shown some attention there. Please have a box of roses sent to his wife at hotel on their arrival in my name and send me bill."[40]

This cordial relationship did not last long. Reports soon reached Giannini that Nolan was running Bank of America of California as a private fiefdom and a vehicle for his own ambitions. One by one, longtime senior executive officers were moved into more subordinate positions, replaced by former Merchants National executives of lesser qualifications. Nolan made other unilateral decisions that considerably annoyed Giannini executives in San Francisco. Six months after the merger Nolan increased the annual salaries of Bell and the Hellman brothers by $5,000 without first obtaining approval from San Francisco. Giannini was immensely displeased with Nolan's unauthorized action, but decided not to make an issue of it.[41]

Then, on May 10, 1929, Giannini received a letter from Bacigalupi with some disturbing news. The evidence was clear, Bacigalupi wrote, that immediately prior to the acquisition of the Merchants National, Nolan had fraudulently inflated the bank's earnings by more than $16 million. Confronted by this accusation in a closed-door meeting with a team of Bank of Italy officials sent down from San Francisco, two of Nolan's closest associates had expressed surprise and denied knowing anything about it. Bacigalupi told Giannini that both men had lied in order to protect Nolan. According to Bacigalupi, "Through a stenographer after the meeting, it was learned that Lacy [one of Nolan's associates] raised the devil with his subordinates and threatened to

find out who it was in the organization who had given . . . the clue."
Bacigalupi characterized the entire matter as a "dirty piece of business"
and told Giannini that it had occurred "with the full knowledge" of
Nolan.[42]

As shocking as these revelations were, Bacigalupi said, no less dis-
quieting was Nolan's behavior following the acquisition and merger of
Merchants National. With the assistance of Bell and Bank of America
of California's cadre of former Merchants National executives, Nolan
had shrouded his management in great secrecy. Bank of Italy executives
sent down from San Francisco had been denied positions of authority
and kept in the dark about the bank's operations. "By degrees," Bacigalupi said, "our boys from the north had either been sent back to San
Francisco or relegated to tasks that are only incidental and in no way
calculated to let them in on the knowledge as to what is going on."[43]
In Bacigalupi's opinion, Nolan's efforts to control the flow of information about the bank's internal affairs pointed to one conclusion: Nolan,
Bell, and the Hellmans were involved in some sort of cover-up.

Bacigalupi urged Giannini to move quickly in purging Bank of
America of California of Nolan's "old Merchants National crowd" and
replacing them with Bank of Italy executives from San Francisco whose
loyalty to the organization was beyond question. "Of course," Bacigalupi said, "this might have the effect of causing Nolan and Bell to
desert the ship, but the feeling here is that even this would be preferable to a continuation of the prevailing 'Star Chamber' and dangerous
regime."[44]

Meanwhile, a team of Bank of Italy examiners headed by P. C. Read,
Bank of Italy's chief examiner, had assembled in Los Angeles in the
summer of 1929 to begin a more thorough examination of the Merchants National loan portfolio. Less than two weeks into the examination, two facts became immediately apparent to Read. The first was
that Merchants National had a nearly unblemished record with state
banking examiners, although there were numerous illegalities in its
books and records that no diligent examiner could possibly have overlooked or approved. The second, far more disturbing fact was that
Merchants National had experienced serious losses in financing a still
unknown number of subdivision schemes during the Los Angeles real
estate boom of the 1920s.[45] The losses from three undeveloped real
estate projects alone came to more than $2 million. There was no doubt
in Read's mind that in acquiring Merchants National, Giannini had also
inherited a considerable amount of bad debt.[46]

As Read pressed on with his examination, he began to uncover even greater losses arising out of Merchants National's participation in a number of highly speculative real estate developments in and around Los Angeles. There was, for example, the Casa del Mar, a private beach club in Malibu built three years earlier as a watering hole and ocean retreat for Los Angeles's rich and socially prominent. The club lost money from the day it first opened its doors and was eventually forced to suspend operations. Merchants National's participation in Casa del Mar had cost the bank nearly $1 million.

Then there was the Carthay Circle Theater, a handsome, cathedral-like structure on the outskirts of Los Angeles. Investors in the project had hoped that the Carthay Circle would eventually rival Grauman's Chinese theater as the site for motion picture premiers and other star-studded affairs. But despite its reputation as the most modern and luxurious theater in southern California, the Carthay Circle suffered badly because of its location thirty miles from the glamour and excitement of Hollywood. Monthly revenues did not come anywhere near expectations. The estimated total loss to Merchants National arising from its participation in the Carthay Circle development project came to an additional $1 million.[47]

Serious as these and other losses were, they paled beside those growing out of Merchants National's participation in an immensely ambitious plan to build a "dream city of the future" in San Clemente, a small coastal town located midway between Los Angeles and San Diego. As visualized by its wildly enthusiastic developers, the plan called for the construction of moderately expensive red-tiled homes, shops, restaurants, tennis courts, and a riding academy spread over the town's five thousand acres of undeveloped land on sun-drenched bluffs overlooking the Pacific. Unknown to Giannini at the time he acquired Merchants National, approximately one thousand of San Clemente's allotted six thousand parcels of land had been sold and work had begun on the construction of streets, pavements, and a sewerage system.[48]

As it turned out, the grandiose expectations of San Clemente's promoters never materialized. After the stock market crash in October 1929, the sale of homes fell far below projections as the nation's descent into hard times made it impossible for most people to afford the high prices. Giannini executives in San Francisco were shocked to learn that Bank of America of California owned all but a small portion of the entire city of San Clemente, including more than four thousand acres of unsold land. The considerable expense of state and local taxes, combined with the cost of carrying the overhead, struck some of them as potentially disastrous.[49]

As Read proceeded with his examination, he kept uncovering additional loan losses that were connected either directly or indirectly to Merchants National's involvement in a variety of high-risk subdivision development schemes. It seemed clear that Merchants National had functioned as a source of easy credit for profit-hungry investors anxious to cash in on the Los Angeles real estate boom of the 1920s. But Read noticed something else far more interesting—and ominous. While subdivision projects like Carthay Circle and San Clemente had attracted a diverse group of investors, the names of the principal holders of the trust deeds on these and other properties were in every instance the same: Nolan, Bell, and the Hellmans. Read immediately sent off an urgent confidential memorandum to Mario Giannini informing him of his findings.

Stunned by Read's disclosures, Mario sent Ferrari to Los Angeles to determine the extent to which Nolan, Bell, and the Hellmans had been either knowingly or unknowingly involved in the apparent endless number of unprofitable real estate loans that had cost Merchants National millions of dollars in losses. With all of the available financial evidence still largely circumstantial, Mario decided not to say anything to his father about Read's findings. A veil of corporate secrecy descended over the entire subject in San Francisco and Los Angeles.

Throughout the remaining months of 1929 and into 1930, Read moved ahead with his examination, loan by loan, trying to pin down the extent of Merchants National's losses. In San Francisco a sense of foreboding gripped Mario and a small number of other Transamerica executives who were privy to what they now called in their private letters and memoranda "the southern situation." How many more defunct subdivision schemes would Read uncover? How high would Merchants National's losses (and consequently Transamerica Corporation's losses) eventually go? Were Nolan, Bell, and the Hellmans illegally tied into the bank's loans?

3

The spring of 1930 was a time of personal anguish for Giannini. During a vacation at the Breakers Hotel in Miami, he began to experience symptoms of polyneuritis, the same disease that had been nearly fatal two years earlier. In mid-March he left Miami for a week-long examination at the Mayo Clinic in Rochester, Minnesota.[50] Despite subjecting Giannini to a battery of neurological tests and a change of diet, doctors could do little for him except to recommend a prolonged period of rest and a greatly reduced work load. Two weeks after checking into the clinic, Giannini returned to his home in San Mateo in almost as much pain as ever.

The news that greeted him was not encouraging. The three-month campaign to increase the number of Transamerica stockholders from 175,000 to 500,000 had fallen far short of the goal.[51] The outcome of the corporation's efforts in California was particularly disappointing: fewer than five hundred new stockholders. Ignoring the worsening state of the economy and the general decline in the market for securities, Mario blamed Transamerica's distributing affiliate in New York for what he perceived as a lackluster performance. "What the hell is the matter with your organization?" he cabled Howard Preston. "They turned only two hundred shares today and have been getting worse each day."[52]

Worse, as far as Giannini was concerned, was Walker and Monnet's leadership of Transamerica, which he began to characterize privately to Bacigalupi and his other Bank of Italy associates as "weak" and "ineffective."[53] From his viewpoint, neither Walker nor Monnet had made any effort to promote the value of Transamerica's underlying assets or to publicize its earnings record, which had increased at the end of 1929 by over $96 million.[54] Giannini's perception was reinforced by a barrage of complaints he began to receive from anxious stockholders after his return to San Mateo. "It seems to me," one disappointed stockholder wrote, that "there has not been a word about earnings even of the vaguest sort. Something to suggest drive and direction—a dirigible instead of a balloon. It seems to me that the silence on earnings has played directly into the hands of the bear crowd."[55]

In this atmosphere Attilio wrote to Mario on March 15, 1930, informing him that Delafield "had created a panic" at Bank of America headquarters in New York by announcing his intention to sell the Transamerica shares of clients who had used them as collateral in obtaining loans from the bank that they were now unable to repay.[56] Calling Delafield's policy "malicious and unnecessary," Attilio predicted that it would almost certainly result in a chain reaction of panic selling among thousands of small shareholders in New York, a great many of whom were Italians. "You know the Italian mind," Attilio said.

"If one man sells it gets around the colony very quickly and our boys are all very excited. . . . All of these stockholders were loyal to Transamerica through the 'crash' . . . among whom are men who have been with us since the beginning."[57]

There was no doubt in Attilio's mind that a "sinister purpose" lay behind Delafield's action, which he connected to a larger effort "to throw us out of the picture" in New York. "The amount of stock that has been sold lately here and in California," he said, "makes me think that there has been an attempt to cause some kind of liquidation. Someone is trying to accumulate the stock at much lower prices."[58] Attilio believed the time had come to launch a challenge to Delafield's authority in New York. "The gang downtown is sticking together pretty well. If you wish to retain control you had better get someone on the job quick. You had better come here and tell these fellows where they head in or else what your Dad built up all these years will very soon go completely into strangers' hands. I do not want to wait for that evil day."[59]

But Giannini was in no shape to involve himself in what would certainly be an ugly battle. Exhausted by the severe pressure he had been working under since his return from Rome nearly two years earlier, and in constant pain from the illness that doctors at the Mayo Clinic had warned could cripple him, Giannini decided to get away. On May 3, 1930, he left San Francisco with his wife and daughter for Karlsbad, a health resort in Czechoslovakia famous for its hot sulfur baths and mineral waters.

Giannini paused long enough in Washington to testify before the House Committee on Banking, which had convened three weeks earlier to hear testimony from a parade of bankers on ways to reform the nation's banking system.[60] At one point in his testimony, annoyed by the charges of "monopolistic power" that some members of the committee leveled against the spread of branch banking, Giannini leaned across the witness table and all but shouted: "Nationwide branch banking is coming, gentlemen. Nothing you can do can stop it."[61]

As Giannini was crossing the Atlantic, the news from San Francisco suddenly turned grim. Transamerica plunged more than seven points in two days—from 45 to 37-3/4. Rumors circulated on Montgomery Street that a "well-organized bear raid emanating out of the east coast" had been responsible for the decline.[62] The fact that the alleged raid coincided with Transamerica's acquisition of the First National Bank of Portland, Oregon, was not lost on some observers of the stock market. As the financial editor of the *San Francisco Chronicle* put it, "Those persons in the east desiring to embarrass the Giannini organization in its expansion program obviously could attempt to do it in no better way than through a raid on the stock."[63]

Simultaneously, reports reached Giannini via a series of urgent radiograms from Mario that a number of prominent San Francisco brokerage firms "were saying derogatory things about our organization . . . urging people to sell their stock, even to the extent of telephoning clients." Rumors had it that Transamerica "was the weakest stock on the market . . . that the Italians are all losing faith in the corporation now that Giannini is out."[64] Giannini began to suspect a connection between the apparent unity of purpose among the corporation's detractors in San Francisco and Walker's silence in New York. It seemed increasingly evident to him that Walker was deliberately avoiding taking any action that could be expected to boost Transamerica's price in the market.

On June 4, 1930, Giannini arrived in London, the first overseas stop on his way to Karlsbad. A few hours later, as he sat reading a copy of the *London Daily Mail* in his room at the Connaught Hotel, he came across an article that both puzzled and angered him. In New York, Walker had released Transamerica's earnings report for 1929. What immediately grabbed Giannini's attention was Walker's figure of $67 million, roughly $30 million less than the figure Giannini had given to the press as an unofficial estimate before leaving San Francisco.[65] The *Daily Mail* stopped short of saying so, but implicit in its comments on the discrepancy between the two figures was the implication that Giannini had deliberately inflated his own estimate in an effort to give a much-needed boost to Transamerica's badly tattered reputation.

Giannini fired off a telegram to Walker requesting an explanation of how he had arrived at the $67 million figure.[66] To protect his own reputation, Giannini said, he intended to "set the record straight" with the *Daily Mail*. But Walker did not share Giannini's eagerness to furnish an explanation for the embarrassing discrepancy. "I have hoped and still hope that it will be possible to avoid any public discussion of this question in the press," he replied.[67]

Giannini immediately concluded that Walker was trying to discredit him publicly by calling his personal integrity into question. "Now fully satisfied," he cabled Mario, "they are trying to cast reflection me."[68]

Panic gripped Bacigalupi in San Francisco when Giannini informed him in a telegram on July 17, 1930, that he had decided to cancel his trip to Karlsbad and return home for a showdown with Walker.[69] Bacigalupi pleaded with him to reconsider. For Giannini to return home suddenly in the midst of Transamerica's steep decline was bound to generate rumors that he was dissatisfied with the way Walker and Monnet were running the corporation. The result would overwhelm stockholders with anxiety and precipitate a selling panic. Desperate to avert a potentially catastrophic crisis of authority within the organization, Bacigalupi enlisted the support of Hale and Pedrini. Both men cabled Giannini, urging him to give Walker and Monnet more time to solve the corporation's problems. Unwilling to be held personally responsible for any further damage, Giannini acquiesced. But he made it plain to Bacigalupi and the others that his patience was wearing thin.[70]

Meanwhile, each week saw a continuous deterioration in Transamerica's price. Giannini, who had begun raising questions about management's apparent inability to lift the corporation out of its decline as far back as March, was now firmly convinced that Walker and Monnet were conspiring with his enemies on Wall Street and in California to seize control of his financial empire. "You folks may think I'm daffy," he cabled Mario from Karlsbad, "but still insist Wall Street gang back whole thing. No great effort has yet been made to boost Transamerica's earnings and none I think is going to be made." Giannini suspected intrigue and treachery all around him. "Don't let anyone put anything over on us," he cautioned. "Be constantly on your guard and at first sign of betrayal from inside expose the culprits."[71]

Three weeks later, on August 7, 1930, Mario cabled his father with more disturbing news. He reported that Belden, whom Giannini had fired three months earlier after accusing him of selling Bancitaly short during the June 1928 crash, had moved from New York to San Francisco to open a brokerage business on Montgomery Street.[72] From the confidential reports of a team of private detectives whom he had hired to tail Belden, Mario said, he was convinced that Belden was involved with Fleishhacker and others in driving down the price of Transamerica stock.[73]

Infuriated, Giannini informed Walker in a telegram on August 11, 1930, that he wanted Belden's manipulations in the market "exposed" and given wide circulation in the press. "According to information just received," Giannini said, "that discharged traitor and tool Belden who deliberately betrayed benefactors when I was taken ill in Rome in 1928 now in San Francisco repeating his dirty work. Accept full responsibility."[74]

Walker rejected Giannini's demand. The last thing Transamerica needed at this point, he replied, was a nasty public quarrel with one of the corporation's former senior executives. Walker told Giannini that he and Monnet were "well aware" of Belden's "bearing operations," but he cautioned that it would be "unwise to dignify his action" with a public statement. "Best way to beat him is by restoring confidence and thru handling of market which is the foremost thing in my mind."[75]

Walker's response displeased Giannini, who saw it not as concern on Walker's part to avoid an embarrassing public quarrel but as more evidence of the chairman's involvement in a conspiracy to lead Transamerica to destruction. Ignoring Walker's own approach to the problem, Giannini sent a telegram to Mario: "Start hitting Belden with a strong statement in the newspapers calling attention to his past doings and past record. Drive him out of the state. When I referred to Belden as tool in cable I should have added prefix contemptible."[76]

The worst blow came on August 8, 1930, when Transamerica plunged to 18. This depressingly low price, which many market analysts believed was far below the corporation's actual value, persuaded Giannini that the continuing downward slide was being personally orchestrated by Walker and Monnet. "Am more than ever convinced that this gang is playing the game with Belden and others there," he cabled Mario. "This is all part of their plan to get price down and buy in so as to wrest control from the old crowd. . . . Mark what I tell you. If you folks allow him [Walker] to get away with this sort of stuff it will mean that the old crowd will stampede itself out and the new crowd will come into control."[77]

Certain that the survival of Transamerica was at stake, Giannini decided that the only solution was for him to return home to reassume control. "Don't you folks think," he cabled Mario, "the time has arrived for calling a spade a spade by telling Elisha [Walker] and Jean [Monnet] take back their original stock and to go ahead out of the organization they have deliberately betrayed so they can be free continue to play the game with their co-conspirators on the corner. . . . If the stockholders and the organization will but so indicate I'll get right back regardless my physical condition and assume my old duties . . . and do my level best to repair damage done."[78]

To Bacigalupi, Pedrini, and other Transamerica executives in San Francisco, Giannini's accusations seemed farfetched, the product of his overly suspicious nature. What neither Giannini nor anyone in San Francisco knew, however, was that for several months past Walker and Monnet had been meeting privately with Thomas Lamont, a senior partner in the firm of J. P. Morgan and Company. On July 30, 1929, Lamont wrote to Monnet informing him that he had discussed the possibility of moving Transamerica Corporation in the direction of "new interests" and a "fresh and changed alignment" with other senior partners in the Morgan firm.[79] In subsequent letters and phone calls between the two men, Lamont furnished Monnet with "supplementary comments" on Transamerica's management practices, particularly in reporting to the corporation's stockholders on business matters.[80]

The scope of the Morgan firm's involvement in the affairs of Transamerica will probably never be known. Walker's stature on Wall Street owed more to his success as a bond broker than it did to banking; it appeared to some in San Francisco that Transamerica's difficulties "can be blamed simply on his own stupidity."[81] At the very least, however, Walker and Monnet's private discussions with Lamont make clear that there was a basis in fact for Giannini's suspicions about a critical link between Transamerica's management and J. P. Morgan and Company and that Walker's conduct as the corporation's chief operating officer could perhaps be traced to policies set in motion by senior Morgan partners like Lamont.

On August 17, 1930, Giannini left Karlsbad for San Francisco, but not for the reasons he would have preferred. The day before, he had received an urgent cablegram from Mario with the news that Lorenzo Scatena was seriously ill with uremic poisoning and that his doctors did not expect him to survive.[82] "Leaving tonight via air and rail," Giannini replied. "Hope this will get me there in time to see grampa alive."[83] Frantic to reach San Francisco before it was too late, Giannini set a Europe-to-California passenger record of six days and six hours. It was not soon enough.[84] Three hours before a bay ferry from San Francisco brought Giannini to his stepfather's home in Sausalito, Scatena had slipped into a coma and died.[85]

On Monday morning, August 25, 1930, Scatena was buried in a family plot alongside his wife in Holy Cross Cemetery on the outskirts of San Francisco. At the church service preceding the burial, he was eulogized as a man "of great energy and ambition, but whose greatest success was as a father who took into his love the three sons of the widow he married."[86] Giannini took Scatena's death hard. "My father broke down at the funeral," his daughter would remember. "It was the first time in my life I had ever seen him cry."[87]

TWELVE

Showdown

On August 22, 1930, three days before Scatena's funeral, Walker and Monnet arrived in San Francisco. To reporters who met them at the train station, Walker explained that he wanted to discuss several matters with the corporation's California executives, including the "simplification of Transamerica's intercorporate relations."[1] A meeting was arranged for the following day at the corporation's downtown headquarters on Montgomery Street. Giannini was there, as were Mario, Bacigalupi, and Pedrini. The discussions went on for days, sometimes well into the night.[2] When they were over, Walker, Giannini, and the others had arrived at a new corporate structure that would, as Mario Giannini later told reporters, put Transamerica in an "ideal position to take advantage of coming developments."[3]

On September 3, 1930, in a large gathering of Bank of America executives, branch managers, and some seven hundred stockholders at San Francisco's Western Women's Club, Bacigalupi announced the merger of Bank of Italy and Bank of America of California under the name Bank of America National Trust and Savings Association. This new consolidation, Bacigalupi said, marked the "culmination of a plan conceived by A. P. Giannini when the Bank of America of California was formed two years ago."[4] Some thought they saw in the merger a portent of things to come. As the *San Francisco Examiner* put it, the name "Bank of America National Trust and Savings Association" was "a tip-off that Giannini anticipated a change in national banking laws that would permit the linking of the newly consolidated western institution with its eastern namesake." Giannini, the *Examiner* said, "has taken another step toward his ambitious goal of establishing a coast-to-coast network of branch banks."[5]

Giannini, who had not expected to be in San Francisco, seized on the occasion to undo his decision that had brought Walker and Monnet into the organization some eighteen months earlier. In a meeting with Bacigalupi, Pedrini, Hale, and a small number of his other old Bank of Italy associates on the board—away from Transamerica headquarters—he urged Walker and Monnet's removal as the corporation's chief executive officers. In what one participant would remember as a "furious assault," Giannini angrily accused both men of "duplicity" and of having deliberately created a crisis of inaction in the organization that "had played directly into the hands of Wall Street."[6]

But neither Giannini's presence in San Francisco nor his considerable powers of persuasion could persuade Bacigalupi and the others to go along with his proposal. Bacigalupi, shocked by the vehemence of Giannini's attack, offered the strongest resistance, accusing him of being "unfair" and "overly suspicious." He would not, he said, participate in a bloody battle for control that would almost certainly send the corporation plunging over the edge. Bacigalupi urged instead that Giannini cooperate with Walker and Monnet in their efforts at rebuilding public confidence in Transamerica by accompanying both men on a statewide promotional tour "so as to put heart into old stockholders whose morale was quite low."[7] Pedrini and Hale, neither of whom shared Giannini's suspicions about the reasons for Transamerica's problems, sided with Bacigalupi. Confronted by the united opposition of his closest associates on the board, Giannini reluctantly agreed.

On September 4, 1930, Giannini left with Walker and Monnet on a ten-day swing across the state, appearing in cities like Sacramento, Fresno, San Jose, Bakersfield, Ventura, and San Diego. The tour ended with an overflow crowd of more than a thousand stockholders at the Biltmore Hotel in Los Angeles.[8] After reaffirming his "faith in the present and future of Transamerica," Walker assured the audience that "every share of Transamerica I have ever had, I still have, and I have never been less disposed to sell them now." Dusting off the pledge he had made on his first visit to San Francisco seven months earlier, Walker then announced his intention to push ahead with plans to expand the corporation's banking operations outside of California. "Transamerica," he said, "will enter the branch banking field in every state and in foreign countries as rapidly as possible."[9]

As Walker spoke, Giannini sat silently nearby, barely able to control his anger. After the speechmaking, he was at his booster best, circulating among shareholders, greeting old friends, expressing confidence and reassurance.[10] Giannini's appearance with Walker and Monnet on the same platform produced the public relations effect Bacigalupi had expected. One stockholder later remembered that when Giannini walked into the convention room of the Biltmore Hotel, "the audience yelled and applauded . . . many with their eyes moist, swarming around him and showering him with questions and praise."[11]

Immediately after the Los Angeles meeting, Walker and Monnet returned to New York. Frustrated and disappointed by the refusal of Bacigalupi, Pedrini, and the others to join forces with him in launching a challenge to Walker's control of the corporation, Giannini retreated to his home in San Mateo. He saw few people and only occasionally appeared at his desk in San Francisco.[12] Still in considerable pain and unable to find relief, he left San Mateo in early November of 1930 for an extended convalescence at the Breakers Hotel in Miami.

By this time—the late fall of 1930—the country was in the throes of a rapidly worsening economic crisis. The depression raged on, "steadily, inexorably, terrifyingly," as the weeks and months went by.[13] Since the spring of the year, the value of all listed stocks had fallen by almost $23 billion. The profits of the nation's two hundred leading industrial corporations—steel, automobile, rubber—had declined from between 45 to 60 percent. Farm income had fallen another 16 percent— the lowest point in forty years—prompting experts to describe the situation as "extremely serious" and "literally ruinous."[14] Unemployment stood at six million, the highest in the nation's history.

Transamerica's deteriorating condition underscored the seriousness of the situation. By the early winter of 1930 the corporation that had once boasted that it stood on the threshold of financial greatness had become the subject of jokes and the target of ridicule. In San Francisco's financial district, the story made the rounds that a local drugstore, well-known for its fire sales, was offering one share of Transamerica stock to any customer who made a five-cent purchase. Another had it that a candy store owner was dispensing the corporation's shares as consolation prizes to losers of his twenty-five-cent punch boards.[15] As an unflattering editorial in the November 1930 edition of *Fortune* explained it, Transamerica's difficulties had moved rapidly from being "an unpleasant prospect to an unpleasant reality."[16]

In San Francisco, meanwhile, the fall and winter of 1930 turned out to be a particularly difficult time for Mario personally. Increasingly, he had come to feel that neither Walker nor Monnet took him seriously as Transamerica's president and were treating him like some faceless junior executive whose advice and recommendations could be freely ignored. Decisions made in New York would invariably be communicated to him through third parties, never by Walker and Monnet themselves, encouraging him to believe that both men were cloaking their deliberations in secrecy.[17] On one occasion Mario was deeply annoyed when he learned that the corporation had paid an unusually high price to take a minority position in several European properties in which Monnet was reported to have a personal financial interest.[18] Despite Mario's strongly worded objections, Walker approved the transactions.[19]

As the relationship between Mario and Walker continued to deteriorate, they barely spoke to one another. Toward the end of the year Mario explained his predicament in a letter to his father. "My situation at the office here is anything but a pleasant one," he wrote. Complaining that his role as Transamerica's president had been reduced to that of being a "chronic objector" to policies in which he had played no part in shaping, Mario said he had come to the conclusion that it would be best for all concerned if he resigned. "Affairs are being handled in a high handed way by W and M and I am rarely, if ever, consulted even in important matters. As far as my part in the management of the affairs are concerned, I feel that they would be better off if I were not around to do the objecting."[20]

On December 3, 1930, Transamerica's price dropped to 14. Mario phoned his father to report that stockholder fears had nearly reached panic level, "most noticeable in the Swiss and Italian population and to a lesser degree among the Portuguese."[21] Ten days later Transamerica went down to 11. That day, December 13, 1930, approximately 360,000 of the corporation's shares were dumped on the New York and San Francisco Stock Exchanges, a rush of liquidation not seen since the disastrous Blue Monday crash in June 1928. The front-page headline in the *Fresno Morning Republican* set the tone for the barrage of negative publicity that followed: "Fortunes Crumble as Transamerica Stock Takes Drop."[22]

In Miami, Giannini met with a group of reporters to place the blame for the selling panic where he thought it really belonged. Without mentioning Herbert Fleishhacker by name, he attributed Transamerica's collapsing price to a "certain California competitor who has been a most active participant in the group conducting market operations."[23] After accusing his enemies of engaging in "the most despicable and malicious tactics," Giannini called for a congressional investigation of the New York Stock Exchange for the purpose of "exposing" the names of those "criminals" whose illegal and self-aggrandizing manipulation of the nation's securities market was costing Transamerica's stockholders such huge financial losses.[24]

Giannini's allegations, which for the first time made public his suspicions regarding Transamerica's financial problems, attracted a good deal of attention in the press, both in California and outside the state as well. The *Los Angeles Times,* the *New York Times,* and the *Wall Street Journal* all carried reports. The *San Francisco Chronicle* published a front-page account of Giannini's sensational allegations under the headline "Giannini Hits Competitor as Stock Raider."[25]

Walker was not pleased. Mario cabled his father with the news that the chairman was "very much disturbed" by his accusations and had gone over to the Anglo-California to offer Fleishhacker his personal apologies. Embarrassed by all the publicity, Mario said, Walker had also prepared a statement to the press saying that "he knew of no such manipulations." Bacigalupi, fearful of Giannini's reaction to what in effect would be a public declaration that at the very least he had acted irresponsibly, had hurried to the chairman's office and pleaded with him not to release it. Walker reluctantly agreed, but only after Bacigalupi had promised to do all that he could to keep Giannini from saying anything more to the press.[26]

None of the chairman's anger mattered to Giannini. As he saw it, Walker and Monnet, acting in the interests of Wall Street, were involved in a "diabolical conspiracy" with market bears like Fleishhacker and Belden to drive small shareholders out of the corporation, thus seizing complete control of Transamerica and silencing once and for all the voice of California in its management. "Hope Congress will take notice and start investigation," Giannini cabled one of the corporation's senior executives in San Francisco, "so that I can get a chance to go on stand and divulge name Fleishhacker and other higher ups and their tools."[27]

Unfortunately for Giannini, neither Washington nor the nation's financial press saw it his way. The public responded to his accusations as another example of his usual habit of diverting attention from distressing news with a display of self-righteous indignation. The sharpest reaction came from *Time,* which urged its readers to "pay no heed" to his wild and unsubstantiated accusations. After pointing out that "Mr. Giannini, 60 and retired," was "no longer official spokesman for Transamerica, having been succeeded by astute Elisha Walker," *Time* disclosed that Walker and Monnet were annoyed and "deeply embarrassed" by the entire affair. The *Time* article concluded: "The Giannini outburst was merely florid sales talk by the aging master of finance."[28]

As Christmas approached, Giannini's rage turned to a dark despondency. "Oh, how I do wish Ped," he wrote to Pedrini in a holiday message, "I could have my old health back again for a while say just a year or so, and be there constantly on the firing line with you all and properly showing up Herbert Fleishhacker et al."[29] A short time later he left Miami with his wife for Badgastein, a health resort in the Austrian Alps.

Such was the situation in late January of 1931 when Mario Giannini, who had written a lengthy memorandum spelling out his dissatisfactions with the way the corporation was being run, scheduled a private meeting with Walker during the chairman's appearance in San Francisco to preside over Transamerica's annual stockholders' meeting.[30] On the day of his arrival, Mario showed up at Walker's outer office but was informed that the chairman was too busy to see him. Mario returned to Walker's office on two successive days. Each time he found himself waiting for hours while the chairman conferred privately with aides or the corporation's other senior executives. Mario eventually ran into Walker as the chairman was leaving the building. Walker promptly announced that he had a luncheon engagement and, in any event, was certain he knew why Mario wanted to see him. He wasn't interested.

Angered and humiliated, Mario returned to his office. "I remember the day I saw Mario sitting alone, slumped back in his chair, minutes after he had been snubbed by Walker," one Transamerica official would later comment. "Hurt and a cold fury were written all over his face. He told me that Walker had treated him like a damn kid."[31]

The next day, February 2, 1931, Mario submitted his resignation. "Responsibility for this action," he wrote in his letter to Walker, "must clearly rest with you. . . . Were it not for the fact that I have always considered the welfare of the corporation and its stockholders over my own physical disadvantage, I should have pursued this course some time ago."[32]

Walker wasted no time in filling the vacancy left by Mario's departure. Not long after his return to New York, he named Bacigalupi as Transamerica's new president. The announcement of this sudden and unexpected change produced a flurry of articles in the press that all but consigned the Gianninis, father and son, to oblivion. "Master of the Transamerica temple for one year now," *Time* reported, "has been Chairman Elisha Walker, a quiet, diplomatic, keen-eyed New Yorker. The great shouts of big, jovial Amadeo Peter Giannini have faded further and further into the distance . . . becoming echoes. Out of the company's presidency went his son, Lawrence Mario Giannini. Into it went one of his oldest and best friends, James Augustus Bacigalupi."[33] The thrust of the *Time* article was clear: three decades of Giannini control had come to an end.

In New York, Attilio was threatening to make the departure of the Gianninis from the corporation complete. "I do not mind the price of the stock," he wrote to Pedrini, "if we had a happy organization where everybody was pulling together—but to be working with people who do not possess the same motives that we do, makes it doubly hard. . . . I will stand it just a wee bit longer and, if there is nothing doing, I will do as Mario did."[34]

2

Early in June 1931, Walker summoned Bacigalupi to New York for an emergency meeting of Transamerica Corporation's executive committee. In a grim voice Walker informed committee members that the situation in the corporation had gone from bad to worse: net earnings were down to one-fourth of what they had been the year before, securities had fallen off dramatically, and the corporation faced a severe debt crisis—more than $50 million, $35 million of which was in loans that national bank examiners had identified as "doubtful" or "outright losses."[35] To make matters worse, Walker said, the comptroller of the currency had begun pressuring him for payment. With the most devastating financial depression in the nation's history raging out of control, he was deeply pessimistic about the chances of turning things around.

Transamerica's best hope for survival, Walker went on, was a drastic program of contraction and liquidation, which "management deemed to be essential to the security and prosperity of the corporation."[36] Walker ran through the details of his restructuring program: sale of Transamerica's interest in Bank of America N.A. (New York), Bank of America N.T. and S.A. (California), and Banca d'America e d'Italia. Also scheduled for sale or merger were the corporation's majority interests in banks outside California and New York. Dividends would be slashed, capital shrunk, and shares marked down to a non-par basis. Giannini's ambitious goal of nationwide branch banking would, of course, be abandoned. No longer was Transamerica to be the nucleus for a coast-to-coast network of banks.

Walker's restructuring program stunned even Bacigalupi. If the plan went through, nearly all of what Giannini had built since the founding of the Bank of Italy thirty years earlier would be evaluated and put up for sale at distressed prices, piece by piece, on the open market.

Immediately after the meeting, Bacigalupi headed for the nearest telegraph office. "Sentiment blue, very blue," he cabled an aide in San Francisco.[37] Returning to the city one week later, Bacigalupi met with Transamerica's board of directors to discuss the general situation and to lay out the details of Walker's reorganization program.[38] The news was instantly relayed to Mario by two board members with whom he kept secretly in touch. Mario cabled his father in Badgastein. Giannini was incensed. "Most extraordinary boldest of bold steals," he replied. "Whole thing framed so they their friends can clean up. Surprising such people out of jail."[39]

Giannini countered with a flurry of telegrams urging Bacigalupi to use his considerable influence on the board to delay approval of Walker's reorganization program at a board of directors' meeting that the chairman had scheduled in San Francisco on June 17, 1930. Accusing Walker of "betrayal," Giannini found it "inconceivable" that "his old friend" had still not "opened his eyes" to the "plot" that he and Mario had suspected Walker and Monnet were involved in more than a year earlier. "Wholly out of sympathy with the plans, procedure of my successor," Giannini wrote. "Plan if carried through as outlined will be found to have cost the stockholders a stupendous sum."[40]

Bacigalupi's reply a few days later disappointed Giannini. He told Giannini that as far as he was concerned, cooperation with Walker was preferable to the total collapse of the corporation. As Bacigalupi saw it, Giannini had two options: either keep his opposition to Walker's program from becoming public, and thus allow him the opportunity to carry it out without the threat of an internal struggle, or return to San Francisco and reassume control of the corporation. Bacigalupi offered no comment on how he expected Giannini to oust Walker and Monnet as Transamerica's chief executive officers or if a majority of board members were prepared to support him in that effort.[41]

Whatever ideas Giannini himself was entertaining on the question of options, remaining silent was certainly not one of them. He was through, he informed Bacigalupi in a coded telegram, with the "scheming New Yorker." Nor did he have any intention of sitting back and allowing Walker to push triumphantly ahead with his reorganization program without permitting the corporation's stockholders to respond in a collective voice. As Giannini perceived it, Walker's crisis proposals were nothing more than the first stage of a cleverly devised plot to seize control of his banking empire in California. "To think that you folks can't see through this scheme is beyond me," Giannini told Bacigalupi. "Simply means the conspirators will get Diocese [Bank of America] without goodwill. How can you stand for such a thing?"[42]

With Bacigalupi obviously unwilling to take the lead in resisting Walker's restructuring program, Giannini tried another approach. Desperate to prevent Transamerica's directors from throwing their weight behind Walker's proposals, Giannini cabled Mario to pressure Bacigalupi into persuading the board to establish an outside committee of prominent businessmen, "independent of management," which would be given "sixty days to study Latern's [Walker's] proposals and submit its recommendations."[43] The sixty-day delaying tactic, Giannini believed, would give him time to get himself into effective physical shape before returning to San Francisco to take on Walker himself.

On June 15, 1931, Walker arrived in San Francisco. Two days later Transamerica's board of directors convened on the tenth floor of the corporation's headquarters on Montgomery Street. Walker reviewed the major points of his program and then asked for the board's approval "in principle."[44] Details of what happened next are sketchy, but several directors would later remember that it was Bacigalupi who exerted the most influence in securing the board's unanimous approval. As one director described the scene, no sooner did Walker call for a vote than Bacigalupi "immediately jumped to his feet and with his notable eloquence threw his support to the Walker plan. His oratory was a deciding factor with the directors. He called for a unanimous vote of confidence in the management and got it."[45]

Before the meeting adjourned, Walker had more to say. Considering the labyrinth of financial transactions that would be required to carry through such a drastic and wide-ranging reorganization, management would need the time free from unnecessary distractions to work out the multitude of uncharted details. Walker then moved that "it was the sense of the meeting that, until the proposed program had been developed to a point permitting the announcement of the plan as a whole, the whole matter should be treated as confidential and no publicity given to the proposed action."[46] The board again approved.

Three blocks away, at Bank of Italy's old headquarters on Clay and Montgomery, Mario continued to hope that his father's interim plan for an independent committee would prevail. Informed by his confidential sources on the board of what had taken place at the directors' meeting, he sent a bitterly worded telegram to Bacigalupi all but accusing him of betrayal. "The forcing of an unanimous approval and vote of confidence in the management of which you were the chief advocate . . . and over the objections of my father, could with a little thought have been foreseen to bring about the result achieved," Mario said. "Thus you have unwittingly, I hope, accomplished for your Wall Street superiors that which they so ardently desired."[47]

Bacigalupi responded with a furious denunciation of Mario's allegations. "Ped, Mount and Ferrari know what I fought for and in the face of this to be put in the light of a deserter *hurts,*" he replied. Given the nearly total paralysis of the nation's economy and the crisis in which the corporation now found itself, Walker's program was clearly "in the best interests of Transamerica and its stockholders." Bacigalupi continued to believe, as he had in September, that Giannini did not appreciate the potentially disastrous consequences of his "harmful agitation." As for the implication that he was Walker's dupe, Bacigalupi said, "Maybe we're all dumb, but at least let us hope that we shall be given credit for being honest in our own dumbness."[48]

Mario believed that Bacigalupi had far more to apologize for than merely being "dumb" when it came to explaining his overzealous support for Walker's program. After learning that at least four members of the board were heavily in debt to the corporation and were strapped for money, he accused Bacigalupi of having conducted a "campaign of intimidation" by privately threatening them with the loss of their positions if they refused to go along with the chairman's proposals.[49] Bacigalupi denied the accusation, but Mario refused to withdraw the charge.[50]

In Badgastein, Giannini was stunned by the board's action and the critical role Bacigalupi was alleged to have played at the meeting. Deprived now of any support on the board, Giannini cabled Mario that it seemed clear that only one course of action was available to them: they would have to lead the fight against the corporation's emasculation on their own. He warned Mario to prepare himself for what promised to be a tough struggle. "Don't let them ruffle you or get your goat," he said. "Maintain dignity keep cool and keep yourself in shape. Above all remember ours was institution with soul working solely interest stockholders. Its right and principle we are battling for . . . and there's no compromise with right or principle regardless consequence. No sir, never my boy."[51]

Two weeks later, on July 2, 1931, Giannini submitted his resignation to Bacigalupi.[52] "It's evident," Giannini said in a coded telegram, "am only one of belief Latern [Walker] isn't on the square and I'll definitely prove my charges if all books records etc. placed my disposal. Hereby tendering my resignation from Clarion [Transamerica] and affiliates effective at Latern's pleasure but in no event beyond date his new plan . . . becomes effective. This should prove extremely pleasant news to Latern and his co-conspirators. My decision irrevocable."[53]

Bacigalupi deeply resented Giannini's innuendo that he was involved as a "co-conspirator" with Walker and Monnet. There was, he said, absolutely no evidence to support that kind of hurtful and malicious accusation. Whether because of personal disappointment over the corporation's financial troubles or the effects of his long and debilitating illness, Giannini was not being "true or fair to us who sticking to firing line trying to do our best for institution and stockholders."[54]

But Giannini yielded no ground. He was convinced that Bacigalupi, Pedrini, and his other "old Bank of Italy pals" on the board had succumbed to the financial allure and intimidating authority of Wall Street. Certainly that was the thrust of a telegram he sent to Bacigalupi on June 14, 1931, that revealed as much about the resentments Giannini had accumulated over the years in his rise to power as it did about his belief that Bacigalupi and the others had traded their loyalty to him for their own self-interest. "I really haven't any business exchanging cables with one of your ability Jim, when, as the New Yorkers have it, I am only a peddler and a lowly one at that," Giannini said. "Perhaps they are right. If there is anything you want to say further . . . do so, but as for me I am through cabling you for good. Good luck to you and to all."[55]

Desperate to regain his health for the struggle ahead, Giannini left Badgastein for a neurological clinic in Berlin where he hoped to find treatment for the pain tormenting his body. "What I am trying to do," he cabled Mario the day after his arrival in Berlin, "is to get myself in shape to give those dirty crooks a battle when the right moment to strike arrives. Believe have some pretty good evidence for a damage suit against those of gang who have betrayed their trust."[56]

3

Back in Badgastein two weeks later, Giannini informed Bacigalupi in a telegram on June 27, 1931, that he had made up his mind to return to San Francisco. He was determined to give Walker his first major show of opposition and, if necessary, the fight of his life. As a first step, Giannini intended to make the chairman's proposals public, thus making the corporation's stockholders privy to policies under consideration that he believed were contrary to their best interests. "Have come to the conclusion it's my duty be on ground at time meeting approves plans, changes, policies, etc.," Giannini said. "Certainly would seem queer with all the reflection being deliberately cast on the policies and the institution it took twenty-seven years hard work build up to be away at such a time. Have every reason to believe shall succeed shortly in unmasking and branding these fellows."[57]

Giannini's telegram sent Bacigalupi into a panic. He was, he said, absolutely certain that Walker and Monnet were doing everything in their power to rescue the corporation from bankruptcy. He accused Giannini of escalating what appeared to him to be a purely personal dispute at the risk of Transamerica's outright collapse. "Assuming you can prove all you charge," Bacigalupi said, "is it going to do the cause or anyone connected with it any good to start an agitation at this critical time? . . . Best interest institution and all concerned let program go through without fuss. Seems to me you are involved in a sideshow."[58] Bacigalupi's charge of personal vindictiveness set off an angry exchange between the two men.

"Don't quite catch the meaning of the sideshow, Jim," Giannini answered. "Let me ask you how you would feel if your model child, say the apple of your eye, would be slowly gradually put to death. . . . You would pursue them to the bitter end to see them justly punished.

Well that is exactly my case. . . . This is one stockholder Jim whom Latern [Walker] can't buy off. No sir, Jim, never."[59]

"Your child illustration good," Bacigalupi replied. "But my point is that if by speaking loudly you would make sure and hasten death you would keep silent. . . . All directors including myself believe Latern is earnest. Calling names does no good. Your intention . . . expressing your sentiments publicly is what I consider detrimental, unconstructive, and unfair to institution to me as well as your other old associates and friends."[60]

"Yes calling names Jim maybe bad," Giannini said, "but haven't I always called a spade a spade and I think you'll admit have hit bullseye hundred percent or pretty close to it."[61]

If Giannini still had any illusions about which side of the struggle his "old Bank of Italy boys" on the board would come down on in a showdown with Walker, Bacigalupi's nearly hysterical reaction to his intentions eliminated them entirely. "Am fully satisfied," Giannini told Mario Giannini in a coded telegram on August 4, 1931, "Lenient [Bacigalupi] is in league with the New Yorkers to do all possible to keep true story from getting to public. . . . Latern apparently puffed boys up with idea corner connection . . . and bought off through social attentions, tips, salary, etc. Useless try change human nature. Selfish fellows will just go their way thinking their interests served readily deserting old for new."[62]

The turning point came on August 12, 1931, when Mario informed his father that Walker had apparently embarked on a smear campaign designed to discredit him personally. The most malicious rumor that had surfaced in recent published news stories, he said, was that "Giannini's salary and fortune were not as modest as the public had been led to believe."[63] To Mario, the motivation behind these and other rumors seemed clear enough: Walker had set out to undermine his father's broad popular appeal among Transamerica's tens of thousands of small shareholders—the one obstacle that could prove difficult to overcome in any confrontation between the two men.[64]

Giannini felt the time had come for him to proceed with his plans to force a showdown with Walker. On August 17, 1931, he instructed Mario to make the necessary travel arrangements for his return to San Francisco and to keep his plans secret. "I value my integrity too highly let them get away with this," Giannini said. "Glad welcome the opportunity to inform public my present net worth which is under half million. Sometimes good strategy do unexpected. Let's call their bluff."[65]

Wanting to gain the advantage of surprise, Giannini slipped out of Badgastein on the evening of August 16 and boarded a train for Cherbourg.[66] From Cherbourg he sent a coded message to Mario to work out the security arrangements for an unpublicized transatlantic crossing on a Canadian ocean liner to Quebec. A few days later Giannini was in Paris, where he remained incommunicado in a hotel room near the offices of the Canadian Pacific Line.[67] A telegram carrying details of the completed arrangements reached Giannini two days later. To minimize the possibility of detection, Giannini had been given the alias "S. A. Williams" for the return trip. "I have taken steps to see that your name does not appear on the passenger list and that it has not been made public in any way," a close aide to Mario wrote. "The Canadian Pacific office in Paris know nothing about it . . . and will not know the name of the real passenger until the night before sailing."[68]

Remaining secluded in his cabin, Giannini reached Quebec five days later. After a transcontinental train trip across Canada, he arrived in Vancouver on the morning of September 4, 1931. Mario had slipped quietly out of San Francisco and was in Vancouver to meet him.[69] Later that same day the two men boarded a ferry to Seattle, then drove the five hundred miles south to Lake Tahoe, a mountain resort on the crest of the Sierra Nevada. They spent the weekend in a rented cabin on the outskirts of town discussing their options in challenging Walker's control of Transamerica. Certain that Walker had been involved with Fleishhacker and Belden in selling Transamerica's shares short, Giannini suggested the possibility of bringing legal action against Walker and Monnet on charges of fraud and misconduct as the corporation's chief executive officers.[70]

Despite the careful precautions he had taken, Giannini's plan to slip quietly into San Francisco was soon aborted. Two days after his arrival at Lake Tahoe, he left the privacy of his cabin for the first time to get a haircut and a shave. As he stepped through the door of a barbershop in the center of town, he suddenly found himself face-to-face with Herbert Fleishhacker, who was vacationing in Lake Tahoe with his family.[71] Fleishhacker, a shocked look pasted across his face, turned and hurried out the door. That evening, San Francisco newspapers carried the news that Giannini was back in California.

THIRTEEN

Rough and Tumble
in the Sunshine State

I

On September 13, 1931, before leaving Lake Tahoe for
his home in San Mateo, Giannini sent a telegram to Bacigalupi and his
other "old business pals" on Transamerica's board that amounted to an
open declaration of war against Walker and Monnet. He was convinced,
he said, that both men were involved in a "gigantic swindle" with his
enemies on Wall Street to seize control of the corporation. Since no one
on the board was prepared to agree with this conclusion, his only
recourse was to take on management himself regardless of the consequences. "I will not recede from my old Bank of Italy policy of
fighting it out to the bitter end, even if I have to go down," he said.
"The charges I have made against Mr. Walker and Mr. Monnet speak
for themselves and I stand behind them. . . . If these two gentlemen do
not like them, why don't they sue me?"[1]

Back in San Francisco two days later, Giannini was greeted at Bank
of Italy's old headquarters on Clay and Montgomery by a small group
of friends and associates from among the ranks of the corporation's
Italian stockholders whom he had not seen in nearly a year.[2] They
were shocked by his appearance. Months of pain and sleepless nights
had left him looking pale, exhausted, and older than his sixty-one
years. As one member of the group later remembered, "I was convinced I was looking at a man who did not have long to live."[3]

One week later, on the morning of September 22, 1931, Transamerica's board of directors convened at the corporation's Montgomery Street headquarters to vote on final approval of Walker's restructuring program. Walker, who had stayed behind in New York, had sent Monnet to the meeting with a two-page "open letter" to stockholders summarizing the major features of his program.[4] No sooner had Bacigalupi opened the meeting than the door to the boardroom burst open and in walked Giannini. There was an awkward silence as board members exchanged embarrassed glances. Looking directly at Bacigalupi, his face flushed with anger, Giannini warned, "If this board goes along with Walker's program it will have a fight on its hands." With that, Giannini submitted his formal resignation from the corporation and walked out of the room.[5]

After a few moments of silence Bacigalupi moved that the board accept Giannini's resignation "with regret"; the motion was approved unanimously.[6]

Bacigalupi then turned the meeting over to Monnet. Reading from Walker's letter, Monnet told the board that "in recognition of business conditions since 1928 . . . and the fact that there is no apparent likelihood that nationwide branch banking will be authorized by the law in the near future," the corporation's management had decided to abandon the effort and "confine itself to minority holdings in amounts not involving a controlling influence." Consequently, the chairman's intention was "to take the necessary steps to dispose of the majority interest in each of the banks which the corporation now controls . . . when conditions are favorable."[7]

As part of management's new financial structure, Monnet continued, Transamerica's board of directors would be "reconstituted with a view to strengthening the position of the corporation as a national institution." All but two of the board's eleven California members—Bacigalupi and Pedrini—would be replaced by new directors from outside the state. Monnet then announced that management had formed a working partnership with the prestigious Wall Street bank investment firm of Lee, Higginson and Company. The chairman was confident, Monnet concluded, that these changes "will best contribute to the growth and prosperity of Transamerica Corporation, and . . . will enable your corporation to participate constructively in the business progress of the country."[8]

Bacigalupi then called for a vote. The outcome was unanimous. The board gave its formal approval to Walker's program. Two days later, before leaving San Francisco for his return trip to New York, Monnet proudly told reporters that Lee, Higginson and Company and "the strong new interests identified with the corporation and the policies now formulated will bring to Transamerica advantages of the first importance."

News of the Walker plan and Giannini's resignation from the corporation flashed across the country. "Walker Ousts Giannini: N.Y. Bankers Get Control of Transamerica" was the page-one headline in the *Denver Post*.[9] New York's financial press responded to Giannini's fall from power as the best thing that could have happened to Transamerica. The *Wall Street Journal* called Walker's plan and the entrance of Lee, Higginson and Company into the management of the corporation "history making . . . the end of the Giannini control of the former billion dollar holding company." The *American Banker* editorialized that with Giannini no longer at the helm, "the majority of bank-wise and financially minded observers will be likely to breathe easier. Giannini's ambitions were excessive and the shortening of his shadow in the banking world will be good for banking in a future that should look askance at too large financial egg-baskets."[10]

On October 2, 1931, moving swiftly with his liquidation program, Walker announced the merger of Bank of America (New York) with Charles Mitchell's National City. To the *New York Post*'s financial editor, Leslie Gould, one consequence of the merger seemed abundantly clear: "It brought to an end the dreams of Amadeo Peter Giannini for creating a chain of banks extending from coast to coast and over the Atlantic to Italy, the land of his forefathers."[11]

Giannini was devastated by the loss of his Wall Street bank but refused any public comment. As one close aide would remember, "He looked like a man who seeing himself being overcome by his enemies, thought it wiser to yield his more distant possessions in order to try to save those closer at hand."[12]

By then Giannini had moved to do just that. On the morning of September 23, 1931, in a fourth-floor office at Bank of Italy's old headquarters building on Clay and Montgomery, he and Mario met with a small group of Italian stockholders to launch a counteroffensive. The obvious response was a proxy battle, but that meant tackling a huge problem: mobilizing support from among the corporation's approximately 200,000 stockholders to gain a majority of the 20 million shares held in private hands. What emerged from their deliberations was the decision to form an organization of "dissident stockholders" that would challenge Walker's reelection as Transamerica's chairman of the board at the corporation's next annual meeting in Wilmington, Delaware, on February 15, 1932.[13]

Events now moved quickly. To give the organization the appearance of a "spontaneous" stockholders' revolt and to discourage the perception of what many might see, as Mario put it, as a strictly "Italian thing," Giannini turned to some of his closest non-Italian friends in San Francisco's business community. Among them was Charles Fay, a Bank of America director and former postmaster of San Francisco. Fay accepted Giannini's offer to serve as the organization's chief officer and spokesman.[14] The next morning, at a hastily called press conference, Fay announced the formation of Associated Transamerica Stockholders (ATS), which he said had been formed in opposition to Walker's reorganization program.[15] "The only way for the directors of Transamerica to find out what the stockholders consider right and fair and advantageous to them," Fay went on to say, "is to submit the question for their approval or disapproval."[16]

Later that same day Fay kicked off ATS's campaign at a meeting of two hundred stockholders in downtown San Francisco.[17] No sooner had the meeting begun than Giannini made a sudden and dramatic appearance and asked to address the gathering. Speaking with great emotion, he charged Walker and "the other enemies of the corporation" with "conspiring to secure the assets of the Bank of America and its 410 branches at less than they are worth." He regarded as unthinkable the possibility that a bank that he had founded to serve the financial interests of the people of California would "fall into the hands of a small group of unscrupulous Wall Street bankers." Although he himself had taken "no direct part" in the formation of ATS, Giannini said, he was nevertheless fully prepared "to throw the full weight of my mental and physical powers to keep Bank of America in the hands of California stockholders."[18]

Reporters, to whom he later repeated his allegations, were quick to sense that in accusing Walker of attempting to "steal Transamerica away from California," Giannini had struck what he had obviously decided to make the dominant theme of the ATS campaign. As a reporter for the *New York Tribune* explained it, "In semi-retirement for several years Giannini never relinquished his hold on the companies he built and in every crisis he has emerged to fight for them. The fight for control of Transamerica will be 'Giannini versus Wall Street' and the struggle will undoubtedly be one of the hardest ever taken by the financier who is now 61 years old."[19]

Toward the end of September, the association's campaign moved into high gear, touching off one of the most dramatic and bitter proxy battles in American financial history. By telephone and telegraph, word went out to stockholders across the state to rally around the ATS banner. Pledge cards were mailed asking for a donation to finance the campaign—"a minimum of five cents for each share owned of Transamerica stock."[20] Stockholders soon began receiving a white proxy, the top portion of which proclaimed: "We Do Not Favor the Election of Elisha Walker as Director or as an Executive at the Annual Stockholders Meeting in Wilmington." Attached to the ballot was a message from Giannini himself, which said: "If a sufficient and prompt response, through proxies, indicates that it is desired that I take the leadership of the association, I stand ready to do so. The decision is yours."[21]

Early in October 1931 Giannini led a large contingent of ATS speakers and volunteers on a whirlwind succession of stockholder rallies that would eventually take them to more than thirty-five towns and cities throughout the state in less than two months. Everywhere Giannini went, he attracted large and enthusiastic audiences. The early evening rally in the rented quarters of Stockton's civic auditorium on November 4, for example, was attended by an audience of more than four thousand stockholders. "We don't intend to allow Wall Street and New York's bluebloods to take Transamerica away from the people of California," one ATS speaker told the wildly cheering crowd. "Do these two or three Wall Street bankers imagine we are a bunch of fools?"[22]

There were similar enthusiastic scenes in scores of other California communities: Fresno, Bakersfield, San Jose, San Luis Obispo, Ventura, Santa Barbara. In Stockton one local reporter called a late afternoon ATS rally—the highlight of which was Giannini's appearance on the stage of a local high school auditorium before a jam-packed audience of some three thousand stockholders—"one of the most unique demonstrations of popular hysteria in the city's history." Giannini was "back again," he wrote, "conferring with stockholders, big and small. They had not been crowded from his memory by the rush of intervening years. Nor had they forgotten him."[23]

As the campaign rolled across the state, Giannini's health improved dramatically. Those closest to him were amazed by the sudden recovery of his energy, stamina, and confidence, as if magically restored by the excitement of corporate combat. By the end of October, Giannini had grown increasingly more confident that the progress of the campaign thus far had gone a long way toward his goal of removing Transamerica's management from power.[24] As he wrote to one associate following a rally in his hometown of San Jose, "Everything is progressing nicely here. The way it shapes up now, nothing can stop us."[25]

In New York, meanwhile, Walker and Monnet met with a small group of Transamerica's top executives to discuss a response to the Giannini-inspired stockholders' revolt in California. In contrast to Giannini's populist, grass-roots, and emotionally charged appeal for support, Monnet recommended that management conduct a low-key campaign, focusing their attention on the minority of stockholders who held the largest blocks of shares. "Quiet, dignified, small meetings with a limited number," Monnet told Walker and the others. "Convince the stockholders who control—the 7,000."[26]

As fall moved into winter, both the number of ATS supporters and the emotional response to the association's appeal for proxies grew dramatically. Toward the end of November, Fay called a press conference in San Francisco to announce that the association had thus far received approximately 150,000 anti-Walker proxies out of the total of 200,000 stockholders. Exactly how many of the corporation's twenty million shares were represented by these proxies, Fay could not say. But he was absolutely certain that "the outcome of the annual election will result in a victory for our association under the leadership of A. P. Giannini."[27]

By then Transamerica executives in New York had come to much the same conclusion. Some weeks earlier Walker had secretly recruited a small team of junior executives from among the corporation's affiliates on the East Coast to trail the Giannini campaign around the cities and towns of California. The message they conveyed in their confidential reports from the field was depressingly the same: the election was slipping away from Walker. "Giannini is winning converts everywhere in the state," one such report said. It ended on a gloomy note: "We are all washed up and soon will be out and finished."[28]

By late November 1931 Walker saw clearly that the time had come to pursue a more aggressive strategy. He appointed Howard Preston as his "campaign generalissimo" and put him in charge of the business of gathering pro-management proxies. Preston approached the assignment with enthusiasm: it was his opportunity to realize his larger ambitions in the corporation. Two weeks later, on December 12, 1931, he cabled Arnold Mount in San Francisco with instructions to "start getting tough." Preston impressed Mount with the importance of concentrating management's efforts on Bank of America's fourteen thousand employees, who held more than 30 percent of the corporation's stock. "Their proxies can and must be changed," he said. "Let's put some speed on the ball."[29]

To that end, Mount sent a confidential memorandum to Bank of America's district vice-presidents ordering them to give "prompt, aggressive, and preferred attention" to the proxy battle.[30] He instructed them to distribute blank pro-Walker proxies to Bank of America's more than four hundred local branch managers. Employees in each of these branches would be given five days to sign the proxies and turn them in. The collected proxies would then be sent via private channels to a designated address in San Francisco. There the names would be cross-checked against a master list of all the bank's employees, a procedure designed to assist headquarters officials in identifying holdouts. Under no circumstance, Mount said, were "letters to be addressed or written by a branch manager to head office in connection with the handling of this matter."[31]

This centralized proxy-gathering operation by no means exhausted Mount's ingenuity in his efforts to ensure management's victory in the proxy battle. By the end of December, with Walker's approval, he had recruited a team of "shock troops" from among Transamerica's affiliates in New York. Sent to California, they were assigned the responsibility of giving "special attention" to Bank of America employees who were having difficulties in coming to terms with Mount's demands. Stockholders outside the bank were subjected to the same kind of pressure and required to furnish proof of their support of management with a signed Walker proxy. "There can be only one side to this question and divided allegiances will not be tolerated," Mount informed Bank of America's regional branch supervisors. "I want 100 percent compliance."[32]

By year's end Bank of America was in complete turmoil. The fear and suspicion that swept through all levels of the organization brought its day-to-day operations dangerously close to paralysis. Employees who refused to sign their pro-Walker proxies or who protested management's harassment were terminated. Stockholders who had loans with the bank became obvious targets for Mount's cadre of "shock troops." One stockholder complained bitterly to state banking officials in Sacramento that he had been "ordered" to sign a pro-Walker proxy or else pay off his $4,500 loan with Bank of America without delay.[33]

Another complained about the same kind of arm-twisting treatment: "People are just now beginning to realize how just is this campaign to roust out Mr. Walker and his associates as the methods for securing proxies well nigh rivals the methods of the infamous Al Capone."[34]

Word of Mount's heavy-handed tactics soon leaked out, triggering a wave of embarrassing publicity.[35] Seizing on an opportunity, Giannini issued a press release denouncing Bank of America's "shocking and reprehensible" policies, which he compared to "Russian methods of control" as a means of determining the outcome of a free election. "Instead of trying to intimidate and coerce employees," Giannini said, "why doesn't Elisha Walker go out and meet the stockholders face to face and find out what they really want?"[36] In New York, Walker instructed Bacigalupi to deny the allegations of employee harassment. Bacigalupi issued a press release accusing Giannini of engaging in a "public relations gimmick," but it did little to repair the damage.[37]

To relieve the pressure on Bank of America's employees, Giannini resorted to a different strategy. Through his supporters inside the bank, he instructed employees to sign the Walker proxies and thus get out from under the intimidation of their immediate superiors and Mount's shock troops. Days or even weeks later, they could then sign a Giannini proxy and send it to ATS's headquarters in San Francisco. Since the proxy votes were not irrevocable, the one carrying the more recent of the two dates would be counted in Wilmington. Transamerica executives would not know until the day of the stockholders' meeting which employees had voted for ATS, and by then, Giannini assured them, he would be back in control.[38]

2

Christmas came and went with both sides exchanging ugly charges and countercharges. Armed with information acquired from Bank of America's confidential files, Giannini's allies circulated a two-page document accusing Bacigalupi of having made profits of $200,000 by using third parties to secretly trade in the corporation's stock during the crash in October 1929.[39] Bacigalupi immediately struck back. At a press conference in San Francisco he criticized Giannini's buy-back efforts during the June 1928 market break, which he said had left the corporation "with a large indebtedness" and severely weakened. "Contrary to the public impression he allowed to be created," Bacigalupi charged, "Giannini in fact has been paid an extraordinary sum of money" as compensation for his services to the corporation. Bacigalupi estimated the amount at approximately $4 million.[40]

On the evening of January 22, 1932, the ATS held its largest and most tumultuous rally in San Francisco's Dreamland Auditorium. Ten thousand stockholders jumped to their feet with wild cheering and applause when one ATS speaker called the campaign against Walker a fight between "home rule for California and foreign rule . . . between California and New York." As small groups of stockholders waved their banners ("Walker Go Home"; "Walker for the Mayflower Bluebloods") he denounced Transamerica's management as a "wrecking crew" that was "trying to coerce us" into reinstating Walker and his "gang of Wall Street cronies" by intimidation. "We've got to win," he shouted. "That bunch can't run the bank."[41]

By this time Bank of America was teetering on the edge of total collapse. Thousands of depositors, their anxieties already heightened by hard economic times and a wave of bank failures across the country, hurried to withdraw their savings. In the three months following the outbreak of the proxy battle, Bank of America lost an average of $3 million a day in deposits—a staggering total of $233 million.[42] The deposit loss was compounded by newspaper reports that national examiners were alarmed by Bank of America's rapidly accelerating loss of capital. The *San Francisco Chronicle* cited the views of these examiners, including the warning from one unnamed San Francisco field examiner who was quoted as saying, "The people of California are going to wake up some morning to receive the greatest shock of their lives when the Bank of America closes its doors."[43]

In Washington, Hoover administration officials watched the internecine struggle in California with mounting alarm. Already plunged in political crisis over the continuing downward spiral in the economy, they feared that the total collapse of California's largest bank would precipitate an even greater panic that would reverberate across the country. On January 8, 1932, John Pole, the fastidious, stiffly formal, British-born comptroller of the currency, sent a confidential telegram to John Calkins, chairman of San Francisco's Federal Reserve Bank, with urgent instructions "to call into conference . . . the two opposing factions and make every effort to bring about a composition of the existing differences as promptly and conclusively as possible."[44]

In the end, Calkins's efforts got nowhere. Confident of victory at the corporation's annual stockholders' meeting a little more than one month away, Giannini was in no mood to compromise. "Please make it clear to Calkins," he cabled Mario Giannini from Los Angeles, "that there can be absolutely no compromise that will include Elisha Walker in the picture. He has no place in a business that wholly depends on public confidence for its success."[45] Calkins was so outraged that in a heated exchange in his office with Mario Giannini, he accused Giannini of "insisting on a result" that would "drag Bank of America into financial ruin and . . . destroy absolutely any value that remains in the stock of Transamerica."[46]

Giannini's unwillingness to cooperate in Calkins's efforts to arrive at a settlement angered administration officials in Washington. Pole thought the situation so serious that he warned Giannini in a telegram on January 19, 1932, that he was prepared to use the authority granted him by Congress to take control of Bank of America.[47] Over the next several weeks Pole put increased pressure on Giannini to settle his differences with Transamerica's management, but without success.[48] Each time Giannini's reply was stubbornly the same: there could be no settlement of any kind until Walker and Monnet had been removed from their positions and were completely out of the picture.[49]

As the proxy battle entered its final phase, the threats and angry rhetoric on both sides produced even greater levels of paranoia. After confiding to associates that he had received threatening letters signed in blood, Bacigalupi concluded that ATS supporters were planning his murder and hired bodyguards to protect him and his family around the clock.[50] Giannini harbored imaginary fears of his own, including the possibility that Walker's forces might be flirting with a plan to steal the association's proxies as they made their way by train on the cross-country trip to Wilmington. He ordered the proxies sealed in heavy wooden boxes bound with leather straps ("Walker's tombs," his aides called them) and hired armed guards to escort them by private railway car to the East Coast.[51] "Have no fear," one of Giannini's aides reassured him from Wilmington. "We know all the rats. As for the proxies we will guard them with our lives."[52]

The proxy battle ended late on the evening of February 15, 1932, in Wilmington, where Giannini and more than a thousand of his supporters had converged on the Dupont Hotel to await the election returns.[53] Walker, Monnet, and a contingent of Transamerica executives, including Bacigalupi, Preston, and Mount, occupied the top floor of the same hotel. By the time half the proxies had been counted, shortly after midnight, it had become obvious to the corporation's management that Giannini had won an overwhelming victory—possibly by a majority of nearly three to one.[54] At 3:00 A.M. Walker's chief legal counsel, Paul Cravath of the prestigious New York law firm of Cravath, Swaine, and Moore, conceded the election to Giannini. As groups of ATS supporters celebrated in the hallways of the hotel, Walker, Monnet, and the others climbed into a chauffeur-driven limousine for the drive back to New York.

Later that morning Giannini made a brief appearance in the convention hall of the hotel, where a thousand Transamerica stockholders had gathered for a breakfast celebration.[55] With tears streaming down his face and his voice hoarse, he told the hushed crowd, "I am grateful for your confidence, and I want to thank each of you. This decisive battle which has been fought and won by Transamerica stockholders against the most formidable financial forces which Wall Street could assemble is inspiring and instructive. It shows after all that right is might and that when stockholders have right on their side they should not be too cowed to fight."[56]

Giannini then left the gathering to meet with ATS leaders to put together a new management team and board of directors for Transamerica and Bank of America. The meeting lasted barely an hour. Giannini was named president of Bank of America and chairman of the board. On his recommendation the board chose John Grant, the former president of Bank of America's international department, to succeed Bacigalupi as Transamerica's president. As a reporter who covered the events in Wilmington for the San Francisco News wrote, "The outcome of the annual stockholders meeting was matched in speed only by the change in command of the parent company and . . . the defeated regime of Elisha Walker was swept out of office with a stroke of a pen."[57]

Giannini's remarkable victory was the talk of the nation's financial community. The San Francisco Chronicle called the outcome of the proxy battle "the greatest Wall Street defeat of all times."[58] Even Giannini's sharpest critics on Wall Street were forced to admit that his victory had been an astonishing achievement, one that few observers could have predicted. As the New York Times put it, "There was general admiration in the street for the fashion in which, at the age of sixty-one, Giannini had returned from retirement to wrest control of the huge holding corporation which he originally created from the men to whom he relinquished the management two years ago."[59]

The day after the meeting, Giannini departed for San Francisco after delegating to Grant the responsibility for overseeing the corporation's affairs on the East Coast. With Bank of America teetering on the edge of financial collapse, Giannini was anxious to return home as quickly as possible. What exactly he had in mind for putting the bank on the path to financial recovery was anyone's guess, but Giannini left no doubt that he was once again firmly in control. "Tear down that damn partition," he cabled Mario, a reference to the private office that corporation officials had built for Walker's use on his trips to San Francisco. Giannini wanted his own office "out in the open on the floor."[60]

On the morning of February 20, 1932, Giannini's train reached Los Angeles's Union Station, where he was treated to a hero's welcome. When Giannini emerged onto the center platform, he was swallowed up by hundreds of his supporters who had broken through police barriers to shower him with praise and admiration. "No reprisals," he told a group of reporters at a press conference inside the station. "Let the mistakes of the past be forgotten. My efforts will be centered on regaining the prestige which has been forfeited within the past several years."[61] Then, escorted by police, he was whisked away in a waiting car to the Biltmore Hotel, where a crowd of more than a thousand employees and stockholders had gathered for a victory celebration.

Two days later Giannini reached the small train station only a short distance from his home in San Mateo. Even though it was Sunday, the welcoming crowd turned out to be just as large and enthusiastic. The scene, as described later by a reporter for the *San Francisco Chronicle,* "was of victorious Caesar returning to Rome—and the Maniscalcos, the Scalmaninis, the Faccis and the Puccinellis were bent on making it a Roman holiday."[62]

After shaking hands with scores of friends and well-wishers, Giannini climbed into the family car for the short drive to his home. "I'll be down at the office eight o'clock Tuesday morning," he shouted to the crowd through the open window of the car as it pulled away. "There is a hard fight before us. We must all work together."[63]

3

Contrary to the "no reprisals" statement he had made to the press in Los Angeles, Giannini returned to San Francisco lusting for revenge. He intended to purge the organization of every senior executive who had sided with Walker during the proxy battle. Attilio Giannini believed that Bank of America's regional headquarters in Los Angeles in particular was a "hotbed of intrigue" and thus a continued threat to his brother's control of the organization. "The sooner you rid the organization of men of questionable loyalty, the better it will be," he warned Mario in a letter of March 15, 1932.[64] Mario, who had complained often about the intrigue and "spy system" that under Walker had come to dominate the upper ranks of the organization, agreed. "Their elimination cannot be too arbitrarily and ruthlessly conducted," he replied.[65]

Throughout the spring and summer of 1932 the purge went on. Some executives paid for their pro-Walker activities with their jobs; others who had tried to play both sides during the proxy battle had their salaries sharply reduced and endured the humiliation of writing letters to Giannini begging for forgiveness. "I am profoundly sorry that I had anything to do with the campaign," one Bank of America senior vice-president wrote in a pleading letter. "I am just a broken old man. I shall accept your salary readjustment. I have wanted, greatly, your respect. I would never betray or be disloyal to you in any way. . . . If you want my sincere friendship . . . it is yours."[66]

Giannini reserved the full force of his well-known penchant for vendetta for the corporation's former top executives like Mount. After submitting his resignation as Bank of America's president, Mount landed a job as a senior vice-president with the Oakland National Bank.[67] Informed of Mount's appointment, Giannini began bidding for the Oakland National's stock in the open market. The price of the stock jumped dramatically—from $60 to $450 a share. The more stock appeared, the more Giannini bought, until he eventually gained working control. He promptly fired Mount, who quickly made plans to leave California. "I'm not going to have Giannini gunning for me for the rest of my life," he told a reporter from *Time*.[68]

Giannini had another motive for probing the scope of disloyalty within the organization. He was certain that during Walker's reign as Transamerica's chief operating officer, the corporation's money had been used to assist the chairman's close friends and allies on Wall Street. Immediately after returning to San Francisco, Giannini instructed aides to examine thoroughly the corporation's books and records.[69]

Uncovering the incriminating evidence Giannini was looking for was not easy. Walker, Bacigalupi, Mount, and other of the corporation's former senior executives had cleaned out their offices and taken their private papers with them.[70] Several employees also reported that when news of Giannini's victory in Wilmington reached San Francisco, corporation officials had spent the night frantically burning documents. "I saw them pulling papers out of desks and the smoke coming out of an open window," one employee said.[71]

Soon after Giannini's return to San Francisco, however, an event occurred thousands of miles from California that seemed to confirm his worst suspicions. On March 13, 1932, the press reported the sensational news that Ivar Kreuger, the Swedish match king, had committed suicide in his Paris apartment. Once described by the *New York Times* as a "genius of finance," Kreuger owned a conglomerate of more than 250 match companies throughout Europe and the United States. In 1922 he turned his sights on the United States, acquiring 240,000 shares of the Ohio-based Diamond Match Company. Kreuger's private banker in this and other financial transactions was Lee, Higginson and Company, the Wall Street bank investment firm that Walker had brought into the organization in the fall of 1931 to run Transamerica.[72]

News of Kreuger's suicide rocked Wall Street. The financial press was quick to attribute his violent death to insurmountable problems arising out of the 1929 crash and "the burden of carrying responsibilities too great for the embrace of the average human being in times of stress and strain."[73] But events soon took an extraordinary turn. After completing a preliminary examination of Kreuger's financial operations, the New York accounting firm of Price, Waterhouse and Company disclosed that at the time of his suicide Kreuger's holding company, Kreuger-Toll, was on the verge of bankruptcy. More startling, the Price, Waterhouse report also revealed that there was indisputable evidence that Kreuger and some of his closest associates had committed forgery, fraud, and embezzlement. All of these illegal activities, the report went on, were designed to cover up years of secret stock market transactions on Wall Street in which Kreuger had suffered huge financial losses.[74]

The Price, Waterhouse disclosures immediately raised a number of disturbing questions. Given the almost epic proportions of Kreuger's personal losses, some began to ask if the match king's private bankers in the corporate boardroom of Lee, Higginson and Company had been, as the firm's senior partners claimed, "completely unaware" of his financial predicament.[75] There was also the question of what had prompted Kreuger to kill himself when he did. On the basis of a second report issued by Price, Waterhouse, the writer of a *Fortune* article later claimed to have solved the mystery. "Why in God's name had he done it?" the writer asked. "Ivar Kreuger killed himself because his companies bankrupt, his credit gone, his forgeries on the verge of discovery . . . he had no decent alternative."[76]

Facing bankruptcy, however, was one thing; being unable to find the money to avoid bankruptcy was another. The *Fortune* article left unanswered the question of when and how Kreuger suddenly discovered that his credit was "gone," except to point out that in the late winter of 1931 he had "reappeared in New York," apparently in search of new sources of money to keep from going under.[77]

In San Francisco, Giannini followed the unfolding drama of the Kreuger debacle with more than ordinary interest. There were, he felt, some intriguing links between Kreuger, Transamerica, and the Lee, Higginson firm, none of which had received attention from the press. Three of the four Lee, Higginson senior partners whom Walker had appointed to Transamerica's board were also on the board of International Match, which was controlled by Kreuger's Stockholm-based company, Swedish Match. Giannini had also learned that soon after Walker and Monnet took over as Transamerica's chief executive officers, both men had gone on the board of Diamond Match, the company Kreuger had sought to control in the 1920s.[78] In addition, contrary to earlier published reports, Kreuger's crippling indebtedness had not been confined to his European creditors. Among Kreuger's largest unsecured creditors was the Lee, Higginson firm itself, which stood to lose $8 million if Kreuger-Toll went into bankruptcy.[79]

John Rovensky, a senior Transamerica loan officer in New York, had plenty to say about the ties between Kreuger, Lee, Higginson, and the corporation. Rovensky told Giannini that toward the end of 1931 a Kreuger associate had come to him with a sizable loan request. For two weeks or more Walker repeatedly made it clear to Rovensky that he wanted him to move as quickly as possible in approving the loan. Suspicious of Walker's anxious intervention, Rovensky decided to drag his feet. "I told him," Rovensky said, "I could not make up my mind in a hurry because of the complex structure of the Kreuger-Toll organization. I knew that once it got into a committee meeting, I did not have a chance of preventing the loan."[80] Rovensky was still reviewing Kreuger-Toll's financial statements when the proxy battle reached its climax at Wilmington.

Rovensky was not alone among Giannini's executives in believing that Walker, under pressure from Lee, Higginson, had been prepared to furnish Kreuger with substantial loans from Transamerica despite a good deal of evidence that Kreuger was in a poor position to repay the money. According to Walter Bruns, a Bank of America senior vice-president who had participated in the investigation of the Kreuger affair, "Walker was involved in something too big for his stature at best or he was a tool of the Lee, Higginson people at the worst. . . . Lee, Higginson had Kreuger around their necks. . . . Let's agree that they didn't know the extent of his crookedness, but they knew he needed money and needed it fast."[81]

Giannini believed that Kreuger had gambled on the possibility that Walker would emerge triumphant at the stockholders' meeting in Wilmington. Had that happened, Giannini speculated, the corporation's money would have been used to relieve Kreuger of the increasing pressure from his creditors, including most prominently the firm of Lee, Higginson. Kreuger's appearance in New York shortly before the Wilmington meeting, therefore, was no mere coincidence. He stayed around long enough to learn about Walker's defeat; then, with all hope for financial rescue gone, he boarded the *Ile de France* for his final voyage back to Paris.[82]

4

In the spring of 1932 Bank of America faced the gravest financial crisis in its history. According to the bank's balance sheet for the fiscal year ending November 30, 1931, it had lost $138 million in deposits during the last six months of the year alone. To make matters worse, the bank was burdened with a staggering amount of debt, including $40 million in loans from the Reconstruction Finance Corporation—and a further $70 million owed to the Federal Reserve.[83] All told, Walker had borrowed a total of $135 million during his slightly more than one-year tenure as Transamerica's chief executive officer, an amount that had proved insufficient to stem the bank's losses.[84] So serious was Bank of America's debt crisis that the comptroller of the currency had warned Walker in the closing months of 1931 that he was seriously considering the possibility of declaring the bank insolvent.[85]

The torrent of mail that flowed into Bank of America headquarters in San Francisco from distraught stockholders underscored the seriousness of the situation. "I am in desperate need of money," wrote one stockholder to Giannini, "not having received any dividend for nearly two years from nearly eleven thousand invested in your stock. I am 82 years old. I sold my ranch and invested every available cent in Transamerica stock. Surely there is a way for me to at least get enough to eat."[86] Wrote another, "I voted for you Mr. Giannini with confidence that you would soon work out a plan by which people like me would be benefited. I am unable to work . . . and it is hard to bear."[87]

On March 3, 1932, Giannini sent a private communication to each of Bank of America's branch managers instructing them "to set a fair quota" in a four-month campaign ending in July aimed at increasing Bank of America's total deposits by $50 million. "This is your campaign and will go far in turning toward prosperity the tide of depression which has enveloped the world," he said. "I would like you . . . to take the initiative in starting at once to achieve the goal which you will set for yourself."[88]

One month later, on April 12, satisfied that his "door-knockers" had moved quickly in roaming the cities and towns of the state soliciting depositors, Giannini launched his Back to Good Times campaign. "Depressions are the product of fear," he told a group of reporters at a press conference in San Francisco kicking off the campaign. "Prosperity, however, is born of confidence. Fear more than any other influence is holding back recovery from the depression and if people could be made to forget their fears and return to normal habits of living the battle would be more than half won."[89]

One week later, breaking a long-held custom of refusing to speak in public, Giannini went on radio to announce that "the hysterical stage of the depression is past." Appearing with Giannini on the broadcast was California governor James Rolph, Jr., who urged the audience to "heed this call going out on the air tonight" by supporting Giannini's Back to Good Times campaign. "Let us cooperate with the banks of this state," Rolph said, "by returning our money to their keeping so that a more generous and free distribution of our wealth may stimulate and encourage our dormant industries."[90]

Giannini's Back to Good Times campaign set in motion one of the most ambitious privately sponsored public relations efforts in California history. Nearly $300,000 of Bank of America's money went into the production of large, colorful cardboard posters, which soon began appearing along highways, on streetcars, and in thousands of movie lobbies and retail store windows across the state. The drawing on the poster featured a smiling and determined "forty-niner" guiding a worried Uncle Sam out of the valley of fear and hard times. The caption read, "California Can Lead the Nation to Sound Prosperity."[91]

It was radio, however, that Giannini chose as the major vehicle for his message of optimism and reassurance. The centerpiece of his Back to Good Times campaign, launched in the spring of 1932, was the production of its weekly thirty-minute "confidence-building" programs, which were carried statewide over NBC station KFI on Wednesday evenings at 8:15.[92] Half of each program was devoted to "the finest music attainable" by a concert orchestra and visiting guest soloists. The other half of each show was set aside for "inspirational talks" by guest speakers representing a cross-section of the state's civic, political, and cultural life.[93] The fifteen-minute talks were then reprinted and distributed free of charge to schools, libraries, local officials, and civic organizations across the state through Bank of America's more than four hundred branch offices.

The high point of Giannini's confidence-building radio campaign occurred on May 16, 1932, when more than one thousand guests gathered at San Francisco's Palace Hotel for a live broadcast of a Back to Good Times luncheon, which had been arranged in tandem with a similar luncheon at the Biltmore Hotel in Los Angeles.[94] The proceedings of both events were broadcast simultaneously into homes, schoolrooms, and workplaces throughout the state. "The luncheon stands out in California history," the *San Francisco Chronicle* commented the next day. "It was the first time on record that two rival cities joined hands over five hundred miles of desert, fertile valleys and mountain ranges through the medium of this uncanny thing we know as radio."[95]

The most widely celebrated event in Giannini's Back to Good Times campaign occurred three months later. Despite the doubts of structural engineers, San Francisco city officials had embarked on an ambitious plan to build a bridge across the bay linking the San Francisco Peninsula with northern California. Although voters in the district had approved a $32 million bond issue six months earlier to finance construction, RFC officials raised serious doubts about the feasibility of the bridge and showed a decided lack of interest in backing the project.[96]

On the morning of August 4, 1932, Joseph Strauss, the bridge's chief engineer, went to see Giannini. For the next thirty minutes Strauss pleaded with Giannini to take the initiative by buying part or all of the bonds. Giannini listened and then agreed. Along with the economic benefits to northern California that the bridge promised, he saw another opportunity to repair Bank of America's tarnished image and to restore public confidence in its management. The bank bought the first $6 million of the bond issue, enough to allow work on the bridge to begin. Later it purchased the remaining $32 million in bonds.[97] It was a masterstroke of finance and public relations. As Giannini expected, when the Golden Gate Bridge was completed four years later, Bank of America shared in the public's acclaim of Strauss's monumental achievement.[98]

Giannini did not depend on headline-making events alone to dramatize Bank of America's road back to recovery. In the fall of 1932 he left San Francisco on a well-publicized tour of each of the bank's 410 branches, traveling more than twenty-six thousand miles in three months. It was a long and exhausting schedule, but Giannini seemed to enjoy every minute of it, crisscrossing the state by car, meeting with civic and business leaders, promoting Bank of America in countless interviews with local reporters.[99] As one close aide who accompanied Giannini on the trip would remember, "We never stopped from morning to night; in a few instances until 3 o'clock in the morning, and then on to another city before the branch manager arrived in the morning."[100]

Meanwhile, Giannini's "door-knockers" at the local branch level did not disappoint their "great leader." The result of the three-month campaign to increase deposits was astonishing. Bank of America's total deposits, which stood at approximately $800 million in March 1932, jumped $22 million in May alone; one month later the figure had climbed to $50 million.[101] By the end of the year the bank's total deposits had increased by nearly $100 million, which represented the savings accounts of 220,000 new customers—an average monthly increase of 27,000.[102] As the *San Francisco Chronicle* pointed out in an editorial praising Giannini's achievement, this figure was approximately the "combined populations of Eureka, Fresno, Bakersfield, Santa Barbara, San Bernardino, Fontana, and Santa Ana."[103]

In the midst of a severe economic depression, Giannini's achievement in California whetted the nation's appetite for success stories. A large number of prominent businessmen and civic and labor leaders sent their congratulations, including General Foods president Charles Chester and AFL president Matthew Well. "Giannini Scores over Deflation" was the headline for an article in the *Wall Street Journal* praising Bank of America's comeback. "A. P. Giannini has demonstrated anew his capacity to inspire confidence among bank customers," wrote the Hearst newspaper's syndicated financial columnist, Merryle Rukeyser. "Bankers of the no, no school might well analyze this new development in mass psychology in banking."[104]

FOURTEEN

A Narrow Escape

I

Throughout the months when Giannini was struggling to repair Bank of America's badly tattered reputation, he found himself increasingly at odds with John Calkins, governor of the Federal Reserve Bank of San Francisco. Some inside the Giannini organization thought the primary reason for the conflict was personal. Two decades earlier Calkins had worked as a cashier in the Mechanics Savings, a small San Francisco bank that Giannini purchased in 1910 and then merged with the Bank of Italy.[1] Angered by the takeover, Calkins resigned, after first telling associates that he had no intention of working for "some damn dago." Giannini never forgot this incident or other occasions over the years when Calkins was reported to have expressed disdain for Italians. He came to believe that Calkins's deep-seated prejudice formed a substantial part of his hostility to him.[2]

There were other, not entirely unrelated, sources of conflict: Calkins was an outspoken critic of branch banking. After Calkins joined the SFFRB as a deputy governor in 1914, he and Giannini became bitter enemies. Things went from bad to worse during the proxy battle, when Giannini learned from sources inside the SFFRB that Calkins was furnishing Walker with tactical advice and critical documents culled from the agency's confidential files. Giannini complained to FRB officials in Washington about Calkins's "abuse and misuse of the power and prestige of his office as Governor of the San Francisco Federal Reserve

Bank."[3] After reviewing Giannini's complaints, the FRB refused to take action.[4]

On March 24, 1932, six weeks after Giannini's victory in Wilmington, Calkins sent him a letter expressing serious concern over Bank of America's monumental debt problems.[5] "Now that you have had time to familiarize yourself with the situation of the Bank of America National Trust & Savings Association and consider policies to be applied in its future conduct," Calkins's letter said, "it will be greatly appreciated if you will write outlining your plans for bringing about a decrease in, and ultimate extinguishment of, its indebtedness for borrowed money."[6]

Given the dimension of the liabilities Bank of America was facing, Calkins's request was not unreasonable.[7] But coming as it did so soon after the proxy battle, Giannini concluded that Calkins was trying to plant seeds of doubt in the minds of regulatory officials in Washington about the soundness of Bank of America and its huge network of branches. Giannini said so in a bristling reply the following day, accusing Calkins of having stood passively by while Transamerica's former management "pursued destructive policies" that had contributed in no small part to the bank's current debt crisis.

"It appears to me," Giannini wrote, "that the bank is being harassed by those who should normally be assisting and cooperating with us in the inherited task of reconstruction in which we are engaged. . . . Why do you find it necessary . . . to continuously suggest the failure of our institution, and why should there be this very evident hesitancy on the part of the Federal Reserve Bank to endorse and recommend our institution?"[8]

The harassment Giannini referred to involved a succession of recent appointments to the Hoover administration's newly established Reconstruction Finance Corporation (RFC), a federal agency whose aim was to promote economic recovery by aiding big business. Giannini was infuriated to learn that in the months immediately following his victory at the Wilmington stockholders meeting, at least seven former top Transamerica executives—among them Mount, Preston, and Talley— had joined the RFC at the highest levels of the agency's policy-making positions.[9]

Giannini complained to the comptroller of the currency that the administration had apparently taken an unusually generous interest in the welfare of a group of men against whom he had struggled to regain control of Transamerica and who now included themselves among his staunchest enemies. "I can't understand how it happens," Giannini wrote, "that so many of our discharged employees find it so easy to secure employment with various government agencies and I'm wondering just what is behind it all. I think you will agree that it could hardly be called a coincidence. It seems to be that the impetus must come from some one person or group of persons influential in circles who is recommending these appointments—possibly Mr. Calkins who appears to have been so close to most of our enemies."[10]

More blameworthy and personally responsible, Giannini also believed, was Eugene Meyer, the stocky, iron-willed, and immensely talented chairman of the FRB and ex officio member of the RFC. A fifty-six-year-old native of Los Angeles, Meyer had worked after graduation from Yale for Herbert Fleishhacker's Anglo-California, moved for a brief time to the London house of Lazard Freres, predecessor bank to the Anglo-California, and then opened his own bank investment firm on Wall Street.[11] Although still in his mid-thirties, Meyer had quickly emerged in Wall Street circles as a "genuine tycoon . . . a shrewd, subtle financier" and still later in the Hoover administration as "a formidable figure in the Washington political-financial establishment."[12]

Meyer's personal and business ties to Fleishhacker and Wall Street convinced Giannini that the FRB chairman had personally intervened in assisting Walker, Mount, Preston, and other former senior Transamerica executives to relocate themselves in the highest levels of Washington's regulatory bureaucracy, where they would be in a strategic position to pursue their opposition to him. "Meyer is rewarding their treachery to us," Giannini wrote to Charles Collins on July 25, 1932. "It's a hell of a state of affairs when such things can be so brazenly put over. Everything possible is being done to block our continued progress."[13]

Throughout the summer of 1932 Giannini could not escape the nagging suspicion that his enemies in California and New York were focusing their energies on a renewed effort to take his banking empire away from him. "The Wall Street gang is still at work trying to put their diabolical conspiracy over," he wrote to Collins, "but it's a fight to the finish and a sorry day for them it will be if they finally succeed in completing the wrecking job they started in the latter part of 1930."[14]

There was yet another reason for Giannini's growing anger toward the Hoover administration. After returning to San Francisco from Wilmington in March 1932, he found a number of serious financial problems awaiting him, not the least of which was the enormous debt accumulated by Bank of America as a direct result of his purchase of Merchants National four years earlier. To understand this development, it is necessary to turn back to the months immediately preceding the outbreak of the proxy battle between Giannini and Walker.

2

Soon after Walker took control of Transamerica in January 1930, he received a summary confidential report from P. C. Read, Bank of America's chief examiner. For more than nine months Read and a team of assistants had been in Los Angeles methodically working their way through Merchants National's books and records. The evidence was clear, Read told Walker, that Nolan, Bell, and the Hellmans, owners and principal stockholders of Merchants National, had been involved over a period of years in massive self-lending activities— the worst instance of an illegal loan operation that Read had ever encountered.

In Read's words, "Four officers of the Merchant's National over a period of years willfully misapplied funds of the bank through the device generally of causing notes to be signed by third persons upon the agreement that such persons would not be liable thereon and applying the funds to the personal use of the officers."[15] Read went on to say that Nolan, in efforts to conceal the illegal use of the bank's money, had altered documents and given "false and misleading information" to state examiners. The precise number of these illicit transactions and the extent of the resulting losses to Bank of America, Read said, was still difficult to estimate. Thus far the losses totaled $12 million, but he warned Walker that this figure could go much higher.[16]

Alarmed by Read's memorandum, Walker arranged a private meeting in New York with Pole, who came up from Washington. Monnet was also at the meeting, along with two other top Transamerica executives. After being appraised of Read's findings, Pole insisted that Walker ask for the immediate resignations of Nolan, Bell, and the Hellmans as Bank of America's president and senior executive officers.[17] Despite the unmistakable evidence of wrongdoing, apparently no serious thought was given to the obvious next step of bringing criminal charges against the four men. On the contrary, in his communications with the corporation's senior executives in San Francisco, Walker made it clear that he wanted Read's disclosures to be kept as confidential as possible.[18] The last thing he or anyone else wanted, Walker said, was a potentially lethal public scandal.

Up to this point Mario Giannini had managed to keep news of Read's investigation from reaching his father. But with such indisputable evidence documenting the criminal activity of Nolan, Bell, and the Hellmans in the creation of the Merchants National's enormous debt, Mario cabled Giannini in Badgastein informing him about the "southern situation" and the continuing progress of Read's investigation. In a telegram to Pole that same day, Giannini demanded that the comptroller's office move as quickly as possible in filing criminal charges against Nolan, Bell, and the Hellmans. Pole replied a few days later that he was fully aware of "the situation" and was "proceeding with the case."[19] Pole said nothing, however, about his meeting with Walker and Monnet in New York, nor did he mention their agreement to keep the scandal from being dragged into the public spotlight.

In Los Angeles, Read spent the remaining months of 1931 uncovering more loan losses arising out of Merchants National's involvement in the Los Angeles real estate boom of the 1920s. Read had seen most of the incriminating evidence before: dummy loans, missing documents, falsified credit records—all designed to cover up a large number of real estate schemes in which Nolan, Bell, and the Hellmans had either a direct or indirect interest. On the basis of these new disclosures, Read revised his previous estimate and notified Walker that Bank of America's financial losses could climb as high as $20 million. In fact, the loss would eventually reach nearly $35 million, a figure that would threaten the very survival of Giannini's branch banking empire.[20]

By this time Giannini had returned to California, where he remained preoccupied over the next seven months in the proxy battle against Walker. Immediately after his victory, however, he instructed Louis Ferrari to pressure Treasury Department officials as never before in bringing criminal charges against Nolan, Bell, and the Hellmans. "For the life of me," he wrote to Mario, "can't see how any good attorney can think of losing such a case unless it's up to some crooked court."[21]

On July 25, 1932, Ferrari informed Giannini about the steps he had taken in complying with his instructions. The good news, Ferrari said, was that he had received a phone call from Pole, who explained that he "knew all about the southern situation" and was prepared to cooperate with Bank of America officials in bringing criminal charges against Nolan, Bell, and the Hellmans. The bad news was that Pole had decided to "postpone" taking any action until "a more opportune" moment presented itself. Given the high level of public anxiety over the integrity of the nation's banking system, Pole said, the last thing anyone wanted was a major scandal that would reverberate far beyond the boundaries of California. He hoped Giannini would understand.[22]

Pole's response infuriated Giannini. Such foot-dragging on the part of administration officials in Washington, he believed, was motivated more by political than national considerations. Nolan and the Hellmans were prominent Republican party fund-raisers in southern California and had participated in the efforts of the Hoover campaign to carry Los Angeles in the presidential election of 1928. Given the already highly charged atmosphere of public resentment over allegations of financial abuse and chicanery in the nation's financial community, Giannini believed that administration officials in Washington, and quite possibly Hoover himself, no doubt saw in the Merchants National scandal a serious threat to the Republican party in Los Angeles and consequently the president's reelection campaign in the fall.

Robert Morrison, a Los Angeles businessman and Giannini loyalist who knew about Read's report, was thinking along similar lines. With the "southern situation" partly in mind, Morrison wrote Giannini on August 21, 1932, that Hoover's selection of personal friends in Los Angeles made it painfully clear that the president was "not in touch with the reaction of great numbers of people toward the financial debauchery of our citizens under Republican administration tactics." Morrison concluded his letter: "The Bank of America and Transamerica Corporation can expect nothing from the present administration if continued in office."[23]

3

Bitter over what he viewed as an attempt on the part of Hoover administration officials to shield Nolan, Bell, and the Hellmans from prosecution, Giannini turned to the fall presidential election as a means for revenge. On September 2, 1931, he sent a confidential letter to Joseph P. Kennedy, the Boston financier and stock market wheeler-dealer who served as Franklin Roosevelt's liaison with the nation's big-business community. "Note in this morning's paper that your friend Franklin Roosevelt will be here in San Francisco on the twenty second," Giannini wrote. "We here at the bank have not as yet decided who we are going to support although a personal representative of

Hoover is doing everything he can to get us on the Hoover band-wagon.[24] Needless to tell you it will give me great pleasure to meet your friend."[25]

Kennedy replied two days later, informing Giannini that he had discussed his letter with Roosevelt, who had expressed great interest in a meeting. Roosevelt, Kennedy said, was very "anxious to have a chat with you."[26]

Giannini's flirtation with Roosevelt's candidacy was given encouragement from another quarter. On September 12, 1932, soon after he had written to Kennedy, Giannini received a confidential letter from Angelo Scampini, a San Francisco attorney and prominent Democratic party activist who sat on Bank of America's board of directors. Scampini told Giannini that he had just returned from a private meeting in Los Angeles with William Gibbs McAdoo, the Democratic candidate for the Senate in California. In return for Giannini's support in the upcoming senatorial campaign, Scampini said, McAdoo "has pledged . . . that your requests will not only be granted but that it shall also apply to representation on the Reconstruction Finance Corporation."[27]

Especially encouraging, in Scampini's view, was McAdoo's assurance that if Roosevelt succeeded in defeating Hoover in the fall election, he planned to name Carter Glass the next secretary of the treasury. Glass, the aging, thin-skinned, and highly respected senior senator from Virginia, was known to be a forceful advocate of branch banking.[28] Scampini was ecstatic when he asked Giannini to consider the advantages that would almost certainly flow to the Bank of America if Roosevelt and McAdoo won in the fall. "Imagine what it means to us in the way of an extension of branch banking," Scampini wrote. "With those thoughts in mind, I want you to make a contribution to the Democratic State Committee of ten thousand dollars. The decision really is in your hands."[29]

Roosevelt arrived in San Francisco on September 22, 1932. The following morning Giannini met with Roosevelt in his suite at the Palace Hotel. Giannini wasted no time in complaining to Roosevelt about Calkins's harassment of him and Bank of America through his position as governor of the SFFRB. The two men then came quickly to terms. Giannini said that while he could not risk the predictable public backlash that would certainly follow an open declaration of support, he could and would actively work behind the scenes to help bring about Roosevelt's victory in California in the fall election.[30] For his part, Roosevelt pledged that he would give serious consideration to the possibility of forcing Calkins's resignation as governor of the SFFRB and promised to consult Giannini "on all matters relating to the banking business in California."[31]

Asked by reporters in the lobby of the Palace Hotel if his meeting with Roosevelt meant that he had decided to support his candidacy, Giannini was noncommittal. "Can't say," he replied, smiling broadly. "Haven't made up my mind yet."[32] A few days later, with Scampini acting as intermediary, Giannini secretly contributed $15,000 of Bank of America's money to the Roosevelt and McAdoo campaigns.[33]

In the presidential campaign Giannini worked quietly and effectively for the Democratic ticket in California. He established warm as well as valuable working relationships with national party leaders, most prominently Roosevelt's campaign manager, James Farley. Giannini had superb political contacts in California, and Farley relied on his reports for information on the effectiveness of the Democratic organization in the state and Roosevelt's voting strength among the electorate.[34] Giannini informed Farley that on the basis of information gathered by his "foreign" missionaries—whom he had instructed to drum up support for the Democratic ticket among Transamerica's tens of thousands of stockholders—he was confident that Roosevelt "should sweep California by 400,000 votes."[35]

For Democratic party leaders in California, Giannini's most important contribution to Roosevelt's campaign occurred in a way that neither he nor they had planned. On November 4, 1932, four days before the end of the campaign, Giannini was on an inspection visit to Bank of America's branch office in Gustine, a small town east of San Francisco. The phone on the branch manager's desk rang, and Giannini was informed that Hoover was on the line and wanted to talk with him. Unnoticed by Giannini, the editor of the town's only newspaper happened to be in the bank, close enough to the phone to overhear the largely one-sided conversation. As reported in the *Gustine Tribune* that same evening and reprinted in newspapers throughout the state the following day, Giannini's harsh reply to what on Hoover's part had obviously been a last-minute appeal for support was as coldly blunt as it was brief.

"Why should I?" Giannini was heard to say. "Every man I've dropped out of my organization you've appointed to some place of honor."

"But I'd like to have your support. You're a man of tremendous influence in California and . . ."

"I'm sorry, Mr. President," Giannini interrupted, "but I'm not in politics at all." Saying nothing more, Hoover hung up.[36]

Democrats, of course, were delighted with the story.[37] They seized on Giannini's rejection of Hoover's plea to ridicule Republican campaign rhetoric that Roosevelt was a threat to the nation's big-business interests and the hope of economic recovery. As the *Los Banos Gazette* editorialized, "The big political hullabaloo being broadcast by Republican spellbinders that the country is going to the dogs if Roosevelt is elected is being kicked into a cocked hat with a single punt. Mr. Giannini's opinion will be greatly respected, and if his banking interests are not afraid of a change in administration, why should other people have any fear?"[38]

Roosevelt swept California by more than 500,000 votes. Characteristically, Giannini lost no time in reminding Farley just how large a role he believed Bank of America's "boys and girls" had played in Roosevelt's victory in the state. "Dear Jim," he wrote to Farley a few days after the election. "It may interest you to know that we were the only bank in the state whose officers and staff as well as one hundred and seventy-five thousand stockholders of Transamerica residing in California were unanimous in support of the Democratic candidate."[39]

In San Francisco, Giannini executives were elated. They felt certain that with Roosevelt's victory they had effectively disposed of dangerous opposition in Washington and had taken an important step toward their "great leader's goal of nationwide branch banking." Alluding to the Jewish ancestry of Walker, Meyer, and Fleishhacker and the expected appointment of Carter Glass to the treasury, one senior Bank of America vice-president viewed Roosevelt's election as the best thing that could have happened to Transamerica Corporation. "Now that the Israelites have been swallowed by the Roosevelt Red Sea," he wrote to Giannini, "perhaps the branch banking system will be allowed to function. Let us hope that the Glasses . . . will have their innings."[40]

"Heartily agree with your views," Giannini replied. "Let us hope we can put our enemies out."[41]

4

By the spring of 1933 the nation's banking system seemed to be headed toward total collapse. To Thomas Lamont, a senior partner in the firm of J. P. Morgan and Company, the situation "could not be worse."[42] In the aftermath of the October 1929 crash, a series of disastrous runs by panicky depositors had drastically reduced the government's supply of gold. Some three thousand banks across the country had failed. The continuing downturn in the economy had become so serious on the eve of Roosevelt's inauguration that twenty state governments had taken emergency measures by declaring a banking moratorium; nearly all others had placed severe restrictions on the amount of money individual depositors could withdraw.[43] Many in the financial community had lost faith in the ability of some of the nation's largest banks to function for more than a few weeks.[44]

Apprehensive that public anxiety caused by the rapidly plunging economy and other financial debacles might result in massive withdrawals, Giannini took steps to increase Bank of America's capital. Early in January 1933 he sent a request to RFC officials in Washington for a loan of $13 million, adding a second request for $35 million a few days later. Although "total deposits of our two banks are about $700,000,000," Giannini wrote, he wanted the loans as a hedge "against possible immediate future eventualities."[45] Simultaneously, he issued an order to Bank of America's branch managers to keep him informed on a weekly basis about "large or unusual withdrawals."[46]

If part of Giannini's concerns stemmed from the public despair over the worsening economy, another part was fueled by fresh rumors of Bank of America's imminent collapse that had spread from the financial community to the general public. One rumor had it that Wall Street was bitter about Giannini's victory over Walker in the proxy battle and was determined to make another effort to take control of Bank of America from him.[47] With the nation deep in a depression seemingly beyond the government's control, such crisis-producing rumors were not unusual. But some Giannini executives believed that evidence suggested a darker side to the spread of disparaging stories concerning Bank of America's financial condition. As one close aide informed him, "These rumors are part of your enemies' villainous and underground campaign to destroy you."[48]

By the end of 1932 Giannini, whose suspicions regarding a renewed assault against his control of Bank of America had already been aroused by the Hoover administration's generous treatment of Transamerica's former senior executives, became obsessed with the notion that his enemies on Wall Street and in California might try to take advantage of the political and economic turbulence to deliver his banking empire a damaging, perhaps fatal, blow. "Take care you fellows to see that the Wall Street racket doesn't put over on us indirectly what it so far hasn't been able to do directly," he cautioned his executives.[49]

On the morning of February 25, 1933, at Roosevelt's invitation, Giannini was aboard a train bound for Washington to attend the inauguration ceremony and to confer with the president-elect about the worsening crisis in the banking system. All during the cross-country trip, the possibility of a counterattack by his enemies was never far from his mind. He warned his executives in a telegram from Chicago to redouble their vigilance in his absence. "Remember enemies still at the helm in [Treasury] department. Don't hesitate to shout from the rooftops. We have the cleanest institution in the United States. . . . Hence every effort is directed toward placing obstacles in our path but so far to little avail."[50]

At a stopover in New York, Giannini met with Roosevelt at the president-elect's East Sixty-fifth Street house. Also at the meeting were three members of the new administration, including William Woodin, the shy, frail, but sharp-tongued president of American Car and Foundry whom Roosevelt had chosen as secretary of the treasury after Glass declined the offer.[51] What Giannini learned during the course of his conversation with Roosevelt and the others pleased him immensely. Minutes after he left the meeting, Giannini sent a telegram to Mario quoting Roosevelt as saying that he was immensely dissatisfied with the performance of the FRB in responding to the crisis in the economy. Roosevelt, Giannini said, planned to ease Meyer out as chairman of the board and to reorganize the entire reserve system with new personnel. "I was so encouraged elimination of our friend C [Calkins]," Giannini said.[52]

Giannini was in Washington one week later when, a few minutes past midnight on March 6, 1933, Roosevelt issued a proclamation declaring a three-day bank holiday. Giannini supported the president's action and said so in a telegram to the White House. That evening Giannini attended a postinaugural Democratic banquet and had a conversation with Roosevelt lasting only a few minutes. His talks with others in the room, including prominent party officials and members of the new administration, were friendly enough; but their rage concerning the desperate state of the economy was everywhere in evidence. Almost everyone felt that the collapse of the nation's banking system pointed to the need for tough new legislation regulating the activities

Illustrations

1. Giannini's birthplace: the Swiss Hotel, San Jose, 1870.

2. "A small corner of the mother country": North Beach and Telegraph Hill at the turn of the century.

3. "A home with a large bay window": Green Street in North Beach, 1906.

4. The Commission District: San Francisco waterfront, 1890.

5. "The handsomest man in North Beach": the young
    Giannini, when he was still a commission merchant.

6. The Gianninis' wedding photo, 1892.

7. Seven Oaks: the Giannini home in San Mateo.

8. Bank of Italy's license, dated September 14, 1904.

9. Bank of Italy's original board of directors, 1904.

10. Birthplace of Giannini's "baby bank," Columbus Avenue, San Francisco.

11. "The Bank of Italy was in ruins": North Beach after the earthquake, 1906.

12. Bank of Italy's first branch office, San Jose, 1909.

13. En route to Europe: (*left to right*) Lawrence Mario Giannini, Clorinda Giannini, A. P. Giannini, Claire Giannini, Virgil Giannini.

14. Conquering rural California: Bank of Italy branch office, 1927.

15. The Bank of Italy's Hollywood connection: Giannini (*top, second from left*) with movie mogul Joseph Schenck (*top, third from left*) and director Cecil B. DeMille (*bottom, center*).

16. Giannini and child star Jackie Coogan, 1923.

To ... Dr...
B... w...
Doug... Fai... 1927

17. A grateful Hollywood: Giannini and Douglas Fairbanks, Sr., 1927.

18. "A bank for women run by women": Giannini's Women's Bank.

ARTHUR REYNOLDS DWIGHT L.CLARKE Dr.A.H.GIANNINI WARNERS EDMUNDS A.P.GIANNINI

19. Even in formal photos, they were never close: Giannini and Attilio
"Doc" Giannini with Bank of America executives, 1930.

20. "The Wild Bull of Montgomery Street."

21. Giannini with wife and daughter, Claire, boarding the train for vacation trip to Italy, three months before the Blue Monday crash of June 1928.

22. Lorenzo "Boss" Scatena on construction site of Bank of America's new headquarters building at One Powell, San Francisco.

23. Giannini and Jean Monnet.

24. "Walker's coffins": Associated Transamerica Stockholders' proxies.

25. On the set of *Gone with the Wind* in Culver City: Giannini and
    Vivien Leigh.

26. Plotting strategy in the struggle against the SEC: Giannini (*second from left*) and Mario Giannini (*third from left*) with legal counsel.

27. At the helm of the USS *Portsmouth*, 1941, a birthday gift from Giannini's "boys and girls" in the Bank of America.

FIFTEEN CENTS · APRIL 15, 1946

TIME

THE WEEKLY NEWSMAGAZINE

CALIFORNIA'S GIANNINI
Along the West Coast, hearts are high.

VOLUME XLVII (REG. U. S. PAT. OFF.) NUMBER 15

28. Founder and chairman of the world's biggest bank.

29. St. Mary's Cathedral, San Francisco, June 9, 1949: Giannini's funeral.

of those who owned or managed financial institutions. Others wanted to see a complete overhaul of the system itself.

Hostility toward the banking and securities industry came as no surprise to Giannini. But some who were promoting a thorough reform of the nation's credit system crossed a line that he thought dangerous. Given this mood of recrimination and the unpredictability of what governmental actions the new administration might eventually decide to take, Giannini believed that his presence was required in San Francisco. Canceling plans to join his family for a vacation at the Breakers Hotel in Miami, he boarded a train for the cross-country trip back to California. [53]

Giannini arrived back in San Francisco on Friday morning, March 9, where he found a group of reporters waiting for him at the train station. They crowded around him, notebooks in hand, anxious for his reaction to the emergency measures Roosevelt had taken in combating the deterioration in the nation's economy. Giannini replied that he was "much impressed with the initiative displayed by the president in dealing with the banking crisis." In his opinion, he added, Roosevelt "was a real leader." [54]

From the train station Giannini went directly to Bank of America's headquarters at 1 Powell. Waiting for him was a telegram from Collins, whom Giannini had instructed before leaving Washington to keep him informed "as to the progress of affairs" in the capital. Collins told Giannini that from private sources inside the administration, he had learned that Roosevelt was about to issue a proclamation authorizing the secretary of the treasury to evaluate banks in the federal reserve system as to their solvency. National banks classified as "sound" would be issued a license and allowed to reopen their doors on the following Monday morning, March 13. Collins assured Giannini that his request for a license would be received favorably by Woodin. [55]

Giannini promptly sent a telegram to Woodin: "Hereby apply for permission to open Bank of America National Trust and Savings Association." [56] A short time later Giannini received a second telegram from Collins. It contained detailed information about the conditions set forth in Roosevelt's proclamation under which member banks in the nation's reserve system would be permitted to reopen. Collins also told Giannini that in trying to keep on top of changing developments at the Treasury, he had learned that Woodin's decision on whether to issue a reopening license to individual member banks would be based in large part on a "recommendation of soundness" from district reserve banks or the comptroller of the currency.[57]

Alarmed by the possibility that more was required of him than the request he had already sent to Woodin, Giannini immediately filed an application for a license with Calkins at the SFFRB. Calkins replied a few hours later that such licenses would be issued "through his office." Calkins went on to add a new and, to Giannini, highly disturbing piece of information: all applications from eligible banks for licenses to reopen, he said, "will be granted in the order received."[58]

Giannini was puzzled. Received where? In Washington or San Francisco? The answer to that question was critical. If San Francisco, Giannini assumed that the delay in filing his second application might mean that it was now lying at the bottom of the pile. Simultaneous with this concern, he was beginning to consider the possibility that Calkins was in a perfect position to use the authority of his office to prevent Bank of America from reopening. There was little doubt that such an objective—if it could be obtained while Giannini's biggest competitors like Crocker, Security First, and Wells Fargo were allowed to reopen their doors—would inflict a potentially fatal blow on Bank of America.[59]

Giannini turned for assistance to California's senior senator, Hiram Johnson, and to William McAdoo, who had only recently taken his seat in the Senate. After informing both men about the steps he had taken in the reopening process, he pointed to the opportunity for dirty tricks that the process itself gave to his enemies like Calkins. "We are only anxious for fair and impartial treatment," he said. "Knowing as you do the unfriendly attitude previously manifest here you can understand that we are concerned lest some influence seek to delay our application so others may open before we do and thereby discredit us. Would consider it a favor if you would check through Washington sources as soon as possible and find out what is being done with our application."[60]

Giannini was at his desk at Bank of America headquarters early the following morning, Saturday, March 11, when an urgent telegram arrived from McAdoo. Contrary to the information Giannini had earlier received from Collins, McAdoo said, the issuance of a license to reopen would be based only "somewhat on recommendation of federal reserve banks each district." The other good news, McAdoo went on to say, was that he had spoken to various officials at the Treasury, including Francis W. Awalt, the acting comptroller of the currency, who had assured him in the strongest terms that Giannini had "many friends in the administration" and had nothing to worry about. "From what I hear I cannot imagine any ground for uneasiness on your part," Mc-Adoo said. "There will be no discrimination."[61]

Giannini's sense of relief was of short duration. Saturday passed by—and still no word from Woodin. Early Sunday morning, March 12, Giannini rushed off a cable to Collins instructing him to inquire about the status of his license with officials at the Treasury and report back to him "as soon as possible."[62] Collins replied a few hours later with the most reassuring news Giannini had heard in over two days. Only a few minutes before, Collins said, he had been informed by officials in the comptroller's office that Woodin had cleared Bank of America to reopen. Giannini could expect to receive the news from the secretary himself momentarily.[63]

Collins's information should have solved the problem for Giannini, but it did not. At seven o'clock that evening (California time) he was still waiting to hear from Woodin. Fearing the worst, Giannini phoned Hiram Johnson at his home in Washington, where he learned that McAdoo had shown up to await news about what had happened in San Francisco. Both men were shocked to learn that Giannini had not yet heard from Woodin. Earlier that afternoon, Johnson said, he and Mc-Adoo had talked on the phone with the Treasury secretary, who had told them that he had cleared the Bank of America to reopen. With time running out, Johnson and McAdoo volunteered to go immediately to the Treasury and find out from Woodin personally what had gone wrong.[64]

It was close to midnight (Washington time) before Johnson and McAdoo were ushered into Woodin's office. What Woodin had to say startled both men. After clearing Bank of America to reopen, Woodin said, he had received an extremely gloomy assessment of the bank's financial condition from Calkins in San Francisco, accompanied by an examination report produced by the comptroller's office. Among other things, the report stated that Bank of America faced a major financial crisis because of a massive number of bad or dubious loans—and it concluded that the bank did not have sufficient cash reserves to cover the losses. Calkins had assured Woodin that Bank of America was "hopelessly insolvent" and warned him against permitting the bank to reopen. In light of the extremely adverse examination report and Calkins's strongly worded recommendation, Woodin told McAdoo and Johnson, he had no choice but to withdraw the license.[65]

Returning to Johnson's home, McAdoo phoned Giannini with the disastrous news. Giannini, badly shaken, asked McAdoo if he could remember the date on the examination report Calkins had sent to Woodin in support of his recommendation. When McAdoo said he could—March 23, 1932—Giannini exploded. Calkins had submitted a copy of an old report that field examiners in the comptroller's office had begun and completed during the height of the proxy battle.[66] He had withheld, no doubt intentionally, the results of Bank of America's latest examination report, completed on November 25, 1932, which had concluded in part that the bank's financial condition had improved considerably in recent months and was stronger than at any time since the October 1929 market crash.[67]

On McAdoo's advice, Giannini phoned Woodin and explained what Calkins had done. Giannini's efforts were frustrated, however, when Woodin repeatedly refused to overrule Calkins's recommendation without sufficient proof to the contrary.[68] With only hours remaining before the Monday morning deadline, Giannini felt desperate. He turned frantically for assistance to William Randolph Hearst, who seemed the best choice for the political handling of a problem that neither Johnson nor McAdoo had succeeded in overcoming. A native Californian who hated Wall Street as passionately as Giannini himself, Hearst had thrown the considerable influence of his newspaper empire behind Roosevelt in the 1932 election. He was also one of Bank of America's biggest corporate clients.

Giannini routed John Francis Neylan, Hearst's personal attorney, out of bed at his home in suburban San Francisco. After listening to Giannini's account of the events that had taken place over the preceding weekend, Neylan phoned Hearst at his mountaintop home in San Simeon. Hearst thought the entire matter extremely serious. He instructed Neylan to phone Roosevelt at once with a clear message of warning from him personally that the failure of Bank of America to reopen "would be a major disaster whose catastrophic results would be with California and the entire Pacific coast for years to come."[69]

Neylan's efforts to reach the president, however, were unsuccessful. Marvin McIntyre, Roosevelt's personal secretary, told him, as Neylan later remembered, that "the president had a cold, was very tired, and had gone to bed." McIntyre suggested instead that Neylan get in touch with Woodin.[70]

Neylan's conversation with Woodin was not an easy one. Woodin responded to Hearst's urgent message by repeating Calkins's assertion "that the bank would not be able to stand on its own" if the Treasury allowed it to reopen. Woodin then asked to see a copy of Bank of America's latest examination report, which Neylan assured him was on its way from San Francisco. Neylan kept hammering away: "Calkins was violently prejudiced . . . his report fictitious . . . the bank had made a remarkable recovery." As he talked, Neylan sensed that Woodin was beginning to have second thoughts. Woodin ended the conversation by telling Neylan that he wanted more time to reconsider the entire situation. He promised to phone Neylan later that morning.[71]

A short time later Woodin summoned a group of Treasury Department officials to his office for a private meeting. Raymond Moley, a member of Roosevelt's "brain trust" who was in Woodin's office at the time, later described the meeting as acrimonious. Two members of the group, both influential holdovers from the Hoover administration, supported Calkins's recommendation and forcefully opposed Bank of America's reopening. In the end, however, Woodin decided to override their objections. "I well remember that the consideration which finally prevailed was the immense importance of Giannini's bank in the whole social structure of California," Moley wrote later. "Untold chaos would result from its fall."[72]

Woodin then phoned Calkins at his home in San Francisco to inform him of his decision. Calkins protested, which produced a heated exchange between the two men punctuated by "strong language." Finally Woodin decided to call Calkins's bluff. "Are you willing to take responsibility for keeping the institution closed?" he asked. Calkins answered no. "Well, then," Woodin snapped, "the bank will open," and he hung up.[73] Woodin then called Neylan.[74]

Giannini was at his desk at Bank of America headquarters when the phone rang and he heard the excitement in Neylan's voice. A Bank of America director, one of a small number of associates who had gathered with Giannini at 5:00 A.M. Monday morning to await the outcome of Woodin's decision, later remembered the "cheers and shouts of relief" that erupted in the room when he told them the news. After waiting to see the doors of Bank of America's headquarters building swing open later that morning, Giannini hurried off on a tour of its branches in and around San Francisco to ensure that the word had gotten around and that it was business as usual.

Later that day Giannini sent a letter of appreciation to Hearst. "Apparently our old enemies have made their last stand and we are deeply grateful to you for the most important part you and Jack Neylan played in defeating their destructive purposes," he wrote. "I am convinced that you have performed one of the most constructive acts for the state of California that has happened in many a day. The conduct of Federal Reserve officials during the period of the Holiday was calculated to lull us into a sense of security. . . . So you can see that if we had not been on the job and if you had not intervened, they would have accomplished their destructive purposes."[75]

5

Not surprisingly, in the weeks immediately following Roosevelt's election Giannini turned his attention toward bringing criminal charges against Nolan, Bell, and the Hellmans. By then, losses to Bank of America as a result of his purchase of the Merchants National had climbed to a staggering $25 million. On November 21, 1932, Giannini filed a formal complaint against the four men with Lee Madland, San Francisco's chief national bank examiner, insisting that "prosecutions . . . be commenced without delay." Giannini told Madland that "the time has surely come when some action should be taken. It is difficult to imagine a situation where an institution taken over with a purported invested capital of twelve million should turn out to be absolutely insolvent."[76]

Months went by before Madland replied, informing Giannini in a letter on June 30, 1933, that he had sent his complaint to the Justice Department "for consideration."[77] Frustrated by the seven-month delay, Giannini wrote to Homer Cummings, Roosevelt's attorney general, urging him to take immediate action against Bank of America's former president and three senior vice-presidents on charges of fraud and embezzlement. With the stalling tactics on the part of Hoover administration officials still fresh in his mind, Giannini concluded his letter to Cummings: "I am confident that your department will not tolerate the delays which hampered the functions of your predecessors."[78]

Two weeks later an official in the Justice Department informed Giannini that his complaint against Nolan, Bell, and the Hellmans had been forwarded to Pierson Hall, U.S. district attorney for Los Angeles. "It is not unlikely," the official wrote, "that a special agent of his department will call upon you at an early date."[79] Vastly encouraged, Giannini wrote to Hall informing him that Bank of America examiners in Los Angeles had put together a large file of highly incriminating evidence against Nolan, Bell, and the Hellmans. He offered to send an associate to Los Angeles "with our data . . . if you prefer."[80]

Then, just as things seemed to be getting off the ground, events took an extraordinary turn. In Los Angeles, Bank of America's examiners suddenly disclosed that Nolan, Bell, and the Hellmans had not limited their illegal activities to Merchants National. Money to finance their speculative real estate investments had also come from a small bank across town, Beverly Hills National, in the form of fake transactions and loans to dummy borrowers.[81] Losses totaled over $2 million, much of it in phony notes that had been transferred to Beverly Hills National from Bank of America. Burdened with so much bad debt, Beverly Hills National had been forced into bankruptcy in June 1932.[82]

As it turned out, at the center of this new evidence of criminal activity stood the figure of none other than Edward Nolan, who had assumed the presidency of Beverly Hills National after being fired from his post as president of Bank of America in February 1931.[83] There were still more disclosures, including evidence that Nolan had been aided in his illegal financial operations in connection with Beverly Hills National by two prominent Los Angeles businessmen and political activists— Richard Hargreaves and Hamilton "Ham" Cotton.

The involvement of Hargreaves and Cotton in the Merchants National debacle attracted an unusual amount of attention at Bank of America headquarters, less for the part both men were alleged to have played as participants in Nolan's wheeler-dealer looting of Merchants National than for their prominence in Democratic party circles in Los Angeles. Hargreaves and Cotton were key figures in the political organization of California's newly elected senator, William McAdoo.[84] Hargreaves, who at one time in his business career had been president of Commercial Bank, predecessor to Merchants National, had helped to manage McAdoo's senatorial campaign in the November election and continued to function as his close political adviser. Cotton had been an influential fund-raiser for McAdoo's campaign and thereafter served as the McAdoo organization's official finance chairman in southern California.[85]

The allegations directed at Hargreaves and Cotton by Bank of America examiners soon received independent confirmation from Robert Morrison, who had close personal and political ties with the McAdoo organization in Los Angeles. On July 26, 1933, Morrison informed

Giannini in a confidential letter that there was absolutely no question in his mind that Hargreaves and Cotton were "tied in with the Bell and Nolan outfit."[86]

Giannini took a hard-line approach, even though it was clear that doing so could jeopardize his relationship with the McAdoo organization in southern California. He instructed Morrison to meet privately with William Neblett, McAdoo's chief of staff and a senior partner in the senator's Los Angeles law firm, McAdoo, Neblett, and O'Connor. He wanted Neblett to pressure Pierson Hall into a more vigorous investigation.[87]

Morrison arranged the meeting but warned Giannini in a coded letter on July 26, 1933, not to expect Neblett to respond favorably to his request. Morrison told Giannini that it was generally known in Democratic party circles that Hall had ambitions that reached well beyond his office as a federal prosecutor and "was extremely indebted to the Chief [McAdoo] politically." A criminal indictment against Nolan, Bell, and the Hellmans, and the subsequent trial, obviously ran the risk of implicating Hargreaves and Cotton in a scandal of major proportions; the consequent publicity obviously had the potential of generating a serious political problem for McAdoo and the Democratic party in southern California. "Chief [McAdoo], Chief II [Neblett] and Ham [Cotton] will exercise a great deal of influence with him [Hall] in the matter," Morrison said.[88]

When Morrison met with Neblett the following day, he went into the magnitude of Bank of America's financial losses as well as the evidence Giannini had submitted to Pierson Hall documenting insider fraud and other criminal activity on a shocking scale. Morrison reminded Neblett that in pursuing charges against Nolan, Bell, and the Hellmans, Giannini at the very least had an ethical obligation to Bank of America's customers and stockholders. Anything less than a vigorous prosecution of the case was unacceptable.

Morrison immediately sensed Neblett's annoyance. Neblett told Morrison that even though he and Hall knew each other on a personal and professional basis, he wanted some time to think about Giannini's request. Neblett said he was reluctant to pressure Hall, not because of his close association with Hargreaves and Cotton but because "he wasn't sufficiently familiar with the facts of the case."[89] Neblett paused and then said that in his opinion Giannini "was foolish to press the matter. . . . The statute of limitations had probably run out . . . and that it was all dead and would serve no good purpose."

Morrison chose not to pursue the matter. As he told Giannini in a coded letter two days later, it seemed clear to him that Neblett's explanation was "a lot of hooey." Neblett's remarks deploring Giannini's determination to pursue the matter further made it equally clear to Morrison that "Ham Cotton is afraid of the investigation, that Dick Hargreaves is afraid of the investigation." Morrison was certain that he knew what was behind Neblett's disappointing response to Giannini's request. "I do not think," he went on to say, "that Chief's [McAdoo's] firm want anything to come up about Nolan, Bell, et al. which may uncover anything concerning Hargreaves."[90]

Given the political threat that the link between Hargreaves, Cotton, and "the Nolan crowd" presented to the McAdoo organization in Los Angeles, Morrison was not optimistic about Hall's willingness to investigate the charges thoroughly. He was certain that powerful outside figures, worried about the political ramifications of an indictment and well-publicized trial, were more than likely to get involved. "There will be considerable pressure to bear to thwart your efforts," Morrison told Giannini. "No doubt great influence will be exercised in Washington to stop . . . any investigation which may effect Hargreaves or Ham directly or indirectly." Morrison predicted that Hall would undoubtedly "dally around" with the investigation for the sake of appearance but would eventually find no basis for indictments and drop the entire matter.[91]

Unknown to Giannini, in fact, soon after his meeting with Morrison, Neblett embarked on a strenuous campaign to keep Hargreaves and Cotton from becoming involved in Bank of America's charges against Nolan, Bell, and the Hellmans. In a letter to McAdoo on November 4, 1933, he warned that the possibility of criminal indictments posed a terrible threat both to the senator's reputation and to the Democratic organization in southern California. Neblett told McAdoo that it would be in the best interests of all concerned if Hargreaves and Cotton "were let alone and allowed to live in peace."[92] Apparently fearing the intense pressures caused by rumors of a Justice Department investigation, Neblett also warned former members of the Beverly Hills National's board of directors that should any of them decide to furnish government investigators with information on the bank's relationship with Hargreaves and Cotton, board members themselves would be vulnerable to the charge of criminal complicity.[93]

It is not known whether Neblett or McAdoo intervened with Hall to prevent him from bringing criminal charges against Nolan, Bell, and the Hellmans.[94] But Morrison's prediction about the outcome of Hall's investigation turned out to be remarkably accurate. Hall took more than five months to comb through the evidence that Bank of America examiners had provided to him, a summary of which he sent to Giannini in late November 1933. Hall told Giannini that after careful consideration he had decided "not to initiate criminal proceedings" because in his opinion a conviction "could not be obtained." In addition, Hall went on to say, since the statute of limitations had run out on the crimes allegedly committed by the four men, further action by his office was in any case irrelevant and unlikely to contribute to any legally satisfying outcome.

Giannini was livid. He immediately sent a bitterly worded letter to Attorney General Cummings, expressing his "keen disappointment" over Hall's "half-hearted interest" in the case.[95] Giannini assured Cummings that the evidence against Nolan, Bell, and the Hellmans was incontrovertible: "As a result of these criminal activities the losses suffered by this institution [Bank of America] have been stupendous."[96] Giannini forwarded a copy of his letter to Marvin McIntyre at the White House, together with an urgent request that "it immediately be brought to the attention of the president."[97]

Giannini's complaint to Cummings led nowhere. The Justice Department took a hands-off approach even though it was clear to many in the Giannini organization that the case itself would not have been difficult to prosecute. On December 5, 1933, Giannini received a letter from an official in the Justice Department informing him that nothing more could be done. Regrettably, the official wrote, the attorney general had no choice but to accept Hall's judgment that "all matters of sufficient importance to warrant investigation and prosecution are now barred from prosecution by the statute of limitations."[98] As far as the department was concerned, the case was closed.

With no other options at the federal level, Giannini decided to bring civil action in state court against Nolan, Bell, and the Hellmans. His problems in this effort soon became obvious. Much to his dismay, the Hellmans had taken the precaution of protecting themselves against a damage suit by declaring bankruptcy. To make matters worse, Bank of America lawyers informed Giannini that Nolan "was so broke" that "any action against him was not worth paying filing fees to commence."[99]

Giannini was eventually more successful in a civil suit against Charles Bell. In 1936 the Bank of America won a judgment of $460,000 for the dummy notes Bell had either signed or endorsed and then deposited in the Beverly Hills National. As things turned out, even in this small and financially insignificant award (when compared to the approximately $35 million in losses the Bank of America had sustained) Giannini was disappointed. Burdened with debt and pursued by creditors, Bell committed suicide.

FIFTEEN

Unaccustomed Disappointments

I

On the cool evening of October 14, 1934, small clusters
of people in formal dress moved through the lobby of San Francisco's
romanesque War Memorial Opera House. They were executives and
employees of Giannini's Bank of America who had gathered for a dinner
party to celebrate the bank's thirtieth anniversary. Not counting spouses
and invited guests, there were more than two thousand participants.
Smaller dinner parties were being held simultaneously in more than
two hundred towns and cities across the state. The guests inside the
spacious rehearsal hall of the opera house were jubilant, responding to
a succession of after-dinner tributes to the bank and its founder with
cheers and applause.

Silence descended over the hall when Giannini, who was attending
a bankers' convention in New York, began speaking over a live telephone and radio hookup carried by eight stations across California and
the entire Pacific coast. "Our president's recovery program has been
assailed by reactionaries who would have us believe that he seeks to
destroy the social order, and by ultra-radicals who have us forsake him
because he does not," he said. "The fact is that our nation as a whole is
much better off than it has been in recent years."[1]

Giannini's voice took on a more urgent tone as he spoke about the
future of branch banking and the continuing relentless opposition of
his enemies to Bank of America's expansion. "We are celebrating here

tonight because we believe that selfish interests can no longer conceal from the public the fundamental improvement that has taken place . . . in our purpose to render to California a statewide banking service appropriate to the needs of all its people, however humble," he said.[2] "The next step will be branch banking in Federal Reserve Districts. Nationwide branch banking will be the final step, giving this country a banking system that will be on a par with the best in the world."[3]

The applause was thunderous after Giannini thanked his employees for their support and dedication and said good-night. Then, as all eyes were directed to the stage, a hugely enlarged photograph of Giannini was lowered slowly from the ceiling and the lights in the hall were turned off. As spotlights from beneath the ceiling illuminated the photograph, the applause and the cheering resumed. "How proud everybody in the room was to be associated with such a leader," wrote one dinner guest to Mario Giannini the next day. "The birthday party had come to an end, but all left with the inspiration to work, work, work, and carry forward the crusade started thirty years ago by the much loved A. P."[4]

Giannini's warm praise of Roosevelt in his banquet speech was not the first time he had used a public forum to express his admiration of the president's leadership. Few inside the nation's business community supported the New Deal more enthusiastically than Giannini. With an eagerness and commitment that surprised administration figures themselves, he seized on every opportunity to defend the New Deal's legislative program against its severest critics in the banking community. In November 1934, for example, the American Bankers Association adopted a resolution at its annual convention in Miami bitterly accusing Roosevelt of leading the nation down the path of "socialized government control."[5] Giannini promptly issued a press release urging the American people to "back up the president" in his efforts to restore prosperity to the nation. "We elected him as our leader," he said. "It is wrong to attempt to block him at every stage."[6]

Giannini was at his most supportive in New Deal efforts at reforming the nation's banking system. In the middle of Roosevelt's first term in office, the administration sent to Congress the Banking Act of 1935, the "most significant banking legislation since the Federal Reserve Act of 1913."[7] The goal of the bill was to move the FRB "from a passive to an active role" by transferring power from district reserve banks to the FRB; it also tied the monetary policies of a "more powerful board to the New Deal's domestic agenda in promoting business stability and

economic recovery."[8] Legislative strategists in the White House generally agreed that the harshest voices raised against the bill would come
from Wall Street's banking investment community, which had long
exercised a large amount of control over the nation's money supply
through an "independent" and decentralized reserve system.[9]

With battle lines drawn, opponents of the bill in the Senate summoned some of Wall Street's most powerful bankers to the capital to
testify against its passage.[10] Winthrop Aldrich, chairman of Chase National, the nation's largest bank, opened the attack. Appearing before
a subcommittee of the Senate, Aldrich called the banking bill "an
instrument of despotic authority."[11] The most effective voice raised
against the bill came from James P. Warburg, a prominent New York
financier and former New Deal adviser who had left the administration
some months earlier to become head of the powerful international
banking firm of Kuhn Loeb and Company. Speaking in defense of the
"American order," Warburg denounced the bill as a thinly disguised
effort to establish a "government owned central bank" and "an essential
step" toward communism. "I am not one who sees a communist under
every bed," Warburg told committee, "but I sometimes wonder if the
authors of these bills realize whose game they are playing."[12]

While Wall Street bankers like Aldrich, Warburg, and others were
using their testimony before the subcommittee to criticize and embarrass the administration, a powerful opposition to the bill was building
up in the Senate. Carter Glass, the imperious, cantankerous, seventy-
six-year-old chairman of the Senate subcommittee, joined forces with
a formidable coalition of conservative senators from both parties in an
effort to divide and then rewrite the measure so as to reduce the
president's reach and power over the federal reserve system. By late
April of 1935 it was clear to many in the White House that the administration's bill was in serious trouble.[13] Roosevelt, who had made
passage of the 1935 banking bill "must legislation for the current session of Congress," instructed aides to generate momentum for its
passage by seeking the assistance of prominent bankers outside of
New York. One of those he specifically mentioned was Giannini.

On April 25, 1935, Giannini unleashed a blistering counterattack
against Warburg's testimony, calling on the distinguished Kuhn Loeb
president to "tell the truth" about his opposition to the administration's
measure. Charging that what Warburg really meant by the "American
order" was the "inalienable right of New York bankers to issue money
and to regulate its value," Giannini said that Warburg "knew only too

well" that the control of money "is a real power for good or evil."[14] Personally, Giannini said, "I take no stock in the political domination argument against the banking bill," adding that he "would rather that this power be exercised by a public body in the public interest than by the New York banking fraternity."[15]

Administration officials were delighted by Giannini's remarks and the publicity they received in the press. In a deeply appreciative letter to Giannini on June 26, 1935, Marriner Eccles, the feisty, blunt, Utah-born chairman of the FRB and the bill's chief author, praised Giannini's efforts at mobilizing public opinion in favor of the administration's overhaul of the federal reserve system. "You have done more than any one person to offset the propaganda of the big bankers that the bill is prejudicial to the interests of the country," Eccles wrote.[16] As the *San Francisco News* editorialized, "Insiders call Amadeo Giannini's wallop at New York bankers in general and Jimmy Warburg in particular a smart New Deal maneuver. It isn't the first time that Giannini came to the New Deal's rescue at a critical moment."[17]

Congress eventually passed the bill, which Roosevelt signed on August 24, 1935. Giannini's contribution toward the administration's victory increased his standing in New Deal circles immensely. "I doubt if we would have been successful against the great weight of banking opinion but for the fact that a few voices—all too few—and yours most notably, were raised in behalf of the bill," Eccles cabled Giannini two days before the bill received Roosevelt's signature. "I do not need to tell you how much I appreciate your efforts and encouragement."[18] Roosevelt was equally appreciative of Giannini's "splendid work" and invited him to the White House for dinner.[19]

Concerned that too close a public identification with the administration might create dissatisfaction among Bank of America's Republican clients, Giannini was uncertain whether to accept. "Should I go?" he cabled his family from New York. "The invitation is quite an honor."[20] Mario urged his father to attend. "Think it splendid thing for you to accept President's invitation," he replied. "While some of our so called friends may not like us any better for it, they will respect us that much more."[21] Giannini's daughter, Claire, was equally in favor, making no secret of the fact which of the two men she considered the more important force in the country. "Of course you should go," she replied, "but the honor is Roosevelt's."[22]

Giannini's admiration for Roosevelt and his outspoken defense of the administration's legislative program was no doubt genuine. But

Giannini also regarded his support of the president as a quid pro quo for favorable treatment from New Deal administrators in his efforts to expand Bank of America under the critical glare of his competitors. One New Deal official whose cooperation he needed was J. F. T. "Jeffy" O'Connor, whom Roosevelt had appointed to replace Pole in the spring of 1933 as comptroller of the currency.[23] A Californian and senior partner in William McAdoo's Los Angeles law firm, McAdoo, Neblett, and O'Connor, the gregarious, politically ambitious, thirty-eight-year-old O'Connor proved sympathetic to Giannini's requests for permits to open new Bank of America branches. By the fall of 1936, three years after assuming control of the comptroller's office, O'Connor had approved a total of ninety-nine permits, increasing the number of the bank's branches to 491.[24]

Giannini's public support of the New Deal increased with considerable effectiveness during the presidential campaign of 1936. James Farley, concerned that there might be some "real difficulties" for Roosevelt in California because of the serious infighting that had developed within the ranks of the Democratic organization, urged Giannini to provide him with a continuing stream of intelligence on the progress of the campaign. "I want the true picture and I want you to go into as much detail as you may feel necessary," Farley wrote. "It is of the utmost importance that we work in close cooperation. Will you please treat this letter confidentially . . . and discuss it with no one except those who are in your confidence."[25]

On August 5, 1936, Giannini sent a confidential report to Farley. He recommended that Roosevelt immediately take steps after the election to withdraw political support from "McAdoo, Neblett, Cotton and the men who follow them." Giannini told Farley that the effectiveness of the McAdoo organization in the state had seriously deteriorated—the result of dissension among rank-and-file Democrats over the excessive concentration of authority in the hands of a small group of men of questionable moral character who lacked the proper credentials for political leadership. "I think the time has come," Giannini said, "for a clean sweep of the old crowd who have been running the affairs of the party in California."[26]

Throughout the fall of 1936 Giannini focused his energy on Roosevelt's reelection. In October he quietly passed the word to his "boys and girls" in Bank of America to begin mobilizing support behind Roosevelt's candidacy among the corporation's more than 200,000 stockholders.[27] The enthusiastic response to his appeal made him certain, as he told Farley, that the president "need not have any worries about California."[28] Dropping the pose of "neutrality" he had adopted four years earlier, Giannini publicly announced his support of Roosevelt's bid for reelection at a press conference in San Francisco on October 22, 1936. He also used the occasion to castigate the president's critics in the financial community. "I say to business: Stop and consider before going on with this anti-Roosevelt campaign. Give Mr. Roosevelt four more years—and he'll leave office with a record that will stamp him as the greatest statesman of his times."[29]

In the closing weeks of the campaign Farley again appealed to Giannini for assistance via Joseph Kennedy, this time for his appearance with Roosevelt on a nationwide radio broadcast to counter the harshly critical attacks against the New Deal from big business.[30] Giannini, who told Farley that he shared the president's public condemnation of the business community's claim to "special financial privilege," agreed. "People would wonder if the administration has anyone backing it except A. P. Giannini," he replied. "However shall hold myself in readiness for broadcast if deemed advisable. . . . There are many things I would like to get to the people of the country and it is the opinion of my associates and myself that just prior to the election would be the right psychological moment."[31]

Roosevelt carried California by more than 500,000 votes. The morning after the president's lopsided victory, Giannini called a press conference to praise the electorate for "putting a man at the helm who is sympathetic to the masses." With the assurance of four more years of Roosevelt's "wise and dynamic" leadership, Giannini said, "the country will move ahead into a new era of higher wages and a higher standard of living."[32] Roosevelt was enormously pleased with Giannini's public flattery of his leadership on this and earlier occasions and responded with a handwritten letter of appreciation. "For your very generous appraisal of my efforts as well as for your public pledge of support," Roosevelt wrote, "I am more grateful than I can say."[33]

As Giannini's popularity in the White House continued to rise, many in California began to perceive that his ties to the New Deal had become closer and more influential in many respects than relationships between the administration and Democratic party leaders in the state—a perception that Giannini lost no time in exploiting to the fullest. Every administration display of political deference or generosity toward California on a wide variety of critical issues from federal appointments to agricultural subsidies to foreign trade invariably generated knowing whispers of Giannini's influence.[34] "A. P.'s name was magic in Washington," one Bank of America executive would remember. "When California wanted something from the New Deal, he was asked to get it."[35]

2

Meanwhile, with the number of Bank of America depositors growing at an ever-increasing rate, Giannini pushed ahead with an aggressive lending program, exploiting opportunities wherever he found them. Soon after reassuming control of Transamerica, he turned his attention to Hollywood, which had been devastated by the nearly total collapse of the economy. By 1932 operating losses in the once glamorous and immensely profitable motion picture industry had climbed to more than $100 million. Paramount-Publix, the giant of the industry with assets of $215 million in 1929, had gone into receivership; talk was widespread that Fox Film and Fox Theater Corporations were headed in the same direction. Four other major studios—Metro-Goldwyn-Mayer, RKO, United Artists, and Universal—had been forced into recapitalization, and Warner Brothers could not find the money to pay its debts.[36]

With Hollywood desperately in need of financing, Giannini moved quickly to increase Bank of America's presence in an industry of enormous importance to the economic vitality of Los Angeles. As early as 1930 he authorized a loan of $3 million for two of Hollywood's most aggressive producers, Darryl Zanuck and Joseph Schenck, to form a new production company, which became 20th Century–Fox two years later.[37] Schenck, who sat on Bank of America's board of directors, persuaded Giannini that Zanuck's drive and talent as a movie producer was justification enough to make loans available to him. With $400,000 in Bank of Italy money, Zanuck worked furiously to rush six films into production, including such financial successes as *The Bowery, The House of Rothschild, Cardinal Richelieu,* and *Bulldog Drummond Strikes Back.* By the end of the decade 20th Century–Fox had expanded into a $60 million studio and was turning out some of Hollywood's biggest box-office attractions.[38]

Hollywood's list of producers who turned to Bank of America for financial assistance grew larger and reached outside the industry's small circle of movie moguls. Among the producers was David Selznick, the brash and talented son-in-law of Louis B. Mayer, head of MGM. Selznick's financial ties to Giannini predated his years at MGM. In the 1920s Selznick had moved from Paramount to become head of production at RKO, where he had played a critical role in developing some of the studio's most successful early films, including *Bill of Divorcement* and *King Kong*. Both films had been financed with Bank of America money. After replacing Irving Thalberg as production boss at MGM in 1932, the energetic Selznick went on to greater heights, turning out such screen classics as *David Copperfield, Dinner at Eight, Anna Karenina,* and *Viva Villa*.[39]

In 1935 Selznick resigned from MGM to start his own production studio, which he named Selznick International Pictures. The following year he paid $50,000 for film rights to Margaret Mitchell's yet unpublished first novel, *Gone with the Wind*. Six months into production, the cost of filming the movie had far exceeded the money Selznick had been able to obtain from private investors. Unable to secure additional financing, Selznick turned to Bank of America. In the fall of 1935 Giannini paid a visit to the production set in Culver City, liked what he saw, and authorized a loan of $1.5 million.[40] Of course, *Gone with the Wind* turned out to be an enormous box-office sensation and launched the Bank of America as the major financier of other Selznick films, including *A Tale of Two Cities, The Prisoner of Zenda, The Adventures of Tom Sawyer,* and *A Star Is Born*.[41]

Another Hollywood beneficiary of Bank of America's aggressive lending policies in the 1930s was Samuel Goldwyn, Jr., the tenacious, balding, flamboyant president of Samuel Goldwyn Productions.[42] Giannini's relationship with Goldwyn dated back to 1925, when the Bank of Italy provided the loans for a string of Goldwyn successes, including *Arrowsmith, Stella Dallas,* and *The Winning of Barbara Worth*. In 1932, at the height of the depression, Goldwyn borrowed $1 million from Bank of America to produce *The Kid from Spain,* starring Eddie Cantor.[43] The picture was a huge commercial success. Shortly afterward Giannini authorized a $4 million line of credit to Goldwyn Productions, part of which Goldwyn used to produce the *Goldwyn Follies* in 1938 and later the Academy Award–winning *Wuthering Heights*.[44]

Increasingly, a succession of Hollywood producers became dependent on Bank of America for outside financing. None leaned more heavily on Bank of America than Walt Disney, the gifted, workaholic producer of animated cartoons. In the early 1920s Disney had used a number of small loans from the Bank of Italy to produce his highly popular but only modestly profitable short-feature Mickey Mouse "Steamboat Willie" cartoons and later *The Three Little Pigs*.[45] Along the way Disney acquired the reputation of being a "spender" and a "perfectionist" whose uncompromising commitment to high-quality productions kept his small studio in Hollywood deep in the red throughout the 1920s and into the 1930s.[46]

After a trip to Paris in the spring of 1935, Disney began to play around with the idea of making Hollywood's first full-length animated cartoon based on an old Grimms' fairy tale called "Little Snow White."[47] Disney pushed rapidly ahead with the project during the summer of 1936, allocating $50,000 of the studio's money for its completion. As usual, he spared no expense in his efforts to achieve greater heights of animated moviemaking. By the end of the year the projected total cost for the movie's photography, musical score, and tens of thousands of individual drawings had climbed to $500,000, a sum far in excess of Disney's ability to pay. There seemed no alternative but to shut down production.

In desperation, Disney turned to Attilio Giannini, who had moved from New York to Los Angeles to become chairman of Bank of America's regional headquarters office in southern California. Unimpressed with the Grimm story and certain that few moviegoers would pay the price of a ticket to sit through a full-length animated cartoon, Attilio turned him down.[48] Undaunted, Disney traveled to San Francisco to take his case personally to A. P. Giannini. After listening to Disney's frantic plea for support, Giannini approved his request for a loan of $630,000.[49] The story later made the rounds that, although Giannini had always been one of Disney's most enthusiastic supporters, his decision was motivated in no small part by the pleasure it provided him in overruling his brother. "My father and his brother disliked each other and never saw eye to eye on anything," Giannini's daughter would remember years later. "When the Doctor refused Disney the loan, my father saw another opportunity to disagree with him."[50]

Snow White cost Giannini and Bank of America executives in Los Angeles some anxious moments. The movie continued to run up huge production costs, which the bank supported. By the fall of 1937 Bank of America's investment in the movie had reached what was then a staggering figure of $1.7 million—the largest individual movie loan any bank in the nation had ever undertaken. In Hollywood accounting terms, this meant that Snow White would have to earn a total gross of

$2.7 million before it could even begin to show a profit. As one senior Bank of America executive in Los Angeles later remembered, "Giannini and Disney knew that *Snow White* was a huge gamble. Had *Snow White* not succeeded, the loss would have bankrupted Disney and hurt the Bank of America enormously."[51]

Rushing to get *Snow White* into theaters in time for the 1937 Christmas season, Disney suddenly found himself in need of an additional $250,000. Alarmed by the huge amount of money that had already gone into the movie's completion, Joseph Rosenberg, a Bank of America senior loan executive who handled the Disney account in Los Angeles, insisted on seeing a print of the movie. Disney later remembered the event as a "nightmare." The movie was still in black and white; many of the scenes were still uncompleted. Rosenberg remained silent during the showing. Later, after walking with Disney to the studio's parking lot and climbing behind the wheel of his car, he turned and spoke the first full sentence Disney had heard from him the entire afternoon. "Goodbye," Rosenberg said. "That thing is going to make a hatful of money." Disney got the loan.[52]

Rosenberg's prediction proved to be something of an understatement. On Christmas Day in 1937, *Snow White* opened at New York's Radio City Music Hall and was an immediate box-office sensation, grossing more than $22 million during its first coast-to-coast showing. *Snow White*'s remarkable success marked a turning point in Disney's moviemaking career as well as in his business relationship with Bank of America. Bank of America went on to finance Disney's next three full-length animated cartoons—*Fantasia, Pinocchio,* and *Dumbo*—and the construction of his new $2.5 million production studio in Burbank.[53]

Throughout the decade of the 1930s and well into the 1940s, Bank of America assumed a larger and larger position of financial leadership in Hollywood, generating handsome profits for the bank and enormous revenues for the movie industry. The list of films financed by Bank of America included such box-office hits as *Cleopatra, Union Pacific* (both by DeMille), *It Happened One Night, Lost Horizons, Mr. Smith Goes to Washington* (Columbia), *Trade Winds* (Walter Wagner), *King Kong* (RKO), *Frankenstein* (Universal), *The Barretts of Wimpole Street,* and *Mutiny on the Bounty* (MGM).[54] In the three years from 1936 to 1939 alone, Bank of America's total loans to the movie business amounted to $55 million; five years later this figure had more than doubled, reaching $136 million.[55]

By spreading more money around than Hollywood had seen in over a decade, Giannini increased the presence of his bank in the motion picture industry enormously. By the late 1940s accounting reports showed that Bank of America loans to independent filmmakers and the major studios—United Artists, Columbia, RKO, 20th Century–Fox, and Warner Brothers—amounted to an incredible $306 million.[56] The inclusion in Bank of America's executive ranks of movie moguls like Schenck, Mayer, Goldwyn, and DeMille as directors or as advisory board members also meant that the payroll accounts of Hollywood's major studios and their more than twenty thousand actors, actresses, designers, construction crews, and other employees would be deposited in the Bank of America.[57] As one industry reporter put it, "The Bank of America was clearly Hollywood's bank."[58]

The key to Bank of America's remarkable comeback and subsequent growth through the decade of the 1930s was not the movie industry, however, but installment financing. By the mid-1930s tight money had created a soaring demand for credit among Americans generally. Partly to satisfy this need, the New Deal had in 1935 sponsored the Federal Housing Act, title I of which guaranteed repayment to banks of loans advanced for home modernization and improvement.[59] The attraction of guaranteed profits was strong, but even with government backing most bankers were reluctant to get involved with installment credit. As a consequence, short-term credit continued to be handled by the nation's more than seventeen thousand independent finance companies at interest rates of between 10 and 30 percent.[60]

Giannini was no stranger to installment credit. One month before the Wall Street crash of 1929 Bank of America had introduced a personal loan department, offering short-term credit to borrowers in amounts ranging from $100 to $1,000. At the end of the first year of operation the total dollar amount of these loans was just over $750,000; thereafter, the results were impressive. Three years later an internal Bank of America audit showed that nearly 200,000 Californians had borrowed a total of approximately $12 million in small, personal loans, with almost no loss to the bank through failure of borrowers to repay.[61]

Giannini quickly saw in the title I provision of the Federal Housing Act an exciting opportunity to aggressively expand this new line of credit. Under a trademark called Timeplan, Bank of America soon began offering installment credit to finance the purchase of such highly sought after consumer goods as stoves, washing machines, vacuum cleaners, refrigerators, and other household appliances. "There is a heavy demand for bank credit which heretofore have [sic] not been regarded by bankers in general as being an effective outlet for loans," he told a group of reporters in San Francisco. "There is money to be made by those bankers who are willing to modify lending policies and recognize the credit standing of the individual."[62]

Giannini's decision to take the aggressive route on installment credit paid handsome dividends. According to an internal Bank of America report dated February 1940, the total dollar amount of these loans had jumped from $22 million in December 1935 to $95 million in December 1937—more than a fourfold increase.[63] Two years later the total dollar amount of Bank of America's small loans stood at $313 million in approximately 278,000 new loans—well over half the total number of loans and nearly half the total dollar amount of all other banks in the state combined.[64]

Giannini was by no means depending entirely on short-term installment credit. Long-term borrowing under the title II provisions of the Federal Housing Act became an increasingly important source of Bank of America's revenues.[65] Title II was intended to revive the nation's sagging housing industry by insuring banks against losses on loans to families who wanted to remodel their homes or to build new ones. As usual, Giannini wasted no time in grabbing the lion's share of the market. Bank of America invested large sums of money in advertising: billboards, posters, newspapers, and radio commercials.[66] In the first year that the Federal Housing Administration (FHA) was in operation, the bank's advertising department spent a total of $500,000. As one FHA regional director in California commented, "We estimate that this institution has expended more money in advertising . . . than it can hope to make out of the loans it has granted."[67]

Giannini's success in selling FHA loans to an eager public was reflected by the astonishing degree to which Bank of America soon came to dominate the market. By 1938, three years after passage of the Federal Housing Act, Bank of America had put $94 million into the hands of 163,000 home buyers; five years later total loans had climbed to $270 million.[68] This figure represented 44 percent of the entire FHA market in California, or eight times the average for banks throughout the rest of the country. By contrast, Giannini's closest competitor for FHA loans in the state was Sartori's Security First, which managed only 17 percent of the market.[69]

Other kinds of installment borrowing quickly followed Bank of America's success with its home modernization and FHA loans. In 1936, against the angry and well-organized opposition of finance companies, the bank began offering installment credit to finance the purchase of automobiles. The demand for the loans at far more favorable rates than buyers had been required to pay from finance companies was astonishing. In only two years the total annual volume of these loans more than doubled, from $20 million in 1936 to just over $49 million in 1938—second only to GMAC, the General Motors subsidiary, in new car financing.[70] As the *San Francisco Examiner* explained, "When Bank of America announced its policy on automobiles at 6 percent the finance companies all over the nation had to come down off their high horses and make much lower rates," adding that Giannini "has saved the people of the United States millions of dollars."[71]

By the early 1940s Bank of America had emerged as California's undisputed leader in consumer credit, with a total loan volume more than half that of all other banks in the state combined.[72] "A veritable department-store bank," said one East Coast financial writer. "It will finance a new home, lend money to cover the medical expense of the new baby born there, see him through college, discount his business notes, sell him insurance or traveler's checks when he needs a vacation. When he dies, it will execute his will. It's a bank that does everything but blow your nose for you."[73]

3

Unfortunately for Giannini, his efforts at increasing the number of Bank of America branches in California was not succeeding nearly as well. Toward the end of 1936 he submitted applications to the comptroller of the currency to open thirty new branch offices, many located in rural towns that offered only minimal banking services.[74] Then he began expanding his banking operations outside California—a path that intensified the concern of his competition. He quickly acquired a dozen or more national banks in four of the seven states—Oregon, Washington, Nevada, Arizona—that constituted the banking system's Twelfth Federal Reserve district. In doing so, Giannini had laid the foundation for a districtwide network of branches along the entire Pacific coast and into two states in the Southwest.[75]

In Washington, J. F. T. O'Connor faced a dilemma. He was acutely aware of Bank of America's organizational strength as a force in Democratic politics in the state. But from California, as elsewhere, O'Connor had come under intense pressure from independent bankers to stem Bank of America's unrelenting advance. Their goal was to prevent—by whatever means necessary—Bank of America's further expansion. After three weeks of stalling, O'Connor decided to approve only some of Giannini's new branch permits, restricting Bank of America's expansion to towns with limited or no banking services.[76]

Giannini was not pleased. Privately he accused O'Connor of pandering to the political alliances in Congress fostered by the independents. In a complaining letter to Farley on October 4, 1936, Giannini made a similar argument. Not only was O'Connor's partial approval of his applications for additional branch permits a short-sighted capitulation to outside pressures, but it was also inconsistent with the New Deal's own much-publicized efforts at putting larger amounts of money into the hands of working-class people. In California, O'Connor's approach would result in slower economic growth. "In many of the towns where we were denied permits," Giannini told Farley, "the other banks do not give federal housing modernization, personal and automobile services and the many other services that our institution gives . . . and these small banks cannot."[77]

With characteristic bluntness, Giannini reminded Farley that Bank of America's expansion into the towns and cities of California had proven to be of considerable value to the administration's political efforts in the state; if Farley could intervene with administration officials to change O'Connor's mind, Democratic party success in the future would be even more certain. "Needless to tell you also, Jim," Giannini said, "that our entry into any town means additional friends for our cause. . . . So, Jim, I should appreciate anything you could do in your own diplomatic way to put these permits through for us without getting 'Jeffy' down on us."[78]

Farley agreed to do what he could, and a few days later he sent a personal appeal to the comptroller's office; but O'Connor held his ground and rejected that as well. "It seems to me," he informed Farley, "that Mr. Giannini should be well pleased at the receptions met by applications of his bank to establish branches since I took office as Comptroller of the Currency."[79]

Although deeply disappointed, Giannini continued to press ahead with his far more ambitious objective: the building of a network of

Bank of America branches within the regional boundaries of the nation's Twelfth Federal Reserve district. "You can't hold this country back," he told Merryle Rukeyser in an interview with the nationally syndicated financial columnist. "Population is moving steadily westward and business has to grow with it. . . . More and more [of] the nation's industries are building plants here. The whole countryside is rich with mineral resources, untapped, and waiting for human enterprise, courage and hard work. Branch banking is a demonstrated success. . . . Let's just keep going ahead."[80]

By the spring of 1937 two proposals aimed at achieving this goal had already taken shape in San Francisco. The first, which would drastically transform the whole of the nation's banking system, was a draft bill modeled closely on the embryonic plans which Giannini had formulated in the late 1920s but which Elisha Walker had later scrapped.[81] Introduced in the Senate by William McAdoo on May 7, 1937, the bill would permit national banks, with the approval of the comptroller of the currency, to open branches within the boundaries of the reserve district in which the parent bank had its headquarters.[82] Passage of the McAdoo legislation would enable Giannini to convert the "independent" national banks he was operating in Washington, Oregon, Nevada, and Arizona into branches of his giant California-based Bank of America system, thus creating in the process the nation's first interstate regional bank.

The second proposal, unanimously approved at a special meeting of Transamerica's board of directors one week later, called for distributing approximately 58 percent of Bank of America's stock among the corporation's 220,000 shareholders.[83] "The day of bank holding companies is gone," Giannini told reporters, who questioned him about his decision to put the stock back into the hands of many of its original owners. "If branch banking is legalized throughout each Federal Reserve District . . . Transamerica will be in a position to establish one of the first districtwide banking systems. The corporation now is interested in national banks in all of the seven states comprising the twelfth Federal Reserve District, except Utah and Idaho."[84]

The reaction of independent bankers across the country to Giannini's plan for districtwide branch banking was intense and immediate. A powerful stream of angry denunciations and protesting letters poured into Congress. In more than twenty states the independents swiftly gained the support of banking superintendents, who regarded districtwide branch banking as an unacceptable threat to their own authority and decision-making powers. "Mr. Giannini's program shall not prevail," a spokesman for the national association of supervisors of state banks announced at a hastily called press conference in Washington on May 16, 1937. "If necessary, we shall summon every state supervisor in the Union to the capital."[85]

In California the independents mobilized their resources for a tough fight, calling McAdoo's interstate banking bill "a further diminution if not elimination of state banking autonomy." Pledging themselves to oppose with every means at their disposal "wider forms of branch banking than now exist," members of the Association of Independent Bankers of San Francisco's Twelfth Federal Reserve District met in San Francisco to adopt a series of resolutions aimed at "preserving the dual system of state and national banks."[86] As the *New York Herald Tribune* explained it, McAdoo's bill "unified, vocalized and energized the forces opposing branch banking as no other single development has in recent years."[87]

For the nation's small independent bankers the issue went deeper still, to New Deal legislation that had contributed in various ways to the consolidating power of bank holding companies, which they believed had begun with the banking bill of 1933. They found sympathetic listeners in the halls of Congress, the most vigorous, outspoken, and politically resourceful of whom was C. Wright Patman, congressman from Texas and a member of the House Committee on Banking and Currency. Disturbed by what he described as the great "domestic evil" of concentrated wealth, Patman called for the strict regulation of bank holding companies in an effort to protect the independents from the seemingly unlimited power of their branch banking competitors.

Giannini, of course, had expected powerful opposition to the McAdoo bill. During the summer of 1937 Bank of America's Washington lobbyists scrambled to work for its passage. Entirely unexpected, however, was the reaction of Leo Crowley, chairman of the New Deal's newly created Federal Deposit Insurance Corporation (FDIC), who quickly emerged as a vigorous opponent of the bill's passage.[88] According to Washington insiders, Crowley, an outspoken critic of the rapid drift throughout the country toward branch banking, had been shocked to learn on assuming the chairmanship of the FDIC that $400 million of the country's $800 million in savings deposits was located in just one bank—Giannini's Bank of America. "If you let Giannini on the loose," he reportedly remarked to aides, "he'd have a thousand banks under his belt before you could say 'stop.' That would kill the little independent banks."[89]

On May 24, 1938, Crowley arrived in Del Mar, California, to address the annual convention of the California Bankers Association. His speech included a harsh attack against the spread of branch banking, which he believed represented a dangerous consolidation of financial power in the hands of a few and a threat to the survival of small-town bankers. "As insurer of the safety of deposits," Crowley said, "the corporation believes that some limits must be placed upon the number of offices and upon the extent of control over banking resources in a given area that are permitted to any corporate entity, be it branch bank or holding company."[90] No one in the audience had any difficulty in identifying Crowley's euphemism "corporate entity" as Giannini's Bank of America.

Informed of Crowley's remarks, Giannini sent a telegram to the FDIC chairman protesting the impact his "unfounded and wildly exaggerated" criticism could have on an already anxious public. "Such a statement by anyone else might not have had serious effects but coming from you . . . the ground is laid for a dangerous inference that depositors' funds in a branch banking institution are not safe," he said. Giannini concluded by saying that should Crowley ever again feel the need "to carry the torch" for California's disgruntled small-town bankers, "my earnest hope is that you will base your arguments on proved facts."[91]

In the Senate, meanwhile, McAdoo and his supporters found themselves unable to muster the votes to overcome the opposition of the bill's critics. Senators were sensitive to the arguments made by Crowley and to the well-organized pressure of a powerful coalition of state banking superintendents. McAdoo withdrew his bill. Giannini felt betrayed. As a zealous supporter of the president, he wrote to Farley, he felt he had earned the right to expect better treatment from administration officials. "May I venture to say, Jim," he said, "I hope you will see to it that true and loyal friends of the administration such as we have been are given a square deal by the government agencies and that they do not go out of their way to harass us, particularly since our reputation for integrity and square dealing is of the highest."[92]

Giannini was disillusioned by the prominent role played by Crowley and other New Deal officials in opposing passage of the McAdoo bill. He was careful, however, to disguise his resentment with renewed pledges to administration figures of continued support and cooperation. "I want you to know," he wrote to Eccles on May 27, 1938, "that you can count on me as ready and willing to serve you and the administration in any way that I consistently can."[93] Privately, however, Giannini made it clear to his executives in San Francisco that what he expected from the White House was a vastly more helpful response to his interstate branch banking ambitions. If he could not succeed in getting that, he was prepared to withdraw his support.

SIXTEEN

Morgenthau Finds a Target

I

Giannini had not been idle during the months when McAdoo was mobilizing his forces in the Senate in support of his districtwide branch banking bill. Throughout the winter of 1937 Giannini had been waiting eagerly for the opportunity to push his banking operations into farm communities yet untouched by his vast network of Bank of America branches.[1] Toward the end of the year he filed a formal application with the comptroller of the currency for permission to open a half-dozen or so new branch offices, beginning with Pinole and Gonzales, two farm towns in northern California.[2] On January 3, 1938, O'Connor gave his "conditional" approval to the Pinole and Gonzales permits, "subject to opening for business during month of January 1938."[3]

A short time later Giannini learned that O'Connor had decided to leave the administration to enter the Democratic primary in California for the party's gubernatorial nomination.[4] Concerned about the status of his Pinole and Gonzales permits, Giannini sent a telegram to Zachariah Cobb, a former national bank examiner who had recently joined Bank of America's team of Washington lobbyists, with instructions to step up the pressure on O'Connor in obtaining formal approval. "Glad to learn Jeffy has thrown his hat in the ring," Giannini wrote. "Hope you will see to it that Jeffy doesn't leave office until after he has squared accounts with us."[5]

As it turned out, O'Connor left Washington in March 1938 without taking final action. For weeks Giannini sought to learn about the status of his permits from Marshall Diggs, a former administrative assistant in the Treasury Department whom Morgenthau had appointed as acting comptroller. "Our premises are completed and ready," Giannini informed Diggs in a telegram on May 4, 1938.[6] "The townspeople are impatient of delay. I shall appreciate it if you would review your files to see if you do not think we are entitled to receive the charters and open for business."[7]

Two months went by. No answer came. The long delay seriously jeopardized Giannini's expansionist objectives in California, joined as they were to his larger and far more ambitious plan for districtwide branch banking. On June 7, 1938, he sent an urgent appeal for assistance to William McAdoo. "We are still being put off from day to day without definite answers," he wrote. "Please talk with Secretary of the Treasury direct."[8]

A short time later McAdoo informed Giannini that his efforts at obtaining the information about the permits had gone nowhere. Diggs had not been available for comment, and officials in the comptroller's office refused to talk about the status of the pending permits without first obtaining the acting comptroller's approval.[9] Frustrated and annoyed by the continuing delay, Giannini turned to the man whom he considered his most powerful ally in Washington—the president himself. "Without criticizing anyone," Giannini wrote to Marvin McIntyre, Roosevelt's personal secretary, on July 5, 1938, "I am writing to ask that you talk with Secretary Morgenthau and convey to him my request that he give these applications personal consideration at the earliest time. . . . I wish you would also inform the President that our joint efforts have gone a long way toward sustaining and increasing business in California."[10]

Henry Morgenthau, Jr., the austere, humorless, self-righteous but also extremely conscientious and hard-working secretary of the treasury, had no sympathy for Giannini's predicament. The son of a wealthy New York real estate executive and a close personal friend of Roosevelt from the president's Hyde Park days, Morgenthau had entered the administration in 1933 as head of the Federal Farm Board.[11] A little more than a year later Roosevelt appointed him to replace William Woodin as secretary of the treasury. Although Morgenthau had only scant knowledge of banking matters, he adhered to a theory for restructuring the nation's credit system that favored locally owned independent banks against the excessive consolidating power of large financial institutions.[12] Bank holding companies like Transamerica were obvious targets.

Beginning in the summer of 1937, Morgenthau had been spending hours conferring with staff members about Bank of America's latest examination report, which had identified a multitude of loan losses and problem loans, particularly in "frozen" real estate.[13] Satisfied that a lack of adequate reserves to cover these losses posed a serious threat to the safety of Bank of America's depositors and stockholders, Morgenthau decided to take strong action. He would insist, he told aides, that Bank of America take immediate steps to improve its financial condition, beginning with the demand that management "either increase its capital or cut its dividends in half."[14]

As head of a cabinet department that had supervisory authority over the Office of the Comptroller of the Currency (OCC), Morgenthau was also extremely critical of what he perceived as a serious dereliction of duty over the years on the part of OCC officials in their dealings with Giannini. At a departmental staff meeting sometime toward the end of 1937, Morgenthau complained to aides that in view of Bank of America's large portfolio of bad loans, he was appalled by the apparent reluctance of federal regulators to take prompt and decisive action in correcting the situation. He accused officials in the comptroller's office of "acting like a bunch of sissies" in allowing Giannini to "run rings around" the examiner's recommendations, thus making the agency look foolish and ineffective.

Morgenthau decided to take charge of a more vigorous supervision of Bank of America himself. Given Bank of America's lack of adequate reserves, Morgenthau told aides at a departmental staff meeting on July 8, 1938, he would not under any circumstances permit Giannini to use current earnings for the purpose of paying dividends. Such a step on the part of Bank of America's management would expose its depositors and stockholders to a potentially serious risk. Giannini's persistent complaints to the comptroller's office about his Pinole and Gonzales permits made no impression on Morgenthau. He was, he said, "personally inclined to 'sit until Hell freezes over' before doing anything in the way of permitting additional branches."[15]

By the spring of 1938 Morgenthau and his aides in the Treasury Department had put together a confidential report critical of Bank of America's aggressive management practices and financial condition. Morgenthau forwarded the report to William O. Douglas, the young,

brash, former Yale Law School professor who had only recently succeeded James M. Landis as chairman of the Securities and Exchange
Commission (SEC).[16] A vigorous and outspoken critic of fraudulent
practices in Wall Street's bank investment and securities business, Douglas had been summoned to Washington a few years earlier to assist the
SEC in bringing reform and financial stability to the stock market.[17]
After assuming the chairmanship of the commission, Douglas lost no
time in leading "the SEC on a crusade" and his "hostility to the 'goddam
bankers' was scathing and passionate."[18]

Douglas, in turn, notified Morgenthau that as part of a broader and
wide-ranging investigation into the financial transactions of some of the
nation's biggest bank holding companies, the SEC for the past several
weeks had been focusing its attention on Giannini's Transamerica Corporation. Although the investigation was still in its earliest stages,
Douglas said, SEC investigators had already uncovered evidence of
abuse of power and financial irregularities on the part of the corporation's management, including the filing of false and misleading information in December 1937 with the New York Stock Exchange.
"It's fragmentary, but it looks very bad," Douglas said.[19]

Morgenthau asked Douglas to keep him informed about the progress
of the SEC investigation, and a few weeks later the two men met privately to discuss the case. Morgenthau pushed for a full-blown investigation of Transamerica and Bank of America. He told Douglas there
was absolutely no doubt in his mind that the evidence that had been
developed thus far by officials in his department warranted prompt
and aggressive government intervention. Douglas agreed, but complained that the SEC was severely handicapped in its investigative
capacity, primarily because Bank of America's confidential examination reports were available only to the OCC and to the treasury.[20]

To assist the SEC in the pursuit of its investigation, Morgenthau took
the highly unusual step of furnishing Douglas with Bank of America's
confidential examination reports, a copy of which he had obtained
from Diggs in the OCC. He also gave Douglas full authority to make
"relevant portions" of the information in the reports public in any
claim the SEC might eventually decide to file against Transamerica.[21]

Not everyone at the treasury agreed with Morgenthau's decision to
force a showdown with Giannini over Bank of America's dividend
policy. Some staff members thought this approach both hardheaded
and excessive. They concluded that the department would be more
likely to get better results by adopting, as one Morgenthau aide put it

in an interoffice memorandum, a less "extreme primitive" solution to the problem.[22] "The situation *must* be cleared up," the aide continued, but suggested that "it may be wise to permit a certain amount of face saving. Expecting Giannini to reduce his dividend all at once . . . is foolhardy, perhaps." But Morgenthau rejected their recommendations. The time had come, he said, when "prompt steps [must] be taken with reference to the Bank of America" in correcting a situation "very much to be worried about."[23]

It was not until July 11, 1938, that Giannini finally heard about the status of his Pinole and Gonzales permits. For whatever reasons, the news came not from Diggs himself but from Marvin McIntyre, who had received a telegram from the acting comptroller in response to the inquiry Giannini had asked McIntyre to make a few weeks earlier. Diggs told McIntyre that his office could not give formal approval to the permits until Giannini took the appropriate steps in eliminating the loan losses that had appeared in Bank of America's latest examination report. McIntyre sent a copy of Diggs's telegram to Giannini, which said in part, "This office cannot act until estimated losses have been charged off."[24]

Giannini, who had obtained a copy of the preliminary examination report two months earlier, had already written to Diggs complaining that the field examiner's evaluation of Bank of America's loan portfolio had been incompetent at best and malicious at worst. "The examiner was in error in the warped picture of the bank's condition presented in the report," Giannini said. "Knowing the condition of the bank as well as I do . . . the writer of the last report either failed to make a proper study of certain matters which he has seen fit to criticize, or he has concocted problems for reasons best known to himself."[25]

As for the denial of his permits, Giannini charged that the unreasonably harsh stance taken by the OCC could not be justified in view of Bank of America's profit gains and strong capital structure. "While certain gross errors in the report could be attributed to lack of understanding on the part of the examiner," Giannini told Diggs, "it has become increasingly apparent to me that the management of this bank is being subjected to undue criticism. . . . Slight consideration is given to the fact that since 1932, not only has the management overcome obstacles that were generally viewed as insurmountable but has carried the institution forward . . . and this in the face of economic conditions which it must be admitted have not favored such an advance."[26]

With the delay on his Gonzales and Pinole permits now moving into its sixth month, Giannini sent Russell Smith, Bank of America's cashier and one of his most valuable senior executives, to Washington. Giannini instructed Smith "to clear up any misunderstanding" over the examination report with Diggs and officials in the Treasury Department. Diggs would later claim that in his meetings with Smith, he had been sharply critical of Bank of America's financial condition and had put off further discussion of Giannini's branch permits "until some $6 million in losses were charged off."[27]

Smith's version of what had transpired in Washington was much different. Smith told Giannini that the day after his arrival in the city, he discussed the disputed examination report with Diggs; later that same afternoon he met with Cyril Upham, Morgenthau's personal assistant on banking matters. The next day, Smith said, he went "round and round" with E. H. Gough, the deputy comptroller of the currency. Gough eventually agreed to reduce Bank of America's alleged credit losses from $6 million to $220,000. Later that same day Smith again met with Diggs, who approved of the reduction and expressed his satisfaction with the terms of the settlement.[28]

"I talked with the acting comptroller," Smith wrote in his report to Giannini, "who gave me assurance that he would discuss our pending branch applications with the Secretary of the Treasury, advising him that the current examination report had been satisfactorily closed, and recommend that everything was all right and I might expect favorable action very soon."[29]

Diggs's promise of "favorable action very soon," however, quickly gave way to new pessimism in San Francisco. More than a month after Smith's return from Washington, Giannini was still waiting for approval from the comptroller's office to open his Gonzales and Pinole branches. Giannini was furious. What made the situation all the more intolerable was Smith's earlier assurance, reinforced by copious notes he had taken in his meetings with Diggs, that the acting comptroller of the currency had given his unqualified approval to the outcome of the negotiations with Gough and Upham and had conferred his blessings on the permits.

With Diggs still unexpectedly intransigent, Giannini became more and more suspicious as the weeks went by; he soon concluded that Secretary Morgenthau was insisting on withholding the permits. On July 11, 1938, Giannini expressed his exasperation to Marvin McIntyre in a telegram that he undoubtedly wanted to reach the president. Despite the fact that he had "satisfactorily disposed" of the comptroller's complaints about "certain items" in Bank of America's examination report, he wrote, "the Treasury has seen fit to withhold the bank's applications." Giannini added that if McIntyre had any knowledge of "further complaints" from the Treasury Department, "please wire me specifically items concerned so that we can clear the way for immediate granting of long pending permit applications."[30]

Despite the conciliatory tone of this telegram, a chill was beginning to develop in the once close and mutually advantageous relationship between Giannini and the White House. On the same day he sent his telegram to McIntyre, Giannini was in Los Angeles when an aide informed him that he had received an invitation from Democratic officials in San Francisco to attend a luncheon for Roosevelt, who was scheduled to arrive in the city in a few days to attend the opening of the Golden Gate Exposition. "Shall I send some nice roses to the president's private car for you?" the aide cabled from San Francisco.[31] "Never mind the roses," Giannini replied. "Extend my sincere regrets."[32]

In Pinole and Gonzales, meanwhile, Bank of America's newly constructed branch offices sat empty and closed, a situation that prompted one senior executive to suggest to Giannini that tenants be found to eliminate the expense of carrying the unused buildings.[33] Giannini defiantly dismissed this recommendation. "Definitely nothing doing," he said. "Our institution didn't get where it is today by giving up so readily. We will be in there some day."[34]

2

Meanwhile, of the list of complaints being compiled by Morgenthau in Washington as an indictment of Giannini and the Bank of America, other items had to do with the shocking mistreatment of farmworkers in California.[35] Morgenthau's allegations dated back to the mid-1930s, when low prices and overproduction turned farm labor into a vicious cycle of debt and chronic unemployment.[36] These conditions were worsened in turn by the unexpected presence of some 300,000 migrant workers who had moved into the state, most of them refugees from the "dust bowl" regions of Arkansas, Oklahoma, and

Texas. By 1934 farmworkers had organized themselves into an independent union for winning wage demands and other concessions with a series of spontaneous strikes throughout the state's agricultural valleys.[37]

California growers responded with a powerful movement to crush the farmworkers' union and defeat its demands. Spearheading the growers' efforts was Associated Farmers, an organization dominated by large landowners whose militant and often violent union-busting activities were financed by many of the most powerful business and corporate interests in the state.[38] Although Giannini privately disapproved of the tactics and demands of the farmworkers' union, he ignored the requests for financial contributions from Bank of America's biggest corporate and agribusiness clients involved with Associated Farmers. He passed the word to his regional executives and branch managers instructing them not to involve themselves or Bank of America in the activities of the organization.[39]

But Giannini's efforts to distance Bank of America from the crisis in the countryside turned out to be unsuccessful. The bank soon became the target of a storm of angry criticism and accusations from extremist groups that found in California's largest and most powerful financial institution a convenient symbol for their populist or socialist rhetoric.[40] Communist party leaders, some of whose members had managed to infiltrate the farmworkers' union, led the attack. *People's World*, the organ of the Communist party, accused Giannini and Bank of America of secretly financing an "unholy war on labor" by granting credit to farmers "contingent upon membership in Associated Farmers."[41]

Far more damaging to Bank of America were the charges contained in two books, the first and most sensational of which was John Steinbeck's best-selling novel *Grapes of Wrath*, which appeared in the spring of 1939. The villains in Steinbeck's melodramatic account of the Joad family's brutal struggle for survival in California were many, but chief among them was the ubiquitous and enormously powerful "Bank of the West."[42] ("This vineyard will belong to the Bank," says one of its spokesmen in the novel. "Only the great owners can survive.")[43] Although Steinbeck had been careful to depict the forces of capitalism arrayed against migrant farm families like the Joads in a broad and inclusive way, many readers instantly recognized his fictitious "Bank of the West" as a thinly veiled disguise for Giannini's Bank of America.

Not long after the publication of Steinbeck's *Grapes of Wrath* came Carey McWilliams's *Factories in the Field*, an incisive, passionately written, nonfiction examination of the "vicious, undemocratic and thoroughly anti-social system of land ownership" in California. In his brutal portrayal of conditions in the state's "feudalistic pattern" of farm labor, McWilliams, a Los Angeles attorney and prominent left-wing political activist, was harshly critical of Bank of America's alleged ties with the state's powerful agribusiness interests.[44] "When one realizes," McWilliams wrote in a widely reprinted passage of his book, "that approximately 50 per cent of the farm lands in Central and Northern California are controlled by one institution—the Bank of America— the irony of these 'embattled' farmers defending their 'homes' against shysters becomes apparent."[45]

In the months following publication of the Steinbeck and McWilliams books, Giannini and the Bank of America came under sharp criticism from a national press sympathetic to the plight of California's struggling migrant workers. The New York Times condemned "the wholesale injustice" in the treatment of farmworkers and deplored the manner in which California had "succumbed to a kind of fascism."[46] On the Berkeley campus of the University of California, hundreds of students gathered to protest Bank of America's "brutal exploitation of farm workers." Splashed across the pages of the campus newspaper, the Daily Bruin, were excerpts from McWilliams's book. McWilliams himself was identified as a "reliable authority" whose careful and meticulous gathering of evidence "provided plenty of proof" to indict Giannini and the Bank of America for their complicity in the oppression of farm workers.[47]

In San Francisco, Bank of America's senior executives were outraged over the Steinbeck-McWilliams allegations. They reserved their harshest criticism for McWilliams, a highly respected scholar and the author of previous works on California history. In mounting his sensational and well-publicized accusations against Bank of America, McWilliams had not bothered to check his figures with the bank or to consult the statistical data on farm mortgages in Sacramento. In fact, Bank of America held mortgages on only 3.6 percent of farmland in northern and central California—considerably less than the 50 percent McWilliams had claimed in his book. In a personal letter to Mario Giannini, McWilliams later admitted his "mistake" and apologized for his allegations, but the damage had been done.[48]

The public uproar infuriated Giannini, tarnishing as it did his and Bank of America's reputation. He contacted the New York public relations firm of Bernays and Bernays with plans for a nationwide counterattack.[49] But aides urged against this course of action. Given the enormous popular appeal of *Grapes of Wrath* in particular, any effort on the part of Bank of America to refute Steinbeck's and McWilliams's allegations in a public forum would be a hopeless mismatch. "We could not hope to reach the same audience Steinbeck did," one Giannini executive wrote in a confidential interoffice memorandum. "Our strategy should be to lie low rather than to muddy the waters by aggressive action on our part."[50] Once this point had been sufficiently impressed on him, Giannini abandoned his plans.

As public outrage over the struggle of California's farmworkers intensified, there were signs that the unfavorable publicity surrounding the Steinbeck-McWilliams allegations had become something of an embarrassment to the White House. On March 17, 1939, James Roosevelt, the president's oldest son, cabled Mario Giannini to inquire about the allegations of a financial link between Bank of America and Associated Farmers. "Any statement accusing the bank of an unfair attitude toward labor is malicious and untrue," Mario replied. "We have never loaned or donated so much as one dollar to Associated Farmers."[51] A few days later Roosevelt replied that he had discussed the entire matter with his father, who was satisfied with Mario's explanation.[52]

Not everyone around Roosevelt was similarly satisfied. Reports soon reached Giannini that Morgenthau was spreading the story in administration circles that Bank of America had joined forces with California's agribusiness interests and had "furnished thousands of dollars to finance Associated Farmers."[53] Giannini was furious and complained to aides that Morgenthau had apparently embarked on a smear campaign to discredit him and the Bank of America organization with the administration. His suspicions were confirmed a short time later in a coded telegram from Louis Ferrari. Ferrari told Giannini that he had learned from a highly reliable source in Washington that the "Hebrew [Morgenthau] trying to turn Roosevelt against you."[54]

To this disturbing turn of events, the Internal Revenue Service suddenly added another embarrassing charge. In May 1938 the IRS informed Giannini that he owed back taxes to the government of $220,000 on the $1.5 million "compensation" he had persuaded Bancitaly's board of directors to donate to the University of California more than a decade earlier. Giannini's response to this complaint was one of puzzlement. No mention was made in the IRS notice that the bureau itself had reviewed the terms of the donation at the time it had been made and had assured him that he owed the government no taxes. Soon thereafter

Giannini was given an explanation for the IRS's action. From Bank of America's chief tax auditor Giannini learned that two IRS agents stationed in San Francisco had reviewed the bureau's complaint before it had been sent to him and had urged cancellation of the government's claim; Morgenthau had rejected their recommendation.[55]

As was his practice in attempting to get a message to Roosevelt, Giannini immediately sent a telegram to Marvin McIntyre angrily appraising the White House of the IRS's complaint. "I don't know what's back of all this," he told McIntyre, "but I certainly am becoming thoroughly 'fed up' regarding the way we have been and are being treated." Although Giannini stopped short of saying so, he made it clear that there was no doubt in his mind who was behind the IRS's action. "The people out here pretty generally think that a mighty good job of rehabilitation has been done since that crooked New York crowd was kicked out of the picture," he went on to say, "and I'll gladly step out of the picture if there's anyone in the Comptroller's Office or the Treasury Department who think differently and will take the job."[56]

Giannini retaliated by filing a claim against the IRS.[57] His feud with tax authorities soon became the subject of a number of unflattering news stories across the state, a development that both angered and embarrassed him. In the end Giannini was victorious. The San Francisco Board of Tax Appeals decided that Giannini was not liable for back taxes on the $1.5 million contribution to the University of California, a decision upheld on appeal by the U.S. Circuit Court for the District of Columbia. "The taxpayer did not receive the money," said the court in its unanimous decision. "All that he did was unqualifiedly refuse to accept any further compensation for his services with the suggestion that the money be used for some worth while purpose."[58]

In San Francisco, Giannini received the news of his victory over the IRS with mixed emotions. He immediately instructed Bank of America's public relations department to reprint a thousand copies of the court's decision and have them distributed to newspaper editors in every city and town in California. "The decision," he wrote in a memorandum to the department's head, "gave me complete clearance and I am awfully anxious that we get as much comment as possible on it in the papers, preferably . . . editorially."[59] At the same time, he was deeply angry about having been thrust into an embarrassing controversy with the IRS in the first place. Not only his own personal integrity but also that of his wife had been thrown into question and made an issue for sensational editorial comment and ugly public gossip. For that, he blamed Morgenthau.[60]

3

On the morning of September 13, 1938, Giannini was in Los Angeles for a regular monthly meeting of the bank's board of directors. Giannini came to the meeting in an angry mood. One week earlier L. H. Sedlacek, a national bank examiner, had given Mario Giannini the preliminary results of an eight-month general examination of Bank of America produced by his team of field examiners. More forcefully than in previous examination reports, Sedlacek repeated the criticisms of the bank's financial condition: undercapitalization, a great many "frozen" real estate loans, too many large lines of credit on collateral of dubious value, and a host of lesser complaints. The report concluded: "The present liberal dividend policy, through which the bank disburses a major portion of its operating earnings, is not warranted by its asset condition."[61]

A few hours before the meeting was scheduled to convene, Mario Giannini was sitting and talking with his father when he received a phone call from Robert Palmer, an official in the comptroller's office stationed in Los Angeles. Palmer asked permission to attend the director's meeting later that day. He would, he said, be carrying a telegram from Diggs, who had instructed him to read it before the entire board.[62] Puzzled and more than a little worried by Palmer's message, Mario phoned Washington to find out from Diggs himself about the contents of the telegram, but without success. He was informed that the acting comptroller was "unavailable."[63] Not without reason, Giannini began to suspect that his enemies were plotting to take his empire away from him. He immediately phoned San Francisco and instructed Russell Smith to catch the first plane to Los Angeles, bringing with him the notes he had made during his meetings with Diggs and Upham in June.[64]

Shortly after one o'clock the meeting convened. Virtually the only item on the agenda was Bank of America's declaration of a quarterly dividend. Following the usual procedure, news of the dividend had been sent to the wire services some days earlier.[65] The board unanimously approved the dividend. A few minutes later Palmer, who had arrived late for the meeting, was ushered into the room. His manner was grave as he proceeded to read Diggs's telegram. Despite "repeated warnings" from the comptroller's office about Bank of America's dividend policy, the telegram began, "the dividend rate has been repeatedly increased." In view of "the unsatisfactory asset condition of the bank . . . [and] of real estate losses in excess of forty million dollars," Diggs said, it "is imperative that the earnings of the bank be used to write off and reduce book value of such assets."[66]

Diggs then dropped a bombshell. He told the board that if Bank of America persisted in ignoring his warnings by declaring a quarterly dividend, he would have no choice but to charge management with having purposely committed an "unsafe and unsound practice" under section 30 of the Banking Act of 1933. Diggs's threat stunned board members. Under the claim of a section 30 violation, the comptroller of the currency was authorized to remove a bank's principal officers and directors from office and to take control of the bank, pending trial.[67] With that, Palmer gave a copy of Diggs's telegram to Giannini and left the room.

Giannini flew into a rage. There was, of course, nothing illegal or improper about the board's action in declaring a dividend. But Diggs had apparently decided that Bank of America's financial condition was so serious as to require prompt corrective action, including the threat of seizing control of the bank and placing it in receivership. Whether intentional or not, Diggs's ultimatum confronted the board with an extremely difficult problem. Announcement of the dividend had already gone out to the press. To rescind the dividend now would risk considerable public embarrassment and generate a good deal of anxiety among Bank of America's depositors and stockholders. Giannini flatly rejected that course of action. "By God this dividend is right and it is going to stand," he told the board.[68]

A few minutes later Russell Smith walked into the room. He was, as he later recalled, "absolutely dumbfounded" by the news. Smith pulled out from his briefcase the notes he had taken in his meetings with Diggs, Gough, and Upham in June, then read through them carefully.[69] There was no hint of any concern on Diggs's part regarding Bank of America's solvency or its real estate portfolio. Nor was there anything in Smith's notes to support Diggs's contention that Bank of America's dividend policy had long been a source of concern to the comptroller's office.[70] Giannini immediately concluded that Diggs's telegram, with its dark threat of placing Bank of America in receivership, had been inspired by Morgenthau.

Morgenthau's role in the drafting of Diggs's telegram in fact had been far more direct than even Giannini had at first suspected. On September 15, two days after the board meeting in Los Angeles, the press carried the news that Morgenthau had replaced Diggs as acting comptroller with Cyril Upham. Sensing an opportunity, Mario Giannini phoned Diggs to obtain information about the origin and contents of his telegram on a strictly confidential basis. He was not disappointed. Diggs told Mario that neither he nor any other official in the comptroller's office had played any part in the drafting of the telegram. Diggs said that he had his "first knowledge" of the telegram on the morning of September 13, when "it was presented to me by Treasury officials for my signature."[71]

More disturbing news soon followed. Four days later Giannini received a confidential letter from Russell Smith with a detailed account of an incident that had occurred on his return flight to San Francisco. Smith told Giannini that all during the trip he carried under his arm a large, brown, "distinctive looking manila envelope," which contained the preliminary examination report that the Diggs telegram had cited. Walking through the lobby of San Francisco's main airport terminal, Smith said, he suddenly found himself face-to-face with none other than Cyril Upham, who was waiting to catch a place to Washington.[72]

According to Smith, Upham turned red. The acting comptroller was clearly embarrassed by the chance meeting and in a nervous, uncertain voice blurted out that he had been in San Francisco "on business." As the two men exchanged polite conversation, Smith suddenly noticed that locked under Upham's arm was an envelope identical in size, shape, and color to the one he himself was carrying. "It was obviously a copy of our examination report," Smith told Giannini. "Each of us instantly recognized what the other was carrying."[73]

The next morning, after sleeping on his suspicions about the apparent coincidence that had brought Upham to San Francisco at the same time Diggs was threatening Bank of America's board of directors with receivership, Smith phoned a source in the comptroller's office. "I learned," Smith told Giannini, "that Mr. Upham had left for San Francisco by plane almost simultaneously with the decision to send our board of directors the telegram and that he was standing by to take over the administration of the bank as conservator if the telegram . . .

caused any disturbance amongst the depositors of the bank. The telegram was undoubtedly calculated to accomplish that purpose. No such disturbance was created and apparently Mr. Upham was recalled to Washington."[74]

The news agitated Giannini in the extreme. Convinced that Morgenthau was intent on "making a prima facie case for legal proceedings to remove the management from the bank and to sue the bank for the forfeiture of its charter," Giannini moved quickly to seize the initiative. On September 21, 1938, a little more than a week after the board meeting in Los Angeles, he instructed Mario Giannini to "ignore his [Morgenthau's] department completely" and to request an immediate hearing before the FRB. "The Treasury is rotten to the core," he wrote. "We positively want that hearing. If we are proud of what's been done and we certainly should be, I see no reason why we should have any hesitancy in smoking out our enemies through a fight in the open and before the world if need be."[75]

Giannini assumed that in appealing to the FRB to conduct an "independent" examination of Bank of America's financial condition, he would receive a complete vindication for his position on the bank's loan portfolio and capital adequacy.[76] Giannini's hopes were grounded on more than brave talk. Since being appointed chairman of the FRB in 1934, Marriner Eccles had joined Jesse Jones among other New Deal administrators as a critic of the "outmoded" evaluation procedures used by field examiners in scrutinizing loans.[77] No less severe was Eccles's criticism of the government's "complex patchwork of overlapping responsibilities" shared by federal and state agencies in regulating banks. Eccles pushed for the consolidation of all bank regulation authority in the FRB, a proposal that Morgenthau opposed as "nothing more than a grab for power at the expense of the Treasury."[78]

Privately Eccles harbored strong doubts about many of the criticisms made by national bank examiners concerning the adequacy of Bank of America's reserves. Even as the OCC was threatening Bank of America with receivership, Lawrence Clayton, Eccles's confidant and administrative assistant, had obtained a copy of Giannini's point-by-point response to Diggs protesting the results of the examination report, a copy of which he sent to Eccles. Clayton told Eccles that Giannini's letter was a "honey" and said that it showed conclusively that "the comments and criticisms of the examiner are misleading either because of ignorance or bad faith."[79] Eccles agreed and sent Giannini a letter critical of the action taken by Diggs and the comptroller's office.[80]

With Morgenthau's responsibility for Diggs's threat of receivership so clearly demonstrated, Giannini unleashed a bitter denunciation of the treasury secretary in a blizzard of telegrams to McIntyre, Jones, Farley, and other members of the administration. To Ambrose O'Connell, the assistant postmaster general with whom Giannini had formed a friendly relationship, he cabled: "I would like you if you will do so to check into what the Treasury Department gang has been trying to do to us of late and you will I am satisfied get an idea just how well the administration treats its loyal friends."[81]

Now that the battle with Morgenthau had been joined, Giannini made it clear in private talks and memoranda to his executives in San Francisco that he would be satisfied with nothing less than unconditional surrender. "Before we should settle this controversy," he told Mario, "they [the Treasury Department] should not only retract the accusations in their telegram but they must also grant us all the permits we applied for. . . . We want to play the same game as Hitler is playing in Germany and have them come to us as Chamberlain did to Hitler, and we in turn will tell them just what we want."[82]

SEVENTEEN

"A Damnable Conspiracy"

I

Giannini's Bank of America was not the only financial institution in California that had become a source of increasing concern to Morgenthau in the spring of 1937. Some months earlier, evidence had begun to surface from two criminal cases, one in San Francisco, the other in Los Angeles, indicating that Herbert Fleishhacker, vice-president of the Anglo-California, had misused the bank's money to finance a variety of personal financial adventures that had resulted in losses to the bank estimated at approximately $14 million.[1]

The news sent a team of treasury officials hurrying to San Francisco. Their reports to Washington were worse than anyone in the department had anticipated: the Anglo-California was in imminent danger of collapse and had been teetering on the edge of bankruptcy since the early 1930s.[2] Alarmed, Morgenthau instructed aides to begin reviewing options to clean up the mess as quickly as possible. "Fleishhacker had his finger in practically every pie on the coast," he wrote to an aide in the department. "This is evidenced by the fact that it took forty-five typewritten pages to list, in detail, his assets and liabilities."[3]

The charges of trial prosecutors in the two Fleishhacker cases were shocking: fraud, falsification of financial statements, misappropriation of funds, and other instances of criminal activity. According to testimony and court documents, Fleishhacker had engaged in a number of self-lending transactions—sometimes hiding his illegal activities behind dummy companies. Also charged with fraud and malfeasance were members of the Anglo-California's board of directors.[4] Despite defense arguments, the verdict of the trial judges in both cases was the same: "Herbert Fleishhacker has violated his trust to the Anglo bank and to its stockholders."[5] In December 1937 the Fleishhacker trials ended with his conviction. Soon after the verdicts Fleishhacker resigned from the Anglo-California and went into bankruptcy.[6]

But serious questions remained. Foremost among these—and the most distressing to Anglo-California's stockholders—was the cozy relationship that had apparently existed between the Anglo-California and the Reconstruction Finance Corporation (RFC).[7] Sources close to the case said that over the years the Anglo-California had become increasingly dependent for its survival on RFC money, even though it was generally known in regulatory circles in Washington that the bank was being sloppily managed and that its future did not look good. The total government loans approached $5 million, most of which had been made available to the Anglo-California in the two-year period following Hoover's selection in 1930 of Eugene Meyer as the RFC's chairman.[8]

According to allegations in a subsequent lawsuit brought against Fleishhacker by a group of incensed Anglo-California stockholders: "The Fleishhacker interests in this bank have been supported with RFC money for years . . . to perpetuate the Fleishhacker control. . . . The examiner's report in 1933 disclosed a situation which should have indicated the necessity of removing Fleishhacker from position of trust and responsibility at the bank . . . [but] the RFC never used its voting power to bring about any improvement until the light of publicity compelled such action. . . . The directors who refused to furnish financial statements or to otherwise comply with the criticisms of the local examiners, appear to be very sure of themselves. Herbert and Mortimer Fleishhacker must have understood when the bank examiners would arrive."[9]

In San Francisco, Giannini was also intrigued by the alleged involvement of the RFC in protecting Fleishhacker's control over the Anglo-California, but for much different reasons. The more he looked, the more convinced he became that a network of close personal and business ties connected Meyer and Fleishhacker with Morgenthau. Eugene Meyer's father, Marc Meyer, had been a partner in the San Francisco branch of Lazard Freres, predecessor bank to the Anglo-California.[10] Eugene Meyer, in turn, had worked for the Fleishhackers before joining the New York banking investment firm of Lazard Freres. Meyer had been a neighbor of the Morgenthaus in Elberon, New Jersey, and had handled business transactions for the family on the New York Stock Exchange.[11]

Out of this pattern of circumstantial evidence Giannini jumped to a disturbing conclusion: Morgenthau was working in collaboration with Meyer to rescue Fleishhacker and the Anglo-California from financial disaster by making Bank of America the target of a government takeover for the purpose of merging the two banks. Giannini was not alone in his suspicions. Russell Smith told Giannini that he had learned from sources inside the Treasury Department that Morgenthau was terribly worried about the possible collapse of the Anglo-California. According to Smith, Diggs's September 13, 1938, letter opposing the board's dividend policy on threat of placing Bank of America in receivership was clearly part of a Morgenthau-inspired scheme "to eliminate the deteriorating financial condition in that institution [Anglo-California] with a consolidation of the two banks."[12]

There is no evidence that Morgenthau and Meyer were involved in a secret effort to prevent the collapse of the Anglo-California because of their personal connections with Fleishhacker; it is most likely that they were not. There is evidence, however, that in the spring of 1938 Morgenthau delayed efforts by the comptroller of the currency to remedy the deteriorating condition of the Anglo-California by instructing Diggs "to lay off the case" until the Treasury Department had completed its investigation of Bank of America.[13] This suggests that in Morgenthau's mind, at least, Bank of America and the Anglo-California had become synonymous as problem banks and that the only solution for averting a potentially devastating financial crisis in California lay in the consolidation of the two banks.

To Giannini, however, the motivation behind Morgenthau's pursuit of Bank of America was clear and unmistakable. The treasury secretary was intent on seizing control of Bank of America for the sole purpose of bailing the Anglo-California out of its financial difficulties. Giannini suggested as much in a letter on November 23, 1938, to E. H. Gough, the deputy comptroller of the currency. The "present situation in some ways," he wrote, "forms a startling parallel" to the proxy battle he had waged against Walker. "Today, as then, men who circulated vicious and mendacious personal attacks on me, attempted secret combinations and endeavored to surrender the Bank and Transamerica to rival bankers, occupy strategic official positions."[14]

As Giannini's difficulties with the Treasury Department dragged on, he became more and more driven by an obsessive hatred for Morgenthau, Meyer, and Fleishhacker, whom he characterized in his private conversations with aides as "a damn pack of Jews."[15] One Bank of America executive later recalled a directors' meeting in Los Angeles when Giannini accused Morgenthau of masterminding a "damnable conspiracy" to take control of Bank of America. "That god-damned Jew is in for a fight to the finish," Giannini shouted across the directors' table.[16] Deeply offended by Giannini's remarks, two Jewish members of the board, movie moguls Louis B. Mayer and Joseph Schenck, got up and left the room. Several days later both men submitted their resignations.[17]

By the late fall of 1938 rumors about Bank of America's difficulties with the Treasury Department and the OCC had begun circulating in the press. Giannini suspected Morgenthau of having leaked the information as part of his efforts to seize control of the bank.[18] The November 9, 1938, issue of the *Kiplinger Washington Letter,* for example, quoted unnamed Treasury Department officials as saying that Giannini and Bank of America had become the target of a government investigation.[19] The Kiplinger story was remarkably accurate in describing the deficiencies cited in Bank of America's confidential examination report, including the most damaging criticism, such as the massive buildup of doubtful loans. It went on to suggest that these problems were serious enough to convince treasury officials that the financial condition of the bank posed an unacceptable threat to the bank's depositors and stockholders.[20]

Giannini immediately responded with a sharply worded telegram to Morgenthau on November 10, 1938, in which he accused the treasury secretary of having leaked confidential information in an effort to discredit Bank of America and its management. "Don't you think, Mr. Secretary that your continued unwarranted and unjustifiable smearing has gone far enough?" he said. "Articles, the source of which is attributed to your department, . . . prompted some of our most valued clients, such as Woolworth's, Penn[e]y's, Safeway, Montgomery Ward . . . to make direct inquiry as to their meaning. . . . To meet a possible emergency arising in consequence of prevalent gossip, the management was obliged to accumulate excessive cash reserves by selling large blocks of government bonds and restricting lending activity, thereby suffering, unnecessarily, a loss in income and prestige."[21]

Morgenthau indignantly denied Giannini's accusations and deplored his tactics of "personal vituperation." He had, he said, "no knowledge" concerning the source of the Kiplinger story and had "authorized no disclosures of any kind about any banking situation. On the contrary, I have enjoined the strictest secrecy. . . . There are matters of grave import pending between the office of the comptroller of the currency, which is a bureau of the Treasury Department, and the financial institutions of which you are the responsible head. Let us not muddy the waters by personal animus or unjust charges."[22]

On the heels of the Fleishhacker disclosures, Giannini was not satisfied with Morgenthau's denial. "In the final analysis," he replied, "someone must take responsibility for the damage caused to Bank of America and its management. I do not propose to sit idly by while thoughtless and inexperienced persons take proceedings which tend to destroy this bank, which is a great public service institution and represents my life's work. I say it is a public institution because it serves over 2,000,000 depositors whose accounts average less than $675."[23]

Giannini was not content to vent his anger in telegrams. A few days later Morgenthau was awakened by the sound of his bedside phone ringing. It was 3:00 A.M. Washington time and Giannini was calling from his home in San Mateo. "You Jew son of-a-bitch," Giannini shouted into the phone, "I'm going to tell the whole world about you and the Fleishhackers."[24]

2

By the winter of 1938 Mario Giannini had decided that there was nothing to be gained by continuing the controversy. He began to seek a settlement with government officials. Early in December he traveled to Washington for a meeting with Preston Delano, whom Roosevelt had recently appointed comptroller of the currency.[25] Also present were Leo Crowley, Jesse Jones, and John Hanes, the undersecretary of the treasury, who came as Morgenthau's personal representative. After several days of intensive discussions, the group succeeded in forging the basis for a settlement. Mario agreed to increase Bank of America's cash reserves to $30 million with a public offering of preferred stock and to refrain from paying dividends until the new capital was raised.[26] To assist the bank with its stock offering, Jones offered to loan Transamerica $25 million in RFC money, which would be used to purchase stock the public did not take.[27]

Acting with great speed, RFC examiners went over Transamerica's books in San Francisco, pronounced the corporation in "satisfactory shape," and approved Bank of America's application to the agency for a $25 million loan. On December 15, 1938, Jones sent a copy of the settlement agreement to Hanes at the treasury, with a covering memorandum. "The memorandum is as agreed upon by you and me over the telephone," Jones wrote. "Leo Crowley has also agreed to it in the same manner, as well as Mr. Delano. . . . I assured Mr. Giannini that he would get fair treatment . . . and I am convinced of his desire to cooperate with the comptroller."[28]

Along with Marriner Eccles, Jones, a former Houston banker, was the most experienced New Deal administrator in banking matters as well as Giannini's strongest supporter in official Washington. "Believe me," Jones said in a phone conversation with Mario Giannini, "you have a great bank and you should go home and attend to business and forget about the situation here."[29] Throughout the remaining months of Bank of America's bitter struggle with Morgenthau, Jones was a constant source of support to Giannini, who relied on the RFC chairman for political and tactical advice. Aware of the delicacy of Jones's position, Giannini assured him that in reaching out for assistance, he would keep the RFC chairman's personal efforts confidential. "I just don't know, Jesse," he wrote, "how I am ever going to repay all your many kindnesses. . . . You have been a wonderful friend."[30]

Back in San Francisco, Mario Giannini sent his formal acceptance of the settlement agreement to Delano on December 15, 1938. Mario told Delano that while he did "not agree to many of the criticisms that have been made in the report of examinations," he had decided to increase Bank of America's cash reserves in an effort to arrive at "a prompt and amicable adjustment of the differences" between the bank and the comptroller's office. "I believe," he said, "that the attached program will be acceptable to my board of directors and I will present it to them for approval with my recommendation."[31] The long controversy between Bank of America and the comptroller's office had apparently been settled.

In the end, however, the settlement fell through. On December 22, 1938, Delano conveyed his personal satisfaction to Mario Giannini over the "corrective measures" that Bank of America had agreed to take. At the same time, Delano said, he wanted it clearly understood that "nothing in the settlement" constituted "an implied agreement on the part of my office that a dividend may be paid . . . [if] it is my judgment that such payment would be an unsafe and unsound practice."[32] Mario was stunned. In his discussions with Delano in Washington, he had assumed that once Bank of America had increased its cash reserves, it would be free to determine its own dividend policy. Jones's December 15, 1938, memorandum to Hanes seemed to confirm that he and Crowley had made the same assumption. Now, less than two weeks after the conclusion of the Washington meetings, Delano had apparently backed away from his own formula for a settlement.

Disappointed but still determined, Mario Giannini pushed ahead to satisfy his end of the agreement as if nothing had happened. In a letter on December 31, 1938, he reminded Delano that the settlement "was not of my authorship but was prepared in the Treasury after the several conferences in which we all participated," and he repeated his "desire to cooperate with your department." Consequently, Mario said, he would prefer ignoring Delano's "apparent reversal" and place his faith instead "in the assurances given to me and my associates by the conferees that they are not going to be unfair to this institution."[33] Shortly thereafter Mario notified Delano that Bank of America's board of directors had approved the settlement and that the bank "was willing to proceed with the capital increase upon the plan agreed."[34]

Delano, however, was in no position to reconsider his decision. Unknown to Mario Giannini, Morgenthau had not been pleased with the terms of the settlement that had come out of the Washington meeting. His dissatisfaction had been conveyed to Delano by James M. Landis, the Treasury Department's chief legal counsel. Landis told Delano that Morgenthau seriously doubted "if merely remedying the existing conditions in the Bank would be a sufficient fulfillment by the Comptroller of his duty." There was, on the contrary, Landis said, "considerable question . . . whether a management that had flagrantly violated the law, as had the present management, should be permitted to continue to operate any national bank."[35] Landis suggested that Delano reconsider the terms of the agreement. He made it clear that in his and Morgenthau's opinion, a section 30 action represented the best way to make Bank of America's management accountable.[36]

Not coincidentally, while all this was going on, the Gianninis received another blow. On November 22, 1938, with almost no advance warning, the SEC issued an order for a public hearing "to determine whether Transamerica stock should be removed from the New York, San Francisco, and Los Angeles stock exchanges." In the complaint the SEC charged that Transamerica officials had filed "false and misleading information" with the New York Stock Exchange in connection with the distribution of the corporation's shares one year earlier. A second charge, related to the first, was that the $22 million in net profits claimed by the corporation in the filing documents was nearly all "fictitious," the result of financial legerdemain in which Giannini had profited personally by $1.4 million.[37]

The SEC allegations, released by Douglas in a blaze of national publicity, had an immediate negative effect on Transamerica and its subsidiaries.[38] The day after the SEC announcement, the corporation's shares dropped four points on the New York Stock Exchange for a total estimated loss of $30 million. Equally damaging was the reaction of Bank of America's best corporate clients, a number of whom promptly withdrew their accounts.[39] Giannini's critics in New York and California had a field day savoring the public humiliation of a man who bragged often and openly about his influence in Washington. *Time* reported that "Wall Street was enormously delighted" with the SEC charges and threat of punitive action "because the New Deal had bit the only big banking hand that ever fed it."[40]

The SEC's allegations elicited a vigorous and wrathful response from Giannini. The day after Douglas's announcement, he issued a statement to the press charging the SEC complaint with being "unjust, unfair, and palpably false . . . a move calculated definitely to prejudice Transamerica in the eyes of the public." Simultaneously, he authorized Ferrari to release a complete statement of his personal net worth, including cash, securities, salary, and insurance. The total came to just over $400,000. Commenting on the SEC charge that Giannini had profited personally from the corporation's securities transactions during the previous year, Ferrari said in a press release that "judged by standards of compensation for comparable activities on the part of other corporation executives, Mr. Giannini's remuneration over a long lifetime of service has been relatively small. . . . The figures speak for themselves."[41]

In the weeks that followed Giannini turned to his favorite method of dealing with an outside attack against his banking empire: a public relations blitz. He hired the prestigious New York public relations firm of Bernays and Bernays to counteract the adverse publicity that the SEC complaint had generated in the press.[42] He quickly stepped up his counterattack by making phone calls and sending letters and telegrams to newspaper editors across California—all designed to produce as much public support as possible for Transamerica. "The SEC people, together with the Secretary of the Treasury, are continuing to feed out subtle publicity," he wrote to the *Los Angeles Times* editor Harry Chandler, "and we have about come to the conclusion that we should combat this. You know, Mr. Chandler, that we are up against a very powerful government agency and it is therefore up to us to see that our side of the case is properly presented to the public."[43]

When the public hearing on the SEC charges convened in Washington, D.C., on February 4, 1949, Transamerica was represented by Donald Richberg. The former legal counsel for the New Deal's National Recovery Administration, the bright, confident, brilliantly aggressive Richberg had left the administration two years earlier for private practice.[44] No sooner had the SEC's chief legal counsel, John Rogge, completed his opening statement defending the merits of the commission's complaint than Richberg launched into a furious attack, accusing the SEC of having made "false and slanderous" statements in announcing its allegations against Transamerica. Charging that the SEC had made a "grave mistake" in making its complaint public, Richberg said that the SEC had no legal authority in the regulation of national banks and had therefore "asserted a right to examine Bank of America's books not conferred on it by Congress."[45] To challenge the SEC's claim to visitorial powers, Richberg then announced that he had filed for an injunction in federal court.[46]

The hearing continued over the next several days and then recessed to await the outcome of Richberg's injunction. Outside the hearing room, Richberg spoke confidently with reporters about the possibility of reaching an accommodation with the SEC. Giannini adopted a far more uncompromising position. Before leaving Washington, he instructed Richberg to stand firm against the developing SEC litigation and to concede nothing without authorization from San Francisco. "I do hope that when you get into conferences with those SEC fellows you will not allow them to bulldoze or blackmail you," he said. "We red-blooded Californians don't stand for this sort of thing. We know that we have nothing to be ashamed of and therefore can stand the light. So do not hesitate for a moment to tell those fellows to go ahead and carry out their threats, no matter what they may be. . . . They have lost the case and they know it."[47]

By now, of course, Giannini's relationship with the New Deal had been ended by the SEC complaint, together with his belief in a Morgenthau-inspired conspiracy against Bank of America. Back in San Francisco, he formalized his break by calling a press conference to launch a bitter attack against Douglas and the SEC and to announce how complete his loss of faith in the administration had become. "I am cured and disillusioned," Giannini said. "I came to Washington expecting to find broad principles of equity and justice. . . . In addition to the scramble for fame through headlines, I found bright young men, fresh from academic halls, completely uninformed of life and experience and the ways of business, dominating councils. I am cured. I am disillusioned."[48]

On May 8, 1939, meanwhile, the Court of Appeals for the District of Columbia handed Giannini a welcome, if only partial, victory. The court upheld Morgenthau's action in furnishing the SEC with Bank of America's confidential examination reports. But the court went on to reprimand Douglas and the SEC severely for making the contents of the reports public and asserting the information in them to be "true . . . before findings are made." More important as far as Giannini was concerned, the court rejected the SEC's claim to visitorial powers over Bank of America's books and records. "If the comptroller's complaints were followed by compliance from Bank of America management," the court said, the SEC "would have no right to substitute its opinion in place of the comptrollers."[49]

Encouraged by the court's decision, Giannini pushed for a larger and more aggressive assault against the Treasury Department. "Am anxious to know . . . if any possibility of congressional investigation," he cabled Collins. "Certainly am anxious to have our case thoroughly aired and brought to attention of people of the country. . . . I am now fully convinced that the senior senator from Virginia [Carter Glass] knew what he was talking about when he said: 'We haven't driven out any money changers, we have only changed bankers.' So, instead of the House of Morgan we have changed to Kuhn, Loeb & Co. of which I am told the venerable father of the present secretary of the Treasury is a major partner."[50]

Mario Giannini, however, adopted a more conciliatory approach. With the controversy between Bank of America and Morgenthau now entering its second year, he went to Washington in the summer of 1939 to try once again to work out a compromise with the comptroller of the currency.[51] He came armed with a point-by-point refutation of the criticisms made by examiners in their November 1938 report. One week later he returned to San Francisco feeling relatively optimistic. In a letter of July 31, 1939, however, Delano informed Mario Giannini that his objections to the much-debated examination report were totally inadequate. "My opinion," Delano wrote, "is that they fail to meet in any particular the criticisms made of the unsafe and unsound practices and violations pursued by your Bank in the face of long continued and persistent warnings." Once again Delano threatened Bank of America with loss of its charter.[52]

Rebuffed by Delano, Mario Giannini turned again to the FRB and renewed Bank of America's request for an outside "objective" examination. "Our bank has been harried and threatened privately and publicly—and we think unfairly and unjustly—until ground is being laid for confusion in the public mind as to its condition," he wrote to Eccles on December 29, 1939. "The great amount of unlawful publication of unproven charges against our bank . . . and the vicious methods pursued by the Commission in cooperation with the Secretary to condemn the bank in the eyes of the public on ex parte data without a hearing would have destroyed any bank whose good will was less strongly entrenched than in the case with our bank."[53]

Mario's plea to Eccles included the warning that more than Bank of America's survival and the integrity of its management was at stake in the event of a section 30 action. Also at stake was the economic stability of California and the entire Pacific coast. "The situation set forth in this letter could possibly result in a grave financial disturbance which would involve the entire Twelfth Federal Reserve District," Mario said. "It would seem therefore that your Board has ample occasion to order an examination of the bank for your information. One of the results . . . would be to give us the benefit of another point of view as to the condition of the bank."[54]

Neither Giannini, however, was depending on a favorable response from Eccles. With the stigma of the Treasury Department's investigation threatening to erode public confidence in Bank of America—confidence that had been in large part restored in the aftermath of the proxy battle—Mario concluded that a far more drastic strategy was needed. He decided that the only way to get out from under Morgenthau's threat of receivership was to remove Bank of America from the national banking system and convert it into a state-chartered institution.[55] On January 3, 1940, Mario cabled his father in Miami to obtain his approval. Confronted by Delano's apparently unbending position, Giannini told Mario to move forward with the reconversion process and to fix the blame publicly on Morgenthau. "We must hit from the shoulders," he replied to one of Mario's advisers. "Nothing in the way of apologies, patronizing or humbling."[56]

On the morning of January 8, 1940, before an audience of more than fourteen hundred stockholders at Transamerica's annual meeting in San Francisco, Mario Giannini opened his attack. He accused Morgenthau and the comptroller's office of "fabricating" an examination report "deliberately calculated to embarrass the bank and prevent its further expansion." Calling on Morgenthau to "tell the whole truth" behind the OCC's threat of receivership as well as the SEC investigation, he challenged Morgenthau to come out from behind the "facade" of bureaucratic officialdom, adding: "Were it not for the privilege that surrounds his office, he would not dare act as he has."[57]

Mario then outlined the strategy he had discussed with his father. The only thing Bank of America "asked from government officials," he said, was "fair consideration and . . . civil treatment" for its directors and officers. But "if this cannot be accomplished and if it appears that Mr. Morgenthau is to be permitted to continue to use his position arbitrarily to harass your bank, we may suggest that you consider its conversion into a state bank."[58] Applause and shouts of approval greeted the announcement. As a reporter for the *San Francisco News* wrote, "It was evident that all the stockholders were 100 per cent in sympathy with the Giannini management."[59]

"Gianninis Open War to End on Morgenthau" was the headline in newspapers across the state the following day.[60] From Miami, Giannini instructed Mario to break off any further contact with Treasury Department officials and to bring pressure on Morgenthau with public statements to defend his harsh criticism of Bank of America's financial condition. "We've got to see this thing through to the finish on our basis," Giannini said. "Now Mario, just don't let those Treasury guys with their special expert legal staff lull you to sleep. Just always figure that Henry hasn't taken on those expert lawyers without thought of placing him in a position to get the best of us and thereby vindication for him, which mustn't be. They've got no case and they know it."[61]

3

Given the angry rhetoric and the sharp personal attacks that both sides had expressed in the controversy, a break in the impasse developed sooner than anyone expected. Toward the end of 1939 the

White House passed the word to officials in the Treasury Department that Roosevelt was extremely unhappy about the long and bitter warfare and "was anxious to have some solution brought about of Giannini's difficulties with government."[62] Some inside the department were quick to attribute Roosevelt's intervention to the influence of Jesse Jones, who had apparently succeeded in convincing the president that the controversy between Giannini and Morgenthau had more to do with personal than strictly banking matters and had the potential for damaging political consequences.[63]

Other influential voices were raised within the administration concerning the merits as well as the tactics of Morgenthau's campaign against Giannini and Bank of America. A Drew Pearson column on April 6, 1939, reported that in the days immediately following the SEC's well-publicized charges against Transamerica Corporation, Eccles had "rushed to the President" at his vacation home in Warm Springs, Georgia, "with an indignant protest that the SEC's action was 'precipitous, ill-advised, and immature.'" Behind the SEC's complaint, the column went on to say, "is one of the bitterest inner-administration feuds in the history of the New Deal."[64]

Whether this explanation is correct or not, there is no doubt that by the fall of 1939 Eccles had grown increasingly critical of the position that Morgenthau had taken against Bank of America. After being persuaded that Delano was serious in his threat to charge Bank of America with a section 30 violation and to put the bank into receivership, Eccles informed Morgenthau in a confidential memorandum on November 4, 1939, that he was not in agreement. He was in fact "frankly dismayed" by such an extreme and inappropriate application of the government's regulatory authority. "On the basis of the facts developed," Eccles said, "I have concluded that it would be a great mistake to proceed along these lines. I ought to let you know how I feel about it personally."[65]

Privately Eccles felt that while certain aspects of Bank of America's lending policies and management practices needed "prompt correction," Morgenthau had precipitated an unnecessary confrontation by relying on examination procedures that were "outmoded . . . and unenlightened."[66] The conflict between Bank of America and the Treasury Department strengthened Eccles's own view that the overlapping responsibilities that had grown up around the government's regulatory agencies—the Federal Reserve Board, the Office of the Comptroller of the Currency, and the Federal Deposit Insurance Corporation—had caused many difficult and self-defeating problems in the nation's banking system.[67] Eccles complained that the federal government's "crazy quilt" of regulatory functions served mainly to produce inefficiency and to inhibit stability in the nation's financial community.[68]

Eccles's goal was to restore confidence in the banking system by placing the regulation of national banks solely under the supervision of the FRB. As Lawrence Clayton, Eccles's personal assistant, informed Giannini in a confidential letter that came close to accusing Morgenthau of having acted irresponsibly, "My chief feels that it is essential to the proper regulation of the banking structure of the country that there be one Federal agency in charge . . . and in particular the Board of Governors of the Federal Reserve System."[69]

One major concern that may have been uppermost in the mind of Eccles and Roosevelt is suggested by a confidential memorandum sent by Russell Smith to Giannini on January 4, 1940. Earlier that day Smith had been summoned to the office of Timothy Day, president of San Francisco's Federal Reserve Bank. Without bringing Eccles into the discussion, Day told Smith that he "was seeking to avoid involving the Federal Reserve Board in any controversies with the Treasury Department." To Smith, "it was apparent" from Day's remarks that Eccles as well as other FRB officials were convinced that an "outside" examination of the Bank of America by the board would produce results "in conflict with those of the Treasury examiners."[70]

FRB officials were not the only ones aware of that possibility. After systematically combing through Bank of America's examination reports for more than a year, a team of government lawyers headed by Jerome Frank, the treasury's special legal counsel, were unable to find the evidence to make the case that Morgenthau wanted for a section 30 charge against Bank of America. "We don't have a case," a close Morgenthau aide wrote in a confidential interdepartment memorandum. "Sufficient evidence to prove the charges made in the examiner's letter is not available. . . . We don't have any case so far as the public is concerned. . . . Frank said he didn't know just what the Treasury could say . . . but he thought it should make a statement."[71]

Early in January 1940 news stories began circulating out of Washington that the Treasury Department's case against Bank of America had been weak from the beginning and that Morgenthau was prepared to reach some kind of settlement. As the Washington correspondent for the *American Banker* explained it, "Treasury authorities were on the wrong track and were advised that they would be unable to prove their points. . . . It can safely be said that the Bank of America has had the 'best of the case.' The case as it now stands seems to indicate that the Treasury has been put in the light of persecutors of the Gianninis for personal reasons."[72]

But it was Eccles, not Morgenthau, who assumed the responsibility of finding a resolution of the controversy. Soon after Transamerica's stockholders' meeting in San Francisco, Eccles summoned Mario Giannini to a meeting in Washington. Informed about Eccles's invitation, Giannini was convinced, more than before, that he had been right in his insistence that an "objective" examination by the FRB would arrive at much different conclusions than had the Treasury Department regarding Bank of America's financial condition—an obvious political embarrassment to Roosevelt in his reelection campaign. "Those fellows are licked, Mario," he cabled from Miami. "So just don't hesitate to pass them up and go home if they persist in their arbitrariness. . . . It looks very much as if neither the FRB or Treasury want a FRB hearing which would be more or less subject to review by others . . . during the campaign."[73]

In Washington, Mario spent the next two weeks in meetings with the administration's interdepartmental banking committee. The group, headed by Eccles, included Delano, Jones, and Crowley. The two sides eventually compromised. At a press conference in Washington on March 15, 1940, Mario Giannini announced that he would recommend to Bank of America's board of directors that it increase the bank's capital by $30 million. In turn, Delano conceded one of Giannini's most insistent points, the right of Bank of America to determine its own dividend policy.[74] With a few minor exceptions, these terms were essentially the same which Mario Giannini had reached with the comptroller of the currency sixteen months earlier but which Morgenthau had rejected.[75]

As part of the settlement, both sides agreed to refrain from issuing a public statement declaring a vindication of the position each had taken during the long months of the controversy.[76] Privately, however, Mario felt that Bank of America had emerged a clear winner. "Everybody here seems think we won out," he cabled his father in San Francisco.[77] Giannini agreed. "Congratulations, Mario," he replied. "You've done a great job and we here are prouder than ever of you."[78] Asked for his reaction to the settlement by a reporter during a press conference in Washington, Morgenthau replied simply, "I am satisfied," and declined to comment further.[79]

With the end of the controversy, New Deal officials like Jones and Eccles hoped that there might be a reconciliation between Giannini and the administration. "I can only wish that banking leaders in the various parts of the country had an equally vigorous and progressive attitude toward the mission of banking in contributing to the solution of our economic problems," Eccles wrote in a soothing letter to Giannini. "If the banks of the country generally were as aggressive as Bank of America in supplying the various needs of the community the Government would be able to reduce its banking activities to a great extent."[80]

Despite these and other efforts at private flattery of Bank of America, Giannini soon made clear how complete his break with the administration had become. In the 1940 presidential election he supported Roosevelt's Republican opponent, Wendell Willkie. "We can phone or wire all of the branch managers to get busy lining up votes for Willkie," he instructed Mario. "If the total vote is around two million then sixty odd thousand votes would turn the state into the Willkie column."[81] Four years later, after publicly criticizing the New Deal for allowing government bureaucrats to hamper the nation's financial system with "arbitrary regulatory policies," Giannini supported the presidential candidacy of Thomas Dewey. "Roosevelt has been in office long enough," he told a group of business leaders in San Francisco, "and a vigorous new leadership is needed to carry on the difficult tasks ahead." To forgive and forget was not in Giannini's nature.

EIGHTEEN

The Final Fight

I

Unlike the opening day ceremony at 1 Powell two decades earlier, the dedication of Bank of America's new headquarters building, held on the morning of December 9, 1941, was a relatively quiet affair. Two days before the Japanese had attacked Pearl Harbor; the nation was now at war, and the one hundred or so senior executives and invited guests who gathered for the dedication ceremony felt that the times called for a proper decorum. Located at 300 Montgomery Street, the twelve-story white-granite structure was only a short distance from where Giannini had opened his Bank of Italy in 1904. Earlier in the year Giannini had laid the cornerstone of the building with a trowel fashioned from a piece of bronze taken from the USS *Portsmouth,* a sloop of war that had sailed into San Francisco Bay in 1846 to claim California for the United States. The symbolism was not lost on his critics.[1]

That same month was also a period of personal grief for Giannini. On December 19, 1941, Clorinda Giannini was sitting at the piano in her daughter's home in San Mateo when she suddenly slumped forward and fell to the floor. Rushed to a hospital, she died three days later of a heart attack.[2] Giannini was devastated by his wife's death. After the funeral he retreated to his home, where he tried to deal with his feelings of loss and depression—a "dark and grieving mood," as one Bank of America executive would later describe it.[3] Giannini had a lifelong aversion to being alone, and the death of his wife exacerbated his fear of solitude. Overcome with loneliness, he threatened to sell his home, Seven Oaks, and move into an apartment in San Francisco, but he eventually persuaded his daughter and son-in-law to move in with him.[4]

With the fever of war mobilization sweeping the country, Giannini did not stay quiet for long. By the end of 1941 California's population had increased by more than 400,000—a figure that would double each year of the war. "Communities of 10,000 to 25,000 sprang up where there had been next to no one before the war."[5] In the first two months of 1942 alone, government contracts to California for the production of airplanes amounted to $1 billion; one year later, employment in the aircraft industry had climbed from 16,000 to 250,000.[6] Nearly 100,000 more defense workers were hard at work building ships, while a survey of Los Angeles at the end of 1943 revealed that one out of every four people had arrived in the city in the two years following the nation's entry into the war.[7]

All this created an unprecedented boom in the economy, placing heavy demands on banking services. Small-town Bank of America branches, which had previously required only $15,000 in available cash for daily business transactions, now found themselves handling deposits and loans in the hundreds of thousands and even millions of dollars. "You have no idea of the terrific pressure we are getting from all parts of California . . . to render some kind of service," one senior Bank of America executive wrote to Giannini.[8]

Always the empire builder, Giannini saw an opportunity for Bank of America's instant expansion into scores of previously small and uneventful communities that were being inundated by a massive influx of war workers.[9] Mario was thinking along similar lines. "This gives us our chance," he wrote to an associate in an interoffice memorandum.[10] As early as January 1940 Giannini had submitted formal applications to the comptroller of the currency to open some twenty Bank of America branches, mostly in and around Los Angeles, which was fast becoming the nation's "major arsenal turning out planes in uninterrupted streams" at aircraft companies like Douglas, Consolidated, Lockheed, North American, and Northrop.[11]

In Washington, Delano flatly rejected the applications, but his response was conveyed by Cyril Upham, whom Morgenthau had appointed deputy assistant comptroller. Upham informed Russell Smith that while the applications "looked like a routine proposition . . . the comptroller's office does not want to see Bank of America use the war as a means of expanding the number of its branches."[12] A short time later Collins informed Giannini that in a private meeting at the OCC, Delano had "frankly admitted" that "he was taking orders" from Morgenthau. "The whole question of the expansion of Bank of America and Transamerica," Collins reported Delano as saying, was one in which "the Treasury was greatly interested."[13]

Blocked by Morgenthau from acquiring additional Bank of America branches, Giannini looked for a method that would enable him to push ahead with his expansionist program. The division of responsibilities among Washington's regulatory agencies provided a solution. Beginning in the spring of 1942, Giannini used Transamerica to purchase a score of national banks, most located in communities in which he had been denied Bank of America permits. He then converted his acquisitions into state-chartered banks, the supervision of which was shared by the state department of banking and the FRB.[14] In this way Giannini freed himself from the supervisory authority of the OCC and the Treasury Department. His next step was to apply to the FRB for permission to open branches.

Giannini's efforts to continue expanding his banking operations by circumventing the OCC infuriated treasury officials. Upham immediately summoned Collins to his office and warned him about Giannini's "attempting to expand Bank of America by means which did not involve the necessity of the comptroller's approval."[15] Upham told Collins that Morgenthau was "greatly concerned" and had begun talking about the need for some kind of disciplinary action. It was clear to everyone concerned, Upham said, that Giannini had foolishly embarked on a course of action that was certain to bring him into serious conflict with government officials—one that was contrary to the "Treasury policy" of "discouraging further expansion of Bank of America and Transamerica upon the ground that they had already expanded too far."[16]

Morgenthau and Delano were not alone among New Deal officials in expressing concern over the aggressive way in which Transamerica had set about gobbling up banks. On January 18, 1942, Leo Crowley wrote to Eccles that "for some time now" the FDIC had been "greatly concerned over rumors that Transamerica intends to establish an additional state branch group" in California. "As the insurer of the Bank of America and other affiliated banks of Transamerica," Crowley wanted to make his position "clearly understood" that the FDIC "was unalterably opposed" to Transamerica's "further expansion," either directly or indirectly through affiliated banks controlled by the corporation. "We feel," Crowley said, "that the financial risk of the Corporation in the California area is already sufficiently concentrated and that further expansion, intensifying this concentration, is highly undesirable."[17]

Anticipating stiff resistance from Morgenthau and Crowley and desperate to get FRB approval of his branch permits, Giannini resorted to methods that had proved effective in similar situations in the past. On November 29, 1941, he wrote to Eccles with the news that he had been presented with the opportunity to purchase the San Francisco-based Bank of California, which had branches in California, Washington, and Oregon. Giannini told Eccles that he had made up his mind to go through with the purchase and appoint him as Bank of California's president. With the approval of the Treasury Department he would then consolidate the Bank of California with Bank of America. To make the transaction even more attractive to Eccles, Giannini went on to say that once the merger had been completed, he would "buy him out" for $250,000 and bring him "into the picture in California" as Bank of America's president.

"Wouldn't it be a good time Marriner," Giannini wrote to Eccles, "to see if a deal couldn't be made in the form of a consolidation . . . which would result in practically a Federal Reserve District wide Branch bank, with offices in Portland, Seattle, Tacoma, San Francisco & Los Angeles. I don't suppose a man of your youth and talents is going to spend much more time in that Washington atmosphere—so let's hope that this note will make you think of getting back actively into the Banking Game out this way."[18]

Eccles was receptive to Giannini's offer. In a personal letter on December 20, 1941, Eccles told Giannini that he found his offer "interesting." In the same letter Eccles also enclosed "excerpts" from federal banking laws "touching on the problem in question," with his own "brief comments" on the methods by which "the consolidated bank could retain the branches of both banks." Eccles informed Giannini that he was planning to spend the Christmas holidays at his home in Ogden, Utah, and he suggested that the two of them get together in San Francisco sometime during his vacation, when "I may possibly have the opportunity of talking it over with you in person."[19]

How far was Eccles prepared to go in pursuing his "interest" in a transaction that would pay such lucrative dividends, both financially and professionally? Giannini could not be certain. But the fact that the FRB chairman had responded favorably to his offer seemed encouraging. Giannini felt he had good reason for assuming that he had found a powerful presence on the board who would adopt a sympathetic attitude toward his expansionist ambitions for Transamerica, whose aggressive penetration into more and more California communities was making Morgenthau and Crowley increasingly anxious.

As it developed, the offer that Giannini had dangled in front of Eccles did not prove to be as valuable as he had hoped. Early in January 1942 Eccles phoned Mario Giannini to say that he was "disappointed" over Transamerica's rapid acquisition of banks.[20] In Eccles's opinion the "sudden change" in the "general character of Transamerica" was a clear violation of "the gentlemen's agreement" that Bank of America had reached with Morgenthau and Delano in Washington in March 1940.[21] As Eccles understood the terms of the agreement, the Gianninis, father and son, had agreed to refrain from acquiring any more national banks for the purpose of converting them into branches without first obtaining approval of the FRB, the FDIC, and the OCC.[22]

Mario Giannini had a far different understanding. "There was never such an agreement made" with the comptroller of the currency, he replied. The terms of the Washington settlement contained "no provisions . . . with regard to Bank of America branches and Transamerica Corporation's expansion." Moreover, not only was the entire notion of obtaining "prior approval" from government regulators inconsistent with his father's "conduct of business," but it was also contrary to the nation's banking laws, which "provided for the establishment of branches for the convenience of patrons and the public."[23]

In a technical sense, Mario Giannini was right. His informal agreement with Delano had prohibited "the further expansion of branch banking activity of national banks in the Transamerica group." But neither Eccles nor Morgenthau apparently had anticipated the possibility that Giannini would try to evade the terms of the agreement by removing Transamerica's new acquisitions from Delano's supervision. In Eccles's view this kind of corporate abracadabra violated the spirit, if not the actual terms, of the agreement. He made clear that his "supervisory responsibilities" as FRB chairman would not permit the Gianninis to make a mockery of the government's regulatory system by conjuring up clever schemes "whereby Transamerica Corporation could avoid the restrictions of the Comptroller of the Currency for further expansion of branch banking activities of national banks in the Transamerica group."[24]

Under pressure from Morgenthau and Crowley, and feeling betrayed by what he believed was a deliberate violation of an agreement in which he had invested a good deal of his personal reputation within the New Deal's top circle of regulatory officials, Eccles decided that something had to be done. He summoned Delano and Crowley to a meeting in his office at the Federal Reserve Building on February 6, 1942, in order "to review the entire situation."[25]

Eccles, personally annoyed by the need for such a meeting, told Delano and Crowley that it had become clear to him that Transamerica "was dominated by a management with a tendency to be more interested in creating an empire than operating a banking institution and more interested in the market price than the soundness of the bank stock." Eccles had other concerns, namely, his belief that Transamerica was being drained of "adequate capital" because of "too rapid an expansion." This massive outflow of capital had created a situation that would make it difficult, if not impossible, for the corporation "to render the necessary assistance to Bank of America" if economic conditions should ever require it.[26]

With Giannini obviously intent on acquiring more banks, despite the warnings expressed to him by the comptroller's office, Eccles felt the time had come for the government's three major regulatory agencies—the FRB, the FDIC, and the OCC—to take decisive action in the face of Giannini's defiance. To this end, Eccles recommended the adoption of a "uniform policy" that would restrain "the further expansion of Transamerica and Bank of America interests," frustrating in the process Giannini's considerable talent for "playing one federal agency against another." Should this policy fail to "meet the situation," Eccles told Delano and Crowley, the three of them should meet again and "undertake to propose legislation which would prohibit further expansion of bank holding companies."[27]

Delano and Crowley agreed. Eccles thought he now had the strategy he needed for stopping Transamerica's bold and unrestrained expansion. In a letter of February 12, 1942, Eccles informed Giannini that "under existing circumstances" the FRB, the FDIC, and the OCC had unanimously decided to "decline permission for the acquisition directly or indirectly of any additional banking offices or any substantial interest therein by Transamerica Corporation and Bank of America N.T. & S.A., or any other unit of the Transamerica group."[28]

This was not, of course, what Giannini had been looking for, particularly in view of the "deal" he had offered Eccles some weeks earlier. A few days later he responded in a frenzy of paranoia and recrimination. "I don't know of any legal justification for such action," Giannini wrote to Eccles. "Frankly, I should like to know what is the cause of this discrimination . . . against us and our attempt to extend our services where the need has been definitely established. . . . I do not think that any bank in the history of this country has been more persistently persecuted than the Bank of America. Can it be due to the fact that we do not represent the vested interests and that throughout our history we have been the bank of the people . . . ? Or are there more sinister motives? I must state to you frankly, Marriner, that I think the position of the supervisory agencies is not sound, and in the long run cannot be sustained under our American system of free enterprise. . . . We should not in these times resort to Nazi-Fascist methods of dictatorship."[29]

"You led us to believe in 1940 that hereafter all contemplated transactions would be presented in advance for prior approval of the respective federal supervising agency interested," Eccles replied in a letter of August 29, 1942. "You will recall that this board played a considerable part in the preparation and conclusion of that agreement. It is with the deepest regret that you have not seemed fit to carry out this promise. . . . It seems rather useless to repeat to you the circumstances that brought about bank holding legislation. . . . We respect your ability as a branch bank operator, but must condemn the methods of expansion you attempt to use."[30]

Eccles reminded Giannini that "time and again attention has been called to the unsatisfactory situation in Bank of America resulting from the policies and practices of the management during its rapid expansion program." Eccles was also critical of Transamerica's "complex corporate structure" and the "unsatisfactory manner in which funds to expand and carry out other activities have been obtained by financing within the group." Eccles wanted no quarrel that was not consistent with the FRB's concern for "the best interest of the general public." But in view of Giannini's apparent indifference to the board's repeated warnings about Bank of America's "lack of sufficient capital," the government's supervisory agencies "would be remiss in discharge of their responsibilities if they permitted the continued expansion of the Transamerica group."[31]

Despite these harsh words, Eccles remained conciliatory. He concluded his letter: "Whenever you or any of your associates feel that you have a just grievance to take up with the board . . . you are always welcome to call in person for a more complete and frank discussion of them than is practical through correspondence. Anytime you are in Washington, I shall be glad to arrange conferences on this matter."[32]

Six months later—in April 1943—Giannini accepted Eccles's invitation. In Washington he met with Eccles and several other FRB members, including John McKee, a critic of bank holding companies who had helped draft Eccles's August 29, 1942, "freeze" letter. Out of these meetings came an informal agreement between Giannini and the board. Giannini promised that neither Transamerica nor Bank of America would acquire an interest in additional banks without first receiving approval of the FRB. The key to the agreement was Eccles's commitment, in return, to obtain a similar pledge from the nation's other bank holding companies.[33]

The agreement soon fell apart. Back in San Francisco, Giannini was angered to learn that McKee and other FRB members felt that since their immediate specific concerns were directed at Transamerica, the board did not think it necessary to obtain the same "no expansion" pledge from the nation's other holding companies. Giannini immediately instructed Collins in a letter on April 13, 1943, to notify Eccles that he no longer felt bound to adhere to the terms of the "stand still" agreement he had reached with him in Washington two weeks earlier.[34]

"It appears that Gov. McKee now assumes that it is unnecessary to secure commitments from other bank holding companies," Giannini told Collins. "If such commitments are unnecessary from other bank holding companies and other banks, they are, of course, not necessary from Transamerica Corporation or Bank of America. What is sauce for the goose is sauce for the gander. We ask only to be placed upon a plane of equality with others."[35]

Giannini's decision angered Eccles and other FRB members. McKee was outraged. On May 13, 1943, McKee took the unusual step of phoning Collins with the warning that "Transamerica and Bank of America were going to be proceeded against in every direction by means of every agency and weapon within the reach of the board." McKee told Collins that he "was aware of the fact that A. P. liked a fight, but the board was now going to give him a fight which he would not like. . . . He said this was going to be an all-out fight through federal legislation, through executive action, through the acts of organized banking, and through building up of public opinion against these institutions and the Gianninis."[36]

McKee's phone message was no empty bluff. By this time the pressure in Congress to enact legislation restricting the activities of bank holding companies had gained new strength.[37] In the spring of 1943 Congressman C. Wright Patman, whose populist roots in Texas fueled his antipathy toward the "consolidation of financial power," introduced a bill in the House to restrict and then eventually abolish all bank holding companies.[38] He made no secret of his concerns arising out of Transamerica's seemingly endless march to greater heights of financial power.

In the spring of 1943 Patman, chairman of the House Committee on Banking, held hearings and wanted to know, among other things, what if any steps the government's regulatory agencies had taken in protecting the "public interest" against the expansive "business activities of banks and bank holding companies" and the creation of new ones. He summoned Eccles to testify before the committee. With his usual blunt manner, Patman lost no time in going after the testimony he wanted by zeroing in on the FRB's apparent "inability" to "get better cooperation" out of Transamerica in controlling the growth of the corporation. "I presume," Patman asked Eccles, "that you would look with favor upon legislation that would curb bank holding companies . . . and that you do not look with favor upon the activities of Transamerica Corporation."

"I do not," Eccles answered. He told the committee that while his concerns over the unrestrained development of bank holding companies were many, the most worrisome among them "was the acquisition by Transamerica of stock in independent unit banks as a means of evading the requirements of the federal agencies who will not permit them to establish further branches." Denying that he or the FRB had in any way "discriminated against" Giannini, Eccles went on to urge that Congress either give the board "powers to deal with this holding company situation, particularly Transamerica, or they should take the responsibility."[39]

Eccles's testimony, of course, came as no particular surprise to Patman and other congressional critics of bank holding companies. But Collins, who attended the committee hearings, believed that Eccles had gone out of his way to damage Transamerica and Bank of America. As Collins saw it, Eccles had used his appearance before the Patman committee to turn Transamerica into a target of those in Congress increasingly dissatisfied with the mounting power of holding companies by providing an ominous picture of the "Giannini interests" in California: a financial juggernaut, uncontrolled and uncontrollable, whose "potential for monopoly" threatened the economic life of the entire Pacific coast.

"Chairman Eccles could have properly declined to be drawn into a discussion," Collins cabled Giannini, "but he seemed to welcome the opportunity to single out Transamerica and Bank of America for destructive and emphatic criticism."[40]

Giannini was furious with Eccles's remarks and said so in a bitterly worded letter to the FRB chairman on May 28, 1943. "I have information that you recently stated that I had broken my word with you," he wrote. "This statement is absolutely untrue and I resent it. . . . You know that the conference understandings were wrecked largely because of a subsequent attempt to bind Transamerica to your so called freezing policies instead of your obtaining similar commitments from other holding companies which you volunteered to undertake personally. I am not concerned with threats, which I have been informed have been made by you, but your intrusive activities in transactions affecting Bank of America are highly detrimental and will be vigorously challenged."[41] Giannini's long and previously friendly relationship with Eccles had ended.

Six months later, in September 1943, Patman's bill was defeated in the House of Representatives. Unable to present a clear definition of what in fact constituted a "holding company" or "potential abuses," Patman's supporters were unable to muster the votes for passage.[42] Notwithstanding congressional failure to come up with some kind of bank holding legislation, Eccles remained firm in denying Bank of America additional branch permits. In June 1945, when Japan surrendered, Bank of America had a total of 492 branches—three less than it had when the nation went to war.[43] Giannini seethed as he watched his branch employees trying to cope with long lines of customers, a great number of whom had come from neighboring communities in which he had been denied permission to open branches. Eventually he was forced to spend over $8 million to enlarge the only existing branches located in the state's most populous communities.[44]

Such developments, however, did not prevent Giannini from wheeling and dealing with an intensity that terrified his opposition. From the spring of 1943 to the end of 1945 Transamerica gained a controlling stock interest in some sixty unit banks—all of which became part of his growing network of "independent" banks.[45] In Washington, Eccles was eyeing Transamerica's feverish acquisition of banks with increased apprehension. To Senator Charles W. Tobey, a New Hampshire Republican and chairman of the Senate Committee on Banking and Currency, he wrote: "It is clear . . . A. P. Giannini and L. M. Giannini mean to do all in their power to defeat regulation of bank holding companies." This suggested to Eccles "the urgent need in the public interest" for the Senate "to prevent the holding company device being used not only to create banking monopolies, but to reach out into wholly unrelated fields . . . to control all sorts of business enterprises."[46]

2

The postwar years were a time of international banking ventures and renewed combative challenge for Giannini. At the regular monthly meeting of Bank of America's board of directors on May 6, 1945, the day before his seventy-fifth birthday, Giannini announced his resignation as Bank of America's chairman of the board. He had, he told the board, "retired" at various times in the past only to reverse his decision. This time, however, he was determined that his resignation "would stick." Before the meeting adjourned, he had accepted the honorary title of founder-chairman.[47]

The next day, at a crowded press conference, Giannini made his resignation public. "My job at Bank of America" in the years ahead, he said, would be limited to "that of a barking watch dog . . . and I find something to bark at every day and always will." When reporters asked Giannini for specifics about immediate problems hindering the growth of Transamerica and Bank of America, he cited "Mr. Morgenthau and other Washington influences," whom he charged "had been unfairly persecuting him and his institutions." Under "Mr. Morgenthau's guidance," Giannini said, "the comptroller's office had denied us the right to establish new branches."[48]

The press conference was brief, but before it concluded Giannini made another announcement that heightened what the *San Francisco News* would call the "high drama" of his resignation.[49] As an investor in a modest amount of stock whose value had increased in recent years, Giannini said, he "seemed to be in danger of getting into the millionaire class." To prevent that, he had decided to turn over more than half his personal wealth—approximately $500,000—to establish the Bank of America–Giannini Foundation, a nonprofit corporation whose purpose was to provide educational scholarships for Bank of America employees and to finance scientific research, particularly in the field of medicine.[50] "I've always vowed I'd never become a millionaire," Giannini said.

To no one's surprise, Giannini did not allow his latest "retirement" to get in the way of looking for every opportunity to push his banking operations into more and more California communities against the opposition of both Morgenthau and Eccles. This goal had obvious limitations. As a result of Eccles's freeze policy during the war years on new branch permits for Bank of America, Giannini had been forced to limit his expansionist activities to the acquisition of Transamerica-owned unit banks. Although Eccles's policy hampered Giannini's free-wheeling ambitions in many ways, he realized that he could do little so long as the Treasury and the OCC stood firm behind the FRB.

Toward the end of 1945, however, Giannini was growing increasingly frustrated with Eccles's freeze. The signs of a continuing economic boom in California were unmistakable. Throughout the state, war priorities had produced a huge backlog of public works projects that directly affected the growth and economic vitality of some three hundred communities. An initial estimate by Bank of America's bond investment department placed the total amount of new building needs at $3.5 billion.[51] At the same time, the demand for new home construction was soaring—a reaction to the continuing movement of people into the state.[52] The FRB's freeze policy put Giannini in a position he detested—unable to take command and turn the postwar momentum of growth and prosperity to Bank of America's advantage. Ironically, it was Morgenthau who would give him the opportunity to break the impasse.

On July 5, 1945, three months after Roosevelt's death at Warm Springs, Georgia, Morgenthau resigned as secretary of the treasury. Moving quickly, Giannini applied to the comptroller of the currency for permission to open thirty-five Bank of America branches, nearly all in and around Los Angeles.[53] A short time later Delano approved two of the applications—the first in more than six years. Although a great deal less than Giannini had requested, it was at least a start. More encouraging was a telegram from Collins in Washington informing him that Delano had actually been prepared to be far more generous but that Eccles was holding him to the terms of the freeze agreement.[54]

Meanwhile, as the number of Bank of America's customers climbed to higher and higher levels, so did the volume of its deposits. At a directors meeting on October 11, 1945, Francis Baer, vice-chairman of the board, spent the first fifteen minutes of the meeting "droning through figures describing the bank's condition."[55] Sitting across from Baer, Giannini shifted impatiently, then suddenly jumped from his chair and began pounding the table. "For God's sake, Frannie," he shouted, "give them the big news." The big news, Baer told the board, was that with total assets of over $5 billion, Bank of America had become the world's largest privately owned bank. Official confirmation came some weeks later when Chase National released its third-quarter figures, which listed total assets of $4.6 billion—$72 million less than Bank of America.[56]

Reaction to the news of Bank of America's status as the new colossus of the financial world was, as Giannini had expected, one of enthusiastic praise from across California.[57] Congratulatory letters and telegrams poured into the bank's headquarters in San Francisco. Giannini, of course, was delighted, but he had no intention of becoming complacent. With California's economy accelerating, he was determined that Bank of America would keep pace and play an even more dominant role in a state that was fast becoming an industrial powerhouse. "Lots of new businesses will be opened," he told one interviewer. "Markets will keep getting bigger. . . . Folks over the country want to settle in California. Jobs, I can't see any lack of them. We'll get bigger."[58]

Giannini had already set plans in motion to do just that. In the late summer of 1945 he completed travel arrangements with the State Department for a business trip to Europe. In a letter of August 29, 1945, he told Secretary of State James Byrnes that the primary purpose of the trip was to inspect Banca d'America e d'Italia, the subsidiary branch banking system that Mussolini had sequestered soon after America's entry into the war.[59] Giannini made no mention about another of his objectives: expansion of his banking operations into western Europe. Bank of America's first foreign branch, which opened in London in 1928, had suffered a severe setback when the stock market crash and hard times through the decade of the 1930s reduced foreign trade to a trickle. But with the end of the war and the urgent need to rebuild western Europe, the economics of foreign trade and international lending looked promising.[60]

After a transatlantic flight, Giannini arrived in London on the evening of October 13, 1945. Accompanied by Russell Smith, Giannini had a long conversation with the British prime minister, Clement Attlee.[61] One week later Giannini and Smith were in Rome, where they conferred with scores of politicians, businessmen, bankers, and industrialists on plans for rebuilding Italy's devastated economy. After a private meeting with Pope Pius XII, the two men left Rome by automobile on an inspection tour of Italian cities—Florence, Pisa, Lucca, Genoa, Naples, Bologna, and Milan.[62]

On November 14 Giannini arrived in Milan, where he received some reassuring news: Banca d'America e d'Italia had functioned more or less normally during the four years it had been under Fascist control and had emerged from the war in much better shape than he had expected. With thirty-one branches and total assets of more than $30 million, it could compete with many other banks in financing the rehabilitation of Italy's devastated economy.[63]

Back in San Francisco, Giannini was eager to demonstrate that the West Coast was no longer dependent on loans from Wall Street to finance foreign trade.[64] Now, however, he turned his attention westward to the Pacific basin and the Far East. The war had transformed California from a largely agricultural state into a rapidly growing industrial power. By forming strong links between Bank of America and the Far East, Giannini saw an opportunity to provide markets and trading partners for California's new plant capacity and industrial products. "Situated as it is on the Pacific Coast," he told a group of reporters, "Bank of America must recognize the responsibility and obligation that such a prominent position carries with it and expand its operations into the Pacific territory and the Far East."[65]

Bank of America's first and most successful postwar foreign branch was in Manila.[66] Giannini's interest in the Philippines had received significant encouragement from the soft-spoken, intensely ambitious Oakland contractor Stephen D. Bechtel, whose wartime shipbuilding projects Bank of America had helped finance.[67] Bechtel, whom Giannini regarded as "tops" among California industrialists, had urged him to move Bank of America into Manila as quickly as possible. Although devastated by the Pacific War, the Philippines had been slow in recovering and developing its economic potential—a delay Bechtel attributed largely to "existing financial institutions . . . so balled up they are unable to handle the situation." The biggest need, Bechtel argued, was capital for industry. He was certain that Bank of America was the only "outfit" that could bring prosperity out of economic chaos in postwar Manila.[68]

In June 1946 the FRB approved Bank of America's application to open a branch office in Manila. The branch soon confirmed the optimistic predictions of Bechtel as well as Giannini executives who had been enthusiastic about the postwar prospects of trade and credit development in the Philippines. By 1949—three years after the Manila branch opened its doors—it had accumulated total resources of $34 million, making it the country's fourth largest bank.[69] Simultaneously with his move into the Philippines, Giannini sent Russell Smith to Thailand to negotiate the possibility of opening a Bank of America office in Bangkok. One year later the Bangkok branch was in operation. Other branch offices in the Far East soon followed: Shanghai, Tokyo, Yokohama, Kobe, Siam (Thailand), and Guam. By the end of 1950 Bank of America had eight foreign branches with total resources of more than $300 million.[70]

3

If the immediate postwar years saw Bank of America emerge as the world's largest privately owned financial institution, they also brought a worsening of Giannini's problems with the FRB. Since the spring of 1943, when Giannini withdrew his commitment to the FRB's "standstill" agreement, Eccles's hostility toward the "Giannini interests" in California had been building.[71] In early October 1945, determined to take action against the threat of Transamerica and Bank of America's "monopolistic development" and to "prevent other abuses," Eccles asked Attorney General Thomas Clark to look into the possibility of bringing antitrust charges against Transamerica Corporation under the Sherman Act.

Clark's response, a short time later, pessimistically recommended against Eccles's course of action. "There was," Clark said, "no persuasive evidence that the Transamerica Corporation was a complete monopoly." Nor was there any convincing evidence that the corporation had "abused its dominant position in the commercial banking field," either through "illegal trade practices as those terms are defined in court decisions interpreting the Sherman Act, or that it abused its dominant position once it was achieved." In the absence of "one or both these types of abuse," Clark said, it would be futile for the Justice Department "to try and make a case under the Sherman Act."[72]

Meanwhile, Eccles had been working quietly on a bank holding bill of his own. Introduced in the Senate in 1947 by Charles Tobey of New Hampshire, Eccles's bill proposed placing the operation of bank holding companies under the strict supervision of the FRB. Despite its broad policy proposals, there was no doubt among observers either in or outside the Senate about the bill's target. "It was, for all intents and purposes," said the *San Francisco Chronicle,* an "anti-Giannini bill."[73]

In San Francisco, Giannini took the position that he was not opposed to legislation restricting the activities of bank holding companies so long as it "was extended on the basis of equality and without discrimination."[74] Privately he was cynical over Eccles's legislative intervention and his new working relationship with influential Republicans and Transamerica critics like Tobey. A few years earlier Eccles had seemed ready to jump at the opportunity to become a major player in Bank of America's proposed takeover of the Bank of California—a financially lucrative transaction that would have, had it been approved by the Treasury Department, added significantly to Giannini's branch banking operations in California.

"I have a letter that if I ever appear before a banking and currency committee, [Eccles has] probably forgotten about it," Giannini confided to a few close friends. "We were going to be all together. The arrangement was, if he wanted to be in the picture, that I would buy him out and pay him 250,000 and he would go out. . . . Now, he's the guy that says we mustn't expand, and yet he was anxious to have us buy the Bank of California, which he was to head, and then come into our picture with it. Mind you, come into our picture if we could get it through Morgenthau's office." To Giannini, the "two-face Mormon," as he had begun referring to Eccles, was a sham and a hypocrite—a "dirty son-of-a-bitch."[75]

By the spring of 1947 Eccles must have felt that among the government's array of bank regulatory agencies, only he and the FRB stood between Transamerica's complete domination of the banking business of the entire Pacific coast as well as a large part of the Southwest. The previous summer Frederick Vinson, who had succeeded Morgenthau as secretary of the treasury, resigned from the cabinet after being nominated by Truman to the U.S. Supreme Court. To replace Vinson, Truman selected John Snyder, a close personal friend and old army buddy with whom he had served in France in World War I.[76]

A former bank president and director of the RFC regional office in St. Louis, Snyder came to Washington in early 1943 to become executive vice-president of the administration's newly formed Defense Plant Corporation (DPC). Soon he developed close personal and professional relationships with a number of New Deal bureaucrats molding the nation's defense effort. One was Sam Husbands, a former RFC director and president of the DPC. Husbands would serve as president of the DPC until the spring of 1944, when he left Washington for San

Francisco to join Transamerica as a senior executive vice-president.[77] With Snyder's elevation to the treasury, Giannini acquired his most important connection to the inner circle of the administration since J. F. T. O'Connor's tenure as comptroller of the currency in the early 1930s.

Giannini soon received more encouraging news. Early in the fall of 1947, after nearly eight years and forty volumes of depositions, charts, and testimony in what had become the most thorough investigation in the history of the SEC, government lawyers put an end to the Transamerica hearings by declaring in effect that they had been unable to prove the commission's charges against the corporation.[78]

In California, Giannini supporters responded to the SEC's admission of defeat with a fierce denunciation of New Deal "bureaucratic zealots" and their failed attempts "to find fault" with the "workings of the free enterprise system" where there had been none to be found. "Although it took the better part of a decade to do so," the San Francisco Call-Bulletin editorialized, "the SEC has said that its accusations against the defendants were wrong. All the work and expense and anxiety involved here—to say nothing of what it cost the American taxpayers—have been officially pronounced unnecessary, invalid and just so much lost motion. The unfortunate aspect of this case is the fact that the defendants ever should have had to go through the ordeal at all."[79]

In Washington, meanwhile, the Husbands-Snyder connection turned out to be more politically advantageous to Giannini than perhaps even he had anticipated. Treasury officials began passing the word that the issuance of branch permits by the comptroller of the currency would henceforth be based in large part on considerations of "public convenience"—exactly the position Giannini had argued in his struggle with Eccles and Morgenthau. The treasury's changed attitude was confirmed when, late in 1947, Delano, who had earlier assured Eccles that he would "continue to restrain as much as possible the growth of monopoly in West coast banking . . . which seems inherent in the expansionist program of Bank of America and Transamerica," suddenly began issuing permits for Bank of America branches.[80]

"We have to keep the free enterprise system working," Delano later told the Senate Committee on Banking and Currency. In a further defense of what to many on the committee seemed a less than convincing justification for his unexpected reversal in policy, Delano said that his decision to grant Bank of America additional branches was "not out of line with the growing population of California."[81]

It was the end of the "uniform policy" toward Bank of America's expansion that Eccles had succeeded in putting together four years earlier. Eccles was both angry and exasperated. Giannini was emerging in the late 1940s with exactly what he had gone after when the decade began, and he was now in an ideal tactical position to carry out the ambitious developmental plans he had envisioned for Bank of America after Pearl Harbor. Equally disappointing as far as Eccles was concerned, signs that the administration had adopted a conciliatory approach toward the "Giannini interests" in Washington seemed to be everywhere in evidence.

Eccles's concern that the administration "had taken sides with the Gianninis" was soon intensified, and in a way that affected him personally. On February 22, 1948, nine days before his term as chairman of the FRB was to expire, Eccles was informed by John Steelman, Truman's special assistant, that the president had decided not to reappoint him as directing head of the board. Stunned, Eccles requested a meeting with Truman the next morning. It was, for both men, a difficult meeting. "When I saw the president," Eccles wrote years later, "it was obvious that he had been influenced to make a distasteful and embarrassing decision." At one point, according to Eccles, he asked Truman point-blank to explain "what was behind his action," but to no avail. "The reasons," Truman replied, "were best known to himself alone."[82]

In an effort perhaps to salve Eccles's badly bruised feelings, Truman offered to reappoint him to the FRB as vice-chairman. To the astonishment of many in Washington (including perhaps Truman himself), Eccles accepted the offer, but he asked that the reappointment be announced in an exchange of letters between the two. On January 22, 1948, in a letter that both men released to the press, Truman made the shift in Eccles's position on the board official. "This decision, I assure you," Truman wrote, "reflects no lack of complete confidence in you . . . or a disagreement with official actions taken by the Board under your leadership."[83]

Unfortunately for the administration, many in the country did not see it that way. In his daily newspaper column on February 6, 1948, Drew Pearson claimed that the solution to "the mystery of who killed Marriner Eccles" was in fact no mystery at all. "Eccles . . . long has

opposed what he described as the 'banking octopus of the West Coast'—
the Giannini chain," Pearson wrote. "Eccles also has frowned on the
approval of Giannini applications for the opening of between 15 and 20
new branches in California." In addition, Giannini's "financial influence in party circles is not to be sneezed at. And it was the question of
campaign contributions to the Democratic Party which finally tilted
the scales against Marriner Eccles."[84]

Similar allegations came from critics of bank holding companies in
Congress. Senator Tobey, who had introduced Eccles's bank holding
bill in the Senate two years earlier, was furious. In the spring of 1948
Tobey was chairman of a Senate committee investigating the qualifications of Thomas B. McCabe, a Philadelphia industrialist whom Truman had named to succeed Eccles as chairman of the FRB. One of the
first witnesses to appear was Snyder. Tobey tried to link the treasury's
post-Morgenthau shift toward a more sympathetic attitude regarding
Bank of America's expansion to a high-paying executive job promised
by Giannini to Snyder whenever he decided to leave Washington.

> *Tobey:* Is it true that A. P. Giannini offered you a job with Bank of America
> whenever you decided to leave the government?
>
> *Snyder:* That is my personal business. I am working for the government and
> have no intention of leaving.
>
> *Tobey:* Did the president consult with you about Mr. Eccles' demotion?
>
> *Snyder:* No. He merely asked me if Mr. McCabe would make a good board
> member and I said yes.[85]

Confronted by Tobey's sensational allegations and news accounts
critical of Bank of America's political clout in Washington, Giannini
issued a press release denying the "absurd columnists' statements" that
"we caused the demotion of Mr. Eccles." The "whole thing," Giannini
said, "would be humorous if it were not so clearly intended as propaganda to influence pending legislation. If we have any influence with
the administration, it is news to us."[86]

Whether Giannini actually made such an offer to Snyder is not
known. It is certain, however, that Giannini had a good deal more
influence in the White House than he cared to admit. In the summer of
1945, soon after Truman took over as president, Giannini turned to
Thomas "The Cork" Corcoran, the influential Washington wheeler-
dealer and "legislative strategist" during the first three terms of the
Roosevelt administration and now a private lawyer in the city. Corcoran's principal job, working closely with a handful of business lob-

byists, was to pressure Democratic party officials into persuading the administration to adopt a more sympathetic attitude toward Giannini's requests for additional Bank of America branch permits.

"Anything you tell me to do, I'll do, because we owe you a favor," Giannini told Corcoran.[87] "I want you to know at any time you want to order us—want to ask us anything, we'll do it. . . . We owe you anything you ask for. . . . You're the only guy that ever delivered a goddamned thing."[88] Corcoran eventually succeeded in coaxing some important concessions out of the Treasury Department, approval of which had come from the president himself.[89]

Whether Truman later bowed to pressure from "the Giannini interests" in Washington to "send Eccles back to Salt Lake City" is unlikely. By the spring of 1948 the relationship between Truman and Eccles had grown increasingly strained for a number of reasons, none related to the negative position Eccles had taken regarding Transamerica's ever-increasing size and power.[90] Despite these other sources of personal conflict, the speculation among Washington's special interest lobbyists was that Giannini, acting through Husbands and Snyder, had "engineered" Eccles's "head-chopping"; in return, Truman had been given assurances of Giannini's support in the fall presidential campaign at a time when California was critical to the president's hopes for reelection.[91]

Chairman of the FRB or not, Eccles wasn't about to abandon his pursuit of Transamerica and Bank of America. As early as the fall of 1947 he had instructed J. Leonard Townsend, who had been the lead government counsel in the SEC's complaint against Transamerica, to begin a preliminary investigation of the "over-all Transamerica situation, together with any suggestions you may have for dealing with the problem." Late in October, Townsend submitted a memorandum to Eccles in which he charged the "Transamerica banking empire" with "monopolistic aspects" and expressing concern over the corporation's "accelerated expansion program."[92]

Like Clark, Townsend told Eccles that there was "insufficient probable evidence" to justify government action under the antitrust provisions of the Sherman Act. The problem with the Sherman Act was that a successful claim by the government required not only proof of illegal trade practices but also clear evidence of monopolization. Instead, he urged that the FRB file a complaint against Transamerica under the Clayton Act, which prohibited stock acquisitions whose effects the government believed *may be* to lessen competition substantially, to restrain trade, or to create a monopoly. "There can be no doubt," Townsend told Eccles, "that Congress intended the board to have primary responsibility for enforcing this phase of national policy in the banking field."[93]

The job of collecting statistical evidence to support the FRB's complaint fell to E. A. Goldenweisar, the board's chief statistician, whom Eccles authorized to document Transamerica's "tendency to monopoly."[94] The result of Goldenweisar's research, which he sent to Eccles on April 22, 1949, was a warning of the potential "harm to the entire economy" as a consequence of Transamerica's "banking monopoly through its control of bank loans." Goldenweisar himself was startled by the findings of his investigation: As of 1947, Transamerica Corporation controlled some 41 banks with 562 branches in California, Washington, Oregon, Arizona, and Nevada. Bank of America's far-flung network of offices in California alone accounted for 500 branches. Transamerica also controlled nearly 40 percent of the total number of banking offices as well as 38 percent of total bank deposits in the same five states. The corporation's total assets exceeded $7 billion.

Goldenweisar cautioned Eccles that Transamerica's size and financial power had reached a point of overwhelming dominance that threatened the very survival of democratic institutions in the United States. "It has been the policy of the United States government since 1890," he wrote, "to foster a competitive system as the greatest safeguard for our free economic development and for the maintenance of our economic and political system. To permit the growth and tightening of a banking and money monopoly would therefore be contrary to established public policy. . . . It would also involve a grave danger to the economy of the region and ultimately to the economic, social, and political institutions of the country."[95]

Eccles decided the time for strong action had come. On July 22, 1948, the FRB issued a complaint against Transamerica charging the corporation with monopolization and antitrust violations under section 7 of the Clayton Act.[96] "For over forty-five years," the complaint said in part, "Transamerica, including its predecessor companies, had been continually expanding its banking interests by acquiring stocks of commercial banks in the five states of California, Oregon, Nevada, Washington and Arizona, and that the effect of such acquisitions may be to substantially lessen competition, restrain trade or tend to create a monopoly of commercial banking offices, commercial banking deposits and commercial bank loans in the five-state area or parts thereof."[97]

After seven years of charges and countercharges, Eccles had succeeded in putting Transamerica on trial.

4

On May 6, 1949, Giannini celebrated his seventy-ninth birthday with his son and daughter and a few close friends at his home in San Mateo. "Sorry, girls," he informed Bank of America's staff of secretaries in San Francisco a few days earlier. "I won't be coming to the office on my birthday. Skip all the flowers this time and the cake."[98] Giannini's cancellation of the birthday celebration came as no great surprise to his employees. In recent months his absences from his desk had become more frequent. He had developed heart trouble and was suffering from a variety of other ailments, the most troublesome of which was chronic bronchitis.[99] "He would telephone from home and say he thought he would 'take it easy today,'" one Bank of America executive would remember. "Then we would hear that he had been 'taking a rest' at some hospital near home."[100]

Despite his declining health, Giannini spent much of his time and energy in the spring of 1949 with a contingent of Transamerica lawyers preparing for the public hearings on the FRB's complaint against the corporation.[101] The signs pointed to a long and furious struggle. In Giannini's view, the legal technicalities over what did or did not constitute a "tendency to monopoly" was not the issue: he planned to concentrate on defending Transamerica with testimony from hundreds of witnesses attesting to Bank of America's long years of service to the people of California. As in his proxy battle with Elisha Walker twenty years earlier, Giannini intended to focus on a single theme: California versus the outsiders.

"Just look the Federal Reserve in the eye and tell them the truth," he told Samuel Stewart, Transamerica's chief legal counsel. "Don't make any excuses either. When they ask why we went into such-and-such a town, say we went there to bring service to the people. Bring in the people, too, and let them tell what we've done. They know and they are our friends. When the Federal Reserve talks about monopoly, you tell them you have to get big to give the best service. And after that you have to keep building better. You die when you stand still."[102]

Giannini, however, would not be among the hundreds of witnesses who testified in defense of the world's largest and most powerful bank holding company when the FRB hearings resumed in Washington a few months later. In the early morning hours of Friday, June 3, 1949, Giannini died in his sleep at his home in San Mateo. The official cause of death was heart failure.[103]

News of Giannini's death was given prominent coverage in newspapers across the country. The *New York Times* wrote, "The rise of Amadeo P. Giannini made pale the tales of Horatio Alger," adding that "no one has had a greater influence on the history of California."[104] The *Los Angeles Times* editorialized that Giannini was "a man of large ideas and the nerve to experiment with them. Money was not an end for him; it was a means. He saw profit where others saw only risk, and from the standpoint of fiscal result he was usually right. His unorthodox methods have been much criticized, but also much copied. That he changed banking in this state, if not in the nation, can never be denied."[105]

Letters and telegrams of sympathy poured into San Francisco from around the country. Many came from ordinary people whose sentiments gave evidence to their feelings about Giannini as a figure of enormous influence, one whose motives and ambitions had differed significantly from others in the world of high finance. "I write so poorly," said one typical letter, "but it is not often that a great man passes away and still rarer when it is someone like A. P. He is the first big businessman for whom many people will grieve or shed any tears. While I have the greatest respect for Morgan, Vanderbilt, Rockefeller and our authentic big shots, AP was the only one of them who had any sincere interest in the average American or any love for the common people."[106]

Condolences also came from the rich and powerful. Winthrop Aldrich, chairman of Chase National, called Giannini "a man of immense ability and courage." Thomas Corcoran wrote a sympathetic letter to Mario defending his father's empire-building obsessions. "All my life," Corcoran said, "I have been lucky to run with the swift and live with the strong. . . . A. P. could trade as well as dream. He was one of the originals who make a difference in their own right—for whose being here the world itself is different. The growth of California and the whole Coast and the shifts of power it has brought in the world— basically, I know, *he* did it. I shall always be indebted to him for his proof to me that a man unafraid could lick anything—and that an intellect great enough to win the prize needs no other food besides success."[107]

Giannini's funeral took place on June 6, 1949, at St. Mary's Cathedral in San Francisco. More than twenty-five hundred people filled the cathedral to overflowing. Thousands more lined the streets outside to watch the funeral procession. A reporter for the *San Francisco Chronicle* was particularly struck by the sharp contrast between the splendor of the cathedral's interior and the simple dress and manners of the hundreds of mourners who attended the service. "On side aisle and in the balcony they sat," he wrote, "men in hard brown suits, the pants legs hitched to reveal high black shoes. Women dressed in stern black, and with black felt hats pulled down low on their foreheads. Just as he had not forgotten them, they had not forgotten him on this day."[108]

At the family's request, the church service was brief. The Reverend John Lally eulogized Giannini as a "big man physically and mentally who rose from humble origins to fame as one of the greatest bankers of our time"; Archbishop John J. Mitty then performed the traditional Catholic sacrament of absolution.[109] As the cathedral choir sang "Benedictus Dominus Deus," Giannini's silver-and-gray casket was carried to a waiting hearse. Accompanied by a police motorcycle escort, a limousine took family members to Holy Cross Cemetery for a private burial service. After graveside prayers, Giannini was lowered into the ground next to his wife.

When Giannini's last will and testament was filed in San Francisco on June 14, 1949, the public was astonished to learn that his personal worth was relatively modest. His estate was valued at $489,254, $50,000 of which he left to various religious charities. The remainder he bequeathed to the Bank of America–Giannini Foundation. "Administer this trust generously and nobly," he instructed Mario, whom he had named executor, "remembering always human suffering. Let no legal technicality, ancient precedent or outmoded legal philosophy defeat the purpose of this trust. Like St. Francis of Assisi, do good—do not merely theorize about goodness."[110]

As had been the case with the SEC hearings ten years earlier, it was Transamerica that would win the last round in the corporation's battle with the FRB. In March 1952 the board's investigation of Transamerica—which had been going on for more than three years—came to an end. By a vote of three to two, the FRB declared Transamerica in violation of the Clayton Act. Transamerica was given two years to divest itself of all of its holdings in more than sixty banks within the five-state area of Oregon, Nevada, Washington, Arizona, and California.[111] The single exception in the board's order was Bank of America. "Divestiture by Transamerica of the stock of other banks," said Roscoe Evans, a member of the FRB, "will place majority holdings of the stock of those banks into new and different hands so that prompt and full disassociation from Transamerica can be expected."[112]

In fact, the FRB's ten-year pursuit of Transamerica had a far different outcome. In June 1952 the board's antitrust verdict against the corporation was rejected by the U.S. Court of Appeals. The court ruled, in part, that the FRB had failed to prove its charges of monopolization—a humiliating defeat for the board. On appeal, the Supreme Court refused to review the case. In Utah, Eccles, who had resigned from the FRB in 1951 to resume his family's banking and business affairs, told one interviewer, "There was no way on earth to keep Bank of America from expanding."[113]

Epilogue

During the first half of the twentieth century, the California economy underwent a remarkable transformation that catapulted the state into one of the fastest-growing regions in the nation. From 1900 to 1950 the population increased more than sevenfold—from 1.5 million to nearly 11 million—making California the nation's third largest state. New subdivisions, schools, shopping centers, bridges, and highways dotted the landscape from the Oregon state line to the Mexican border. California ranked first in farm production, growing enough in a wide variety of fruits and vegetables to supply the needs of the entire nation. Along with a remarkable increase in agricultural production, there was a corresponding growth in industrial production. The country's entry in World War II gave a tremendous boost to the state's industrial base, triggering an enlargement of production not exceeded anywhere else in the country. In Los Angeles County alone, aircraft plants turned out more than half the nation's total production of airplanes. Other industries, such as oil, steel, rubber, and shipbuilding, added to the remarkable growth. By war's end the total annual value of factory production in all industries had climbed to a remarkable $10 billion.

No one has a larger claim as the architect of these momentous changes than Amadeo Peter Giannini. He was eager to promote Bank of America as a huge, sympathetic source of credit to ordinary Americans and quick to open branches in his relentless effort to increase the bank's influence. He missed few opportunities to extend the financial power of his bank into every emerging enterprise that seemed to hold out new prospects for invigorating the economy, sometimes initiating but more often than not encouraging and accelerating that change. As an editorial writer for *Fortune* magazine expressed it at the end of World War II, "Giannini took full advantage of the forward motion all around him. Take away one of a score of U.S. impulses toward twentieth century growth, ranging from the Model T, the nickelodeon, and the telephone, to world wars and the broadening of the U.S. economy— take away any of these and the Bank of America, and California, would not be what they are today."[1]

From the beginning, Giannini wanted to achieve big things, first as a commission merchant on the San Francisco waterfront, later as a branch banker, still later as the builder of a nationwide network of banks. Seizing on branch banking as a way to grow and prosper, Giannini democratized the banking industry in California, developing with his energy and ambition an extensive network of branches that promoted a more vigorous and productive economy. As one financial writer put it, "Giannini was not the only banker who smelled the opportunity in the favorable attitude of California law toward the acceptance of savings accounts by commercial banks. Others could also see that California banking should look for its major growth to small deposits, and for its major profits to the retailing of credit to home builders, small units of farm and business enterprise, and consumers. But A. P.—because he sensed both the branch and the savings money opportunities more vividly than anyone else—exploited the relation between them more successfully than anyone else. Only branches could build savings accounts in huge quantities, and only branches could use savings accumulation on such a scale."[2]

Over the years Giannini's branch building ambitions generated bitter opposition, first from his competitors and state banking officials and later from an array of forces ranging from the federal reserve system and the secretary of the treasury to Wall Street. He had many powerful enemies, and he had to fight against repeated assaults against his bank, a fact that added to his acute awareness of being a minority member in a world of WASP establishment bankers. He manifested this sense of embattled outsider throughout his business career. "A. P. was quick to ascribe" any unusual delay in his expansionist ambitions "to an enemy's plot," one close associate would remember. "With him, a suspicion could grow quickly, and his reaction was apt to be more forceful than diplomatic. Because it was foreign to his nature to run away from a fight, he undoubtedly precipitated a few which more patience and tact might have avoided."[3] He seemed to thrive on controversy. He was, by his own admission, a "roughneck" who again and again expressed his pleasure at having aroused the enmity of the high and the mighty, whether in business or government. If this behavior created much unfavorable comment about Giannini's overly suspicious and overly combative nature, it nevertheless would prove more of a source of strength than a liability to him, at least from his perspective. "For whatever success I have attained," he would say toward the end of his life, "I give the bulk of the credit to my enemies. They stimulated me. They kept me going. I am thankful to them."

Giannini's driving ambition was yoked to a ferocious temper, an exalted sense of his own rectitude, an insatiable need to dominate his competitors, and a forcefulness in his relations with others that often bordered on intimidation. He could not tolerate criticism that seemed to reflect unfavorably on his business judgment, nor could he accept the opposition of public officials who wanted to frustrate his ambitions. He was convinced that he ran the best, most honest, and most public-minded banking institution in the country; anyone who took exception to these assertions would come to regret his dissenting opinions. Giannini was, as one financial writer would remember, a "good hater."[4]

"Giannini was ahead of his time in instinctively grasping the importance of integrating his business activities into the social interests of large numbers of people," said the financial columnist Merryle Rukeyser. "His concept of banking for the little people was more than a slogan."[5] As the son of immigrant Italian parents and a self-made man, Giannini shared with working-class families the folkloric American belief that success was achieved through a few essential elements: hard work, personal merit, and free enterprise. He had an exceptional sense of other people's hopes and ambitions. He genuinely believed that Bank of America was the bank of the people, the institutional support for those in search of a more productive and materially satisfying life; he saw himself as a social and economic hero, ready to assist ordinary people in enjoying the benefits of the free market system. "It has been my aim to distribute as much good as possible," he said on one occasion, "to make as many people as possible happy."[6] Through Bank of America, he had the idea of creating a greatly expanded middle class, making it larger and more accessible to more socially diverse groups of people. More important, he wanted to make this new middle class the foundation of a revitalized democracy. "He wanted them to have the more abundant life," one close associate would remember, "and more than any one man of his time he consciously engineered just that."[7]

Giannini was also more aware than other bankers of California's enormous potential for growth. He believed that what economic historians now call human capital—motivation, discipline, personal sacrifice, and the ethic of self-betterment associated with them—was nowhere more apparent than in California. What he saw, as he traveled throughout the state, was an immensely enterprising people and a region of rich and varied resources joined together in the creation of a huge new social and economic powerhouse whose influence would eventually be felt throughout the nation. The economic possibilities, he believed, were limitless. He was convinced that California and the West generally, in contrast to the Northeast, with its crusty and entrenched corporate and business practices, was on the eve of moving very rapidly into a position of great prominence over other regions of the country. He promoted this vision of the future relentlessly. "Big things are ahead for California," he told an interviewer. "California really is just starting to grow. All young men should live in the West. That's where the space is, that's where our future will be."[8]

Giannini's influence over the way banks conducted their business was enormous. Over the years that followed his founding of Bank of Italy in 1904, he financed much of California's rise to agricultural ascendancy with his liberal loan policy and the far-flung branch banking system he created to sustain it. California's remarkable industrial development in the twentieth century—manifested in the rise of Kaiser, Bechtel, Douglas, and Lockheed, among many others—benefited significantly from Giannini's determination to free the state's aggressive and newly emergent community of industrialists from their dependency on Wall Street. He was a major figure in the transformation of Los Angeles into a major metropolis and an ideal location for new industries, including the Hollywood film industry. As Giannini helped finance the growth of agriculture and small businesses, he simultaneously financed hundreds of films whose production stimulated the local economy significantly and added to the city's appeal to tourists and new waves of home buyers. At a time when most bankers were unwilling to become involved with consumer financing, Giannini plunged enthusiastically into the field of installment credit, thus creating a wide market in consumer goods for borrowers who had no other sources of credit.

Despite the enormous success of his bank, Giannini himself had no interest in accumulating money. He repeatedly resisted opportunities to cash in on profitable ventures; nor did he take pleasure from those things that money could buy. In contrast to other powerful businessmen, he collected no valuable art or priceless antiques; he lived quietly and modestly in the suburban enclave of San Mateo, shunning the glamour of San Francisco society. Giannini's ambitions were fed not by the privileges of wealth but by the exercise of power and the creation of a gigantic bank. He was the quintessential empire builder, a corporate titan whose departure from traditional banking practices not only remolded permanently the American financial system but also connected great numbers of ordinary people in a direct and personal way to one of society's most essential institutions. Many Americans had long hoped that private enterprise would help build a society offering equal economic opportunity and greater freedom for the many. By providing easy credit to the working class, the Bank of America expanded the boundaries of life for millions. This was A. P. Giannini's dream, and its realization was no small achievement.

Notes

Prologue

1. Moira Johnson, *Roller Coaster: The Bank of America and the Future of American Banking* (1990), 11–16.
2. Claire Giannini Hoffman, interview with the author.
3. See, for example, Roger Boschetti to Rudolph Peterson, April 23, 1969; see also Ernest E. Tabscott to Rudolph Peterson, May 6, 1969; Frank Longo, June 6, 1969, Bank of America Archives (BAA).
4. Rudolph Peterson to George F. Getty II, September 10, 1969, BAA.
5. "World's Biggest Bank," *Fortune,* July 1947, 69–72 (Man of Adventure series); see also "A Hall of Fame for Business Leadership," *Fortune,* January 1975, 64–74; Gary Hector, *Breaking the Bank: The Decline of BankAmerica* (1988), 17.
6. Matthew Josephson, "A. P. Giannini: Big Bull of the West," *Saturday Evening Post,* September 13, 1947, 15.
7. Fred Yeates, *The Gentle Giant* (1954), 6–7.
8. Matthew Josephson to A. P. Giannini, July 7, 1947, BAA.
9. Josephson, "Giannini," September 13, 1947, 16.
10. *New York City World,* February 12, 1928. See also *Forbes,* November 10, 1932; *Coast Banker,* August 1924.
11. Quoted in Matthew Josephson, *The Money Lords: The Great Financial Capitalists, 1925–1950* (1972), 69.
12. *Wall Street Journal,* May 9, 1939.
13. Johnson, *Roller Coaster,* 20.
14. "World's Biggest Bank," *Fortune,* July 1947, 69.
15. *San Francisco News,* March 1928 (BAA).
16. Yeates, *Gentle Giant,* 46.

17. *New York City World,* February 12, 1928; see also *Sunset,* February 1928 (BAA).

18. Josephson, "Giannini," September 27, 1947, 74.

19. Gordon Thomas and Max Morgan-Witts, *The Day the Bubble Burst: A Social History of the Wall Street Crash of 1929* (New York: 1979), 14.

20. Ettora Della Giovanna, "The Day the Pope Smiles," *BankAmerican,* 5.

1. Waterfront Entrepreneur

1. A. P. Giannini, interview with Jane Conant, *San Francisco Call-Bulletin,* June 6, 1949.

2. A biographical portrait of Luigi Giannini is found in Julian Dana, *A. P. Giannini: Giant in the West* (1947), 7–14. Dana's information was based in part on interviews with friends of the Giannini family from the old days. Notes on his interviews are found in the Julian Dana Papers, Bancroft Library, University of California, Berkeley.

3. For Luigi Giannini's plans to settle in California, see G. B. Cordano, interview with Bessie James, Bank of America Archives (BAA). An excellent discussion of Italian immigration to California is Dino Cinel, *From Italy to San Francisco: The Immigrant Experience* (1982); see also Deanna Paoli Gumina, *The Italians of San Francisco, 1850–1930* (1978), and Andrew Rolle, *The Immigrant Upraised* (1968), 251–95. For the physical similarity between Italy and California, see Mario Spinello, "Italians of California," *Sunset* 14 (January 1905): 256–58; Andrea Sbarboro, "Wines and Vineyards of California," *Overland Monthly,* January 1900, 65–96; Doris Wright, "The Making of Cosmopolitan California: An Analysis of Immigration, 1840–1870," *California Historical Society Quarterly* 19 (December 1940): 65–79.

4. Giannini seldom talked about his father. But in the years immediately following World War II, while traveling in Italy, he tried to find out more about the Giannini family's roots in Chivaki. His search took him to a convent outside Genoa, where he located his mother's sister. For information on Luigi Giannini's courtship and marriage, see Teresa DeMartini to George Solari, February 9, 1947, BAA.

5. Ibid. Additional information on the Gianninis' marriage and immigration to California can be found in the brief biographical sketch of Virginia Giannini, "In Memoriam," *Bankitaly Life,* September 1920.

6. On the hardships endured by immigrants to California via the Panama route, see John Haskell Kemble, "The Panama Route to California, 1848–1869," Ph.D. diss., University of California, Berkeley, 1937.

7. For social and economic developments in San Jose in the years following the gold rush, see Oscar Osburn Winther, *The Story of San Jose* (1935); Francis McCarthy, *The History of Mission San Jose California, 1797–1835* (1958), 223–37.

8. For scattered biographical material, see "World's Biggest Bank," *Fortune;* Julian Dana, "The Biggest Banker in the World," *Cosmopolitan,* June 1947; Grady Johnson, "Giannini—America's Best-Loved Banker," *Facts,* June 1945; "The True Story of Giannini," *Finance,* May 1944; "A. P. Giannini: Phenome-

nally Successful Banker of San Francisco," *Advance Bio-Bulletin,* October 1912; "The Phenomenon of the Bank of Italy," *Coronet,* August 1944; "A. P. Giannini, Banker to the West," *Look,* May 1927; "Men Who Developed the West—The Story of A. P. Giannini: A Trailblazer in Banking and Finance," *Goodall News,* August 1949.

9. Italian immigration to California is the topic of Hans C. Palmer, "Italian Immigration and the Development of California," Ph.D. diss., University of California, Berkeley, 1965; see also Ernest S. Falbo, "State of California in 1856: Federico Biesta's Report to the Sardinian Ministry of Foreign Affairs," *California Historical Society Quarterly* 42 (December 1963): 311–33; Arthur Inkersley, "The Vintage in California and Italy," *Overland Monthly* 54 (October 1909): 406–11; Ernest Peixotto, "Italy in California," *Scribner's,* July 1910, 75–84; Andrew Rolle, "Italy in California," *Pacific Spectator* 9 (Autumn 1955): 408–19.

10. Dana, *Giannini,* 7–9.

11. Hostility toward Italians in San Jose found frequent expression in the *San Jose Mercury and Herald,* the town's leading newspaper. For a discussion of anti-immigrant prejudice generally, see Lucile Eaves, *A History of California Labor Legislation* (1910); Gladys H. Waldron, "Anti-Foreign Movements in California, 1919–1929," Ph.D. diss., University of California, Berkeley, 1945; Spencer C. Olin, Jr., "European Immigrant and Oriental Alien: Acceptance and Rejection by the California Legislature of 1913," *Pacific Historical Review* 35 (October 1958): 305–15. On discrimination against Chinese, see Gunther Barth, *Bitter Strength: A History of the Chinese in the United States, 1850–1870* (1964); Elmer C. Sandmeyer, *The Anti-Chinese Movement in California* (1939); S. C. Miller, *The Unwelcome Immigrant* (1970).

12. Clyde Arbuckle, *History of San Jose* (1986), 236–37. There is a quite melodramatic and largely erroneous discussion of Luigi Giannini's murder in Dana, *Giannini,* who mistakenly dates the event as occurring in 1877. This date was repeated by Marquis and Bessie James in their *Biography of a Bank* (1954). A lengthy account of the incident appeared in the *San Jose Mercury and Herald,* August 14, 1876.

13. Dana, *Giannini,* 15–16. In 1925, shortly after the death of his mother, Giannini established the Virginia Scatena Memorial Fund for needy San Francisco schoolteachers. He contributed to the foundation 100 Bank of Italy shares, then worth $25,000.

14. For Giannini's early years in Alviso, see his interview with Jane Conant, *San Francisco Call-Bulletin,* June 3, 1949; see also Pauline Jacobson, "How I Began Life: Amadeo P. Giannini Tells Pauline Jacobson," *San Francisco Call,* November 26, 1921; Thane Wilson, "Look Ahead! Then Back Your Judgment to the Limit," *American Magazine,* August 1921; "The True Story of Giannini," *Finance,* May 1944; "A. P. Giannini, Banker Extraordinary," *Baltimore Sun,* February 26, 1928; A. C. Moore, "Giannini—Native Son and Native Genius," *The Citizen,* October 1926.

15. River transportation along the peninsula is discussed in Jerry MacMullen, *Paddle-wheel Days in California* (1944); see also Wallace Smith, *Garden of the Sun: A History of the San Joaquin Valley, 1772–1939* (1939); Julian P. Dana, *The Sacramento: River of Gold* (1942).

16. John Leale, *Recollections of a Tule Sailor* (1939), 64.

17. For biographical information on Lorenzo Scatena, see "Lorenzo Sca-tena," Personnel Records, BAA; see also "A Tribute to 'Boss' Scatena," *Bankitaly News,* 1930; Challis Gore, "A. P. Giannini—Biographical" (newspa-per collection), BAA; *San Francisco Call-Bulletin,* August 23, 1930; "Remarks and Motion Made by Louis Ferrari in Relation to the Death of Past President L. Scatena," in Board of Directors, Bank of Italy National Trust and Savings Association, Minutes, September 10, 1930, Transamerica Corporation Papers, BAA.

18. See Giannini, interview with Walter Bruns, March 31, 1949, BAA; see also Giannini, interview in B. C. Forbes, "Giannini—The Story of an Unusual Career," in his *Men Who Are Making the West* (1923), 204–27.

19. Giannini, interview with Jane Conant, *San Francisco Call-Bulletin,* June 6, 1949; see also Paul Dias (principal of the Alviso Grammar School), interview with Julian Dana, January 27, 1938, Julian Dana Papers; *San Jose Mercury and Herald,* June 21, 1925.

20. For a discussion of California's "terrible seventies," see Walton Bean, *California: An Interpretative History* (1968), 219–32. The relationship between water and the California economy is the focus of Frederick D. Kershner, "George Chaffee and the Irrigation Frontier," *Agricultural History* 27 (October 1953): 115–32.

21. Dana, *Giannini,* 17.

22. Robert O'Brien, *This Is San Francisco* (1948), 3.

23. For information on the Giannini-Scatena family in San Jose, I have relied on interviews with neighbors gathered by a team of researchers employed by the Bank of America to assist Marquis and Bessie James in the writing of *Biography of a Bank.* Given the institutional nature of the James's study, most of these recollections did not make their way into their book and were later collected and deposited in the Bank of America Archives in San Francisco. See file folder "Giannini—Before 1904," BAA.

24. The Gianninis lived in a number of homes in and around North Beach before moving to San Mateo. For a complete listing, see file folder "A. P. Giannini—Residences," BAA.

25. For Giannini's early years on the waterfront, see Reed Hayes, "A Real Romance of San Francisco: The Story of the Bank of Italy and A. P. Giannini," a seven-part series that appeared in the *San Francisco News* beginning on March 6, 1928. Hayes, a reporter for the newspaper, interviewed Scatena, Giannini, and numerous friends and relatives who reminisced about the old days on the waterfront. For the Scatena quote, see *San Francisco News,* March 6, 1928.

26. Ibid.

27. Ibid. "During the first month," Scatena told Hayes, "I earned $1500 for myself. Ever after that, I have been in business for myself except since we started the Bank of Italy."

28. James and James, *Biography of a Bank,* 6.

29. For the history and development of North Beach, see Raymond S. Dondero, *The Italian Settlement of San Francisco* (1953); Paul Radin, *The Italians of San Francisco: Their Adjustment and Acculturation* (1935); Gumina, *Italians of San*

Francisco: 1850–1930; Cinel, *From Italy to San Francisco.* See also Gladys Hansen, ed., *San Francisco: The Bay and Its Cities,* American Guide Series (1974), 223–36.

30. Hansen, *San Francisco,* 223.

31. Gumina, *Italians of San Francisco,* 41. For contemporary descriptions of the Italian community in North Beach, see Falbo, "State of California in 1856"; see also Frederick G. Bohme, ed. and trans., "Vigna Dal Ferro's 'Un Viaggio Nel Far West Americano,'" *California Historical Society Quarterly* 41 (June 1962): 148–61; Peixotto, "Italy in California"; Spinello, "Italians of California," 256–58; Francesco M. Nicosia, *Italian Pioneers of California* (1960).

32. For Giannini's recollections of his school days at the Washington Street Grammar School, see Giannini, interview with Walter Bruns, March 31, 1949, BAA; see also Giannini, interview with Jane Conant, *San Francisco Call-Bulletin,* June 6, 1949.

33. C. B. Cordano, interview with Bessie James, undated, BAA. Other useful material on Giannini's early activities in the Scatena firm may also be found in the *San Francisco Chronicle,* February 23, 1927; Moore, "Giannini— Native Son and Native Genius."

34. Giannini, interview with Walter Bruns, March 31, 1949, BAA.

35. Giannini, interview in *Oakland Press Enquirer,* March 16, 1928; see also *Forbes,* November 1923; Hayes, "Real Romance," March 8, 1928; *San Francisco Bulletin,* January 13, 1928.

36. Quoted in Hayes, "Real Romance," March 8, 1928; see also *San Francisco Chronicle,* February 27, 1927; "Meet America's Best Loved Banker," *National Public Affairs,* February–March 1946; "Giannini: Little Man's Banker," *Coronet,* April 1945; "APG—The Banker Who Knew His Onions," *The Gregg Writer* (March 1946); "The True Story of APG," *Finance,* May 10, 1944.

37. Quoted in Hayes, "Real Romance," March 9, 1928.

38. For material on the commission trade, see William Figari, "San Francisco and the Waterfront, 1900–1965" (interview conducted by Ruth Teiser), in *Regional Oral History Office,* Bancroft Library, University of California, Berkeley, 1969, 1–162; Thomas Crowley, "Recollections of the San Francisco Waterfront" (interview conducted by Karl Kortum and Willa Klug Baum), *Regional Oral History Office,* University of California, Berkeley (1967), 1–282; see also O'Brien, *This Is San Francisco;* George Harlan, *San Francisco Bay Ferryboats* (1967); John Kemble, *San Francisco Bay* (1957).

39. Quoted in Hayes, "Real Romance," March 8, 1928.

40. George Webster quoted in Hayes, "Real Romance," March 9, 1928.

41. For Giannini's recollections of his commission days on the waterfront, see APG to John Campedonico, September 23, 1938; see also APG to J. W. Sefton, July 23, 1944; Giannini, interview with Bessie James, October 7, 1947; Charles Grondona to Bessie James, undated memorandum; James Dougherty to APG, June 8, 1945, BAA. See also Frank Cooley to Mario Giannini, September 18, 1947, Lawrence Giannini Papers, BAA. Giannini's prowess as a commission merchant is also discussed in some detail in Dana, *Giannini,* 20–28, and in Hayes, "Real Romance," March 9, 1928.

42. George Webster quoted in Hayes, "Real Romance," March 9, 1928.

43. Charles Grondona to Bessie James, undated memorandum, BAA.

44. Giannini, interview with Bessie James, undated, BAA. "I was the most ignorant man about farming in the produce business," Giannini recalled later in life. "I was only interested in one thing. I was interested in the business of selling fruits and vegetables. It has been the same way for me at the bank. I don't know much about banking. I only know what I need to know to build the bank into a good business. My life is my business. I think all the time about my business" (APG to Albert Haase, undated memorandum, but sometime in 1947, BAA; see also *American Magazine,* August 1921; *Forbes,* November 1923).

45. Russell Smith and Virgil Dardi, interviews with the author; plus other interviews.

46. Giannini, interview with Walter Bruns, March 31, 1949, BAA.

47. G. B. Cordano, undated letter to Bessie James, BAA.

48. Giannini, interview with Walter Bruns, March 31, 1949, BAA; see also Hayes, "Real Romance," March 9, 1928.

49. Hayes, "Real Romance," March 9, 10, 1928.

50. For a good account of Giannini's days in the Sacramento Valley, see Josephson, "Giannini," September 20, 1947. For Giannini's own recollections, see Fred Yeates to APG, February 10, 1947; APG to Fred Yeates, February 12, 1947, BAA.

51. For descriptions of the produce commission trade in the Sacramento, see Dana, *Sacramento;* Smith, *Garden of the Sun;* Carey McWilliams, *California: The Great Exception* (1979); MacMullen, *Paddle-wheel Days in California;* Jack McNairn and Jerry MacMullen, *Ships of the Redwood Coast* (1945); William M. Camp, *San Francisco: Port of Gold* (1947); W. H. Hutchinson, *California: Two Centuries of Men, Land, and Growth in the Golden State* (1969), 157–75.

52. Quoted in Hayes, "Real Romance," March 9, 1929; see also Giannini, interview with Walter Bruns, March 31, 1949, BAA. For additional information on the commission trade in produce, see Rodman Paul, "The Beginnings of Agriculture in California: Innovation vs. Continuity," *California Historical Society Quarterly* 28 (1970): 19–27.

53. Quoted in *Forbes,* November 1923.

54. Dana, *Giannini,* 22–40. For recollections of Giannini's customers of his competitive work habits, see Frank Cooley to APG, September 18, 1947; Harold Stonier to Mario Giannini, June 4, 1949, BAA.

55. Giannini, interview in *Forbes,* November 1923; for other anecdotal material, see Giannini, interview in *Personal Efficiency,* November 10, 1925; *American Magazine,* August 1921; *New York Journal,* June 21, 1930; Dana, *Giannini,* 26–27; Hayes, "Real Romance," March 10, 1930.

56. On farmers' complaints and attempts to organize, see Paul S. Taylor, "Foundations of California Rural Society," *California Historical Society Quarterly* 24 (1945): 139–61; R. M. McCurdy, *The History of the California Fruit Growers Association* (1924); E. Kraemer and H. E. Erdman, *History of Cooperation in Marketing California Fresh Deciduous Fruits* (1933); Charles C. Teague, *Fifty Years A Rancher* (1944).

57. For comments on Giannini's personal conduct as a commission merchant, see Hayes, "Real Romance," March 8, 1928.

58. Russell Smith, interview with the author; other interviews by author; see also Russell Smith, Oral History Program, BAA; George Marvin, "De-Bunking Banking," *Sunset*, February 1928.

59. Giannini, interview with Walter Bruns, March 31, 1949, BAA; see also Hayes, "Real Romance," March 10, 1928; Josephson, "Big Bull of the West," September 13, 1947.

60. See Eda Beronio, interview with Bessie James, undated, BAA; see also James and James, *Biography of a Bank*, 6.

61. For biographical information on Joseph Cuneo, see APG and Clarence Cuneo to Bessie James, undated memoranda in file folder "A. P. Giannini—Before 1904," BAA.

62. Giannini's courtship of Clorinda Cuneo is discussed in some detail in Dana, *Giannini*, 33–35.

63. Giannini, interview with Bessie James, September 22, 1947, in file folder "Giannini—Before 1904," BAA.

64. See Giannini, interview with Walter Bruns, March 31, 1949; see also material in file folder "Giannini—Before 1904," BAA.

2. A New Career

1. Yeates, *Gentle Giant*, 8.

2. Winther, *Story of San Jose*, 43. For the boom in California agriculture and the expansion of the fruit and vegetable market, see Joseph McGowan, *History of the Sacramento Valley* (1939); Paul, "Beginnings of Agriculture in California"; H. J. Webber and L. D. Batchelor, eds., *The Citrus Industry* (1967); McCurdy, *History of the California Fruit Growers Exchange;* H. E. Erdman, "The Development and Significance of California Cooperatives, 1900–1915," *Agricultural History* 32 (July 1958): 179–84; Sidney H. Burchell, *Jacob Peek, Orange Grower: A Tale of Southern California* (1915).

3. Giannini, interview with Walter Bruns, March 31, 1949, BAA; see also Dana, *Giannini*, 31–32.

4. On these and other aspects of Giannini's activities in the commission trade, see Frank Cooley to APG, September 18, 1947, BAA. For anti-Catholic sentiment in the countryside, see Priscilla F. Knuth, "Nativism in California, 1886–1897," M.A. thesis, University of California, Santa Barbara, 1947.

5. Hayes, "Real Romance," March 10, 1928. For details on the Scatena firm's ascendancy in the commission trade, see Giannini, interview with Walter Bruns, March 31, 1949; see also Giannini, interview with Matthew Josephson, February 22, 1947; Giannini, interview with Bessie James, October 7, 1947, BAA. On other important aspects of the commission trade, see *San Francisco Wholesale Fruit and Produce Market* (1926); W. T. Calhoun et al., *Improving the San Francisco Wholesale Fruit and Vegetable Market* (1943); John Brucato, *The Farmer Goes to Town* (1948).

6. Hayes, "Real Romance," March 12, 1928.

7. Louis Bacigalupi (no relation to James Bacigalupi) later became one of the original stockholders in Giannini's Bank of Italy. For a biographical sketch of Bacigalupi, see Louis Bacigalupi file under acquisition file marked "People," BAA.

8. On the influence of the Irish in San Francisco generally, see R. A. Burchell, *The San Francisco Irish, 1848–1880* (1980), 116–54.

9. For factual information on Buckley and San Francisco politics at the turn of the century, I have relied on numerous sources, including William Bullough, *The Blind Boss and His City* (1979); Alexander Callow, Jr., "San Francisco's Blind Boss," *Pacific Historical Review* 25 (August 1956): 261–79; for additional information on Buckley's political career and turn-of-the-century politics in San Francisco, see also William Bullough, "The Steam Beer Handicap: Chris Buckley and the San Francisco Municipal Election of 1896," *California Historical Quarterly* 54 (1975): 245–59; William Bullough, "Hannibal Versus the Blind Boss: Chris Buckley, the 'Junta,' and Democratic Reform Politics in San Francisco," *Pacific Historical Review* 46 (May 1977): 181–206; Curtis Grassman, "Prologue To Democratic Reform: The Democratic Impulse, 1886–1898," *Pacific Historical Review* 42 (November 1973): 518–36; Hal R. Williams, *The Democratic Party and California Politics, 1880–1896* (1973).

10. On the "isolation" of North Beach Italians from larger San Francisco social and political issues, see Cinel, *From Italy to San Francisco,* 196–228.

11. On the use of fraud and intimidation in San Francisco politics, see Callow, "San Francisco's Blind Boss," 269–73; see also Walton Bean, *Boss Ruef's San Francisco: The Story of the Union Labor Party, Big Business, and the Graft Prosecution* (1952).

12. Bullough, *Blind Boss,* 236–37.

13. Bullough, *Blind Boss,* 234; see also William Issel, "The Reform Charter of 1898," *Labor History* 18 (Summer 1977): 341–59.

14. Hayes, "Real Romance," March 13, 1928.

15. Hayes, "Real Romance," March 12, 1928.

16. Ibid.

17. Ibid.

18. Ibid.

19. Ibid.

20. Ibid.

21. For additional genealogical data, see file folder "Giannini Family," BAA.

22. On APG's financial situation and retirement from the commission trade, see Gore, "A. P. Giannini—Biographical" (newspaper collection); see also Giannini, interview with Walter Bruns, March 31, 1949; Giannini, interview with Matthew Josephson, February 12, 1947, BAA.

23. See Giannini, interview with Bessie James and statement on his retirement in file folder "Giannini—Before 1904"; see also Bessie James, memorandum to Marquis James, September 22, 1947; APG to Fred Yeates, February 12, 1947, BAA.

24. See file folder "Residences"; see also Giannini, interview with Walter Bruns, May 29, 1949, BAA. For a published history of Seven Oaks, see Betty

L. Hoag, "A Man of Charisma: A. P. Giannini in San Mateo, California," *Journal of the San Mateo County Historical Association*, Spring 1973, 1–6.

25. For Giannini's real estate activities during his commission days, see Giannini, interview with Walter Bruns, March 31, 1949; see also Charles Grondona, interview with Bessie James in file folder "Giannini—Before 1904," BAA.

26. On details of the Cuneo will, see Clarence Cuneo, interview with Bessie James, in file folder "Giannini—Before 1904," BAA.

27. Giannini's financial arrangement with the Cuneo family was that he would receive a 25 percent commission on increases in the value of the real estate holdings he was directly responsible for. Fifteen years later, when the J. Cuneo Company was liquidated, Frank Cuneo, a brother-in-law, sued Giannini for the return of $36,994.24, which the family had paid him in commissions. Frank Cuneo argued that Giannini's commissions had been "excessive." He lost his case in a lower court decision, which was upheld on appeal. See James and James, *Biography of a Bank,* 523.

28. For additional information on Cuneo family property holdings, see Clarence Cuneo, interview with Bessie James, undated, but sometime in 1947, BAA.

29. For Cuneo's relationship with the Columbus Savings and Loan, see Minute Books of Fugazi's bank, which are located in the Bank of America Archives. Giannini acquired the Columbus Savings and Loan in 1926.

30. For biographical material on James Fugazi, see Ira B. Cross, *Financing an Empire: History of Banking in California,* 4 vols. (1927), 2:613; see also "James F. Fugazi," in *The Bay of San Francisco* 2 (1892): 54; "Bank President Fugazi, Donor, Highly Honored," *San Francisco Call,* February 13, 1913; Ettore Patrizi, *Gl'Italiani in California* (1911), 65.

31. On the establishment of Fugazi's bank in North Beach and a description of its activities, see Gumina, *Italians of San Francisco,* 141–42; see also Cinel, *From Italy to San Francisco,* 234–35. Cinel estimates that by 1901 Italian savings deposited in the Columbus Savings and Loan came to approximately $1.5 million. See also Raymond Dondero, *The Italian Settlement of San Francisco* (1950), 52–53. For hints about the disagreements among the bank's management, see pamphlet published by North Beach's leading Italian-language newspaper, *L'Italia,* translated by Dorothy Sturla in BAA; see also Charles Grondona, interview with Bessie James, in file folder "Giannini—Before 1904," BAA.

32. On these and other "conservative" aspects of Fugazi's bank policies, see Jesse McCargar, "Notes," Bank of Italy File; see also Charles Grondona, interview with Bessie James, in file folder "Giannini—Before 1904," BAA.

33. For a discussion of Sbarboro's life and career, see Deanna Paoli Gumina, "Andrea Sbarboro, Founder of the Italian Swiss Colony Wine Company," *Italian Americana,* August 1975, 1–17.

34. For biographical information on Andrea Sbarboro, see *Crocker-Langley San Francisco Directory for 1900* (1900), 533; see also Andrea Sbarboro, "Life of Andrea Sbarboro: Reminiscences of an Italian American Pioneer," manuscript,

Bancroft Library, University of California, Berkeley; Sbarboro, "Wines and Vineyards of California"; Hans C. Palmer, "Italian Immigration and the Development of California Agriculture," Ph.D. diss., University of California, Berkeley, 1965; Frank Norris, "Italy in California," *The Wave,* October 24, 1896; "Death Takes a Sbarboro," *San Francisco Examiner,* March 1, 1923; M. B. Levick, "Interesting Westerners: A Man with Three Thousand Monuments," *Sunset,* January 1913.

35. In twenty-five years of operation, Sbarboro's bank helped approximately twenty-five hundred Italian families in San Francisco, Oakland, Berkeley, and Alameda to become home owners. See *San Francisco Examiner,* March 1, 1923. Other information on the activities of Sbarboro's bank is found in H. L. Peraso, interview with Bessie James, in file folder marked "Giannini—Before 1904," BAA.

36. For population statistics, see Radin, *Italians of San Francisco,* 36.

37. See Giannini, interview with Bessie James, in file folder "Giannini—Before 1904"; see also Giannini, interview with Matthew Josephson, February 12, 1947, BAA.

38. James and James, *Biography of a Bank,* 11–12.

39. See Parker B. Willis, *The Federal Reserve Bank of San Francisco: A Study in American Central Banking* (1937), 16–18; see also Edmund H. Galvin, "Bank Capital on Trial," Ph.D. diss., University of Washington, Seattle, 1954, 10–13.

40. Cross, *Financing an Empire* 1:425–26.

41. James and James, *Biography of a Bank,* 11–12. According to the *New York Post* for July 6, 1906: "The wall of the Rocky Mountains made the California banks dependent on their own resources. . . . San Francisco is the metropolis and commercial heart of California. California is a State whose natural wealth may perhaps most strikingly be indicated by the statement that it has produced since 1849, $1,425,000,000 (this is 1906 figure) of gold, equaling the estimated stock of gold in the world on January 1, 1849. . . . The community was a creditor community; that is to say, the California banks never borrowed from New York or Chicago institutions, but constantly had large sums of money in New York and Chicago to their credit."

42. Cross, *Financing an Empire* 1:425–26.

43. As Giannini said later, "There isn't any good reason why a bank should have the temperature of a fish market. When you walked into some of them years ago you felt as if you'd got into an undertaking parlor"; quoted in George Marvin, "De-Bunking Banking," *Sunset,* February 1928, 13; see also Giannini, interview in *Personnel Efficiency,* January 8, 1925.

44. Giannini's ideas for the banking possibilities of the Columbus (and later his Bank of Italy) were stimulated in part by the success of San Francisco's two largest "immigrant" banks: the Hibernia and the German Savings and Loan. Both of these banks pursued depositors well beyond the confines of a single ethnic group—a policy Giannini had included in his recommendations to Fugazi and the Columbus's directors. See Giannini, interview with Bessie James, in file folder "Giannini—Before 1904," BAA.

45. See G. B. Cordano, interview with Bessie James, October 31, 1947, BAA.

46. See Charles Grondona, interview with Bessie James, in file folder marked "Giannini—Before 1904"; see also Giannini, interview with Bessie James, September 9, 1947. In addition to Giannini's testimony, see also statements by M. L. Perasso, Dr. Guido E. Caglieri, Charles Grondona, G. B. Cordano, V. L. Puccinelli, and George Chiappari, all in file folder "Giannini—Before 1904," BAA.

47. Quotation in Josephson, "Giannini," September 13, 1947, 138.

48. For biographical material on Fagan, see "James Fagan," Personnel Records, BAA. Additional material on the relationship between Giannini and Fagan is found in Jesse McCargar, interview with Bessie James, February 13, 1948; James Fagan to APG, July 27, 1923; Armando Pedrini to APG, July 30, 1923, BAA.

49. In addition to Fagan's testimony, this incident was later confirmed by three other sources—Jesse McCargar, Charles Grondona, and Gian Cordano—in interviews with Bessie James. See file folder "Giannini—Before 1904," BAA.

50. Challis Gore, "Bank of America N.T. & S.A. Chronology," 1905 (unpublished account of early history of the bank based on bank records and conversations with Giannini and other contemporary sources), in Challis Gore Papers, BAA; see also Bank of Italy, First Minute Book, 1904–1905, August 9, 1904, BAA.

51. Bank of Italy, First Minute Book, 1904–1905, August 9, 1904, BAA. See also other entries for 1904.

52. See Giannini, interview with Bessie James, in file folder "Giannini—Before 1904"; see also Eda Beronio, interview with Bessie James, October 7, 1947, BAA.

53. Hayes, "Real Romance," March 15, 1928.

54. For detailed information on change of name to Bank of Italy, see Giannini, interview with Bessie James, September 26, 1947; see also Bank of Italy, First Minute Book, 1904–1905, August 9, 1904, BAA.

55. Grondona was involved in selling shares in the bank at its beginnings. According to notes taken from his later testimony, "Grondona and A. P. went out to sell the shares of the Bank of Italy before it had been chartered. They had no difficulty with making sales because of their known successful business careers. Besides, they were well liked in the Italian settlement. Grondona said they sold the bank shares, one or two at a time; sometimes 25 in a block; to fishermen, peddlers, policemen, saloonkeepers—to people from every walk of life. He said the shares went like hot cakes which was why the bank was able to increase its capitalization so quickly after opening for business. . . . The Bank of Italy was located about a block from the city jail. . . . Some of the police from the jail bought shares and made deposits in the bank. With the police interested . . . the Bank of Italy received special attention from the coppers who covered the beat at night" (Charles Grondona, interview with Bessie James, October 2, 1947, BAA). Grondona's testimony that the shares went like "hot cakes" is confirmed by the minutes of the Bank of Italy's annual stockholders' meeting on February 28, 1906. Some ninety stockholders, representing 2,594 shares, attended the meeting, which suggests an average holding of approximately 20 shares. See Gore, "Bank of America," for year 1906.

56. For discussion of the bank's location, see Bank of Italy, Stockholders' Meeting, August 12, 1904, Bank of Italy, First Minute Book, 1904.

57. For Giannini's activities regarding the acquisition of the Drexler Building and Fugazi's reaction, see Bank of Italy, First Minute Book, 1904, August 12 and August 31, 1904; see also Armando Pedrini, interview with Bessie James, September 26, 1947; Eda Beronio, interview with Bessie James, dated October 7, 1947, BAA.

58. The Bank of Italy's address was 1 Montgomery Street, which was located on the northwest corner of Montgomery Avenue and Washington Street. Montgomery Avenue was later changed to Columbus Avenue. See James and James, *Biography of a Bank,* 15.

59. For biographical information on Armando Pedrini, see "Armando Pedrini," Personnel Records, BAA. See also Bank of Italy, First Minute Book, 1904–1905, 11, and entry from *Who's Who in California,* 1928–1929, BAA.

60. As it turned out, this agreement touched off a minor argument between Giannini and the bank's directors. They could not understand why he had agreed to give Pedrini twice the salary he was earning at the Columbus. "Because he knows his business and because he is polite and has a following," Giannini replied. "The women are crazy about him, he kisses their hands Continental fashion, and he gives a man in overalls as much attention as a big depositor." Giannini's explanation did not impress his directors, who opposed the increase. The problem was solved when Giannini agreed to pay the additional $150 out of his own pocket until Pedrini proved his worth to the bank. On Giannini's decision to hire Pedrini and the board's reaction, see Giannini, interview with Bessie James, September 26, 1947; Eda Beronio, interview with Bessie James, October 7, 1947; see also Gore, "Bank of America," entry dated September 17, 1904; Bank of Italy, First Minute Book, 1904, BAA.

61. See Giannini, interview with Bessie James, in file folder "Giannini— Before 1904"; see also *Bankitaly Life,* February 1921, BAA.

3. A People's Bank

1. Challis Gore, "Bank of America," January 18, 1905; see also APG to Bessie James, undated, but sometime in 1947, BAA. See also James and James, *Biography of a Bank,* 17.

2. For biographical data on Charles Grondona, see "Charles Grondona," Personnel Files, BAA; see also Grondona, interview with Bessie James, October 2, 1947, BAA.

3. See data on Bank of Italy's first depositors and financial statements supplied by G. O. Boardwell in file folder "Bank of Italy—Financial, 1904–1907," BAA.

4. Charles Grondona, interview with Bessie James, October 2, 1947; see also Gore, "Bank of America," January 18, 1905; Bank of Italy, First Minute Book, 1904, BAA. Giannini accepted no salary for the first fifteen months of the Bank of Italy's existence. He was voted a salary of $200 a month by the

board at a director's meeting on February 1, 1906 (Bank of Italy, First Minute Book, 1906, BAA). Giannini's door-to-door campaign in North Beach soon paid off. By the end of November 1904, the bank's savings accounts had jumped to 156, representing deposits of slightly more than $44,000. See Bank of Italy, First Minute Book, October 31, 1904, BAA.

5. For information on the failure of the French Mutual, see Cross, *Financing an Empire* 1:439. As some North Beach Italians would remember, "Our experience in the past has not been happy with so-called bankers of our race. A good many of them have for some reason failed, and our people became skeptical." See *Sons of Italy Magazine* 11, no. 3 (September 1938). For the repercussions of the French Mutual's failure in North Beach, see Grondona, interview with Bessie James, October 2, 1947, BAA.

6. Grondona, interview with Bessie James, October 10, 1947, BAA.

7. According to the testimony of one Bank of Italy executive and a Giannini aide, Giannini "was quick to sense the need of rural California for a more democratic and helpful banking system that would in due course bring to even the remotest corners of his native State the boon of a more resourceful and adequate metropolitan bank. There was nothing original in this thought, because San Francisco even then possessed several successful branches of Canadian branch banks and his reading and reasoning had convinced him that there must have been sound merit in the fact that practically all other civilized nations, much older in banking experience than our own, after trying out every form and type of banking system, had uniformly adopted nation-wide branch banking" (James A. Bacigalupi, statement, *Hearings Before Committee on Banking and Currency*, House of Representatives, May 1930, 2d sess., part 2, p. 1340).

8. The way Giannini later told it, "There were big merchandising houses all through the valley—a lot of Jewish firms—and they sold groceries and supplies to the farmers on credit. That would go on until he had a bad year, and then he would lose everything. A lot of them were always in debt. . . . We had run a branch business in the produce line, and I didn't see why it wasn't a good thing for banking. I don't see why a bank shouldn't have as many branches as can make money. We will go into any town where we can make money" (Giannini, interview with Walter Bruns, March 31, 1949, BAA).

9. Quoted in Josephson, "Giannini," September 13, 1947, 30.

10. On occasion, San Francisco banks published the names of their officers and directors, but that was the extent of their efforts to solicit customers. Giannini himself did not begin advertising in English-language newspapers until 1906, but he did place large ads in *La Voce del Popolo, L'Italia,* and other North Beach Italian-language newspapers. Announcement of the Bank of Italy's opening, for example, was advertised in *L'Italia.* See *L'Italia* ads for October 15, 16, and 17, 1904, translated by Dorothy Sturla, BAA. As Giannini later remembered, "A banker is never popular. People are always suspicious of bankers. You never hear of them being elected to office. The old idea of a banker was that he must hold himself aloof, wear a silk hat and shut himself up in fancy quarters. He thought he couldn't solicit trade. If trade's worth having it's worth going after. The tendency when a man gets on top is to shut himself off from the masses, forget the little fellow who made him. It isn't the big fellow who's

your friend. As a rule the big fellow is looking to use you, and when he has no more use for you he throws you over." See Giannini interview, *San Francisco Bulletin*, November 26, 1921.

11. Quoted in Josephson, "Giannini," September 13, 1947, 16.

12. Grondona, interview with Bessie James, October 10, 1947, BAA.

13. See Bank of Italy, First Minute Book, January 17, 1906, BAA.

14. See Gian Cordano, interview with Bessie James, October 3, 1947; see also Grondona, interview with Bessie James, October 2, 1947, BAA. Several Bank of Italy directors held "extra" shares of stock, which Giannini kept in reserve to supply the demand. In addition to his own 100 shares, for example, Fagan carried some 1,900 shares that were later sold to 149 new stockholders, most of whom lived in North Beach. See Bank of Italy, General Ledger, 1904, BAA. See also Bank of Italy, First Minute Book, December 27, 1904, BAA.

15. See list of 159 Bank of Italy shareholders, nearly all of whom were Italians, in Gore, "Bank of America," taken from booklet published by the bank in Italian, undated, but sometime in 1904, BAA. Shareholders included, for example, Charles Maggini, 25 shares; Antonio Chichizola, 60 shares; L. Demartini, 100 shares; G. Garibaldi, 25 shares; G. B. Legaggi, 100 shares; G. Granucci, 25 shares; and Clarence Musto, 30 shares. See Bank of Italy, Financial Statement, June 30, 1905, furnished by G. B. Boardwell, BAA.

16. Joseph Giovinco, "Democracy in Banking: The Bank of Italy and California's Italians," *California Historical Society Quarterly* 47 (September 1968): 207.

17. Giannini kept Bank of Italy open on Sundays. See Giannini, interview with Bessie James, September 22, 1947; see also Charles Grondona, interview with Bessie James, October 2, 1947, BAA. For comments on Giannini's service to North Beach residents, see *L'Italia*, July 12, 1906.

18. Giannini, interview with Bessie James, September 26, 1947, BAA.

19. See Clarence Cuneo, interview with Bessie James, September 25, 1947, BAA.

20. See Bank of Italy, First Minute Book, 1905, for commercial and savings deposits in the period from July 1, 1905, to December 31, 1905. See also Bank of Italy, General Ledger, entry dated April 17, 1906, BAA. For additional information, see financial statements supplied by George Boardwell in file folder marked "Bank of Italy—Financial, 1904–1906," BAA; *L'Italia*, July 2, 1906.

21. Bank of Italy, First Minute Book, June 29, 1906, BAA.

22. Hayes, "Real Romance," March 16, 1928.

23. See Giannini, interview with Bessie James, September 22, 1947, BAA.

24. For Giannini's efforts to reach San Francisco, see Giannini, interview with Bessie James, September 26, 1947; see also recollections of an unidentified clerk in the Scatena firm dated April 14, 1937; first draft of an article by John Cooney, dated September 10, 1944, BAA.

25. For information on the earthquake's devastation, see Gordon Thomas and Max Witts, *The San Francisco Earthquake* (1971); William Bronson, *The Earth Shook, the Sky Burned* (1959); John Kennedy, *The Great Earthquake and Fire* (1963).

26. See Giannini, interview with John Cooney, August 23, 1944, BAA.

27. The two employees were Ettore Avenali and Armando Pedrini, who roomed together in North Beach. According to Avenali, the two men "had decided to follow the usual daily custom of calling at the Crocker National Bank to withdraw bank monies left there each night in a safe deposit box." See Ettore Avenali, interview with Julian Dana, June 7, 1937, Julian Dana Papers.

28. Doctor Guido E. Caglieri, interview with Bessie James, undated, but sometime in 1947, BAA.

29. Giannini, interview with Bessie James, September 22, 1947, BAA; see also recollections of an unidentified clerk in the Scatena firm, April 14, 1937.

30. See Charles Grondona, interview with Bessie James, September 25, 1947; see also recollections of an unidentified clerk in the Scatena firm, April 14, 1937, BAA. Quotation from Giannini, interview with John Cooney, August 18, 1944, BAA. For additional material on the trip back to San Mateo, see Charles Grondona and Clarence Cuneo, interviews with Bessie James, September 25, 1947, BAA.

31. Giannini, interview with Bessie James, September 22, 1947; see also Giannini, interview with John Cooney, September 10, 1944, BAA.

32. On Giannini's return trip to San Francisco, see Giannini, interview with Bessie James, September 22, 27, 1947, BAA.

33. On the damage to the city, see John McGloin, *San Francisco: The Story of a City* (1978), 132–53; see also Thomas and Witts, *San Francisco Earthquake,* 229–30; "San Francisco Prostrate But Courageous," *The Outlook,* May 26, 1906, 157–71; "San Francisco Rising from the Ashes," *The Outlook,* July 7, 1906, 562–70.

34. For a description of the meeting, see Leroy Armstrong and J. C. Denny, *Financial California: An Historical Review of the Beginnings and Progress of Banking in the State* (1916), 134; see also *San Francisco Chronicle,* April 28, 1906; Giannini, interview with Bessie James, September 22, 1947, BAA.

35. In his monumental four-volume history of banking in California, Ira Cross estimates that approximately $76 million in cash lay in bank vaults made inaccessible by the fire. For problems facing bankers in the days immediately following the earthquake and fire, see Cross, *Financing an Empire* 2:670–85; see also *San Francisco Examiner,* April 27, 1906.

36. For Pardee's proclamation and other actions, see *San Francisco Examiner,* April 21, 1906.

37. See Armstrong and Denny, *Financial California,* 134; see also Cross, *Financing an Empire* 2:686; *San Francisco Examiner,* April 27, 1906; *San Francisco Recorder,* June 23, 1906.

38. See, for example, Dana, *Giannini,* 58–59; see also James and James, *Biography of a Bank,* 27–28.

39. William Crocker, president of the Crocker-Woolworth, had succeeded in getting most of the bank's cash and securities out of its vaults before the fire reached the financial district. A few days after the earthquake the Crocker-Woolworth opened for business on a "limited basis" in Banker's Row along San Francisco's Lafayette Square. See Jesse McCargar, interview with Bessie James, February 13, 1948, BAA. See also Thomas and Morgan-Witts, *San*

Francisco Earthquake, 119. For other bank openings, see George Boardwell, interview with Bessie James, September 22, 1947, BAA; *San Francisco Examiner,* April 21, 28, 1906; *San Francisco Chronicle,* May 8, 1906.

40. For Giannini's circular letter to the bank's depositors, see Giannini, interview with Bessie James, September 22, 1947, BAA; see also Wilson, "Look Ahead!"; "The True Story of Giannini," *Finance,* May 1944; "The Bank of Italy, San Francisco," *Bankers Magazine,* March 1918. For similar public announcements of the bank's reopening, see *L'Italia,* May 19, 1906, translated by Dorothy Sturla, BAA.

41. For additional information on Giannini's "waterfront bank," see Giannini, interview with Walter Bruns, March 31, 1949, BAA. As Giannini told another interviewer, "I used to come up every day (from San Mateo) with gold and currency in a satchel to put up cash for the little fellows who wanted it to get started again. . . . We paid on cash books and on character. We paid on cash books of other banks—Crocker bank, for instance" (Giannini, interview with Bessie James, September 22, 1947, October 2, 7, 1947, BAA).

42. Giannini later moved his banking operations to Charles Grondona's real estate office at 632 Montgomery Street. See Charles Grondona, interview with Bessie James, October 14, 1947; see also John Burns, interview with Bessie James, July 9, 1948, BAA. See also Bank of Italy, First Minute Book, May 1, 1906, BAA; *San Francisco Examiner,* May 12, 1906.

43. See article in *L'Italia,* July 2, 1906, translated by Dorothy Sturla, BAA; see also Charles Grondona, interview with Bessie James, October 2, 1947, BAA.

44. For example, Cirisco and Rosania Addiego ($1,500); A. and D. Stegnaro ($5,000); Antonio and Maria Perata ($4,000); Marano and Santo Tortorce ($500); Philip DeMartini ($13,000); Celeste and Adalada Gallia ($4,000). For list of loans made by Giannini in the days following the earthquake and fire, see Bank of Italy, First Minute Book, July 10, 1906, BAA.

45. Charles Grondona, interview with Bessie James, October 2, 1947, BAA.

46. Ibid.

47. See Charles Grondona, interview with Bessie James, September 22, 1947, BAA. One such firm was J. B. Schiaffino and Company. According to Grondona, the firm "would borrow $10,000 at a time, assigning its fire insurance policy to the Bank of Italy to secure the loan. Before his importations reached San Francisco, they would have been sold and he was in a position to borrow more from Bank of Italy. After the fire . . . Schiaffino had $80,000 in goods floating between Europe and the United States, all financed on $10,000 from Bank of Italy" (Charles Grondona, interview with Bessie James, October 6, 1947, BAA).

48. *L'Italia* estimated that during the period from April 1906 to April 1907, some seven hundred building permits valued at approximately $4 million were granted to North Beach's Italian residents (*L'Italia,* "Facts and Figures Worthy of Consideration" [editorial], April 18, 1916, translated by Dorothy Sturla, BAA).

49. *L'Italia,* July 2, 1908; see also *L'Italiani in California,* pamphlet published by *L'Italia* in 1911, translated by Dorothy Sturla, BAA.

50. *San Francisco Call,* October 4, 1906; see also *San Francisco Chronicle,* September 1, 1906, and April 13, 1907. "The busiest portion of the city today," the *Chronicle* said, "is the northern, or what was known as the Italian quarter. . . . Mr. Giannini . . . is taking a large part in the reconstruction of the northern part of the city." See also *San Francisco Examiner,* October 21, 1906.

51. For discussion of the bank's new location, see Bank of Italy, First Minute Book, June 12, July 21, and September 1, 1906, BAA.

52. *San Francisco Chronicle,* August 17, 1908.

53. For the Gianninis' trip to the East Coast, see Gore, "Bank of America," January 8, 1907.

54. For discussion of these issues, see Milton Friedman and Anna Schwartz, *A Monetary History of the United States, 1867–1960* (1963); Robert Sobel, *Panic on Wall Street: A History of American Financial Disasters* (1972); Fredrick Lewis Allen, *The Big Change: 1900–1950* (1952); Andrew Sinclair, *Corsair: The Life of J. Pierpont Morgan* (1981).

55. Schiff's talk was delivered to a meeting of New York's Chamber of Commerce. See Alexander Noyes, *Forty Years of American Finance* (1938), 128–29.

56. On the weakness in the American banking system, see Paul Warburg, *The Federal Reserve System—Its Origins and Growth,* vol. 1 (1930); see also Anthony Sampson, *The Money Lenders: Bankers and a World in Turmoil* (1982); Seymour Harris, *Twenty Years of Federal Reserve Policy* (1933); Richard Sayers, *Modern Banking* (1938); Martin Mayer, *The Bankers* (1974).

57. For the relationship between San Francisco banks and their correspondents in the San Joaquin Valley, for example, see Jesse McCargar, interview with Bessie James, February 13, 1948, BAA; see also Carl C. Phelin, "The San Francisco Clearing House Certificates of 1907–1908," *Publications of the Academy of Pacific Coast History,* January 1909, 3–4; *Proceedings of the Fourteenth Convention of the California Bankers Association,* May 14–18, 1908, 83; *San Francisco Call,* October 29, 31, 1907.

58. See, for example, *Daily Journal of Commerce,* May 15, 1907; see also *Commercial and Financial Chronicle,* May 16, 1907.

59. See Giannini, interview with Bessie James, undated, but sometime in 1947, BAA.

60. Giannini's success in this regard is reflected in Bank of Italy's first quarter statement for 1906, which showed an increase of $300,000 in deposits, bringing total deposits to nearly $1 million. See Bank of Italy, First Minute Book, January 17, 1906, 94, BAA. For other indications of growing confidence among Italians in Giannini's bank, see the editorial in *L'Italia,* January 2, 1908.

4. On the Move

1. Bank of Italy closed the year 1906 with 2,644 depositors; see Bank of Italy, First Minute Book, January 16, 1907, BAA. Other San Francisco banks responded to the rumors of an imminent crisis by sharply reducing their real estate loans. See *The Recorder,* November 5, 1907.

2. See Giannini, interview with Bessie James, undated, but sometime in 1948, BAA.

3. See Charles Grondona and Clarence Cuneo, interviews with Bessie James, undated, but sometime in 1948, BAA; see also Hayes, "Real Romance," March 19, 1928; *San Francisco Call,* January 9, 1949.

4. Following the policy he recommended to the board at the June directors' meeting, between the end of the month and the end of September the bank increased its real estate loans by only $40,000 and its personal loans by less than $16,000. See Bank of Italy, General Ledger, 1907, nos. 1–2, BAA.

5. See James and James, *Biography of a Bank,* 36; Charles Grondona and Clarence Cuneo, interviews with Bessie James, undated, but sometime in 1948; see also Jesse McCargar, interview with Bessie James, February 14, 1948, BAA.

6. By the time the panic hit San Francisco in the late fall of 1907, Giannini had "hoarded" approximately $50,000 in gold in the vaults of the Crocker-National. See figures supplied by George Boardwell in file folder "Bank of Italy, Financial, 1904–1907," BAA. On Giannini's campaign to reduce loans, see Bank of Italy, General Ledger, 1907, nos. 1–2, BAA.

7. James and James, *Biography of a Bank,* 36. For the board's approval of the Mission Street "branch," see Bank of Italy, First Minute Book, 1907, 108; see also Gore, "Bank of America," August 13, 1907, BAA.

8. Gumina, *Italians of San Francisco,* 142.

9. For a discussion of the "mixed-multitudes" of California's immigrant population, see McWilliams, *California,* 63–88.

10. For Giannini's promotional activities in the Mission district, see *Mission Times,* August 3, 1907.

11. See collection of clippings from *L'Italia* for similar advertisements in Advertising and Publicity Department, Bank of America, translated by Dorothy Sturla, BAA.

12. See *San Francisco Chronicle,* October 17, 1907; see also *Dun's Review,* January 21, 1908.

13. On the 1907 panic, see Sobel, *Panic on Wall Street;* Dana L. Thomas, *The Plungers and the Peacocks* (1967); Noyes, *Forty Years of American Finance;* Charles Colman, *Our Mysterious Panics, 1830–1930* (1931); Richard Wycoff, *Wall Street Ventures and Adventures Through Forty Years* (1930). For weaknesses in the banking system, see *Report of the Comptroller of the Currency for 1908,* 64; *San Francisco Commercial and Financial Chronicle,* October 20, 1907, and November 2, 1907; *Dun's Review,* January 11, 1908.

14. *San Francisco Chronicle,* October 24, 31, 1907. A state banking examination later disclosed that the California Safe Deposit and Trust had made more than $11 million in loans to its directors and management. Loans to one director amounted to $4 million. See *Report of Bank Commissioners of California for 1908,* 20–23.

15. *San Francisco Chronicle,* October 31, 1907; *San Francisco Examiner,* October 31, 1907. See also Phelin, "San Francisco Clearing House Certificates," 3–4. For other emergency measures taken by San Francisco banks, see *San*

Francisco Chronicle, October 30, November 1, 1907. A good general account of the panic in San Francisco is found in Cross, *Financing an Empire* 2:700–706.

16. It was customary for all California banks to stack piles of gold inside the teller cages, but on this occasion Giannini "piled his stacks higher than ever . . . on the theory that his depositors would go away reassured by the sight of so much money" (Mario Giannini, interview with Bessie James, undated, but sometime in 1948, BAA).

17. For favorable comment about the Bank of Italy, see editorial in *L'Italia,* November 1, 1907, translated by Dorothy Sturla, BAA. By contrast, the Crocker National was forced to pay some $50,000 in premiums to obtain gold from New York and Chicago to satisfy the demands of its correspondent banks in the San Joaquin Valley. See Jesse McCargar, interview with Bessie James, February 13, 1948, BAA.

18. Along with the California Safe Deposit and Trust, three other San Francisco banks—the Citizens State, the Market Street Bank, and the Bank of Greater San Francisco—went into bankruptcy. See Cross, *Financing an Empire* 2:705–6.

19. See *San Francisco Daily Commercial News,* December 12, 1907; see also *San Francisco Examiner,* October 30, 1907. Bank of Italy finished the year with approximately $1.5 million in deposits—an increase of $300,000 over the previous year. Real estate loans also increased by nearly $500,000. See figures supplied by George Boardwell in file folder "Bank of Italy—Financial, 1904–1907"; see also Bank of Italy, General Ledger, nos. 1 and 2, BAA.

20. Among other things, an investigation of the state's banking industry disclosed that, although banks in cities of over 200,000 were required by law to keep a cash reserve equivalent equal to 25 percent of deposits, hardly any of them had done so. See speech by Governor J. N. Gillette, in *Proceedings of the Fifteenth Convention of the California Bankers Association, 1908,* 70–72; see also *San Francisco Examiner,* November 19, 1907; *San Francisco Chronicle,* November 20, 1907.

21. See Gerald D. Nash, *State Government and Economic Development: A History of Administrative Politics in California, 1849–1933* (1964), 228–32.

22. Quoted in Mansel G. Blackford, *The Politics of Business in California, 1890–1920* (1977), 101.

23. Cross, *Financing an Empire* 3:128–30.

24. See Giannini, interview with Bessie James, undated, but sometime in 1948, BAA.

25. At the time of Giannini's visit, there were some 35 banks in Canada with 1,841 branches in 1,016 towns and cities. As one writer explained it, "None of the branch banks could make a run on the parent or reserve banks as was occurring in 1907 in the United States. No parent bank would make a run on another even if it could. A common interest bound them together" (Hayes, "Real Romance," March 19, 1928).

26. Giannini later contrasted the Canadian system with the U.S. banking system, in which, "until branch banking was brought about, most every banker felt he had to stand alone; had to protect himself, no matter what might happen

to another" (quoted in Hayes, "Real Romance," March 19, 1928). For a fuller statement on Giannini's attraction to Canada's branch banking system, see *Wall Street Journal*, June 21, 1925. See also APG to Charles Collins, March 2, 1927, BAA.

27. See Giannini's statement in unidentified clipping, December 1927, BAA.

28. See Giannini, interview in *San Francisco Examiner*, May 23, 1927. As Giannini put it, "The development of our nation's resources demands big capital and large institutions to handle it in mobile form like the direction of an army in the field, so that forces can be shifted from place to place where most needed. The small banks, even in interior towns, can no longer meet the requirements of intricate and far-reaching business demands." See also Giannini, interview in *Wall Street Journal*, June 21, 1935.

29. See Giannini's statement in the *Sacramento Bee*, January 2, 1936; see also *San Francisco Commercial News*, February 23, 1944; *San Francisco Examiner*, August 1, 1941.

30. See Giannini's statement in *San Francisco Examiner*, August 21, 1937.

31. *San Francisco News*, March 19, 1928.

32. John P. Wernette, "Branch Banking in California," Ph.D. diss., Harvard University, 1932, 30–31.

33. See George Dowrie, "History of the Bank of Italy in California," *Journal of Economic and Business History* 2 (1930): 277–78; see also H. H. Preston, "Bank of America," *Journal of Economic and Business History* 4 (1932): 200–201.

34. See *San Francisco Examiner,* October 30, 1907, November 18, 1907.

35. See speech of Governor J. N. Gillette, in *Proceedings of the Fifteenth Convention of the California Bankers Association, 1908,* 70–72; see also *San Francisco Examiner*, November 18, 19, 1907; *San Francisco Chronicle*, November 20, 1907.

36. Nash, *State Government and Economic Development,* 281.

37. See *Proceedings of the Fifteenth Convention of the California Bankers Association, 1908,* 79–88; see also *Statutes and Amendments to the Codes of California,* Thirty-eighth Session, chap. 76. For a full discussion of the 1909 Banking Act, see *Coast Banker*, March 1909, 105–7.

38. Section 9 of the 1909 Banking Act provided: "No bank in this state, or any officer or director thereof, shall thereafter open or keep an office other than its principal place of business, without first having obtained the written approval of the Superintendent of Banks to the opening of such branch office, which written approval may be given or withheld in his discretion, and shall not be given by him until he has ascertained to his satisfaction that the public convenience and advantage will be promoted by the opening of such branch office"; see *Coast Banker*, March 1909, 105–7.

39. In preparation for his move outside San Francisco, Giannini increased the bank's capital from $500,000 to $1 million. See Gore, "Bank of America," March 10, 1908, BAA.

40. F. C. Mitchell, interview with Bessie James, undated, but sometime in 1948, BAA.

41. By 1910 there were approximately thirty thousand Italians living in the Santa Clara Valley.

42. On San Jose's development from a frontier outpost to a major farm center by the end of the nineteenth century, see Oscar O. Winther, *The Story of San Jose, 1777–1869* (1935); John Caughey, *California: A Remarkable State's Life History* (1970); Ralph J. Roske, *Everyman's Eden: A History of California* (1968), 257.

43. From 1878 to 1896 the Commercial and Savings assets had declined by more than $150,000. Real estate foreclosures in 1896 alone came to approximately $80,000. See Cross, *Financing an Empire* 2:670, 892, 909.

44. For loans to various members of the Murphy family, see Commercial and Savings Bank of San Jose, Minute Book, 1869–1907, BAA.

45. For Lion's efforts to keep the Commercial and Savings from bankruptcy, see Commercial and Savings Bank of San Jose, Minute Book, 1909–1910, 12, BAA. Biographical information on Lazard Lion appears in Amaury Mars, *Reminiscences of Santa Clara Valley* (1935), 58.

46. See James A. Bacigalupi, statement, *Hearings Before Committee on Banking and Currency,* House of Representatives, May 1930, 2d sess., part 2, p. 1340.

47. "There was a great need in the community—or rather a great group in need," Giannini later recalled. "That was one of the conditions I had in mind when I thought of entering the banking field. It didn't look too technical, for there was a human need, and human folks don't let technicalities stand in the way of accomplishing what should be done" (Giannini, interview in *Personnel Efficiency,* January 11, 1925).

48. For biographical material on Bacigalupi, see "James A. Bacigalupi," Personnel Files, BAA.

49. Giannini's efforts to recruit Bacigalupi into the bank are told in Giannini, interview with Bessie James, October 1, 1947, BAA.

50. James and James, *Biography of a Bank,* 50–51. Acting as individual buyers, Scatena or other Bank of Italy directors would borrow the money from the Crocker National (renamed from Crocker-Woolworth in 1907), using the purchased bank's assets as collateral.

51. "It was easy to merge banks," Giannini said later. "People didn't understand that as soon as you have bought a bank you have assets and cash, and as soon as you take over, you get your money back" (Josephson, "Giannini," September 13, 31).

52. For the board's approval of Giannini's request for a branch permit, see Bank of Italy, Minute Book, October 12, 1909, BAA.

53. *San Jose Mercury and Herald,* November 14, 1909.

54. For Giannini's promotional activities, see Bank of Italy, Minute Book, December 14, 1909, BAA.

55. See George Zaro, interview with Bessie James, undated, but sometime in 1948, BAA.

56. For biographical material on Attilio Giannini, see *San Francisco Examiner,* February 8, 1943.

57. Russell Smith, interview with the author.

58. Bacigalupi to APG, November 17, 1909, BAA.

59. The two San Francisco banks were the Bank of San Francisco and the Mechanics Savings Bank. See *Coast Banker,* December 1910, 416; see also Bank

of San Francisco, Minute Book, 1907–1910, BAA. Giannini later merged the Mechanics Bank with his Mission Street branch. See Bank of Italy, First Minute Book, 1910, 216, BAA. For purchase of the Bank of San Francisco and the Bank of San Mateo, see Gore, "Bank of America," September 13, 1910, December 10, 1912, BAA.

60. See Charles Grondona, interview with Bessie James, January 28, 1948. Gian Cordano, who worked as a clerk in the bank, later remembered a conversation he had with Giannini shortly after the opening of the San Jose branch. "George," Giannini said to Cordano, "if I succeed with what I am doing, I am going to put the Bank of Italy on the map" (Gian Cordano, interview with Bessie James, February 16, 1948, BAA).

61. For Italian immigration to New York, see Richard Gambino, *Blood of My Blood* (1974); Federal Writers Project, *The Italians of New York* (1938); Nathan Glazer and Patrick Moynihan, *Beyond the Melting Pot* (1963); Joseph Lopreato, *Italian Americans* (1970).

62. See James Cavagnaro, interview with Bessie James, February 16, 1948, BAA.

63. Giannini's interest in breaking into New York actually began on a trip to the East Coast with Fagan in the fall of 1911. See Bank of Italy, Minutes, November 11, 1911, BAA.

64. *Coast Banker,* March 1913.

65. James Cavagnaro, interview with Bessie James, undated, but sometime in 1948, BAA.

66. Bank of Italy, First Minute Book, November 11, 1911, BAA.

67. Giannini himself did not doubt that Cavagnaro and the others would eventually see things his way. In a letter to Pedrini on a trip to New York five years later, Giannini said: "They're all talking Bank to me here and of course I'm telling them all that we are coming some day—just as soon as we can spare a couple of good men from California and not until then it doesn't do any harm to let them keep on talking Bank of Italy" (APG to Armando Pedrini, May 5, 1918, BAA).

5. Going South

1. *Annual Report of the California Development Board,* 1902, 13; see also R. W. Durrenberger, *Geography of California* (1960), 132–42; Miller and Hyslop, *California,* 208–32.

2. Carey McWilliams, *Southern California Country* (1946), 128–37.

3. On California's agricultural development, see Claude B. Hutchinson, ed., *California Agriculture* (1946); John Weaver, *Los Angeles: The Enormous Village, 1781–1981* (1980); John Caughey and LaRee Caughey, *Los Angeles: Biography of a City* (1976); Robert Cleland, *From Wilderness to Empire: A History of California* (1959).

4. Kevin Starr, *Material Dreams: Southern California Through the 1920s* (1990), 85, 87.

5. See Cleland, *From Wilderness to Empire*, 299–301; see also Hutchinson, *California;* Gerald White, *Formative Years in the Far West: A History of the Standard Oil Company of California and Predecessors Through 1919* (1962); Earl Wetty and Frank Taylor, *Black Bonanza* (1958).

6. Winfield Scott, "Old Wine in New Bottles: When Italy Comes To California Through the Panama Canal—What Then?" *Sunset,* May 1913, 519–26; see also Peixotto, "Italy in California," 367–78; Rolle, "Italy in California."

7. For Giannini's decision to open a branch in Los Angeles, see Gore, "Bank of America," April 8, 1913; see also Bank of Italy, Board of Directors' Meeting, Minutes, April 8, 1913, BAA.

8. In 1910 white, native-born Protestants totaled nearly 54 percent of the city's population. The "foreign born" composed only 27 percent of the population, in contrast to 78 percent in San Francisco (McWilliams, *Southern California Country,* 156–64).

9. Los Angeles's "big seven" banks were the Security Trust and Savings, First National, German-American Trust and Savings, Farmers and Merchants National, Los Angeles Trust and Savings, Citizens National, and the Merchants National (*Los Angeles Daily Tribune,* January 2, 1913).

10. For additional information on Sartori, see John McCarthy, *Joseph Francis Sartori, 1858–1946: A Biography Published by the Security First National Bank of Los Angeles* (1948); see also Cross, *Financing an Empire* 3:202–3.

11. Starr, *Material Dreams,* 45.

12. Kays was a Los Angeles businessman and the bank's largest stockholder. With resources of close to $2 million, the Park Bank ranked eighteenth among the city's thirty-six banks (*Los Angeles Daily Tribune,* January 2, 1913). For additional information on Kays, see Gore, "Bank of America," May 5, 1913, BAA.

13. For the poor financial condition of many smaller banks in the state like the Park, see Jackson A. Graves, *My Seventy Years in California, 1857–1927* (1927), 311–26. On the condition of the Park specifically, see William Williams, interview with Bessie James, undated, but sometime in 1948, BAA.

14. Sartori was not alone in his opposition to Giannini's plans to move into Los Angeles. See Donald B. Thorburn, *The Story of Transamerica* (1931), 7–8.

15. See William Williams, interview with Bessie James, undated, but sometime in 1948, BAA.

16. For biographical information on Williams, see "William R. Williams," Personnel Files, Bank of America, BAA.

17. See William Williams, interview with Bessie James, undated, but sometime in 1948, BAA.

18. Ibid.

19. See William Williams, letter to Bessie James, June 30, 1944, BAA.

20. Giannini acquired the Park in late April of 1913. See Gore, "Bank of America," April 30, 1913, BAA. For early public discussion of the purchase, see *San Francisco Daily Journal of Commerce,* April 12, 1913.

21. Dana, *Giannini*, 15; see also Giannini, interview in *Forbes*, November 1923.

22. For some of the hostile reaction, see Graves, *My Seventy Years*, 330–32. What further infuriated Los Angeles bankers was Giannini's attempt, soon after his takeover of the Park, to purchase a second bank in the city. His efforts were frustrated, however, when a group of his competitors bid up the price of the bank's 2,000 outstanding shares beyond his ability to pay for them. See *Los Angeles Stock Exchange Bulletin*, January 1, 1913–July 1, 1913; see also *Los Angeles Daily Tribune*, March 29, 1913; *San Francisco Daily Journal of Commerce*, April 22, 1913.

23. *Los Angeles Daily Tribune*, May 8, 1913.

24. *Los Angeles Daily Tribune*, May 10, 1913; see also Giannini, interview with Bessie James, undated, but sometime in 1948; Jal Stonier, interview with Bessie James, undated, but sometime in 1948, BAA. Over the years Giannini maintained a discreet silence on the anti-Italian prejudice he encountered in the banking profession, only occasionally expressing his resentment privately. See APG to Albert Haase, undated, but sometime in 1948, BAA.

25. *Los Angeles Daily Tribune*, July 26, 1913; see also *Los Angeles Evening Herald*, July 26, 1913.

26. *Los Angeles Evening Herald*, July 26, 1913; see also *Los Angeles Daily Tribune*, August 7, 24, 1913; James and James, *Biography of a Bank*, 65.

27. Quoted in Hayes, "Real Romance," March 27, 1928.

28. See Hal Stanton, memorandum to Bessie James, undated, but sometime in 1948. Stanton was a former employee of the Park Bank who stayed on to work for Giannini. In statements to the press, however, Giannini could not have been more optimistic on the financial condition of his Los Angeles branch. See *Los Angeles Times*, January 2, 1914; see also *Coast Banker*, August 1913, 349.

29. Giannini, interview with Bessie James, undated, but sometime in 1948, BAA.

30. By the end of 1914, for example, Sartori's Security Trust had lost nearly $2 million in deposits. See Security Trust's semiannual figures in *Los Angeles Times*, December 3, 1914; see also Thorburn, *Story of Transamerica*, 7–8.

31. Giannini, interview with Bessie James, undated, but sometime in 1948, BAA.

32. See Gore, "Bank of America," January 13, 1914, BAA.

33. The growing dispute between Giannini and the bank's board of directors over the Los Angeles "venture" is told in some detail in a sanitized version by the Jameses in their *Biography of a Bank*, where they write that the disagreement was in "good humor." In fact, Giannini bitterly resented the board's criticism and their loss of confidence in his leadership. See, for example, Gore, "Bank of America," January 12, 1915, BAA.

34. Giannini was partly attracted to the Seventh and Broadway corner because of its location directly across the street from Bullock's department store (Irving Metzler, interview with Bessie James, undated, but sometime in 1948, BAA).

35. See Bank of Italy, Board of Directors, Minutes, January 13, 1914, BAA.

36. Ibid.

37. See Bank of Italy semiannual figures published in the *Los Angeles Times,* January 2, 1914; see also *Coast Banker,* January 1914, 35.

38. For the complete text of Giannini's resignation, see Gore, "Bank of America," February 10, 1914, BAA.

39. See Bank of Italy, Board of Directors, Minutes, February 10, 1914, BAA.

40. See Bank of Italy, Board of Directors, Minutes, March 12, 1914, BAA.

41. See Gore, "Bank of America," January 12, 1915, BAA.

42. See Special Meeting, Bank of Italy Board of Directors, Minutes, November 14, 1914, BAA.

43. Ibid.

44. Giannini also offered to take over the bank's San Mateo branch, which had also become a target for criticism by several board members (Gore, "Bank of America," November 14, 1914, BAA).

45. Ibid.

46. Asked about the episode some months later, Giannini said simply: "I made them see it" (Gore, "Bank of America," January 12, 1915, BAA).

47. Special Meeting, Bank of Italy Board of Directors, Minutes, November 14, 1914, BAA.

48. G. B. Cordano, interview with Bessie James, undated, but sometime in 1984, BAA. The month following the board's vote of confidence, Giannini withdrew his resignation (Gore, "Bank of America," January 15, 1915, BAA).

49. The Seventh and Broadway branch opened in April 1915. For comment and opening day celebration, see Hugh Pye to Bessie James, undated, but sometime in 1948, BAA.

50. The combined value of California field crops, fruits, vegetables, poultry, and livestock jumped to $664 million (*Pacific Rural Press,* December 23, 1916).

51. Quotation in *Pacific Rural Press,* October 7, 1916. As Giannini would remember, "No one could have foreseen the enormous increase in spring planting that followed the declaration of war" (*The Financier,* January 1, 1918; see also *Pacific Rural Press,* December 28, 1916). For nationwide increase in farm production, see Robert Cleland and Osgood Hardy, *The March of Industry* (1929), 57.

52. In 1916 small-town independent bankers held 45 percent of California's farm mortgages. See R. L. Adams, *Farm Management Notes* (1926), 246–47; see also B. T. Cunningham and Thomas Jones to Bessie James, undated, but sometime in 1948, BAA. The average nationwide interest on farm mortgages in 1916 was 7.6 percent (C. W. Thompson, "Costs and Sources of Farm Mortgages," in *United States Department of Agriculture Office of Market and Rural Organization* [1916], bulletin no. 384).

53. As one Fresno farmer complained, "There are many banks which refuse to loan directly upon county property but will loan upon the same property to a broker who charges from two to five per cent for his services. Besides the mortgage, the farmer must pay an interest rate of eight per cent or more from three to five times the actual cost of sending a man to appraise the property" (*Pacific Rural Press,* March 4, 1916).

54. Quotation in *Pacific Rural Press*, February 12, 1916; see also B. T. Cunningham to Albert Haase, undated, but sometime in 1948, BAA. It was not uncommon for the management of a local bank and its officers to turn down requests for loans from small borrowers to finance their own investments. See C. B. Hutchinson (dean of the College of Agriculture, University of California, Berkeley), "California Agriculture in Relation to Banking," quoted in California Bankers Association, Minutes, Pasadena, May 25, 1944.

55. For purchase of the Santa Clara bank, see Gore, "Bank of America," February 8, 1916. For Giannini's additional purchases in the valley, see Challis Gore, "Bank of America Family Tree," table 2, "Growth of Bank of America Branch System," BAA.

56. For the growth and development of the San Joaquin, see Smith, *Garden of the Sun;* see also Lilbourne Winchell, *History of Fresno County and the San Joaquin Valley* (1933); Hutchinson, *California Agriculture.*

57. One unique feature of California's farm population was the large number of immigrants from southern and central Europe who had settled in the countryside, a feature Giannini understood quite well. As one historian later commented, "In other parts of the country outside the South, the most mixed populations, racially and culturally, are commonly found in the large cities; and the farm populations are, by comparison, relatively homogeneous. Exactly the opposite pattern prevails in California, where the most heterogeneous population is to be found in the rural areas, on the farm. . . . On the other hand, the 'small town' population in rural California is very largely made up of native born 'white' elements" (McWilliams, *California,* 74–76).

58. APG to Charles F. Stern, February 9, 1921; Charles F. Stern to APG, June 18, 1921, BAA.

59. Angelo J. Scampini, interview with the author.

60. For additional biographical information on Hale, see "Prentice Hale," Personnel Files, BAA.

61. Giannini, interview with Bessie James, undated, but sometime in 1948, BAA.

62. Quoted in Josephson, "Giannini," September 20, 1947, 113.

63. As with Giannini's other banking innovations, the evening banking hours proved to be so popular with customers that competitors were forced to follow his example. See *Bankitaly Life,* September 1918.

64. Quoted in *San Francisco Bulletin,* November 26, 1921.

65. See House Committee on Banking and Currency, *Congressional Hearing on Branch, Chain and Group Banking,* May 6, 1930, 1547.

66. See Giannini's statement in *The Citizen,* October 1926.

67. See, for example, the favorable editorial in the *Fresno Morning Republican,* which said in part: "With the entrance of the Bank of Italy into the city, the standard rate of interest has been lowered from 8 per cent to 7 per cent, and the announcement made yesterday by Giannini has resulted in a realignment of the interest table" (*Fresno Morning Republican,* October 29, 1916). Giannini reduced interest rates on loans in other towns in the region where he had established a branch of his bank. See, for example, announcement in the *Napa Weekly Journal,* February 2, 1917; see also *Madera Daily Tribune,* June 22, 1917.

68. For Giannini's statement, see House Committee on Banking and Currency, *Congressional Hearings on Branch, Chain, and Group Banking,* 1547.

69. Thus, for example, one month after Giannini's interest reduction announcement, the *Fresno Morning Republican* reported: "The Farmers National Bank, which was to give the Bank of Italy its stiffest competition, rushed out a statement saying it had several hundred thousand dollars to loan on this basis" (*Fresno Morning Republican,* October 21, 1916).

70. See R. B. Imberton to Bessie James, undated, but sometime in 1948, BAA.

71. See Giannini quote in *Forbes,* November 1923.

72. *San Francisco Chronicle,* September 10, 1921.

73. See Josephson, "Giannini," September 20, 1947, 31.

74. Claire Giannini Hoffman, interview with the author.

75. See figures for Stockton, Fresno, and Santa Rosa compiled by Roscoe Evans from Bank of Italy Ledgers for 1915–1918, BAA.

76. The director was P. C. Hale (Giannini, interview with Bessie James, undated, but sometime in 1948, BAA).

77. For some of the difficulties in this cumbersome procedure, see Bacigalupi's testimony before the House Committee on Banking and Currency, *Congressional Hearings on Branch, Chain, and Group Banking,* 1543.

78. See James Bacigalupi to Frank Jordan (California's secretary of state), June 9, 1917, James A. Bacigalupi Papers, BAA.

79. See James Bacigalupi to Garret McEnerney, April 30, 1925, Bacigalupi Papers, BAA.

80. For Giannini's statement of denial and complaints from his competitors, see Hayes, "Real Romance," April 3, 1929.

81. APG to James Bacigalupi, May 20, 1917, BAA. At the first meeting of the Stockholders Auxiliary, Giannini was elected president and P. C. Hale vice-president. See Stockholders Auxiliary Corporation, Minutes, Transamerica Corporation Papers, Bank of America Archives.

82. See figures compiled by Roscoe Evans from Bank of Italy Ledgers for 1915–1919, BAA.

6. A Storm of Opposition

1. See, for example, *Coast Banker,* January 1918, 71.

2. For these and other remarks about the danger of branch banking, see *California Bankers Association Bulletin* no. 11, December 1921.

3. In 1909, when Giannini opened his first branch office in San Jose, only twelve states in the nation permitted branch banking (usually with restrictions); twenty-seven states had no statutes providing for branch banking, and nine states prohibited it entirely. See John M. Chapman and Ray B. Westerfield, *Branch Banking in California* (1942), 84. For Giannini's remark about "horse and buggy" bankers, see Josephson, "Giannini," September 20, 1947. For a survey of hostile opinion, see *Coast Banker,* January 1918, 71; see also *Annual Report of*

the Comptroller of the Currency, 1923, 10. Although the vast majority of California's small-town independents were enraged with branch banking, a few quietly wrote to Giannini asking for information on how to start branches of their own. See, for example, R. H. Roseberry to James Bacigalupi, April 23, 1919, James Bacigalupi Papers, BAA.

4. As his friendship with Giannini grew, Williams publicly expressed his defense of branch banking. "The establishment of these branches [Bank of Italy]," Williams wrote, "immediately accomplished a public good. Smaller communities . . . found themselves the beneficiaries of larger loans and more substantial credit facilities. Interest rates were reduced and stabilized" (California Superintendent of Banks, *Ninth Annual Report* [1918], 10). Many years later Williams told an interviewer: "I hadn't been superintendent very long before I had a theory that branch banking would be good for California. My time in the banking department was spent in an elaboration of this theory" (William Williams, interview with Bessie James, undated, but sometime in 1948, BAA).

5. For a biographical sketch of Stephens and a brief discussion of his career in California politics, see Howard A. DeWitt, *Images of Ethnic and Radical Violence in California Politics, 1917–1930* (1975), 10–22; see also Brett Melendy and Benjamin Gilbert, *The Governors of California* (1965), 323–24.

6. For Stephens's hostility toward Giannini and the Bank of Italy, see James Bacigalupi to Garret McEnerney, April 30, 1925, James Bacigalupi Papers, BAA.

7. Charles F. Stern, interview with Bessie James, undated, but sometime in 1948, BAA.

8. For a discussion of Stephens's "loan" practices in Los Angeles, see Hayes, "Real Romance," April 3, 1928; see also Dana, *Giannini*, 90–91.

9. Asked by a reporter later in life about his actions in pursuing the repayment of Stern's loan, Giannini replied: "I know nothing about what other banks may or may not have done. I was interested in getting what was owed us and that was all" (Hayes, "Real Romance," April 3, 1928).

10. Giannini later defended his appointment of Williams by saying: "Williams was easily the best superintendent California ever had. . . . I knew when I appointed him that it was about the poorest move, if considered purely from a political standpoint, that I could make, but I was in the banking business and not in politics" (ibid.).

11. On Stern's close relationship with California's small-town independent bankers, see Bacigalupi's report in file folder "Charles Frank Stern," December 5, 1918, James Bacigalupi Papers, BAA.

12. Giannini also applied for a permit to open a branch in the town of Santa Maria, located about 160 miles north of Los Angeles (Bank of Italy, Minutes, January 14, 1919, BAA).

13. Charles F. Stern to Bank of Italy, June 23, 1919, BAA.

14. Acting on Giannini's instructions, Williams replied to Stern with a point-by-point refutation of his numerous criticisms, which said in part: "We do not claim that we have reached perfection but we do claim that we are rendering a service which could not have been rendered by any independent bank whose business we have acquired nor could it have been rendered by all

such banks collectively" (William Williams to Charles F. Stern, August 12, 1919, BAA).

15. As the former superintendent of banking, Williams was not unaware of these deficiencies. "A. P. was moving so fast his accounting department could not keep up with him," Williams said later. "My department had to keep up with him because our job was to make sure bank depositors were protected. . . . When Giannini started his branch expansion nobody in California, excepting him possibly, knew much about branch banking" (William Williams, interview with Bessie James, undated, but sometime in 1948, BAA).

16. James Bacigalupi to Garret McEnerney, April 30, 1925, BAA. According to Bacigalupi, "Stern opened the interview by telling us to set one thing down in our minds and that was that so long as he was superintendent of banking we could hope for no permission to expand—not even to the extent of one single, solitary branch—by purchase, consolidation or otherwise" (Hayes, "Real Romance," April 4, 1928).

17. For Giannini's complete statement, see Bankitaly Life, October 1919, 3–4.

18. Charles F. Stern to APG, November 10, 1919, BAA.

19. The Federal Reserve Act, signed into law on December 23, 1913, divided the country into twelve reserve districts administered by the Federal Reserve Board in Washington, whose members were appointed by the president. The Twelfth Reserve District, which had its headquarters in San Francisco, included California, Oregon, Washington, Idaho, Nevada, Utah, and Arizona.

20. Before joining the federal reserve system, Giannini asked for and received assurances from John Perrin, chairman of San Francisco's Federal Reserve Bank, that the board would not oppose the expansion of his branch banking system. See APG to John Perrin, September 18, 1917, Federal Reserve Bank of San Francisco Papers; see also A. C. Miller to APG, September 26, 1917, BAA. Further assurances also came from W. P. G. Harding, governor of Federal Reserve Board (W. P. G. Harding to John Perrin, October 23, 1917, BAA).

21. See Transamerica Corporation Papers, Stockholders Auxiliary Corporation, Minutes, 1 (1919), 61.

22. See, for example, Giannini's statement in the pages of Bankitaly Life: "The Bank of Italy will take care of all proper loans, which these National banks may be unable to handle. Arrangements will be made whereby the Bank of Italy will provide the necessary machinery for taking applications for the loans . . . in order that all such loans may be just as effectively handled as though they were through the medium of a Branch Office of the Bank of Italy" (Bankitaly Life, October 1919); see also James Bacigalupi to Garret McEnerney, April 30, 1923, BAA.

23. See Josephson, "Giannini," September 20, 1947, 113.

24. See Gore, "Bank of America Family Tree," June 10, 1942, BAA.

25. San Francisco Chronicle, December 25, 1920.

26. See James Cavagnaro, interview with Bessie James, February 16, 1948, BAA.

27. "By all means," Giannini cabled his brother, Attilio, "let nothing interfere with our acquiring East River so make sure give this matter your first attention" (APG to Attilio Giannini, November 18, 1918, BAA). By now

Giannini was obsessed with the idea of breaking into New York. As he cabled Bacigalupi, "Unquestionably greatest thing ever if we can effect proper organization Italians there" (APG to James Bacigalupi, July 20, 1918, BAA).

28. APG to James Bacigalupi, July 20, 1918; see also APG to G. Granata, July 2, 1918; APG to Ernest Stauffen, July 9, 1918; APG to Antonio Stella, July 10, 1918, BAA.

29. "In other words," Giannini added, "I can more briefly cover what I mean . . . as follows: personal equation or personal touch. This is the one thing that is lacking in most of New York's banking institutions" (APG to James Bacigalupi, undated, but sometime in June or July 1918; see also APG to James Bacigalupi, July 12, 1918; APG to Ernest Stauffen, July 11, 1918; APG to J. Freschi, August 1, 1918, BAA).

30. On Bacigalupi's solicitation efforts, Giannini cabled: "It has occurred to me that it would be well if it could be arranged for you folks to meet all the Italian doctors there. . . . To start off with the priests, doctors and lawyers 'pulling for us' would surely give us a big advantage" (APG to James Bacigalupi, July 26, 1918; see also APG to Salvatore D. Antoni, July 26, 1918, BAA).

31. From San Francisco, Giannini sent telegram after telegram urging greater effort. "There's nothing to it, Jim," he cabled Bacigalupi, "if only each and everyone of those we've picked as good timber . . . will get out and hustle among their own friends each ought be able line up at least hundred subscribers . . . each section of the city being well represented" (APG to James Bacigalupi, July 16, 1918, BAA).

32. Anonymous interview with the author. "You have to admit, Doc, that I haven't had the educational advantages that you have had. You were born several years after me and, during those years, I worked very hard (getting up at midnight and in the early hours of the morning) to do my part toward laying the foundation that made those advantages possible for you" (APG to Attilio Giannini, August 14, 1936, BAA).

33. Russell Smith, interview with the author.

34. By the end of 1920 the East River National had 6,500 savings accounts; one year later the number had climbed to 10,700. See "Giannini to All Stockholders," May 6, 1921, Transamerica Corporation Papers, BAA.

35. APG to James Bacigalupi, undated, but sometime in August 1918, BAA; see also APG to H. Grassi, August 15, 1918; APG to G. Franata, October 31, 1918; Carlo Del Pino to APG, November 27, 1918, BAA. Giannini's Brooklyn bank generated a good deal of resentment from other Italian banks in New York. See Martin Wechsler to F. A. Zunio, August 13, 1918, BAA.

36. See Gore, "Bank of America," entry dated May 13, 1919, BAA. In 1922 the name of the bank was changed to Banca d'America e d'Italia.

37. See Armando Pedrini to Bancitaly Corporation, June 9, 1922, Bancitaly Corporation Papers, BAA. "These changes," Pedrini informed Giannini, "made a very good impression on the public, giving an absolute assurance of the responsibility of the members of the Board." See P. C. Hale to Armando Pedrini, January 9, 1922; see also APG to Armando Pedrini, January 20, 1922, Bancitaly Corporation Papers, BAA.

38. As Pedrini wrote to Giannini: "After the general stockholders meeting . . . the news spread out through the local newspapers that new capital from North America was coming in, and that the policy and general administration of the bank would be changed. This strengthened so much the credit of the institution . . . which shows that with the proper management, organization and good locations and with our American business added to it, there is a big possibility ahead of us" (Armando Pedrini to APG, October 15, 1919, Bancitaly Corporation Papers, BAA).

39. In 1918 Bank of Italy had approximately 160,000 depositors and deposits of nearly $86 million. By the end of 1920 it had 220,000 depositors and more than $140 million in deposits. See *Bankitaly Life,* August 1920; see also *Coast Banker,* July 1919, 92; *San Francisco Bulletin,* February 28, 1921.

40. For newspaper accounts of the run, see *Santa Rosa Democrat,* January 8, 1921; *San Francisco Chronicle,* January 7, 1921; *Coast Banker,* January 1921; *Bankitaly Life,* January 1921. With only minor changes, the events surrounding the Santa Rosa run were used many years later by Joseph Mankiewicz in his film *House of Strangers,* starring Edward G. Robinson. The movie was released over strong protests from Giannini family members, who were outraged by Robinson's portrayal of Gino Monetti, a barber turned banker, who bullied and intimidated his family. See Kenneth L. Geist, *Pictures Will Talk: The Life and Films of Joseph L. Mankiewicz* (1974), 149-51.

41. Hysteria because of decline in farm production had already forced local bankers to tighten credit. See *Pacific Rural Press,* January 14, 1920; see also C. W. Douglas, "The Bean Situation," *Coast Banker,* March 1921; California State Superintendent of Banks, *Twelfth Annual Report* (1921), 9; A. B. Hendricks to Farm Loan Board, May 18, 1921, BAA.

42. L. B. McGuire, interview with Al Haase, November 24, 1948. On the efforts of Giannini's branch manager to persuade depositors to leave their money in the bank and the loss of deposits during the first few hours of the run, see C. B. Wingate to Charles Stern, January 10, 1921; see also J. A. Lombardi, interview with Al Haase, November 24, 1948.

43. For recollections of the Santa Rosa run, see Bessie James's interviews with Walter Bruns, February 17, 1948; with John Burns, February 19, 1948; and with James Cavagnaro, February 16, 1949, BAA.

44. Cuneo and Scatena were accompanied by Jake Fisher, who began his career in the bank as a messenger boy and later made his way up the ranks to become a senior vice-president. According to Fisher's recollections, "Two detectives accompanied them in the closed Hudson car. The money was put in the back of the car and the curtains drawn. They cut down the time of their trip by getting on the Sausalito Ferry. The Golden Gate Bridge was not built at the time. The ferry took only passengers and Fisher and the detectives were able to persuade the captain to put the Hudson aboard" (Jake Fisher, interview with Bessie James, February 19, 1948, in file folder "Santa Rosa Incident," BAA; see also Jake Fisher, interview with the author).

45. In Sacramento, Stern was also concerned about the ripple effect of the panic and released a statement to the press the next day reassuring the public

that the Bank of Italy was "in splendid shape" (statement by Charles F. Stern, January 8, 1921, James Bacigalupi Papers, BAA).

46. See James A. Bacigalupi, "To All Branch Managers," January 7, 1921, James Bacigalupi Papers, BAA.

47. On the arrival of Scatena and the others in Santa Rosa, see Al Haase, interviews with L. B. McGuire, November 24, 1948, and J. A. Lombardi, November 24, 1949. See also Jake Fisher, interview with the author.

48. For Scatena's actions, see file folder "Santa Rosa Incident," BAA. Scatena informed local reporters that he had brought $5 million in gold from San Francisco, a wildly inflated figure designed to reassure depositors. "This money," the press dutifully reported. "is far in excess of any amounts that could be withdrawn from the bank, and their officials are ready and willing to pay depositors who really wish to withdraw their money" (*Santa Rosa Republican,* January 11, 1921; see also C. B. Wingate to Charles F. Stern, January 18, 1921, BAA).

49. "Let them come," Scatena told the press after he and the others had completed their preparations for the next day's business. "We are ready for everybody and any depositor wanting his money can have it. We are also ready to make loans to anyone having the proper security" (*Santa Rosa Democrat,* July 8, 1921; see also Armando Pedrini's statement in the *Santa Rosa Republican,* January 11, 1921; John Burns, interview with Bessie James, February 19, 1948; J. A. Lombardi, interview with Al Haase, November 24, 1948, BAA).

50. It took Giannini's Santa Rosa branch more than three years to regain much, but not all, of the money that had been withdrawn during the run and deposited in other local banks. See J. A. Lombardi, interview with Al Haase, November 24, 1948, BAA.

51. For Giannini's arrival in Santa Rosa and his efforts to limit the panic, see file folder "Santa Rosa Incident," February 17, 1949, BAA; see also *San Francisco Chronicle,* January 8, 1921.

52. *Santa Rosa Republican,* January 11, 1921.

53. Giannini's competitors in Santa Rosa blamed the run on the operating practices of the Bank of Italy itself. According to a statement filed with the state department of banking by an examiner in the office: "Mr. Edward, president of the Savings Bank of Santa Rosa, informs me that in his judgement the Bank of Italy has largely developed this situation for itself by two errors in its Santa Rosa policy: The first, an insistent, irritating, and aggressive campaign for depositors, particularly with the foreign element. It is alleged that their soliciting often takes the form of a deprecation of the other banks and that extravagant promises of a future accommodation are made which are not fulfilled" (C. B. Wingate to Charles Stern, January 10, 1921, BAA).

54. For this version of the run, see San Francisco Operative 403, Special Report, January 8, 1921, James Bacigalupi Papers; see also *Santa Rosa Press Democrat,* January 8, 1921; *San Francisco Chronicle,* January 8, 1921; *Bankitaly Life,* January 1921.

55. See Hayes, "Real Romance," April 7, 1928.

56. See San Francisco Operative R-1, Special Report, January 10, 1921; see also San Francisco Operative R-2, Special Report, January 21, 24, 1921; for more detailed information and notes on interviews with various sources, see

San Francisco Operative L-44, Special Report, January 12, 1921; San Francisco Operative L-1, Special Report, January 19, 1921, James Bacigalupi Papers, BAA.

57. See San Francisco Operative R-2, Special Report, January 24, 1921, James Bacigalupi Papers, BAA.

58. See statistical papers prepared for James A. Bacigalupi, 1930. On the Bank of Italy's loan policy for farmers, see W. T. Rice, District Supervisor, Memorandum, March 25, 1930; Arnold J. Mount to Charles Collins, August 21, 1929, Charles Collins Papers, BAA.

59. For biographical material on Paganini, see "Robert Paganini," Personnel Files, BAA; see also Giovinco, "Democracy in Banking," 211.

60. In a period of fifteen months Paganini himself brought in more than eight hundred new accounts ranging from $10 to $20,000 and totaling nearly $500,000. See Business Secured by Robert Paganini, report dated December 31, 1925, Italian Department Papers, Bank of America Archives. By 1927 Paganini was able to report, "We have practically all of the Italian business in Ventura, San Pedro, Venice, Descondido, Burbank, San Diego, Imperial Valley and Bakersfield." See Robert Paganini to James Bacigalupi, July 10, 1927; see also R. Crisci, "Italian Department Report," November 9, 1927, and reports from Louis Perna, Amadeo Ponzio, and Louis Ostaggi in file folder "Italian Department," Italian Department Papers.

61. Armando Pedrini to APG, March 15, 1923, BAA.

62. For the activities of Paganini's missionaries in various regions of the state, see Louis Perna, Memorandum, undated, but sometime in 1923; see also A. Ponzio, Report on Monterey, October 28, 1922; W. H. McGinnis, Jr., Memorandum, February 11, 1925; Louis Valperga, Memorandum, April 8, 1925; Robert Paganini, Memoranda, October 9 and November 7, 1925, Italian Department Papers, BAA.

63. See J. J. Taverna to Robert Paganini, September 17, 1921, Italian Department Papers, BAA.

64. R. Crisci, "Italian Department Report," November 9, 1927; see also Petro Romeo to Robert Paganini, September 26, 1926; I. J. Andreani to Robert Paganini, March 31, 1924, Italian Department Papers, BAA.

65. See Paganini's instructions to his missionaries in Paganini to F. A. Marinette, November 22, 1922; see also J. P. Weller to Armando Pedrini, November 25, 1922, Italian Department Papers, BAA.

66. Armando Pedrini to J. Onetu, October 25, 1927; see also A. M. Ghio to Robert Paganini, August 5, 1927, Italian Department Papers, BAA.

67. Josephson, "Giannini," September 13, 1947, 16.

68. See Robert Paganini to W. W. Hoover, October 22, 1922; see also Robert Paganini to C. L. Monge, August 24, 1927; Robert Paganini to J. Onetu, October 25, 1927; A. M. Ghio to Robert Paganini, August 5, 1925, Italian Department Papers, BAA.

69. Cinel, *From Italy to San Francisco,* 239; see also, for example, Robert Paganini to J. A. Lombardi, June 3, 1924; Robert Paganini to C. Cattori, June 3, 1924; Robert Paganini to J. Onetu, October 25, 1927, Italian Department Papers, BAA.

70. See, for example, Robert Paganini to E. T. Cunningham, May 20, 1925;

see also J. J. Taverna to Robert Paganini, December 15, 1927; Robert Paganini to Vincent Enea, September 15, 1924; Robert Paganini to C. M. Hartley, January 15, 1923, Italian Department Papers, BAA.

71. For these kind of activities, see Robert Paganini to C. Cattori, September 15, 1924; see also J. A. Lombardi to Robert Paganini, January 3, 1924; W. P. Wente to Robert Paganini, July 28, 1924; A. M. Ghio to Robert Paganini, August 10, 1925; J. D. Harlings to Robert Paganini, December 13, 1922, Italian Department Papers, BAA.

72. L. Niccoli to Robert Paganini, October 1, 1927, Italian Department Papers, BAA.

73. See C. B. Wingate to Charles F. Stern, January 18, 1921, Business Extension Papers, BAA.

74. For a variety of promotional activities at the local level, see Robert Paganini to A. M. Ghio, March 20, 1925; see also Robert Paganini to J. A. Lombardi, January 9, 1925; P. E. Manfreidi to Robert Paganini, May 28, 1923; Robert Paganini to Armando Pedrini, August 2, 1924; A. M. Ghio to Robert Paganini, March 9, 1925; L. G. Perna to Robert Paganini, April 2, 1925, Italian Department Papers, BAA.

75. See, for example, Robert Paganini to L. Ostaggi, December 12, 1925; see also Robert Paganini to Louis Perna, December 9, 1925; Robert Paganini to Joseph Marsili, December 28, 1926; Robert Paganini to A. M. Ghio, July 28, 1925, Italian Department Papers, BAA.

76. Robert Paganini to L. Ostaggi, December 12, 1925, Italian Department Papers, BAA.

77. Robert Paganini to Joseph Marsili, December 28, 1926; see also Robert Paganini to A. M. Ghio, July 28, 1925, Italian Department Papers, BAA.

78. L. Niccoli to Robert Paganini, October 1, 1927; see also A. M. Ghio to Robert Paganini, August 5, 1925; Robert Paganini to F. A. Marinette, December 9, 1922; Joseph Marsili to Robert Paganini, July 26, 1926; Robert Paganini to A. Sola, October 31, 1925; Robert Paganini to L. Ostaggi, October 3, 1925, Italian Department Papers, BAA.

79. Robert Paganini to F. A. Marinette, December 9, 1922; see also Robert Paganini to J. Onetu, October 25, 1927; Robert Paganini to C. L. Monge, August 18, 1927; Robert Paganini to L. Ostaggi, May 11, 1925, Italian Department Papers, BAA.

80. Paganini's missionaries were under instructions to sell Bank of Italy stock at every opportunity, mostly in small blocks of from two to ten shares. See J. J. Taverna to Robert Paganini, September 26, 1927; see also Petro Romeo to Robert Paganini, December 3, 1927; Robert Paganini to C. Cattori, June 3, 1924; Robert Paganini to J. A. Lombardi, June 3, 1924; I. J. Andreani to Robert Paganini, April 18, 1925, Italian Department Papers, BAA. For Giannini's early stock promotion activities, see General Ledger, Bank of Italy, 1904; see also Bank of Italy, First Minute Book, December 27, 1904; Gore, "Bank of America," undated, but sometime in late 1904, BAA.

81. Robert Paganini to C. Cattore, June 3, 1924; see also Robert Paganini to J. A. Lombardi, June 3, 1924; F. A. Ferroggiaro to Robert Paganini, Sep-

tember 5, 1924; Petro Remeo to Robert Paganini, December 3, 1927, Italian Department Papers, BAA.

82. Giannini to Armando Pedrini, September 3, 1924, Italian Department Papers, BAA.

83. See statistical data collected by the Italian Department for the period 1920–1930 in Armando Pedrini Papers, Transamerica Corporation Papers, BAA.

84. See W. H. McGinnis, Jr., "Survey of the Business Extension Department for 1926," Business Extension Papers, BAA.

85. With the exception of the Italian Department, all of the other "foreign divisions" of Bank of Italy came under the supervision of William Douglas, who had once managed Giannini's Market Street branch in San Francisco. See McGinnis, "Survey." During the 1920s the number of Yugoslavian accounts rose to 20,000; Greek, 4,000, and Russian, 10,000, for a combined total of $30 million in deposits. San Francisco had several Chinese banks, including the Bank of Shanghai and the Bank of Hong Kong. Nevertheless, Giannini's Bank of Italy had more Chinese depositors than any other bank in the city. For Yugoslavian and Russian accounts, see Antone Pilcovich to James Bacigalupi, October 22, 1922; see also Reports, Slavonian Department, May 7, 1924, October 21, 1925, January 6, 1927; C. Chanowsky to Armando Pedrini, December 4, 1929; W. H. McGinnis to Arnold J. Mount, April 11, 1927, Business Extension Papers, BAA. For statistical information on Greek accounts, see B. Metropulos to Armando Pedrini, January 22, 1929. For Portuguese accounts, see L. G. Perna, Memorandum, November 17, 1927. For Spanish and Mexican accounts, see Emilio L. Dominquez to Robert Paganini, May 6, 1930; see also W. H. McGinnis to Armando Pedrini, January 11, 1928, Business Extension Papers, BAA.

86. See McGinnis, "Survey"; see also Morgan Gunst to Armando Pedrini, January 22, 1928; "Yearly Survey of Foreign Divisions, 1930," Business Extension Papers, BAA.

87. The idea of school savings was not new. Originating in western Europe in the 1830s, it was introduced in the United States in Beloit, Wisconsin, in the late 1870s and then quickly spread to other states. By 1900 school savings programs had been adopted by more than one thousand schools in some twenty-two states. See Sara L. Oberholtzer, "School Savings Banks," *United States Bureau of Education Bulletin* 46 (1914): 10–14; see also Andrew Price, "Teaching Thrift as a Branch of Public Education," *Education,* October 1916, 191. Giannini introduced the program at a directors' meeting in June 1911. See Bank of Italy, Minutes, June 1911, 267, BAA.

88. See Giannini's statement in *American Magazine,* August 1921.

89. As one Bank of Italy executive put it, "It may be argued that School Savings is expensive and a little philanthropic, but it is considered a number one public relations activity in that every child in school has an opportunity to carry a bank account. Many stay with us through life, becoming our best depositors and customers" (H. C. White, Memorandum, undated, in file folder "The School Savings Bank System," Business Extension Papers, BAA).

90. See Philip Lawler to Armando Pedrini, December 21, 1920, Pedrini Papers, BAA; see also *Bankitaly Life,* February 1918, 14; see also *Coast Banker,* November 1911, 90.

91. Philip Lawler to George Webster, May 29, 1931, Business Extension Papers, BAA.

92. As Philip Lawler, who ran the Bank of Italy's school savings program, explained it: "Just to illustrate what we are doing in just one big agricultural area of our state, the San Joaquin Valley: In that valley . . . we have over 48,000 depositors in its schools, we have standing to their credit in excess of $480,000.00. That, it is true, represents only an average of $10.00 per pupil, but just think of the immeasurable potential value of 48,000 contacts with San Joaquin homes. . . . Then, when he completes his course at school and takes his place in the busy world, what could be more natural for him than to remain with us, as a loyal client of the bank that *showed him how to save*" (Philip Lawler to George Webster, May 29, 1931, BAA; see also Philip Lawler to William F. Morrish, June 25, 1931, William Morrish Papers, BAA).

93. For the opening of Giannini's "Women's Bank" in San Francisco, see *Bankitaly Life,* June 1921.

94. See Memorandum, "To Mr. A. P. Giannini from Women's Banking Department," August 1, 1922, BAA.

95. See, for example, Memorandum, "To Mr. A. P. Giannini from the Women's Banking Department," April 1928, BAA; see also Delphia Phillips, "A Bank for Women Run by Women," *Progress: A Magazine for the New Day,* July 1924, 198–99; T. A. Gallagher, "The Women's Bank," *Sunset,* January 1929, 24–53.

96. See Women's Banking Department, Financial Report, June 30, 1924, BAA.

97. See Women's Banking Department, Statement of Savings, April 1928, BAA. Shortly thereafter Giannini established a "Women's Bank" in Los Angeles. For financial and statistical information on the Los Angeles bank, see "Report for the Years 1926–1928," by Grace S. Stoermer, Director, Women's Banking Department, Southern California Headquarters, October 1928, BAA.

98. Gallagher, "Women's Bank," 25.

99. See B. C. Forbes's column in the *San Francisco Examiner,* May 24, 1924. Forbes was the financial editor for the Hearst newspapers.

7. Winning at Any Cost

1. See David A. Alhadeff, *Monopoly and Competition in Banking* (1954), 173–94; see also Nash, *State Government and Economic Development,* 290–91.

2. On the development of branch banking in California, see Chapman and Westerfield, *Branch Banking in California.*

3. For the branch banking activities of Sartori's Security Trust, see George M. Wallace, *Joseph Francis Sartori, 1858–1946* (1948), 92–98. Biographical infor-

mation on Henry Robinson and his relationship with Hoover is found in Richard Norton Smith, *An Uncommon Man: The Triumph of Herbert Hoover* (1984), 115; see also Jordan A. Schwarz, *The Interregnum of Despair: Hoover, Congress, and the Depression* (1970), 94; Guy W. Finney, *The Great Los Angeles Bubble* (1929), 72.

4. See Gore, "Bank of America Family Tree," June 10, 1943, BAA.

5. See Charles F. Stern, interview with Bessie James, undated, but sometime in 1949, BAA.

6. Beginning in 1920, for example, Henry Robinson, president of the Los Angeles Trust (which changed its name in 1922 to the Pacific-Southwest Bank of Los Angeles) had increased the number of his bank's branches from twenty-one to thirty-five, all in and around Los Angeles. On branch banking in Los Angeles generally, see *Coast Banker,* September 1919, 284.

7. For the number and location of Giannini's branches in 1920, see Bank of Italy, Minutes, January 21, 1920, BAA.

8. See *Bankitaly Life,* June 1921, BAA; Hayes, "Real Romance," April 11, 1928.

9. Quoted in Hayes, "Real Romance," April 11, 1928.

10. First National had formerly been named Pacific-Southwest Bank of Los Angeles. On Stern's resignation and a summary of his career as bank superintendent, see *California Bankers Association Bulletin* 2, no. 6 (June 1921), BAA.

11. On assuming office, Dodge told reporters that California was "proud" of the Bank of Italy. Giannini responded to this compliment with a letter to Dodge that said in part: "We were greatly pleased to read the statement in your letter of acceptance that 'California is proud of this institution.' Coming from you at the very outset of your term as Superintendent of Banks, it would appear that our efforts and intentions are somewhat better understood and appreciated by your office than has recently been the case" (APG to Jonathan S. Dodge, June 23, 1921, BAA).

12. Giannini's campaign to break into Sacramento actually began in 1920, when three prominent Italian businessmen carried a petition to Stern with the names of 232 residents asking for a permit to open a branch of the Bank of Italy in the city. Stern denied the petition, saying that Sacramento already had too many banks. For Giannini's early campaign, see *Coast Banker,* January 1921, 27.

13. See James Bacigalupi to Garret McEnerney, April 30, 1925, BAA. For the hostile reaction of Sacramento bankers and their anti–Bank of Italy activities, see John Chambers to Leo V. Belden, July 11, 1921; see also *Bankitaly Life,* December 1921, 19.

14. See *Bankitaly Life,* July 1921, 19.

15. Jonathan Dodge to Bank of Italy, July 5, 1921, BAA. In his letter granting the permit, Dodge wrote: "Pursuant to my own independent investigations personally made, it is my belief that the public convenience and advantage will be promoted by the operation of the branch office of your institution at the location described."

16. James Bacigalupi to Garret McEnerney, April 30, 1925, BAA. Among other things, farmers were excited by the stories they had heard about Giannini's

generous credit policy; the Bank of Italy held nearly $100 million in farm mortgages in the early 1920s. See A. W. Hendrick to APG, February 18, 1932, BAA.

17. Letter quoted in District Supervisor W. T. Rice, Memorandum, March 25, 1921, BAA.

18. See *California Bankers Association Bulletin* 2, no. 9 (September 1921), BAA; see also *Coast Banker,* October 1921, BAA; *San Francisco Journal,* August 10, 1921. For enthusiastic local reaction, see *Los Banos Enterprise,* June 25, 1921; *Lompoc Review,* June 8, 1921; *Marysville Appeal,* October 1, 1921; *Chico Record,* November 8, 1921; *Santa Clara Journal,* June 29, 1921.

19. Josephson, "Giannini," September 20, 1947, 113; see also Hayes, "Real Romance," April 10, 1928.

20. For the great outburst of branch banking expansion in the early 1920s, see Petition for Writ of Mandate, *Bank of Italy vs. John Franklin Johnson,* in *Records of the Supreme Court of California,* vol. 3726, 16, BAA.

21. As Bacigalupi later explained the situation: "The natural effect of the sudden conversion to the cause of branch banking on the part of so many, and not a few of them, old-line conservative bankers; the feverish haste with which each was endeavoring in a couple of years to overtake and outdistance the Bank of Italy; and the agitation which ensued; was to arouse the unit bankers of California and the country generally" (Bacigalupi to Garret McEnerney, April 30, 1925, James Bacigalupi Papers, BAA).

22. See *Literary Digest,* October 28, 1922. "If this sort of thing goes unchecked," the *Digest* quoted Giannini's critics as saying, "before long a few gigantic banks will control the credit of the country, even more completely than the Steel Corporation controls steel or the Standard Oil controls petroleum." For additional anti-branch-banking sentiment, see Howard Whipple, interview with Albert Haase, September 26, 1948; see also *California Bankers Association Bulletin* 2 (December 1921): 505–7.

23. Charles F. Stern, interview with Bessie James, undated, but sometime in 1949, BAA; see also *California Bankers Association Bulletin* 3 (December 1922): 541, BAA.

24. James Bacigalupi to Garret McEnerney, April 30, 1925; see also C. E. Gruhler, Bank of America District Supervisor, March 14, 1939, BAA. See also *California Bankers Association Bulletin* 2 (December 1921): 505–7, BAA; *Coast Banker,* February 1923, 206–7.

25. For Schuler's remarks, see *California American,* April 1, 1927.

26. Jonathan Dodge to Bank of Italy, July 12, 1921, BAA.

27. For Dodge's increasingly hard line toward the Bank of Italy, see Jonathan Dodge to W. R. Williams, September 23, 1921; see also Dodge to APG, November 21, 1921, BAA.

28. Jonathan Dodge to Bank of Italy, November 22, 1921, BAA.

29. See Bacigalupi's testimony in House Banking and Currency Committee, *Hearings on Branch, Chain, and Group Banking,* 1930, 2d sess., part 2, p. 1506. "Los Angeles was growing so fast," Giannini later told an interviewer, "and the center was becoming so congested that banks and business establishments had to follow the trend of things in order to hold their own and get

their share of new business. Of course, Mr. Dodge said in his letter . . . announcing the policy, that we had nothing to do with causing its formulation or adoption. That was true, but we were the institution against which it was aimed" (Hayes, "Real Romance," April 21, 1928).

30. Giannini believed that his branch banking rivals in Los Angeles had pressured Dodge to come up with his de novo ruling. "That was necessary from their viewpoint," Giannini said later, "otherwise the Bank of Italy would grow apace and the late converts to branch banking could not hope to catch up" (quoted in Hayes, "Real Romance," April 21, 1921).

31. For biographical information on Perrin, see John Calkins, interview with Bessie James, undated, but sometime in 1949, BAA; see also Cross, *Financing an Empire* 4:184.

32. See *Bank of Italy v. John Franklin*, 16; see also James Bacigalupi to Garret McEnerney, April 30, 1925, BAA.

33. For the FRB's concern about the loss of banks from the national banking system, see *Coast Banker*, September 1923, 298, BAA. "A great battle is now going on in banking and the effect will be of tremendous import," the *Coast Banker* editorialized. "The fight is between the banker who believes in branch banking and the banker who believes in individually owned and managed banks. Of course there has been more or less friction between the two parties to the branch banking controversy in California for several years, but now it has developed into a controversy between the Federal Reserve Board on one side and those who favor branch banking . . . on the other."

34. As one angry independent complained: "The situation is such that country bankers in many parts of the state are disposed to think that it is hopeless for them to try to continue in business as independent bankers and expedient for them to sell out to one of the institutions now actively engaged in buying banks for conversion into branches at the first opportunity" (quoted in *Coast Banker*, September 23, 1923, 298, BAA).

35. For Giannini's plans to establish the Liberty Bank, see James Bacigalupi to Garret McEnerney, April 30, 1925, James Bacigalupi Papers, BAA.

36. For the bank's opening, see Bank of Italy, Minutes, 1921, 3:354, BAA; see also *Coast Banker*, August 1921, 191, BAA. Giannini turned the Liberty into the state's first "day and night" bank, with banking hours from 9:00 A.M. until midnight.

37. See, for list of officers and directors, *San Francisco Examiner*, June 14, 1921. Despite Giannini's efforts to "disguise" the ownership of the Liberty Bank, state banking officials were well aware of the connection between the bank and Giannini. See, for example, Jonathan Dodge to Giannini, June 4, 1926; see also Jonathan Dodge to Liberty Bank, August 3, 1921, BAA.

38. Quoted in Hayes, "Real Romance," April 13, 1928.

39. For background material on Giannini's difficulties with Perrin, see W. R. Williams to S. G. Sargent, July 8, 1921; see also John Perrin to W. R. Williams, July 11, 1921, BAA.

40. James Bacigalupi to Garret McEnerney, April 30, 1925, BAA.

41. See Stockholders Auxiliary Corporation, Minutes, 1921, 104, Transamerica Corporation Papers; see also Bank of Italy, Minutes, 1921, 3:355; John

Perrin to APG, August 25, 1921; James Bacigalupi to John Perrin, August 28, 1921; BAA.

42. James Bacigalupi to Garret McEnerney, April 25, 1930, BAA.

43. John Perrin to APG, November 25, 1921, BAA. "Permit me to assure you," Perrin added in his letter, "that we not only have no desire to harm your institution, but are most solicitous to protect it. That is the fundamental occasion of the care which is being exercised in this matter."

44. John Perrin to APG, November 29, 1921, BAA. Perrin received the support of the FRB, which promptly informed Giannini of that fact. See W. P. G. Harding to APG, December 1, 1921, BAA.

45. See Charles Stern, interview with Bessie James, undated, but sometime in 1949, BAA; see also Hayes, "Real Romance," April 18, 1928.

46. To Giannini, the injunction also represented the betrayal of a promise Perrin had made to him when he brought the Bank of Italy into the reserve system in 1913. See *Coast Banker,* September 1923. For other unfavorable comments about the FRB's apparent reversal of policy, see House Committee on Banking and Currency, *Hearings,* April 24, 1924; see also *Bankitaly Life,* December 1923; *Commercial and Financial Chronicle,* November 10, 1923.

47. See Hayes, "Real Romance," April 18, 1928.

48. See Galvin, "Bank Capital on Trial," 9–14.

49. For the attitude of Dawes and other FRB members toward branch banking, see *Annual Report of the Comptroller of the Currency,* December 3, 1923, 10; see also *Coast Banker,* August 1923, 246; *Bankitaly Life,* December 1923, 18–19.

50. For biographical sketches of McAdoo, see James S. Olson, ed., *Historical Dictionary of the New Deal* (1986), 319–20; Otis Graham, Jr., "William P. McAdoo," in *Dictionary of American Biography,* supplement, part 3, 479–82.

51. Angelo Scampini, interview with the author.

52. Quoted in Hayes, "Real Romance," April 19, 1921.

53. See, for example, Armando Pedrini to APG, June 14, 1922; see also Armando Pedrini to APG, August 21 and September 26, 1922, BAA.

54. For details of McAdoo's settlement with the FRB, see William McAdoo to APG, December 23, 1921, BAA.

55. See W. P. G. Harding to APG, January 18, 1922, BAA. The agreement read: "The Bank of Italy agrees that for the future it will not either directly or indirectly, through affiliated corporations or otherwise, acquire an interest in another bank in excess of 20 per cent or indirectly promote the establishment of any new bank for the purpose of acquiring such an interest in it, nor make any engagement to acquire such an interest, without first having received the approval of the Federal Reserve Board."

56. For the political career of Richardson, see DeWitt, *Images of Ethnic and Radical Violence,* 95–108.

57. A brief biographical sketch of Johnson appears in *California Bankers Association Bulletin,* January 1923, 9.

58. See John Chambers to James Bacigalupi, December 30, 1922, James Bacigalupi Papers, BAA.

59. For Giannini's interest in San Luis Obispo, see Bank of Italy, Minutes, January 14, 1919, in Gore, "Bank of America," BAA. Giannini had earlier applied for a permit to open a branch in Santa Maria when Dodge was superintendent of banking. Dodge denied his request (Jonathan S. Dodge to Giannini, November 23, 1921, BAA). In addition to its thriving agricultural economy, San Luis Obispo was also home to large numbers of Swiss-Italians and Portuguese, another fact that encouraged Giannini's interest in the region. On San Luis Obispo's growth and development, see Annie L. Morrison and John H. Haydon, *San Luis Obispo and Environs* (1917).

60. See W. T. Rice, interview with Bessie James, undated, but sometime in 1949; see also F. C. Mitchell to Walter E. Bruns, October 28, 1949, BAA.

61. For Giannini's acquisition of the Biaggini shares, see F. C. Mitchell to Walter Bruns, October 28, 1949; see also James Bacigalupi to M. C. Elliot, January 8, 1924, BAA.

62. See W. T. Rice, interview with Bessie James, undated, but sometime in 1949, BAA.

63. E. C. Aldwell to Armando Pedrini, January 26, 1921, BAA.

64. For letters to Giannini from Santa Maria Swiss Italians and Portuguese pleading with him to open a branch of the Bank of Italy in town, see, for example, Swiss-Portuguese-Americans to James Bacigalupi, November 15, 1918. "Establish an [*sic*] here and you will get all the business you can take care of from the start," the letter began. "All the banks here (they are the same really) have got into a mess. . . . Come on down and look the field over, just on the quiet. No need to ring a bell or blow a horn to let people know you are in town. This is the best opening in the State of California for a branch of a good strong institution." See also B. E. James to Louis Ferrari, March 16, 1921; George Smith to William McAdoo, December 19, 1922, BAA.

65. For biographical material on Teitzen, see W. H. Nuss, Jr., to Marquis James, September 4, 1949, BAA; see also Morrison and Haydon, *San Luis Obispo*, 371.

66. For Bacigalupi's version of events, see James Bacigalupi to M. C. Elliot, January 8, 1924, BAA.

67. According to the testimony of a Bank of Italy examiner who went over the books and records of the Bank of Santa Maria, Teitzen's bank was holding between $300,000 and $400,000 in bad loans. In a confidential memorandum to Bacigalupi, the examiner reported: "Mr. L. P. Scaroni [the Bank of Santa Maria's chief cashier] admitted to me in my room at the Santa Maria Inn that my analysis of the assets was substantially correct but that he could not face Mr. Teitzen with conditions as they were. He made an offer to me of a new Cadillac automobile if I would put through on behalf of the Bank of Italy a tentative proposition which was then under their consideration" (W. H. Nuss, Jr., to Bessie James, September 4, 1948, BAA). For the sale of Teitzen's bank to the Pacific-Southwest Bank of Los Angeles, see James Bacigalupi to John S. Chambers, November 13, 1922; see also James Bacigalupi to William McAdoo, November 2, 1922; C. L. Preisker to Jonathan Dodge, December 10, 1922, BAA.

68. See Howard Whipple's testimony, House Committee on Banking and Currency, *Hearings,* 1924, 1511-20.

69. Ibid.; see also James Bacigalupi to APG, September 13, 1923, BAA.

70. See House Committee on Banking and Currency, *Hearings,* 1924, 1511-22.

71. Quoted in Russell Posner, "State Politics and the Bank of America, 1920-1934," Ph.D. diss., University of California, Berkeley, 33.

72. For allegations against Giannini, see House Committee on Banking and Currency, *Hearings,* 1924, 176-84.

73. See James Bacigalupi to M. C. Elliot, January 8, 1924, BAA.

74. John S. Chambers to Giannini, March 8, 1923, BAA.

75. See editorial in *Coast Banker,* September 1923, BAA.

76. See W. T. Rice, interview with Bessie James, undated, but sometime in 1949, BAA.

77. George Smith to Friend W. Richardson, December 20, 1922, BAA.

78. John S. Chambers to James Bacigalupi, August 6, 1923; see also James Bacigalupi to John S. Chambers, August 8, 1923, BAA.

79. For Johnson's remarks, see *San Francisco Chronicle,* October 27, 1926.

80. John S. Chambers to APG, October 24, 1923; see also APG to John S. Chambers, October 26, 1923, BAA.

81. Willis, *Federal Reserve Bank of San Francisco,* 212-13.

82. See, for example, George Smith to L. M. McDonald, July 16, 1923, BAA.

83. See APG to William McAdoo, November 10, 1923; see also APG to James Bacigalupi, November 14, 1923, BAA.

84. On the Federal Reserve Board's action, see James Bacigalupi to R. H. Pearce, November 1, 1923; see also James Bacigalupi to Garret McEnerney, April 30, 1925, BAA.

85. See *Annual Report of the Comptroller of the Currency,* 1923, 10; see also *Coast Banker,* August 1923, 246; *Commercial and Financial Chronicle,* November 10, 1923; *Bankitaly Life,* December 1923, 18-19.

86. After Giannini moved his Bancitaly Corporation from New York to Los Angeles, the Federal Reserve Board accused him of violating the agreement he had signed with the board one year earlier, a charge Giannini denied. Unlike his Stockholders Auxiliary, he pointed out, Bancitaly was in "no sense affiliated legally or otherwise with Bank of Italy." See *Report of the Federal Reserve Committee on Branch, Group, and Chain Banking,* 1930, 2d sess., 74; see also James Bacigalupi to Garret McEnerney, April 30, 1925, BAA.

87. On Giannini's various acquisitions, see Americommercial Corporation Papers, Minutes, September 15, 1924, Transamerica Corporation Papers, BAA; see also *Coast Banker,* March 1923, BAA; *Los Angeles Examiner,* March 10, 1923; *San Francisco Chronicle,* September 2, 1925.

88. *San Francisco Chronicle,* July 11, 1925; see also *Los Angeles Times,* March 31, 1925.

89. For the concerns of Giannini's competitors, see James Bacigalupi to Garret McEnerney, April 24, 1925; John F. Johnson to Bank of America, March

5, 1926, BAA; see also *San Francisco Bulletin,* July 25, 1925; *San Francisco Call,* December 14, 1925.

90. For editorial comment on Giannini's use of the Liberty Bank and his evasion of Dodge's de novo ruling, see *Wall Street Journal,* September 18, 1925; see also *Palo Alto News,* November 5, 1925; *Sonoma Tribune,* December 19, 1925.

91. *San Francisco Bulletin,* September 17, 1925.

92. Quoted in *San Francisco Chronicle,* October 22, 1925.

93. James Bacigalupi to APG, January 6, 1924, BAA.

94. See Bank of Italy, Minutes, 1924, 4:332, BAA.

95. Quoted in Forbes's column, *San Francisco Examiner,* May 24, 1924.

96. *San Francisco Chronicle,* September 2, 1925.

8. The Octopus

1. Petition for Writ of Mandate, *Bank of Italy v. Johnson,* in *Records of the Supreme Court of California,* vol. 3726, 27; see also *San Francisco Chronicle,* June 19, 1925; *Independent Banker,* August–September 1925, 2.

2. For details of the merger and Bacigalupi's request to Johnson, see Americommercial, Minutes, 99, Transamerica Corporation Papers, BAA; see also Louis Ferrari to Walter J. Braunschweiger, June 15, 1925, BAA; APG to Charles Collins, August 7, 1925, Charles Collins Papers, BAA. Initially Giannini's executives were optimistic that Johnson would approve the merger and encouraged the press to think the same. See, for example, *Los Angeles Examiner,* December 14, 1925; *San Francisco Examiner,* December 14, 1925.

3. APG to James Bacigalupi, June 27, 1926, BAA.

4. One reason for Johnson's long delay, perhaps, was his uncertainty over whether he had either the legal authority or the political support in the state legislature to halt the expansion of branch banking. In a maneuver aimed at curbing Giannini, he and Joseph Sartori, president of Security First, had tried to push a bill through the legislature giving the superintendent of banking the power to prohibit the spread of branches affiliated with a holding company. They were unsuccessful. See *California Bankers Association Bulletin,* March 1925, 88, BAA.

5. John Franklin Johnson to Bank of America, March 5, 1926, BAA; also quoted in Nash, *State Government and Economic Development,* 288.

6. See draft letter, Bacigalupi to John Franklin Johnson, April 1926; see also Bacigalupi to Orra E. Monnette, March 19, 1926; Eustace Cullinan to Garret W. McEnerney, March 9, 1926, BAA.

7. Bank of America–Liberty Bank to John Franklin Johnson, July 12, 1926, BAA.

8. Section 31-A of the state's 1909 Banking Act explicitly granted to "going banks" the right to consolidate. Giannini believed that nothing in this section of the act would allow Johnson to fall back on the "public advantage and

convenience" provision in the de novo ruling to prevent him from consolidating his various banking systems. See Eustace Cullinan to John Franklin Johnson, December 30, 1926, BAA.

9. Bank of America–Liberty Bank to John Franklin Johnson, July 12, 1926, BAA. In a not-so-subtle barb aimed at Johnson's defense of the de novo rule, Bacigalupi added: "The Pacific Southwest Trust and Savings Bank, with head office in Los Angeles, has a branch as far north as San Luis Obispo; and why not? . . . The Bank act recognizes no such theory of tributary territory as you lay down."

10. Johnson was reported to have told several of his deputies in the department that the Bank of Italy had gotten a "bad case of indigestion" trying to swallow too many branches and that he intended to cure it. See Orra Monnette to APG, April 3, 1926, BAA.

11. Addendum, Brief for Respondent, VII, May 22, 1926, *Bank of Italy v. Johnson*.

12. See, for example, Orra Monnette to APG, April 3, 1926, BAA.

13. James Bacigalupi to APG, July 26, 1926, BAA.

14. For Young's early career in education and politics, see Alice H. Rose, interview with Young, May 9, 1938, in Borel Collection, Stanford University. On Young's nomination and the split in the ranks of the Republican party, see Posner, "State Politics," 193–205. For a discussion of California's progressive movement, see George Mowry, *The California Progressives* (1951), 278–303; see also Royce D. Delmatier, Clarence McIntosh, and Earl G. Waters, *The Rumble of California Politics, 1948–1970* (1970), 220–29; Bean, *California*, 326–40, 363–65.

15. James Bacigalupi to APG, July 26, 1926, BAA.

16. Ibid. By late July, Bacigalupi had also learned that the state supreme court seemed certain to decide against Bank of Italy in Giannini's mandamus suit—another reason to oppose Richardson's renomination. See Giannini, interview with Bessie James, April 6, 1949, BAA. While Bacigalupi was pleading his case for Young, other Giannini executives were urging Giannini to see Richardson privately to discuss his difficulties with Johnson, a course Giannini rejected. See APG to Orra Monnette, April 8, 1926, BAA.

17. For Neylan's career in California politics, see "John Francis Neylan: San Francisco Irish Progressive," typescript, Bancroft Library, University of California, Berkeley. For Neylan's relationship with Hearst, see Lindsay Chaney and Michael Cieply, *The Hearsts: Family and Empire: The Later Years* (1981), 63, 81–84, 172–75.

18. See Hayes, "Real Romance," April 25, 1928; see also Posner, "State Politics," 212–13.

19. See Giannini, interview with Bessie James, undated, but sometime in 1949, BAA.

20. Rumors soon began circulating in Republican circles that Giannini and Young had made a deal. See Franklin Hitchborn to Herbert Jones, June 11, 1926, Franklin Hitchborn Papers, Bancroft Library, University of California, Berkeley. For Richardson's concern, see postscript dated April 27 in James Bacigalupi to APG, April 26, 1926, BAA.

21. See Giannini, interview with Bessie James, April 6, 1949, BAA.

22. See Frank F. Merriam to Garret McEnerney, undated, but sometime in August 1926, Frank Merriam Papers, Bancroft Library, University of California, Berkeley.

23. See Posner, "State Politics," 217; see also Posner, "The Bank of Italy and the 1926 Campaign in California," *California Historical Society Quarterly* 37 (December 1958): 347–58.

24. Young's political allies were in fact increasing pressure on Giannini to jump into the campaign on their candidate's behalf. "I realize that the Bank of Italy is not in politics," a Young aide wrote to Bacigalupi, "but the fact remains that all the opposition banks in southern California are in politics and are directing their activities against the Bank of Italy" (Kent Parrott to James Bacigalupi, July 28, 1926, James Bacigalupi Papers, BAA).

25. Giannini statement quoted in Hayes, "Real Romance," April 25, 1928. Giannini later sent a personal check to the Young campaign for $500. See John F. Neylan to APG, August 17, 1926, BAA.

26. See Mario Giannini to Leo Belden, August 24, 1926, BAA; see also Testimony of James A. Bacigalupi, in House Committee on Banking and Currency, *Hearings* (1930) 2:1472–78.

27. For the split in the ranks of the Republican party's progressive wing, see Hiram Johnson to Herbert C. Jones, March 19, 1926, Herbert C. Jones Papers, Stanford University; see also Posner, "State Politics," 225–26.

28. See Testimony of James A. Bacigalupi, in House Committee on Banking and Currency, *Hearings* (1930) 2:1472.

29. For Bank of Italy's support of Young, see Franklin Hitchborn, "California Politics, 1891–1939," typescript, 4:2312, Franklin Hitchborn Papers, University of California, Los Angeles.

30. See Orra Monnette to APG, August 27, 1926; see also Mario Giannini to Leo Belden, August 24, 1926, BAA.

31. Orra Monnette to APG, August 27, 1926, BAA.

32. *Los Angeles Times,* August 25, 27, 1926.

33. *Los Angeles Times,* August 29, 1926.

34. *Los Angeles Times,* August 29, 1926. Aside from any damage it may have done to Giannini, the Richardson advertisement also produced some dissatisfaction among Young's supporters in the progressive wing of the party in northern California who were not pleased to learn that Giannini had jumped into the campaign on behalf of their candidate. See, for example, Franklin Hitchborn to C. C. Young, September 1, 1926, Herbert Jones Papers, Stanford University; see also Posner, "State Politics," 224.

35. See Mario Giannini to Leo Belden, August 24, 1926, BAA.

36. For reports on the progress of the bank's campaign, see V. Dardi to L. M. McDonald, August 27, 1926; see also W. E. Blauer to APG, August 27, 1926; L. D. McDonald to APG, August 26, 1926; Orra Monnette to APG, August 27, 1926, BAA.

37. See APG to Leo Belden, August 30, 1926, BAA.

38. For the reaction among Young's forces to his victory, see Franklin Hitchborn to John Haynes, September 3, 1926, John Haynes Papers, University

of California, Los Angeles; for a breakdown of the vote and a discussion of Giannini's influence on the outcome of the election, see Posner, "State Politics," 226–28.

39. See congratulatory letters and telegrams, Joseph Schenck to APG, January 1, 1926; Charles McMorran to APG, September 2, 1926; Orra Monnette to APG, September 3, 1926, BAA.

40. Orra Monnette to APG, September 20, 1926, BAA. Among others, the *California Christian Advocate*, a fundamentalist newspaper, accused Giannini of "placing his wealth at the disposal of Mussolini to aid in the furtherance of the latter's plans to promote fascism in the United States" (quoted in John Knowles to APG, November 5, 1926, BAA).

41. See Heflin's statement in the *New York Times*, February 16, 1927.

42. Giannini's statement is quoted in the *Santa Rosa Republican*, February 17, 1927.

43. These acquisitions enabled Giannini to enter thirty-two additional California communities. See *San Francisco Chronicle*, January 27, 1927; see also *Coast Investor*, February 1927, BAA.

44. *San Francisco Chronicle*, January 27, 1927. For additional comment, see *Wall Street Journal*, December 15, 1926; *San Francisco Examiner*, January 5, 1927; *Stockton Record*, January 5, 1927.

45. For biographical information on Wood, see Posner, "State Politics," 196–98; see also Cross, *Financing an Empire* 3:261–62; Delmatier, McIntosh, and Waters, *Rumble of California Politics*, 209, 214, 223.

46. For Giannini's expectations, see James Bacigalupi to APG, September 7, 1927, BAA.

47. For Wood's recollections, see Will C. Wood, Memorandum, undated, but sometime in the spring of 1927, BAA.

48. See Charles W. Collins, *The Branch Banking Question* (1926), 83–84; see also Cross, *Financing an Empire* 2:920.

49. See LeRoy M. Edwards to A. J. Mount, March 27, 1926; see also Leo Belden to A. J. Mount, February 17, 1926, BAA.

50. Will C. Wood, Memorandum, undated, but sometime in the spring of 1927, BAA. For a discussion of Wood's meeting with Williams, see Russell M. Posner, "State Politics," 244–45.

51. Will C. Wood to M. B. Harris, May 15, 1930, BAA; Posner, "State Politics," 240–45.

52. Will C. Wood, Memorandum, undated, but sometime in the spring of 1927, BAA.

53. Posner, "State Politics," 240–45.

54. Ibid. For a good general discussion of these events, see ibid., 241–46.

55. Ibid., 240–45. For a press report on Wood's actions, see *San Francisco Chronicle*, January 27, 1927. The *San Francisco Examiner* (January 27, 1927) mistakenly reported that Wood's announcement "was made without advance warning and came as a surprise to Giannini officials." The day after Wood's announcement, the Liberty Bank of America was operating, as Bacigalupi put it, "at full force" (James Bacigalupi to Leo Belden, January 28, 1927, BAA).

56. APG to Clorinda Giannini, January 25, 1927, BAA.

57. *San Francisco Call*, February 10, 1927; *San Francisco Examiner*, February 10, 1927.

58. "The present Superintendent," Wood said, "will not attempt to write into the law a limitation on branch banking which the law clearly does not contemplate or countenance" (*Wall Street Journal*, March 24, 1927). As Giannini would recall years later, "Wood, a school teacher all his life, may not have known much about banking, but he was a mighty good Superintendent for us" (quoted in Josephson, "Giannini," September 20, 1947, 114).

59. Collins, *Branch Banking Question*, 102.

60. See Leo Belden to Arnold J. Mount, February 17, 1927; see also Leo Belden to APG, February 17, 1927, BAA.

61. For the last-ditch effort of the opponents of branch banking in the Senate, see Carter Glass, "The Battle for the Banking Bill," *Nation's Business*, April 1927, BAA.

62. See *The Participant*, March 1927, 1.

63. Josephson, "Giannini," September 20, 1947, 117; Bacigalupi expressed his own reaction with a two-word telegram to Leo Belden: "Some Bank" (James Bacigalupi to Leo Belden, February 19, 1927, BAA).

64. *San Francisco Examiner*, February 22, 1927; *San Francisco Call*, February 21, 1927. See also *San Francisco Chronicle*, February 20, 1927.

65. *New York Commercial and Financial Chronicle*, March 26, 1927.

66. For admiring press reports, see *New York Herald Tribune*, May 4, 1927; see also *Wall Street Journal*, September 10, 1935; *New York Times*, October 30, 1927; *San Francisco Call*, October 17, 1927; *San Francisco Examiner*, October 7, 1927.

67. Quoted in Josephson, "Giannini," September 27, 1947, 126; see also *Forbes*, February 1928, BAA.

68. Quoted in David Warren Ryder, "A. P. Giannini–Bancitaly," reprint of undated article, BAA.

69. Among the first of these new acquisitions was San Francisco's French-American Bank, which Giannini quickly merged with his state-chartered United Bank and Trust Company. See French-American Bank, Minutes, March 1, 22, 1927; see also United Bank and Trust Company, Minutes, March 22, 1927, BAA; *San Francisco Examiner*, March 22, 1927.

70. See William Cavalier and Company, "Bank of America N.T. & S.A.," in "Comparative Bank Statistics," June 30, 1928, BAA.

71. Quoted in Josephson, "Giannini," September 27, 1947, 114. Commenting on Giannini's unexpected achievement, one Bank of Italy executive wrote: "The Bancitaly Corporation is the talk of two continents—Europe and America. . . . When we compare California with New York, or San Francisco with New York City, the Bank of Italy is ten times larger than the National City Bank. . . . Then add to the power of the Bank of Italy the prestige and latent support of the Bancitaly Corporation, and we have a combination that is not duplicated anywhere in the world" (John Grant to James Bacigalupi, May 31, 1927, BAA).

72. Janet Wasko, *Movies and Money: Financing the American Film Industry* (1982), 13.

73. Neal Gabler, *An Empire of Their Own: How the Jews Invented Hollywood* (1988), 5.

74. See Attilio's remarks made during a symposium at Harvard University in the 1920s, quoted in Joseph Kennedy, ed., *The Story of the Films* (1927), 78–79.

75. See Benjamin B. Hampton, *History of the American Film Industry* (1970), 110–45.

76. For the financial difficulties of early motion-picture producers, see Wasko, *Movies and Money,* 13.

77. Quoted in Frank Taylor, "He's No Angel," *Saturday Evening Post,* January 14, 1939, 46; see also Wasko, *Movies and Money,* 13.

78. See "All in Fifty Years," unpublished and undated report on Bank of Italy's role in the growth of the motion-picture industry, BAA; see also article on Attilio Giannini and motion-picture financing in *Wall Street Journal,* September 10, 1935; *San Francisco Examiner,* February 8, 1943; *San Francisco Chronicle,* February 8, 1943.

79. Wasko, *Movies and Money,* 12. For the important part Attilio played in the financing of films, see Taylor, "He's No Angel." An exaggerated but interesting claim was made by the gossip columnist Sheila Graham: "Without Doc, there would be no Hollywood" (Sheila Graham, "Story of First Banker to Accept Film as Collateral," *San Francisco Chronicle,* December 6, 1936).

80. See *Wall Street Journal,* September 10, 1935; see also *Motion Picture Daily,* May 17, 1934; Jack Carleton, "The Films Are Financed Here," *Los Angeles Times Sunday Magazine,* April 21, 1935; *San Francisco Examiner,* February 8, 1943.

81. In Kennedy, *Story of the Films,* 80–81.

82. See statistics compiled for the Bank of America by Robert L. Tollefson, "Summary of Motion Picture Financing, Bank of America," May 12, 1950, BAA.

83. See Gerth von Ulm, *Charlie Chaplin* (1940), 125; see also Ken Howe, "Hollywood and B of A: Yesterday and Today," *BankAmerican,* March 1980, 4–5. *The Kid* cost $500,000 to make and grossed around $2.5 million. See Charles J. Maland, *Chaplin and American Culture* (1989), 58–59. Many years later Chaplin singled out Giannini for praise (*My Autobiography* [1964], 186).

84. See "All This in Fifty Years" (anonymous manuscript), BAA; see also Graham, "Story of First Banker"; Kennedy, *Story of the Films,* 85–86.

85. Quoted in Carleton, "Films Are Financed Here." Aside from profits to banks and to the industry, the boost to the economy of southern California was considerable. In 1919 alone, for example, the industry invested more than $500,000 in film production and employed 20,000 people. See J. E. Barber, "The Banker and the Motion Picture Industry," *Coast Banker,* June 1921, 664; see also *New York American,* June 14, 1925.

86. H. R. Erkes to Arnold J. Mount, September 19, 1930; see also Attilio Giannini to Arnold J. Mount, June 8, 1931; APG to James Cavagnaro, July 13, 1938, BAA.

87. See L. M. McDonald to APG, December 3, 1926; Attilio Giannini to Arnold J. Mount, June 8, 1931, BAA; see also *California Bankers Association Bulletin,* April 1925, 127; *Coast Banker,* January 1928, 112.

88. See Attilio Giannini to James Phelan, September 30, March 14, 1928, Attilio Giannini Papers, Bancroft Library, University of California, Berkeley.

89. See David McClintock, *Indecent Exposure: A True Story of Hollywood and Wall Street* (1982), 129–30.

90. See *New York City Telegraph,* October 11, 1934; see also *New York Journal,* July 6, 1935.

91. Will Rogers, who called Attilio Giannini a "wop entirely surrounded by Jews and Gentiles," acknowledged that as far as his personal finances were concerned, "everything was up to Giannini" (Jack Lait, "The Life Story of Will Rogers," *San Francisco Examiner,* August 20, 1935).

92. Stephen Birmingham, *The Rest of Us: The Rise of America's Eastern European Jews* (1985), 206.

93. Taylor, "He's No Angel," 22.

94. See series of letters from Armando Pedrini to APG, April–September 1926, Transamerica Corporation Papers, BAA.

95. See Armando Pedrini to James Bacigalupi, November, undated, 1926; see also Armando Pedrini to APG, May 24, 1926, Transamerica Corporation Papers, BAA.

96. For additional biographical information on Belden, see "Leo Belden," Personnel Files, BAA; see also *New York Evening Post,* March 3, 1928; *San Francisco Call,* September 17, 1928.

97. Quoted in *New York Herald Tribune,* May 4, 1927.

98. For a statistical breakdown of Bancitaly's profits from 1921 to 1930, see Transamerica Corporation, Semi-Annual Report, July 12, 1930, Transamerica Corporation Papers; see also APG to John Lagomarsino, August 28, 1925; APG to R. P. Lathrop, December 11, 1926, BAA. On figures reported in the press, see San Francisco Chronicle, July 14, 1927; *San Francisco Examiner,* July 26, 1927; *San Francisco Call,* July 25, 1927.

99. *San Francisco Examiner,* April 10, 1928.

100. For a report on Giannini's annual salary as president of Bank of Italy and later Bancitaly, see Guy R. Helvering, Commissioner of Internal Revenue, in the U.S. Circuit Court of Appeals for the Ninth District, Docket No. 87128, BAA.

101. Written statement of Louis Ferrari, Sr., vice-president and general counsel of the Bank of Italy, dated February 15, 1939, BAA.

102. Ibid.

103. See Bank of Italy, Press Release, January 23, 1928, BAA.

104. Bancitaly's gift to the University of California was reportedly the country's first philanthropic endowment in the field of agricultural research. See *Coast Banker,* April 1928; see also *Literary Digest,* January 1929, BAA.

105. For press reaction, see *San Francisco Chronicle,* May 21, 1929; *Oakland Post Enquirer,* March 26, 1928; *New York Times,* March 1, 1928.

106. For Will Rogers's statement, see *San Francisco Chronicle,* January 5, 1928.

107. For Giannini's interview and statement, see *San Francisco Examiner,* January 24, 1928.

9. Morgan's Rules

1. Leo Belden to APG, November 22, 1927, BAA.

2. APG to Leo Belden, November 30, 1927, BAA.

3. New York's Bank of America was the country's second oldest bank, successor to the Bank of the United States, which became the target in the 1830s of Andrew Jackson's much-celebrated "war against the banks." See Bray Hammond, *Banks and Politics in America: From the Revolution to the Civil War* (1957), 161–64.

4. For a brief but informative history of Bank of America, see *San Francisco News*, March 6, 1928.

5. *New York Telegram*, February 29, 1929; see also *New York Times*, February 28, 1928.

6. For press discussion of the Delafield-Jonas struggle, see *New York Times*, February 15, 1928; see also *Brooklyn Eagle*, February 15, 1928.

7. For Edward Delafield's background and business career, see profiles in *New York Journal of Commerce*, February 26, 1928; *New York Times*, February 28, 1928; *Brooklyn Standard Union*, February 26, 1928; *San Francisco Chronicle*, February 25, 1928.

8. An informative but highly admiring biography is John Douglas Forbes, *J. P. Morgan, Jr., 1867–1943* (1981). A more critical and far more useful account of Morgan's importance on Wall Street can be found in Ron Chernow, *The House of Morgan: An American Banking Dynasty and the Rise of Modern Finance* (1990).

9. Word soon went out—leaked by Jonas, perhaps—of Giannini's interest in acquiring a controlling interest in Bank of America. Giannini denied the rumor. See *New York Journal of Commerce*, February 17, 1928; see also *San Francisco Call*, February 18, 1928.

10. Leo Belden to APG, November 2, 1927, BAA.

11. Belden warned Giannini: "There seemed to be a good deal of doubt, uncertainty, and misinformation in their minds regarding our general picture and I understand that this was particularly true of some of the older partners" (ibid.).

12. "I don't want to give you the impression that there is any well-defined doubt or fear concerning us, but it is rather a matter of not knowing what it is all about," Belden later wrote Giannini. "Our rapid growth and increase in capital has caused a good many of the old-timers to 'sit up and take notice' and wonder what was happening and also how it could happen. You can guess that I welcomed the opportunity of explaining to them in detail the foundations upon which our organization rests and tracing its growth from the beginning to the present time" (ibid.).

13. Belden clearly enjoyed being part of New York's financial scene and played up the success he seemed to be having in his negotiations with Bartow. "I am working here along a very definite policy trying to form close relationships with the real crowd, which I think will pay extremely well in the long run," he informed Giannini. "I feel that I know what you want and what you

would like to have in this situation and I am sure it has been handled in line with your desires" (ibid.).

14. Leo Belden to APG, December 21, 1927.

15. APG to Leo Belden, November 30, 1927; see also APG to Leo Belden, December 30, 1927, BAA.

16. Leo Belden to APG, December 30, 1927, BAA.

17. Quoted in Josephson, "Giannini," September 27, 1947, 14.

18. For press coverage of Giannini's arrival in New York, see *New York Times*, February 24, 1928; *Wall Street Journal*, February 28, 1928; *New York Journal of Commerce*, February 25, 1928; *New York Evening Post*, March 3, 1928; *New York Mid-Week Pictorial*, March 17, 1928; *New York Sun*, February 23, 1928; *New York Telegram*, February 29, 1928.

19. For Giannini's denial, see *New York Times*, February 10, 1928; see also *New York Journal of Commerce*, February 17, 1928.

20. See *New York Mid-Week Pictorial*, March 17, 1928; *New York World*, March 14, 1928; *Commercial and Financial Chronicle*, March 3, 1928; *Financial Age*, March 3, 1928; *Manufacturers Record*, March 8, 1928.

21. *New York Times*, March 1, 1928. For California reaction to Giannini's "spectacular" reception in New York, see *San Francisco Call*, March 1, 1928: "That Giannini has cut a wide swathe in Wall Street goes without question," the financial editor of the San Francisco *Call* wrote. "All of New York's newspapers for weeks have been devoting columns of space to stories of Giannini's activities. From a purely local figure he has flashed across the horizon of international finance." See also *San Francisco Bulletin*, February 21, 1928; *San Francisco News*, March 6, 1928; *San Francisco Examiner*, February 21, 1928.

22. *New York City Telegram*, March 13, 1928; see also *New York Mid-Week Pictorial*, March 17, 1928; *New York Sun*, February 23, 1928.

23. *New York Sun*, March 14, 1928; see also *New York Journal of Commerce*, February 25, 1928; *Wall Street Journal*, February 28, 1928; *New York Evening Post*, March 3, 1928; *Wall Street News*, March 5, 1928.

24. This aspect of Giannini's meeting with Morgan was omitted from the account furnished by John Rovensky, a Bank of America senior vice-president, who wrote later: "A. P. was informed that his acquiring control of the Bank of America would be favorably received by the management of the bank and have the blessing of J. P. Morgan and Company" (John Rovensky to L. M. Giannini, September, undated, 1949, BAA).

25. In addition to these demands, Morgan also thought it would be "most helpful" if Giannini increased Bancitaly's account with J. P. Morgan and Company by $1 million. Giannini agreed to only half this amount. See Leo Belden to APG, March 5, 1928; APG to Belden, March 6, 8, 1928, BAA.

26. For Giannini's concessions to Morgan, see Leo Belden to APG, March 5, 6, 7, 8, 1928, BAA.

27. Giannini's executives later justified his reasons for wanting working control of the Bank of America. "This bank," said one associate, "was selected because: (1) it had the ideal name to express its intended nationwide character; (2) it . . . was consistently one of the most liquid and one of the oldest banking institutions in the city of New York; (3) it had established tremendous goodwill

in banking circles and among people everywhere; (4) it had developed one of the foremost trust businesses in New York" (Goldwater, Memorandum, February 13, 1929, BAA).

28. See the undated, handwritten account of his meeting with NYFRB officials that Giannini wrote soon after he returned to San Francisco (Celestine Sullivan Papers, BAA).

29. See Mario Giannini's handwritten note scrawled at the bottom of a letter from Gates McGarrah to Leo Belden, March 23, 1928, BAA.

30. APG to Leo Belden, March 14, 1928, BAA.

31. On details of Giannini's purchase agreement with Jonas, see *New York Times*, February 28, 1928; see also *Wall Street Journal*, February 28, 1928; *New York Sun*, February 28, 1928; *Brooklyn Standard Union*, February 26, 1928.

32. For details of Giannini's consolidation program, see *New York Times*, February 25, 1928; *New York Journal of Commerce*, February 25, 1928; "What Is Ahead for Bancitaly Corporation?" *Magazine of Western Finance*, March 15, 1928, 9.

33. *New York Herald Tribune*, March 14, 1928, BAA.

34. *San Francisco Chronicle*, March 23, 1928; see also *San Francisco News*, March 16, 1928; *San Francisco Call*, March 16, 1928; *San Francisco Examiner*, March 23, 1928. For press comment in other parts of the country, see *Cleveland Plain Dealer*, May 4, 1928; *Chicago Daily News*, April 14, 1928; *Pittsburgh Press*, April 17, 1928; *Portland [Oregon] Journal*, April 13, 1928.

35. *San Francisco Bulletin*, February 17, 1928; see also *Wall Streeter*, March 1928.

36. Quotation in Fred Yeates, "Lawrence Mario Giannini: A Memorial," manuscript, BAA.

37. For biographical information, see profile in *Time*, January 27, 1936; see also *Business Week*, April 7, 1950; *Fortune*, August 1951; *American Banker*, April 20, 1948; *Commercial and Financial Chronicle*, January 23, 1947; *Los Angeles Times*, January 22, 1930; *Pacific Coast Business and Shipping Register*, March 17, 1952.

38. Quotation in Yeates, "Lawrence Mario Giannini," BAA.

39. Jake Fisher, interview with the author.

40. Claire Giannini Hoffman, Russell Smith, and Virgil Dardi, interviews with the author.

41. By mid-April Bank of America was selling at $1,475 a share. See *New York Evening Post*, April 12, 1928; see also *New York Journal of Commerce*, April 4, 1928; *Wall Street News*, January 27, 1928; *San Francisco Call*, February 9, 1928.

42. *Forbes*, March 1, 1928. See also *San Francisco News*, March 16, 1928; *San Francisco Chronicle*, March 23, 1928; *San Francisco Call*, March 16, 1928.

43. See *New Yorker*, May 5, 1928; see also *Wall Street News*, May 16, 1928; *San Francisco Examiner*, February 21, 1928; *San Francisco Call*, May 8, 1928.

44. *San Francisco News*, April 23, 1928; see also *Forbes*, March 1, 1928; *San Francisco Examiner*, April 10, 1928.

45. See George O. Boardwell, interview with Bessie James, undated, but sometime in 1949, BAA. For Giannini's press warnings, see, for example, *Wall Street Journal*, March 31, 1928; see also *San Francisco Examiner*, February 10, 1928. Angered by reports that many of the bank's employees were borrowing

money to speculate in his stocks, Giannini instructed Bacigalupi to order an end to all such activities (San Francisco Board of Management, Minutes, April 9, 1928, BAA).

46. Quotation in Thomas H. Gammack, "Giannini Comes to Wall Street," *The Outlook,* March 14, 1928, BAA. Commenting on Giannini's actions, the *Wall Street Journal* (March 31, 1928) wrote: "The California banker's attitude in this connection has gone a long way to recommend his entrance into New York banking circles through the purchase of the Bank of America. A few days ago, he wrote a personal letter to the president of every large bank and trust company and investment banking house in the East requesting no loans be made on Bancitaly stock, where the money was to be used for speculation. It was the first time anything like that had been done by the head of a banking institution."

47. See, for example, a confidential report written after the bubble burst by H. C. Carr, a Bank of Italy vice-president in the San Joaquin Valley. "Tony Sala (assistant cashier at Bank of Italy branch in Fresno) tells me that the greater part of the loss of accounts . . . was because of a dissatisfaction on the part of our clients, occasioned by a feeling they had against some of our officers and employees who advised them to buy bank stock . . . during the first months of this year. In fact, Sala frankly states that he, himself, urged the purchase of the stocks not only when he was asked, but volunteered the advice that the stocks were a good buy. He stated he did this because he had been instructed to do it by someone over him, and had even a list presented to him of his own countrymen that he might solicit, and that he actually inaugurated a selling campaign and followed it up until he finally sold most of his people" (H. C. Carr to R. B. Burmister, August 17, 1928, BAA).

48. See *San Francisco Call,* March 27, 1928; see also William R. Bacon, interview with Bessie James, undated, but sometime in 1949, BAA.

49. *San Francisco Chronicle,* April 23, 1928.

50. These arrangements were in accordance with the agreement Giannini had signed with the FRB two years earlier. See Charles Collins to R. A. Young, October 6, 1927, Charles Collins Papers, BAA. Along with trust powers, Giannini also wanted the initials "S.A." (savings association) attached to Bank of America. "Am assuming," he wrote to Leo Belden on his return to San Francisco, "that nationalization plan provided for S.A. being added to the title. . . . It would certainly serve to advertise to the people of New York generally that strong institution now doing a savings business." Morgan, however, rejected Giannini's request, making it clear that he had no intention of allowing a Wall Street bank to advertise the fact that it was soliciting the deposits of ordinary people. See APG to Leo Belden, March 5, 1928; Belden to APG, March 5, 1928, BAA. On Morgan's hostility toward "small banking" activities, see Ken Auletta, *Greed and Glory on Wall Street: The Fall of the House of Lehman* (1986), 28–29; Cary Reich, *Financier: The Biography of Andre Meyer— A Story of Money, Power, and the Reshaping of American Business* (1983), 20–21; Vincent Carosso, *Investment Banking in America* (1970), 89–90.

51. See Leo Belden to APG, March 22, 23, 1928; see also APG to Leo Belden, March 24, 1928, BAA.

52. See Transamerica Corporation to Federal Reserve Agent, New York, Memorandum, February 13, 1929, Transamerica Corporation Papers.

53. Ibid.

54. APG to Leo Belden, March 26, 1928, BAA.

55. Leo Belden to APG, March 23, 1928; see also APG to Leo Belden, March 23, 1928, BAA.

56. Leo Belden to APG, March 23, 1928, BAA.

57. APG to Leo Belden, March 23, 1928, BAA.

58. For Giannini's suspicions, see his handwritten personal reaction in the files of Dr. Celestine Sullivan, Celestine Sullivan Papers; see also Charles Collins to Arnold J. Mount, December 2, 1931, BAA.

59. Charles Collins to Arnold J. Mount, December 2, 1931; see also Charles Collins to Marquis James, December 22, 1949, BAA.

60. See Charles Collins, Memorandum no. 11, May 4, 1929, BAA.

61. Leo Belden to APG, March 24, 1928, BAA.

62. See Charles Collins to Arnold J. Mount, December 2, 1928, BAA.

63. Attilio Giannini to Armando Pedrini, January 18, 1929, Armando Pedrini Papers, BAA; see also Attilio Giannini to APG, March 10, 1928, BAA.

64. Attilio Giannini to Lorenzo Scatena, March 14, 1928, BAA.

65. Attilio Giannini to Lorenzo Scatena, March 10, 1928; see also Attilio Giannini to Armando Pedrini, January 10, 18, 1928, Armando Pedrini Papers, BAA.

66. Attilio Giannini to APG, March 10, 1928, BAA.

67. APG to Leo Belden, March 12, 1928, BAA.

68. Leo Belden to APG, March 13, 1928, BAA.

69. APG to Leo Belden, March 12, 1928, BAA. As Giannini informed Belden, "It will be best to fill the additional places with men of wide business which will mean business for us not only in New York but in California and in other parts of the country."

70. APG to Attilio Giannini, March 15, 1928; see also APG to Leo Belden, March 20, 1928; Lorenzo Scatena to Attilio Giannini, March 15, 1928, BAA.

71. For Giannini's appointments, see APG to Attilio Giannini, March 21, 1928; see also APG to Leo Belden, March 19, 1928, BAA. For press reports, see New York Times, April 27, 1928; San Francisco Call, April 28, 1928.

72. APG to Leo Belden, March 15, 20, 1928, BAA.

73. APG to Attilio Giannini, March 15, 1928, BAA. As Giannini explained it to Belden, "The bank will need plenty of motive power. . . . Capable business men and very well informed and interested in the success of the bank" (APG to Leo Belden, March 20, 1928, BAA).

74. Attilio Giannini to Lorenzo Scatena, March 14, 1928, BAA.

75. Lorenzo Scatena to Attilio Giannini, March 15, 1928; see also the series of letters between Lorenzo Scatena and Attilio Giannini written between March 12 and March 21, 1928, BAA.

76. Lorenzo Scatena to Attilio Giannini, March 21, 1928, BAA.

77. For Giannini's denials, see, for example, the interview in the San Francisco Chronicle, April 4, 1928.

78. APG to Leo Belden, March 20, 1928, BAA.

79. See *Chicago Journal of Commerce,* April 13, 1928; see also press reports in *San Francisco Chronicle,* April 15, 1928; *San Francisco Bulletin,* April 24, 1928.

80. *American Banker,* April 25, 1928; see also *San Francisco Examiner,* May 2, 1928.

81. On Giannini's arrival in Milan, see *Boston News Bureau,* May 5, 1928; see also *San Francisco Call,* May 3, 1928; *San Francisco News,* May 3, 1928.

82. Quotation in *San Francisco Bulletin,* May 5, 1928.

83. For Giannini's announcement, see *Washington Evening Star,* May 10, 1928; see also *New York Evening Post,* May 7, 1928; *San Francisco Bulletin,* May 10, 1928.

84. *San Francisco Chronicle,* May 8, 1928.

85. For Giannini's efforts to discourage speculation, see Bank of Italy Publicity Department, Press Release, May 1928, BAA.

86. For Bacigalupi's statement, see *San Francisco Chronicle,* May 11, 1928; see also *San Francisco Examiner,* May 11, 1928; *Wall Street News,* May 14, 1928.

87. *Wall Street Journal,* May 23, 1928.

88. *San Francisco Examiner,* May 5, 1928.

10. Season of Troubles

1. See reprint of the paper's column in *E. F. Hutton & Co. Bulletin,* May 11, 1928.

2. See Giannini's statement in *San Francisco Daily News,* December 4, 1925; see also APG to Dr. Edward Taussig, December 8, 1933, BAA.

3. See reports in *Washington Evening Star,* May 10, 1928; *San Francisco Bulletin,* May 10, 1928.

4. Giannini, interview with Bessie James, undated, but sometime in 1948, BAA.

5. Claire Giannini Hoffman, interview with the author.

6. See Bacigalupi's statement in the *San Francisco Call,* May 29, 1928. Bank of Italy's identification as a one-man bank had been well established in the public mind at this time, a fact that worried many of Giannini's executives, who felt that the connection would cause serious problems for the bank if Giannini was no longer around to direct its operations. See W. H. McGinnis, Jr., to Arnold J. Mount, March 21, 1928, BAA.

7. For stock market decline, see *Wall Street Journal,* June 8, 1928; see also *San Francisco Bulletin,* May 14, 1928; *San Francisco Call,* May 18, 1928; *San Francisco Chronicle,* May 23, 1928.

8. See Hale's long and detailed report to Giannini on the events preceding and immediately following the dramatic market break on June 8 (Prentice Hale to APG, August 2, 1928); see also James Bacigalupi, "To Whom It May Concern," February 2, 1932, BAA.

9. For price fluctuations in Giannini's stocks, see *San Francisco Call,* June 7, 1928; see also *San Francisco News,* June 8, 1928; *Wall Street Journal,* June 8, 1928.

10. See Mario Giannini, Memorandum to Bessie James, undated, but sometime in 1948, BAA.

11. Mario Giannini, interview with Bessie James, undated, but sometime in 1949, BAA.

12. Virgil Dardi, interview with the author.

13. Prentice Hale to APG, August 2, 1928, BAA.

14. Ibid.

15. See James Bacigalupi, "To Whom It May Concern," February 2, 1932, James Bacigalupi Papers.

16. See copy of Giannini's telegram in *San Francisco Call,* June 12, 1928.

17. *Barron's,* August 13, 1928.

18. See James Bacigalupi's letter to an IRS agent stationed in San Francisco, undated, in file folder marked "Stock Speculation"; see also Bessie James, "Hurdle 10," part 2, BAA.

19. Prentice Hale to APG, August 2, 1928, BAA.

20. According to Giannini's personal physician, "Always, even on his most painful days, he kept up with his business affairs, averaging fifty-five to sixty cable message daily" (*San Francisco Examiner,* July 6, 1928).

21. James Bacigalupi to APG, July 25, 1928, BAA.

22. In an effort to curtail speculation in the stock market, the FRB increased the discount rate from 4 to 4-1/2 percent, a step that many felt also contributed to the June market break. See Prentice Hale to APG, August 2, 1928, BAA.

23. Prentice Hale to APG, July 25, 1928, BAA.

24. For Giannini's accusations, see Charles Collins, Memorandum, undated, but sometime in the summer of 1928, Charles Collins Papers.

25. See typed copy of Giannini's account in the file of Dr. Celestine Sullivan, BAA.

26. G. Andreini, "Battle of the Giants," manuscript in possession of the author. (Andreini was an aide to Mario Giannini.)

27. James Bacigalupi to APG, July 25, 1928; see also Prentice Hale to APG, August 2, 1928, BAA.

28. Louis Ferrari to Charles Collins, undated, but sometime in June of 1928, BAA.

29. Collins later revealed to Giannini that on the weekend preceding the March 26, 1928, stockholders' meeting, Belden had made no mention to him of Gates McGarrah's letter, although he and Belden were working together in the same office in New York. Collins, who had developed personal contacts with a number of highly placed officials in the Washington bureaucracy, informed Giannini: "Had I known about it . . . I would have easily blocked it [the McGarrah divestiture demand] in Washington." The implication of Collins's testimony is that Belden had deliberately withheld the information from him to ensure Giannini's acquiescence. See Charles Collins, interview with Bessie James, undated, but sometime in 1949, BAA.

30. Charles Collins to Louis Ferrari, June 26, 1928, BAA.

31. APG to James Bacigalupi, June 28, 1931, BAA.

32. As Giannini explained it, "Belden made frequent visits to the home of Francis D. Bartow . . . [and] entered into the Morgan office getting tips on the

market to his personal advantage and hobnobbing with Bartow and others of his partners and friends, joining their Country and City Clubs etc." See Giannini's undated handwritten notes in the file of Dr. Celestine Sullivan, BAA.

33. As the *Kansas City Star* explained the significance of Morgan's "preferred list," "Those favored by Morgan were placed under obligation to him" (quoted in Arthur Schlesinger, Jr., *The Coming of the New Deal* [1959], 435–37).

34. James Bacigalupi to APG, August 1, 1928, BAA.

35. For Giannini's press conference, see *New York Times*, September 5, 1928; see also *New York World,* September 5, 1928; *San Francisco Examiner,* September 5, 12, 1921.

36. *San Francisco Daily News,* September 12, 1928; see also *San Francisco Examiner,* September 12, 1928.

37. *New York Times,* September 5, 1928; see also *Brooklyn Eagle,* September 7, 1928.

38. G. Andreini, "Battle of the Giants."

39. Leo Belden to APG, August 27, 1928, BAA.

40. For the meeting with Bartow, see the typed copy of Giannini's handwritten account in the file of Dr. Celestine Sullivan, BAA.

41. Ibid.

42. For Giannini's interview, see *San Francisco Bulletin,* September 11, 1928; see also *San Francisco Examiner,* September 11, 1928.

43. Quotation in Gordon Thomas and Max Morgan-Witts, *The Day the Bubble Burst: A Social History of the Wall Street Crash of 1929* (1979), 18.

44. For early discussions between Giannini and his executives along these lines, see James Bacigalupi to APG, July 25, 1928; see also APG to Leo Belden, October 13, 1928, BAA. For early newspaper speculation, see *New York Tribune,* October 12, 1928; *New York Times,* October 13, 1928; *San Francisco Chronicle,* October 12, 1928.

45. James Bacigalupi to APG, July 25, 1928; see also APG to Leo Belden, July 25, 1928; Leo Belden to APG, October 5, 10, 13; William Snyder to APG, November 13, 1928, BAA. For a complete description of Bancitaly's stock holdings, see "The Transamerica Corporation to the Federal Reserve Agent in New York," February 13, 1929, Transamerica Corporation Papers, BAA.

46. See "A. P. Giannini to Stockholder Addressed," October 24, 1928, Transamerica Corporation Papers, BAA.

47. A brief account of Transamerica's formation can be found in George H. Koster, *The Transamerica Story* (1978), 9–10. For Mario Giannini's statement, see *New York Times,* October 13, 1928; see also *San Francisco Chronicle,* October 12, 1928; *San Francisco Examiner,* October 13, 1928.

48. Angelo Scampini, interview with the author; see also J. Tosi, interview with Al Haase, undated, but sometime in 1948, BAA.

49. For press reaction to the formation of Transamerica, see *New York Times,* October 13, 1928; *New York Journal of Commerce,* October 15, 1928; *New York Tribune,* October 12, 1928; *San Francisco Chronicle,* October 13, 1928; *San Francisco News,* October 24, 1928.

50. Goldwater, Memorandum, BAA.

51. APG to Leo Belden, January 4, 7, 1929, BAA.

362 NOTES TO PAGES 144-47

52. Leo Belden to APG, January 7, 1929, BAA.

53. Leo Belden to APG, January 8, 1929, BAA.

54. APG to Leo Belden, January 17, 1928; see also APG to Carl Stamer, January 18, 1929, BAA.

55. Leo Belden to APG, January 28, 1929, BAA.

56. For a detailed account of Giannini's meeting with Bartow, see personal affidavit dictated by Prentice Hale, March 13, 1933. Hale agreed to submit this affidavit on the condition that it be kept classified until his death; see also Charles Collins, Memorandum no. 11, March 4, 1929, in Charles Collins Papers, BAA; Charles Collins to Bessie James, December 22, 1949, BAA.

57. George Whitney later denied this version of the story, writing to Giannini that the Morgan firm had in no way influenced the action of New York's Federal Reserve Bank (George Whitney to APG, June 12, 1947, BAA).

58. For additional information on Giannini's meeting with Bartow and Reynolds, see Giannini's handwritten notes in file of Dr. Celestine Sullivan; Charles Collins to Jean Monnet, December 2, 1931, Charles Collins Papers, BAA; James Rovensky, interview with Bessie James, November 1949, BAA.

59. James Rovensky, interview with Bessie James, November 1949, BAA.

60. See Charles Collins, "Events tending to show a conspiracy to wrest control of Transamerica Corporation from the Giannini interests and to bring about its liquidation," August 10, 1934, BAA.

61. On Giannini's allegations about Morgan's influence over New York's Federal Reserve Bank, see Charles Collins to APG, December 3, 1928, BAA. "The Morgan control of the Federal Reserve System is exercised through control of the management of the Federal Reserve Bank of New York and the mediocre representation and acquiescence of the Federal Reserve Board in Washington" (New York Times, July 4, 1930).

62. Charles Collins, Memorandum no. 11, May 4, 1929, in Charles Collins Papers, BAA. As Collins put it, "I took the position that Transamerica was morally and legally right in the matter and that the Fed's position was high handed, improper, and unlawful."

63. Transamerica Corporation to Gates McGarrah, February 15, 1929; see also Transamerica Corporation to J. P. Morgan and Company, February 13, 1929, Transamerica Corporation Papers, BAA.

64. G. Andreini, "Battle of the Giants."

65. See Giannini's undated handwritten notes in the file of Dr. Celestine Sullivan, BAA.

66. Virgil Dardi, interview with the author.

67. See Attilio Giannini to APG, December 12, 1928, and March 12, 1929; see also Attilio Giannini to Armando Pedrini, January 10, 1929, BAA. See also collection of letters and telegrams marked "private and confidential" that Attilio Giannini sent to various Bank of Italy executives between January and March of 1929 (Attilio Giannini Papers, BAA).

68. Attilio Giannini to Armando Pedrini, January 13, 18, 23, 25, 1929; see also Attilio Giannini to APG, December 12, 1928, and January 9, 1929; Armando Pedrini to Attilio Giannini, January 10, 1929, BAA.

69. Attilio Giannini to APG, December 12, 1928, BAA.

70. Attilio Giannini to APG, March 12, 1929; also Attilio Giannini to Armando Pedrini, January 25, 1929, BAA.

71. APG to Attilio Giannini, January 29, 1929; see also Lorenzo Scatena to Attilio Giannini, March 14, 1929; Armando Pedrini to Attilio Giannini, January 10, 1929, BAA.

72. APG to Edward Delafield, March 16, 1929, BAA.

73. For biographical material on Elisha Walker, see *Coast Investor,* May 1929; see also *The Participant,* April 1929; *New York Times,* March 22, 1929; *New York World,* May 20, 1929.

74. For a summary of Walker's business career, see *New York Times,* March 22, 1929.

75. For details of the Giannini-Walker agreement, see Proceedings of Transamerica Meeting, February 27, 1930, Transamerica Corporation Papers, BAA; see also *Fortune,* March 1930; *New York Times,* April 1, 1929; *Wall Street Journal,* September 29, 1929; *New York Tribune,* May 22, 1929; *San Francisco Chronicle,* May 22, 1929.

76. For biographical material on Monnet, see *Bankitaly News,* October 1930; see also "Jean Monnet," Personnel Files, Transamerica Corporation Papers, BAA.

77. Quoted in "Mr. Giannini, Branch Banker, and Mr. Walker of Blair & Co.," *Fortune,* August 1930; for additional press comment, see *New York World,* May 20, 1929; *Coast Investor,* March 1929, BAA.

78. Quoted in *The Participant,* July 7, 1929.

79. For Giannini's plans, see *Wall Street News,* April 1, 1929; see also *American Banker,* January 14, 1929, BAA; *San Francisco Chronicle,* February 16, 1929; *San Francisco Examiner,* March 15, 1929.

80. Giannini called his "selling organization" Intercoast Trading Company. Its purpose, he said, "was to carry on all trading and other activities not properly the function of a holding company" ("A. P. Giannini to the Stockholders of Transamerica Corporation Addressed," August 26, 1929, Transamerica Corporation Papers, BAA).

81. Howard Preston to APG, October 19, 1929; see also APG to William Snyder, October 15, 1929; William Snyder to APG, October 17, 1929, Transamerica Corporation Papers, BAA. For press reaction, see *Wall Street Journal,* May 21, 1929; see also *New York Journal of Commerce,* May 24, 1929; *San Francisco News,* May 9, 1929; *San Francisco Examiner,* July 30, 1929.

82. *San Francisco Examiner,* March 29, 1929; see also *New York Financial World,* October 9, 1929; *New York Tribune,* May 20, 1929; *Chicago Journal of Commerce,* May 22, 1929; *Coast Banker,* October 20, 1929; *San Francisco Examiner,* September 3, 1929.

11. The Downhill Slide

1. Giannini statement in an unidentified clipping dated December 1927, BAA.

2. For press accounts of the dinner and Bacigalupi's retirement, see *San Francisco Call-Bulletin,* October 18, 1929; see also *San Francisco Chronicle,* October 17, 1929; *San Francisco News,* October 17, 1929.

3. For Giannini's announcement, see *San Francisco Examiner,* May 23, 1929; see also *New York City Tribune,* May 22, 1929.

4. For biographical sketch of Mount, see "Arnold J. Mount," Personnel Files, BAA; see also *Oakland Tribune,* October 17, 1929; *Reedley Exponent,* October 22, 1929.

5. *San Francisco Chronicle,* October 17, 1929; see also *San Francisco Examiner,* October 18, 1929; *San Francisco Call-Bulletin,* October 17, 1929.

6. For general information on the crash, see Kenneth S. Davis, *FDR: The New York Years, 1928–1933* (1979); John Kenneth Galbraith, *The Great Crash: 1929* (1972); John A. Garraty, *The Great Depression* (1987); L. V. Chandler, *America's Greatest Depression* (1970).

7. Davis, *FDR: The New York Years,* 147–48; see also *New York Times,* October 30, 1929; *San Francisco News,* October 30, 1929; *San Francisco Call-Bulletin,* October 29, 1929; *San Francisco Chronicle,* October 29, 1929.

8. For Giannini's market support of Transamerica, see Elisha Walker, "To the Stockholders of Transamerica," January 30, 1933, Transamerica Corporation Papers, BAA.

9. As Giannini wrote to Cavagnaro about his decision to withdraw his support, "It would be folly to continue buying in view of present market situation. Prices ought to get back to former level and even much higher once general situation becomes normal" (APG to James Cavagnaro, October 29, 1929, Transamerica Corporation Papers, BAA). For comments in the press, see *Sacramento Bee,* October 29, 1929; *San Francisco Examiner,* November 1, 1929.

10. See *San Francisco News,* October 30, 1929; see also *San Mateo Times,* October 29, 1929; *San Rafael Independent,* October 29, 1929.

11. APG to Howard Preston, October 29, 1929, Transamerica Corporation Papers, BAA. "Everything is tiptop," Giannini wrote to Cavagnaro. "All our stockholders are for us one hundred percent" (APG to James Cavagnaro, October 29, 1929, BAA).

12. On Giannini's Oakland acquisition, see W. F. Morrish to J. E. Byrnes, January 23, 1930, BAA. The five New York branches came with the acquisition of the Nassau National Bank and the Traders National Bank, both of which were located in Brooklyn. See Bank of America Executive Committee, Minutes, December 10, 1929; see also Attilio Giannini to APG, May 2, 1930, Transamerica Corporation Papers, BAA.

13. For favorable press comment, see *San Rafael Independent,* December 4, 1929; see also *Organized Labor's Friend,* December 28, 1929, BAA.

14. *San Francisco Chronicle,* December 4, 1929.

15. For Mario Giannini's negotiations with Walker and Monnet, see exchange of telegrams between him and his father, November 25, 1929–December 29, 1929, BAA.

16. APG to L. M. Giannini, November 29, 1929, BAA.

17. See exchange of telegrams between Giannini and Mario Giannini from November 25, 1929–December 29, 1929, BAA; see also "Contract Signed by Elisha Walker and Jean Monnet," January 16, 1930, BAA.

18. Two sections of the contract dealt specifically with nationwide branch banking: "1. Transamerica shall develop its policy of nation-wide branch banking. . . . 2. Bank of America to be developed so that it will be one of the principal institutions of New York. An outstanding institution in New York is necessary for the proper upbuilding of Transamerica and for nationwide branch banking." See "Contract Signed by Elisha Walker and Jean Monnet," January 16, 1930, BAA.

19. See APG to Mario Giannini, November 29, 1929, BAA.

20. For Walker's remarks, see L. M. Giannini to APG, February 8, 1930, BAA. For press reports on the Walker and Monnet appointments, see *San Francisco Examiner,* January 19, 1930; *Los Angeles Times,* January 21, 1930; *Sacramento Bee,* January 20, 1930; *Oakland Tribune,* January 21, 1930; *New York City World,* January 21, 1930.

21. L. M. Giannini to APG, February 8, 1930, BAA.

22. For Walker's address to stockholders and press reports on his arrival in San Francisco, see Proceedings at Transamerica Meeting, February 27, 1930, BAA; see also *San Francisco News,* February 19, 1930; *San Francisco Examiner,* February 19, 1930; *Wall Street Journal* (Pacific coast edition), February 19, 1930.

23. L. M. Giannini to Howard Preston, February 24, 1930. For similar expressions, see George Armsby to Giannini, January 20, 1930, BAA.

24. Attilio Giannini to Armando Pedrini, January 25, 1930, BAA.

25. Attilio Giannini to Armando Pedrini, January 29, 1930; see also Attilio Giannini to L. M. Giannini, March 14, 1930, Transamerica Corporation Papers, BAA.

26. See "Memorandum about Merchants National Deal," confidential files of Walter Bruns, Walter Bruns Papers, Bank of America; see also memorandum of an interview between Louis Ferrari and James Byrnes, July 23, 1928, Bank of America Legal Department Files; *Cushing v. Cushing,* June 28, 1935, and Deposition of Louis Ferrari, April 20, 1936, in Louis Ferrari Litigation Files, Louis Ferrari Papers, BAA; William Snyder to L. M. Giannini, April 23, 1928, Transamerica Corporation Papers, BAA.

27. James and James, *Biography of a Bank,* 230. The Merchants National Bank of Los Angeles was merged with the Hellman brothers' Hellman Commercial Trust to form the Merchants National Trust and Savings Bank of Los Angeles. For biographical material on the Hellman brothers, see "Marco Hellman" and "Irving Hellman," Personnel Files, BAA; see also Ira Cross, *Financing an Empire* 2:536; *Western Livestock Journal,* January 22, 1948.

28. For Nolan quotation, see *Los Angeles Examiner,* November 17, 1928. For additional biographical information, see "Edward J. Nolan," Personnel Files, BAA; *Bancamerica News,* November 1930, BAA; James and James, *Biography of a Bank,* 231.

29. For additional biographical information, see "Charles Bell," Personnel Files, BAA; see also *San Francisco Chronicle,* December 19, 1928; *Bancamerica News,* February and May 1931, BAA.

30. Byrnes was so terrified that Giannini would turn his back on the deal that he bombarded him with telegrams urging him not to let the opportunity slip by. See James Byrnes to APG, June 2, 7, and 15, 1928; see also James Bacigalupi to APG, May 5, 16, and 24, 1928, BAA.

31. See "Acquisition of Merchants National Trust and Savings Bank," Louis Ferrari Legal Files, Louis Ferrari Papers, BAA. For press speculation on Giannini's interest in Merchants National, see *San Francisco Examiner,* October 21, 1928; *San Francisco Chronicle,* October 10, 1928; *Stockton Independent,* November 29, 1928.

32. William Snyder to L. M. Giannini, June 2, 7, 1928, BAA.

33. Charles Collins to Bessie James, November 14, 1949, BAA.

34. William Snyder to L. M. Giannini, April 25, 1928. See also William Snyder to L. M. Giannini, June 15, 1928, Transamerica Corporation Papers; James Bacigalupi to Giannini, May 5, 16, and 24, 1928, BAA.

35. Giannini, interview with Bessie James, undated, but sometime in 1949, BAA.

36. See APG to Louis Ferrari, November 29, 1928, Louis Ferrari Papers, BAA.

37. See Giannini, interview with Bessie James, undated, but sometime in 1949, BAA.

38. See Bank of America, Press Release, December 10, 1928, BAA.

39. See, for example, Edward Nolan to APG, December 12, 1928, BAA.

40. APG to Leo Belden, January 22, 1929, Transamerica Corporation Papers, BAA.

41. APG to Louis Ferrari, Louis Ferrari Litigation Files, July 12, 1929, Louis Ferrari Papers, BAA. For complaints from Giannini executives about Nolan, see Will Morrish to Edward Nolan, July 8, 1930, Arnold J. Mount Papers; see also Russell Smith to Arnold J. Mount, June 16, 1931, Transamerica Corporation papers, BAA.

42. James Bacigalupi to APG, May 10, 1929, BAA.

43. Ibid.

44. Ibid.

45. See Bank of America, "Report on Subdivision Trusts," May 31, 1923; see also APG to Lee Madland, June 10, 1933; Arnold J. Mount to James Bacigalupi, November 8, 1931, Transamerica Corporation Papers; Los Angeles Real Estate and Blue Book, 1924, BAA.

46. See Deposition of P. C. Read, April 21, 1936, Transamerica Corporation Papers, BAA; see also Charles Collins to J. W. Pole, August 5, 1931; P. C. Hale to Giannini, September 7, 1933, Charles Collins Papers, BAA; Arnold J. Mount to R. A. Laird, July 22, 1931, Arnold Mount Papers, BAA.

47. See Ralph Groner, interview with Bessie James, undated, but sometime in 1949, BAA; for subdivision activities in Los Angeles during the 1920s, see Bank of America, "Report on Subdivision Trusts," BAA; *California Real Estate Magazine,* June 1929, 129.

48. See Mario Giannini to R. E. Trengrove, August 12, 1929, BAA; see also *Los Angeles Times,* May 11, 1930.

49. See letters and memoranda in Bank of America, "San Clemente File," January 8, 1928–January 29, 1949, BAA.

50. See Gore, "Bank of America," March 26, 1930, BAA.

51. On the campaign itself, see Arnold J. Mount, "To My Fellow Officers and Co-Workers," April 4, 1930, BAA.

52. L. M. Giannini to Howard Preston, March 18, 1930; see also Howard Preston to L. M. Giannini, April 1930. The results of the campaign in California were particularly disappointing. After a strenuous three-week effort, only 77 of Giannini's 288 branches were able to report sales of Transamerica stock, for a total of only 415 new stockholders. See W. H. McGinnis, Report, April 19, 1930, Transamerica Corporation Papers, BAA.

53. Andreini, "Battle of the Giants," 70–71.

54. See earnings statement in *San Francisco Chronicle,* March 27, 1930.

55. C. T. Hallinan to John Grant, January 30, 1930; see also Robert McCrea to James Bacigalupi, May 9, 1931, James Bacigalupi Papers, BAA.

56. See Edward C. Delafield to George E. Hoyer, undated, but sometime in March 1930, BAA.

57. Attilio Giannini to Mario Giannini, March 14, 1930; see also Attilio Giannini to Jean Monnet, March 13, 1930, BAA.

58. Attilio Giannini to Mario Giannini, March 15, 1930, BAA.

59. Ibid.

60. Giannini accepted the invitation in part because, as he told Collins, it would give him an opportunity to "open up on that Wall Street crowd with little history of their rotten raw methods and system" (APG to Charles Collins, March 20, 1930, BAA). For Giannini's appearance before the committee, see Fred Kerman to L. M. Giannini, May 10, 1930; see also "Statement of James A. Bacigalupi, Vice Chairman of Advisory Committee, Transamerica Corporation, May 6, 1930," Transamerica Corporation Papers, BAA.

61. See House Committee on Banking and Currency, *Hearings,* May 8, 1930, 1539.

62. See Elisha Walker to Stockholder Addressed, July 12, 1930, BAA. For press reports on the alleged raid, see *San Francisco Chronicle,* June 6, 1930; see also *Los Angeles Times,* July 12, 1930.

63. *San Francisco Chronicle,* June 6, 1930; see also *Portland Oregonian,* June 5, 1930; *The Participant,* June 30, 1930.

64. Arnold J. Mount, Memorandum, June 12, 1930; see also Will F. Morrish to Guy W. Brundage, June 10, 1930, BAA. Alarmed by the rumors, Mount sent a "personal word" from Walker to Bank of Italy's branch managers: "You can confidentially advise stockholders who may make inquiries, that their best interests are served by holding the stock" ("Arnold J. Mount to All Branch Managers," June 9, 1930, BAA).

65. For Walker's earnings statement, see Ernst and Ernst to Jean Monnet, July 24, 1930, BAA; see also *Wall Street Journal,* August 21, 1930; *San Francisco Chronicle,* July 12, 1930; *Los Angeles Times,* July 12, 1930.

66. Giannini's earnings figure of $96 million did not include such items as undistributed earnings, taxes, employee compensation, and real estate depreciation, items which, among others, accounted for the discrepancy but which Walker did not explain to the press when he released his own statement. For Giannini's explanation, see *Wall Street Journal,* August 21, 1930; see also APG to L. M. Giannini, August 10, 1930, BAA.

67. Elisha Walker to APG, August 5, 1930, BAA.

68. APG to L. M. Giannini, July 20, 1930, BAA.

69. APG to James Bacigalupi, July 17, 1930, BAA.

70. APG to L. M. Giannini, August 9, 1930, BAA. To Bacigalupi, Giannini cabled: "Cancelled reservations. Satisfied return unwelcome. Likely cause friction. Still believe friends participated recent raid. Continued short selling. Simply make other raids easily possible minimum risk" (Giannini to James Bacigalupi, July 17, 1930, BAA).

71. APG to L. M. Giannini, August 10, 1930, BAA.

72. L. M. Giannini to APG, August 7, 1930, BAA.

73. L. M. Giannini to APG, August 7, 1930, BAA.

74. APG to Elisha Walker, August 11, 1930, BAA. Giannini's letter to Walker also included some of his hard evidence to support his charge of "treachery" on Belden's part in selling Transamerica short. "If Belden friends . . . will tell what they told Mario and me in my own home shortly before my departure," Giannini wrote, "you'll learn he had several millions in his drive against TAC in 1929 when I was stubbornly supporting it couple days to prevent general California panic in which I succeeded as you well know."

75. Elisha Walker to APG, August, undated, 1930, BAA.

76. APG to L. M. Giannini, August 10, 1930, BAA.

77. APG to L. M. Giannini, August 9, 10, 19, 20, 1930, BAA.

78. APG to L. M. Giannini, August 6, 10, 20, 1930, BAA.

79. Thomas W. Lamont to Jean Monnet, April 2, 1931, Thomas Lamont Papers, Baker Library, Harvard Business School, Harvard University.

80. See, for example, Thomas Lamont to Jean Monnet, July 21, 1930, Thomas Lamont Papers.

81. See Bessie James to Marquis James, undated memorandum, BAA.

82. L. M. Giannini to APG, August 17, 1930, BAA.

83. APG to L. M. Giannini, August 19, 1930, BAA.

84. For press reports about Giannini's record-setting trip, see *San Francisco News,* August 21, 1930; see also *Chicago Tribune,* August 22, 1930; *Philadelphia Ledger,* August 20, 1930.

85. See *Sausalito News,* August 29, 1930; see also *San Francisco Examiner,* August 26, 1930; *San Francisco News,* August 23, 1930; *Wall Street Journal,* August 22, 1930.

86. See *San Francisco Examiner,* August 26, 1930; *San Francisco Chronicle,* August 26, 1930.

87. Claire Giannini Hoffman, interview with the author.

12. Showdown

1. *San Francisco Chronicle,* August 26, 1930.

2. See "Memorandum of Matters Discussed at Conference Held by Transamerica Executives," August–September 1930, Transamerica Corporation Papers, BAA; see also *Bankitaly News,* September 1930, 3, BAA.

3. *San Francisco Chronicle,* September 5, 1930; see also *Wall Street Journal* (Pacific coast edition), September 5, 1930; *San Francisco News,* September 6, 1930.

4. See reprint of Bacigalupi's remarks in *Bankitaly News,* September 1930, 3, BAA.

5. See press reports in *San Francisco Examiner,* September 3, 1930; see also *Heraldsburg Enterprise,* September 5, 1930.

6. Andreini, "Battle of the Giants," 91–92. Giannini's suspicions were also aroused by rumors he had picked up on his return trip to San Francisco that Walker was planning to sell Bank of America (New York) to Charles Mitchell's National City. "This is all part of their plan to get price down and buy in so as to wrest control from the old crowd," he cabled Mario (APG to Mario Giannini, August 19, 1930, BAA).

7. James Bacigalupi, Memorandum, July 1930, BAA.

8. See Transamerica Corporation, Press Release, September 12, 1930, Transamerica Corporation Papers, BAA.

9. Ibid.; see also *Fresno Bee,* September 6, 1930; *Hollister Free Lance,* September 6, 1930.

10. Ralph Hayes to Fred Kerman, September 10, 1930; Roy Cullian to W. H. McGinnis, September 6, 1930, BAA.

11. Andreini, "Battle of the Giants," 94.

12. Ibid.

13. See Davis, *FDR: The New York Years,* 221–26, 236–39.

14. Ibid. See also Bessie James, notes, "Hurdle 14," 67, BAA.

15. See W. E. Rose to L. M. Giannini, November 17, 1930; see also W. H. McGinnis, Memorandum, December 17, 18, 1930; Robert Paganini to Arnold Mount, October 14, 1930, BAA. There were runs on two Bank of America branches at this time, both the result of rumors that the bank "was on the edge of bankruptcy" (A. C. Dimon to Al Haase, undated, 1930, BAA).

16. *Fortune,* November 1930, BAA.

17. In addition, Mario was upset over Walker's handling of Transamerica shares on the market, which he characterized as "bungling" and which he charged had cost the corporation hundreds of thousands of dollars. See L. M. Giannini, Memorandum, March 9, 1931; see also L. M. Giannini to APG, January 17, 1931, BAA.

18. Mario Giannini to Elisha Walker, September 24, 1930; see also Mario Giannini to Jean Monnet, September 24 and October 4, 1930, BAA. Equally annoying to Mario was Walker's decision to drastically reduce the corporation's quarterly dividend. "Feel I should tell you that I am not in sympathy with what you propose regarding dividend," Mario protested in a letter to Walker. "After all that is the purpose for which surpluses are created" (L. M. Giannini to Elisha Walker, July 3, 5, 1930, BAA).

19. See, for example, L. M. Giannini to Elisha Walker, September 24, 1930, October 4, 1930, BAA. "I fear you will feel," Mario wrote to Monnet, "I am taking the role of chronic objector but . . . it seems to me desirable to again frankly state my attitude. . . . Would like to have you show this to Elisha so

that he may be informed of my continuing opinion in these matters" (L. M. Giannini to Jean Monnet, October 4, 1930, BAA).

20. Mario Giannini to APG, undated, probably December 1930 or January 1931, BAA.

21. L. M. Giannini, Memorandum, January 20, 1931; see also W. E. Nuss, Jr., to Arnold Mount, December 10, 1930; "Arnold Mount to All Branch Managers," December 12, 1930; Will Morrish to Dwight L. Clarke, December 12, 1930, BAA.

22. *Fresno Morning Republican,* December 14, 1930; see also T. B. Whipple to W. F. Morrish, December 27, 1930; W. H. McGinnis, Jr., Memorandum, December 17, 1930, BAA. For Bank of America's efforts to combat these rumors, see "Arnold J. Mount to All Branch Managers," December 30, 1920, BAA. "As people come into the bank to make deposits or to cash checks—make or repay loans—to transact other business," Mount wrote, "give them copies of the bank's statement and talk with them about it."

23. See Giannini's statement in *San Francisco Chronicle,* December 17, 1930. See also Mario Giannini's handwritten memorandum concerning his father's suspicions, undated, but sometime in December 1930, BAA.

24. See Mario Giannini's handwritten memorandum concerning his father's suspicions, undated, but sometime in December 1930, BAA.

25. *San Francisco Chronicle,* December 17, 1930.

26. L. M. Giannini to APG, undated, January 1931, BAA.

27. APG to Fred Kerman, December 18, 1930; see also APG to Howard Preston, May 16, 1930, BAA.

28. *Time,* December 15, 1930.

29. APG to Armando Pedrini, December 25, 1930, BAA.

30. For Mario's objections, see L. M. Giannini to Jean Monnet, October 4, 1930; see also L. M. Giannini, Memorandum, March 9, 1931; L. M. Giannini to APG, January 17, 1931, BAA.

31. Virgil Dardi, interview with the author.

32. L. M. Giannini to Elisha Walker, December 2, 1930; see also L. M. Giannini to Elisha Walker, January 24, 1931, BAA. In response to a personal plea from Hale, Mario delayed making a public announcement of his resignation until after the March 1931 annual stockholders' meeting. See L. M. Giannini to P. C. Hale, February 7, 1931, BAA. When Mario finally did make his announcement, he told reporters that "personal views" had forced him to cut his ties with the corporation (*San Francisco Call,* March 27, 1931).

33. *Time,* April 6, 1931; see also Transamerica Corporation Annual Report, 1930, 3, Transamerica Corporation Papers, BAA.

34. Attilio Giannini to Armando Pedrini, April 12, 1931, BAA.

35. See Transamerica Corporation, Minutes, September 22, 1931, Transamerica Corporation Papers, BAA; see also Elisha Walker to Fred Kerman, June 8, 1931, BAA.

36. For a summary of Walker's reorganization proposals, see James Bacigalupi to APG, June 18, 1931, BAA.

37. James Bacigalupi to Fred Kerman, June 3, 1931, Bacigalupi Papers, BAA.

38. Bacigalupi gave a much different evaluation of the situation to the press. "While I cannot say truthfully that I found sentiment enthusiastically hopeful with respect to a rapid termination of the depression," he said, "I did gain the general impression that the counsel of cool heads in responsible positions prevails, and that much thought is being given to the solution of the many problems which have perplexed the world during the past two years" (James Bacigalupi, Press Release, June 11, 1931, BAA).

39. APG to L. M. Giannini, June 13, 29, 1931; see also July 11, 1931, BAA. "Game being played," Giannini cabled an associate in New York, "try get Bacigalupi such position as to furnish cause enable gang take away from Trans-america on terms its eastern unit as the J P Morgan Co by very same detestable methods acquired . . . effective control Manufacturers thereby depriving stock-holders" (APG to Howard Preston, May 18, 1931, BAA).

40. APG to James Bacigalupi, July 17, 1931; see also APG to L. M. Giannini, June 14, 1931, BAA.

41. James Bacigalupi to APG, June 19, 1931, BAA.

42. APG to James Bacigalupi, June 18, 1931, BAA.

43. See APG to L. M. Giannini, June 13, 1931, BAA.

44. Transamerica Corporation, Minutes, June 17, 1931, Transamerica Cor-poration Papers, BAA.

45. See L. M. Giannini to James Bacigalupi, June 25, 1931, BAA.

46. Transamerica Corporation, Minutes, June 17, 1931, Transamerica Cor-poration Papers, BAA.

47. L. M. Giannini to James Bacigalupi, June 25, 1931, BAA.

48. James Bacigalupi to L. M. Giannini, June 20, 1931, BAA. "First of all," Bacigalupi said in a second letter to Mario Giannini one week later, "I resent your insinuation that I, or anyone else, was guilty of indirection or dishonesty in the presentation of the new plan to the Board or in any of the discussions or deliberations by the Board, at the meeting in question" (Bacigalupi to L. M. Giannini, June 27, 1931, BAA).

49. L. M. Giannini to James Bacigalupi, June 25, 1931, BAA.

50. James Bacigalupi to L. M. Giannini, July 6, 1931, BAA. For Bacigalupi's denial that "anyone used any force or coercion at the meeting or that any director voted in fear of losing his job," see Bacigalupi to L. M. Giannini, June 27, 1931, BAA.

51. APG to L. M. Giannini, July 6, 1931, BAA.

52. To Walker and Monnet, Giannini wrote: "In the interest of all Trans-america Corporation stockholders, I feel it is my duty to communicate to you the contents of this letter. The situation that has developed in the affairs of the Bank of America N.T. & S.A. and its affiliated State bank over a period of approximately the last year and a half, during your administration of the affairs of Transamerica Corporation, is most disappointing to me, the founder of this institution, and I must again express most emphatically to you my objection to your manner of managing the affairs of the Corporation" (APG to Elisha Walker and Jean Monnet, undated, BAA).

53. APG to James Bacigalupi, July 2, 1931, BAA.

54. James Bacigalupi to APG, June 22, 1931; see also James Bacigalupi to

L. M. Giannini, June 29, 1931, BAA.

55. APG to James Bacigalupi, June 30, 1931, BAA.

56. APG to L. M. Giannini, June 20, 1931, BAA.

57. APG to James Bacigalupi, June 27, 1931, BAA. "Please note this," Giannini had written in an earlier telegram to Bacigalupi, "am just going to play absolutely lone hand expect and want you fellows play along with your chiefs the same as you did with me so long as you continue believe in them. Time am sure will prove me right" (APG to James Bacigalupi, June 20, 1931, BAA).

58. James Bacigalupi to APG, June 29, 1931, BAA.

59. APG to James Bacigalupi, June 30, 1931, BAA.

60. James Bacigalupi to APG, July 3, 1931, BAA.

61. APG to James Bacigalupi, July 6, 1931, BAA.

62. APG to L. M. Giannini, July 4, 1931, BAA.

63. L. M. Giannini to APG, July 24, 1931, BAA.

64. L. M. Giannini to APG, July 29, 30, 1931, BAA.

65. APG to L. M. Giannini, August 17, 1931, BAA.

66. APG to L. M. Giannini, August 19, 1931, BAA.

67. See series of cables sent from Giannini to L. M. Giannini, August 17–August 18, 1931, BAA.

68. C. T. Hanington to John Grant, August 21, 1931, BAA.

69. For Mario's rendezvous with his father, see series of cables from Giannini to L. M. Giannini, August 27–September 3, 1931, BAA.

70. APG to L. M. Giannini, August 20, 25, 26, 1931, BAA.

71. For the Giannini-Fleishhacker meeting, see Dana, *Giannini,* 201. Contrary to Dana's account, neither Bacigalupi nor Belden was in Lake Tahoe at the time.

13. Rough and Tumble in the Sunshine State

1. "Giannini to James A. Bacigalupi and My Other California B of I and B of A Coworkers Resident California Directors of Transamerica Corporation," September 13, 1931; see also APG to James Bacigalupi, September 14, 1931, Transamerica Corporation Papers, BAA. Giannini added: "Submission at the point of a gun tactics of the representatives of Wall Street is assuredly a wide deviation from our old and well established policy of fighting it out to the bitter end for the right knowing that if we had to go down we would do so with the consciousness that our motives had been clean and honest and our principles right."

2. For newspaper reports of Giannini's appearance in San Francisco, see *San Francisco Chronicle,* September 15, 1931; *San Francisco Call-Bulletin,* September 15, 1931.

3. Virgil Dardi, interview with the author; see also Andreini, "Battle of the Giants," 162–63.

4. Only eleven of Transamerica's twenty-nine directors, all Californians with the exception of Monnet, showed up at the meeting. See Transamerica Corporation, Minutes, September 22, 1931, Transamerica Corporation Papers, BAA.

5. Ibid.

6. Bank of America, Minutes, September 22, 1931, BAA.

7. Ibid.

8. Elisha Walker to Stockholders Addressed, September 22, 1931, Transamerica Corporation Papers, BAA. See profile of the Lee, Higginson firm in *Wall Street Journal,* March 20, 1931. Among Transamerica's new East Coast directors were Fredrick W. Allen, Charles E. Cotting, and George Murnans, all of whom were partners in the Lee, Higginson firm. Charles W. Nash, president of Nash Motors and another new Transamerica director named by Walker, also sat on Lee, Higginson's board. For a rundown on Transamerica's new board of directors, see *San Francisco Chronicle,* September 23, 1931; *San Francisco News,* September 22, 1931.

9. *Denver Post,* September 23, 1931; see also *Los Angeles Times,* September 23, 1931; *San Francisco Chronicle,* September 23, 1931; *Oakland Tribune,* September 23, 1931.

10. *Wall Street Journal,* September 23, 1931; *American Banker,* October 2, 1931. See also *San Francisco Argonaut,* September 25, 1931; *New York Times,* September 24, 1931; *Chicago Tribune,* September 23, 1931; *Business Week,* September 30, 1931.

11. *New York Post,* October 3, 1931; see also *New York Times,* October 3, 1931; *Commercial and Financial Chronicle,* October 2, 1931; *San Francisco Examiner,* October 2, 1931.

12. Andreini, "Battle of the Giants," 216.

13. Angelo Scampini and Virgil Dardi, interviews with the author. One participant at the meeting later recalled Giannini as saying, "All my boys have deserted me; we have no money and many powerful enemies" (Andreini, "Battle of the Giants," 201–3).

14. Virgil Dardi, interview with the author.

15. See "Associated Transamerica Stockholders," undated; see also APG to James Bacigalupi, September 26, 1931, BAA; Andreini, "Battle of the Giants," 201–3.

16. For Fay's interview with the press, see *San Francisco Chronicle,* September 25, 1931; *San Francisco Examiner,* September 25, 1931; *San Francisco News,* September 25, 1931. On news reports outside California about the "stockholders revolt," see *New York City American,* September 24, 1931; *New York Journal of Commerce,* September 24, 1931; *Wall Street Journal,* September 26, 1931.

17. See confidential report on the meeting written to one Transamerica director, Herbert Soher to George Webster, October 7, 1931, BAA; see also Andreini, "Battle of the Giants," 204.

18. For press reports of the meeting, see *San Francisco News,* September 24, 25, 1931; *Oakland Tribune,* September 24, 1931; *San Diego Union,* September 24, 1931; *Wall Street Journal,* September 24, 26, 1931.

19. *New York Tribune,* September 27, 1931.

20. See Amerigo Bozzani to Mario Giannini, October 14, 1931; see also R. B. Hayes to Jean Monnet, October 21, 1931, BAA.

21. Charles Fay to the Stockholders of Transamerica Corporation, November 7, 1931, Transamerica Corporation Papers, BAA.

22. *Stockton Independent,* December 4, 1931.

23. See, for example, *Fresno Bee,* November 4, 1931; *Del Norte Triplicate,* January 1, 1932; *Bakersfield California,* January 14, 1932; *Marysville Appeal-Democrat,* January 21, 1932; *L'Italia,* January 18, 1932; *San Francisco News,* December 6, 1931; see also Herbert Soher to Arnold J. Mount, Memorandum, December 8, 1931, BAA.

24. Virgil Dardi, interview with the author.

25. APG to C. Buttaranoli, November 19, 1931; see also APG to Angelo Scampini, December 6, 1931; APG to Joseph Carmini, December 19, 1931; BAA.

26. See W. H. McGinnis, Memorandum, December 10, 1931; see also W. H. McGinnis to the District Executive Vice President Addressed, November 10, 1931, Transamerica Corporation Papers, BAA.

27. For Fay's statement to the press, see *San Francisco News,* November 30, 1931.

28. For this and other pessimistic reports, see Orra Monnette to Arnold J. Mount, November 16, 1931; see also Peter Michelson to W. F. Morrish, October 4, 1931; J. T. McClellan to A. E. Carpenter, November 4, 1931, BAA.

29. Howard P. Preston to Branch Manager Addressed, December 11, 1931; see also W. H. McGinnis to the District Executive Vice President Addressed, December 10, 12, 1931, Transamerica Corporation Papers, BAA.

30. See Robert Morrison to APG, December 17, 1931; see also James Cavagnaro to APG, December 21, 1931; Louis Scaramelli to APG, December 23, 26, 1931; Amerigo Bozzani to APG, December 22, 1931, BAA.

31. W. H. McGinnis to the District Executive Vice President Addressed, December 10, 1931, Transamerica Corporation Papers; see also Arnold J. Mount to Branch Manager Addressed, December 17, 1931; Arnold J. Mount to Branch Managers and Advisory Board Members, October 29, 1931; W. J. Kieferdorf to George D. Schilling, December 12, 1931, BAA.

32. Arnold J. Mount to Branch Managers and Advisory Board Members, October 29, 1931, BAA.

33. See, for example, Carlo Del Pino to William Noonan, January 6, 1932; see also Henry Scaramelli to APG, February 4, 1932, BAA.

34. Amerigo Bozzani to APG, December 22, 1932; see also B. R. Rodman to APG, February 3, 1932, BAA.

35. For angry reaction from the corporation's stockholders, see L. Depaoli to James Bacigalupi, December 16, 1931; see also H. E. White to Arnold J. Mount, December 17, 1931, BAA.

36. For Giannini's statement, see *Fresno Bee,* December 15, 1931; see also *San Francisco News,* December 15, 1931.

37. For Bacigalupi's statement, see *Fresno Bee,* December 15, 1931.

38. For Giannini's instructions, see Edmund Rossi to Charles Fay, December 16, 1931, BAA.

39. See "To Whom It May Concern, Condensed Statement Concerning Bacigalupi's Stock Transactions Based on an Examination of Certain of His Accounts," February 2, 1932, BAA.

40. Elisha Walker and James Bacigalupi to the Stockholders of Transamerica Corporation, December 9, 1931; James Bacigalupi to Banker Addressed, December 9, 1931, Transamerica Corporation Papers; see also *San Francisco Examiner*, December 12, 1931; *San Jose Mercury and Herald*, December 11, 1931; *New York City Tribune*, December 14, 1931.

41. *San Francisco Chronicle*, January 23, 1932.

42. See, for the bank's loss of deposits, L. M. Giannini, Memorandum, July 1930; see also Statement of Condition, Bank of America, N.T. & S.A., December 31, 1931; "Statistics Compiled by Bank of America, N.T. & S.A., Analysis and Research Department," April 1941; Hugh L. Clary to W. F. Morrish, January 6, 1932, BAA.

43. *San Francisco Chronicle*, January 15, 1932.

44. John Pole to John Calkins, January 8, 1932; see also John Calkins, Transcript of Proceedings, January 9, 1932, San Francisco Federal Reserve Board Papers.

45. APG to L. M. Giannini, January 9, 1932, BAA.

46. John Calkins, Transcript of Proceedings, January 9, 1932, Federal Reserve Bank of San Francisco Papers.

47. See U.S. Federal Judge Herbert Erskine to Albert Haase, Memorandum, undated, but sometime in 1949, BAA.

48. Secretary of the Treasury Ogden Mills and Federal Reserve Bank Chairman Eugene Meyer sent Pole to San Francisco to talk with Fay and other leaders of Associated Transamerica Stockholders. Acting on Giannini's instructions, however, they rejected a compromise. See Charles Fay to J. W. Pole, January 29, 1932; see also Charles Collins to Bessie James, undated, but sometime in 1949, BAA.

49. See, for example, John Pole to Associated Transamerica Stockholders, January 28, 1932; see also John Calkins to Associated Transamerica Stockholders, February 5, 1932, BAA.

50. Albert Haase, Memorandum, undated, but sometime in 1949, BAA.

51. APG to Thomas Walker, February 6, 1932; see also APG to Ernest Zerga, February 8, 1932; Mario Giannini to APG, February 10, 1932; BAA.

52. Thomas Walker to APG, February 7, 1932; see also A. Fanelli to APG, February 10, 1932; Henry Scaramelli to APG, February 4, 1932, BAA.

53. Virgil Dardi and Angelo Scampini, interviews with the author; see also Virgil Dardi to C. P. Cuneo, February 15, 1932, BAA. Giannini's supporters outside California had done their work well. On the morning of the meeting, a delegation of Italians from New York arrived in Wilmington carrying boxes of ATS proxies said to represent more than two million shares of Transamerica stock. "It suddenly became apparent," one ATS supporter would later recall, "that the victory over Walker would be overwhelming" (Andreini, "Battle of the Giants," 286).

54. Associated Transamerica Stockholders received 15,371,578 proxies out of 24,153,900 voted. "Son, it's all over," Giannini immediately cabled Mario

Giannini in San Francisco. "We win by more than seven million shares. Tell mother and all" (APG to Mario Giannini, February 15, 1932, BAA).

55. For press reports on the celebration, see *San Francisco News*, February 15, 1932; see also *San Francisco Chronicle*, February 15, 1932; *Investment News* (New York), February 15, 1932; *Santa Rosa Republican*, February 15, 1932.

56. See *Wall Street Journal*, February 20, 1932; see also *New York World-Telegram*, February 16, 1932; *Pittsburgh Independent*, February 16, 1932.

57. See *San Francisco News*, February 15, 1932; see also *New York Times*, February 16, 1932; *New York Journal of Commerce*, February 16, 1932.

58. *San Francisco Chronicle*, February 16, 1932; see also *San Francisco Argonaut*, February 19, 1932.

59. *New York Times*, February 16, 1932.

60. APG to Mario Giannini, February 16, 17, 1932.

61. *Los Angeles Times*, February 20, 1932; see also *San Francisco News*, February 20, 1932; *San Francisco Call-Bulletin*, February 20, 1932.

62. *San Francisco Chronicle*, February 22, 1932; see also *San Mateo Times*, February 22, 1932.

63. *San Mateo Times*, February 22, 1932.

64. Attilio Giannini to Mario Giannini, March 15, 1932, BAA.

65. Mario Giannini to Attilio Giannini, March 23, 1932, BAA.

66. Orra Monnette to APG, August 27, 1932, BAA.

67. See "Arnold J. Mount," Personnel Files, BAA; for Mount's appointment, see also *California Banker*, September 1932, 480.

68. *Time*, May 9, 1932.

69. APG to A. Fanelli, February 25, 1932; see also John Grant to APG, March 12, 1932, BAA.

70. Virgil Dardi and Angelo Scampini, interviews with the author. Giannini's aides discovered a similar collection of empty file cabinets in Monnet's office. A confidential memorandum to Mario Giannini informed him that two days before the Wilmington meeting, "Mr. Howe, secretary to Mr. Monnet, spent some time removing certain papers from Mr. Monnet's file at Transamerica. In the same manner, Mr. Cook was known to have extracted and destroyed numerous papers from the Cook Carpenter-Purdy file" (A. L. Elliott Ponsford to L. M. Giannini, February 24, 1933, BAA).

71. A. L. Elliott Ponsford to L. M. Giannini, February 24, 1933, BAA.

72. For Kreuger's business career and suicide, see the three-part series "Ivar Kreuger," *Fortune*, May 1933, 51–57, 78–84; June 1933, 59–63, 78–95; July 1933, 68–76. See also Arthur N. Plummer, *The Great American Swindle Incorporated* (1932), ch. 11; John L. Parker, *Unmasking Wall Street* (1933), 156–73.

73. Quoted in *Fortune*, May 1933, 52.

74. See Report of Duncan U. Fletcher, Chairman, U.S. Senate Committee on Banking and Currency, *Hearings to Investigate Banking and Stock Exchange Practices*, April 1932–May 1934, 123.

75. See John T. Flynn, *New Republic*, May 25, 1932; *Time*, January 23, 1933, BAA.

76. *Fortune*, May 1933, 57–58.

77. Ibid., 92–93.

78. See Elisha Walker to Stockholder Addressed, September 22, 1931, Transamerica Corporation Papers; see also *Wall Street Journal*, March 20, 1931; *New York City Journal*, September 26, 1931; *Business Week*, September 30, 1931.

79. The collapse of Kreuger's fortunes had such a devastating effect on Lee, Higginson that on June 14, 1932, the firm was forced into liquidation. See Edward Weeks, *Men, Money, and Responsibility: A History of Lee, Higginson Corporation, 1848–1962* (1962), 27.

80. See John Rovensky to Bessie R. James, November 1949, BAA.

81. See Walter Bruns to Bessie James, undated, but sometime in 1949, BAA.

82. See Giannini, interview with Bessie James, September 26, 1947, BAA; see also APG to Marvin McIntyre, April 25, 1933, BAA.

83. For RFC loans to Bank of America, see Reconstruction Finance Corporation Papers, National Archives; see also Walter L. Vincent to APG, February 26, 1932; Lynn P. Talley to John U. Calkins, January 29, 1932; APG to Charles A. Miller, March 3, 1933; APG to W. A. Day, March 24, 1932; W. A. Day to Walter L. Vincent, March 28, 1932, BAA.

84. This figure also includes $20 million that Walker borrowed from a syndicate of five New York banks in the closing months of 1931.

85. For Bank of America's financial difficulties, see "Comparison of December 31, 1930 Statement with June 30, 1931 Statement, Bank of America"; see also W. H. McGinnis, Memorandum, December 17, 1930; Walter L. Vincent to APG, February 26, 1932; T. B. Whipple to Will Morrish, December 27, 1930, BAA.

86. M. F. Hachatt to APG, April 10, 1932, BAA.

87. M. E. Ivory to APG, April 7, 1932, BAA.

88. APG to All Branch Managers, March 3, 1932, BAA.

89. See announcement in *Fresno Times*, March 30, 1932. The success of Giannini's Back to Good Times campaign was given a significant boost by the size of Bank of America's "family" in California. By the spring of 1932 Bank of America had 410 branches in 243 towns and cities, 200,000 stockholders, 6,000 employees, and 1,800 advisory board members. Taking these together with their families, the bank's publicity department estimated that approximately 1 million people in the state—or roughly one out of every five Californians—had either direct or indirect ties to Bank of America. See Peter Michelson, "Radio as a Medium for Financial Institutions," paper delivered to the American Institute of Banking, June 9, 1932, BAA. Michelson was manager of advertising and publicity with Bank of America.

90. See Bank of America, Press Release, March 29, 1932, BAA; see also *Humboldt Times*, April 10, 1932.

91. For the advertising campaign, see Doremus and Doremus to APG, August 30, 1932, BAA.

92. See Will F. Morrish to L. Bacqueraz, July 18, 1932, BAA.

93. See *Los Angeles Times*, June 15, 1932; see also *Los Angeles Examiner*, June 22, 1932; *Los Angeles Evening Herald*, May 11, 1932; *San Francisco Call-Bulletin*, July 2, 1932.

94. For the Palace Hotel luncheon, see Michelson, "Radio as a Medium."

95. *San Francisco Examiner*, May 17, 1932.

96. See Allen Brown, *Golden Gate: Biography of a Bridge* (1965), 61–66; see also Paul Bryan Israel, "Spanning the Golden Gate: A History of the Highway Bridge in California," M.A. thesis, University of California, Santa Barbara, 1980, 91–92.

97. For Bank of America's participation in financing construction of the Golden Gate Bridge, see Memorandum to Syndicate Members, Golden Gate Bridge Bonds, undated, but sometime in late 1932, BAA. The bank purchased the last block of bonds one month before the bridge was completed for $35.5 million.

98. Golden Gate Bridge and Highway District, *The Golden Gate Bridge* (1938), 47.

99. For newspaper reports about Giannini's appearance in various California communities, see *Dinuba Sentinel,* July 26, 1932; *Santa Cruz News,* September 16, 1932; *Willows Transcript,* September 15, 1932; *Sutter Independent,* September 12, 1932; *King City Herald,* September 27, 1932.

100. Will Morrish, interview with Bessie James, undated, but sometime in 1947, BAA.

101. See Report of Charles P. Partridge, Bank of America's Extension Department, July 18, 1932. During the first four months of the campaign, Partridge reported, Giannini's "door-knockers" made more than 150,000 calls and averaged $455 in deposits for every five calls made.

102. Will F. Morrish to James E. Byrnes, September 6, 1932; see also Giannini to Advisory Board Members, July 16, 1932, BAA. See also *San Francisco News,* July 1, 1932; *Wall Street Journal,* July 25, 1932; *Los Angeles Examiner,* July 9, 1932; *New York Herald Tribune,* July 3, 1932. In June 1932 Bank of America reported total deposits of $710,903,867, of which $51,600,000 had come in since March 1932. By comparison, during this same period the Chase National, National City, and Continental Illinois reported a significant decrease in deposits. See Giannini to Advisory Board Members, July 16, 1932, BAA.

103. *San Francisco Chronicle,* September 26, 1932.

104. *Wall Street Journal,* July 25, 1932; see also *Los Angeles Times,* July 6, 1932; *New Republic,* July 6, 1932. One senior Giannini executive wrote to Herbert Hoover: "Your home state is indeed displaying the pioneer spirit of courage and cooperation which prompted us to assert that California can lead the nation to a sound prosperity" (Will Morrish to Herbert Hoover, April 8, 1932, BAA).

14. A Narrow Escape

1. For a biographical sketch of Calkins, see Cross, *Financing an Empire* 2:144–45.

2. For the "damn dago" incident, see APG to Eugene R. Black, July 12, 1934; see also APG to James Farley, December 31, 1933, BAA.

3. APG to Charles Miller, August 25, 1932; see also APG to Charles Collins, August 2, 1932, Charles Collins Papers, BAA.

4. Charles Collins to APG, September 6, 1932, BAA.

5. Walter Vincent to W. A. Day, March 24, 1932, BAA. For Transamerica's debt crisis, see Walter L. Vincent to APG, February 26, 1932. On Bank of America's RFC loans, see Lynn P. Talley to John Calkins, January 29, 1932; see also W. D. Yealland to Will F. Morrish, September 12, 1932; APG to Charles A. Miller, March 3, 1933; APG to W. A. Day, March 24, 1932; W. A. Day to Walker A. Vincent, March 28, 1932, BAA.

6. John Calkins to APG, March 24, 1933, BAA. For RFC loans to Bank of America, see Reconstruction Finance Committee, Minutes, Applications and Loans, 1933, 1070, Records of the Reconstruction Finance Corporation, 1932–1964, National Archives.

7. Calkins's inquiry was also prompted in part by Giannini's application to the Reconstruction Finance Corporation for a new loan of $10 million. See Walter Vincent to W. A. Day, March 24, 1933, BAA.

8. APG to John Calkins, March 25, 1933, BAA.

9. Will F. Morrish, Memorandum, August 31, 1932; see also APG to J. Sessa, October 31, 1932; J. C. Gallaher to T. A. Campbell, December 7, 1933, BAA. Giannini was also annoyed by Bank of America's lack of representation on local RFC committees. In San Francisco, for example, the local RFC committee included representatives appointed by the FRB from Wells Fargo, Bank of California, Crocker First National, and the Anglo and London Paris. By contrast, not a single Bank of America executive received an appointment to the RFC committee for either northern or southern California, although it was the state's largest and the nation's fourth largest financial institution. See *American Banker,* March 1932, 92.

10. APG to J. F. T. O'Connor, November 15, 1934, BAA.

11. In 1892, while pursuing his career as a banker in San Francisco, Marc Meyer, Eugene Meyer's father, became a partner in Lazard Freres of New York and Lazard Brothers of London. For a discussion of the Lazard firm's influence over the years in international finance, see Thomas Wise, "In Trinity There Is Strength," *Fortune,* August 1968. As a key figure in the Hoover administration, Eugene Meyer played an important role in the establishment of the Reconstruction Finance Corporation. Hoover appointed him chairman of the Federal Reserve Bank in 1930. See Gerald D. Nash, "Herbert Hoover and the Origins of the Reconstruction Finance Corporation," *Mississippi Valley Historical Review* 46 (December 1959): 455–68; see also Schwarz, *Interregnum of Despair,* 88–99. Meyer resigned as chairman of the FRB in May 1933 and then purchased the *Washington Post.* See "The Rise of the Washington *Post,*" *Fortune,* December 1944.

12. David Halberstam, *The Powers That Be* (1979), 160. For Meyer's career in banking and government service, see Tom Kelly, *The Imperial Post* (1983), 15–66; Howard Bray, *The Pillars of the Post* (1980), 3–9; Chalmers M. Roberts, *The Washington Post: The First Hundred Years* (1977), 196–200.

13. APG to Charles Collins, July 25, 1932, Charles Collins Papers, BAA.

14. Ibid.

15. Read's original report was later reported missing. On Giannini's request, Read repeated much, if not all, of what he had reported to Walker in the spring

of 1931. See P. C. Read to APG, September 7, 1933, BAA. See also James and James, *Biography of a Bank,* 315–16.

16. P. C. Read to APG, September 7, 1933, BAA.

17. Pole later repeated his advice in a letter to Bank of America's board of directors. "I am forced to the conclusion," Pole wrote, "that it is not only desirable but very necessary that as a Board you give careful consideration to a complete change of management in your Los Angeles Branch with as little delay as possible" (John W. Pole to Board of Directors, Bank of America, June 8, 1931, BAA). Mount immediately agreed: "I assume it is unnecessary for me to say that the practices and policies evidenced at that office antidated [*sic*] the absorption into our organization of the business under criticism and in no way reflects the present or past policies of this institution" (Arnold J. Mount to John W. Pole, June 13, 1931, BAA).

18. See, for example, Arnold J. Mount to R. A. Laird, July 22, 1931, BAA.

19. Quoted in APG to T. E. Harris, November 21, 1932, BAA.

20. APG to Homer Cummings, November 22, 1933, BAA.

21. APG to Mario Giannini, January 26, 1935, BAA.

22. Louis Ferrari to APG, July 25, 1932, BAA.

23. Robert Morrison to APG, September 21, 1932, BAA.

24. Hoover's "personal representative" was Harry Chandler, editor of the *Los Angeles Times,* who had written to Giannini asking for a $5,000 contribution. See Harry Chandler to ʾAPG, undated, but sometime in early September 1932, BAA. For Chandler's political influence in southern California, see Halberstam, *Powers That Be,* 105–18; see also Kevin Starr, *Inventing the Dream: California Through the Progressive Era* (1985), 246–82.

25. APG to Joseph Kennedy, September 6, 1932; see also September 10, 1932, BAA. Giannini added: "Roosevelt can carry California if pains are taken to see to it that his fight is put into proper hands. As you know there are several factions here and if they can be gotten together under the leadership of someone in whom they have absolute confidence there should not be any doubt of Roosevelt carrying the state." Joseph Kennedy's biographer, David E. Koskoff, writes that Kennedy "was credited with feats like that of immobilizing the powerful Italian-American banker, A. P. Giannini, who was under tremendous pressure to endorse incumbent Republican president Herbert Hoover for reelection, but on Kennedy's urgings refrained from doing so and instead gave silent backing to Roosevelt" (Koskoff, *Joseph P. Kennedy: A Life and Times* [1974], 46). In fact, Kennedy did neither of these things. Giannini had no intention of supporting Hoover. Moreover, as his letter to Kennedy makes clear, it was he who initiated the move toward Roosevelt.

26. Joseph Kennedy to APG, September 10, 1932, BAA.

27. Angelo J. Scampini to APG, September 12, 1932, BAA.

28. See Rixley Smith and Norman Bearsley, *Carter Glass: A Biography* (1939), 234–37.

29. Angelo J. Scampini to APG, September 12, 1932, BAA. McAdoo needed help. The state's Democrats had not sent one of their own to the Senate in nearly twenty years, Republicans had a better than three to one advantage in registration, and McAdoo was considered something of a "carpetbagger"

from New York. For a discussion of McAdoo and the Democratic party in the 1932 election, see Robert Burke, *Olson's New Deal for California* (1953), 1–5; Delmatier, McIntosh, and Waters, *Rumble of California Politics*, 230–69; Russell Posner, "California's Role in the Nomination of Franklin D. Roosevelt," *California Historical Society Quarterly* 39 (June 1960): 121–39.

30. As Giannini wrote to one Democratic party activist in Los Angeles, a public declaration of support for Roosevelt "might do considerable harm to our institution, even though . . . [it represented] an entirely personal standpoint" (APG to Robert Morrison, October 19, 1932, BAA).

31. For details of Giannini's arrangement with Roosevelt, see APG to James Cavagnaro, December 20, 1932, BAA.

32. *San Francisco News,* September 25, 1932, BAA.

33. Angelo J. Scampini, interview with the author.

34. For Giannini's behind-the-scenes campaign activities, see APG to Robert Morrison, October 19, 1932; see also APG to Joseph Sessa, October 31, 1932; Robert Morrison to APG, October 14, 1932, BAA.

35. APG to James Farley, November 8, 1932, BAA.

36. For confirmation of the conversation between Giannini and Hoover, see Will F. Morrish to R. L. Underhill, November 5, 1932, BAA. Giannini later issued a press release in which he denied having an active connection with the Roosevelt campaign. "I very much deprecate the publicity given to a private conversation between the President and myself," he said. "Naturally I have my opinion on political affairs but it is only a personal one which I hold as a private citizen. Any implication that I or any of the institutions with which I am associated have taken a political stand is wholly unauthorized" (Bank of America, Press Release, November 5, 1932, BAA).

37. See, for example, Robert Morrison to APG, November 7, 1932; see also Louis Rossi to APG, November 5, 1932, BAA.

38. *Los Banos Gazette,* November 4, 1932.

39. APG to James Farley, November 8, 1932; see also APG to James Cavagnaro, December 20, 1932, BAA. See, for Farley's appreciation of support, James Cavagnaro to APG, November 9, 1932, BAA. Giannini also let Roosevelt's political advisers know that he expected to hold the president-elect to the terms of the agreement they had reached in San Francisco. To James Cavagnaro, a close friend of Farley's, Giannini wrote: "While it has been understood that because of our support of Roosevelt our institution would be consulted with reference to all matters pertaining to California banking, after an election promises are sometimes overlooked. I hope that you will keep an eye on the situation and make sure that our friends back there, including Joe Kennedy and Mr. Farley, will see to it that we are at least given an opportunity to express our views concerning any proposed appointments which may be made that have any bearing on our situation out here" (APG to James Cavagnaro, December 20, 1932, BAA).

40. A. H. Hendrick to APG, November 8, 1932, BAA.

41. APG to A. H. Hendrick, November 10, 1932, BAA.

42. For a discussion of J. P. Morgan and Company and the growing economic crisis in the country, see Chernow, *House of Morgan,* 346–77.

43. The event that precipitated the bank holiday in Nevada, for example, was the failure of the Winfield-Reno National, the state's largest bank. See *Pacific Banker,* November 1932, 226. When the governor of the state failed to obtain a loan from the RFC to keep the Winfield-Reno open, he appealed to Giannini to take it over, an offer that Giannini declined. See "Hearing Before Board of Governors of the Federal Reserve System in the Matter of Transamerica Corporation," October 21, 1949, 6186, BAA. Giannini did not go into Nevada until 1934.

44. For information on the banking crisis in the spring of 1933, see Susan Estabrook Kennedy, *The Banking Crisis of 1933* (1973); Kenneth S. Davis, *FDR: The New Deal Years, 1933–1937* (1986); Arthur Ballantine, "When All the Banks Closed," *Harvard Business Review* 26 (March 1948): 129–43.

45. APG to Charles A. Miller, March 3, 1933, BAA.

46. For reports from Bank of America branch managers, see, for example, J. F. Flaherty to Will Morrish, January 24, 1933, BAA.

47. These rumors were in large part responsible for a run on Bank of America's four branch banks in Sacramento in January 1933. See G. W. Peltier to Will Morrish, January 30, 1933, BAA; see also Will C. Wood to Will Morrish, February 7, 1933, BAA.

48. Robert Morrison to APG, November 7, 1932; see also Robert Morrison to APG, March 30, 1933, BAA. According to Morrison, "Another rumor I have heard is that New York interests in the past three months have several times put pressure on you for control of Transamerica, which you have steadily refused, and that their interests had only recently advised you that some action would be taken which would force you to acquiesce to their request and result in such things as cutting the branch banks down to two hundred, etc., etc." (Arthur Reynolds to Will Morrish, February 3, 1933, BAA).

49. APG to Will Morrish, March 4, 1933, BAA.

50. APG to Mario Giannini, March 8, 1932; see also APG to Will Morrish, March 4, 1933, BAA.

51. Giannini was familiar with William Woodin. Three years earlier Giannini had solicited an account in Bank of America from Woodin's company American Car and Foundry. See APG to Marvin McIntyre, March 16, 1933, BAA.

52. APG to Mario Giannini, March 6, 1933, BAA.

53. APG to Will Morrish, March 8, 1933; see also APG to Marvin McIntyre, March 16, 1933, BAA.

54. *San Francisco News,* March 10, 1933.

55. Charles Collins to APG, March 10, 1933, BAA.

56. APG to William Woodin, March 10, 1933, BAA.

57. Charles Collins to APG, March 10, 1933, BAA.

58. Charles Collins to APG, March 10, 1933, BAA.

59. See "Events Tending to Show a Conspiracy to Wrest Control of Transamerica Corporation from the Giannini Interests and to Bring about Its Liquidation," August 10, 1934; see also APG to John Calkins, March 25, 1933, BAA. Giannini had long harbored suspicions that Calkins would take advantage of any opportunity to inflict serious damage on Bank of America. Soon after

regaining control of Transamerica, Giannini wrote to Calkins: "The feeling I have had that there has been a conspiracy to bring about the ultimate liquidation of our institution for a selfish interest, has been strengthened by happenings since we have taken charge and through knowledge of the destructive policies by the former management with the apparent acquiescence of the Federal Reserve Bank" (APG to John Calkins, March 25, 1933, BAA).

60. APG to Hiram Johnson, May 10, 1933, BAA.

61. William McAdoo to APG, March 11, 1933; see also Charles Collins to APG, March 11, 1933, BAA.

62. See APG to Prentice Hale, August 15, 1933, BAA.

63. Charles Collins to APG, March 12, 1933, BAA.

64. See Bessie James, notes in file folder "The Banking Holiday—March, 1933," 34, BAA.

65. APG to Will Morrish, April 14, 1933, BAA; see also Thomas Storke, *California Editor* (1958), 344–46; *Los Angeles Times,* June 10, 1949.

66. APG to Prentice Hale, August 15, 1933, BAA.

67. See A. R. Price, "Report of National Bank Examination, Commenced on March 31, 1932," BAA. Among other things, the more recent report showed that Bank of America's net income in early 1932 was just over $5.7 million—a decline of $5 million since 1930. Less than one year later, however, net income had climbed to $32 million, and it increased an additional $2.75 million the following year. See A. R. Price, "Report of National Bank Examination Commenced February 11, 1935," BAA.

68. For Giannini's conversation with Woodin, see APG to Marvin McIntyre, April 16, 1933; see also APG to Prentice Hale, August 15, 1936, BAA.

69. John F. Neylan to APG, October 13, 1947, BAA.

70. Ibid.

71. Ibid.

72. Raymond Moley, *After Seven Years* (1939), 154–57; see also Raymond Moley, *The First New Deal* (1966), 192–93.

73. Raymond Moley, "Five Years of Roosevelt and After," *Saturday Evening Post,* July 29, 1939, 55; see also Storke, *California Editor,* 346–47.

74. Roosevelt later applauded Woodin's decision and took great delight in telling others how he and Woodin had "outbluffed Calkins." There is no evidence, however, that the president played a part in Woodin's decision to permit Bank of America to reopen. For Roosevelt's claim to the contrary, see Diary of J. F. T. O'Connor, September 11, 1933, Bancroft Library, University of California, Berkeley.

75. APG to William R. Hearst, March 13, 1933, BAA. In a letter to a member of the Roosevelt administration many years later, Hearst wrote of Giannini and Bank of America: "We all know them in the West and admire them and have confidence in them. They have a broad-minded viewpoint—the wider Western vision. We will be out of the stifling atmosphere of Wall Street and Broad Street—which ought by rights to be called Narrow Street. . . . I was interested in keeping California for Californians, free from the contagious touch of Wall and Narrow streets. I suspect Mr. Giannini has the same sentiments" (William R. Hearst to John Hanes, November 22, 1942, BAA).

384 NOTES TO PAGES 218-22

76. See APG to T. A. Harris, June 10, 1933; see also APG to Lee Madland, June 30, 1933, BAA.

77. Lee Madland to APG, June 30, 1933, BAA.

78. APG to Homer Cummings, July 29, 1933, BAA; see also Homer Cummings Diary, November 5, 1933, Homer Cummings Papers, University of Virginia (microfilm copy, Library of Congress); APG to Lee Madland, July 8, 1933; APG to A. M. Chaffey, July 8, 1933, BAA.

79. Pat Malloy to APG, July 14, 1933, BAA.

80. APG to Pierson Hall, July 26, 1933, BAA.

81. For information on the Beverly Hills National, see Cross, *Financing an Empire* 4:158-59.

82. See William H. Neblett to Bank of America National Trust and Savings Association, June 15, 1931; see also Russell Smith, interview with the author; Russell Smith to Arnold J. Mount, June 16, 1931, BAA.

83. Nolan resigned from the presidency of the Bank of America on June 15, 1931, and accepted the presidency of the Beverly Hills National five months later. See Edward J. Nolan to Board of Directors, Bank of America National Trust and Savings Association, July 7, 1931; see also Al Fenton to Will Morrish, December 28, 1931, BAA.

84. See Eustace Cullinan to Louis Ferrari, September 7, 1933; see also W. E. Blauer to Eustace Cullinan, July 15, 1931; Eustace Cullinan to W. E. Benz, July 22, 1931, BAA; Russell Smith, interview with the author.

85. See Delmatier, McIntosh, and Waters, *Rumble of California Politics*, 244-62.

86. Robert Morrison to APG, July 26, 1933, BAA.

87. See Louis Ferrari to Edmund Nelson, July 26, 1933, BAA.

88. Robert Morrison to APG, July 26, 1933, BAA.

89. Neblett, in fact, was very familiar with the "facts of the case." By the spring of 1933 word of Hargreaves and Cotton's involvement with Nolan, Bell, and the Hellmans had leaked to his office. On April 10, 1933, he wrote to William McAdoo that "the whole thing" for Hargreaves and Cotton "looks very bad" (William Neblett to William McAdoo, April 10, 1933, William McAdoo Papers, Library of Congress).

90. Robert Morrison to APG, July 29, 1933, BAA.

91. Robert Morrison to APG, July 29, 1933, BAA.

92. William Neblett to William McAdoo, June 13, 1933, William McAdoo Papers.

93. William McAdoo to William Neblett, June 17, 1933, William McAdoo Papers.

94. Not surprisingly, soon after Neblett learned about Hargreaves and Cotton's involvement in the Beverly Hills National scandal, he began pressuring McAdoo to find both men a job in Washington. See William Neblett to William McAdoo, May 29, 1933; see also William Neblett to William McAdoo, April 25, 1933, William McAdoo Papers. A similar plea for assistance also came from Hargreaves's wife, Helen Hargreaves, who was the daughter of William Jennings Bryan. "I appeal to you from the bottom of my heart to help Dick today," she wrote to McAdoo. "This ghastly spite inspired persecution should not

succeed in depriving an honest man of his livelihood and the ability to support his children. I know your great heart and breadth of vision and deep understanding will. Answer my prayer for justice and I shall be forever grateful for your help" (Helen Hargreaves to William McAdoo, May 24, 1933, William McAdoo Papers). Neblett no doubt concluded that it would be best for all concerned if Cotton and Hargreaves were out of California. McAdoo responded by writing to Roosevelt and various New Deal officials, recommending both men for a position in the Washington bureaucracy. See Franklin Roosevelt to William McAdoo, February 23, 1933; see also William McAdoo to Jesse Jones, February 23, 1933; William McAdoo to Daniel C. Roper, March 23, 1933, William McAdoo Papers.

95. Giannini also complained to other members of the administration, including J. F. T. O'Connor. See Diary of J. F. T. O'Connor, entry dated September 6, 1933.

96. APG to Homer Cummings, November 22, 1933, BAA; see also Homer Cummings Diary, November 23, 1933, Homer Cummings Papers, University of Virginia.

97. APG to Marvin McIntyre, November 22, 1933, BAA.

98. J. B. Keenan to APG, December 5, 1933, BAA.

99. See James notes, "Hurdle 19," 41.

15. Unaccustomed Disappointments

1. For Giannini's remarks, see *San Francisco Enquirer*, October 17, 1934.

2. Giannini had good reason for self-congratulation. By the fall of 1934 deposits had climbed to $300 million, or about twice what they had been when he had regained control of Transamerica three years earlier. With more than two million depositors and total resources of $1 billion, Bank of America had become the fourth largest financial institution in the country. See Howard Whipple, Memorandum, November 6, 1939; see also APG to Marvin McIntyre, May 23, 1933; Research Council, American Bankers Association, *Bank Lending Activity*, February 1940, BAA.

3. For a more detailed discussion of Giannini's plans for nationwide branch banking, see *Bancamerica Deposit Builder*, October 17, 1934.

4. Reynolds Barbieri to Mario Giannini, October 18, 1934; see also Sydney Clark to Reynolds Barbieri, October 17, 1934, BAA.

5. For the association's attack against the New Deal, see *San Francisco Examiner*, October 23, 1934; see also *New York Post*, October 11, 1934.

6. *San Francisco Call-Bulletin*, November 8, 1934. For other public declarations of support, see *Wall Street Journal*, July 10, 1934; *San Francisco Call-Bulletin*, March 16, 1934.

7. For a first-rate discussion of the 1935 reform bill, see Davis, *FDR: The New Deal Years*, 537–41; see also Donald F. Kettl, *Leadership at the Fed* (1986), 48–55.

8. Kettl, *Leadership at the Fed*, 8.

9. As an article in *Nation* explained it, "Woodrow Wilson thought he had triumphed over the money trust when he created the Federal Reserve System, but it was later discovered that he was wrong: the Federal Reserve allowed control of the system to slip away to New York" (*Nation*, August 14, 1935; see also Transamerica Corporation, Annual Report, 1934, Transamerica Corporation Papers, BAA).

10. For the struggle over passage of the bill, see John Morton Blum, *From the Morgenthau Diaries: Years of Crisis, 1928–1938* (1959), 343–54; see also the series of articles in *Nation*, February 27, 1935, May 29, 1935, June 26, 1935, and August 14, 1935; see also *Time*, February 18, 1935.

11. *Time*, February 18, 1935.

12. *New York Herald Tribune*, April 28, 1935.

13. Davis, *FDR: The New Deal Years*, 450.

14. For the full text of Giannini's attack, see *New York Times*, April 28, 1935; see also *San Francisco News*, May 4, 1935.

15. For Giannini's strong support of the 1935 bill, see APG to Hiram Johnson, July 8 and July 24, 1935; see also APG to William McAdoo, May 30, 1935, BAA.

16. See letter from Eccles's personal assistant, Lawrence Clayton, to APG, June 26, 1935, BAA. For Eccles and the 1935 bill, see Marriner Eccles, *Beckoning Frontiers: Public and Personal Recollections*, edited by Sidney Hyman (1951), 222–29; see also "Marriner Stoddard Eccles," *Fortune*, February 1935, 63–65.

17. *San Francisco News*, May 4, 1935.

18. Marriner Eccles to APG, August 22, 1935, BAA. "It was a job extraordinarily well done," Giannini replied, "and no one but you could have put it over. Our good little Senator from Virginia I don't believe knew what it was all about" (APG to Marriner Eccles, August 21, 1935, BAA).

19. "I hope to be in your state within a week or so," Roosevelt wrote, "and hope very much that it will be possible for us to meet once again" (Franklin Roosevelt to APG, September 24, 1935, BAA).

20. APG to L. M. Giannini, November 29, 1935, BAA.

21. L. M. Giannini to APG, November 29, 1935, BAA.

22. Claire Giannini Hoffman to APG, November 30, 1935, BAA.

23. For a biographical sketch of J. F. T. O'Connor, see *American Banker*, February 2, 1938.

24. See J. F. T. O'Connor to James Farley, September 4, 1936, BAA. "It seems to me that Mr. Giannini should be well pleased at the receptions met by applications of his bank to establish branches since I took office as Comptroller of the Currency," O'Connor wrote to Farley.

25. James Farley to APG, July 1, 1936, BAA.

26. APG to James Farley, August 5, 1936; see also APG to Lawrence Clayton, November 2, 1936, BAA.

27. For Giannini's campaign activities in the state's Italian communities, see APG to O. R. Angelillo, October 29 and November 30, 1936; see also APG to James Farley, November 2, 1936, BAA.

28. APG to James Farley, October 14, 1936, BAA.

29. See *Santa Rosa Press Democrat,* November 8, 1936; see also *Pittsburgh News,* October 15, 1936; *Buckley Register,* November 1, 1936; *Cameron Observer,* October 16, 1936.

30. Joseph Kennedy to APG, October 20, 1936, BAA. The *Wall Street Journal* commented that it could think of only "two prominent bankers" in the country whose views on public finance were similar to the president's—Marriner Eccles and A. P. Giannini (reprinted in *Chicago Tribune,* November 30, 1935).

31. APG to Joseph Kennedy, October 20, 1936, BAA.

32. *San Francisco Chronicle,* November 5, 1936.

33. Franklin Roosevelt to APG, July 8, 1936, BAA.

34. See, for example, APG to Attilio Giannini, January 9, 1936; see also George Saunders to APG, January 21, 1936; APG to James Farley, July 9, 1936; APG to Ambrose O'Connell, July 28, 1936; APG to R. S. Heaton, August 10, 1936, BAA.

35. E. A. Rossi to Al Haase, undated, but sometime in 1949, BAA.

36. See Barrie A. Wigmore, *The Crash and Its Aftermath: A History of Securities Markets in the United States, 1929–1933* (1985), 61–63, 168–75, 264–66, 370–72; see also Wasko, *Movies and Money,* 47–89; Gertrude Joves, *Motion Picture Empire* (1966), 283–300. For a good general discussion of the stock market crash and its effects on Hollywood, see Carosso, *Investment Banking in America,* 300–321.

37. "Twentieth Century-Fox," *Fortune,* December 1935, 85–93; see also Leonard Mosley, *Zanuck: The Rise and Fall of Hollywood's Last Tycoon* (1984), 129–32; Norman J. Zierold, *The Hollywood Tycoons* (1969), 256–72.

38. For the close financial relationship between Zanuck and the Bank of America, see APG to Joseph Rosenberg, August 5, 1937, BAA. Some years earlier Giannini had financed the start of United Artists, which was formed in 1919 by Mary Pickford, Douglas Fairbanks, Charles Chaplin, and D. W. Griffith. Through Joseph Schenck, chairman of the board of United Artists and a Bank of America director, the association between the Giannini organization and United Artists continued well into the 1940s. See Tino Balio, *United Artists: The Company Built by the Stars* (1976), 36, 44, 52, 79, 140–44; see also Steven Bach, *Final Cut* (1985), 21–28. By the early 1940s United Artists had a $4 million line of credit with the bank (Joseph Rosenberg to Fred Ferroggiaro, May 31, 1944, BAA).

39. For Selznick's career at Paramount, RKO, and later at MGM, see "Paramount Pictures Inc.," *Fortune,* June 1947; "RKO: It's Only Money," *Fortune,* May 1953; "MGM: War among the Lion Tamers," *Fortune,* August 1956; Richard Jewell with Vernon Harbin, *The RKO Story* (1982); Gary Carey, *All the Stars in Heaven: Louis B. Mayer's M-G-M* (1981).

40. Bob Thomas, *Selznick* (1970), 158–59.

41. For the Bank of America–Selznick relationship, see "Report on Motion Picture Lines and Loans to the General Finance Committee and the Los Angeles Loan Committee," May 16, 1938, BAA.

42. For Goldwyn's life and career in the movie industry, see A. Scott Berg, *Goldwyn: A Biography* (1989); see also Alvin H. Maril, *Samuel Goldwyn Presents*

(1976); Arthur Marx, *Goldwyn: A Biography of the Man Behind the Myth* (1976); Lawrence J. Epstein, *Samuel Goldwyn* (1981).

43. See Howe, "Hollywood and B of A," 3–7; see also Sidney Skolsky's column, "Behind the News," in *Los Angeles Times,* January 17, 1933; Peter Geiger, "The Bank and Feature Financing," in Jason E. Squire, ed., *The Movie Business Book* (1983), 107–10; Peter Geiger, "The View from the 48th Floor," *Hollywood Reporter,* November 29, 1974.

44. For the Bank of America–Goldwyn relationship, see "Samuel Goldwyn, Inc.," in Bank of America, Los Angeles Loan Committee, Minutes, December 13, 1938; see also "Report on Motion Picture Lines," May 26, 1938; "Loan Memorandum from Los Angeles Main Office, Samuel Goldwyn Productions Inc.," May 20, 1949, BAA.

45. For Disney's early movie career, see "The Big Bad Wolf," *Fortune,* November 1934; John McDonald, "Now the Bankers Come to Disney," *Fortune,* May 1966; Jack Alexander, "The Amazing Story of Walt Disney," *Saturday Evening Post,* October 31, 1953; John Bright, "Disney's Fantasy Empire," *Nation,* March 1967; Bosley Crowther, "The Dream Merchant," *New York Times,* December 16, 1966.

46. Joseph Morgenstern, "Walt Disney (1901–1966): Imagineer of Fun," *Newsweek,* December 20, 1966; see also Herbert Russell, "Of L'Affaire Mickey Mouse," *New York Times Magazine,* December 26, 1937; "Father Goose," *Time,* December 17, 1954; Bill Davidson, "The Fantastic Walt Disney," *Saturday Evening Post,* November 7, 1964.

47. Richard Schickel, *The Disney Version* (1968), 56, 208–9.

48. Francis Herwood and Jake Fisher, interviews with the author.

49. Wasko, *Movies and Money,* 172–73.

50. Claire Giannini Hoffman, interview with the author.

51. Keith Carver, interview with the author.

52. Schickel, *Disney Version,* 207–8.

53. For the Bank of America–Disney relationship, see "Walt Disney Productions, Bank of America Credit Files," Motion Picture Loans, April 19, 1942; see also Reconstruction Finance Corporation Loan Agreement, Walt Disney Productions, April 1939, BAA. Bank of America loans to finance *Fantasia, Dumbo, Bambi, The Reluctant Dragon,* and other Disney films are found in Joseph Rosenberg to APG, February 14 and March 1, 1941, BAA.

54. Giannini had a particularly close relationship with Columbia, whose owners, Harry and Jack Cohn, had used a loan from the Bank of Italy to start the studio in 1920. For the Bank of America–Columbia relationship, see McClintock, *Indecent Exposure,* 129–30; see also Frank Capra, *The Man and His Films* (1975), 29; Frank Capra, *The Name above the Title: An Autobiography* (1971), 136–40. By the early 1940s Columbia had an unsecured line of credit with the Bank of America for $2 million. See W. F. H. to L. M. Giannini, "Columbia Pictures Corporation," June 14, 1943; see also Russell Smith, "Motion Picture Distributors—Columbia," May 28, 1948, BAA.

55. On the bank's involvement in motion-picture financing, see Taylor, "He's No Angel"; see also Attilio Giannini, "Financing the Production and Distribution of Motion Pictures," *Annals of the American Academy of Political and*

Social Sciences 128 (November 1926): 45–50; Sheilah Graham, "Story of First Banker to Accept Film as Collateral," *San Francisco Chronicle,* December 6, 1936; Carleton, "Films Are Financed Here."

56. This figure of $306 million is based on a thorough and detailed survey of Bank of America's motion-picture loans conducted in 1950 by Robert R. Tollefson, a staff member in the bank's legal department; see Tollefson, "Summary of Motion Picture Financing, Legal Department, Bank of America," May 12, 1950, BAA.

57. The most influential Hollywood director whom Giannini brought into the organization was Cecil B. DeMille, who had used a loan from the Bank of Italy in 1923 to film *The Ten Commandments.* Giannini made DeMille president of Bank of Italy's Culver City branch, which handled most of the bank's motion-picture loans. See Donald Hayne, ed., *The Autobiography of Cecil B. DeMille* (1959), 243–46, 256, 258; see also Charles Higham, *Cecil B. DeMille* (1984), 114–15; Phil A. Koury, *Yes, Mr. DeMille* (1978), 92–98. For Bank of America's studio accounts, which averaged $1 million annually, see Glenn E. Carter, "Survey of Motion Picture Pay-Roll Accounts," April 17, 1946; see also Walter Braunschweiger to F. M. Dana, April 19, 1946, BAA.

58. Quoted in Wasko, *Movies and Money,* 124.

59. Davis, *FDR: The New Deal Years,* 431–33.

60. For consumer dependence on finance companies for short-term loans, see Irving S. Michelman and Leon Henderson, *Consumer Finance: A Case History in American Business* (1966), 112–30; see also William L. Wilson, *Full Faith and Credit: The Story of C.I.T. Financial Corporation, 1908–1975* (1976), 173–83.

61. See Bank of America, Consolidated Report of Personal Loans as of October 31, 1934, BAA. From 1929 to 1935 the bank's total volume in personal loans amounted to $11,490,000; one year later this figure had climbed to over $23 million. See *Wall Street Journal* (Pacific coast edition), March 31, 1938. Throughout the first two years of the depression, the bank's losses from its personal loans averaged one-eleventh of 1 percent; delinquencies averaged 2 percent (*The Participant,* March 28, 1930).

62. Quoted in *San Francisco Chronicle,* July 24, 1936.

63. See Bank of America Annual Report, July 24, 1936, BAA.

64. According to a survey by the American Bankers Association, in the first half of 1939, 104 California banks accounted for 510,000 new loans for a total dollar amount of $650 million. Bank of America was responsible for 277,906 new loans, for a total of $313,270,345, or over half of the total number of loans and nearly half of the total dollar amount. See Howard Whipple, "Bank Lending Activity," November 6, 1939; see also Testimony of E. A. Mattison, Transamerica Hearing Before Board of Governors of the Federal Reserve System, October 11, 1949, 61, 5485, Transamerica Corporation Papers, BAA.

65. Under title II of the Federal Housing Act, individuals were entitled to borrow up to $16,000 to buy or build a home or to refinance an existing mortgage.

66. L. E. Townsend to Zack Cobb, February 21, 1938; see also APG to Henry Luce, September 21, 1928; Arthur Reynolds to Spencer S. March, October 29, 1935, BAA; *Bankamerican Deposit Builder,* January 3, 1935. By June

1939 Bank of America had made more than 150,000 FHA modernization loans, or roughly 60 percent of all such loans in the state. Under title I of FHA, Bank of America's average remodeling loan was about $392. See Arthur Reynolds to Spencer S. March, October 29, 1935, BAA; see also *Wall Street Journal,* June 26, 1939.

67. Alfred B. Swinerton to APG, December 18, 1934, BAA.

68. K. S. McBride to W. Dunn, December 12, 1940; see also Bank of America, Publicity Release, August 19, 1940, BAA; *Wall Street Journal,* January 10, 1938.

69. J. A. Purdy to F. M. Dana, September 3, 1942, BAA. On the eve of World War II the volume of title II loans climbed even higher—60,000 by the end of 1941, for a total dollar amount of $250 million. Out of every ten homes purchased in the United States with FHA financing, one was a California home financed through the Bank of America. Astonishingly enough, out of Bank of America's tens of thousands of FHA-financed loans, only forty-eight borrowers defaulted. See Bank of America, Annual Report for 1941, BAA; see also *San Francisco News,* August 16, 1941; James, *Biography of a Bank,* 417–18.

70. See H. L. Clary to Joshua Garrison, Jr., January 6, 1937, BAA. Prior to 1938 only a few banks in the United States had experimented with new car loans on a very limited basis. Bank of America's interest on new car loans was 5 percent for the first $400 and 4 percent above that amount. Giannini later added a "letter of credit" to his loan program, which enabled buyers to pay the full purchase price for the car, thus eliminating the dealer's customary service charges. See *Los Angeles Daily News,* October 23, 1935; James and James, *Biography of a Bank,* 419.

71. *San Francisco Examiner,* October 31, 1935. See also the favorable publicity in *Los Angeles Daily News,* October 31, 1935; *Coronada Citizen,* November 12, 1939; *Woodland Democrat,* October 31, 1935.

72. A. C. Dimon to L. M. Giannini, January 4, 1939, BAA.

73. Josephson, "Giannini," September 13, 1947, 16.

74. See Transamerica Corporation, Annual Report, December 31, 1937, Transamerica Corporation Papers, BAA; see also Russell Smith to APG, August 28, 1936, BAA.

75. For Giannini's bank acquisitions in Washington, Oregon, and Nevada, see *San Francisco Call-Bulletin,* October 28, 1936.

76. See Russell Smith to APG, August 28, 1936, BAA.

77. APG to James Farley, September 14, 1936, BAA.

78. Ibid.

79. J. F. T. O'Connor to James Farley, September 4, 1936, BAA.

80. See Rukeyser's column in the *San Francisco Examiner,* March 25, 1938.

81. APG to William McAdoo, May 25, 1937, William McAdoo Papers; see also Charles Collins to APG, November 27, 1936, BAA; Chapman and Westerfield, *Branch Banking in California,* 124–25.

82. "A much clearer presentation could be made [in Congress]," Collins advised Giannini, "if the Federal Reserve District is adhered to. If these districts do not represent business or trade areas they should be changed in order that they will so conform. They were certainly intended by the Federal Reserve Act

to mark the grand division of the flow of commerce and trade in the area of the United States" (Charles Collins to APG, November 27, 1936, BAA).

83. See Transamerica Corporation, Annual Report, May 14, 1937, and June 17, 1937; see also John Grant to the Stockholders of Transamerica Corporation, May 14, 1937, Transamerica Corporation Papers, BAA.

84. See Giannini's statement in *New York Herald Tribune,* May 16, 1937. For the new distribution of Bank of America stock, see Transamerica Corporation, Annual Report for 1937, Transamerica Corporation Papers, BAA; see also *Time,* December 6, 1937.

85. *New York American,* May 16, 1937.

86. For the anti-branch-banking resolutions adopted at the convention, see *Wall Street Journal* (Pacific coast edition), May 14, 1937; see also *New York Herald Tribune,* October 10, 1937.

87. *New York Herald Tribune,* January 6, 1938.

88. For Crowley's anti-branch-banking attitudes, see John E. Miller, *Governor Philip F. La Follette, the Wisconsin Progressives, and the New Deal* (1982), 10-13, 18-19.

89. Josephson, "Giannini," October 4, 1947, 128.

90. For Crowley's Del Mar speech, see *San Francisco Chronicle,* May 26, 1938; see also *San Francisco News,* May 26, 1938.

91. APG to Leo Crowley, June 2, 1938, BAA.

92. APG to James Farley, July 13, 1938, BAA.

93. APG to Marriner Eccles, May 27, 1938, Marriner Eccles Papers, University of Utah, Salt Lake City, Utah.

16. Morgenthau Finds a Target

1. For Giannini's push for additional Bank of America branches, see Transamerica Corporation, Annual Report, December 31, 1937, Transamerica Corporation Papers, BAA. Although ranked as the nation's fourth largest bank in 1937, Bank of America's earnings of $16,584,270 exceeded those of any other bank. Second was the Chase National, with earnings of $15,340,000. See *Los Angeles Evening Express,* January 17, 1938.

2. Not surprisingly, word of Giannini's intentions produced a hostile reaction from independent bankers. See anti-branch-banking resolutions adopted by the Association of Independent Bankers of the Twelfth Federal Reserve District in *Wall Street Journal* (Pacific coast edition), May 14, 1937; see also *New York Herald Tribune,* October 10, 1937. For background on Giannini's branch expansion activities, see APG to James Farley, September 4, 14, 1936; see also Russell Smith to APG, August 28, 1936, BAA.

3. J. F. T. O'Connor to APG, January 3, 1938, BAA.

4. *American Banker,* February 2, 1938; see also APG to Zack Lamar Cobb, January 19, 1938, BAA. For a discussion of Democratic politics in California in the late 1930s, see Delmatier, McIntosh, and Waters, *Rumble of California Politics,* 272-94.

5. APG to Zack Lamar Cobb, January 20, 1938, BAA.

6. Construction delays on the Gonzales and Pinole branches had forced Giannini to ask the comptroller's office for a sixty-day extension on the original deadline, which was granted. See Russell Smith to E. H. Gough, January 24, 1938, BAA.

7. Russell Smith to E. H. Gough, January 24, 1938; see also APG to E. H. Gough, May 4, 1938, BAA.

8. APG to William McAdoo, June 7, 1938, BAA.

9. On McAdoo's efforts, see Bessie James, notes, "Hurdle 22," BAA.

10. APG to Marvin McIntyre, July 5, 1938, BAA.

11. For a biographical sketch of Morgenthau, see Olson, *Historical Dictionary of the New Deal,* 338–40.

12. John Morton Blum, *From the Morgenthau Diaries: Years of Urgency, 1938–1941* (1965), 4–5.

13. See, for example, report from Henry Oliphant to Henry Morgenthau, October 8, 1937, General Records of the Department of the Treasury, Office of the Secretary, 1933–1956, Treasury Department Papers, National Archives.

14. Excerpts from memorandum prepared by Cyril Upham covering meeting with Morgenthau, July 8, 1938, Treasury Department Papers.

15. Ibid.

16. William O. Douglas to Henry Morgenthau, January 21, 1938, Treasury Department Papers.

17. For Douglas's commitment "to pull an oar" in bringing reform and stability to the securities business, see William O. Douglas to A. A. Berle, January 3, 1934, William O. Douglas Papers, Library of Congress; see also Joel Seligman, *The Transformation of Wall Street: A History of the Securities and Exchange Commission and Modern Corporate Finance* (1982), 110–11.

18. Ralph F. DeBedts, *The New Deal's SEC: The Formative Years* (1964), 156–69; see also Michael E. Parrish, *Securities Regulation and the New Deal* (1970), 180–83.

19. Department of the Treasury Staff Meeting, Minutes, January 19, 1938, Treasury Department Papers.

20. William O. Douglas to Henry Morgenthau, November 17, 1938; see also William O. Douglas to John Hanes, November 10, 1938; Treasury Department Papers.

21. Henry Morgenthau to William O. Douglas, November 23, 1938; see also E. H. F., Jr., to Henry Morgenthau, May 19, 1939; Henry Oliphant to Henry Morgenthau, November 23, 1938; Memorandum of Conference in Cyril Upham's Office, dated November 19, 1938, Treasury Department Papers.

22. "For the Secretary," unsigned staff memorandum, September 12, 1938, Treasury Department Papers.

23. Minutes of Group Meeting in Henry Morgenthau Office, January 28, 1938, prepared by Donald J. Sherbondy, Treasury Department Papers.

24. Marvin McIntyre to APG, July 11, 1938, BAA. The examination, begun in July of 1937, was completed in August of 1938.

25. APG to Marshall Diggs, May 6, 1938, BAA.

26. Ibid.; see also W. N. Wholey, "Dispute with Comptroller of the Currency," undated; "Statement Dictated by A. B. Giannini," undated, but sometime in the fall of 1938, BAA.

27. Quoted in a telegram from Marvin McIntyre to APG, July 11, 1938; see also APG to Marvin McIntyre, July 11, 1938, BAA.

28. Russell Smith, Memorandum, October 9, 1941, BAA.

29. Ibid.; see also Board of Governors in the Matter of Transamerica, "Memorandum on the 1938 Plot," Charles Collins to Samuel Stewart, March 10, 1949; see also Wholey, "Dispute," BAA.

30. APG to Marvin McIntyre, July 11, 1938, BAA.

31. Jake Fisher to APG, July 11, 1938, BAA.

32. APG to Jake Fisher, July 11, 1938, BAA.

33. I. D. Wright to Russell Smith, May 26, 1939, BAA.

34. APG to Reynolds Barbieri, February 24, 1941, and March 20, 1945, BAA.

35. See, for example, Herman Oliphant to Henry Morgenthau, September 16, 1938, Treasury Department Papers.

36. On California's "dust bowl" migration, see Carey McWilliams, *Ill Fares the Land* (1955); Lloyd Fisher, *The Harvest Labor Market in California* (1953); Davis McEntire, *The Labor Force in California* (1952); "Migratory Labor," *Fortune*, April 1939.

37. See Paul S. Taylor, *Adrift on the Land* (1940); see also Paul S. Taylor and Clark Kerr, "Uprisings on the Farms," *Survey Graphic* 24 (January 1935): 19–22; Harry Schwartz, "Organization Problems of Agricultural Unions," *Journal of Farm Economics* 23 (May 1941): 456–66.

38. On the formation of Associated Farmers, see Cletus E. Daniel, *Bitter Harvest: A History of California Farmworkers, 1870–1941* (1981), 141–66; see also Walter J. Stein, *California and the Dust Bowl Migration* (1973), 18–22; Sidney C. Sufrin, "Labor Organization in Agricultural America, 1930–1935," *American Journal of Sociology* 43 (January 1938): 544–59.

39. To Joseph DiGiorgio, one of the state's largest growers and a Bank of America client, Giannini wrote: "Sorry, Joe, I can't do it. We've got to stay out of such things." See copy of the letter reprinted in *Sacramento Bee,* December 16, 1939.

40. For a discussion of California's extremist movements, see Alan Brinkley, *Huey Long, Father Coughlin, and the Great Depression* (1983), 222–24.

41. *People's World,* March 20, 1939; see also July 14, 1939, and December 1, 1939.

42. John Steinbeck, *Grapes of Wrath* (1939), 205–6, 387, 476.

43. Ibid., 193, 306, 364. See also Tetsumaro Hayashi, ed., *A Study Guide to Steinbeck: A Handbook to His Major Works* (1974), 35–41; see also Warren French, *A Companion to "The Grapes of Wrath"* (1972), 105–43.

44. For McWilliams's career as a political activist, see Carey McWilliams, *The Education of Carey McWilliams* (1979), 67–86.

45. Carey McWilliams, *Factories in the Field: The Story of Migratory Farm Labor in California* (1939), 233.

46. See, for example, review of McWilliams's book by Ralph Thompson in the *New York Times,* July 24, 1939; see also *New York Post,* July 2, 1939; Allens Press Clipping Bureau, June 16, 1939.

47. See, for example, "Explanation Wanted" (editorial), *Daily Californian,* September 1939 (copy in BAA).

48. McWilliams to L. M. Giannini, quoted in L. M. Giannini to James Roosevelt, December 4, 1939, BAA. Out of a total of 150,000 farms in the state, Bank of America held mortgages on 7,398 farms, or 4.9 percent. See W. N. Wholey, "Report to the Comptroller of the Currency," undated, but sometime in 1939; see also R. B. Evans, General Ledgers of Bank of America; Segregation of Real Estate Loans, 1931 and 1941; Memorandum, Farm Operations of California Lands and Bank of America, undated, but sometime in 1939, BAA; James and James, *Biography of a Bank,* 411–13.

49. Russell Smith to Edward Bernays, August 1, 1939, BAA.

50. Howard Whipple to Russell Smith, June 26, 1939, BAA.

51. L. M. Giannini to James Roosevelt, September 19 and December 4, 1939; see also L. M. Giannini to James Roosevelt, April 4, 1940, BAA.

52. See L. M. Giannini to APG, March 17, 1939, BAA.

53. L. M. Giannini to James Roosevelt, April 4, 1940, BAA; see also Blum, *From the Morgenthau Diaries* 2:345.

54. Louis Ferrari to APG, June 8, 1938; see also APG to Charles Collins, September 21, 1938, BAA.

55. APG to Winfield Buckley, August 28, 1940, BAA.

56. APG to Marvin McIntyre, May 5, 1938, BAA.

57. See *A. P. Giannini v. Commissioner of Internal Revenue,* U.S. Board of Tax Appeals, Docket No. 9931, September 1940; see also *Los Angeles Daily Journal,* September 12, 1940; George H. Koster to John Enrietto, December 23, 1940; Henry Mazzera to APG, September 4, 1940, BAA.

58. See *Commissioner of Internal Revenue v. A. P. Giannini,* U.S. Circuit Court of Appeals for the Ninth District, Docket No. 87128, December 1940; see also Harry Friedman to Andrew Burke, July 15, 1942; Mary McGoldrock to APG, July 11, 1942; George Koster to APG, March 31, 1942, BAA.

59. APG to Wiley Reynolds, August 17, 1940, BAA.

60. APG to L. M. Giannini, September 20, 1938; see also APG to A. O. Stewart, September 20, 1938; APG to R. A. Everard, September 21, 1938, BAA.

61. Report of National Bank Examiner L. H. Sedlacek on condition of Bank of America N.T. & S.A. commenced on April 28, 1938, and closed on September 15, 1938, BAA.

62. Wholey, "Dispute"; see also Bank of America, Special Meeting of the Board of Directors, Minutes, September 30, 1938, BAA.

63. Board of Governors in the Matter of Transamerica, "Memorandum on the 1938 Plot," Charles W. Collins to Samuel Stewart, March 10, 1949, BAA.

64. Russell Smith, Memorandum, October 9, 1941, BAA.

65. Bank of America, Board of Directors' Meeting, Minutes, September 13, 1938, BAA; see also R. P. A. Everard, Secretary of the Board, Bank of America, to Comptroller of the Currency, October 11, 1938, BAA.

66. Marshall R. Diggs to R. E. A. Palmer, September 13, 1938, BAA.

67. Board of Governors in the Matter of Transamerica, "Memorandum on the 1938 Plot," Charles W. Collins to Samuel Stewart, March 10, 1949, BAA.

68. Virgil Dardi, interview with the author.

69. Smith, interview, in Oral History Program, BAA; see also Wholey, "Dispute."

70. Russell Smith, Memorandum, October 9, 1941; see also Russell Smith to John M. Grant, February 3, 1941, BAA.

71. L. M. Giannini to James Roosevelt, March 2, 1941, BAA.

72. Russell Smith, Memorandum, October 9, 1941, BAA; see also Russell Smith, interview with the author.

73. Russell Smith, interview with the author.

74. Ibid.

75. APG to L. M. Giannini, September 21, 1938; see also APG to R. P. A. Everard, September 20, 1938, BAA.

76. APG to L. M. Giannini, September 21, 1938; see also L. M. Giannini to Marriner S. Eccles, September 17, 20, 1938; Board of Directors, Bank of America to Board of Governors of the Federal Reserve System, September 17, 1938, BAA.

77. For a discussion of Eccles's attitudes, see Dean L. May, *From New Deal to New Economics: The Liberal Response to the Recession* (1981), 59–81.

78. Kettl, *Leadership at the Fed,* 55–59.

79. Lawrence Clayton to Marriner Eccles, May 12, 1938, Treasury Department Papers. "What we really need today," Clayton wrote to Giannini, "is less examination, less restriction, and a broadening of the lending and investment field for the banking system" (Lawrence Clayton to APG, May 11, 1938, Marriner Eccles Papers).

80. Marriner J. Eccles to APG, May 20, 1938; Marriner J. Eccles to APG, March 22, 1940; Lawrence Clayton to APG, May 10, 1939; Marriner J. Eccles Papers.

81. APG to Ambrose O'Connell, September 21, 1938, BAA.

82. APG to L. M. Giannini, September 21, 1938, BAA.

17. "A Damnable Conspiracy"

1. *E. W. Denicke v. Anglo-California National Bank of San Francisco, Herbert Fleishhacker, et al.,* U.S. Circuit Court, Northern Department, California, Docket No. 21033-S, 1942, Reply Brief, col. 45, 38.

2. Jesse Jones to Henry Morgenthau, December 7, 1938, Treasury Department Papers.

3. Henry Oliphant to Henry Morgenthau, December 7, 1938; see also Henry Morgenthau to Jesse Jones, December 8, 1938, Treasury Department Papers.

4. For published reports about a handful of these financial transactions, see *Time,* December 20, 1937, and November 7, 1938.

5. *Denicke v. Anglo-California;* see also *Time,* November 7, 1937, December 27, 1937; *San Francisco News,* December 6, 1937; *Bank Trends,* November 12, 1940.

6. News of Fleishhacker's resignation prompted Giannini to send a tongue-in-cheek telegram of "congratulations" to Morgenthau for his department's "belated housekeeping" of the Anglo-California. "I hope, however," Giannini said, "that the institution itself didn't have to undergo such unprecedented treatment as was recently accorded a certain other institution"—meaning, of course, Bank of America (APG to Henry Morgenthau, October 28, 1938, BAA).

7. See, for example, Mortimer Fleishhacker to Henry Morgenthau, November 2, 1938, Treasury Department Papers.

8. For published reports on RFC loans to the Anglo-California, see *Time,* December 20, 1937.

9. See *Denicke v. Anglo-California,* quoted in Dana, *Giannini,* 283–84.

10. Russell Smith, Memorandum, October 9, 1941, BAA. For background information on the Lazard Freres's banking family, see Reich, *Financier;* Wise, "In Trinity There Is Strength."

11. For the Morgenthau-Kuhn connection, see Stephen Birmingham, *"Our Crowd": The Great Jewish Families of New York* (1967), 306; see also Kelly, *Imperial Post,* 18–19.

12. Russell Smith, Memorandum, October 9, 1941, BAA; see also Russell Smith, phone conversation with the author.

13. Diggs told this story to Giannini several months after he was replaced as acting comptroller of the currency by Preston Delano. See APG to Lawrence Clayton, February 8, 1940, Marriner Eccles Papers.

14. APG to E. H. Gough, November 23, 1938, BAA.

15. See *Fortune,* June 1939; see also Dora Olinsky to APG, June 1, 1939, BAA.

16. Virgil Dardi, interview with the author.

17. "There are two reasons why I am resigning," Schenck wrote in his letter to Giannini. "The number one reason is because of the expression that you made regarding the Jews being against you. I know you are possibly of a suspicious mind and in looking for a reason for the unjustified criticisms which have been made by the comptroller's office, you discovered the international fall guy—the Jew. However, I happen to be a Jew and it didn't sit well with me. It was very embarrassing and I, therefore, feel that I am better off out of the bank" (Joseph Schenck to APG, October 11, 1938, BAA).

18. See, for example, APG to Russell Smith, October 24, 1938, BAA.

19. Similar stories also appeared in *Washington Banking Trends and Background,* a widely read industry magazine. For these and other rumors concerning Bank of America's "troubles" with the Treasury Department, see *Time,* December 26, 1938.

20. APG to E. H. Gough, November 23, 1938; see also Charles Collins to L. E. Birdzell, October 18, 1938, BAA.

21. APG to Henry Morgenthau, November 1, November 10, 1938, Treasury Department Papers.

22. Henry Morgenthau to APG, November 5, 1938, BAA.

23. APG to Henry Morgenthau, November 10, 1938, Treasury Department Papers. Not surprisingly, Giannini's anger toward the administration at this time was steadily growing. After a private interview with Giannini, a reporter for the *New York Times* wrote: "Remarking that he had been known as a New Dealer among bankers, Mr. Giannini said that he was getting 'fed up' with some of the people down in Washington and with their antagonistic attitude toward the bigness of business" (*New York Times,* November 18, 1938).

24. Claire Giannini Hoffman, interview with the author.

25. See Lawrence Giannini, "Remarks of the President of the Bank of America N.T. & S.A to Shareholders," January 9, 1940, BAA.

26. See "Memorandum, re. Bank of America and Comptroller's Office," December 15, 1938, BAA.

27. "You have advised me that upon request of the Secretary of the Treasury and approval of the President you would lend our stockholders, individually or in group, the money necessary to finance the increase," Mario wrote to Jones. "Upon receipt of advice that this application is approved, our directors will, I am sure, take definite action to put the plan in operation. . . . Our earnings are such that it will be easy for us to return the preferred stock within a much shorter time than your usual terms and we will want the privilege of retiring it as rapidly as earnings are available for this purpose" (L. M. Giannini to Jesse Jones, April 3, 1939, BAA).

28. Board of Directors, Bank of America, to the Comptroller of the Currency, December 12, 1939; see also Jesse Jones to J. W. Hanes, December 15, 1938, BAA.

29. See APG to James Cavagnaro, December 17, 1938, BAA.

30. "My associates and I are deeply indebted to you for your words of encouragement yesterday," Giannini wrote. "This is again evidence of true friendship on your part. Thank you sincerely" (APG to Jesse Jones, November 26, 1938, BAA).

31. L. M. Giannini to Preston Delano, December 15, 1938. As part of the settlement with the comptroller's office, Mario agreed to increase Bank of America's capital structure to a ratio of one to ten, although, as he told Delano, he was not pleased by the fact that this same ratio "did not apply to other banks." See also "Remarks of the President of the Bank of America N.T. & S.A to the Shareholders," January 9, 1940, BAA.

32. Preston Delano to L. M. Giannini, December 22, 1938, BAA.

33. L. M. Giannini to Preston Delano, December 31, 1938, BAA.

34. "We are just closing the best year in the history of the Bank," Mario added. "Our net earnings will be more than $24,000,000. Of this amount approximately $1,200,000 has been allotted to the Bank's personnel under a profit-sharing bonus plan and $8,900,000 has been paid to stockholders in dividends, leaving more than $13,000,000 for reserves and increase in capital funds" (ibid.; see also Board of Directors, Bank of America, Minutes, January 10 and March 14, 1939; L. M. Giannini to Jesse Jones, April 3, 1939, BAA).

35. See E. H. Foley, Jr., to Henry Morgenthau, December 17, December 22, 1938, Treasury Department Papers.

36. For Landis's own belief that Bank of America's troublesome examination reports required prompt corrective action, see James Landis to Bank of America, Board of Directors, August 8, 1939, James Landis Papers, Library of Congress.

37. See *Wall Street Journal* (Pacific coast edition), November 28, 1938; *Oakland Free Press,* December 13, 1938; *San Francisco Chronicle,* November 23, 1938. Bank of America officials were critical of the SEC's sudden and unexpected announcement. In written testimony given years later Collins explained: "On November 25, 1938, the Securities and Exchange Commission gave nationwide publicity to its Order of November 22, 1938, and on the same day served the same upon Transamerica Corporation in San Francisco. This was the first information that Bank of America and Transamerica Corporation had about the contents of the order. In fact, it was released to the press and was sent out to various financial houses throughout the United States before any of the officers of these two corporations had any knowledge of it" (Charles Collins, "Chronological Digest of Events in the Treasury Department and Securities and Exchange Commission Relations with Bank of America National Trust and Savings Association, 1938–1941," October 15, 1941, BAA). To Jesse Jones, Giannini wrote: "Can't understand how a government agency should give such wide publicity to such bank smearing without first advising us" (APG to Jesse Jones, November 26, 1938, BAA).

38. For information on Douglas's career as an SEC commissioner prior to his appointment as the agency's chairman, see DeBedts, *New Deal's SEC,* 154–67; see also Fred Rodeli, "Douglas over the Stock Exchange," *Fortune,* February 1938; Harry Newman, "Redhead from Carolina," *Saturday Evening Post,* January 13, 1940; William T. Raymond, "Big Year for the SEC," *Barron's,* January 6, 1936.

39. James Cavagnaro to APG, December 13, 1938, BAA. "Today," Cavagnaro informed Giannini from New York, "I had Jimmy Smith go up to see Mr. Frisch, Treasurer of Lerner's Stores, regarding the publicity in the papers in connection with the SEC matter. Mr. Hirsch was much concerned, and said he was confidentially told to reduce his balance in the bank, and that the impression was getting around in circles that the bank was under-capitalized, and that the proper reserves were not being carried for possible losses." See also *Time,* December 12, 1938.

40. *Time,* December 12, 1938; see also *Wall Street Journal,* January 19, 1939; *San Francisco News,* November 29, 1938.

41. See Louis Ferrari, Press Release, December 15, 1939; see also A. P. Giannini, Statement of Net Worth as of December 31, 1938; A. P. Giannini, Statement of Securities, December 31, 1938; "Information Relative to Surplus and Undivided Profits and New Profit of Bancitaly Corporation–Transamerica Corporation and Subsidiaries and Amounts Drawn by A. P. Giannini from Date of Organization, Taken from Reports of the Respective Companies"; APG to Robert Everard, January 3, 1938, BAA. *Time* commented on the Ferrari press release: "Banker Giannini himself took a bold propagandistic step. To squelch S.E.C. charges that he took more money from his empire than he admitted,

A. P. released a complete statement of his net worth, including cash, securities, salary, and insurance. Instead of the millions most people would have guessed, it totaled only $407,798.46" (*Time,* December 15, 1938; see also *Time,* February 27, 1939).

42. APG to Harry Chandler, December 16, 1938, BAA.

43. Giannini also enclosed copies of the letters and telegrams that had been exchanged between Bank of America and the comptroller's office since the September 15, 1938, board meeting in Los Angeles, adding, "Despite the fact that Bank of America had received full one hundred per cent clearance from . . . Mr. Delano, Comptroller, Mr. Jones, Chairman of the Reconstruction Finance Corporation, and Mr. Eccles, Chairman of the Federal Reserve System, the SEC had gone ahead with its investigation. It is difficult to believe that the subsequent action taken was not a deliberately planned conspiracy. . . . If you feel that you need the enclosed papers for future reference, will you please have them placed in your confidential files, not to be used without the approval of either yourself or your son Norman" (APG to Harry Chandler, December 21, 1938, BAA).

44. For a biographical sketch of Richberg, see Otis Graham, Jr., and Meghan Robinson Wander, eds., *Roosevelt: His Life and Times* (1985), 275–78.

45. For a detailed account of Richberg's statement, see *New York Times,* January 17, 1939; *Wall Street Journal,* January 17, 1939; *San Francisco Examiner,* January 18, 1939; *Los Angeles Times,* January 18, 1939.

46. Collins, "Chronological Digest," BAA; see also *Business Week,* January 21, 1939.

47. APG to Donald Richberg, March 25, 1939; see also APG to L. M. Giannini, March 20, 23, 1939, BAA. Giannini was equally aggressive in his public statements. "I'm glad to see you mad this morning," he told Richberg as reporters swarmed around the two men after one morning session. "I want you to stay mad" (*New York Times,* January 17, 1939; see also *New York World-Telegram,* January 28, 1939; *New York Herald Tribune,* January 30, 1939).

48. See Bank of America, Press Release, February 14, 1939; see also *San Francisco Call-Bulletin,* February 14, 1939; *New York Herald Tribune,* February 15, 1939; *New Republic,* February 1, 1939.

49. For a digest of the court's decision, see Charles Collins to Louis Ferrari, May 8, 1939; see also L. B. Birdzell to William Malone, April 2, 1942, BAA. In a statement to the press Mario Giannini called the court's ruling "an outstanding victory for the bank" and expressed his satisfaction with a decision that would "keep inviolate the confidential relations between the bank and its clients" (Bank of America, Press Release, sent by Richard Bernays to Russell Smith, May 8, 1939; see also APG to Richard Bernays, May 22, 1939, BAA).

50. APG to Charles Collins, May 10, 1939, BAA. To Henry Steagall, chairman of the House Committee on Banking, Mario wrote: "The public interest demands that these matters be given the widest publicity at this time to protect the future of the American public, the entire banking structure of America, the economic welfare of California . . . , and our own two million one hundred thousand depositors and our 145,000 stockholders. We will be

happy to supply hitherto unpublished startling information. The unwarranted, unjust and biased action of one governmental agency in harassing a national bank . . . induces us to make this request of you" (L. M. Giannini to Henry Steagall, May 1939, BAA).

51. L. M. Giannini to Preston Delano, July 28, 1939; see also Russell Smith to R. M. Hanes, July 6, 1939; APG to Drew Pearson, November 25, 1939, BAA. Although Giannini went along with Mario's decision, he made clear his own preference for pursuing the attack against Morgenthau and the comptroller's office. "Am certainly and definitely against our easing up on this gang," he wrote to Ferrari. "I have no faith in them. Past experience has certainly taught us to place no reliance in what they say or promise" (APG to Louis Ferrari, July 14, 1939; see also APG to John Grant, July 14, 1939, BAA).

52. Preston Delano to L. M. Giannini, July 31, 1939, BAA.

53. See Bank of America to Board of Governors, Federal Reserve System, December 29, 1939, BAA.

54. Ibid.

55. L. M. Giannini to APG, January 13, 1940, BAA. Giannini was not altogether enthusiastic about Mario's conversion plan. "The American Banker has a nice article on the subject," he wrote to Mario, "saying that for us to retreat by going into the state system would be regarded as our capitulation and that we should fight it through to the end in the national system and off hand I should say thems my sentiments too" (APG to L. M. Giannini, January 29, 1940, BAA). "Do not be concerned about the conversion," Mario replied. "As I see it, Federal Reserve Bank would make examination before approving continuation of our membership. Superintendent of Banks will make examination or review of condition. Approval of plan for conversion would therefore provide for vindication of the position we have taken with Treasury by two impartial agencies. If we can succeed in getting these impartial examinations . . . we shall be perfectly satisfied with results of conversion proceedings and may see fit then not to go through with actual conversion" (L. M. Giannini to APG, January 13, 1940, BAA).

56. APG to R. A. Everard, January 1, 1940, BAA.

57. See "Remarks of the President of the Bank of America to the Shareholders," January 9, 1940, BAA.

58. Ibid.

59. *San Francisco News,* January 10, 1940.

60. See *San Francisco News,* January 10, 1940; *San Francisco Chronicle,* January 10, 1940; *Wall Street Journal,* January 12, 1940.

61. APG to L. M. Giannini, February 8, 1940; see also APG to Russell Smith, January 13, 1940, BAA.

62. See, for example, Jerome Frank to James Rowe, October 13, 1939; see also Franklin Roosevelt to James Rowe, September 18, 1939, Franklin Roosevelt Papers, Hyde Park, New York.

63. According to Edward C. Eicher, a member of the SEC, Jones had reportedly informed Roosevelt that, as far as the government's case against Bank of America was concerned, the SEC was acting in a "somewhat overzealous, legalistic and impractical" manner (Edward C. Eicher to Franklin Roo-

sevelt, October 11, 1940; see also "In re: Gianninis [Transamerica]," Franklin Roosevelt Papers).

64. See Drew Pearson's column in the *San Francisco Chronicle,* April 6, 1939; see also *Time,* December 12, 1938.

65. Marriner Eccles to Henry Morgenthau, November 4, 1939, Treasury Department Papers. There is no doubt that in the hostility between Bank of America and the Treasury over the bank's examination report, especially after Giannini's response to the examiner's criticism, Eccles felt that Giannini's views were largely correct. "You don't know how much I appreciated your having written me so fully about my letter to the Acting Comptroller," Giannini wrote to Lawrence Clayton. "I was very much pleased also to receive such a fine letter from your Chief on the subject. You have both always been mighty good friends" (APG to Lawrence Clayton, May 27, 1938, Marriner Eccles Papers).

66. Lawrence Clayton to APG, May 11, 1938, Marriner Eccles Papers. "My Chief," Clayton told Giannini, "has received a copy of your letter of May 6 addressed to Mr. Diggs, Acting Comptroller of the Currency, in which you comment on certain comments and criticisms of the examiner in connection with the report of examination of your bank. . . . I have had the pleasure of reading this letter and certainly compliment you on the forceful manner in which you have answered practically every criticism. In fact, I should think the Comptroller's face would be just a little bit red. The attitude of the examiner in the case mentioned above is a sample of the unenlightened approach to the banking problem generally, which is manifested by the majority of the supervisory authorities as well as the majority of important bankers in the country. In spite of the fact that every study shows a trend in commercial banking away from the old lines of commercial lending, these people still live in the past and criticize a bank for adjusting itself to this trend."

67. "It seems to me," Eccles wrote to Giannini, "that you have made an excellent, if not devastating, answer to the criticisms contained in the examiner's report, as set forth in your letter. . . . Since your letter involves certain questions of examination policy I wanted it to get the attention of the responsible heads at the Treasury. Therefore I called up Wayne Taylor, Assistant Secretary of the Treasury, who represents the Secretary in banking matters, and told him of the gist of your letter and the points you had made. He seemed much impressed, as I was" (Marriner Eccles to APG, May 20, 1938, Marriner Eccles Papers).

68. Kettl, *Leadership at the Fed,* 58–59.

69. Lawrence Clayton to APG, October 19, 1938, Marriner Eccles Papers. "My Chief," Clayton went on to say, "has espoused the consolidation program on the broad principle that there should not be overlapping, duplicating, and sometimes conflicting functions with reference to bank supervision and regulation exercised by several Federal agencies. He feels that it is essential to the proper regulation of the structure of the country that there be one Federal agency in charge."

70. Russell Smith, Memorandum, January 31, 1940, BAA.

71. See "Conversation Between Mr. Foley and Jerome Frank," November 17, 1939, Treasury Department Papers.

72. *American Banker,* January 29, 1940; see also *Bank Trends,* February 8, 1940.

73. APG to L. M. Giannini, February 25, 1940, BAA. "Now just be yourself keep cool as you always do," Giannini wrote in another telegram to Mario, "and give and take if you find they're on the square and not trying to hamstring you in the interest of their diabolical conspiracy" (APG to L. M. Giannini, February 22, 1940, BAA).

74. See Board of Directors, Minutes, March 14, 1940, 199; see also "Requirements of the Comptroller of the Currency," March 6, 1940; A. P. Giannini to the Stockholders, April 30, 1940, BAA.

75. Associated Press Dispatch, March 18, 1940, BAA.

76. Marriner Eccles to L. M. Giannini, March 22, 1940; see also Lawrence Clayton to APG, March 19, 1940, Marriner Eccles Papers.

77. L. M. Giannini to APG, March 14, 1940, BAA.

78. APG to L. M. Giannini, March 15, 1940, BAA. For the predictably positive view on the part of Treasury Department officials that the settlement represented a "swell victory" for their side in the controversy, see John M. Blum, *Roosevelt and Morgenthau* (1970), 250-51. Blum obviously agrees with this view; he fails to mention, however, that the terms of the agreement were essentially the same as those that Morgenthau had rejected as insufficient many months earlier.

79. See Associated Press Dispatch, March 18, 1940.

80. Marriner Eccles to APG, November 2, 1940, Marriner Eccles Papers; APG to L. M. Giannini, October 16, 1940, BAA.

81. APG to William R. Daly, June 30, 1944; APG to George L. Radcliffe, November 2, 1944.

18. The Final Fight

1. *San Francisco Chronicle,* May 7, 1941; *San Francisco News,* May 8, 1941; *American Herald,* December 27, 1941.

2. *San Francisco News,* December 22, 1941; *San Francisco Chronicle,* December 22, 1941; *Daily Commercial News,* December 23, 1941.

3. Yeates, *Gentle Giant,* 22-24.

4. Claire Giannini Hoffman, interview with the author.

5. James and James, *Biography of a Bank,* 458.

6. Bank of America, Annual Report, 1940, 20. See also *War Production Series 1942-1943,* California State Chamber of Commerce Publication no. 1; *Bank of America Business Review,* March 1942, 1. For Bank of America's participation in loans to aircraft companies, see, for example, Consolidated-Vultee Aircraft Credit Agreement, April 1943, BAA; W. F. Huck to L. M. Giannini, *Memorandum,* June 29, 1943, BAA.

7. California State Chamber of Commerce, Research Department, *Report on Shipbuilding in California, September 1939-July 1941;* California State Chamber

of Commerce, *California Profile* (1946), 4; Memorandum, Survey and Analysis of Banking in the Richmond Area by the Standards Department, September 21, 1946; California State Chamber of Commerce, *Survey of the Housing Problem in California* (1946), 3, BAA.

8. Russell Smith, Memorandum, March 10, 1942, BAA.

9. Bank of America, *Bank of America a War Industry* (pamphlet; April 7, 1943), BAA; Bank of America, "Building the Bank" (dividend enclosure, June 1941), 3.

10. See W. M. Hale to R. G. Smith, June 3, 1942, BAA.

11. Donald W. Douglas, "One Big Assembly Line," in Caughey and Caughey, *Los Angeles*, 374–75. For Bank of America permit applications, see APG to Edward J. Flynn, October 30, 1940; see also R. G. Smith to Charles Collins, March 10, 1942; A. M. Twomey to L. E. Birdzell, January 4, 1941, BAA.

12. Russell Smith, Memorandum, March 10, 1942; see also Cyril Upham, Memorandum, October 9, 1941, BAA.

13. C. W. Collins to APG, August 26, 1941; see also E. L. Kelly to L. M. Giannini, August 27, 1941, BAA.

14. See A. P. Giannini, handwritten note, September 9, 1941; see also APG to E. L. Kelly, October 14, 1941; E. L. Kelly to APG, October 16, 1941; Charles Collins to APG, August 26, 1941, BAA.

15. See Cyril Upham, Memorandum, October 9, 1941, BAA.

16. Charles Collins to APG, August 26 and 27, 1941; Charles Collins to Louis Ferrari, January 28, 1942; see also E. L. Kelly to APG, August 26, 1941; Preston Delano to APG, January 15, 1942, BAA.

17. Leo Crowley to Board of Governors, Federal Reserve System, January 18, 1942, Marriner Eccles Papers.

18. APG to Marriner Eccles, November 29, 1941, Marriner Eccles Papers.

19. Marriner Eccles to APG, December 20, 1941; see also Eccles's comments in "Right of Two National Banks to Consolidate and Status of Consolidated Institution with Respect to Branches," Marriner Eccles Papers.

20. APG to Marriner Eccles, November 25, 1942; see also W. L. Andrews to Board of Governors, Federal Reserve System, March 17, 1942.

21. Marriner Eccles to APG, September 29, 1942; see also Chester Morrill to APG, October 13, 1942, Marriner Eccles Papers.

22. Marriner Eccles to APG, October 15, 1942, Marriner Eccles Papers.

23. See *Transamerica Corporation v. Board of Governors of the Federal Reserve System*, Appendix, 1:578a, Transamerica Corporation Papers, BAA.

24. Marriner Eccles to APG, August 29, 1942, Marriner Eccles Papers.

25. Extract from Minutes of the Board, Meeting of February 6, 1942, Marriner Eccles Papers.

26. Ibid.; see also Chester Morrill to APG, October 13, 1942, Marriner Eccles Papers.

27. Marriner Eccles to APG, August 29, 1942, Marriner Eccles Papers.

28. Ibid.

29. APG to Marriner Eccles, August 17, 1942, Marriner Eccles Papers.

30. Marriner Eccles to APG, August 24, 1942, Marriner Eccles Papers.

31. Marriner Eccles to APG, October 13, 1943; see also Marriner Eccles to APG, October 15, 1942, Marriner Eccles Papers.

32. Marriner Eccles to APG, October 15, 1942, Marriner Eccles Papers; see also Marriner Eccles, Memorandum to the Files, November 12, 1942; Marriner Eccles to APG, November 13, 15, 1942, Marriner Eccles Papers.

33. "Draft of Report of Informal Conference with A. P. Giannini on February 18, 1943," Marriner Eccles Papers; Giannini, "Memorandum, for the Personal Use of Mr. Charles Collins," March 30, 1943, BAA; *Transamerica Corporation v. Board of Governors of the Federal Reserve System,* Appendix, 10:716a.

34. APG to Charles Collins, April 13, 1943, BAA.

35. Ibid.; see also Collins to APG, April 15, 1943, BAA.

36. Charles W. Collins, "Memorandum, Conversation with Governor John McKee of the Federal Reserve Board," May 13, 1943, Charles Collins Papers, BAA.

37. For a discussion of this development, see Gerald C. Fischer, *Bank Holding Companies* (1961), 59–85.

38. Extracts from Hearings Before the Committee on Banking and Currency, House of Representatives, 78th Congress, 1st sess., on H.R. 2634, BAA; *San Francisco Commercial News,* September 20, 1943.

39. Extracts from Hearings on H.R. 2634, BAA.

40. Charles Collins to Russell Smith, May 10, 1943; see also Charles Collins to APG, May 19, 1943, BAA.

41. APG to Marriner Eccles, June 16, 1943; see also Charles Collins to Thomas F. Ford, June 22, 1943, BAA.

42. Edward S. Herman, "Board of Governors v. Transamerica: Victory Out of Defeat," *Antitrust Bulletin,* July–August 1959, 521–25.

43. Federal Reserve Bulletin, June 1946, 673; see also L. E. Birdzell to Willkie, Owen, Otis, Farr, and Gallagher, June 19, 1943, BAA.

44. See "Address Delivered by L. M. Giannini at Management Conference," April 17, 1948, BAA.

45. Leonard Townsend to Board of Governors of the Federal Reserve System, October 31, 1947, Marriner Eccles Papers; see also Herman, "Board of Governors v. Transamerica," 523.

46. Marriner Eccles to Charles W. Tobey, June 13, 1947, Marriner Eccles Papers.

47. *San Francisco News,* May 5, 1945.

48. Ibid.

49. Ibid.

50. See L. M. Giannini to M. Muzi Falconi, January 30, 1950, BAA.

51. See statement submitted by Dr. Otto Jeidels to State Committee on Public Buildings and Grounds, February 8, 1944, BAA; see also statistics furnished to Al Haase by Bank of America Bond Investment Department.

52. On home construction, see Testimony of E. A. Mattison, Transcript of Transamerica Hearing Before Board of Governors of the Federal Reserve Sys-

tem, October 12, 1949, 62:5574; see also E. A. Mattison to All Branches, December 20, 1945; *Bankamerican,* April 1945, 1.

53. See APG to Mary Ottoboni, May 26, 1948, BAA; see also Herman, "Board of Governors v. Transamerica," 525.

54. See *American Banker,* August 19, 1948.

55. *Time,* October 15, 1945.

56. See V. C. Dickinson to APG, October 10, 1945; see also *San Francisco Chronicle,* October 10, 1945.

57. See, for example, J. L. Cauthorn to APG, January 11, 1945; V. C. Dickinson to APG, October 10, 1945; George Smith to APG, October 11, 1945, BAA.

58. See Giannini's statement in the *San Francisco Chronicle,* November 3, 1945.

59. APG to James F. Byrnes, August 29, 1945; see also Russell Smith, "Memorandum re European Trip," June 27, 1945; Russell Smith to Joe Rodrigo; Charles Collins to APG, June 12, 1945, BAA.

60. See Bank of America, Annual Report for 1945, BAA.

61. See Smith, "Memorandum re European Trip."

62. Conversation between A. P. Giannini and Vittorio de Fiori, December 1945, BAA.

63. Transamerica Corporation, Annual Report for 1945, Transamerica Corporation Papers, BAA; see also J. H. Callarate to Alvise Spineda de Cattaneis, January 29, 1949; Mario Scerni to L. M. Giannini, "Report on the Italian Situation," June 22, 1947, BAA.

64. Bank of America, Annual Report for 1945, 11.

65. *San Francisco News,* September 14, 1945; see also Bank of America, Annual Report for 1946, 13.

66. See, for example, F. S. Baer, "Report on Manila," March 4, 1946, BAA.

67. At their wartime peak, Bank of America loans to the Bechtel Corporation reached nearly $3 million (see W. F. Huck to L. M. Giannini, June 25, 1943, BAA).

68. F. S. Baer to F. A. Ferroggiaro, October 11, 1945, BAA.

69. T. B. Coughran to Al Haase, undated, but sometime in 1949, BAA; see also *Bankamerican,* June 1947, 1.

70. See L. E. Davis to F. S. Baer, September 6, 1948; L. E. Davis to D. Lapham, August 9, 1948, "Monthly Comparative Record of Deposits, Loans, etc., November, 1950," Branch Financial Statements, December 30, 1950, BAA. See also James and James, *Biography of a Bank,* 480–82.

71. See, for example, Marriner Eccles to Charles W. Tobey, January 13, 1947; Marriner Eccles to Preston Delano, November 24, 1947, Marriner Eccles Papers; see also *San Francisco Examiner,* October 11, 1944; *Wall Street Journal* (Pacific coast edition), October 11, 1944.

72. Thomas Clark to Marriner Eccles, October 31, 1945, Marriner Eccles Papers.

73. *San Francisco Chronicle,* March 31, 1948.

74. APG to Leo Crowley, February 1, 1943, BAA.

75. FBI, Memorandum, November 15, 1945, Federal Bureau of Investigation Files, Washington, D.C.

76. For the Truman-Snyder relationship, see Richard S. Kirkendall, *The Harry S. Truman Encyclopedia* (1991), 103–6; see also Richard Laurence Miller, *Truman: The Rise to Power* (1983), 324–25; Cabell Phillips, *The Truman Presidency* (1987), 156.

77. Koster, *Transamerica Story*, 29; *American Banker*, October 15, 1948.

78. *Time*, July 12, 1948; Charles Molony, "Two Years of Transamerica Case Hearings Move to Final Phase," undated article, BAA.

79. *San Francisco Call-Bulletin*, April 17, 1947.

80. For Delano's assurances to Eccles, see Preston Delano to Marriner Eccles, August 31, 1945, Marriner Eccles Papers. For Delano's changed position, see *American Banker*, August 19, 1948; *San Francisco News*, March 21, 1950; *San Francisco Examiner*, June 24, 1950.

81. *American Banker*, August 19, 1948.

82. Sidney Hyman, *Marriner S. Eccles: Private Entrepreneur and Public Servant* (1976), 334–39.

83. Ibid.

84. See Drew Pearson's column in *Washington Post*, February 6, 1948; *Oakland Tribune*, February 6, 1948.

85. *San Francisco News*, August 19, 1948; *San Francisco Chronicle*, March 31, 1938; *American Banker*, August 19, 1948; see also Drew Pearson's column in *Los Angeles Daily News*, May 7, 1948.

86. See Bank of America, News Dispatch, February 6, 1948; see also APG to Earl Lee Kelly, February 10, 1948; APG to Drew Pearson, July 14, 1948, BAA.

87. Some years earlier Corcoran had furnished Giannini with legal assistance in the SEC case against Transamerica and Bank of America. See Mario Giannini to Thomas Corcoran, February 3, 4, 1941, Thomas Corcoran Papers, Library of Congress.

88. FBI, Memorandum, December 4, 1945, Federal Bureau of Investigation Files.

89. FBI, Memorandum, December 12, 1945, Federal Bureau of Investigation Files.

90. Hyman, *Marriner S. Eccles*, 337–38.

91. See Drew Pearson's column, *Oakland Tribune*, February 6, 1948.

92. J. Leonard Townsend to Marriner Eccles, October 31, 1947, Marriner Eccles Papers.

93. Ibid.

94. See Ralph A. Young to Marriner Eccles, April 22, 1949, Marriner Eccles Papers.

95. See "Outline of Economic Testimony on the Trans-America Case," April 11, 1949, E. A. Goldenweisar Papers, Library of Congress.

96. Thomas B. McCabe to Thomas Clark, June 24, 1948, Marriner Eccles Papers.

97. Quoted in Fischer, *Bank Holding Companies*, 66.

98. Yeates, *Gentle Giant* (1954), 77.

99. See, for example, *San Francisco Chronicle,* October 11, 1947; *Oakland Tribune,* October 13, 1947, *San Francisco Examiner,* October 12, 1947.

100. Yeates, *Gentle Giant,* 77.

101. See, for example, A. P. Giannini, Statement, Annual Meeting of Stockholders, San Francisco, April 28, 1949; see also Fred Yeates, Memorandum, June 20, 1950; Glen E. Carter to R. P. A. Everard, October 28, 1949, BAA.

102. Giannini, interview with Bessie James, undated, but sometime in early 1949, BAA.

103. *San Francisco Chronicle,* June 9, 1949; *San Francisco Examiner,* June 9, 1949.

104. *New York Times,* June 5, 1949.

105. *Los Angeles Times,* June 5, 1949.

106. Charles Chambers to L. M. Giannini, June 3, 1949, BAA.

107. Thomas Corcoran to L. M. Giannini, August 13, 1949, BAA; Charles Chambers to L. M. Giannini, June 3, 1949.

108. *San Francisco Chronicle,* June 6, 1949.

109. *San Francisco Chronicle,* June 6, 1949.

110. Last Will and Testament of Amadeo P. Giannini, BAA.

111. Koster, *Transamerica Story,* 28–29.

112. For Evans's remarks, see *New York Times,* June 14, 1951; see also *New York Herald Tribune,* June 14, 1951.

113. Hyman, *Marriner S. Eccles,* 339.

Epilogue

1. "World's Biggest Bank," *Fortune,* 69.

2. Ibid.

3. Dwight L. Clarke, "The Gianninis—Men of the Renaissance," *California Historical Society Quarterly* 49 (September 1970): 256; see also Memorandum of conference with Mr. Charles W. Collins, September 21, 1938, Treasury Department Papers.

4. Josephson, *Money Lords,* 144.

5. *Los Angeles Examiner,* June 12, 1949.

6. APG to Mr. H. Vollmer, October 3, 1927, BAA; see also APG to J. Gilmarten, September 20, 1927, BAA.

7. Yeates, *Gentle Giant,* 55.

8. *San Francisco News,* May 7, 1948; see also *San Francisco Call-Bulletin,* September 2, 1941.

Selected Bibliography

Archival Sources

Bacigalupi, James. Papers. Bank of America Archives (BAA), San Francisco.
Business Extension. Papers. BAA.
Corcoran, Thomas. Papers. Library of Congress, Washington, D.C.
Cummings, Homer. Papers. Library of Congress (microfilm copy).
Dana, Julian P. Papers. Bancroft Library, University of California, Berkeley.
Douglas, William O. Papers. Library of Congress.
Eccles, Marriner. Papers. University of Utah, Salt Lake City.
Ferrari, Louis, Sr. Papers. BAA.
Giannini, Amadeo P. Papers. BAA.
Giannini, Attilio. Papers. BAA.
————. Papers. Bancroft Library.
Giannini, Lawrence. Papers. BAA.
Goldenweisar, E. A. Papers. Library of Congress.
Gore, Challis. Papers. BAA.
Grondona, Charles F. Papers. BAA.
Hoover, J. Edgar. Papers. Federal Bureau of Investigation Archives, Washington, D.C.
Italian Department. Papers. BAA.
Jones, Herbert C. Papers. Stanford University.
Lamont, Thomas. Papers. Baker Library, Harvard University School of Business, Harvard University.
Landis, James. Papers. Library of Congress.
McAdoo, William P. Papers. Library of Congress.
Merriam, Frank. Papers. Bancroft Library.

Morrish, William. Papers. BAA.
Mount, Arnold. Papers. BAA.
O'Connor, J. F. T. Papers. Bancroft Library.
Paganini, Robert. Papers. BAA.
Pedrini, Armando. Papers. BAA.
Reconstruction Finance Corporation. Papers. National Archives, Washington, D.C.
Roosevelt, Franklin. Papers. Franklin D. Roosevelt Memorial Library, Hyde Park, N.Y.
Rowell, Chester. Papers. Bancroft Library.
San Francisco Federal Reserve Board. Papers. San Francisco Federal Reserve, San Francisco.
Smith, Russell. Oral History Program. BAA.
Stockholders Auxiliary Corporation. Papers. BAA.
Sullivan, Celestine. Papers. BAA.
Transamerica Corporation. Papers. BAA.
Treasury Department. Papers. National Archives.
Women's Banking Department. Papers. BAA.
Wood, Will C. Papers. BAA.

Secondary Sources

Alhadeff, David A. *Monopoly and Competition in Banking*. Berkeley, 1954.
Allen, Frederick Lewis. *The Big Change: 1900–1950*. New York, 1952.
Andreini, G. "Battle of the Giants." Manuscript in possession of the author.
Arbuckle, Clyde. *History of San Jose*. San Jose, 1986.
Armstrong, Leroy, and J. C. Denny. *Financial California: An Historical Review of the Beginnings and Progress of Banking in the State*. San Francisco, 1916.
Auletta, Ken. *Greed and Glory on Wall Street: The Fall of the House of Lehman*. New York, 1986.
Bach, Steven. *Final Cut*. New York, 1985.
Balio, Tino. *United Artists: The Company Built by the Stars*. Madison, 1976.
Ballantine, Arthur. "When All the Banks Closed." *Harvard Business Review* 26 (March 1948): 129–43.
Barber, J. E. "The Banker and the Motion Picture Industry." *Coast Banker*, June 1921, 664–67.
Barth, Gunther. *Bitter Strength: A History of the Chinese in the United States, 1850–1870*. Cambridge, Mass. 1964.
Bean, Walton. *Boss Ruef's San Francisco: The Story of the Union Labor Party, Big Business, and the Graft Prosecution*. Berkeley, 1952.
———. *California: An Interpretative History*. Berkeley, 1968.
Berg, Scott. *Goldwyn: A Biography*. New York, 1989.

Birmingham, Stephen. *"Our Crowd": The Great Jewish Families of New York.* New York, 1967.

———. *The Rest of Us: The Rise of America's Eastern European Jews.* New York, 1985.

Blackford, Mansel G. *The Politics of Business in California, 1890–1920.* Columbus, Ohio, 1977.

Blum, John M. *From the Morgenthau Diaries.* 3 vols. Boston, 1959–1967.

———. *Roosevelt and Morgenthau.* Boston, 1970.

Bohme, Frederick G., ed. and trans. "Vigna Dal Ferro's 'Un Viaggio Nel Far West Americano.'" *California Historical Society Quarterly* 41 (June 1962): 149–62.

Bray, Howard. *The Pillars of the Post.* New York, 1980.

Brinkley, Alan. *Huey Long, Father Coughlin, and the Great Depression.* New York, 1982.

Bronson, William. *The Earth Shook, the Sky Burned.* New York, 1959.

Bullough, William. *The Blind Boss and His City.* Berkeley, 1979.

———. "Hannibal Versus the Blind Boss: Chris Buckley, the 'Junta,' and Democratic Reform Politics in San Francisco." *Pacific Historical Review* 46 (May 1977): 181–206.

———. "The Steam Beer Handicap: Chris Buckley and the San Francisco Municipal Election of 1896." *California Historical Quarterly* 54 (1975): 245–62.

Burchell, R. A. *The San Francisco Irish, 1848–1880.* Berkeley, 1980.

Burke, Robert. *Olson's New Deal for California.* Berkeley, 1953.

Calhoun, W. T., et al. *Improving the San Francisco Wholesale Fruit and Vegetable Market.* Berkeley, 1943.

Callow, Alexander, Jr. "San Francisco's Blind Boss." *Pacific Historical Review* 25 (August 1956): 261–79.

Camp, William M. *San Francisco: Port of Gold.* New York, 1947.

Capra, Frank. *The Name above the Title: An Autobiography.* New York, 1971.

Carey, Gary. *All the Stars in Heaven: Louis B. Mayer's M-G-M.* New York, 1981.

Carleton, Jack. "The Films Are Financed Here." *Los Angeles Times Sunday Magazine,* April 21, 1935.

Carosso, Vincent. *Investment Banking in America.* Cambridge, Mass., 1970.

———. *The Morgans: Private International Bankers, 1854–1913.* Cambridge, Mass., 1987.

Caughey, John, and LaRee Caughey, eds. *Los Angeles: Biography of a City.* Berkeley, 1976.

Chandler, L. V. *America's Greatest Depression.* New York, 1970.

Chaney, Lindsay, and Michael Cieply. *The Hearsts: Family and Empire: The Later Years.* New York, 1981.

Chaplin, Charles. *My Autobiography.* London, 1964.

Chapman, John M., and Ray B. Westerfield. *Branch Banking in California.* Berkeley, 1942.

Chernow, Ron. *The House of Morgan: An American Banking Dynasty and the Rise of Modern Finance.* New York, 1990.

Churchill, Allen. *The Incredible Ivar Kreuger.* London, 1957.

Cinel, Dino. *From Italy to San Francisco: The Immigrant Experience.* Stanford, 1982.

Cleland, Robert. *From Wilderness to Empire: A History of California.* New York, 1959.

Cleland, Robert, and Osgood Hardy. *The March of Industry.* Los Angeles, 1929.

Collins, Charles W. *The Branch Banking Question.* New York, 1926.

Collman, Charles. *Our Mysterious Panics, 1830–1930.* New York, 1931.

Cross, Ira B. *Financing an Empire: History of Banking in California.* 4 vols. San Francisco, 1927.

Crowley, Thomas. "Recollections of the San Francisco Waterfront." (Interview conducted by Karl Kortum and Will Klug Baum.) In *Regional Oral History Office,* 1–282. Bancroft Library, University of California, Berkeley, 1967.

Dana, Julian P. *A. P. Giannini: Giant in the West.* New York, 1947.

———. *The Sacramento: River of Gold.* New York, 1939.

Daniel, Cletus E. *Bitter Harvest: A History of California Farmworkers, 1870–1941.* Ithaca, 1981.

Davis, Kenneth S. *FDR: The New Deal Years, 1933–1937.* New York, 1986.

———. *FDR: The New York Years, 1928–1933.* New York, 1979.

DeBedts, Ralph F. *The New Deal's SEC: The Formative Years.* New York, 1964.

Delmatier, Royce D., Clarence McIntosh, and Earl G. Waters. *The Rumble of California Politics, 1948–1970.* New York, 1970.

DeWitt, Howard A. *Images of Ethnic and Radical Violence in California Politics, 1917–1930.* San Francisco, 1975.

Dondero, Raymond S. *The Italian Settlement of San Francisco.* Berkeley, 1953.

Douglas, Donald W. "One Big Assembly Line." In John and LaRee Caughey, eds., *Los Angeles: Biography of a City,* 347–78. Berkeley, 1976.

Dowrie, George. "History of the Bank of Italy in California." *Journal of Economic and Business History* 2 (1930): 271–98.

Durrenberger, R. W. *Geography of California.* Palo Alto, 1960.

Eaves, Lucile. *A History of California Labor Legislation.* Berkeley, 1910.

Eccles, Marriner. *Beckoning Frontiers: Public and Personal Recollections.* Edited by Sidney Hyman. New York, 1951.

Epstein, Lawrence J. *Samuel Goldwyn.* Boston, 1981.

Erdman, H. E. "The Development and Significance of California Cooperatives, 1900–1915." *Agricultural History* 32 (July 1958): 179–84.

Falbo, Ernest S. "State of California in 1856: Federico Biesta's Report to the Sardinian Ministry of Foreign Affairs." *California Historical Society Quarterly* 42 (December 1963): 311–33.

Federal Writers Project. *The Italians of New York.* New York, 1938.

Figari, William. "San Francisco and the Waterfront, 1900–1965." (Interview conducted by Ruth Teiser.) In *Regional Oral History Office,* 1–162. Bancroft Library, University of California, Berkeley, 1969.

Finney, Guy W. *The Great Los Angeles Bubble.* Los Angeles, 1929.

Fischer, Gerald C. *Bank Holding Companies.* New York and London, 1961.

Fisher, Lloyd. *The Harvest Labor Market in California*. Cambridge, Mass., 1953.

Forbes, B. C. "Giannini—The Story of an Unusual Career." In his *Men Who Are Making the West*, 204–27. New York, 1923.

Forbes, John Douglas. *J. P. Morgan, Jr., 1867–1943*. New York, 1981.

Freidel, Frank. *Franklin D. Roosevelt: Launching the New Deal*. Boston, 1973.

Friedman, Milton, and Anna Schwartz. *A Monetary History of the United States, 1867–1960*. Princeton, 1963.

Gabler, Neal. *An Empire of Their Own: How the Jews Invented Hollywood*. New York, 1988.

Galbraith, John Kenneth. *The Great Crash: 1929*. Boston, 1961.

Gallaher, T. A. "The Women's Bank." *Sunset*, January 1929, 24–53.

Galvin, Edmund H. "Bank Capital on Trial." Ph.D. diss. University of Washington, Seattle, 1954.

Gambino, Richard. *Blood of My Blood*. New York, 1974.

Gammack, Thomas H. "Giannini Comes to Wall Street." *The Outlook*, March 14, 1928, 428–31.

Garraty, John A. *The Great Depression*. San Diego, 1987.

Geiger, Peter. "The Bank and Feature Financing." In Jason E. Squire, ed., *The Movie Business Book*, 108–12. Englewood Cliffs, N.J., 1983.

———. "The View from the 48th Floor." *Hollywood Reporter*, November 29, 1974, 46–49.

Geist, Kenneth L. *Pictures Will Talk: The Life and Films of Joseph L. Mankiewicz*. New York, 1974.

Giannini, Attilio. "Financing the Production and Distribution of Motion Pictures." *Annals of the American Academy of Political and Social Sciences* 128 (November 1926): 45–50.

Giovinco, Joseph. "Democracy in Banking: The Bank of Italy and California Italians." *California Historical Society Quarterly* 47 (September 1968): 195–218.

Graham, Otis, Jr. "William P. McAdoo." In *Dictionary of American Biography*, supplement, part 3.

Graham, Otis, Jr., and Meghan Robinson Wander, eds. *Roosevelt: His Life and Times*. Boston, 1985.

Grassman, Curtis. "Prologue to Democratic Reform: The Democratic Impulse, 1886–1898." *Pacific Historical Review* 42 (November 1973): 518–36.

Graves, Jackson A. *My Seventy Years in California, 1857–1927*. Los Angeles, 1927.

Gumina, Deanna Paoli. "Andrea Sbarboro, Founder of the Italian Swiss Colony Wine Company." *Italian Americana*, August 1975, 1–15.

———. *The Italians of San Francisco, 1850–1930*. Staten Island, 1978.

Halberstam, David. *The Powers That Be*. New York, 1979.

"A Hall of Fame for Business Leadership." *Fortune*, January 1975, 64–74.

Hammond, Bray. *Banks and Politics in America: From the Revolution to the Civil War*. Princeton, 1957.

Hampton, Benjamin B. *History of the American Film Industry*. New York, 1970.

Hansen, Gladys, ed. *San Francisco: The Bay and Its Cities*. American Guide Series. New York, 1974.

Harlan, George. *San Francisco Bay Ferryboats*. Berkeley, 1967.

Harris, Seymour. *Twenty Years of Federal Reserve Policy*. Cambridge, Mass., 1933.

Hayashi, Tetsumaro, ed. *A Study Guide to Steinbeck: A Handbook to His Major Works*. Metuchen, N.J., 1979.

Hayes, Reed. "A Real Romance of San Francisco: The Story of the Bank of Italy and A. P. Giannini." *San Francisco News*, March 6, 1928.

Hayne, Donald, ed. *The Autobiography of Cecil B. DeMille*. Englewood Cliffs, N.J., 1959.

Hector, Gary. *Breaking the Bank: The Decline of BankAmerica*. 1988.

Herman, Edward S. "Board of Governors v. Transamerica: Victory Out of Defeat." *Antitrust Bulletin*, July–August 1959, 521–39.

———. "The Transamerica Case." University of California, Berkeley, 1953.

Higham, Charles. *Cecil B. DeMille*. New York, 1984.

Hitchborn, Franklin. "California Politics, 1891–1939." Typescript, 5 vols. University of California, Los Angeles, 1949.

Hoag, Betty L. "A Man of Charisma: A. P. Giannini in San Mateo, California." *Journal of the San Mateo County Historical Association*, Spring 1973, 1–6.

Hoffman, Claire Giannini. "The Giannini Family in Banking and Public Service." (Interview conducted by Ruth Teiser.) In *Regional Oral History Office*, 204–82. Bancroft Library, University of California, Berkeley, 1976.

Howe, Ken. "Hollywood and B of A: Yesterday and Today." *BankAmerican*, March 1980, 3–7.

Hutchinson, Claude B., ed. *California Agriculture*. Berkeley, 1946.

Hutchinson, W. H. *California: Two Centuries of Men, Land, and Growth in the Golden State*. Palo Alto, 1969.

Hyman, Sidney. *Marriner S. Eccles: Private Entrepreneur and Public Servant*. Stanford, 1976.

Inkersley, Arthur. "The Vintage in California and Italy." *Overland Monthly* 54 (October 1909): 406–11.

Issel, William. "The Reform Charter of 1898." *Labor History* 18 (Summer 1977): 341–59.

James, Marquis, and Bessie James. *Biography of a Bank: The Story of Bank of America*. New York, 1954.

Jewell, Richard, with Vernon Harbin. *The RKO Story*. New York, 1982.

"John Francis Neylan: San Francisco Irish Progressive." Manuscript. Bancroft Library, University of California, Berkeley.

Johnson, Moira. *Roller Coaster: The Bank of America and the Future of American Banking*. New York, 1990.

Josephson, Matthew. "Big Bull of the West." *Saturday Evening Post*, September 13, September 20, September 27, October 4, 1947.

———. *The Money Lords: The Great Finance Capitalists, 1925–1950*. New York, 1972.

Joves, Gertrude. *Motion Picture Empire*. Hamden, Conn., 1966.

Kelly, Tom. *The Imperial Post: The Meyers, the Grahams, and the Paper That Rules Washington.* New York, 1983.

Kemble, John Haskell. "The Panama Route to California, 1848–1869." Ph.D. diss. University of California, Berkeley, 1937.

————. *San Francisco Bay.* Cambridge, Md., 1957.

Kennedy, John. *The Great Earthquake and Fire.* New York, 1963.

Kennedy, Joseph, ed. *The Story of the Films.* Cambridge, Mass., 1927.

Kennedy, Susan Estabrook. *The Banking Crisis of 1933.* Lexington, Ky., 1973.

Kershner, Frederick D. "George Chaffee and the Irrigation Frontier." *Agricultural History* 27 (October 1953): 115–22.

Kettl, Donald F. *Leadership at the Fed.* New Haven, Conn., 1986.

Kirkendall, Richard S. *The Harry S. Truman Encyclopedia.* Boston, 1991.

Knuth, Priscilla F. "Nativism in California, 1886–1897." M.A. thesis. University of California, Santa Barbara, 1947.

Koskoff, David. *Joseph P. Kennedy: A Life and Times.* Englewood Cliffs, N.J., 1974.

Koster, George H. *The Transamerica Story.* San Francisco, 1978.

Koury, Phil A. *Yes, Mr. DeMille.* New York, 1978.

Kraemer, Erich, and H. E. Erdman. *History of Cooperation in Marketing of California Fresh Deciduous Fruits.* Berkeley, 1933.

Leale, John. *Recollections of a Tule Sailor.* San Francisco, 1939.

"L. M. Giannini of the Bank of America." *Fortune,* August 1951, 13.

McCarthy, John R. *Joseph Francis Sartori, 1858–1946: A Biography Published by the Security First National Bank of Los Angeles.* Los Angeles, 1948.

McClintock, David. *Indecent Exposure: A True Story of Hollywood and Wall Street.* New York, 1982.

MacCurdy, Rahno M. *The History of the California Fruit Growers Association.* Los Angeles, 1924.

McEntire, Davis. *The Labor Force in California.* Berkeley, 1952.

McGloin, John. *San Francisco: The Story of a City.* San Rafael, 1978.

McGowan, Joseph. *History of the Sacramento Valley.* New York, 1939.

MacMullen, Jerry. *Paddle-wheel Days in California.* Stanford, 1944.

McWilliams, Carey. *California: The Great Exception.* Santa Barbara and Salt Lake City, 1979.

————. *The Education of Carey McWilliams.* New York, 1979.

————. *Factories in the Field: The Story of Migratory Labor in California.* Hamden, Conn., 1939.

————. *Ill Fares the Land.* New York, 1942.

————. *Southern California Country.* New York, 1946.

Maland, Charles J. *Chaplin and American Culture.* Princeton, 1989.

May, Dean L. *From New Deal to New Economics: The Liberal Response to the Recession.* New York, 1981.

Mayer, Martin. *The Bankers.* New York, 1974.

Melendy, Brett, and Benjamin Gilbert. *The Governors of California.* Georgetown, 1965.

Michelman, Irving S. *Consumer Finance: A Case History in American Business.* New York, 1966.

Miller, Crane, and Richard Hyslop. *California: The Geography of Diversity.* Palo Alto, 1983.

Miller, John E. *Governor Philip F. La Follette, the Wisconsin Progressives, and the New Deal.* Columbia, Mo., 1982.

Miller, Richard Laurence. *Truman: The Rise to Power.* New York, 1983.

Miller, S. C. *The Unwelcome Immigrant.* Berkeley, 1970.

Moley, Raymond. *After Seven Years.* New York, 1939.

————. *The First New Deal.* New York, 1966.

Morrison, Annie L., and John H. Haydon. *San Luis Obispo and Environs.* Los Angeles, 1917.

Mosley, Leonard. *Zanuck: The Rise and Fall of Hollywood's Last Tycoon.* Boston, 1984.

Mowry, George. *The California Progressives.* Chicago, 1951.

Nash, Gerald D. "Herbert Hoover and the Origins of the Reconstruction Finance Corporation." *Mississippi Valley Historical Review* 46 (December 1959): 455–68.

————. *State Government and Economic Development: A History of Administrative Politics in California, 1849–1933.* Berkeley, 1964.

Nicosia, Francesco M. *Italian Pioneers of California.* 1960.

Norris, Frank. "Italy in California." *The Wave,* October 24, 1896.

Noyes, Alexander. *Forty Years of American Finance.* New York and London, 1909.

Oberholtzer, Sara L. "School Savings Banks." *United States Bureau of Education Bulletin* 46 (1914): 10–14.

O'Brien, Robert. *This Is San Francisco.* New York, 1948.

Olin, Spencer C., Jr. "European Immigrant and Oriental Alien: Acceptance and Rejection by the California Legislature of 1913." *Pacific Historical Review* 35 (1958): 305–15.

Olson, James S., ed. *Historical Dictionary of the New Deal: From Inauguration to Preparation for War.* Westport, Conn., 1986.

Palmer, Hans C. "Italian Immigration and the Development of California." Ph.D. diss., University of California, Berkeley, 1965.

Parrish, Michael E. *Securities Regulation and the New Deal.* New Haven, 1970.

Paul, Rodman. "The Beginnings of Agriculture in California: Innovation vs. Continuity." *California Historical Quarterly* 28 (1970): 19–27.

Peixotto, Earnest. "Italy in California." *Scribner's,* July 1910, 75–84.

Phelin, Carl C. "The San Francisco Clearing House Certificates of 1907–1908." *Publications of the Academy of Pacific Coast History,* January 1909, 3–4.

Phillips, Cabell. *The Truman Presidency.* New York, 1987.

Phillips, Delphia. "A Bank for Women Run by Women." *Progress: A Magazine for the New Day,* July 1924, 198–99.

Posner, Russell. "The Bank of Italy and the 1926 Campaign in California." *California Historical Society Quarterly* 37 (December 1958): 347–58.

————. "California's Role in the Nomination of Franklin D. Roosevelt." *California Historical Society Quarterly* 39 (June 1960): 121–39.

————. "State Politics and the Bank of America, 1920–1934." Ph.D. diss. University of California, Berkeley, 1957.

Preston, H. H. "Bank of America." *Journal of Economic and Business History* 4 (1932): 197–223.

Radin, Paul. *The Italians of San Francisco: Their Adjustment and Acculturation.* San Francisco, 1970.

Reich, Cary. *Financier: The Biography of Andre Meyer—A Story of Money, Power, and the Reshaping of American Business.* New York, 1983.

Roberts, Chalmers M. *The Washington Post: The First Hundred Years.* Boston, 1977.

Rolle, Andrew. *The Immigrant Upraised.* Norman, Okla., 1968.

————. "Italy in California." *Pacific Spectator* 9 (Autumn 1955): 408–19.

Sampson, Anthony. *The Money Lenders: Bankers and a World in Turmoil.* New York, 1981.

Sandmeyer, Elmer C. *The Anti-Chinese Movement in California.* Urbana, Ill., 1939.

Sbarboro, Andrea. "Life of Andrea Sbarboro: Reminiscences of an Italian American Pioneer." Manuscript. Bancroft Library, University of California, Berkeley.

————. "Wines and Vineyards of California." *Overland Monthly,* January 1900, 65–76, 95–96.

Schapsmeier, Edward. *Encyclopedia of American Agricultural History.* Westport, Conn., 1973.

Schickel, Richard. *The Disney Version.* New York, 1968.

Schlesinger, Arthur, Jr. *The Coming of the New Deal.* Boston, 1959.

Schwartz, Harry. "Organization Problems of Agricultural Unions." *Journal of Farm Economics* 23 (May 1941): 456–66.

Schwarz, Jordan A. *The Interregnum of Despair: Hoover, Congress, and the Depression.* Urbana, Ill., 1970.

Scott, Winfield. "Old Wine in New Bottles: When Italy Comes to California Through the Panama Canal—What Then?" *Sunset,* May 1913, 519–26.

Seligman, Joel. *The Transformation of Wall Street: A History of the Securities and Exchange Commission and Modern Corporate Finance.* Boston, 1982.

Sinclair, Andrew. *Corsair: The Life of J. Pierpont Morgan.* Boston, 1981.

Smith, Richard Norton. *An Uncommon Man: The Triumph of Herbert Hoover.* New York, 1984.

Smith, Wallace. *Garden of the Sun: A History of the San Joaquin Valley, 1772–1939.* Los Angeles, 1939.

Sobel, Robert. *Panic on Wall Street: A History of American Financial Disasters.* New York, 1972.

Spinello, Mario. "Italians of California." *Sunset,* January 1905, 256–58.

Starr, Kevin. *Inventing the Dream: California Through the Progressive Era.* New York, 1985.

————. *Material Dreams: Southern California Through the 1920s.* New York, 1990.

Stein, Walter J. *California and the Dust Bowl Migration.* Westport, Conn., 1973.

Steinbeck, John. *Grapes of Wrath*. New York, 1939.

Storke, Thomas. *California Editor*. Los Angeles, 1958.

Sufrin, Sidney C. "Labor Organization in Agricultural America, 1930–1935." *American Journal of Sociology* 43 (January 1938): 544–59.

Taylor, Frank. "He's No Angel." *Saturday Evening Post,* January 14, 1939, 45–48.

Taylor, Paul S. *Adrift on the Land*. New York, 1940.

———. "Foundations of California Rural Society." *California Historical Society Quarterly* 24 (1945): 139–61.

Teague, Charles C. *Fifty Years a Rancher*. Los Angeles, 1944.

Thomas, Dana L. *The Plungers and the Peacocks*. New York, 1967.

Thomas, Gordon, and Max Morgan-Witts. *The Day the Bubble Burst: A Social History of the Wall Street Crash of 1929*. New York, 1979.

———. *The San Francisco Earthquake*. New York, 1971.

Thorburn, Donaldson B. *The Story of Transamerica*. San Francisco, 1931.

von Ulm, Gerith von. *Charlie Chaplin*. Caldwell, Idaho, 1940.

Waldron, Gladys H. "Anti-Foreign Movements in California, 1919–1929." Ph.D. diss. University of California, Berkeley, 1945.

Warburg, Paul. *The Federal Reserve System—Its Origins and Growth*. 2 vols. New York, 1930.

Wasko, Janet. *Movies and Money: Financing the American Film Industry*. Norwood, N.J., 1982.

Weaver, John. *Los Angeles: The Enormous Village, 1781–1981*. Santa Barbara, 1980.

Weeks, Edward. *Men, Money, and Responsibility: A History of Lee, Higginson Corporation, 1848–1962*. New York, 1962.

Wernette, John P. "Branch Banking in California." Ph.D. diss. Harvard University, 1932.

Wetty, Earl, and Frank Taylor. *Black Bonanza*. New York, 1958.

White, Gerald. *Formative Years in the Far West: A History of the Standard Oil Company of California and Predecessors Through 1919*. New York, 1962.

Wigmore, Barrie A. *The Crash and Its Aftermath: A History of Securities Markets in the United States, 1929–1933*. Westport, Conn., 1985.

Willis, Parker B. *The Federal Reserve Bank of San Francisco: A Study in American Central Banking*. New York, 1937.

Wilson, William L. *Full Faith and Credit: The Story of C.I.T. Financial Corporation, 1908–1975*. New York, 1976.

Winchell, Lilbourne. *History of Fresno County and the San Joaquin Valley*. Fresno, Calif., 1933.

Winther, Oscar Osburn. *The Story of San Jose, 1797–1895*. San Francisco, 1935.

Wright, Doris. "The Making of Cosmopolitan California: An Analysis of Immigration, 1840–1870." *California Historical Society Quarterly* 19 (December 1940): 65–79.

Wycoff, Richard. *Wall Street Ventures and Adventures Through Forty Years*. New York, 1930.

Yeates, Fred. *The Gentle Giant*. San Francisco, 1954.

Zierold, Norman J. *The Hollywood Tycoons*. London, 1969.

Index

Compositor: Dharma Enterprises
Printer: BookCrafters, Inc.
Binder: BookCrafters, Inc.
Text: 10/13 Bembo
Display: Bernhard Modern